Tom Swan's GNU C++ for Linux

Tom Swan

A Division of Macmillan USA
201 W. 103rd Street
Indianapolis, Indiana 46290

Contents at a Glance

Tom Swan's GNU C++ for Linux

Copyright © 2000 by Que Corporation

International Standard Book Number: 0-7897-2153-8

Library of Congress Catalog Card Number: 99-63268

Printed in the United States of America

First Printing: December, 1999

01 00 99   4   3   2   1

TRADEMARKS

WARNING AND DISCLAIMER

Associate Publisher
John Pierce

Development Editor
Erik Dafforn

Managing Editor
Thomas F. Hayes

Copy Editor
Geneil Breeze

Indexer
Bill Meyers

Proofreader
Maribeth Echard

Technical Editor
Rich Blum

Team Coordinator
Julie Otto

Media Developer
Michael Hunter

Production
Dan Harris
Brad Lenser

TABLE OF CONTENTS

PREFACE

This book was born at sea—literally. One lazy day, I was aboard my home and sailboat anchored in the Bahamas, where I had planned to spend a leisurely winter. It was one of the first times in two decades that I wasn't writing at least one computer book and working at it almost every day. After writing thirty-some books, I told myself I needed a break. I *deserved* a vacation. Maybe I'd dust off that novel I've always threatened to finish.

So, instead of spending the day glaring at a computer screen, I went fishing, one of my many talents. Unfortunately, catching is not another and, late that night, after a hearty meal of rice and beans (and, you know, the fish laugh at me, but that's another story), I started reading a couple of books about Linux that I had brought along.

I was familiar with UNIX, having used it to install networks and database systems years ago. I remember thinking that all computers would eventually run UNIX or something like it, a thought that returned as I read about Linux. The more I read, the more intrigued I became. After digging out the laptop from under the life raft, I installed Linux, tried the GNU C++ compiler, and in a couple of hours a gale could have blown through and I wouldn't have noticed. Nothing could have excited me more than discovering the fantastic GNU C++ compiler! Okay, catching a really big fish would have done it. But not much else.

At my fingertips, I realized, was not merely a great C++ compiler, but a full-featured, professional software development system. Along with GNU C++ comes an impressive suite of programming tools including the Emacs editor (which I used to write this book's sample programs), a revision control system, debuggers, a profiler, and a host of other tools and libraries for console and X development. In a word—Wow!

That moment started me on a journey through GNU C++ that is just now coming to a close as I write these words. The result is this book, a complete guide to the ANSI C++ programming language using GNU C++ for Linux. In these chapters, you will find information on creating finished Linux software from console utilities to X graphical applications. Numerous sample programs pepper these pages, and as with all of my books, you are welcome to incorporate this book's listings into your own programs without restriction. On the book's CD-ROM is the full Linux-Mandrake 6.0 Red Hat operating system, the GNU C++ compiler, various tools and utilities, plus all of this book's sample program files.

Now that the book is finished, I realize that my voyage into the world of Linux programming, GNU C++, and other related topics has only just begun. Like all programmers, the more I know about a programming language, the more I realize how much more I have to learn, and I welcome your comments and suggestions for future editions of this book. Please contact me by sending email to TomSwan@compuserve.com, or write to me in care of the publisher.

Perhaps now I'll have time for a little more fishing. I might even catch something this time. But you know what? I've grown kind of fond of rice and beans. Enjoy!

Tom Swan

Key West, Florida

ABOUT THE AUTHOR

Tom Swan (www.tomswan.com) is an internationally popular author of more than 30 books on computer programming in C++, Pascal, Delphi, and assembly language. His books are favorites in classrooms and have been translated into numerous languages worldwide. Professional developers have cut their programming teeth on Tom's bestselling books—such as *Mastering Borland C++ 5.0, Mastering Turbo Assembler, Learning C++,* and *Delphi™ 4 Bible.* Tom is a frequent contributor and former columnist for *Dr. Dobb's Journal, PC World,* and *PC Techniques* magazines. He is an avid Linux enthusiast who is building a new name by supporting free software distribution to the Linux community.

DEDICATION

To Maureen Walsh Hunt, for believing in me.

ACKNOWLEDGMENTS

So many people contribute to a book of this size and scope, it is impossible for me to thank them all. A mere thank you seems inadequate to folks such as Linus Torvalds who brought us Linux, and to Richard Stallman for starting the free-software ball rolling that led to the GNU project, and hence to Linux. I don't know these two gentlemen personally, but I am indebted to them as well as to the hundreds if not thousands of programmers worldwide who have improved Linux and GNU C++, and who continue to contribute to this amazing project. I also thank Bruce E. Wampler for developing the V C++ class library for X programming, introduced in this book's final two chapters.

On a personal note, warm thanks to Barbara Paré for encouraging me to begin this project and see it through (and for keeping the bad weather at bay); to Larry Weeldreyer for the use of his scanner and for many tips and suggestions (plus the lunches and good company); to George Shetzley for helping me run errands and for friendship; to my friends at Sunset Marina for package handling, getting my phone service woes solved, and especially for the air conditioner; to Anne Swan for emotional support and for forwarding my mail while I travel around; to John Windholtz for reminding me to tell readers what a.out means (and to Patty Windholtz for the sundowners and company); to Barry Braverman for helping me maintain my sanity and improve my guitar playing; to my brother David Swan for encouraging me to knuckle down and do the work; and to my mother Mary Swan and my father Reyer Swan for the care packages and loving support not only during the time I wrote this book, but always.

I am particularly grateful to the employees and associates of Que and Macmillan USA, and even though I don't know all your names, your hard work shines on every page. I especially thank (in alphabetical order) Richard Blum, Geneil Breeze, Erik Dafforn, Tom Hayes, Dean Miller, Julie Otto, John Pierce, Katie Robinson, and Mandie Rowell. My name might be on the cover, but without the help of these fine people and everyone at Que and Macmillan USA, this book would simply not exist.

PART

I

Getting Started

Introducing This Book

Learning a new subject is like taking a trip, although the destination in a book is not a park or an island, but knowledge. Not everyone, however, likes to travel the same way. Some prefer to hop in a vehicle and just go. Others meticulously plan in advance every aspect of their journey.

If you're the take-off-now-and-the-consequences-be-damned type, you might want to skip to Chapter 2, "Installing Linux." Jet-setters who have already installed Linux and want to start programming right now should turn to Part II, "C++ Fundamentals." For the rest of us who opt for a more leisurely course through life's adventures, consider this chapter as a road map (or a nautical chart) and equipment list for the chapters in this book.

Read this chapter to understand the styles used in the text, for overviews of this book's six parts and 30 chapters, and for a general feel of the book's layout. In addition, I include here some notes about the hardware and software you need to make the most of this book's information.

TEXT STYLES

To help make this book easier to read, the text is set using three distinct styles. Normal text looks like this. Programming words such as `string` and `while` are set in `monospace`. This typeface should closely, although perhaps not perfectly, match the characters you see on your screen when viewing source code listings. Any commands you are to type are set in ***bold italic*** when appearing in a sentence, or they are set apart and preceded by console-shell dollar signs as in the following two commands that compile and run one of the book's sample programs:

```
$ g++ welcome.cpp
$ ./a.out
```

Three other text items—notes, tips, and warnings—appear at numerous places throughout this book. Here's an example of a note, which typically expands on a topic or suggests how to find additional information:

Note

If you have Internet access (and who doesn't these days?), use a Web search engine such as Lycos or Google to look for sites containing the key words Linux and UNIX. Remember, Linux *is* UNIX, so for the most information, search both types of locations.

A tip gives more specific advice and is usually short and to the point:

Tip

If you are browsing this book in a bookstore, purchasing a copy would be a really great idea!

A warning tells you about a questionable or harmful programming technique that might lead to a hard-to-find bug in a program's source code:

Tip

> Learning to program in C++ might be hazardous to your vacation time and personal life. During your quest to master GNU C++, don't forget to put this book aside every so often and go smell the roses.

REQUIREMENTS

In general, if you can run any version of Linux, you can use this book to learn GNU C++ programming. Every Linux installation comes complete with the full GNU C++ development system, so unless you intend to upgrade your operating system, if you have already installed Linux, you can skip to the part and chapter summaries at the end of this chapter. For readers who are installing Linux for the first time using this book's CD-ROM, or a version from another source, following are minimum and suggested hardware and software requirements.

Note

> GNU stands for *GNU is Not UNIX*—an intentionally recursive definition. GNU C++ is one of many pieces of the GNU project, which, through the Free Software Foundation (FSF), encourages the free distribution of computer software.

HARDWARE REQUIREMENTS

Linux runs on just about any 80386, 80486, or 80586 (Pentium) based PC. However, the Mandrake-Linux 6.0 CD-ROM included with this book is optimized for, and therefore requires, a Pentium-class system. Linux does not require a color display, but if you plan to run X (as do most Linux users), a 16- or 24-bit color video card and suitable monitor are recommended. There are reports of Linux running on 8086- and 80286-based systems, although these older-model PCs are not likely to take full advantage of the operating system. Tantalizing news also floats around concerning Linux installations on 68000 and other systems, but at the present, Linux is generally an Intel-processor-based operating system.

UNIX users might be able to use much of this book's information along with a version of GNU C++. This may require obtaining and installing the compiler and libraries, but these are readily available over the Internet (see Appendix C, "Web and FTP Sites"). This book's information on X and Xlib programming should also apply to any X installation, and the V class library discussed in Chapter 29, "Introducing the V Class Library," and Chapter 30, "Developing X Software with V," comes with support for numerous UNIX and Linux platforms, plus (with a suitable compiler, not included) Microsoft Windows and OS/2. Because readers of this book probably have a wide range of hardware, I can't make any guarantees that the programs listed in the coming chapters will work on any particular system, but if you encounter any system dependencies or quirks, please let me know by dropping a line in care of the publisher.

Note

I wrote this book and all sample programs on my Dell Pentium-Pro system with 32MB RAM, 24-bit true-color video, and a bunch of disk drives with the total capacity of an average bottomless pit. It's a great system, but being more than two years old, it is nowhere near state of the art. I developed most of this book's programs and text using Red Hat Linux version 5.1. I also tested all programs and information using Linux-Mandrake (Red Hat) 6.0 as supplied with this book. The program's listings were also tested using Caldera Linux 2.2. Most other flavors of Linux should work equally well.

Authorities differ on minimum memory requirements for running Linux, but as always in computer programming, the more memory you have, the better. For best results, you should have at least 2MB RAM, but 16MB or even 32MB is needed to compile really big projects and to run the X windowing system at a reasonable speed. If you merely want to learn GNU C++ programming, as long as Linux runs, you can probably compile and run most of this book's sample programs.

There are also differing reports on how much free disk space you need, but this is probably not much of a concern for most readers, especially those with relatively new computers that typically include huge disk drives. Based on a totally unscientific rough guess, 500MB is a rock-bottom minimum size, but at least one gigabyte is better. You'll need at least two gigabytes of hard drive space if you want to install both Linux and Microsoft Windows on the same system. (Chapter 2 explains how to do that.)

A keyboard is required, of course, but a mouse is optional. However, X applications require a mouse. You don't need a printer. A tape drive or other backup system is highly recommended. A CD player is required to install this book's CD-ROM.

Although not strictly required, a UPS (uninterruptible power supply) is an essential piece of gear on any Linux (and UNIX) installation. Linux maintains file directories in memory until the associated disk or other device is unmounted, which in the case of hard drives, does not occur until the system is properly shut down. This means that a power loss might be disastrous. I use an APC power supply with my computer to prevent interruptions, which happen regularly in my tropical-storm-prone area. For more information, check out APC's Web site at http://www.apcc.com.

SOFTWARE REQUIREMENTS

Linux and GNU C++ are freely distributed under the GNU General Public License (see Appendix E, "Copyright Information—The GNU General Public License"). This fact makes it possible for the publisher to offer on this book's CD-ROM the entire Linux-Mandrake 6.0 operating system, an enhanced version of Red Hat Linux 6.0. The CD-ROM includes the complete GNU C++ development system, all libraries, and all tools you need to create C++ programs from small to large. Also on the CD-ROM are the source code files for this book's sample programs as well as the V C++ class library for X programming.

In short, you don't need any other software to make full use of this book—everything you need is on the included CD-ROM. If you already have Linux installed, simply copy this book's files to your hard drive along with the V C++ class library if you want to learn X programming techniques (see also Chapter 3, "Installing GNU C++," and Chapter 29, "Introducing the V Class Library.").

LISTINGS

This book's listings are numbered by chapter and also named—for example, Listing 4.1, welcome.cpp. To find a listing's source code file on disk, change to that chapter's directory such as src/c04. (See Chapter 3 for instructions on how to install this book's listing files.)

Any line numbers mentioned in reference to a listing—for example, in this book's hands-on sessions with the GNU debugger—might differ for you. This is because, to save space in the book, I deleted extraneous comment lines, divided long lines to fit on the printed page, and removed duplicate programming. Future updates to any listings on disk may also cause line numbers to change. Of course, the complete sources for all programs are on the CD-ROM.

Note   Follow the instructions in this book to compile and run each sample program. Some programs are divided into separate modules that require linking together. Just because a source code file ends with the filename extension .cpp doesn't mean it is a complete program.

PART SUMMARIES

This book is organized into six parts and 30 chapters, covering the entire ANSI C++ programming language as implemented by GNU C++, plus other topics. Read the following for overviews of each part:

- Part I, "Getting Started," Chapters 1 to 3, provides overviews of this book and instructions for installing and configuring Linux and GNU C++.

- Part II, "C++ Fundamentals," Chapters 4 to 11, covers the basics of C++ programming and explains how to create programs using GNU C++.

- Part III, "Object-Oriented Programming," Chapters 12 to 17, explains object-oriented C++ techniques using classes, encapsulation, and inheritance.

- Part IV, "Advanced C++ Techniques," Chapters 18 to 21, expands on the preceding part with advanced object-oriented programming methods using C++.

- Part V, "C++ Class Libraries," Chapters 22 to 27, details the standard C++ string class and the standard template container and algorithm library.

- Part VI, "X Window Development," Chapters 28 to 30, introduces X and Xlib programming and concludes with a hands-on tutorial for the V C++ class library for X software development for Linux, Microsoft Windows, and other platforms.

CHAPTER SUMMARIES

This book's numerous topics are covered in 30 chapters and include details on installation, C++ programming, standard libraries, and X application development. Read the following for overviews of each chapter:

- Chapter 1, "Introducing This Book," as you are discovering, suggests how to make the most of this book.

- Chapter 2, "Installing Linux," gives tips for installing Linux using this book's CD-ROM and explains how to set up a dual boot system for Linux and Microsoft Windows.

- Chapter 3, "Installing GNU C++," suggests how to install and configure GNU C++, how to install this book's listing files, and also compares the C and C++ programming languages.

- Chapter 4, "Introducing GNU C++," covers the basics of C++ programming using the GNU C++ compiler.

- Chapter 5, "Compiling and Debugging C++ Programs," suggests numerous ways to compile and debug programs (using the provided GNU debugger), and also explains how to deal with many common types of errors and warning messages.

- Chapter 6, "Creating Data Objects," explains how to create variables and other structures for storing data in C++ programs.

- Chapter 7, "Applying Fundamental Operators," illustrates many of the ways to create expressions using C++ operators.

- Chapter 8, "Controlling Input and Output," introduces standard C++ methods for programming input and output statements and also compares these methods with standard C techniques.

- Chapter 9, "Controlling Program Flow," documents C++ flow-control statements such as `for` and `while` loops.

- Chapter 10, "Creating and Calling Functions," explains how to write functions and use them to divide programs into manageable pieces.

- Chapter 11, "Managing Memory with Pointers," gives a detailed account of the tricky subject of pointers and memory management using the C++ `new` and `delete` operators.

- Chapter 12, "Introducing the Class," introduces the major contribution of C++ to programming: the class, and shows how to use classes to encapsulate data and functions.

- Chapter 13, "Creating and Destroying Objects," shows the nuts and bolts for using C++ classes to create and use objects in object-oriented programming.

- Chapter 14, "Investing in Inheritance," makes clear the mechanics and advantages of using inheritance to build C++ class hierarchies.

- Chapter 15, "Programming with Virtual Functions," explains the technique of runtime-binding of objects to functions, a feature that sometimes goes by the term *polymorphism*.

- Chapter 16, "Handling Exceptions," covers in detail how to deal with program errors using C++ exceptions.

- Chapter 17, "Creating Class Templates," illustrates how to create and use class and function templates, one of the unique features in C++.

- Chapter 18, "Overloading Your Friends," shows the methods and purpose of friend functions and how overloaded functions work.

- Chapter 19, "Overloading Operators," expands on the preceding chapter with a look at overloading C++ operators such as + and / for use with new data types.

- Chapter 20, "Customizing I/O Streams," uses overloaded operator techniques to program I/O stream statements to recognize new data types and to read and write objects in disk files.

- Chapter 21, "Honing Your C++ Skills," covers a number of advanced C++ programming techniques, such as reference counting and the copy-on-write method, and completes this book's tutorial information on C++ programming.

- Chapter 22, "Mastering the Standard string Class," explains how to create and use string data with the standard C++ string class template.

- Chapter 23, "Using the Standard Template Library (STL)," introduces the ANSI C++ standard template container library provided with GNU C++ and other ANSI C++ compilers.

- Chapter 24, "Building Standard Containers," shows examples of storing data in standard C++ template container objects such as vectors and lists.

- Chapter 25, "Applying Standard Algorithms," lists and explains numerous examples showing how to apply ANSI C++ standard algorithms such as sort() on standard template containers and other data structures.

- Chapter 26, "Introducing X Programming," takes a close look at the complex world of programming for X (incorrectly but popularly known also as X Windows), provided with every Linux installation, and also widely available on UNIX systems. This chapter provides the basics for creating an X client that connects to an X server to provide a graphical user interface (GUI).

- Chapter 27, "Controlling Xlib Input and Output," details how to create graphical output using Xlib functions and also how to respond to keyboard and mouse input events sent from an X server.

- Chapter 28, "Breaking Out of Xlib Fundamentals," carries the introduction of Xlib programming into advanced areas including the tricky subject of using X colormaps.

- Chapter 29, "Introducing the V Class Library," introduces V, a portable, object-oriented, class library included on the CD-ROM for X, Microsoft Windows, and OS/2 application development using GNU C++ and other ANSI C++ compilers.

- Chapter 30, "Developing X Software with V," covers many of the features found in V for creating fully developed X client applications complete with pull-down menus, toolbars, graphics, and status bars.

SUMMARY

This book's CD-ROM provides the full Linux-Mandrake 6.0 operating system, including GNU C++, plus all utilities and programming tools. Also on the CD-ROM are this book's source code files and the V C++ class library for programming X windowed client applications for Linux and Microsoft Windows. This chapter gives hardware and software requirements for running Linux and GNU C++. It also lists overviews of the book's six parts and 30 chapters. The next two chapters provide additional tips and instructions for installing and configuring Linux and GNU C++.

2

INSTALLING LINUX

Because this book describes programming for Linux using GNU C++, I don't want to waste your time or mine with a lengthy tutorial on installing and using Linux. Consider this chapter, then, as more of a personal account than a reference. It is by no means a complete guide to installing and configuring Linux, but some of the tips in this chapter might prove useful, especially if you run into difficulties.

If you are new to Linux, you are fortunate because most CD-ROM distributions such as Linux-Mandrake 6.0 included with this book now come with auto-installation utilities. Chances are excellent that you can simply boot to the CD-ROM, install Linux, and turn to the next part to begin learning your way around C++ programming. This wasn't always the case, however, and in the recent past, getting a Linux system up and running usually took much trial and error.

Tip

If you already have Linux installed, try using your existing system. *Don't upgrade without good reason*.

HOW TO INSTALL LINUX

Before installing Linux, a little homework will save you many hours of grief. Linux is complex software, and a successful installation requires more effort than when installing an application or a simpler operating system such as Microsoft Windows. Following are some tips that saved my skin on numerous occasions when installing Linux:

- Back up all existing application, data, and operating system files. Don't just trust your backup software—be sure that you can also restore your files from the backup copies. For safety, make two backups and print out any critical data. As with any operating system software, installing Linux removes all existing files on your system, and a reliable backup is absolutely essential to a successful installation, especially if you intend to create a dual-boot system for Linux and Microsoft Windows.

- Keep a detailed log of every step that you perform during installation. Don't neglect to write down the steps that failed and any solutions you discovered. If you have to reinstall from scratch, or if you need to install Linux on a different computer, these notes will be extremely valuable and can save you hours of frustration. (If you have a spare laptop, consider using it to create this log file.)

- Write down as much information as you can about your system, its hard drive parameters, video system, monitor, video refresh frequencies, processor type and speed, memory capacity, BIOS version, and other facts. Run all available system and setup utilities to obtain facts about your modem, sound card, and other adapters. If possible, print these screens for future reference. *You can't collect too much information*. Keep in mind that, during installation, it might not be possible to obtain essential facts about your hardware, so spend as much time on this step as you can.

- Decide now whether you want to install a standalone Linux system or create dual-boot partitions for Linux and another operating system such as Microsoft Windows. In this chapter are suggestions for creating dual-boot Linux installations using standard MS-DOS tools. Expend some mental energy figuring out the best arrangement for your needs. After you install Linux, it might be difficult to make changes such as converting a single-boot to a dual-boot system, or allocating more or less space to a specific disk partition.

- Turn off your screen blanker. Many users aren't aware that they have such a blanker enabled because it's overridden by a screen saver—for example, one in Microsoft Windows. Boot your computer and press Delete to enter your computer's setup utility. On some systems, you might have to press a different key such as F1 or F2. Look for a command that disables the screen blanker. If you can't find this command, don't worry—not all systems have this feature.

Warning

Did you back up your system? Remember, installing a new operating system such as Linux wipes out *all* existing files. If you didn't back up your system, do so now before continuing.

CD-ROM Booting Trouble

On some systems, the default device boot order prevents booting to a CD-ROM. (My NEC laptop exhibits this problem.) The usual boot order is drive A: (floppy disk), C: (primary hard drive partition), followed by a CD-ROM or, perhaps, an Iomega zip drive. This means that, if the system has an installed operating system on drive C:, it might never attempt to boot to the CD-ROM even if one is inserted, thus causing the automatic installation to fail before it even begins.

The solution is to change the default boot order to boot to the CD-ROM before the primary partition. Usually, you can do this by rebooting the computer and pressing the Delete key. (Remember, on some systems, this might be another key—it's F2 on my laptop.) This should bring up a setup utility with an option to arrange the device boot order. Set your CD-ROM drive to boot *after* drive A: (so you can still recover by booting to a floppy disk) but before drive C:. After installing Linux, you can change the boot order back to its original configuration.

If your system doesn't permit changing the device boot order, and if you can't boot to the CD-ROM included with this book, you'll have to use another method to install Linux. If you can boot to MS-DOS, do that and then insert the CD-ROM (I assume here that it's in drive D:). Enter these commands:

```
d:
cd \dosutils
autoboot.bat
```

You must be running *only* MS-DOS for those commands to work—you cannot, for example, use these commands from a DOS window opened in Microsoft Windows. If you can't boot to MS-DOS, you have to create a special boot floppy disk to install Linux. Complete instructions for creating this disk are in the file Readme on the CD-ROM. View this file using the Microsoft Windows WordPad accessory application.

Note

When booting to plain MS-DOS, you might need to load a driver to access the CD-ROM. You'll also need a copy of the Microsoft mscdex.exe utility for accessing the CD-ROM's file system. This file is included with most MS-DOS and Microsoft Windows software.

STANDALONE INSTALLATIONS

Most current Linux CD-ROMs, including the one packaged with this book, provide automatic setup utilities that make installation a snap, especially if you are creating a dedicated Linux system. Simply boot to the CD-ROM and follow onscreen instructions. The Mandrake-Linux 6.0 automatic installer includes utilities for partitioning your hard drive—you don't need to do this before installation.

If you want to install both Linux and Microsoft Windows, read the next section. Otherwise, turn now to "Installing Mandrake-Linux 6.0" later in this chapter.

DUAL-BOOT INSTALLATIONS

Many software developers need to create dual-boot systems for Linux and Microsoft Windows. This is not as difficult as you might have heard, but it does take a little more work. The most critical part of the process is correctly partitioning your hard drive or drives.

The following steps are from my notes that I kept while installing a dual-boot configuration on the system I used to write this book and its sample programs. The details might be a little different for your system, but the following suggestions should help you puzzle through any difficulties you encounter.

Warning

If you already have a dedicated Linux system installed, and the Linux loader (Lilo) is stored in your system's master boot record (MBR), attempts to reinstall DOS or Microsoft Windows might fail. In such cases, you must low-level-format your hard drive and restore the original MBR before proceeding. On some systems, however, you might be able to use the following steps to delete all disk drive partitions and then use a system CD-ROM to recover the MBR.

First, back up your Windows directories. If possible, back up everything, including the operating system, all applications, and your data files. If you have multiple drives such as C: and D:, be sure that you back up the files in both locations—many backup utilities do not automatically back up multiple drives. However, if it isn't practical to back up every file, you might back up only your data files and then use your Windows CD-ROM and other application source disks to reinstall.

Even after making a complete backup, you still need an original Microsoft Windows CD-ROM or the equivalent set of floppy disks for reinstallation. That might not be true if you can back up over a network, or if you are running MS-DOS backup software. But if your backup software runs under Windows, you must first install the operating system from its original source, install your backup software, and *then* restore your files from your backups.

Warning

Do not perform the following steps until you are sure that you can reinstall Microsoft Windows from an original CD-ROM or set of floppy disks, and that you can restore your backed-up application and data files.

After creating and verifying your backups, the next step is to create an MS-DOS boot disk. Insert a blank disk into drive A:, and from an MS-DOS prompt or a DOS window opened in Microsoft Windows, enter the following command (this erases all files on the disk):

```
format a: /s
```

The /s option copies system boot files to the disk. After formatting is done, copy to the disk the utility programs fdisk.exe, format.com, sys.com, and scandisk.exe that are probably located in C:\DOS or C:\Windows\Command. You might also want to save copies of your autoexec.bat and config.sys files, but be sure to rename them (or place them in a subdirectory on the disk) so that they aren't referenced during booting.

Next, boot to the MS-DOS disk. You are now going to allocate your hard-drive partitions and permanently erase all files on your hard drives. *This is your last chance to back up your files.* When you are ready to proceed (you should be seeing an A: prompt), enter *fdisk* to run the MS-DOS disk partitioning program. If you are asked whether to enable large disk support, answer no.

Select option 4 and write down all existing partition information in your installation log. Now, follow the next steps, which should be generally correct for most readers. However, depending on how many drives you have and their sizes, you might need to make specific changes to suit your system and needs. The following steps assume that you are dividing your system equally between Linux and Microsoft Windows:

1. Delete all logical drives one by one from the extended DOS partition, if there is one.

2. Delete the extended DOS partition.

3. Delete the primary DOS partition.

4. Create a new Primary DOS Partition using 25% to 50% of the hard drive. This *must* be the first partition. You will install Microsoft Windows to this partition.

5. Set the active partition to the Primary DOS Partition that you just created.

6. Optionally create a new extended DOS partition using 25% of the hard drive, or however much space you want. I like to do this to create a separate partition for my data files.

7. If you created an extended DOS partition, also create a logical drive (D:) in the extended DOS partition. You can create more than one logical drive at this time—for example, to divide an extended partition among multiple drive letters.

8. Exit fdisk. If you are asked whether to write the new partition data, answer yes.

9. Leaving the floppy disk in drive A:, reboot by pressing Ctrl-Alt-Del.

You are still booted to the floppy disk, and at this stage in the game, the new partitions are not yet usable. All you've done so far is to apportion your hard drive's disk space. Next, from the A: prompt, you need to format the primary DOS partition to make it usable for MS-DOS and Windows. Do this by entering the following command:

```
format c:
```

The format program warns that you are about to destroy all data on your hard drive C:. Answer yes and wait for formatting to finish. When prompted for a volume label, enter *dos* or another name if you want. If you partitioned any extended logical drives, you must also format each of these. For example, to format drive D:, enter this:

```
format d:
```

Again, answer yes to the warning prompt. When you are finished formatting each logical drive, you are ready to install Microsoft Windows. This should be easy. Remove the floppy disk and insert your original Windows CD-ROM or "setup" floppy disk into the drive. Reboot by pressing Ctrl-Alt-Del. Because there is no operating system on drive C:, booting should automatically transfer to the CD-ROM drive even if it comes after C: in the boot sequence.

The rest should be automatic. Because you formatted only selected drive partitions, Windows "sees" only the space allocated to the primary and, if you created one, an extended partition. The rest of the space is reserved for Linux.

After the Windows installation finishes, and you reboot, you might install auxiliary drivers, applications, and perform other setup chores as you want. However, I suggest you postpone any further steps until you finish installing Linux. If something goes wrong, you might have to start over, so don't waste too much time configuring Windows now. You can do that and restore your backups later after you are finished installing Linux. Continue to the next section to complete your installation.

INSTALLING MANDRAKE-LINUX 6.0

Assuming that you can boot to the included CD-ROM (see the preceding sections if you need help), and after partitioning your drive if you are creating a dual-boot system, you are ready to install Linux. Boot the CD-ROM's automatic installation program and follow instructions onscreen. Most steps are well explained, and you should be able to complete most sections without help. However, the following notes answer some questions that might arise during installation.

Note

Before proceeding, try to find out the refresh frequency of your video monitor and the amount of RAM in your video card. Also determine whether your system clock stores the time in local or GMT (Greenwich Mean Time), also known as Zulu or UTC (Universal Coordinated Time). Most PCs store local, not GMT, time.

Do not select *expert mode* unless you are truly an expert. The installation program performs "auto probing" to determine various facts about your system, and if you disable this feature by selecting expert mode, you must enter system parameters manually.

Three control keys operate all installation screens. Press Tab to move from one item to another. Press Enter to select a highlighted item. Press the spacebar to select or deselect options such as check boxes. The automatic installer does not use a mouse. The bottom of the display also displays function and other keys you can press from time to time.

Tip

Virtual screens are supported during installation. To see them, press Alt-F1 through Alt-F4. Various messages are displayed on these screens, and on them you might find useful information in case of trouble.

After you select some obvious items such as the language to use, and your keyboard type, you'll be asked whether to use Disk Druid or fdisk to partition your drive. Unless you are familiar with the Linux fdisk utility (this is not the same as the MS-DOS fdisk program), you should use Disk Druid. Even if you already partitioned your drive, you need to use this utility to complete the partitioning information for Linux.

Depending on whether you already have any partitions set up, you might need to use the Delete command to delete an existing partition to make room for Linux. Use the Add command to create two partitions—one of type *Linux Swap* and one of type *Linux Native*. The swap partition should be 128MB if you have less than 64MB of RAM, or no less than 80MB if you have more than 64MB of RAM. The native partition should be as large as possible.

You must specify a *mount point* for each partition except for the swap space, which has no mount point. For most users, the *Linux Native* partition's mount point should be named / (a single forward slash, *not* a backslash). If you are setting up multiple partitions—for example, to correspond with multiple hard drives—you may specify other mount points such as /home for user directories.

When you are finished creating partitions and specifying their mount points, continue to the next screen. Save the partition table information, and if you see an option to "Check for bad blocks...," select it by pressing the spacebar. This takes some extra time, but is a wise choice. Formatting of the Linux partitions now takes place. If you have installed Microsoft Windows, those partitions are not affected.

Eventually, you are asked about the components you want to install. This is a lengthy list, and because you probably don't know what many of the components are, you might have trouble deciding which to install. If you have at least one gigabyte of disk space available, the easiest solution is to install everything—enable that option at the end of the component list and go on to the next screen. However, if you choose to install only some components, in addition to the default selections, add at least the following items (items marked with an asterisk are required for this book's sample programs):

- Printer Support
- X Window System* (Chapters 28-30 only)
- KDE or Gnome X Interface or Other Window-managers*
- Emacs (console only), Emacs with X windows (console for X), or XEmacs (graphical interface), or all three programming editors*
- C Development*
- Development Libraries*
- C++ Development*
- Kernel Development
- X Development*
- X Games (recommended)
- KDE and Gnome Development
- Extra documentation (recommended)

Note

You may see an option for installing individual *packages*—archives containing files, patches, and installation information for different pieces of Linux and related software. Don't select this option unless you are an experienced Linux user. Various components need multiple, dependent packages, and not selecting the correct packages might cause installation to fail. You can install individual packages at any time after you install Linux (see Chapter 3, "Installing GNU C++").

When you are finished selecting the components you want to install, the automatic installer creates a file system on your drive partitions. This might take several minutes, especially if you elected to check for bad blocks. There is little or no indication that something is happening during this process, so unless you can see a flashing drive light or other indicator, be patient, even if the computer appears to have fallen asleep.

Soon, you will see numerous installation screens that display all sorts of text, progress bars, and other items while individual components are unpacked and installed. There's nothing for you to do except watch, so you might want to get up, stretch, eat lunch, or have a cup of tea. On a slow system, this stage of the installation might take a half hour or more.

After all selected components are installed, "auto probe" looks for a mouse. Read the resulting screen and make any necessary changes. If you have a two-button mouse, enable the Emulate 3 Buttons check box. Some Linux programs, particularly X software, use three mouse buttons, and unless you have a three-button mouse, it's a good idea to select this feature now.

The next few steps are fairly obvious. You can set up a network at this point, configure your system clock, and select some other services such as printer support. Choose the default settings unless you have good reasons for doing otherwise.

Finally, you come to a most important step—entering the root password. For those who have never used Linux or UNIX, "root" is the name of the so-called super user. When logging in as root, you have privileges to write to, move, change, and delete all files, including system files. This power can be dangerous to the health of the operating system—a single accidental command can easily wipe out an entire file system. So, enter the root password carefully, and if others will use this system, be sure that the password you select can't be easily discovered. You must enter the password twice to ensure you typed it correctly.

After entering the root password, you are asked to create one "normal" user. That's you at most times, except when you become the super user to perform system tasks. Enter a short login name (for example, I use tswan), your real name (just for identification purposes), and a password, which you need to type twice for verification. You can also select a *shell*. This is the software that runs the console, lets you run other programs, and accepts file-system commands. Unless you are familiar with UNIX or Linux shells, select the default, Bash (Bourne Again Shell).

Note

You must enter one normal user at this point so that you can log on to Linux. The super user can add other users later on—for example, if you are setting up a network installation.

After you continue, you are eventually asked where to install the "boot loader." (If you see other screens beforehand, select the default settings for any options you are unsure about.) The boot loader, or Lilo (Linux system loader) is a small utility that boots the Linux or other operating system *kernel*. Usually, the best choice of locations for Lilo is the master boot record (MBR). This is true for standalone and dual-boot systems. In the former case, Lilo automatically boots Linux after a brief pause. On dual-boot setups, Lilo gives you the chance to type *dos* to boot to Microsoft Windows (or another operating system), or just press Enter to boot to Linux. The only reasons for not installing Lilo in the MBR is if you are running another networking operating system such as Windows NT, or if you use another utility to boot to multiple operating systems.

The next and final steps configure X, if you elected to install this graphical interface. The first step in the process installs XFree86—a collection of X servers written for Intel 80x86 processors. After that, you are asked for information about your video system. With luck, your monitor is listed in the lengthy database displayed onscreen. In that case, just select your monitor and continue. If your monitor is not listed, you have to enter its sync frequencies manually. To do that, select Custom and follow onscreen instructions.

Warning

If you do not know your monitor's sync frequencies, do not just try values at random. Entering the wrong frequencies can permanently damage your monitor!

It's okay to select Custom even if you are unsure about the exact sync frequencies for your monitor. In that event, however, you should select a relatively safe entry such as Standard VGA, 640x480 @ 60 Hz or Super VGA, 800x600 @ 56Hz and go on to the next step. At least, this will let you start using Linux until you can figure out the proper settings, which you can specify later.

Select the Probe command to begin an auto-detection phase of the installation that attempts to identify your video hardware. This is done in addition to configuring your monitor—auto-detection probes your video card or circuitry to determine how much memory is available and what display modes are supported. Most modern video systems are correctly identified, and if the displayed test screen looks right, you can proceed. However, if auto-detection fails, you must enter the amount of memory in your video system, the number of bit planes, and select one or more resolutions. If you are unsure about these settings, try the highest values that seem to work. (For best results, X needs a resolution of at least 800-by-600. It works only marginally with a 640-by-480 display.)

Finally, you are asked whether to start Linux in graphics or console mode. I prefer console mode because it shortens boot time, but this requires me to log in and then enter *startx* to run X. If you want to run X at startup, that's fine.

Tip After installation, a complete log of the steps taken is stored in the file /tmp/install.log.

BOOTING LINUX

You have now installed Linux and are ready to begin using your new operating system. Remove all floppy disks and CD-ROMs, and reboot. If you set up your computer as a stand-alone system, Lilo boots directly into Linux after a 5-second pause. If you have a dual-boot system, Lilo waits briefly for you to select an operating system. Enter *dos* to boot into Microsoft Windows, or just press Enter to boot to Linux. If Lilo times out, it automatically boots the Linux kernel (but see the tip at the end of this section to change the pause time).

The first step after booting is to log in as a user. You must do this even if you are running Linux on a standalone workstation. During installation, you were given the opportunity to create a login name and password. Enter these now at the login prompt.

Some users see a graphics display for logging in; others log in at a character-based terminal. Either way, after logging in, you should see a prompt of some kind in a terminal window, probably ending with a dollar sign ($). If not, look for a button, a command, or an icon of some sort that opens a terminal window. This might be called a console or a terminal. You'll use this console mode to compile and run the sample programs in this book, as explained in the coming chapters.

If you see a character prompt after logging in, and you want to run the X windowing system, enter *startx* at the prompt. Because of the many configurations and window managers available, I can't predict what you'll see at this point. Probably, you see a graphics screen with a terminal window, or a desktop manager of some sort. After X starts, if you don't see a terminal or console window, look for a command or button to open one so that you can compile and run this book's sample programs.

If your graphics display doesn't suit you, exit X (or choose a "logout" option if you find one), and get back to a login prompt. (Try typing *exit* if you are still logged in.) Enter *root* to log in as the super user, and then from a console shell prompt, enter *Xconfigurator* to configure X. This is the same configuration program that you ran during installation. Select a different resolution or enter new video parameters until you are satisfied.

> **Tip**
>
> To extend the time that Lilo waits before booting, log in as root and edit the file /etc/lilo.conf. Enter or edit a command such as `delay=5000` to specify a pause time in tenths of seconds. For some reason, this command is misnamed `timeout=` in countless versions of Linux.

SHUTTING DOWN

When you are finished using Linux, you must shut down your system properly. Failing to shut down can cause the loss of files because of the way Linux and UNIX systems keep their directory information in memory. Although this provides for a faster file system (a necessity in a networked environment), it means that a power loss can have serious consequences—all the more reason to attach a UPS to your system.

To shut down Linux, there might be a button you can click or a command to select from a menu. Some X window managers provide an *Exit* command that returns you to a character-based console; others return you to the login screen. In any case, to shut down, you must log in as root (the super user). Do that and enter the root password you specified during installation, and then enter the following command to shut down Linux:

```
$ shutdown -h now
```

The `-h` option halts the computer. The word `now` performs the command right away. You can instead enter the number of minutes to wait before shutting down—but that's necessary only if you are the system administrator in a network environment, and you want to give users fair warning of an imminent shutdown. After you see the message "System halted," or similar, you can switch off power. (If you have power-management facilities on your system, it might turn off automatically at this point.) To reboot instead of shutting down, enter the following:

```
$ shutdown -r now
```

After Linux shuts down, the `-r` option reboots the computer. When you see the Lilo prompt, you can enter *dos* to boot to Microsoft Windows, or press Enter to get back to Linux.

Tip

Press the usual PC reboot keys, Ctrl-Alt-Del, to reboot if you halted the computer and want to continue. Some Linux systems permit shutting down by pressing these keys, but for better safety, you should always log in as root and enter a proper shutdown command.

MOUNTING DISKS AND DRIVES

One of the most perplexing subjects for Linux newcomers is how to mount and use disks of various kinds. Even getting Linux to recognize a floppy disk might take some wrangling. I end this chapter with some additional information that should help answer any questions you have about mounting different types of disks. If you want to start using GNU C++, however, you can turn to the next chapter now and read the following information later.

GENERAL DISK USAGE

Keep in mind that under Linux you cannot simply insert a disk and use it. Unlike with MS-DOS and Microsoft Windows, Linux requires you to *mount* a disk before you can access its files. To ensure that all directory information is updated on a disk, you must *unmount* it before removing the physical disk. Failing to unmount a disk before removing it may cause a loss of information.

Tip

Some computers lock the drive door until a disk is unmounted; however, this isn't true for all computers nor for all types of disk drives. If you can't remove a disk from a drive, try unmounting it as explained in the following sections.

Mounting a disk attaches it to the file system and makes the disk's files available as though they existed in a subdirectory. In Linux, there are no A:, C:, or D: drives—all disks appear as directories in the *same* file system as your hard drive. On most installations, mounted disks appear in the /mnt directory, but it's possible to mount a disk in a different location named anything you want.

The default mount directory, /mnt, is just an empty subdirectory in your Linux file system. Mounting a disk *attaches* it to that directory. For example, after mounting a CD-ROM to /mnt/cdrom, that directory references the files on the disk. To store files on the mounted disk (assuming that you can write to this type of media), simply copy the files to the mount location. When you unmount the disk, Linux updates the directory. The actual writing of large files might not take place until this time.

MOUNTING MS-DOS PARTITIONS

If you created a dual-boot system for Linux and Microsoft Windows, you can make your Windows file systems available under Linux. (However, you cannot access Linux files from Windows, or at least there is no straightforward way to do so.) The first step is to create directories for the mount points. Do this in Linux by logging in as root and then entering commands at a console prompt such as the following:

```
$ cd /mnt
$ mkdir msdosc
$ mkdir msdosd
```

You now have two directories, /mnt/msdosc and /mnt/msdosd, that you can use to mount your MS-DOS partitions. You need to know the device names for each partition, which you can find using fdisk or the equivalent utility. (You must be the super user to run the Linux /sbin/fdisk utility.) For example, to mount my C: and D: drives, I can enter these commands:

```
$ mount -t msdos /dev/hda1 /mnt/msdosc
$ mount -t msdos /dev/hda5 /mnt/msdosd
```

PART

I

CH

2

Tip

To become the super user, instead of logging off and back in, you can simply enter *su* at a console prompt and enter the root password. Type *exit* to give up your super powers and return to normal status.

The -t option specifies the disk type (msdos here). The last two arguments give the device name and mount point directories. If the commands are successful, you should now have access to all files on C: and D:. (However, depending on the type of file access table, or FAT, in use on your MS-DOS or Microsoft Windows partitions, long filenames might be truncated to the old MS-DOS 8.3 format.)

Determining the proper device names might take some digging. On my system, /dev/hda1 is the first partition and references my C: drive. This should be the same for all users. The /dev/hda5 device is the first *logical* drive (my D: drive), which is actually stuffed inside an extended partition. *That* partition's device name is /dev/hda2, but we don't want to mount the partition; we want to mount the logical drive *inside* the partition (which might contain multiple logical drives). Because only four primary partitions are permitted, logical partitions begin with /dev/hda5, /dev/hda6, and so on.

Hard drive partitions are unmounted automatically when you shut down Linux. Because you can't physically remove hard disks from their drives, it isn't necessary to unmount them. However, you may do so by issuing the following commands (again, you might have to be the super user):

```
$ umount /mnt/msdosc
$ umount /mnt/msdosd
```

AUTOMATIC MS-DOS DRIVE MOUNTING

If you want to have Linux automatically mount your MS-DOS partitions at boot time, log in as root and edit the file /etc/fstab with the necessary mounting information. Unless specified as noauto, all devices in /etc/fstab are mounted if possible when Linux starts. The information in the file also makes using the mount command easier. After entering the correct data in /etc/fstab, you can simply specify the mount point to mount any device. The mount utility retrieves the drive's type and its device name from the information in /etc/fstab.

Listing 2.1 shows the /etc/fstab file on my system. Do *not* blindly copy this data to your file! Before creating an entry in your file, you should have tested the command thoroughly as suggested in the preceding section. After successfully mounting a disk in a drive, you can enter that device's information into /etc/fstab. Copy and preface any modified lines with # to turn them into comments for future reference. For safety, make a copy of the unmodified file and also note in your installation log any changes you make.

LISTING 2.1 THE AUTHOR'S /ETC/FSTAB FILE

```
/dev/hda4    /            ext2     defaults        1 1
/dev/hda3    swap         swap     defaults        0 0
/dev/fd0     /mnt/floppy  ext2     noauto,user     0 0
/dev/cdrom   /mnt/cdrom   iso9660  noauto,ro,user  0 0
/dev/hda1    /mnt/msdosc  msdos    defaults        0 0
/dev/hda5    /mnt/msdosd  msdos    defaults        0 0
/dev/hdd4    /mnt/zip     ext2     noauto,user     0 0
none         /proc        proc     defaults        0 0
```

Warning

Listing 2.1, /etc/fstab, is for reference only. It is not included on this book's CD-ROM. Do not copy or use this file on your system. Use it only as a guide for configuring the actual file-system devices listed in your installation's /etc/fstab file.

In addition to adding entries for /mnt/msdosc and /mnt/msdosd, I also changed the entries for /dev/fd0 (floppy drive 0, otherwise known as A:) and /dev/cdrom to include the word user in the fourth column. This change allows me to mount these devices while logged in under my username instead of root. I also specified noauto for these entries to prevent them from being mounted automatically during booting because I normally don't keep disks in the drives. (See the sections on Iomega zip drives near the end of this chapter for the meaning of the next-to-last entry.) With my /etc/fstab file, to mount a Linux floppy disk, I can insert it and simply type the following:

```
$ mount /mnt/floppy
```

This causes the mount utility to read the device information for that mount point from /etc/fstab. I can similarly mount a CD-ROM by inserting it and then typing this:

```
$ mount /mnt/cdrom
```

To unmount either type of disk is equally simple. The following commands unmount a floppy and CD-ROM, making it safe to remove the floppy and, because my system locks the door for a mounted disk, to spit out the CD-ROM disk:

```
$ umount /mnt/floppy
$ umount /mnt/cdrom
```

Tip

The correct command is spelled *u*mount, not *un*mount, which I frequently type and then waste several minutes trying to figure out why the command no longer works.

Use the preceding commands to mount and unmount *only* Linux formatted disks. Do not mount MS-DOS disks this way. Instead, you can simply insert an MS-DOS formatted disk into A: and run the Linux DOS utility programs such as mdir and mcopy to access your files. MS-DOS disks never have to be mounted and unmounted.

For CD-ROMS, you don't have to be concerned about the type of file system because most all CDs, except for some very old ones, are formatted using the ISO9660 standard. This is true whether the contents of the CD-ROM are intended for use with Microsoft Windows, Linux, or another operating system. ISO9660 CD-ROM disks are directly usable from MS-DOS, Linux, and other operating systems.

MOUNTING A CD-ROM

See Listing 2.1 for the /etc/fstab entry to enable a CD-ROM drive. If you install this book's CD-ROM, a similar entry is created automatically, but you might want to add user to the fourth column so that ordinary users can mount CD-ROM disks. Read the other notes in the preceding section for mounting instructions. The mount point for CD-ROMs is usually /mnt/cdrom.

USING FLOPPY DISKS

As mentioned, it's important to know whether a disk is formatted for MS-DOS or Linux. Be sure to label all disks accordingly. MS-DOS disks can be used without mounting—but you must run utilities such as mdir and mcopy to access files on them.

To create a native Linux disk requires two steps. First, you need to format the disk. Next, you have to install a file system. There's more than one way to give these commands, so try them on a scratch disk and make extensive tests copying files before trusting the disk to store important information.

You must be the super user to format a floppy disk, so the first step is to upgrade yourself using the *su* command and entering root's password (you could alternatively log in as root):

```
$ su
Password:
```

Insert a blank 3.5-inch disk into the A: drive and format it with the following command (this erases all files on the disk). For reference, I show the formatting program's output:

```
$ fdformat /dev/fd0H1440
Double-sided, 80 tracks, 18 sec/track. Total capacity 1440 kB.
Formatting ... done
Verifying ... done
```

When formatting is complete, you must install a file system to be able to use the disk to store Linux files. (However, a "raw" disk utility could now be used to transfer a binary image to the formatted disk—a technique often employed to quickly manufacture copies of system disks.) To create a file system, use the mkfs utility in the /sbin (system binaries) directory. You must specify this directory unless you actually logged in as root. Again, I show some of the program's output:

```
$ /sbin/mkfs -t ext2 -m 0 /dev/fd0H1440 1440
mke2fs 1.10, 24-Apr-97 for EXT2 FS 0.5b, 95/08/09
Linux ext2 filesystem format
360 inodes, 1440 blocks
0 blocks (0.00%) reserved for the super user
...
8192 blocks per group, 8192 fragments per group
360 inodes per group
Writing inode tables: done
Writing superblocks and filesystem accounting information: done
```

The -m 0 option in the command reserves zero bytes for the super user. Normally, 10% is set aside, but this is probably not necessary when formatting small floppy disks. Carefully specify the device name fd0H1440—in that name, 0H is the digit zero and a capital H.

Alternatively, try the following simpler command, which runs the mke2fs utility, also located in /sbin:

```
$ /sbin/mke2fs /dev/fd0 1440
```

Whichever command works for you, when you are finished creating file systems, be sure to relinquish super-user status by typing the following command:

```
$ exit
```

That logs you out, or it causes you to lose your super powers and return to a normal, mild-mannered human being who, of course, cannot be trusted to format floppy disks.

MOUNTING IOMEGA ZIP MS-DOS DISKS

If you have an Iomega zip drive, you can use zip disks in much the same way as you do disks. Ordinarily, a zip disk comes formatted for use with MS-DOS and Microsoft Windows. Internally, the disks are formatted and recognized as hard drives, but they are configured as logical drives in the same way as drives such as D: and E: in an extended hard-drive partition.

The trick for mounting one of these disks is to discover the drive's Linux device name. Watch during booting for a line that mentions IOMEGA ZIP DRIVE or something like that and note the device name. This is probably /dev/hdd, but don't count on it. You can't mount that device directly because, as in all extended hard-drive partitions, the file system is actually encased in a logical drive. On my system, that logical drive's device name is /dev/hdda, and so to mount the disk, I can enter commands such as the following (the first command is needed only once to create the mount-point directory):

```
$ mkdir /mnt/zip
$ mount -t msdos /dev/hdd4 /mnt/zip
...
$ umount /mnt/zip
```

Because this makes the zip disk appear to be an msdos hard drive, you can use Linux commands to access files and directories just as you can with a mounted hard drive partition such as /mnt/msdosc. You don't have to use the mcopy and mdir commands, which are intended for use only with MS-DOS floppy disks.

CREATING LINUX ZIP DISKS

Although you can use MS-DOS-formatted Iomega zip disks with Linux commands, better performance is possible by installing a Linux file system. This also makes zip disks ideal for backups. For example, to back up the directory and all its files for this book, I simply enter these commands:

```
$ mount /mnt/zip
$ cp -a gpl /mnt/zip
$ umount /mnt/zip
```

The gpl—GNU Programming for Linux—in this command is the directory where I store this book's files. The -a option, for "archive," is just a simple way to copy many files and directories with one command. To use a zip drive this way on your system, you need to install a file system on the disk. You also might want to modify /etc/fstab so that you can mount and unmount zip disks without having to become the super user. However, you must be root to perform these steps, so enter this command first:

```
$ su
Password:
```

Note

Do *not* mount a zip disk before formatting. If you are not sure whether it's mounted, unmount the disk by typing ***umount /mnt/zip***.

Next, follow these steps to install a Linux file system on a zip disk. This removes all existing files from the disk, so be sure you want to do that before continuing. I assume here that the Iomega drive device name is /dev/hdd, which might be different for you. Because zip disks are configured as hard drives, they have partition tables that you can examine using the Linux fdisk utility. With a zip disk inserted but not mounted, enter this command:

```
$ /sbin/fdisk /dev/hdd
```

Warning

Be *extremely* careful when running the fdisk utility. Some of its commands permanently erase files. Remember also that you are the super user, and your powers include read and write permission for *all* files. Finally, be aware that the fdisk utility might understand different commands than described here, or it might have an entirely different display depending on the version of Linux you are running. Consider the following instructions as suggested guidelines only and proceed with caution.

Type *m* for a list of fdisk commands. Type *p* to print the zip disk's partition information, which should look something like this:

```
Disk /dev/hdd: 64 heads, 96 sectors, 32 cylinders
Units = cylinders of 6144 * 512 bytes
Device    Boot Begin Start End Blocks Id System
/dev/hdd4 *    1     1      32  98288  6  DOS 16-bit >=32M
```

You might also see some error messages about block number discrepancies. If so, ignore them. This step merely verifies that you are operating on your zip disk and haven't accidentally specified a primary hard-drive partition.

Next, use the *d* command to delete partition number 4 (the only one allocated). Create a new primary partition with the *n* command, making it number 4 and specifying cylinders 1 to 32. If your disk is a different size, get the correct cylinder numbers from the Start and End columns in the original partition table. Finally, use the *w* command to write the partition table to the disk and then type *q* to quit.

You can now run /sbin/mke2fs to create a new file system on the zip disk. Do that by entering the following command:

```
$ /sbin/mke2fs /dev/hdd4
```

You should see a bunch of information onscreen, which might help you verify that the disk is formatted correctly. After the command finishes (it doesn't take long), test the disk by mounting it. First create a mount point if you haven't already done so by typing this:

```
$ mkdir /mnt/zip
```

You can name the mount point anything you want, but /mnt/zip seems logical enough. Mount the native Linux zip disk by issuing the following command:

```
$ mount -t ext2 /dev/hdd4 /mnt/zip
```

So that you can more easily mount a zip disk, and also so that you don't have to become the super user to do that, add commands such as the following to /etc/fstab:

```
/dev/hdd4    /mnt/msdoszip  msdos  noauto,user  0 0
/dev/hdd4    /mnt/zip       ext2   noauto,user  0 0
```

I purposely specify different mount points for my MS-DOS zip disks and those formatted with a native Linux file system, although this isn't strictly necessary. Simply use the mount command described in the preceding section. (If you mount the wrong type of disk, the mount utility displays an error message.) I know I've said this before, but do remember to unmount your zip disk when finished using it, and if you are still the super user, also return to your normal login rank:

```
$ umount /mnt/zip
$ exit
```

GETTING ONLINE INFORMATION

Use the Linux info utility to view online information about operating system commands, GNU C++, and dozens of other topics. The info utility is intended to replace the age-old UNIX man program—not a sexist reference, but an abbreviation for "manual." Although man is available in Linux, the info program generally gives more up-to-date information.

To use info, type its name at a console prompt optionally followed by the name of the item you want to know more about. For example, enter the following command for information about the Emacs programmer's editor:

```
$ info emacs
```

When you are finished viewing information, type *q* to quit info and return to a console prompt. Some info topics seem to be case sensitive, so if an info command doesn't work, check the exact spelling of the item you are trying to find. For a tutorial on using the info utility, type *info info*. For help using man, type *man man* or *info man*.

Throughout this book, I suggest various info pages you might like to view for more information about a subject. However, don't wait for me to suggest using info to answer any questions you might have while reading this book. In time, you'll find info to be one of the most useful information utilities at your disposal.

SUMMARY

It is my sincere wish that you are reading this summary after happily and successfully installing Linux on your computer. It's difficult in one small chapter to provide a complete guide to installing and configuring an operating system as large and as capable as Linux, but this chapter should have given you a springboard for getting started as well as providing tips for formatting and using hard drives, floppy disks, and Iomega zip disks. Steps in this chapter suggested ways to create standalone Linux systems, and dual-boot systems for Linux and Microsoft Windows. The next chapter explains how to install the GNU C++ compiler, if necessary, along with this book's listing files.

## CHAPTER 3

Installing GNU C++

Because GNU C++ comes with Linux, installing the operating system may already have installed the compiler and other necessary files. In that case, you can skip to "How to Install This Book's Sample Programs" in this chapter. However, depending on the options you selected during installation, you might have to install additional files using one of the methods explained here.

WHERE TO GET GNU C++

The best source for GNU C++ is right here, on this book's CD-ROM. However, if you want to upgrade to a newer release, or if you already have Linux or UNIX running and you want to add GNU C++ to your system, begin your search for the necessary files at the following Web site:

`http://www.gnu.org/`

You'll have to hunt for the page that offers the release files, and because this is a very busy server, you might need to download the files using a mirror FTP (file transfer protocol) site. At this writing, the FTP location of the files is `ftp://ftp.gnu.org/gnu/gcc`. At the minimum, you need the GCC compiler, all associated library files, and preferably, any documentation files you come across. These files are provided in "tarred and zipped" format. For example, a recent release of GNU C++ comes in a file cryptically named something like gcc-g++-2.95.1.tar.gz. Files for upgrading an installed compiler also are available. These are generally smaller than the full system and take less time to download.

The "gz" filename extension indicates the file is compressed using GNU's gzip file compression utility. You can unzip the file by using gunzip. The "tar" in the filename indicates that the files are packed using the age-old UNIX tar (tape archive) utility, which despite its name, works just fine with disks and other media, not only tape. For more information on these utilities, read their online documentation by entering the commands *info tar*, *info gzip*, and *info gunzip*. Also read the following sections for more installation suggestions.

How to Install the GNU C++ Compiler

Before you go to the trouble of installing GNU C++, check whether the compiler is already installed. To do that, get to a console prompt and enter the following command (notice that the correct command is not *c++* but **g++**, the *g* referring to GNU C++):

```
$ g++ -v
Reading specs from /usr/lib/gcc-lib/i686-pc-linux-gnu/
➥pgcc-2.91.66/specs
gcc version pgcc-2.91.66 19990314 (egcs-1.1.2 release)
```

If you see a similar response—don't worry about the version number or exact filename spellings—you are ready to go. However, if the compiler's version number is earlier than 2.3, you might need to install an upgrade to make full use of this book's advanced chapters. If all seems well, turn to "How to Install This Book's Sample Programs."

If you receive an error message such as "bash: g++: command not found," you need to install GNU C++ before continuing. Basically, you have four choices:

PART

I

CH

3

- Reinstall Mandrake-Linux 6.0 from scratch using this book's CD-ROM.
- Upgrade your installation to add GNU C++ and associated library files, using the upgrade option on this book's CD-ROM automatic installer.
- Install individual packages from this book's CD-ROM using the Red Hat Package Manager (RPM), either from a console window or using an X window manager.
- Download the GNU C++ compiler release files from the Internet and install the files manually (not recommended unless you know your way around Linux and UNIX).

The following sections discuss each of these installation methods. The first three methods are relatively simple. Of these, the first two methods can be used by anyone. The third requires you to know your system's root password. The last method might require additional research into how your system is organized and also requires you to know the root password.

Reinstalling Everything

This is the easiest method. Reboot to the attached CD-ROM, and follow instructions in Chapter 2, "Installing Linux," to install the operating system and GNU C++. Be sure to select the proper components during installation, as suggested in the chapter. GNU C++ is *not* installed by default unless you select that component. If you have the room, install Everything.

Upgrading an Existing Installation

If you have already installed Mandrake-Linux 6.0, but neglected to install the GNU C++ compiler, you can add the necessary files without affecting existing user directories and files. Follow these steps:

1. Back up all files. Even though upgrading your installation doesn't affect user directories, making a complete backup before upgrading is a good idea in case something goes wrong.

2. Insert the CD-ROM and reboot. If Linux is running, to reboot, log on as root and enter the command *shutdown -r now*.

3. When you see the opening installation screen, press Enter for a normal installation—do not select expert mode. Select various options such as your keyboard type and language.

4. Eventually, you are shown a window titled Installation Path. Choose the *Upgrade* button (press Tab and Enter). This bypasses the drive-partitioning parts of the installation and proceeds straight to building a database of installed packages. This takes a few minutes.

5. Eventually, you see another window titled Upgrade Packages. Answer *Yes* to customize the set of packages already installed. Unfortunately, this part of the installation is not the same as the original that presents components for installation—instead, you must specify each package. Select a listed entry to display the individual packages. At the least, select *Development/Debuggers* (gdb, xxgdb), *Development/Languages* (cpp, libstdc++-devel, pgcc, pgcc-c++), *Development/Libraries* (glib-devel, glibc-devel, gtk+-devel, readline-devel, Xaw3d-devel, XFree86-devel), and *Development/Tools* (automake, make, patch, and others). You may also select other packages at this time. Select the *Done* command when you are finished, but review all your selections before selecting Done—the only way to return to this step is to start over.

> **Tip**
>
> A log of the upgraded packages is saved in /tmp/upgrade.log. Read and save this file after the upgrade installation finishes.

The rest of the upgrade-installation is automatic, although you might have to enter responses in a few more display screens. When installation finishes, Linux reboots. Be sure to remove the CD-ROM when this happens.

After logging on, enter the test command *g++ -v* to check that GNU C++ is properly installed. If so, you can skip to "How to Install This Book's Sample Programs."

INSTALLING PACKAGES WITH RPM

Another way to install packages is to run the Red Hat Package Manager (RPM). This utility has become a standard on many different types of Linux, so even if you aren't using Red Hat's version, you probably have RPM on your system. (The included CD-ROM comes with RPM for console and X display modes.) RPM maintains a database of installed packages, so you can use it also to check whether a particular file is installed.

A *package* is an archive that contains the files for a single program, or for a group of programs. A package might also contain updates in the form of patches, and it includes directory and installation information. You can find packages on various Linux Web sites and also on most Linux CD-ROMs. They are typically located in directories named RPMS (binary packages) and SRPMS (source file packages). These directories are probably located inside one or another subdirectory, so you might have to hunt for them.

> **Note**
>
> RPM package files on this book's CD-ROM are located in the directory /mnt/cdrom/Mandrake/RPMS.

To install a package from a CD-ROM, you first have to mount the disk (see Chapter 2, "Installing Linux," for help if you get stuck with this step). Probably, you can simply insert the CD-ROM and enter this command at a console prompt.

```
mount /mnt/cdrom
```

If you are running X, you might find a CD-ROM icon that you can click with the mouse. This should also mount the CD-ROM and display its files.

After mounting the CD-ROM, you can run RPM and install package files, which end with the filename extension .rpm. Depending on your version of Linux, however, the package filenames for GNU C++ and associated libraries are probably different. Look for package files beginning with the words pgcc and pgcc-c++, or if you are not using this book's CD-ROM, those beginning with gcc and egcs. You also need to install various library files, particularly those beginning with the words libc, libelf, and libstdc++.

> **Note**
>
> To save space here, I don't always show complete package filenames. For example, the egcs package file on one of my Linux systems is named egcs-1.0.2-12.src.rpm. Here, I might refer to that file as egcs.rpm without the embedded version numbers. Remember to press the Tab key to more easily type filenames such as these. For example, type *egcs-1* and press Tab to automatically complete the rest of the filename.

If you are running X and a window manager installed by this book's CD-ROM, log in as root, and then to install GNU C++, follow the steps listed next. You might have to repeat these steps to install other packages such as any library files needed to compile various programs in this book:

1. Insert this book's CD-ROM and click on the icon labeled CDROM to mount the disk.

2. Start RPM by clicking its icon.

3. Select RPM's *File*, *Open* command.

4. Click the up arrow to find the directory path /mnt/cdrom.

5. Open the /mnt/cdrom directory, and then go to the Mandrake or Red Hat subdirectories.

6. From there, go to the subdirectory RPMS. This should open a window listing numerous package files. (The complete pathname of the directory is /mnt/cdrom/Mandrake/RPMS.)

PART

I

CH

3

7. Package filenames keep changing with every release of Linux, and they differ among vendors. For the GNU C++ compiler on this book's CD-ROM, find the file pgcc-c++.rpm. On another disk, this might be named gcc-c++.rpm or perhaps egcs-c++.rpm (minus any version numbers in the filenames).

8. Open the package file by double-clicking its name, and then from the resulting dialog box, select the *Install* button.

9. If you did not log on as the super user, you see an error message and are asked for the root password. (This window might be confusingly hidden behind another.) Enter the password and try again. Installation of the package files should proceed.

10. Repeat the preceding steps to install any other packages you need. You can use these steps also to install components such as games, utilities, and source code files.

You should now be able to run the GNU C++ compiler. Log out and then log back in using your normal username. Enter *g++ -v* to check whether GNU C++ has been successfully installed. Table 3.1 lists the package filenames (not including version information) that you need to install to compile this book's sample programs.

TABLE 3.1 PACKAGE FILES NEEDED FOR THIS BOOK

Filename	Description
cpp.rpm	Compiler preprocessor
emacs.rpm	Emacs programming editor
gdb.rpm	GNU debugger
gtk+.rpm	X toolkit
libstdc++.rpm	Standard C++ library
make.rpm	Auto-compilation make utility
pgcc.rpm	The GNU C compiler
pgcc-c++.rpm	The GNU C++ compiler
readline.rpm	Text readline tools
Xaw3d.rpm	Athena X widgets
X11R6.rpm	X libraries and tools

You can also install packages from a console prompt. This works whether you run Linux using X or a plain text-only display. Log in as root, or issue the command *su* and enter the root password to become the super user. Then, follow these steps (for demonstration, the instructions explain how to install the GNU C++ standard C++ development libraries in the package files libstdc++.rpm and libstdc++-devel.rpm):

1. Insert the CD-ROM, and enter the following command to mount the disk (the dollar sign is the shell prompt; don't type it):

```
$ mount /mnt/cdrom
```

2. Change to the directory containing the package file you want to install (you might have to replace Mandrake with Red Hat or another vendor name if you are not using this book's CD-ROM). Enter the following command:

```
$ cd /mnt/cdrom/Mandrake/RPMS
```

3. To display an information header for a package (always a good idea before installing the files), run the RPM utility program by typing a command such as the following. Remember to type only part of the filename and press Tab to automatically complete its version information:

```
$ rpm -qip libstdc++-dev
```

4. Replace -qip with -qlp to list the package's files. In some cases, however, the files might be further compressed. See "How to Install This Book's Sample Programs" for help unpacking these types of files if you find them in a package. When you are finished looking at a package, install it by giving the command (again, press Tab to complete the full filename):

```
$ rpm -i libstdc++-dev
```

PART
I
CH
3

Note If you receive an error during installation, did you remember to log on as root? To check, type ***whoami***.

If the package is already installed, RPM detects that fact and displays an error message; otherwise, it installs the files. In some cases, you might have to follow the installation with a build command that further unpacks the necessary files. The details for this step differ among Linux vendors, but in general, after installing a package, look for a SPECS subdirectory that contains a package specification file ending with the name .spec. For example, using a Red Hat Linux distribution, change to the SPECS directory and use the following RPM command to build the package:

```
$ cd /usr/src/redhat/SPECS/
$ rpm -bp filename.spec
```

You might need to use a similar command to complete the installation of various source code packages. The resulting files might be found in another directory named BUILD or SOURCE. When you are finished installing and building any packages you need, be sure to type ***exit*** to log off, and then log back in using your normal username. For online instructions about the RPM utility, type ***info rpm***.

DOWNLOADING GNU C++ FROM THE INTERNET

Unless you are an experienced Linux or UNIX programmer, I suggest using one of the preceding methods to install GNU C++ and other packages. However, if you want to download the files and install the compiler manually, follow these instructions. In addition to the suggestions here, you will need to select various options, enter configurations, copy files, and change system settings specific to your system. The following notes will help you get started, but because every system is different, it's not possible to give complete installation instructions here. (You can use the following commands to install other files such as a program written in C++, or development source code files.)

After downloading a "tarred and zipped" file, you need to unpack it into a directory. Always create a temporary directory for this purpose to prevent accidentally installing a few hundred files in your home or other directory. After unpacking, look for Readme or similarly named files for additional instructions.

> **Note**
>
> MS-DOS and Microsoft Windows users who download Linux and UNIX files might find their filenames scrambled. This happens because Microsoft operating systems do not like filenames with multiple extensions. One solution is to rename your files—for example, from filename.tar.gz to filename-tar.gz (the hyphen may also be an underscore). If you copy a "tarred and zipped" file from a DOS or Windows directory to a Linux directory, you might find the filename truncated to something like file~1.gz. In that case, note the original filename and use the Linux mv command to rename the file before proceeding.

To decompress and unpack a "tarred and zipped" file, copy it to an empty directory, and then enter commands such as the following:

```
$ gunzip gcc-g++-2_95_1_tar.gz
$ tar -tf gcc-g++-2_95_1_tar
$ tar -xvf gcc-g++-2_95_1_tar
```

The first command decompresses the file and automatically removes the .gz filename extension. The second command, which you can skip if you want, lists the tarred files before unpacking them. The third command unpacks the files and creates any necessary subdirectories. You don't have to type the full filenames—just type the first few letters and press Tab to complete the names automatically (assuming that your shell supports this feature).

At this point, you need to look for a Readme or other file containing compilation and additional installation instructions. In many cases, you merely need to set up a configuration file, and then run the make utility to compile and copy files to their final resting places. (If you have trouble, check the Web sites listed in Appendix C, "Web and FTP Sites," for help. Look for FAQ sheets and other online help files.)

Caldera OpenLinux Users

If you are using Caldera's OpenLinux, especially version 2.2, you might discover that the automated installation does not properly install the GNU C++ compiler. This is so even if you select the option All Recommended Packages. Following is an email message from this book's technical editor, Richard Blum, describing the problem and explaining the steps he took to resolve it. Perhaps his account will help you install GNU C++ if you experience the same difficulty. Rich writes…

"I decided to upgrade to Caldera OpenLinux 2.2. After a couple of failed attempts, I was finally able to get it running on my PC. When I tried to compile the first program, I received a 'command not found' error. I checked, and sure enough, g++ was not on the system. The GNC C compiler, gcc, was installed and worked fine, but not g++. I checked the installed programs, and the egcs c++ module was not loaded (even though I had selected the Install All Packages option). I tried to manually install the package, but RPM claimed that it failed on 'dependencies.' Thinking that I must have seriously messed something up, I reinstalled the entire operating system, but received the same result. By now, I was getting worried. I checked the Caldera Web site, and discovered a 'KnowledgeBase' article on fixing egcs dependencies (REF#990524-0005). The site offers several new .rpm files to download and install. After I did that, everything worked fine."

How to Install This Book's Sample Programs

All this book's sample programs are provided on the CD-ROM packaged with this book. All files are provided in full source code form and must be compiled before you can run them. In addition, see Chapter 29, "Introducing the V Class Library," for instructions on installing the V C++ class library for X programming, also provided on the CD-ROM.

Note

> Listings printed in this book do not include extraneous comments, and in some cases, have been stripped of duplicated programming to save space. This might cause line numbers shown in the text—for example, in descriptions of how to use the GNU debugger—to differ from those line numbers on your screen. The full source code for all listings is on the CD-ROM. For best results, use the CD-ROM files to compile the programs as instructed in the chapters.

Mounting the CD-ROM

This book's source code files are packed into a single "tarred and zipped" file, named gplsrc-tar.gz (that's gpl for GNU Programming for Linux). To find this file, insert the CD-ROM and then mount it by issuing the following command:

```
$ mount /mnt/cdrom
```

If you have trouble, see Chapter 2, "Installing Linux." for detailed instructions on mounting disks. (On some systems, you might have to become the super user by typing *su* and entering the root password to give the preceding command.)

Unpacking the Files

After mounting the CD-ROM, locate the gplsrc-tar.gz file (it might be in a subdirectory), and copy it to your home directory or to a new one created using mkdir:

```
$ cp gplsrc-tar.gz /home/yourname
$ cd /home/yourname
```

To unpack the archive, issue the following two commands. This creates, inside the current directory, a single new directory named src, with subdirectories containing the source files organized by chapter:

```
$ gunzip gplsrc-tar.gz
$ tar -xvf gplsrc-tar
```

The first command decompresses the .gz file and removes the filename extension. The second command unpacks the archive using the Linux tar utility and creates all chapter subdirectories such as C04 and C05. After unpacking the files, you can remove the original archive, unmount the CD-ROM, and if you are logged in as the super user, return to a normal user by issuing these commands:

```
$ umount /mnt/cdrom
$ exit
$ cd /home/yourname
$ rm gplsrc.tar
```

You can now change to a chapter subdirectory and compile the programs found there (in some cases, you might have to look further into other subdirectories to find listing files):

```
$ cd src/c04
$ g++ welcome.cpp
$ ./a.out
```

COMPARING C AND C++

C programmers reading this book might want to hunt for information specific to C++. Following is a list of key differences between C and C++ that will help you focus on the topics you need to learn to begin programming "the C++ way." Beginners and newcomers to C and C++ can skip this section, which uses terms familiar to C programmers but not yet introduced in this book. You might find the following information useful also for upgrading C programs to C++, or just for deciphering a C program's source code statements:

- C and C++ generally use the same syntax, operators, expressions, built-in types, structures, arrays, unions, loops, functions, and pointers. These fundamental elements are used identically in both languages.

- C and C++ support the same kinds of preprocessor directives such as #include, #define, and conditional expressions such as #ifdef.

- C++ has several new reserved words (a total of 97 in my version of GNU C++), many of which are the same in C and C++. See Chapter 6, "Creating Data Objects," and also Appendix A, "GNU C++ Reserved Words," for a complete list of GNU C++ reserved words.

- C++ introduces a few operators that are not found in C. For example, the "put-to" operator << is used to write data to objects. This book fully explains how to use all C and C++ operators. See Appendix B, "C++ Operator Precedence and Associativity," for a complete list.

- C++ supports minimum and maximum operators. The expression (X <? Y) returns the lesser of X and Y. The expression (X >? B) returns the greater of X and Y. Not all C++ compilers support this feature.

- C++ requires all functions to have formal prototypes. C encourages, but does not require, function prototypes. Functions that are used before being declared (that is, if there are any implicit function declarations) generate a compiler error.

■ Type checking in expressions is more strictly enforced in C++ than in C. In general, values in expressions must be of the same types, or they must be readily convertible to appropriate types. Where C gives an incompatible type warning, C++ tends to generate a compiler error. However, objects are implicitly cast from one type to another, an action that is easily missed. Be careful in assignment statements to use objects and values either of the same types or, if different, of types that are assignment compatible.

■ C++ reduces the need for `typedef` declarations. You can declare a `struct` such as

```
struct mystruct {
   ...
};
```

and then declare variables such as `mystruct x;`. To do the same in ANSI C, you need to write `struct mystruct x;`, or you need to use a `typedef` alias for `struct mystruct`.

■ In C++, a `char` object is an 8-bit byte. In C, a `char`'s size is not defined. In C, character constants are of type `int`, and the expression `sizeof('X')` equals `sizeof(int)`. In C++, character constants are of type `char`, and the expression `sizeof('X')` equals `sizeof(char)`. (However, tests indicate that, in GNU C++ and GNU C, `sizeof('X')` always equals 1.)

■ C++ permits local object declarations in compound statement blocks. For example, in C++, if you declare a local variable inside a `while` loop, that variable's scope is limited to the loop's statement block. In C++, you can also create local variables inside a `for` statement.

■ C++ provides `const` (constant) objects. Any object declared `const` cannot have its value changed at runtime. (This feature is also available in ANSI C, but not in precursor C compilers.)

■ C++ supports comments beginning with `//` and extending to the end of the line. C++ also recognizes C-style comments delimited with `/*` and `*/`. C++-style comments are found more and more in ANSI C compilers (GNU C and C++ recognize both types of comment styles).

■ In C++, function parameters may be given default values. In addition, functions can be overloaded—that is, a program may have two or more functions of the same name provided that they differ in at least one parameter data type.

■ C++ supports object-oriented programming, a main focus of this book. The primary tool for C++ OOP is the `class`, an enhanced `struct` that encapsulates data and functions, and that supports the concept of inheritance. C++ classes can use single inheritance (one class derived from another base class) and multiple inheritance (one class derived from two or more base classes).

■ Because on some systems C++ programs might need to be linked using a standard system linker, C++ supports an internal convention known as *name mangling*. In brief, this creates unique identifiers by combining an object's type and name information. However, because of name mangling, standard C functions need to be specially declared so that the linker can find them. If you have trouble linking to a standard C library, try including its function and other declarations inside the directive `extern "C" { ... }`.

- C++ supports inline functions. Calls to inline functions are replaced at compile time with the function's statements. Using inline functions can greatly speed performance in time-critical loops. (In GNU C++, you must compile with optimizations using option -O to enable inline function expansion.)

- C++ supports virtual functions, which in classes, are used to create polymorphic objects. The classic example of polymorphism is a graphics object that "knows" how to draw itself. Drawing a full screen of such objects is a simple matter of telling them to do their thing. Virtual functions do not exist in C.

- C++ supports templates, a facility for automatically generating classes and functions. With templates, you can write completely general code that is molded at compile time into specific forms from which objects and functions are then created.

- C++ supports exceptions, a powerful means for intertwining error handling in programs. Exceptions are particularly useful for dealing with critical errors such as a memory shortage that occurs during a deeply nested function call. By providing an automatic method for handling error conditions, exceptions reduce the need to write explicit error-checking flow-control statements.

- C++ provides a standard template library (STL) plus a string class, both described in this book. The STL combines algorithms such as sorting and searching with data structures—vectors, stacks, queues, and others—in completely general ways.

- ANSI C++ allows nested functions—that is, one function declared and used inside another. However, GNU C++ does not yet support this feature.

SUMMARY

Most likely, you do not have to install GNU C++. Most Linux automated installation programs install the compiler, especially if you elect to install "all packages" or "everything." If you followed the installation instructions in Chapter 2, you probably have GNU C++ installed and ready to go. However, if you experience trouble running the compiler, this chapter offered several alternative methods and tips for installing GNU C++ (and other files) by using this book's CD-ROM, the Red Hat Package Manager (RPM), or by downloading the necessary files from the Internet. This chapter also explained how to unpack and install this book's sample programs. In addition, at the end of this chapter was a comparison of features in C and C++ that might be of interest to C programmers. Now, turn to the next chapter to begin learning how to use GNU C++ for Linux programming.

PART **II**

C++ FUNDAMENTALS

## CHAPTER 4

INTRODUCING GNU C++

By now, you have installed Linux and GNU C++. You've tweaked files and poked settings to configure the operating system to your heart's content. You're ready to start learning how to program Linux software with GNU C++. Where should you begin?

Right here. Even if you know C, C++, or another language, don't skip this and the following GNU C++ tutorial chapters. Most chapters build on the preceding chapters, and even C++ gurus can benefit from reading them in order. Along the way, you pick up valuable techniques for compiling, optimizing, debugging, maintaining, and modularizing GNU C++ programs. Armed with this information, you not only learn programming techniques but also acquire the tools and knowledge for creating and maintaining many different types of Linux programs from the lowliest console utilities to the most complex X graphical applications.

WELCOME TO C++ PROGRAMMING

Many programming books begin with a program named "hello" that prints a message onscreen. Although simple, the hello program introduces the fundamentals of a programming language, and it verifies that your system is properly configured. Being the contrary sort, however, I name my hello program "welcome." Running it welcomes you to GNU C++ programming.

THE WELCOME PROGRAM

Listing 4.1 shows the *source code* listing for the welcome program. The program file is named welcome.cpp, and it is located in the src/c04 directory along with other numbered listings in this chapter. Files from other chapters are similarly organized in directories by chapter number.

LISTING 4.1   WELCOME.CPP

```
#include <iostream.h>

int main()
{
  cout << "Welcome to GNU C++ for Linux programming!" << endl;
  return 0;
}
```

Note

If you did not copy the src directory and its files from this book's CD-ROM to your hard drive, do so now by following the instructions in Chapter 3, "Installing GNU C++," in the section "How to Install This Book's Sample Programs."

The welcome program's filename ends with .cpp, which, of course, stands for "C plus plus." C++ filenames can end with other extensions such as .cc, .cxx, .cpp, or .c++. I prefer .cpp because that's the default for Borland C++, but you can use one of the other filename endings if you prefer. Filenames ending with .c (lowercase c) contain standard C source code, not C++. However, GNU C++ can compile C *and* C++ programs, and it lets you combine C and C++ techniques as you want. With C, you get only C; with GNU C++, you get the best of both worlds.

COMPILING THE WELCOME PROGRAM

Before examining welcome.cpp, compile and run the program. *Compiling* a C++ program in source-code form creates an executable code file that you can run by typing its name. There are many ways to compile programs (I explain more in Chapter 5, "Compiling and Debugging C++ Programs"). The easiest method, and the one to use for most of this book's sample programs, is to change to the file's directory and then run the GNU C++ compiler. To do that, enter commands such as

```
$ cd /home/username/src/c04
$ g++ welcome.cpp
```

The dollar signs represent the shell prompt, which might be different for you, and might show a different character. In this book, lines preceded with dollar signs are those you type at the console. *Don't type the dollar signs.* To run the compiler, you may type either *g++* or *c++*. In some versions of Linux, those commands actually run the GNU C compiler, gcc, with options selected for C++ programming. In newer releases, GNU C++ is the standalone compiler, egcs (Experimental GNU Compiler System), which does not rely on gcc.

Note

> GNU C++ selects the correct compiler depending on the filename extension. The commands *g++ filename.c* and *gcc filename.c* run the GNU C compiler. The command *g++ filename.cpp* automatically selects GNU C++.

After you compile welcome.cpp, a directory listing produced by the ls command shows a new file named a.out. This file contains the executable code that g++ created. It's a finished code file, ready to run. However, because the src/c04 directory is probably not in your environment path, to run the program, preface its name with a period and slash. This tells the shell to look for the file in the current directory. For example, enter this command:

```
$ ./a.out
Welcome to GNU C++ for Linux programming!
```

The two lines show your typing and the program's output. I often reproduce screen output this way so that you can compare your screen with mine. But don't merely read this text. To learn a programming language, there's no substitute for entering, compiling, and running programs on your own computer.

Note

You might come across documentation that states a.out is an "old format" replaced by the ELF executable code format. Nowadays, a.out is in ELF format, and you don't need to do anything special to enable the newer system. To be sure, however, enter a Linux file command as follows and check the reported message:

```
$ file ./a.out
./a.out: ELF 32-bit LSB executable, Intel 80386,
➥ version 1, dynamically linked, not stripped
```

THE OUTPUT FILE OPTION

Compiling programs to a.out is convenient for quick tests, but subsequent compilations overwrite the output file. To save a.out, you can rename the file using a mv command, but it's easier to specify an output filename in the first place. To do that, use the compiler's -o option in a command such as

```
$ g++ -o welcome welcome.cpp
```

Follow -o with the output filename. It's conventional to use the same filename as the source with no extension. You may specify a different name if you want. Some authorities say not to add a space after -o; others show the command as I do. If the preceding command fails for you, try -owelcome. After compiling, you can run the program by entering

```
$ ./welcome
Welcome to GNU C++ for Linux programming!
```

Warning

Be especially careful when using the -o option to supply a filename. If you type a command such as *g++ -o xxx.cpp, the compiler overwrites xxx.cpp!* Always double check that you have supplied the name of a file after -o and that you are sure it is safe to overwrite the file.

UNDERSTANDING THE WELCOME PROGRAM

Now that you know how to compile and run a C++ program, take a look at the source code in welcome.cpp (refer to Listing 4.1). The first line is a *preprocessor directive*. This is a command to the compiler that, in this case, tells it to include the declarations from a file named iostream.h, one of hundreds of similar *header files* that come with GNU C and C++. Include directives are usually in the following form:

```
#include <filename.h>
```

Although include directives might appear just about anywhere in a program's source code file, they are normally best located near the top above any other programming. The directive begins with #include, and is followed by a filename enclosed in angle brackets) (otherwise known as less-than and greater-than signs). The filename doesn't have to end with .h, but it almost always does. The brackets tell GNU C++ to look in standard directories for the named file. To include a header file of your own making, use double quotes like this:

```
#include "local.h"
```

GNU C++ stores standard header files in the directories /usr/include, /usr/include/g++, and others. Different versions of Linux and GNU C++ might store header files elsewhere. Place your own header files in your program's directory or in a subdirectory named include.

Warning

Never store your own header files in the standard include directories. You might lose them when upgrading or reinstalling GNU C++.

Including a header file imports its declarations as though they were typed at the location of the #include directive. Through a somewhat roundabout process, this also causes the compiler to link into the finished code various subroutines and data that, in this case, implement the GNU C++ I/O stream library. In due course, you learn more about how to link code to libraries, and what exactly happens when you include a header file. Here, you need to understand only that including iostream.h provides input and output capabilities for C++ programs.

Next in welcome.cpp is a *function* named main(). Functions group one or more *statements*, written in a *statement block* between a pair of matching braces. The statements run when another part of the program calls the function. In this case, however, it's the shell that calls main(). (I explain the main() function more fully in the section "Program Entry and Exit" later in this chapter.) All C and C++ programs must have one and only one main() function.

Note

To distinguish them from other program elements, in this book, function names such as main() end with a pair of parentheses.

The main() function in welcome.cpp contains two statements. The first one writes a string to the standard output, usually the console. Examine this statement closely:

```
cout << "Welcome to GNU C++ for Linux programming!" << endl;
```

The C++ output operator << passes the quoted string plus an end-of-line object (endl) to cout. The c in cout stands for "character." It's an output object, provided by the C++ I/O stream library, that can accept character data such as strings and end-of-line objects. Writing to cout sends text to the system's standard output file, most often the user's console. Another output object, cerr, writes to the standard error output file. Notice that a semicolon terminates the statement. Function declarations, statement blocks, preprocessor directives, and some other items you meet throughout this book are not statements, so they don't end with semicolons.

The second and last statement in `main()` (notice that it too ends with a semicolon) *returns* a
value to the function's caller:

```
return 0;
```

A return value of 0 indicates that the program ran and finished successfully. A nonzero
value, which must be in the range of 1 to 255, indicates that an error occurred. See
"Program Entry and Exit" later in this chapter for more information on `main()` return
statements.

MORE ABOUT SEMICOLONS

Semicolon placement in C and C++ programming confuses everyone at first. Always
remember that semicolons terminate *statements*, not lines of text. Semicolons also terminate
some other elements such as variable definitions, but more on that in Chapter 6, "Creating
Data Objects."

The best way to learn where to type semicolons is to understand that the compiler needs
them to locate the ends of statements and declarations. This is because the compiler ignores
whitespace, or more specifically, extraneous blank lines, spaces, and tabs. Programmers write
most statements on separate lines and use indentation to make source code readable, but the
compiler is no literary connoisseur, and it doesn't care how the text looks. The following
rearranged welcome.cpp compiles correctly because the compiler understands its syntax perfectly well (notice the locations of the semicolons):

```
#include <iostream.h>
void main(){cout<<"Welcome to GNU C++ for Linux programming!"
<<endl;return 0;}
```

If you write code like that, you will incur the wrath of all who have to read your programs.
You'll deserve it too.

CALLING C LIBRARY FUNCTIONS

Because the C++ programming language is based on C, anything you can do in C, you can
do in C++. The same is generally true with most C++ compilers, but GNU C++ makes it
particularly easy to switch between the two languages. You can also combine C and C++
programming methods in the same program.

Those capabilities are important to C++ programmers for several reasons. For one, numerous Linux programs are written in C. To understand the source code statements in those
programs, you need to know C programming techniques. For another, GNU C++ provides
an extensive standard library of C functions that perform all sorts of services such as working with dates and times, performing mathematical calculations, and manipulating character

strings. The GNU C library implements all functions defined in the ANSI C specification, also known as ISO C. Also available in the library are IEEE POSIX standard functions and other declarations. This book explains how to use many GNU C library functions in C++ programs.

Note

> POSIX stands for a mouthful. It's the Portable Operating System Interface for Computer Environments, an attempt to standardize the function libraries from many different versions of UNIX, hence the X in the acronym.

A good example of how C and C++ differ is in printing character strings and other data. As you have learned, in C++, you can write strings to the cout object with a statement such as

```
cout << "The write stuff" << endl;
```

Listing 4.2, cwelcome.cpp, shows two other ways to print strings to the standard output using methods commonly found in C programming but also available to C++ programmers. For comparison, the program also shows the C++ method.

LISTING 4.2   CWELCOME.CPP

```
#include <iostream.h>
#include <stdio.h>

int main()
{
  puts("A string written by puts()");
  printf("A string written by printf()\n");
  cout << "A string written to cout" << endl;
  return 0;
}
```

PART

II

CH

4

Compile and run the cwelcome program by typing the following two commands:

```
$ g++ cwelcome.cpp
$ ./a.out
A string written by puts()
A string written by printf()
A string written to cout
```

Running the program writes three output lines three different ways. The first technique calls the *library function*, puts(). This function, along with several others, is declared in the stdio.h header file. So that it can call the function, the program includes stdio.h in addition to iostream.h. As usual, the two include directives are placed near the top of the source code file. Calling puts() as follows prints a quoted string to the standard output and also starts a new line:

```
puts("A string written by puts()");
```

The second output technique in cwelcome calls another library function, printf(), also declared in stdio.h. The f in printf() stands for "formatted." Although used in simple fashion here, printf() can perform highly complex formatting on its output, as explained in

Chapter 8, "Controlling Input and Output," in the section "Formatting Output with the sprintf() Family." As with puts(), calling printf() as follows is another perfectly acceptable way to print a string to the standard output:

```
printf("A string written by printf()\n");
```

Look closely at the end of the quoted string. The double-character symbol \n is called an *escape code*. A backslash begins the code, which is followed in this case by a lowercase n. Together, the two characters represent the "new line" character. Written to the standard output, this starts a new line on the display. To write a backslash, type two of them like this:

```
printf("Write a backslash \\ and start a new line\n");
```

Some other escape codes are \t, which prints a tab, \e for <esc> (this might be specific to GNU C++), and \a, which is supposed to "alert" the user by ringing a bell, but don't count on it. You can use escape codes in any literal string. For example, the following C++ statement writes a string to the standard output followed by two new lines:

```
cout << "Give me some space!\n\n";
```

It is clearer, although not necessarily better, to use the endl object in place of \n. The technically correct way to write the preceding line in C++ is

```
cout << "Give me some space!" << endl << endl;
```

Note

See Chapter 6, "Creating Data Objects," in the section "Character Escape Codes" for a complete list of escape codes you can insert into strings.

You might wonder which C or C++ output method to use. All work perfectly well, but I favor the C++ method for several reasons. As explained in this book's more advanced chapters, in C++ you can create customized output objects for use in I/O stream statements (see for example Chapter 20, "Customizing I/O Streams"). You can also use the << operator to write file data along with >> to read input, and you can even reprogram those operators to recognize other types of objects. C is not as flexible. In the standard C library, the puts() function is strictly limited to writing string data. Other functions in the C library are similarly restricted to using data of a specific type. That's not *bad*, but in practice, the inflexibility of standard C library functions creates barriers to writing easily maintained code.

Another good reason to favor C++ over C output techniques is that C++ uses *exceptions* for error handling. Because the C language does not implement exceptions, standard C library functions can't use them to report errors. Chapter 16, "Handling Exceptions," explains how to use exceptions for creating robust programs that safely handle even the trickiest error conditions.

COMMENTS ABOUT COMMENTS

A *comment* in a program is text intended strictly for human consumption. The compiler ignores any comments it finds in source code and header files.

Use comments liberally to document your program's source code, credit the program's authors, keep a history of modifications, and for other notes. For instance, I usually keep a list of unfinished business in a comment at the beginning of my program files. This helps jog my memory about what needs doing, especially when I haven't looked at the file recently.

The following sections explain how to write comments using two different styles—one for C and C++ programs, and one for C++ only.

C-STYLE COMMENTS

You may use C-style comments in C and C++ programs. This type of comment begins with the double-character symbol /* and ends with its mirror image, */. The compiler ignores both symbols and all text in between, even if that text stretches for two or more lines. For example, this single-line comment might appear at the beginning of a source code file:

```
/* Fishing Database System: by Grouper Tom */
```

Note   Any relation to Grouper Tom and the author is strictly wishful thinking.

You may also write C-style comments on multiple lines. Even so, you need only one set of comment delimiters. For example, you might create a file with commented text that you can insert into new source code files:

```
/*  Program name:  */
/*  Author:        */
/*  Purpose:       */
```

Rather than type all those comment delimiters, you can more easily write those lines this way:

```
/*  Program name:
    Author:
    Purpose:
*/
```

That looks a little strange; so many programmers pretty things up with some fancy footwork, writing the preceding comment as

```
/*
 *  Program name:
 *  Author:
 *  Purpose:
 */
```

For some reason, this style confuses many programmers when they first see it. But look—there's a starting comment delimiter /* on the first line and an ending delimiter */ on the last. The compiler ignores all the text in between, including the three asterisks in the middle, there only for the sake of neatness. For a fancier effect, many programmers box their comments using text such as this:

```
/* ==========================
 * Program name:
 * Author:
 * Purpose:
 * ========================== */
```

That's still just one comment to the compiler. The comment generates no code, and it produces no effect in the compiled program. Even so, it's amazing how much time programmers spend getting their comment file headers *just right!*

C-style comments don't have to appear on their own lines. They can appear ahead of or even in the middle of statements and other declarations. However, the most common use for comments is to document a statement such as this:

```
cout << "Press Enter..."; /* Tell user to press the Enter key */
```

In this case, the statement's purpose is fairly obvious, and it probably doesn't need commenting, but too many comments are better than too few. Don't hesitate to use comments to document even the obvious statements and declarations in your code.

Comments usually document what the program does, but you can also use them for *commenting-out* portions of source code that you don't want to erase completely, perhaps because you are chasing down a bug. Examine this statement:

```
cout << "One " /*<< endl*/ << "Two" << endl;
```

Because of the comment delimiters, the compiler "sees" that statement as though written:

```
cout << "One " << "Two" << endl;
```

Compiling and running that statement writes the text "One Two" on a single line. Removing the comments and changing the statement to the following inserts an endl object between the two strings, thus writing them on separate lines:

```
cout << "One " << endl << "Two" << endl;
```

Using C comments as demonstrated here is a simple, but vital, technique to learn. You will frequently comment-out unfinished sections of code or statements that you've copied to try out variations or optimizations. To restore the original code, simply delete the comment delimiters.

C++-STYLE COMMENTS

C++ adds to C another kind of comment delimiter that works a little differently. In a C++ program, a double slash // begins a comment. The compiler ignores every character from // to the end of the line. To use a C++-style comment, type // followed by the comment's text:

```
// Fishing Database System: by Grouper Tom
```

Unlike C comments, C++ comments use only one double-character symbol. They begin at // and continue to the end of the line. Multiple C++ comments must all begin with //. Using C++ comments, you can write the file header from the preceding section like this:

```
// ===========================
// Program name:
// Author:
// Purpose:
// ===========================
```

C++ comments typically document statements and other declarations. Here's the same statement from the preceding section, but this time ending with a C++ comment:

```
cout << "Press Enter...";  // Tell user to press the Enter key
```

This type of comment looks clean and is easy to type. The compiler ignores all text from // to the end of the line. For this reason, you can't use C++ comments to comment-out code in the middle of a statement, but you can use them to temporarily delete a statement such as

```
// cout << "This doesn't do anything!" << endl;
```

Removing the comment delimiter from the beginning of the line enables the statement.

Note

History buffs might like to know that C++-style comments are resurrected from C's predecessor language, BCPL. The GNU C compiler, gcc, recognizes C++-style comments in C programs, but not all C compilers do the same.

This Book's Source File Comments

As you might have noticed, all source code files on this book's CD-ROM begin with several comments that document the file's name and purpose, give compilation instructions, and, in many cases, show how to use or run the compiled code. The comments also include my copyright notice to satisfy the legal beagles.

Note

You may use any of this book's sample listings in your own programs as you want. See Appendix E, "Copyright Information—The GNU General Public License," for details.

Listing 4.3 shows the welcome.cpp program's opening comments. To save space, most printed listings in this book do not show these comments.

```
//=============================================================
// welcome.cpp -- A simple C++ program
// Time-stamp: <1999-02-10 10:24:17 tswan>
// To compile:
//   g++ -o welcome welcome.cpp
// To run:
//   ./welcome
// Copyright (c) 1999 by Tom Swan. All rights reserved.
//=============================================================
```

Each comment line in welcome.cpp is a C++-style comment that begins with a double slash. Various comments identify and describe the program. On the third line is a time stamp in a form that the Emacs editor recognizes (more on this in the next section). Other comments show compilation and running instructions, and the ubiquitous copyright notice. In some files, you might find additional comments at the end where I like to keep a revision history of modifications and bug fixes.

CREATING AN AUTOMATIC TIME STAMP

If you use the Emacs text editor, you can track modifications to files with an automatic time stamp comment such as in welcome.cpp. To create a time stamp, insert the following comment in any of the first eight lines of a source code file:

```
// Time-stamp: <>
```

A similar entry works the same in any text file, but in a non-source-code file, the C++ comment delimiter, //, isn't needed. You may also write the line as a C-style comment. To enable automatic time stamping for Emacs, insert the following command into a text file named .emacs (preceded by a period) saved in your home directory:

```
(add-hook 'write-file-hooks 'time-stamp)
```

Now every time Emacs saves a file to disk, it inserts the date, time, and your login username between the time stamp's angle brackets. Saving welcome.cpp, for example, changes the time stamp to something like this:

```
// Time-stamp: <1999-02-10 10:24:17 tswan>
```

An automatic time stamp is a great way to note when you last modified a file. Later in this book (see Chapter 20, "Customizing I/O Streams"), you examine a program that prints the names of files and their automatic time stamps.

PROGRAM ENTRY AND EXIT

Two important aspects of all programs, large and small, are how they start and how they end. As a programmer, you have certain responsibilities to ensure that your programs start correctly, but more important, to make certain they end in high style. Following are proper methods for correctly starting and ending C++ programs.

THE main() FUNCTION

All C and C++ programs have one and only one main() function. The first statement inside main() is the first to run. When main() ends, control passes back to the process that started the program—for example, the shell. Programming main() is how you control the way a program starts and, most often, but not always, how it ends.

There are slightly different ways to construct the main() function. In its simplest form, main() looks like this:

```
int main()
{
}
```

That's also the shortest possible, syntactically complete, C++ program. The word int ahead of the function name indicates that the function returns an integer value to its caller. Because of that declaration, it is more correct to end main() with an explicit *return statement*. Following is the shortest possible, *correctly written*, C++ program:

```
int main()
{
   return 0;
}
```

The zero value indicates the program ended with no errors, but more on this technique under "Returning Values from main()." Sometimes, you might see main() declared with void in place of int:

```
void main()
{
}
```

The word void here indicates that main() returns no value, and therefore, a return statement isn't needed. (Only a programmer can appreciate the beauty of using something like void to indicate nothing.)

The empty parentheses in main() tell you that the function receives no parameters from its caller. Actually, as C or C++ programmers in the audience probably know, main() can receive parameters, but if they are not declared, they effectively don't exist. Chapter 11, "Managing Memory with Pointers," in the section "Passing Arguments to main()," explains how to add parameters to the main() function. All forms of main() shown here are correct, but it is more proper to declare main() as returning int and to end the function with an explicit return statement. Whatever its form, when main() ends, so does the program.

PART

II

CH

4

Tip

When browsing through source code files, try to find the file that contains main(). Because main() is where all C and C++ programs start running, finding this function often provides a useful key for unlocking the program's secrets. Many programmers place their program's main() function in a file named main.cpp or main.c.

C-STYLE main() FUNCTIONS

While browsing C source code files, you might see main() declared this way:

```
int main(void)
{
  return 0;
}
```

The word void in parentheses is an ANSI C technique for indicating that a function receives no input parameters. GNU C++ doesn't seem to mind this type of declaration, but other C++ compilers might complain, so it's best not to use this form of main() in C++ programs.

C programmers also seem to favor writing the function return type on a separate line. You will often see a C program's main() function (and others) written like this:

```
int
main(void)
{
  return 0;
}
```

Placing the return type on its own line is purely a matter of style. C++ programmers tend to place the data type ahead of the function name.

RETURNING VALUES FROM main()

You can use a shell script to run a program and examine its return value. This is often a simple, but effective, way to indicate whether a program succeeded or failed. Listing 4.4, error.cpp, combines what you know so far about C++ to display a message and return an error result code. No real error occurs, of course.

LISTING 4.4 ERROR.CPP

```
#include <iostream.h>

int main()
{
  cout << "This program simulates an error" << endl;
  return 12;
}
```

Listing 4.5, runerror, is a sample bash (Bourne Again Shell) script that intercepts a program's return code. Script programming is too far afield from this book's subject matter, so I won't go into it here. Use the info command or consult a Linux reference for help with writing scripts for the shell of your choice.

LISTING 4.5   RUNERROR

```
if ./a.out
then
  echo "Program terminated successfully"
else
  echo "Error result code = $?"
fi
```

To make the shell script executable, enter a command such as

```
$ chmod a+x runerror
```

Next, compile the error.cpp program, and then run it by executing the shell script. For example, type the following two commands:

```
$ g++ error.cpp
$ ./runerror
This program simulates an error
Error result code = 12
```

The program displays the first message. The shell script displays the second, which indicates that the program returned an error code of 12. Change the return value in error.cpp from 12 to 0, and then recompile and run the program as before. This time, it displays:

```
$ ./runerror
This program simulates an error
Program terminated successfully
```

GOING OUT IN STYLE

When main() ends, so does the program. However, there are other ways to end programs. A useful method is to call the standard library's exit() function, declared in the stdlib.h header file. For example, to end a program and return the error code 1, call exit() like this:

```
#include <stdlib.h>
...
exit(1);
```

The value in parentheses is called an *argument*, and it is passed to the exit() function. To try out exit(), include the stdlib.h header file in a copy of error.cpp and insert the preceding line in place of the return statement. Listing 4.6, exiterr.cpp, shows the finished program.

LISTING 4.6   EXITERR.CPP

```
#include <iostream.h>
#include <stdlib.h>

int main()
{
  cout << "Calling exit() to simulate an error..." << endl;
  exit(1);
}
```

To compile exiterr.cpp and run it using the runerror shell script, enter the following two commands:

```
$ g++ exiterr.cpp
$ ./runerror
Calling exit() to simulate an error...
Error result code = 1
```

Unlike a return statement in main(), the exit() function can terminate a program at any place in its execution. This is valuable because, in larger programs, it is often necessary to "bail out" somewhere in the middle of a deeply buried function. In such cases, calling exit() is one of the best ways to end a program immediately when a serious error crops up—for example, if the program can't open a critical file.

Along with exit(), stdlib.h also defines two *constants*, EXIT_FAILURE and EXIT_SUCCESS, intended for use with the function. Constants are values that cannot be changed at runtime, and by convention, they are typed in all capital letters. Use one of the two constants in an exit() statement such as this:

```
exit(EXIT_FAILURE);
```

That returns the value 1 to the shell. Use the other constant to end the program and return the value 0, which means no error occurred:

```
exit(EXIT_SUCCESS);
```

Obviously, the descriptive constants make the program much clearer than literal values such as 0 and 1. You learn more about constants in Chapter 6, "Creating Data Objects." If you are following along, use the runerror script to examine the values returned by the preceding two statements.

You may use either constant also in main() return statements. For example, either of the following two statements is a good way to end main():

```
return EXIT_FAILURE;
return EXIT_SUCCESS;
```

Notice that, with exit(), the constant is in parentheses, but not so with return. This is because exit() is a function; return is a fundamental C++ operative. You *call* functions such as exit(), and you *pass* them arguments in parentheses. You don't call operatives such as return; you simply use them. Technically, though, parentheses group *expressions*, and because even a simple value is an "expression," the following works perfectly well with parentheses added:

```
return (EXIT_FAILURE);
```

Note

This may be nit-picking at its worst, but as a convention, I insert a space after return to indicate that the statement is *not* a function call. No space as in exit(1) indicates the statement calls a function. This is purely my own choice of styles, not a C++ requirement, and many C++ programmers insert a space between the function name and its parentheses. Some even get real huffy about these sorts of concerns. No doubt I'll hear from them.

GOING DOWN IN FLAMES

To end a program and indicate that a more serious error occurred, you can call abort() declared in stdlib.h along with exit(). The abort() function does not accept an argument value. Call it as follows with empty parentheses:

```
abort();
```

Warning
Calling abort() is a drastic measure that is rarely necessary. It causes no permanent damage, but it is not a recommended way to end C or C++ programs. Because many existing programs call abort(), you should be aware of its effects, but it's probably best never to use this function.

To examine what happens when a program calls abort(), enter the preceding statement into a copy of the welcome.cpp program, save it as atest.cpp (or use another filename), and then type the following commands:

```
$ g++ atest.cpp
$ ./a.out
Aborted (core dumped)
```

The last line tells you the process—that is, the running program—was aborted, and that core memory, including the system stack, was dumped to a file named core. Such *core dumps* tend to be huge (often 200KB or more) and nearly impossible to decipher. If you want to take a look at a core dump, use the Linux hexdump utility by typing the following command (if *less* isn't on your system, use *more* instead):

```
$ hexdump -bc core ¦ less
```

Type *q* to quit. More power to you if you can understand the output of a core dump. There are other, and vastly more sophisticated, ways to *debug* errant code, as you learn starting in Chapter 5, "Compiling and Debugging C++ Programs." If you are following along, you can remove the core-dump file with the command *rm core*.

Note
Yet one more way to exit a program is to throw an *exception*. Exceptions are extremely valuable for dealing with error conditions, but you need to learn more about C++ programming before using them. Exceptions are available only in C++, not in C.

REVIEW OF ENTRY AND EXIT TECHNIQUES

As you have learned in this chapter, starting a program is easy. Simply create a main() function and insert the program's first statement into the function's statement block. You also learned five ways to end a C++ program. Here they are in a list for review:

- Do nothing. After its last statement, main() simply ends, returning the user to the shell or to whatever process started the program.

- Execute a `return` statement in `main()`, optionally passing a return value in the range 0 to 255 back to `main()`'s caller—for example, a shell script.

- Call `exit()` to end the program at any time or place. To make `exit()` available to your program, include the stdlib.h header file. Pass to `exit()` a literal value in the range 0 to 255, or use one of the two stdlib.h constants `EXIT_SUCCESS` or `EXIT_FAILURE`.

- Call the `abort()` function, also declared in stdlib.h, from anywhere in the program. Calling `abort()` ends the program immediately and creates a core dump file. This is a drastic measure that is rarely necessary and is not considered good programming.

- Throw an exception, but don't try this yet.

SUMMARY

This chapter introduced GNU C++ programming with a simple program, welcome.cpp, that shows elements common to all C++ programs large and small. The chapter also explained how to compile and run C++ programs, display text on the console using a variety of methods, call C library functions, create and use C- and C++-style comments, write `main()` functions, and properly begin and end programs.

For more information on subjects introduced in this chapter, turn to the following chapters:

- Chapter 6, "Creating Data Objects"
- Chapter 8, "Controlling Input and Output"
- Chapter 10, "Creating and Calling Functions"
- Chapter 11, "Managing Memory with Pointers"
- Chapter 16, "Handling Exceptions"
- Chapter 20, "Customizing I/O Streams"

## CHAPTER 5

COMPILING AND DEBUGGING C++ PROGRAMS

Compiling is the process of translating source code text into executable code. *Debugging* is the art of making that code run error free. These are the mechanical aspects of programming, and as a mechanic needs to know how to use shop tools, so you need to know how to run compilers and debuggers—the essential tools of a programmer's trade.

This chapter introduces key mechanics of GNU C++, such as warnings, errors, portable code generation, and performance optimizations. Using specific options, you learn how to interrupt compilation so that you can study the compiler's output at different stages and understand more about the compilation process.

This chapter also introduces the GNU C++ debugger. By learning how to run the debugger now, you'll be ready to use it when the time comes to squash bugs in your code. And that time will come, just as surely as ants to a picnic. It has been said that all programs have bugs. Maybe that's true, but with the help of the GNU C++ debugger, you can learn to find and fix most kinds of errors so that your program's users don't bug *you* with complaints.

WARNINGS AND ERRORS

Although all programmers make mistakes, the most skillful developers know how to find and fix most kinds of errors before they cause bugs. To identify mistakes in source code so that you can repair them, the compiler prints warnings and errors about any problems it discovers.

Note

> There's a world of difference between a warning and an error. A *warning* is a message the compiler prints when it discovers a potential problem in the source code. An *error* is a mistake in syntax that prevents the compiler from finishing its job.

Warnings are frequently caused by missing declarations, values of inappropriate types, and various kinds of improper constructions. Despite the warning, the program's source code is syntactically complete, so these types of problems don't prevent the compiler from creating a finished code file. However, that code might not run correctly.

Errors are caused by syntactical mistakes in source code such as typographical errors, missing semicolons, and other kinds of faulty constructions. Because these types of problems make it impossible for the compiler to create a finished code file, you must fix all reported errors before completing the compilation.

Warnings and errors are sometimes called *compile-time bugs*. Later in this chapter in the section "Introduction to Debugging," you learn about another class of errors that the compiler does not identify. These are called *runtime bugs* and are caused by faulty logic in your program. Runtime bugs are your responsibility to find and fix.

The next sections show examples of warnings and errors, and further explain the differences between these two types of compiler messages.

YOU'VE BEEN WARNED

A typical warning comes about when a program fails to supply code that satisfies an earlier declaration. For example, if you declare a function that returns an integer value but you neglect to write a statement to perform that action, the compiler warns you of your mistake. Technically, because the source code is syntactically complete, this is not an error. However, the resulting program almost certainly fails to produce expected results.

For example, suppose that you write a main() function to return an integer value. But inside main(), you insert a return statement that simply ends the function. Here's the faulty code:

```
int main()
{
  return;  // ???
}
```

In this book, the C++-style comment, // ???, at the end of a line indicates a questionable practice or a faulty construction that might cause a bug. Type those lines into a text file named atest.cpp and then compile with the following command:

```
$ g++ atest.cpp
atest.cpp: In function 'int main()':
atest.cpp:3: warning: 'return' with no value,
➥ in function returning non-void
```

You receive two messages from the compiler. The first message identifies the name of the function in which GNU C++ found a problem. The second message is the warning. It tells you several important facts:

- The name of the file (atest.cpp)
- The line number that caused a problem (3)
- That this is a warning message
- The nature of the problem

The text of the warning message tells you that the compiler found a plain return statement in a function that is declared to return a value—that is, one declared as "non-void." That warning message might seem a bit cryptic, and you will frequently have to interpret messages to understand them. However, GNU C++ tends to give helpful messages that are far more descriptive than those of other C++ compilers.

Despite the warning, the compiler creates the finished executable code file. In this case, running that code causes no harm because, as you learned in the preceding chapter, the shell ignores main()'s return value. But in another situation, that same warning might indicate a serious problem. *Never ignore any warnings you receive from the compiler.* You've been warned.

TO ERR IS HUMAN

You're human. You're a programmer. You are going to make mistakes. Even experts make plenty of them. Those that confuse the compiler cause compilation to end prematurely with an error message. For example, type the following atest.cpp program exactly as follows:

```
int main()
{
  return EXIT_SUCCESS;
}
```

In the preceding chapter, returning the EXIT_SUCCESS constant seemed to work, but now when you compile the program, the compiler reports an error:

```
$ g++ atest.cpp
atest.cpp: In function 'int main()':
atest.cpp:3: 'EXIT_SUCCESS' undeclared (first use this function)
atest.cpp:3: (Each undeclared identifier is reported only once
atest.cpp:3: for each function it appears in.)
```

As it does for warnings, the compiler tells you the filename, line number where the problem occurred, and name of the function. Because the word "warning" does *not* appear in the messages, this is an error, and the compiler does not create a finished code file. Even though you see several message lines, they refer to only one error. Read the text carefully to become familiar with the GNU C++ format for error messages, many of which provide lengthy explanations that can help you figure out what's wrong. Here, the compiler tells you that EXIT_SUCCESS is an "undeclared identifier," and that line 3 is where the compiler *first* found this problem.

You probably realize what's wrong. Because in C++ you must *declare* items such as constants, variables, and functions before you can use them, the compiler has no idea what EXIT_SUCCESS is. As the preceding chapter explains, the stdlib.h header file declares that constant. The problem arose because the programmer neglected to include the header file. To fix the bug, insert the following directive above main():

```
#include <stdlib.h>
```

> **Note**
>
> The single most likely cause of an undeclared identifier error is a forgotten include file. This often happens when the programmer assumes that one header includes another. For example, in my version of GNU C++, iostream.h includes stdio.h, so it might seem unnecessary to include both headers. However, the same might not be true with all GNU C++ versions or with another compiler. By the way, don't worry about including a header file more than once. All headers are designed so that the compiler ignores them if they are included two or more times.

An even more common mistake is a simple typographical error that causes compilation to halt. The compiler is an unforgiving taskmaster, and even the tiniest mistake results in an error message. For an example, try this test program, which does not use a semicolon to terminate a statement:

```
#include <iostream.h>
int main()
{
  cout << "Where's my semicolon?" << endl  // ???
}
```

Even though the preceding code lacks only one teensy character, when you compile the program with the following command, the compiler reports a "parse error" (the line number might be different for you):

```
$ g++ atest.cpp
atest.cpp: In function 'int main()':
atest.cpp:4: parse error before '}'
```

Parsing is part of the process the compiler undertakes to translate C++ source code into executable code. The compiler *parses* the program's text into a symbolic form suitable to the compiler's tastes. When the compiler finds a mistake in the text, it can't go on because it no longer "comprehends" the program's expression. Errors in parsing confuse the compiler the way a missing word in a sentence might confuse you. Of course, you might be able to figure out an incomplete sentence's meaning. But the compiler isn't so intuitive, and it must have a complete program, or it refuses to go on.

In this case, the compiler found a closing brace before it finished parsing a statement. Notice that the error message indicates that the error is located at some place *before* the unexpected character. The compiler doesn't explain what the mistake is or its precise location, but only that it found an unexpected character. The source of the error might be many lines back from where the compiler became confused, and this can make finding the cause of parsing errors difficult.

Tip

If you have trouble locating the cause of a parsing error, comment-out preceding statements one at a time and recompile. When you can compile the program successfully, the error is in the last statement that you converted into a comment.

WARNING AND ERROR OPTIONS

Although GNU C++ warns about most kinds of common problems, by specifying selected options, you can control how picky the compiler is about parsing a program's source code. Increasing the compiler's warning level this way might help you find and fix subtle bugs. The technique is also helpful if you are just learning C++, when, of course, you are apt to make more mistakes.

To increase the level of warnings issued, use the -Wall option. Despite the "all" in that option's name, you can add even more warnings by specifying -W. For a full load of all possible warnings, combine the two options with a command such as

```
$ g++ -Wall -W atest.cpp
```

Be careful to type a capital W in both cases. The following command turns *off* all warnings:

```
$ g++ -w welcome.cpp  // ???
```

Don't ever do that! It tells the compiler not to report any warnings, and this command could cause you to miss a serious bug.

You can also turn on specific warnings. A good one is -Wreturn-type. This tells the compiler to warn you about functions that declare a return value but don't include a return statement. To use this option, compile the program with a command such as

```
$ g++ -Wreturn-type atest.cpp
```

Another specific warning finds a subtle problem that can easily occur when using C-style comments. Insert these two statements into a atest.cpp file's main() function:

```
cout << "Hello "; /* write a string *\
cout << "there!" << endl; /* write another string */
```

When you compile and run the program, it prints only the "Hello" string, but does not print "there" and does not start a new line (notice that the dollar sign prompt appears after "Hello"):

```
$ g++ atest.cpp
$ ./a.out
Hello $
```

Look closely at the end of the first statement and you'll see the problem. The careless programmer typed a backslash instead of a forward slash. When the compiler parses the opening comment bracket, /*, it searches for the ending bracket, */, which here appears at the end of the *second* statement. Everything in between has been accidentally commented-out by the typo. Because the program is syntactically complete, it compiles with no warnings or errors. But it fails to run as expected.

In similar cases, especially when a program compiles without error but runs strangely or not at all, use the -Wcomment warning to find whether you have made this type of mistake. Compiling the code with the following command shows the warning message:

```
$ g++ -Wcomment atest.cpp
atest.cpp:6: warning: '/*' within comment
```

The warning tells you that a starting comment delimiter was found inside another C-style comment. Often, when using C comments, this indicates that a section of the program was mistakenly commented-out. By the way, this same error isn't possible with C++-style comments.

Tip

Specifying -Wall enables the -Wcomment and -Wreturn-type warnings along with others. See the info gcc pages for more information on the specific warnings enabled by -Wall and -W.

TURNING WARNINGS INTO ERRORS

Many developers rightly insist on a clean compilation before they release their code. The most careful among them switch on all warning levels with -Wall and -W.

However, despite issuing a warning, the compiler still creates the finished code file, and it is easy to miss a warning message on a busy screen. This is especially so when compiling large

programs using a *Makefile script*. To prevent the creation of the output code [...]
ings are discovered, use the -Werror option as follows:

```
$ g++ -Wall -Werror atest.cpp
atest.cpp:6: warning: '/*' within comment
```

With -Werror in effect, the compiler considers any warnings to be er[...]
not create the executable code file. Notice, however, that it still sho[...]
"warning."

Warning

My tests indicate that with -Werror in effect, the comp[...]
file from the directory. This could cause you to assum[...]
successfully, when in fact, it did not create the finish[...]
always remove a.out (or a differently named outp[...]

INTERA SYSTEMS, INC.

kevinco@InteraSystems.com
tel: (408) 395-7788
fax: (408) 395-4548

20 S. Santa Cruz Ave.
Suite 107
Los Gatos, CA 95030-5917

Kevin Covey
Member of
Technical Staff

www.interasystems.com

COMPILE-AND-GO SCRIPT

I highly recommend using the -Wall and -W options to compile your progr[...] if
you are just learning C++. These options point out potential trouble spots. They [...] o
invaluable for helping you write code that has a good chance of compiling with other C++
development systems.

Rather than type those options over and over, you might want to create a shell script for
compiling programs using selected options. Listing 5.1, cg (compile and go), shows a sample
bash shell script that you can use to compile and run many of this book's sample programs
using the -Wall and -W options.

LISTING 5.1   CG

```
g++ -Wall -W $1 $2 $3 $4 $5 $6 $7 $8 $9
./a.out
```

Enter or copy the script (it's in the src/c05 directory) to a directory listed in your environment path. Make the file executable by entering the following command:

```
$ chmod a+x cg
```

Use cg as follows to compile and run programs such as welcome.cpp in the preceding chapter:

```
$ cg welcome.cpp
Welcome to GNU C++ for Linux programming!
```

Note

If cg is not in a directory listed in your PATH environment variable, to run the program
in the current directory, precede it with a period and slash—for example, enter
./cg welcome.cpp.

COMPILER OPTIONS

GNU C++ offers a virtual mountain of options that you can specify to select from a diverse set of features. However, after you learn which options you need, you can probably ignore most of the others. Many options have little or no effect on executable code but merely satisfy an esoteric ANSI C++ rule or select a feature of interest only to that particular option's author.

For a complete list of options, use the commands *info g++* and also *info gcc*. You need to examine both sets of info pages for the complete story of options available in GNU C++. Take a moment to browse the compiler's info pages so that you know where to find specific options, but don't be overwhelmed by the number of choices. (Press *q* to get out of the info program.) I cover various compiler options at the appropriate times throughout the book. However, the next sections introduce a few options you might want to start using right away.

> **Note**
>
> Because some options have long names, you must enter multiple options individually. For example, to specify the -c (compile only) and -W (extra warnings) options, you must type -c -W. Combining the two options into -cW does not work as it might for some other programs.

PORTABILITY OPTIONS

Writing *portable* code is a concern to many programmers, especially those who develop function and class libraries. By restricting source code to strictly defined ANSI C++ constructions, you increase the potential market for your software.

Although writing portable code is a worthy goal, it is difficult to achieve in practice. Even if your programming is ANSI *compatible*, it still might not be *portable*, a fact that Microsoft Windows developers soon realize when they attempt to move their programs to X. Still, the following GNU C++ options help promote, if not guarantee, portability. First, try the -Wtraditional option using a command such as

```
$ g++ -Wtraditional atest.cpp
```

This option warns about constructions that are either nontraditional or not allowed in the ANSI C++ and ANSI C specifications. Specify -traditional without the capital W if you want the compiler to treat all nontraditional items as errors:

```
$ g++ -traditional atest.cpp
```

If the program compiles with that command, it has a good chance of compiling with other ANSI C++ systems. Another option, -pedantic, prints warnings if a program uses GNU-specific features. With this option in effect, the compiler warns you if the program uses GNU features that another compiler is unlikely to recognize.

Finally, you can try the -ansi option. This instructs the compiler to accept only ANSI defined constructions. Programmers who write real software in the real world probably won't ever use -ansi. It's of value, however, for testing GNU's adherence to the standard, comparison testing of GNU C++ versions, and identifying discrepancies between GNU C++ and other ANSI implementations. The -ansi option might appeal to instructors who need to test whether student programs adhere to the ANSI standard. It's also useful for students who have finicky professors.

> **Note**
>
> If you specify -traditional or -ansi when compiling C programs, GNU C reportedly no longer recognizes C++-style comments, although this might not be true for all compiler versions.

INTERMEDIATE COMPILATIONS

When you compile a C++ or a C program, several intermediate processes take place behind the scenes. It is often useful, and always informative, to halt the compiler at one or more of these intermediate steps. This can provide insight into a compilation problem and also help you better understand how the compiler operates. To halt compilation at various intermediate stages, GNU C++ provides the following three options:

- -E   Stop after preprocessing; do not compile.
- -S   Stop after compiling; do not assemble.
- -c   Stop after assembling; do not link.

USING THE -E OPTION

The -E option shows the text of the program after the *preprocessor* expands directives such as #include. Because the output of this command is sent to the standard output, usually the console, you need to pipe the output to the less or more utilities, or store the results in a file for later viewing. For example, enter one of the following two commands to compile the welcome.cpp program from the preceding chapter:

```
$ g++ -E welcome.cpp ¦ less
$ g++ -E welcome.cpp > tmp.txt
```

If you try the second command, load tmp.txt into a text editor to see the program's expanded text. This option is particularly useful when compilation fails to complete because of missing elements. By compiling with -E, you see all the included header files, along with their expanded *macros*. A macro is a preprocessor command that is expanded into a C or C++ declaration or statement. Macros can be exceedingly complex and are often difficult to understand. Running them through the preprocessor with the -E option makes them much more readable, if not perfectly plain.

> **Tip**
>
> For more information on the GNU preprocessor, view the info pages for cpp. In this case, cpp doesn't mean "C plus plus," but "The GNU C-Compatible Compiler Preprocessor."

The -E option is also useful for discovering the names of various objects that the compiler adds to programs. For example, the preprocessor output created by using the -E option on welcome.cpp shows the following three declarations:

```
extern _IO_istream_withassign cin;
extern _IO_ostream_withassign cout, cerr;
extern _IO_ostream_withassign clog
```

At this point, you might not understand those lines—see Chapter 20, "Customizing I/O Streams." However, you have seen the cout and cerr objects shown here on the second line. The GNU preprocessor creates that declaration as a result of the program including the iostream.h header file. When you need to find the type of an included object, examining the preprocessed text is often useful. In this case, the preprocessed text tells you that cout and cerr are external objects of type _IO_ostream_withassign. The word extern in these declarations indicates that the actual objects exist somewhere else, most probably in a library file that is combined—that is, *linked*—to the compiled output code file.

USING THE -S OPTION

Linking is the process of combining various files and libraries of compiled code to create a final executable file such as a.out. The intermediate code is called *object code.* Use the -S option to halt compilation just before the compiler creates object code for a program's source text. For example, enter this command:

```
$ g++ -S welcome.cpp
```

After that, the directory contains a new file, welcome.s, which you can examine with less or more (or load it into your editor). In this file are the *assembly language* statements that GNU C++ creates. This might come as a surprise, but as the file shows, the compiler outputs assembly language statements in text form, not executable code as you may have assumed. Yet another intermediate step calls on the GNU assembler (as) to create the program's intermediate object code, which the GNU linker (ld) combines with library files and other object code files to create a finished executable code file.

USING THE -c OPTION

The -c option halts compilation after the assembler creates object code for the specified source file. Without this option, GNU C++ links that code to other libraries to create a finished executable code file such as a.out. Use the -c option to create separate modules that you intend to link later on. See "Separate Compilation" in this chapter for more about using the -c option.

THE COMPILATION PROCESS

As you can tell from the preceding section, a lot goes on when compiling even a simple program such as welcome.cpp. You can normally ignore the details of the intermediate stages, but it's useful to understand the basic steps. Using the aforementioned options and inspecting the output reveals that compilation involves from one to four separate processes that always take place in the following order:

1. The GNU preprocessor, cpp, expands directives such as `#include`. This output is piped directly to the compiler. Use option `-E` to halt compilation after this stage.

2. The GNU compiler, egcs, translates the preprocessed C and C++ statements into assembly language, stored in an intermediate file ending in .s. Use option `-S` to halt compilation after this stage.

3. The GNU assembler, as, translates assembly language statements into object code, stored in an intermediate file ending in .o. Use option `-c` to halt compilation after this stage.

4. The GNU linker, ld, combines the program's object code files with any required libraries to create the finished executable code. This output is stored as a.out or in a file named in an `-o` option.

For simplicity, the preceding four processes are collectively known as "compiling." However, understand that more than one process is needed to translate a C++ program from text into executable code and that there are actually three symbolic languages involved: preprocessing directives, C++ (or C), and assembly language. Fortunately for you and me, GNU C++ easily handles all the intermediate steps with hardly a whimper.

Tip

For more information on the GNU assembler, view the info pages for as and gasp— respectively, the GNU assembler and assembly preprocessor. For more information on the GNU linker, view the info pages for ld.

To examine all the commands issued at each intermediate stage during compilation, use the `-v`, verbose, option. Try this:

```
$ g++ -v welcome.cpp
```

Using the `-v` option displays each intermediate compiler command and also shows all the files referenced during preprocessing, compilation, assembling, and linking. When you can't figure out why a program won't compile, `-v` can often help pinpoint the cause. At such times, however, you might want the compiler not to produce real output. To merely inspect the compiler's commands, combine `-v` with another option, `-fsyntax-only`, to perform a syntax check of the program's source code. For example, enter this command:

```
$ g++ -v -fsyntax-only welcome.cpp
```

The `-fsyntax-only` option alone is useful also for viewing any warnings or errors the compiler generates. Because no output is actually created, compilation might go faster with this command. You can use the `-v` option also to determine your compiler version. On my system, the compiler reported the following:

```
$ g++ -v
Reading specs from /usr/lib/gcc-lib/i386-redhat-linux/
➥egcs-2.90.27/specs gcc version egcs-2.90.27 980315
➥ (egcs-1.0.2 release)
```

PART

II

CH

5

SEPARATE COMPILATION

One of the most widely used compiler options is -c, compile only. This option halts compilation after the GNU assembler creates a source file's object code. With -c in effect, the GNU linker does not combine that object code to create a finished executable code file. Using the -c option is called *separate compilation*.

> **Tip**
>
> You *must* use the -c option when compiling a module that does not have a main() function.

With separate compilation, you can divide programs into multiple source code files. Using the -c option, GNU C++ compiles each module separately, and then at some later point, another compilation command combines the resulting object code files to create the finished executable code. Dividing the source code among separate files this way makes it more convenient to edit and debug large programs. Separate compilation also saves time that would be wasted by unnecessarily recompiling finished and tested modules.

For example, suppose that your program is stored in three source code files named first.cpp, second.cpp, and main.cpp. So that you can follow along, sample files of those names are in the CD-ROM's src/c05 directory but aren't listed here. Only main.cpp has a main() function. The other files contain functions that the program uses. Use the -c option to compile the first.cpp and second.cpp source code files:

```
$ g++ -c first.cpp
$ g++ -c second.cpp
```

Given those commands, the compiler creates two new object code files, first.o and second.o, in the working directory. The files contain the object code created from their respective source code files, but the program isn't yet ready to run because it lacks a main() function. Also, the intermediate code files are not linked to any required libraries. You can also separately compile multiple source code files with a single command such as

```
$ g++ -c first.cpp second.cpp
```

That also creates first.o and second.o in the current directory. To create the finished executable program, issue the following command without the -c option:

```
$ g++ main.cpp first.o second.o
```

That tells the compiler to translate main.cpp into main.o and then to link the three object code files—main.o, first.o, and second.o—along with any needed library code to create the finished executable code file, a.out. Because -c is not specified, the compiler removes the intermediate main.o file, but it does not erase first.o and second.o because those files already exist. To keep all three object code files, you can compile all files separately and then link them into the finished code file by using commands such as these:

```
$ g++ -c main.cpp
$ g++ -c first.cpp second.cpp
$ g++ -o runme main.o first.o second.o
```

The first command compiles main.cpp, creating main.o. The second command compiles first.cpp and second.cpp, creating the object code files first.o and second.o. Finally, the third command specifies runme as the output code filename and links the three object code files along with any needed library code to create the finished program. In the third command, g++ is used merely as an executive—a kind of supervisor—for running the linker. Because no source files are specified, the preprocessor, compiler, and assembler stages are skipped. It is possible to run the GNU linker directly, but using g++ as an executive is usually easier and ensures that all proper linking options are selected.

TO QUOTE OR NOT TO QUOTE

Programmers new to C or C++ are usually confused when writing `#include` directives whether to quote header filenames as in `"header.h"` or to bracket them like this: `<header.h>`. But the mystery is easily explained by two rules:

- Use brackets to include standard C and C++ header files such as iostream.h and stdlib.h.
- Use double quotes to include your own program's header files. You may name them as you like, but it's common to use the .h filename extension.

Most programs use a mix of standard and program headers. For example, the following two directives include two header files:

```
#include <time.h>
#include "graphics.h"
```

In the first instance, the compiler looks in its standard paths for the bracketed time.h file. In the second instance, the compiler looks for a file named graphics.h in the current directory.

INCLUDE-FILE OPTIONS

Several useful options alter the directories where the compiler searches for files named in `#include` directives. By using these options, you can tell the compiler to look in alternate directories for your program's header files. Wild and crazy programmers cleverly name their include directories *include*.

The option `-I` (it must be a capital I) tells the compiler to search a named directory *ahead* of those it normally examines for quoted header files in directives such as

```
#include "myheader.h"
```

The following command, for example, tells the compiler to search in the /include directory for the program's quoted header files before searching the current directory:

```
$ g++ -I /include atest.cpp
```

If you specify multiple directories using `-I` options, they are scanned in left-to-right order. The following command looks in two directories, include1 and include2, for the program's quoted header files:

```
$ g++ -I/include1 -I/include2 atest.cpp
```

There may or may not be a space between the -I option and the named directory. To specify an include directory to be searched *after* the compiler searches the current directory, use the -idirafter option. The following command searches /include after the compiler finishes looking in the current directory for the program's quoted headers:

```
$ g++ -idirafter /include atest.cpp
```

Neither -I nor -idirafter has any effect on the compiler's search for standard header files such as stdlib.h and iostream.h. The two options affect only the header files that belong to your program. They help you organize a large program's many files and are also useful for trying test compilations using modified copies of header files, or for compiling different versions of a program using alternate declarations.

CONTROLLING THE INCLUDE PATHS

Selected options specify all the paths the compiler searches for header files, including standard ones in locations such as /usr/include. These additional measures are useful for testing custom versions of the standard header files, perhaps if one is found to cause a compilation problem. Experienced programmers also sometimes streamline standard headers by removing extraneous declarations, although this is a tremendous undertaking and not for the fainthearted. If you think you're ready, feel free to skip to the next section. But if you are experiencing problems with a standard header, or you need to modify one for some reason, read on.

The first step is to use option -I- to change the way the compiler treats quoted and bracketed filenames in #include directives. Specifying -I- (the option is preceded and followed by hyphens) causes the compiler to search for both forms of header filenames, <header.h> and "header.h", in any *subsequent* -I paths. For example, examine this command:

```
$ g++ -I- -I /myinclude atest.cpp
```

Given those options, the compiler looks for <header.h> and "header.h" in the /myinclude directory. Another option, -idirafter, specifies whether the compiler searches the specified include directory before (-I) or after (-idirafter) it searches the standard locations. However, even with the -I- option in effect, the compiler still looks for standard headers in the standard places.

If you don't want the compiler to do that, specify the -nostdinc (no standard includes) option. Combined with -I- and -I, -nostdinc gives you total control over where the compiler looks for standard and program header files. When using these options, you assume responsibility for telling the compiler where to find all the header files it needs. This can be a little confusing. The correct command to give is in the following general form (but don't type this yet). The option order is critical:

```
$ g++ -nostdinc -I ./ -I- -I /myinclude atest.cpp
```

Take that a piece at a time. The option -nostdinc tells GNU C++ not to search its standard include-file directories. Option -I- specifies that the subsequent -I directory, /myinclude, should be searched for both forms of headers, <header.h> and "header.h", rather than just the quoted form as usual. With these options, the compiler no longer looks in the current directory for quoted filenames, so if that's also necessary, you must specify that location using -I ./. This must *precede* -I- to prevent the compiler from looking for bracketed headers also in the current directory, which is probably not what you want.

If you try the preceding command on a test file, it almost certainly fails because even small programs require searching for numerous header files in various locations. You must find out what those locations are. Using the -v option explained in this chapter, for example, compiling a test program provided the following information:

```
$ g++ -v atest.cpp
...
#include "..." search starts here:
#include <...> search starts here:
 /usr/include/g++
 /usr/i386-redhat-linux/include
 /usr/lib/gcc-lib/i386-redhat-linux/egcs-2.90.27/include
➥/usr/include End of search list.
```

From this and other information reported by the -v option, you can write down all the directories and referenced header files the compiler needs. You can then copy those files to a new directory and tell the compiler to hunt for its files there. If that directory is named /test/include, the command to compile the program becomes

```
$ g++ -nostdinc -I ./ -I- -I /test/include atest.cpp
```

Now that the compiler uses copies of its standard headers, you can edit them without fear of damaging the original files. To go back to using the standard headers in their rightful places, simply compile normally.

Warning	Don't take this section as an endorsement for modifying standard header files. Although this is sometimes necessary to check out an assumption about a problem that seems to involve a standard declaration, it's dangerous to fiddle around with the standard headers. Needless to say (but I'll say it anyway), the steps outlined here are vastly safer than becoming the super user and editing standard header declarations. Don't ever do that! I provide the foregoing information specifically so that you won't be tempted to do something so potentially harmful to the compiler's health.

OPTIMIZING CODE

GNU C++ is an *optimizing compiler*. This means that, given certain options, the compiler attempts to produce code that runs faster than the code it normally generates. Unless you tell GNU C++ to optimize, it takes no such action.

Why doesn't the compiler simply produce the fastest, tightest code possible in the first place? There are several reasons. For one, some optimizations are more appropriate than others depending on the type of program. For example, the -ffast-math option can speed math calculations at the expense of violating stringent IEEE rules such as ensuring that parameter values passed to the sqrt() (square-root) function are always positive. Because these tests can degrade the program's performance, you might choose not to make them if you are writing an action game, but you'd probably want to perform the standard checks in a mathematical subroutine library.

Another reason the compiler does not normally optimize code is time. Each level of optimization increases compilation time and expands the amount of memory required during compilation. Also, with no optimizations selected, the compiler produces code that the GNU debugger can synchronize with the program's source text so that you can view statements and data. Because optimizations rearrange compiled code, use processor registers, and perform other tricks, it is more difficult to debug optimized code.

Other optimizations speed performance but can greatly expand the size of the executable code file. Depending on your needs, you might opt to have smaller code files in return for a small degradation in performance. On the other hand, if you have plenty of disk space, you probably want your programs to run as fast as possible regardless of how much real estate they stake out. The following sections describe various options that you can use to select different levels and types of optimizations.

OPTIMIZATION LEVELS

General optimization options begin with -O (that's the capital letter O) either alone or followed by one of the digits 0, 1, 2, or 3. For example, to compile welcome.cpp from the preceding chapter using the first level of optimizations, specify -O1 to the compiler with this command:

```
$ g++ -O1 welcome.cpp
```

Level one is the default, so that's the same as typing -O alone. The equivalent command is

```
$ g++ -O welcome.cpp
```

Specify -O2 or -O3 to select additional levels of optimizations, which might result in even faster running code, but which also makes the compiler work a lot harder. The option -O0 (a capital O and a zero) is the same as not specifying any optimizations. Because the compiler normally performs no optimizations, you rarely have to specify -O0, but it might come in handy in a Makefile script that selects among optimization levels.

You can also select specific optimizations such as -ffast-math. These options begin with -f and are followed by the option name. There must be no space after -f. For example, the following command tells the compiler to ignore the inline keyword:

```
$ g++ -fno-inline
```

Inline functions, which you meet in Chapter 10, "Creating and Calling Functions," can greatly speed up some kinds of programs. They are an excellent example of the kinds of optimizations that *you* can perform in the program's source code. However, inline functions can also greatly expand the program's executable code file. Using the preceding option might cause the program to run a little slower, but it might also reduce its code file size significantly.

Inline functions are actually compiled as such only when using at least the first level of optimization, -O or -O1, so specifying -fno-inline alone has no effect. GNU C++ does not integrate inline functions in nonoptimized code, and therefore, you must combine the -fno-inline option with an option-level selector, as in this command:

```
$ g++ -O1 -fno-inline welcome.cpp
```

That specifies optimization level one but does not expand inline functions. Most GNU C++ optimization and other options have similar "no-" forms. The opposite option, -finline, for example tells the compiler to recognize the inline keyword. However, because that's the default action, you probably never need to specify -finline.

TO OPTIMIZE OR NOT TO OPTIMIZE

Just before releasing a program, many developers compile using the highest level of optimization and then ship the beast out the door (or, more likely these days, over the Internet). However, there is a great danger in doing this. If you don't optimize until just before releasing your program, this means that you have spent the last several weeks or months testing and debugging code that is *different* from the code you release. You are sending your users a version of a program that is virtually untested!

For that reason, some programmers advise always compiling with the same level of optimizations to be used in the finished code. That's good advice, but these are the folks who have access to the university's Cray supercomputer at 2 a.m. For those of us developing on PCs, optimizing makes debugging too difficult, and it wastes compilation time that can be better spent on other activities. (Sleeping comes to mind. Eating is useful, too.)

I suggest a compromise. Start optimizing when your program begins to resemble its expected final form. Use optimizations periodically from then on—at each level of beta release, for example, or whatever you call your program's test versions. At other times, and especially for debugging sessions, turn off all optimizations. Certainly, you should test optimized code at selected intervals and not just before you send out the finished program. But you don't have to optimize every single time you compile. With a little care, this scheme lets you use optimizations safely and still have time left for dinner and a little shut-eye.

PART
II

CH
5

INTRODUCTION TO DEBUGGING

At the beginning of this chapter, you learned about errors and warnings—messages the compiler issues for problems it discovers in a program's source code. These are examples of compile-time bugs. Another type of error is called a runtime bug. This is a problem caused, not by an error of syntax, but by faulty logic in your program's operation. For example, a runtime bug might result from a statement multiplying two values when it should have added them. The compiler can't help you there. It comprehends the program's symbolic expression, but it doesn't understand what the program is supposed to do.

When a program fails to operate as expected, it's time to dig out the debugger, roll up your sleeves, and investigate the cause. Don't waste time staring at the source code. After all, you have spent hours slaving over that code, and if it doesn't work, staring at it some more is unlikely to reveal the problem. Learn instead to use the GNU debugger to peer inside the program similar to the way you can use a microscope to observe a plant or animal's normally invisible cell structures. Viewing a program this way at a "microscopic" level is the best way to find out why it isn't working.

This chapter introduces the GNU debugger and explains how to load a program into the debugger for investigation. Mastering the art of debugging, however, can take a lifetime. To help you learn debugging techniques, and not merely the debugger's commands, throughout this book I point out C++ debugging methods.

> **Note**
>
> In addition to C and C++ programs, the GNU debugger can debug programs written in Pascal, Modula-2, and Fortran, but support for these and other languages is currently incomplete.

COMPILING FOR DEBUGGING

Before you can run a program under the control of a debugger, you must compile it using special options that add information to the compiled object code. This information makes it possible for the debugger to synchronize the executing program with its source code. After compiling for debugging, you can perform various commands such as running the program a single statement at a time while viewing each statement's effect, a process called *single-stepping*. You can also inspect the values of variables, and you can set *breakpoints* to halt the program automatically at strategic locations.

Future chapters explain all those commands in association with appropriate C++ programming techniques. Here, you learn how to compile a program for debugging and how to run it under the debugger's control. To compile code for debugging, specify the -g option. For example, compile welcome.cpp from the preceding chapter using this command:

```
$ g++ -g welcome.cpp
```

Compiling with debugging information takes longer than usual, so be patient. Using -g produces a medium-level amount of debugging information in the object code. Usually, this is adequate, but for even more information (and a longer compilation time), jump to level 3 using this command:

```
$ g++ -g3 welcome.cpp
```

At level 3, the highest available, the output includes macro definitions and, perhaps, other helpful data. Because GNU versions undoubtedly differ on this, you might have to experiment to find out what each level does on your system. For quick tests, you can jump down a level with -g1 using a command such as

```
$ g++ -g1 welcome.cpp
```

The -g1 option does not produce line number information, nor does it allow inspection of local variables, but compilation finishes more quickly and you might use this for simple investigations. For best results in most cases, you can ignore the subject of levels and simply compile using the option -g.

If your versions of GNU C and C++ are installed with multiple debugging formats, you might need to compile for debugging by using the options -ggdb (same as -g normally), -gstabs+, -gstabs, -gxcoff+, -gxcoff, -gdwarf+, or -gdwarf. For most readers of this book, the -g option is all that's needed. (See the info gcc pages for more information on this topic.)

If you compile with optimizations, the debugger might not be able to synchronize the running program with the source code. However, the GNU debugger allows you to specify the first level of optimization (-0 or -01) and still be able to debug the results. Use this command to optimize and prepare a program for debugging:

```
$ g++ -O -g welcome.cpp
```

That might cause some parts of the program to be out of synch with the source code, but at least you can debug the optimized code. This is so largely because, unlike some other compilers such as Cfront, which translates C++ into C for compiling with the system's C compiler, GNU C++ is a true compiler. It translates C++ source code directly into object code (in the form of assembly language), and as a result, the debugging information added to that code more closely tracks the original source even with some optimizations. However, with -0, inline functions are more difficult to trace.

Tip

To debug inline functions as normal, callable functions, compile using -g but without the -0 option. Or, you can use -0 along with -fno-inline.

The GNU C++ compiler creates debugging information in a format known as *stabs*, which stands for Symbol Tables. Given the -g option, the compiler stores stabs directives in the intermediate assembly language file. The assembler and linker transfer the data in those directives to the object code and executable code files. Debugging information includes the source code file's line numbers and symbols, such as the names of functions and variables. To view this information, compile with the -g and -S options, and then load the resulting .s assembly language file into your editor. Hunt for directives such as .stabs, .stabn, .stabd, and .stabx. For more information on these directives, read the info stabs pages.

CHOOSE YOUR WEAPON

The GNU debugger is an excellent example of how freely distributed software can produce quality results. By my count from the debugger's info pages, more than 60 programmers contributed to the GNU debugger, and the resulting software is top-notch. It's hard to imagine any software company, even the biggest, spending as much effort on a commercial debugger.

PART

II

CH

5

GNU provides two debugger interfaces, one that runs in console mode and one in X. These aren't different debuggers; just different ways to issue debugging commands and view their output. Which interface to use boils down to whether you prefer to run a console shell or an X graphical interface. Try them both as the following sections suggest and then use the interface you prefer. The Emacs editor can also run the GNU debugger. I show all these methods in the next sections.

Tip

You can use the console debugger in a shell window opened under X. This is the method I used to debug most of the sample programs listed in this book.

Using the gdb Console Debugger

The basic GNU console debugger, gdb, understands numerous commands entered at a shell prompt, and it displays its output on the console. To begin learning how to use gdb, try the following commands on the welcome.cpp program from the preceding chapter. First, compile the program and load it into the debugger using the two commands:

```
$ g++ -g -o welcome welcome.cpp
$ gdb welcome
```

The first command compiles welcome.cpp for debugging and specifies welcome as the executable code filename. The second command starts the debugger and loads the compiled welcome code. Onscreen, gdb displays its version number and copyright notice:

```
GNU gdb 4.17
Copyright 1998 Free Software Foundation, Inc.  GDB is free
software, covered by the GNU General Public License, and you
are welcome to change it and/or distribute copies of it under
certain conditions.  Type "show copying" to see the
conditions. There is absolutely no warranty for GDB. Type
"show warranty" for details.
This GDB was configured as "i386-redhat-linux"...
(gdb)
```

The final line (gdb) is the debugger's command prompt. To prevent the debugger from displaying its wordy preface, you can use the -quiet option:

```
$ gdb -quiet welcome
(gdb)
```

The option -silent, though not listed officially, also works. However you start it, the debugger comes up quickly because it loads only a minimum amount of information from the specified program. For help with the debugger's commands, simply type *help* like this:

```
(gdb) help
```

That displays an impressive list of debugging commands, organized into categories such as breakpoints, data, and running. For help on a specific category, type *help* followed by its name. The following command requests help on the debugger's data-inspection commands:

```
(gdb) help data
```

You might want to browse through some of gdb's help pages—if you do, you'll discover that the GNU debugger offers a full suite of commands for inspecting programs in just about any way imaginable. Now let's get back to running welcome, which is paused inside the debugger, waiting for a command. To run the loaded program, type ***run***:

```
(gdb) run
Starting program: /src/c05/welcome
Welcome to GNU C++ for Linux programming!
Program exited normally.
Current language:  auto; currently c
(gdb)
```

When you give the run command, the debugger reads the program's code and debugging information into memory. This takes a few moments. Eventually, the program runs and, in this case, displays the welcome string shown here on the third line. The debugger tells you the program exited normally and that the language recognized is auto; currently c. (This is correct for C++.) The program remains loaded into the debugger. To run it again, type another run command.

Some debugger commands require a source file line number. To find line numbers, use the list command. For example, type

```
(gdb) list
13 int main()
14 {
15   cout << "Welcome to GNU C++ for Linux programming!" << endl;
```

To save space, I show only three lines. Onscreen, you see more. Type a second list command to view more lines. Type ***list n***, where ***n*** is a line number, to center that line in the output. Armed with the program's line numbers, you can use commands such as break, which sets a *breakpoint*. With a breakpoint set, the debugger halts the program just before reaching the specified breakpoint location. You may set as many breakpoints as you need.

To try out breakpoints, find the line number of the statement where you want to pause execution. To set a breakpoint at line 15, enter the following command:

```
(gdb) break 15
Breakpoint 1 at 0x804868b: file welcome.cpp, line 15.
```

The debugger tells you the number of the breakpoint (1) and its address in memory. It also identifies the source code filename and the line number associated with this breakpoint. Run the program by giving the run command:

```
(gdb) run
Starting program: /home/tswan/mgcc/c05/welcome
Breakpoint 1, main () at welcome.cpp:15
15 cout << "Welcome to GNU C++ for Linux programming!" << endl;
```

When execution reaches the breakpoint, the program pauses. The debugger tells you that Breakpoint 1 stopped the program, and you see onscreen the line of code at that location. To execute only that statement, issue a next command:

```
(gdb) next
Welcome to GNU C++ for Linux programming!
16 return 0;
```

PART

II

CH

5

You first see the result of the executed statement—in this case, the message printed on the console. After that, the debugger displays line 16, indicating the statement to be executed next. The program is again paused. To make it go on, you could type another next command to execute this single statement, or you can type continue to run the program normally from this point onward. Try continue:

```
(gdb) continue
Continuing.
Program exited normally.
```

In this case, continuing the program causes it to end. However, if another breakpoint were reached, the program would again halt. Setting a breakpoint, running the program to that spot, and then single-stepping the program's statements with next are useful commands for running a program in slow motion, one step at a time. The commands work like the editing buttons on a video camera for inspecting a recording one frame at a time. By single-stepping a program, you can often find the cause of a problem obscured by running at full speed.

Breakpoints and single-stepping are good techniques also for learning C++ programming. A debugger makes a great programming teacher! Don't wait for me to suggest using the debugger. Load any of this book's sample listings into the debugger and use its commands to investigate how the program works. To quit the debugger and return to the console, use this command:

```
(gdb) quit
$
```

Tip

You can also press Ctrl-D to quit. Or, simply type *q*. The gdb command prompt recognizes tab completion, so you can type *q* and press Tab to complete the quit command. Many commands require only an initial letter or two. Type *r* to run, *c* to continue, *n* to execute the next statement, and *b 15* to set a breakpoint at line 15. Experiment with these and other abbreviations, and develop your own shorthand of the debugging commands you use most often.

USING THE XXGDB X WINDOW DEBUGGER

The xxgdb program is not a different debugger. It's merely a graphical interface for gdb. You must be running X to use xxgdb. There are two ways to start the debugger using xxgdb. The easiest is to type a command at a console prompt in a shell window. First compile the program for debugging and then load it into xxgdb. Enter these two commands:

```
$ g++ -g -o welcome welcome.cpp
$ xxgdb welcome
```

In a short moment, you see the graphical debugger's display as shown in Figure 5.1. At top is the program listing. In the middle is a window of commands you can select by pointing and clicking with the mouse. At bottom are the commands and messages that gdb displays. This window resembles a console terminal, but you can't type into it.

Figure 5.1
GNU's graphical
debugger, xxgdb.

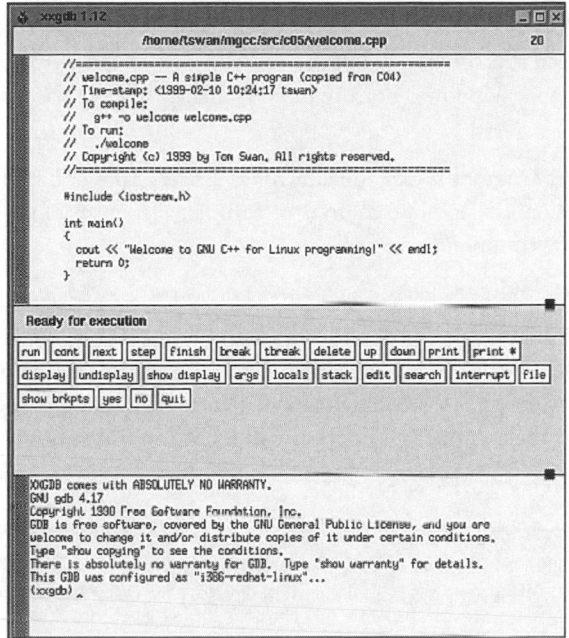

Another way to start xxgdb is to select it from the Start menu, or if you don't use the Fvwm Windowslike interface, from whatever program menu your window manager provides. Be prepared to hunt for the debugger's parent menu. On my system, this was Start/Programs/Utilities/Mail. Obviously, the debugger has nothing to do with Mail utilities, and it took me a while to find it. I think it's all-around easier just to run xxgdb from the console. In fact, I prefer to run many X programs this way.

Tip

Start xxgdb from a console prompt without specifying a filename. When the debugger's window appears, click the File button and select a compiled program for debugging.

The graphical debugger's commands are similar to the console commands but are in the form of clickable buttons. To run the program, click the Run button. To set a breakpoint, click the line in the top window's source code and then click the Break button. You see a red hand next to the line—at least, that's what my version of xxgdb shows.

Click Run to execute up to a breakpoint, and observe the bottom window for any messages. The debugger's output is the same as explained in the preceding section. However, it's much handier to see the source code at the same time. Click Continue to continue the program after it halts at a breakpoint.

PART
II

CH
5

RUNNING GDB IN EMACS

The Emacs editor can run the gdb debugger and show its output along with associated source code files in split windows. For my money, this is the best way to run the GNU debugger.

To start debugging a program under the control of Emacs, first compile the program with debugging information. It's possible to do this from Emacs, but for simple programs, this is more easily done at a command prompt:

```
$ g++ -g -o welcome welcome.cpp
```

After compilation finishes, switch back to Emacs and select Tools, Debugger from the menu. At the bottom of the Emacs display, an incomplete gdb command is shown. Complete it by typing the program's executable code filename (the one that contains the debugging information created with the compiler's -g option). The bottom line looks like this:

```
Run gdb (like this): gdb welcome
```

Tip

For best results, load at least one of the program's source code file's into Emacs. This makes the program's path the current directory for the preceding gdb command.

Emacs starts gdb and prepares two buffer windows, one showing the program's source code and the other showing gdb's output. Figure 5.2 shows the Emacs display while debugging welcome.cpp.

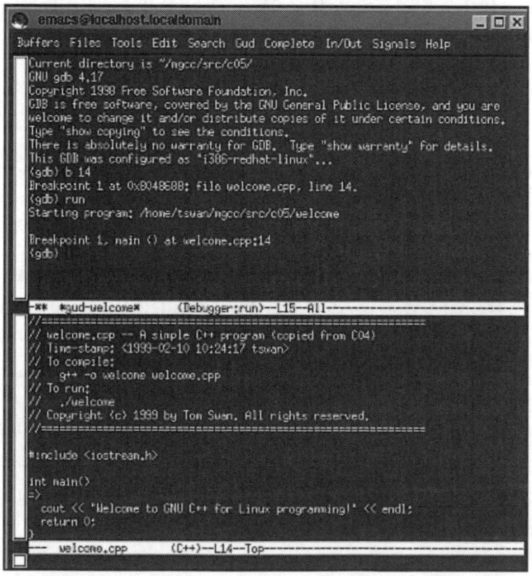

Figure 5.2
Debugging
welcome.cpp in
Emacs.

The top Emacs window operates like a console terminal. The other window shows the program's source code. (The order of the windows might be reversed.) To issue debugger commands, type them as you do when running gdb in console mode. The advantage of using Emacs is that it shows you the program's source code and also highlights the current line and any breakpoints. Also, you can write, compile, and debug programs without switching away from Emacs.

If you are following along, repeat the steps in "Using the gdb Console Debugger" to see how Emacs displays the results of various commands. Another advantage of running gdb in Emacs is that the debugger's output is saved in a buffer (in this case, named gud-welcome). Use the buffer to scroll back through commands and their output. You might even save or print the entire debugging session. When tracking a difficult bug, it's helpful to have a record of debugging commands issued.

USEFUL DEBUGGER OPTIONS

Use -h (or --help) to list available options you can specify when starting gdb. Following are explanations of some of the options that you might find useful.

Specify --command=FILE where FILE is the name of a text file containing gdb commands. This is a great way to repeat debugging sessions without typing the same commands over and over. For example, create a text file named commands containing the following two lines:

```
break 15
run
```

To debug the welcome.cpp program and execute the file's commands, type the following at the console prompt (this assumes that you compiled welcome.cpp using the -g option). This command loads welcome and then executes the break and run commands in the commands file:

```
$ gdb --command=commands welcome
```

If you store your program's source code in a directory that is different from where you store the executable code, use the --directory option to tell gdb where to find the source code files. Use a command such as

```
gdb --directory=/home/you/source yourprogram
```

You might need to do that when using Emacs to run gdb if the current directory does not contain the compiled program. To send the program's output to a terminal that is different from the one you are using to view gdb's messages, use the --tty command as follows:

```
gdb --tty=/dev/ttyp0 welcome
```

This works the same in the console, X, and Emacs debugger interfaces. To find the device name of a terminal, type the following tty command at a shell prompt:

```
$ tty
/dev/ttyp0
```

Switch to another terminal—or under X, open a new shell window—and then specify the reported device name to gdb using the --tty option. The program's output appears on the other console window. This is particularly useful when debugging programs that display

PART II
CH 5

formatted output. With this option, you can run the debugger in one window and see the program's output in another. Although this works equally well with dumb terminals, and also with Linux virtual terminals selected on supported systems by pressing Alt-F*n*, where F*n* is a function key from F1 to F6, it is especially handy under X because you can arrange the two windows for simultaneous viewing.

Tip

Use the --tty option when debugging from Emacs to send the program's output to a separate console window instead of an editor window pane.

For stalwart gurus in the audience who can decipher core dumps, the --core option loads a core file into the debugger for analysis. For test purposes, I ran a test program that calls the standard abort() function as explained in the preceding chapter and then I loaded the resulting core dump file into the debugger with the following command:

```
$ gdb -q --core=core
Core was generated by './testerr'.
Program terminated with signal 6, Aborted.
#0  0x40088781 in ?? ()
```

The reported information indicates what program caused the abnormal termination and how that process was terminated. The final line in the debugger's output is a good example of why I don't like to read core dump files. (Type *q* to quit the debugger if you are following along.)

Finally, one of the commands I like best in the GNU debugger is stop. Its help entry tells all you need to know about this command:

```
stop -- There is no 'stop' command
```

Only in Linux....

SUMMARY

Like a good mechanic, a skillful GNU C++ programmer needs to master the mechanical aspects of running the compiler and debugger. This chapter explained the differences between the compiler's warning and error messages and showed examples of several common errors. The chapter also demonstrated a variety of compiler options you can use to create portable code; optimize runtime performance; separately compile modular programs; halt the preprocessor, compiler, and assembler at intermediate stages; and perform other useful services. The chapter ended with an introduction to the GNU debugger and included examples of three debugger interfaces, one for console mode, one for X, and one for the Emacs editor.

For more information on subjects introduced in this chapter, turn to the following:

- Chapter 10, "Creating and Calling Functions"
- Chapter 20, "Customizing I/O Streams"

CREATING DATA OBJECTS

Data are the facts a program knows or can calculate. A program's data can take many forms, such as character strings, integers, floating point values, arrays, and structs. This chapter explores these fundamental types of data objects and also includes suggestions for debugging a program's data.

| Note | The word "object" as I use it here does not necessarily refer to object-oriented programming. All data items are correctly called objects. See Part III, "Object-Oriented Programming," for an introduction to object-oriented programming techniques that use objects created from C++ *classes*. |

DATA DECLARATIONS

C++ requires you to *declare* data objects before their first use in a program. To declare a data object, specify its type and name, and terminate the declaration with a semicolon. Here's a sample:

```
int counter;
```

That declares a *variable* named counter of type int. Running the program creates space in memory to hold the variable's value. It's a *variable* because, although it can hold only one value at a time, the program is free to change that value as often as necessary. One way to do that is to use a statement that *assigns* a value to the variable. The following statement assigns the value 100 to counter:

```
counter = 100;
```

Assigning a value to counter replaces whatever value the variable previously held. It's especially important to understand that the equal sign does *not* state that counter is equal to 100; it performs the runtime action of moving the value 100 *into* counter (or technically, into the memory that the program reserves for the variable). You can also assign the results of expressions to variables. The following statement increases the current value of counter by ten:

```
counter = counter + 10;
```

A shorthand way of writing that same statement is

```
counter += 10;
```

The shorthand references counter only once, and in some cases this might be more efficient (for example, if counter is a complex expression and not merely a simple variable). You can also use type-compatible variables in expressions. If you declare another int variable like this:

```
int total;
```

the program can *initialize* total to 10 and then add counter to it with statements such as the following:

```
total = 10;
total = total + counter;
```

If `counter` equals 100 before those statements, `total` now equals 110. As with all assignments, the result of the expression (`total` + `counter`) must be of a type that is compatible with the object that receives the value. The preceding statement can also be written using the shorthand

```
total += counter;
```

This simply avoids having to type `total` twice. Either form is correct, but the shorthand version is popular, and as mentioned, possibly more efficient.

TYPE CONVERSIONS

An assigned value must be of an appropriate type. If you try to assign a value of one type to a variable of another type, as in the following statement, the compiler attempts to convert that value to a compatible type. This is important to understand, especially if you are familiar with other programming languages such as Pascal, in which data types in assignments must strictly match their target object types. Consider these statements:

```
double pi = 3.14159;
int counter = pi;    // ???
```

The `double` type specifies `pi` as a floating point value. Assigning `pi` to the `int` counter variable sets its value to 3, but because the assignment refers to objects of different types, the compiler issues the following warning:

```
x.cpp:8: warning: initialization to 'int' from 'double'
```

It's possible to "fix" warnings about incompatible data types by using a *type cast expression*. Changing the preceding assignment to the following gets rid of the warning:

```
int count = (int)pi;
```

Specifying the data type of an object in parentheses this way converts its value to the specified type. It also tells the compiler that you realize the objects are of different types, and that you are intentionally assigning the one value to the other. However, you can't use casts to perform type conversions willy-nilly. For example, you can't use a type cast expression to convert a string into an `int` value—for that, you must call a library function (see "String Conversions" later in this chapter for more information).

> **Note**
>
> The data type `double` is so named from the term "double precision," a reference to the internal storage format used for floating point values.

IDENTIFIERS: GOOD, BAD, AND UGLY

An object's name, or *identifier*, must conform to certain rules. A properly formed identifier must begin with an alphabetic character or an underscore, and it must contain only alphabetic characters, digits, and underscores. It may contain upper- and lowercase letters. Identifiers may be from one to 255 characters long, but the compiler recognizes only the first 32 characters. It's common to use single-letter identifiers such as `i` and `x` for general purpose variables, but longer names such as index and x_coordinate can make programs more understandable.

Tip

Although the legal length limit for identifiers is 255, in practice, identifiers should not be any longer than about 15 to 20 characters.

There are some esoteric, and mostly useless, variations to the GNU C++ identifier naming rules. You can, for example, use dollar signs in identifiers, but this may or may not be acceptable with other compilers. You are best advised to use only characters, digits, and underscores. Some examples of good identifiers are

```
counter
y2k_fix
date_of_birth
speedOfLight
```

Many C programmers object to uppercase characters in identifiers and prefer speed_of_light to speedOfLight. Whatever your preference, you must be consistent. This is because C++ is *case sensitive*, and the compiler considers the identifiers speed_of_light, speedOfLight, and speedoflight to be three different objects. Here are some examples of bad identifiers:

```
10times
user-name
xq29b
```

The first identifier begins with a digit, and that's never allowed. The second includes a hyphen, but only letters, digits, and underscores are permitted. The third identifier is merely ugly. If you create identifiers like that, when it comes time to debug the program, you'll wonder what you could possibly have meant by xq29b. Always choose identifiers that describe their purposes. Don't be cryptic; be clear.

Tip

Although identifiers may begin with one or more underscores as in _username and _ _uservalue, this convention is used by the standard library to avoid conflicts with user-program identifiers. For that reason, do not begin your own identifiers with underscores.

GNU C++ RESERVED WORDS

C++ reserves 97 identifiers for its own use (this number might differ depending on your compiler version). Table 6.1 lists all reserved words in GNU C++. Do not use any of the words in the table for your own identifiers.

TABLE 6.1   GNU C++ RESERVED WORDS

_ _alignof	_ _const _ _	_ _inline	reinterpret_c	try
_ _alignof_ _	const	_ _inline_ _	return	typedef
and	const_cast	inline	short	typeid
and_ _eq	continue	int	_ _signature_ _	typename
_ _asm	default	_ _label_ _	signature	_ _typeof
_ _asm_ _	delete	long	_ _signed	_ _typeof_ _
asm	do	mutable	_ _signed_ _	typeof
_ _attribute	double	namespace	signed	union
_ _attribute_ _	dynamic_case	new	_ _sigof_ _	unsigned
auto	else	not	sigof	using
bitand	enum	not_eq	sizeof	virtual
bitor	explicit	operator	static	void
bool	_ _extension_ _	or	static_cast	_ _volatile
break	extern	or_eq	struct	_ _volatile_ _
case	false	overload	switch	volatile
catch	float	private	template	_ _wchar_t
char	for	protected	this	while
class	friend	public	throw	xor
compl	goto	register	true	xor_eq
_ _const	if			

Tip

If you receive a "parse error" from the compiler but the source code appears to be correct, check whether you have accidentally used one of the words in Table 6.1.

SIMPLE DATA OBJECTS

Simple data objects hold numerical values such as integers or floating point values. Other simple data types include Boolean values that represent true or false conditions, characters, and *enumerations*. An enumeration is simply a set of names given to values in a series such as the days of the week.

This section introduces C++'s simple data types and lists a few programs that explain related subjects, such as how to determine the size and type of an object, and how to calculate the results of expressions.

INTEGER VARIABLES

There are seven numerical data types in C++: char, short, int, long, float, double, and long double. GNU C++ adds an eighth type, long long, but more on that in the section "Double Wide Integers" later in this chapter.

> **Note**
>
> Although the char type usually represents alphanumeric characters, it is internally just an integer value and can be used to represent byte values as well as characters.

Listing 6.1 shows how to declare variables of all seven C++ integer data types. The program also demonstrates how to determine the size of an object using the C++ sizeof operator.

LISTING 6.1   INTEGERS.CPP

```
#include <iostream.h>

// Global variables

char c;
short s;
int i;
long l;
float f;
double d;
long double ld;

int main()
{
  cout << "Sizeof char        == " << sizeof(c) << endl;
  cout << "Sizeof short       == " << sizeof(s) << endl;
  cout << "Sizeof int         == " << sizeof(i) << endl;
  cout << "Sizeof long        == " << sizeof(l) << endl;
  cout << "Sizeof float       == " << sizeof(f) << endl;
  cout << "Sizeof double      == " << sizeof(d) << endl;
  cout << "Sizeof long double == " << sizeof(ld) << endl;
  return 0;
}
```

The integers.cpp program declares seven *global variables*, one for each of the C++ numerical data types. They are called global variables because they are declared outside any function and are therefore available for use globally throughout the program. (Chapter 10, "Creating and Calling Functions," in the section "Functions and Variables" explains how to create and use *local variables* inside functions. See also "Global and Local Variables" later in this chapter.) Global variables are initially zeroed—in other words, the bytes that compose the variables are set to zero at runtime. Compile and run the integers.cpp program with the following two commands:

```
$ g++ integers.cpp
$ ./a.out
Sizeof char        == 1
Sizeof short       == 2
```

```
Sizeof int         == 4
Sizeof long        == 4
Sizeof float       == 4
Sizeof double      == 8
Sizeof long double == 12
```

> **Note**
>
> The double equal sign (==) means "is equal to." A single equal sign (=) means "assign value to." Don't confuse them.

The program's output shows the size in 8-bit bytes of each numerical object. A char occupies one byte, an int takes 4, and a double takes 8. A long double variable takes 12 bytes of memory. These sizes are defined by ANSI C++. Unlike in C, where the size of fundamental types depends on the whim of the compiler, you can depend on these simple objects taking the same space with any up-to-date ANSI C++ compiler.

LIMITS

The size of a numerical data type limits its range of values. The range is further determined by whether it is *signed* or *unsigned*. Signed objects can hold negative and positive values. Unsigned objects can hold only positive values. All numerical objects can represent the value zero.

Of the seven numerical data types, only char, short, int, and long may be specifically signed or unsigned. Unless specified otherwise, these four types are signed by default. Floating point objects of the types float, double, and long double are always signed. To specifically state whether an object is signed or unsigned, precede it by the reserved words signed or unsigned. Here are some samples:

```
unsigned int average;   // Must be positive or zero
signed long total;      // Can be negative, zero, or positive
long total;             // Same as preceding declaration
unsigned char byte;     // Must be in the range 0 ... 255
```

The variable average is declared unsigned, and so it might hold only positive int values and zero. The variable total is declared as signed, so it can hold positive and negative values (and zero), but because the long type is normally signed, there's no practical reason to declare it this way, and the third line is more commonly used. The variable byte is declared as an unsigned char, and because a char is 8-bits in length, the byte object as defined here can hold values in the range of 0 to 255.

> **Note**
>
> Whether char variables are signed by default is an important consideration. Because the rules on this differ among various C and C++ compilers, this obscure fact is also the source of many frustrating bugs. In ANSI C++, char is signed by default, and as such can represent values in the range of –128 to +127 including zero. If you want unsigned chars, you must explicitly declare them so.

The short and long data types are actually abbreviations for short int and long int, respectively. You may declare variables using these unabbreviated names like this:

```
short int shorter;
long int longer;
```

But the following declarations are equivalent and more common:

```
short shorter;
long longer;
```

You can combine unsigned and signed with short and long int declarations. For example, the following statements declare two unsigned variables of types short int and long int:

```
unsigned short int short_n_sweet;
unsigned long int long_n_tall;
```

Constants As Macros

A *constant* is an object or other value that a program can't change at runtime. In C++ (and in ANSI C), there are two types of constants—those defined by macros and those defined as data objects. The simplest constant is a macro created by a #define directive. For example, this defines a constant named MAXIMUM equal to 100:

```
#define MAXIMUM 100
```

A symbol such as MAXIMUM is known as a *macro* because the C++ preprocessor replaces it with its associated value wherever the symbol appears (but not inside strings or comments). By convention, constants defined this way are written in all uppercase, but that's not required.

The single most important reason for defining constants such as MAXIMUM is to avoid strewing literal values throughout the program's source code. For example, even if MAXIMUM is used in a hundred different places, a simple change to the #define directive is all that's needed to change the associated value. Well-named constants also make the program's source code more understandable.

You can use a constant such as MAXIMUM anywhere its value (100) is appropriate. By "value," I do not mean its integer value—despite appearances, MAXIMUM is *not* an integer object. It's a symbolic macro representation of the characters 1, 0, and 0. You can display MAXIMUM using an output statement such as

```
cout << "MAXIMUM == " << MAXIMUM << endl;
```

After preprocessing, that statement is compiled as though it were written this way:

```
cout << "MAXIMUM == " << 100 << endl;
```

In expanding the MAXIMUM macro, the C++ preprocessor inserts the characters 1, 0, and 0 into the program text *before* compilation.

When using #define to create constants, there are two other important rules to remember. First, never end the directive with a semicolon. In GNU C++, that common mistake produces the following warning and error messages:

```
x.cpp:5: warning: missing white space after '#define MAXIMUM'
x.cpp:9: parse error before ';'
```

Second, keep in mind that a constant created with #define is merely a symbolic representation of whatever follows (ignoring leading whitespace). It's up to you to use constants appropriately. Listing 6.2, defines.cpp, shows a few examples of constants of various types created with #define.

LISTING 6.2   DEFINES.CPP

```cpp
#include <iostream.h>

#define CHARACTER    '@'
#define STRING       "I'd rather be programming!"
#define MAX_VALUE    100
#define PI           3.14159

int main()
{
  cout << "CHARACTER == " << CHARACTER << endl;
  cout << "STRING    == " << STRING    << endl;
  cout << "MAX_VALUE == " << MAX_VALUE << endl;
  cout << "PI        == " << PI        << endl;
  return 0;
}
```

Compiling and running defines.cpp produces this output:

```
CHARACTER == @
STRING    == I'd rather be programming!
MAX_VALUE == 100
PI        == 3.14159
```

As this program demonstrates, constants created with #define can represent any kind of data that you can type into the program's text, including characters, strings, integers, and floating point values, just to name a few.

CONSTANTS AS OBJECTS

Another way to declare a constant value is to precede an object's declaration by the reserved word, const. This tells the compiler to disallow the program from attempting to change the constant's value. The const identifier is a C++ innovation, but it has been adopted back into ANSI C, so you can now use const in C and C++ programs.

Declaring objects as const throws a force field around them, preventing changes to their values at runtime. If you declare an integer count to be const like this:

```cpp
const int count = 1234;
```

the compiler rejects the statement:

```cpp
count = count + 100;  // ???
```

The initial value of count is locked in, and a later program statement cannot change it.

There are good reasons for using const to create fixed values, and there are some not-so-good reasons. Some authorities would have you use const in place of any #define-d macros. According to this advice, instead of using this MAX_COLORS macro:

```
#define MAX_COLORS 16
```

you are advised to declare MAX_COLORS using const this way:

```
const int MAX_COLORS = 16;
```

With MAX_COLORS declared as a const int object instead of a #define-d macro, you gain two supposed advantages:

- The compiler can perform stricter type checking on the constant. C++ knows that MAX_COLORS is an integer constant, but it doesn't possess any information about the type of a #define-d macro.

- The GNU debugger can examine the value of MAX_COLORS. Because the preprocessor expands #define-d macros, the macro is not entered into the symbol table that the debugger uses to locate the program's data.

Those are important considerations. However, there's nothing wrong with using #define-d macros, especially for simple values such as buffer sizes and title strings. As you learn more about C++ programming in future chapters, though, you'll appreciate the value of const. It can be applied to class objects, function return values, and function parameters, and when used in these ways, const is an invaluable tool for writing robust code that prevents modifying any values that should never change.

Predefined Constants

GNU C++ provides several useful predefined constants. Especially helpful are a set of constants that define the allowable ranges of values for numerical objects. Listing 6.3, ranges.cpp, uses some of these constants to display the allowable ranges of all integer and floating point, signed and unsigned, data types. Most of the program is repetitious, so I list only its first two output statements here (the complete listing is on the CD-ROM). I used the data from this program to create Table 6.2, which shows the range of values for each standard numerical data type.

Listing 6.3   ranges.cpp (partial)

```
#include <iostream.h>
#include <limits.h>
#include <float.h>

int main()
{
  cout << "signed char   : "
       << SCHAR_MIN
       << " ... "
       << SCHAR_MAX
       << endl;
```

```
    cout << "unsigned char : "
         << 0
         << " ... "
         << UCHAR_MAX
         << endl;
    ...
    return 0;
}
```

TABLE 6.2   INTEGER AND FLOATING POINT RANGES

Data Type	Minimum	Maximum Range
signed char	−128	127
unsigned char	0	255
char	−128	127
signed short	−32768	32767
unsigned short	0	65535
int	−2147483648	2147483647
unsigned int	0	4294967295
long	−2147483648	2147483647
unsigned long	0	4294967295
float	1.17549e−38	3.40282c+38
double	2.22507e−308	1.79769e+308
long double	3.3621e−4932	1.18973e+493200

GLOBAL AND LOCAL VARIABLES

A global variable is always declared outside main() or any other function—usually, but not always, in a header file. A local variable is declared inside a function, typically immediately after the statement block's opening brace. Listing 6.4, default.cpp, demonstrates some of the differences between global and local variables.

LISTING 6.4   DEFAULT.CPP

```
#include <iostream.h>

int global = 100;
int globalDefault;

int main()
{
  int local = 200;
```

continues

LISTING 6.4 CONTINUED

```
  int localDefault;

  cout << "global....... == " << global        << endl;
  cout << "local........ == " << local         << endl;
  cout << "globalDefault == " << globalDefault << endl;
  cout << "localDefault  == " << localDefault  << endl;
  return 0;
}
```

There are two key differences between global variables such as global and globalDefault declared outside any function, and local variables such as local and localDefault, here declared inside main(). The differences are

- Global variables are potentially available to any statement throughout the program. Local variables are available only to statements inside their declaring function.

- Global variables are automatically initialized to zero when the program is started. Local variables are not initialized until the program assigns them values.

Compiling and running the sample default.cpp program demonstrates these differences. Enter these lines and take a look at the program's output:

```
$ g++ default.cpp
$ ./a.out
global....... == 100
local....... == 200
globalDefault == 0
localDefault  == 1
```

Function main() can refer to both the global and local variables. However, if there were another function in the program, it would not be able to refer to the two local variables, local and localDefault, because these are inside main(). The variables' *scope* extends only to their declaring statement block.

Note   See Chapter 10, "Creating and Calling Functions," for more information on local variables.

MULTIPLE VARIABLE DECLARATIONS

When declaring multiple variables of the same type, you can write them one after the other separated by commas this way:

```
int v1, v2, v3, v4;
```

Or you can create them individually by stacking their declarations on separate lines:

```
int v1;
int v2;
int v3;
int v4;
```

Whichever style you choose, you may assign initial values to variables, or you may leave them uninitialized. (If they are global, however, remember that they are automatically initialized to zero.) The following statement declares four `int` variables and initializes two of them, v2 and v4, to the values 123 and 321, respectively.

```
int v1, v2 = 123, v3, v4 = 321;
```

That looks jumbled to me, so as a general rule, I use the shorthand declaration style only for uninitialized variables. If I intend to assign initial values, I prefer to write them on separate lines as follows:

```
int v2 = 123;
int v4 = 321;
```

ENUMERATED TYPES

An enumerated type is a symbolic representation of a series of values such as the colors of the rainbow, the days of the week, or any other series that can be represented in a program using integers. For instance, suppose that you want to represent a rainbow's seven fundamental colors. To give a name to each color, you could define symbolic constants such as these:

```
#define RED     0
#define ORANGE  1
#define YELLOW  2
#define GREEN   3
#define BLUE    4
#define INDIGO  5
#define VIOLET  6
```

The values are meaningless—they just give the program a convenient way to represent color names as unique integer values that might be stored in variables, written to disk files, or used in other ways. Given these symbols, a program can declare an `int` variable like this:

```
int color;
```

and then assign to `color` any of the color symbols:

```
color = GREEN;
```

The compiler replaces GREEN with that symbol's associated text, in this case the single digit 3. In effect, the statement is compiled as

```
color = 3;
```

Obviously, the symbol GREEN is more meaningful than the literal value 3. But typing a long series of color names and other relatively fixed symbols (the months of the year, for instance) is drudge work. Also, there's nothing in the program to indicate that the individual color symbols are related.

To make creating such lists easier, C++ provides a helpful device, called an *enumerated type*. Using the reserved word `enum`, you can create the preceding seven color constants using a single declaration:

```
enum { RED, ORANGE, YELLOW, GREEN, BLUE, INDIGO, VIOLET };
```

PART

II

CH

6

This has the identical effect as the #define directive listed earlier. The enum reserved word is followed by a list of identifiers (typically in uppercase) separated by commas, delimited by curly braces, and ending with a semicolon. Each symbol is assigned a sequential integer value, beginning with 0. In this example, RED equals 0, ORANGE is 1, YELLOW is 2, and so on, up to VIOLET, which equals 6.

Given the preceding declaration, to declare an int variable named color and assign it the color value for BLUE, you can write

```
int color = BLUE;
```

Rather than use an object of type int to store enumerated values, it is clearer to give the enumerated type a name. To do that, use the reserved word typedef (for "type definition") as in the following enumeration for the colors of the rainbow:

```
typedef enum
{
  RED, ORANGE, YELLOW, GREEN, BLUE, INDIGO, VIOLET
} TColors;
```

The typedef reserved word creates the new data type name, TColors, associated with the enumerated list of color names. Now that TColors is defined as a new data type, a program can declare variables of that type like this:

```
TColors oneColor;
```

That makes oneColor a variable of type TColors and makes it possible to assign color symbolic constants to oneColor with statements such as

```
oneColor = INDIGO;
```

The compiler automatically enumerates the elements in an enum declaration. Sometimes, however, it's necessary to take over that job and assign explicit values to one or more symbols. For example, consider the problem of creating an enumerated type for the months of the year. You might try this:

```
enum { JAN, FEB, MAR, APR, MAY, JUN,
       JUL, AUG, SEP, OCT, NOV, DEC };
```

The trouble is, because the first symbol in the enumerated list is assigned the value 0, JAN equals 0 not 1—the normal value associated with the first month of the year. To fix that problem, you can assign an explicit starting value to a member of the enumerated list. For example, to set JAN to 1, change the preceding declaration to

```
enum { JAN = 1, FEB, MAR, APR, MAY, JUN,
       JUL, AUG, SEP, OCT, NOV, DEC       };
```

The expression JAN = 1 assigns 1 to the symbol JAN. Subsequent symbols continue the sequence from that point, making FEB equal to 2, MAR to 3, APR to 4, and DEC to 12. You may similarly initialize any elements of an enumerated type.

One fact to keep in mind when using enumerated variables is that symbolic names such as RED, ORANGE, SEP, and DEC are merely preprocessor symbols, similar to those declared in #define directives. As such, the symbols exist only in the program's source code, and they are replaced with their underlying numerical values in the compiled code. Many programmers who are unfamiliar with enumerations wrongly assume that writing them displays their associated names, but as Listing 6.5, enum.cpp, demonstrates, that's not what happens.

LISTING 6.5   ENUM.CPP

```
#include <iostream.h>

typedef enum
{
  RED, ORANGE, YELLOW, GREEN, BLUE, INDIGO, VIOLET
} TColors;

int main()
{
  TColors acolor = INDIGO;
  cout << "acolor == " << acolor << endl;
  return 0;
}
```

Compile and run the program with the following commands. The program creates and displays the value of a TColors enumerated variable, acolor:

```
$ g++ enum.cpp
$ ./a.out
acolor == 5
```

As you can see, the program reports that acolor equals 5. It does not write the associated symbolic name INDIGO as you might expect because that symbol is replaced during compilation by its enumerated value. Enumerated symbols can help clarify a program's logic, but the symbols exist only at the source code level.

Tip

This chapter's section "Initializing Arrays of Strings" explains a technique that you could use to provide alphabetic names for enumerated types such as TColors.

BOOLEAN VARIABLES

C++ provides the bool data type for representing one of two symbolic values, true or false. Also called Boolean, or true-false, variables, bools are frequently used as *flags* to indicate various conditions. They become more important when you learn about control statements such as while and if in Chapter 9, "Controlling Program Flow." To create a Boolean variable, use a statement such as

```
bool error = false;
```

That declares a variable error of type bool and assigns it the initial value false. Assuming that error is a global variable, elsewhere in the program if an error condition is detected, a statement could assign true to error:

```
error = true;
```

Back in `main()`, another statement can inspect `error` and use it as a flag to select one of two ways to end the program:

```
int main()
{
  if (error)
    return 1;
  else
    return 0;
}
```

You haven't met `if` statements yet, but the code's effect should be obvious. If the `error` variable is `true`, the program returns 1 as an error code; otherwise, it returns 0, signifying no error.

> **Note**
>
> C programs use integer variables to represent true (any nonzero value) and false (0). You may do the same in C++; however, it is clearer to use the `bool` type. Also, the size of a `bool` variable is one byte. An `int` takes a relatively wasteful four bytes.

LITERAL VALUES

You may specify literal integer values using a decimal, hex, or octal radix. Except for the value 0, decimal constants must begin with a nonzero digit. Constants that start with a leading 0 are octal values that may include only the digits 0 through 7. Constants that start with `0x` or `0X` are hexadecimal and may include the digits 1 though 9 plus A though Z in upper- or lowercase. Listing 6.6, literal.cpp, declares `int` variables initialized with hexadecimal, octal, and decimal literal values.

LISTING 6.6 LITERAL.CPP

```
#include <iostream.h>

int main()
{
  int hexValue = 0xF9AC;
  int octalValue = 0724;
  int decimalValue = 255;

  cout << "hexValue == " << hexValue << endl;
  cout << "octalValue == " << octalValue << endl;
  cout << "decimalValue == " << decimalValue << endl;

  return 0;
}
```

Compiling and running literal.cpp effectively converts the octal and hexadecimal values in the sample program to decimal. Enter these commands to compile and run the program:

```
$ g++ literal.cpp
$ ./a.out
hexValue == 63916
```

```
octalValue == 468
decimalValue == 255
```

As the output indicates, the default output format is decimal. Although the literal value 0xF9AC is expressed in hexadecimal, internally it's just an integer value like any other. Because the default output format for integers is decimal, writing hexadecimal and octal values to cout displays them in decimal.

Note

Chapter 8, "Controlling Input and Output," explains how to display integer values using hexadecimal, octal, and decimal output formats.

LITERAL CONSTANT RANGES

In addition to radix, you can specify the data type of a literal value, which is sometimes necessary for ensuring that GNU C++ internally represents a literal value the way you want. For example, to ensure that the compiler treats 100 as a long int, add the suffix L. The following declaration assigns the long integer value 1234L to a variable named bigValue:

```
long bigValue = 1234L;
```

To specify an unsigned long value, add UL. For example, the following assigns the unsigned long value 1234UL to bigValue. The values are the same, but internally they are represented in memory according to their specific types:

```
unsigned long bigValue = 1234UL;
```

Note

Because GNU C++ normally represents integer constants as long or unsigned long values, the suffixes L and UL are rarely needed. However, they might be required by other C and C++ compilers that represent integer constants as type int. For better portability, it's a good idea to attach L or UL to all constants that should be treated as long or unsigned long values.

DOUBLE WIDE INTEGERS

GNU C++ permits a special type of "double wide" integer named long long that can store truly huge values. Listing 6.7, verybig.cpp, demonstrates how to declare long long integers and determine the minimum and maximum values they can represent.

LISTING 6.7   VERYBIG.CPP

```
#include <iostream.h>

long long min_signed, max_signed;
unsigned long long max_unsigned;

main()
```

continues

LISTING 6.7   CONTINUED

```
{
  // Assign minimum and maximum values to var1 and var2
  // Assign maximum value to unsigned var3
  min_signed   = 0x8000000000000000LL;
  max_signed   = 0x7FFFFFFFFFFFFFFFLL;
  max_unsigned = 0xFFFFFFFFFFFFFFFFULL;

  cout << "Signed long long range" << endl;
  cout << "   " << min_signed << " ... ";
  cout << max_signed << endl;
  cout << "Unsigned long long range" << endl;
  cout << "  0 ... " << max_unsigned << endl;
  cout << "long long size in bytes == ";
  cout << sizeof(max_unsigned) << endl;
  return 0;
}
```

When you compile and run the verybig.cpp program with the following commands, it reports the minimum and maximum values of signed and unsigned long long integer values, and also shows the size in bytes of a long long variable:

```
$ g++ verybig.cpp
$ ./a.out
Signed long long range
  -9223372036854775808 ... 9223372036854775807
Unsigned long long range
  0 ... 18446744073709551615
long long size in bytes == 8
```

The program's output shows that a signed long long integer is capable of representing huge values in the range of plus or minus 9-thousand trillion and change. Unsigned long long integers double the maximum value to more than 18 thousand trillion. That's certainly big enough for my bank balance, with no danger of overflow.

Tip

By assuming a decimal place, long and long long integers are appropriate for accounting and spreadsheet software. (See Chapter 8, "Controlling Input and Output," for information on formatting values as strings—for example, to insert a decimal point into a long or long long integer value.)

Because GNU C++ represents literal integer constants as type long or unsigned long, the hexadecimal assignments in the sample program must end with LL and ULL to prevent an out-of-range warning. Despite appearances, the third constant does not end with the word "FULL." That's a hexadecimal F followed by ULL, meaning unsigned long long:

```
min_signed   = 0x8000000000000000LL;
max_signed   = 0x7FFFFFFFFFFFFFFFLL;
max_unsigned = 0xFFFFFFFFFFFFFFFFULL;
```

The constants take advantage of the fact that, in binary, a signed integer's minimum value is an initial 1 bit followed by all zeros (in hexadecimal, 0x80...). A signed integer's maximum value is a zero bit followed by all ones (in hexadecimal, 0x7F...). An unsigned integer value's maximum value in binary is all ones (in hexadecimal, 0xFF...). Of course, the minimum value for all unsigned integers is zero.

Warning

Double wide integers of type `long long` are probably unique to GNU C and C++. Using this type might make your programs incompatible with other C and C++ compilers.

IT'S A WRAP

A trouble area to watch out for, especially with integer variables, is a wrap-around effect that resembles how an odometer returns to all zeros after reaching its upper limit. It's a kind of internal Y2K effect that at times is useful, but might cause a bug. Listing 6.8, wrap.cpp, demonstrates the problem.

LISTING 6.8   WRAP.CPP

```
#include <iostream.h>

short int value;

int main()
{
  value = 32767;
  cout << "value      == " << value << endl;
  value = value + 10;
  cout << "value + 10 == " << value << endl;
  return 0;
}
```

Compile and run wrap.cpp with the commands:

```
$ g++ wrap.cpp
$ ./a.out
value      == 32767
value + 10 == -32759
```

The second line of output appears to be a bug. How can 32627 + 10 equal –32759? The apparent problem occurs because GNU C++ stores integer values in a fixed number of bytes. Because they are fixed in size, the variables' bits can represent values only in a limited range—in this case, –32768 to +32767 for `short ints` including zero (refer to Table 6.2). Expressions that exceed a variable's range cause the value to "wrap around," just like a typical automobile odometer does upon reaching 999999. Because this happens at runtime, the compiler is unable to issue a warning or error message for calculations that cause a wrap-around. To fix the problem, simply choose a larger data type. For example, changing value's type from `short int` to `int` increases the potential range of values the variable can represent, and the wrap-around no longer occurs.

Inconsequential code, such as a game, might use wrap-around for some reason (perhaps as a graphics device), but production software should never rely on this effect. This rule is especially important in C programs because many C compilers define the same integer types using different internal byte sizes and value ranges.

FLOATING POINT VARIABLES

A floating point value (sometimes referred to as a real number) is written with a decimal point. Floating point values are best considered to be approximations. For instance, the currently known value of pi is an unwieldy mass of digits, but the approximate floating point value 3.14159 is close enough for many applications.

You can also write literal floating point values using scientific notation. The value 3.755E+02 is equivalent to the decimal value 375.5. (Mathematicians would write that same value as 3.755×10^2.) To form the decimal equivalent of a scientific value, move the decimal point right for positive exponents, left for negative ones. Thus, 5.123E+03 equals 5123.0, and 6.5E-03 equals 0.0065.

GNU C++ and other ANSI C++ compilers provide three floating point data types: float, double, and long double. (There's no such thing as a long float except in a parade.) Table 6.3 lists the memory sizes and approximate value ranges for the three floating point types. Most programs use the double type for floating point variables, but you can use float to save space at the expense of a loss of precision, or use long double for more precision and a greater range of values but with a possibly longer execution time for evaluating complex expressions.

TABLE 6.3   FLOATING POINT DATA TYPES

Data Type	Bytes	Bits	Minimum	Maximum
float	4	32	1.17549e–38	3.40282e+38
double	8	64	2.22507e–308	1.79769e+308
long double	12	96	3.3621e–4932	1.18973e+4932

See the standard library header file float.h for exact ranges and other details about GNU C++ floating point values. The constants in this file tend to be highly compiler- or machine-specific, and for that reason, float.h is probably not located in /usr/include along with other standard headers. Use the Linux find or locate commands to find float.h on your system. On my installation, I found float.h in the following obscure path:

```
/usr/lib/gcc-lib/i386-redhat-linux/egcs-2.90.27/include/
```

Create floating point variables the same way you do any others, but specify one of the types from Table 6.3. For example, to declare a variable named balance, use the declaration:

```
double balance;
```

As with integer variables, if balance is a global variable, its value is initialized to zero (0.0) at runtime. If balance is declared in a function's statement block, it's your responsibility to assign it an initial value. As with integers, you can do that with a single statement such as

```
double balance = 525.49;
```

Note

Floating point constants such as 525.49 and 99.99 are of the double type unless followed by f or F, in which case they are represented as floats. The value 3.14159F is type float. Use l or L to tell the compiler that a value should be a long double as in 3.14159L.

Listing 6.9, tax.cpp, shows how to use floating point variables to calculate values. The program calculates the amount of tax paid and the retail price of an item given its total purchase price and the local tax rate. I wrote it because I sometimes need to backtrack a purchase and figure how much tax I paid. For example, if I come across a bill for $13.96, the program can tell me how much of that was tax.

LISTING 6.9   TAX.CPP

```cpp
#include <iostream.h>
#include <stdio.h>      // need printf()

double list, paid, rate, tax;

main()
{
  cout << "Price paid? ";
  cin >> paid;
  cout << "Tax rate (ex: .06)? ";
  cin >> rate;

  list = paid / (1 + rate);
  tax = paid - list;

  printf("List price = $%8.2f\n", list);
  printf("Tax paid   = $%8.2f\n", tax);
  return 0;
}
```

Compile and run tax.cpp in the usual way, and then enter the price you paid for an item plus your local tax rate. Here's a sample run:

```
$ g++ tax.cpp
$ ./a.out
Price paid? 13.96
Tax rate (ex: .06)? 0.075
List price = $   12.99
Tax paid   = $    0.97
```

Given a bill of $13.96 and my local tax rate of 7.5%, tax.cpp calculates that I paid $12.99 retail for this item and $0.97 in sales tax. The program's source code contains some new elements not yet introduced. This statement reads input into a variable:

```
cin >> paid;
```

The cin object is similar to cout, but directs standard input to a variable, in this case, the double paid. The C++ I/O-stream input operator >> looks like an arrow that "shoots" cin's input into the target variable. You may use similar statements to read input into other simple types of variables. (See also Chapter 8, "Controlling Input and Output," for other ways to read user input.)

After obtaining input values for paid and rate, the program calculates the list price and tax paid by using these statements:

```
list = paid / (1 + rate);
tax = paid - list;
```

Parentheses in the first statement's expression ensure that the addition is performed before the division. This is necessary because division has a higher *precedence* than addition and would therefore be performed first in the absence of parentheses. In other words, the following statement would cause a bug in the program:

```
list = paid / 1 + rate;  // ???
```

That incorrectly divides paid by 1 and then adds rate to the intermediate result. Always use parentheses to ensure that your mathematical calculations are performed as you want. See Appendix B, "C++ Operator Precedence and Associativity," for details on GNU C++ operator precedence.

Note

Extra parentheses never do any harm or add any unnecessary object code to compiled programs. Use parentheses lavishly to clarify all your program's expressions—for the compiler and for you.

CHARACTER STRINGS

Strings give computer programs the gift of speech. With strings, programs can display error messages, prompt for input, and report facts about internal events. Strings can also hold filenames, database search keys, and other text information. The following sections explain how to create C-style strings and some related topics such as how to convert strings to binary integer and floating point values.

Note

GNU C++ provides the string class for constructing string objects, explained in Part V, "C++ Class Libraries." However, many C++ programmers continue to use C-style strings described in the following section, and it's good to know how to create strings of both types.

CHARACTERS

Use the char type to create variables that can hold individual characters. For example, the following statement creates a char variable c and assigns it the letter Q:

```
char c = 'Q';
```

Delimit single literal characters with single quotes (the apostrophe character on most PC keyboards). As mentioned, the char type is internally just an integer value. Because 81 is the letter Q's ASCII value, the following is equivalent to the preceding statement:

```
char c = 81;
```

C-STYLE STRING CONSTANTS

A C-style string is a series of one or more chars, each taking one byte in memory, and ending with a null character, equal to ASCII 0. Quote literal strings using double quote marks. For example, you might define a constant named TITLE associated with a literal string like this:

```
#define TITLE "My Program"
```

You can then write the program's title to the console, and start a new line, using the following statement:

```
cout << TITLE << endl;
```

C-STYLE STRING VARIABLES

A C-style string variable typically holds user input—for example, a filename. Use the char type to create a C-style string variable with a statement such as

```
char filename[] = "datafile.txt";
```

The square brackets tell the compiler that filename is an *array* of multiple characters. The size of the array equals the number of characters in the quoted string plus one for a terminating null. Precede the declaration with const to create a constant string that cannot be changed at runtime:

```
const char mypath[] = "/home/yourname";
```

If you don't want GNU C++ to calculate a string's size automatically, specify the size you want in brackets:

```
char input[128];
```

That creates an uninitialized string variable named input capable of holding 127 characters plus a terminating null. You may specify a size and an initial string value:

```
char input[128] = "/home/yourname";
```

That sets input to the stated string and makes the variable large enough to hold up to 127 characters. If a string declaration is global, GNU C++ automatically sets all its bytes to zero.

There's no practical limit to a string's size, and it's often useful to use them for large buffers, perhaps for performing "raw" disk operations. The following declares a buffer of 1,028 bytes:

```
char buffer[1028];
```

Warning

> Never create large string variables or buffers inside functions! This places the variable on the relatively limited system stack and is not good programming. See Chapter 11, "Managing Memory with Pointers," for other ways to create string variables and large buffers without using global declarations.

Because C-style string variables are actually arrays of individual characters, you cannot assign new strings to them using assignment statements. The following does not work:

```
pathname = "/etc/scripts";  // ???
```

That fails to compile because the assignment operator is not defined for C-style string variables. To copy one C-style string to another requires calling a standard *string function*, such as strcpy(). To do that, include the standard string.h header file with the following directive:

```
#include <string.h>
```

You can then call strcpy() to copy a string into the variable using a statement such as

```
strcpy(pathname, "/usr/yourname");
```

That copies "/usr/yourname" into pathname. Be careful that the source string isn't larger than the target variable. A similar, but safer, function, strncpy(), limits how many characters are copied. If source and destination are the names of C-style string variables, the following statement copies up to 10 characters from source to destination:

```
strncpy(destination, source, 10);
```

Note

> Generally, string functions with an extra *n* in their names declare a numeric parameter that limits the function's action in some way. These functions tend to be safer or more restrictive than their n-less counterparts. Examples include strcpy() and strncpy(), strcat() and strncat(), and strcmp() and strncmp(). See the info pages for online documentation on these functions.

SIZE MATTERS

The *size* of a string determines how many characters it can hold. The *length* of a string is equal to how many characters the string currently holds. Listing 6.10 demonstrates the difference between string size and length.

LISTING 6.10   PROMPT.CPP

```cpp
#include <iostream.h>
#include <string.h>    // Need strlen()

char username[64];

main()
{
  cout << "What's your name? ";
  cin >> username;
  cout << "Hello " << username << '!' << endl;
  cout << "size    == " << sizeof(username) << endl;
  cout << "length  == " << strlen(username) << endl;
  return 0;
}
```

Compile and run the program in the usual way and enter a string when prompted. Here's a sample run:

```
$ g++ prompt.cpp
$ ./a.out
What's your name? Rumpelstilzchen
Hello Rumpelstilzchen!
size    == 64
length  == 15
```

The size in bytes of the username string variable is 64, the same as its declared size in the program's source code. However, the length of the string depends on how many characters it holds, in this case 15. Use the C++ sizeof operator as shown to determine the size of a string or any other variable. Call the strlen() function to count the number of characters in a string. The standard header file string.h declares strlen() along with other C-style string functions.

Note

Chapter 8, "Controlling Input and Output," discusses other ways to read user input into string variables.

MUCH TO DO ABOUT NOTHING

All C-style strings must end with an ASCII null character, equal to zero. This marks the end of the string for various string functions such as strcpy() and strlen(). If a string lacks a terminating null, string functions merrily operate on data beyond that reserved for the string variable, causing a serious bug.

To represent null, you can specify its ASCII value in a character expression like this:

```cpp
char anull = '\0';
```

The backslash specifies that the following digits represent a character's ASCII value. Be sure to use single quotes to specify a single character. The string "\0" is a two-byte *string* that contains two null characters.

Another way to represent a null character is to use the standard library's NULL symbol, written in all uppercase. Unfortunately, the nature of this symbol is as fickle as the weather. In some ANSI C and C++ systems, NULL is defined as equivalent to zero usually with a #define directive such as

```
#define NULL 0
```

However, ANSI C declares NULL differently using the following macro definition:

```
#define NULL ((void *)0)
```

This makes NULL equal to a "void pointer to zero." (See Chapter 11, "Managing Memory with Pointers.") Although GNU C++ appears to make an attempt to redefine NULL as equivalent to zero, other standard headers seem to ignore that effort, causing NULL to be defined as in ANSI C. As a result, even simple statements such as the following cause GNU C++ to issue a warning about the lack of a cast:

```
char cnull = NULL;  // ???
```

Many C++ compilers accept that statement, but GNU C++ doesn't like it. If using NULL causes this trouble, to repair the problem, *after* including standard headers, you can try to redefine NULL using the following directives:

```
#ifdef NULL
#undef NULL
#endif
#define NULL 0
```

That's a lot to do about nothing, but it might be necessary to compile some existing programs that expect NULL to be defined simply as zero. However, because of the potential for causing trouble in standard library functions that might expect NULL to be defined differently, it might be best simply to avoid using this symbol in new code. If I need to represent the null character, I make up my own constant using a directive such as

```
#define ANULL 0
```

Or, even better, you can define it as a character constant:

```
#define CHNULL '\0'
```

COMPARING STRINGS

To compare two strings, call the strcmp() function, which returns one of three integer values: -1, 0, or +1. Suppose that you create two string variables such as the following:

```
char stringA[] = "Oranges";
char stringB[] = "Apples";
```

The following statement alphabetically compares "Oranges" to "Apples":

```
int result = strcmp(stringA, stringB);
```

Use the resulting integer, assigned in this case to the int variable result, to determine the results of the comparison according to these three rules:

- If `result` equals -1, then `stringA` is alphabetically less than `stringB`.
- If `result` equals 0, then the two strings are identical.
- If `result` equals +1, then `stringA` is alphabetically greater than `stringB`.

Function `strcmp()` is case sensitive. It considers lowercase letters to be alphabetically greater than their uppercase equivalents (because lowercase letters have higher ASCII values than uppercase letters). For a caseless (but not tasteless) comparison between two strings, call `strcasecmp()`. The `strcasecmp()` function works identically to `strcmp()` but ignores differences in case. When compared using `strcmp()`, "Apple" is alphabetically less than "apple." When compared using `strcasecmp()`, "Apple" and "apple" are considered identical.

To compare only a portion of two strings, use `strncmp()`. For example, this statement

```
int result = strncmp(s1, s2, 2);
```

sets `result` to zero only if the first two characters of the strings addressed by s1 and s2 match exactly. For a caseless comparison, call function `strncasecmp()`.

> **Tip**
>
> Some other C and C++ standard libraries define functions with an "i" in their names to indicate that they "ignore" case. For example, `stricmp()`, sometimes spelled `strcmpi()`, is the caseless version of `strcmp()`. GNU C++ uses the word "case" to indicate a caseless string function. If an older program gives an error for the use of functions such as `stricmp()`, `strncmpi()`, or similar, simply change the "i" to "case."

CONCATENATING STRINGS

Concatenating two strings joins them, creating a new, longer string. Given an existing string declared like this:

```
char original[128] = "Testing ";
```

the following statement sets the original string to "Testing one, two, three!":

```
strcat(original, "one, two, three!");
```

Add spaces as needed to prevent concatenated strings from running together. For example, the first string, `"Testing "`, ends with an extra space.

SEARCHING FOR SUBSTRINGS

Often, a program needs to search strings for characters and substrings in C-style string variables. One of the most common uses for the technique is to examine filenames for a certain extension. For example, after prompting users to enter a filename, you might want to check whether they entered the extension .txt, and if so, display the file onscreen. Listing 6.11, extension.cpp, uses string functions to detect a filename extension and, if missing, add a default name.

PART
II

CH
6

LISTING 6.11 EXTENSION.CPP

```cpp
#include <iostream.h>
#include <string.h>    // Need strstr(), strcat()

char filename[128];

int main()
{
  cout << "File name (.txt)? ";
  cin >> filename;
  cout << "Original input    : " << filename << endl;
  if ( !strstr(filename, ".txt") )
    strcat(filename, ".txt");
  cout << "Resulting filename : " << filename << endl;
  return 0;
}
```

Function strstr() locates a substring in another string. The function returns a *pointer* to char, written in C and C++ as char*. (Chapter 11, "Managing Memory with Pointers," covers pointers thoroughly.) In this case, we don't care where the substring is located; we want only to know whether it exists. This statement accomplishes the task:

```cpp
if ( !strstr(filename, ".txt") )
  strcat(filename, ".txt");
```

The exclamation point negates the result of strstr() and in effect states that if ".txt" is not found in filename, then the subsequent statement should be executed. Here, that statement calls another string function, strcat(), to add the missing filename extension.

CHARACTER ESCAPE CODES

In addition to the characters you can type, strings and characters may also contain escape codes. These are special symbols that represent control codes and other ASCII values, which can't be typed using a text editor, or that conflict with string and character quote marks. Table 6.4 lists the full set of GNU C++ character escape codes, most of which are probably recognized by most ANSI C and C++ compilers.

TABLE 6.4 STRING ESCAPE CODES

Code	Meaning	Decimal	ASCII Value(s) Hexadecimal	Symbol(s)
'\a'	Bell ("alert!")	7	0x07	BEL
'\b'	Backspace	8	0x08	BS
'\f'	Form feed	12	0x0C	FF
'\n'	New line	10	0x0a	LF
'\r'	Return	13	0x0d	CR
'\t'	Horizontal tab	9	0x09	HT

Code	Meaning	Decimal	ASCII Value(s) Hexadecimal	Symbol(s)
'\v'	Vertical tab	11	0x0b	VT
'\\'	Backslash	92	0x5c	\
'\''	Single quote	39	0x27	'
'\"'	Double quote	34	0x22	"
'\?'	Question mark	63	0x3f	?
'\000'	ASCII octal 000	n/a	n/a	n/a
'\x00'	ASCII hex 00	n/a	n/a	n/a

Each of the escape codes in Table 6.4 is a single character, stored internally as an int value and composed of a backslash followed by a letter, punctuation symbol, or octal digits. The octal and hex codes make it possible to enter any ASCII code into a string or character constant. For example, the following declaration assigns the ASCII value 0x27 (a single quote) to cquote:

```
char cquote = '\x27';
```

Because a single quote delimits a literal character, that's one way to assign a single quote character to a variable such as cquote. Another way is to use the single quote escape code like this:

```
char cquote = '\'';
```

You may use escape codes as individual characters also in strings. As an example, and also to demonstrate a useful technique for pausing to prompt users to press the Enter key, see Listing 6.12, enter.cpp.

LISTING 6.12   ENTER.CPP

```
#include <iostream.h>

const char prompt[] = "Press the \"Enter\" key now...";

main()
{
  char temp;
  cout << prompt;    // Display prompt
  cin.get(temp);     // Wait for user to press Enter
  return 0;
}
```

PART II CH 6

Compiling and running the program in the usual way results in the program pausing for you to press Enter. Notice that the program's output displays "Enter" quoted by virtue of the \" string escape codes in the constant prompt:

```
$ g++ enter.cpp
$ ./a.out
Press the "Enter" key now...
```

STRING CONVERSIONS

As mentioned, you can write statements to read user input directly into integer and floating point variables. For example, the following statements create a `double` variable and prompt users to enter a value:

```
double value;
cout << "Enter value: ";
cin >> value;
```

That's not always possible or convenient. In many cases, a program inputs data in text form, perhaps from a file downloaded over a network. To use the string data in binary form—in calculations, for example—you must convert the strings to binary values. Listing 6.13, convert.cpp, shows how to do this for integer and floating point values entered in string form.

LISTING 6.13   CONVERT.CPP

```
#include <iostream.h>
#include <stdlib.h>

char input[128];
long lvalue;
double dvalue;

main()
{
  cout << "Enter an integer value: ";
  cin >> input;
  lvalue = atol(input);
  cout << "Value in binary == " << lvalue << endl;

  cout << "Enter a floating point value: ";
  cin >> input;
  dvalue = atof(input);
  cout << "Value in binary == " << dvalue << endl;

  return 0;
}
```

Include the stdlib.h header file and call function `atol()` (ASCII to `long`) to convert a string into a `long` int value. The program assigns the result of `atol()` to `lvalue`, a variable of type `long`. To the function, pass a C-style string, such as `input`:

```
lvalue = atol(input);
```

Similarly, use `atof()` (ASCII to float) to convert a floating point value in string form to a `double` binary value:

```
dvalue = atof(input);
```

Another function, `atoi()` (ASCII to integer), not used in the sample program, converts a string to an `int` value:

```
int ivalue = atoi(input);
```

Note

The stdlib.h declares other string to binary functions such as `strtod()` (string to `double`), `strtol()` (string to `long`), and `strtoul()` (string to `unsigned long`), described online in Linux info pages. Using these functions requires an understanding of pointers, introduced in Chapter 11, "Managing Memory with Pointers."

STIR-FRIED STRINGS

If you like stir-fried vegetables, you'll love the GNU C++ `strfry()` function. It scrambles the characters in any string by randomly shuffling them. Although this might seem frivolous, it might be used in a program to mix up the byte values in a string or other buffer—for example, to prepare blocks of randomized test data, or for use in encryption algorithms. Listing 6.14, scramble.cpp, demonstrates the `strfry()` function.

Note

The `strfry()` function is probably unique to Linux and the GNU C standard library.

LISTING 6.14   SCRAMBLE.CPP

```
#include <iostream.h>
#include <string.h>

// The following three lines may be required if strfry()
// is not declared in string.h.

extern "C" {
  char *strfry(char *string);
}

char alpha[] = "abcdefghijklmnopqrstuvwxyz";

main()
{
  cout << "before : " << alpha << endl;
  strfry(alpha);
  cout << "after  : " << alpha << endl;
  return 0;
}
```

Compile and run the program to scramble the `alpha` character string. Try running it several times as a test of the system's random number generator (but wait a second between trials because the generator uses the current time as a starting seed). Enter these commands:

```
$ g++ scramble.cpp
$ ./a.out
before : abcdefghijklmnopqrstuvwxyz
after  : niaoldtpswbqkfejzghvcruymx
```

Because `strfry()` is documented as being unique to Linux and GNU C and C++, you probably won't find the function in other standard C libraries. Also, it is apparently not declared

PART

II

CH

6

in the standard string.h header files shipped with the compiler, a bug that results in this warning in any program that calls strfry():

```
warning: implicit declaration of function 'int strfry(...)'
```

Note Later versions of GNU C++ apparently do declare the function properly in string.h, so you might not see this warning.

If you receive the warning, the program still works correctly because strfry() is located in a compiled library even though it is not declared as it should be in string.h. However, you can use the following lines to declare the function and get rid of the warning:

```
extern "C" {
  char *strfry(char *string);
}
```

Note The extern "C" directive encases a C function declaration for use in a C++ program. This is necessary because the C++ compiler "mangles" function names and other identifiers to create unique symbols during compilation. The extern "C" directive disables name mangling so that the linker can find the declared C function's compiled code.

ARRAYS AND STRUCTS

An *array* is simply a series of objects, all of the same type, stored next to each other in memory. A struct is a collection of objects possibly of different types, also stored next to one another. The following sections introduce these types of *complex data structures*.

SINGLE-DIMENSIONAL ARRAYS

You've already seen one example of a single-dimensional array—a C-style string declared as

```
char input[128];
```

That creates a variable named input as an array of 128 char values. Similarly, you can create arrays of other data types. Here's an array of 10 double objects:

```
double values[10];
```

To use the array in a statement, specify the index of the element you want. You can assign a value to an array element:

```
values[5] = 3.14159;
```

You can also use array elements in other ways. The following statement, for example, writes the sixth element of the values array to the standard output:

```
cout << values[5] << endl;
```

Because all C and C++ arrays begin with the first element at index [0], the index value 5 locates the sixth element in the array. The key to using arrays properly is to remember that an expression such as values[5] is a single object of the array's stated type—a double value in this case. As such, an expression such as values[5] may be used in any context where a double value is appropriate.

> **Note**
> The maximum array index is always one less than its declared size. For example, the indexes for an 100-element array range from 0 through 99.

MULTIPLE-DIMENSIONAL ARRAYS

To create arrays with two or more dimensions, specify an additional size in brackets. For example, the following creates a 10 by 20 matrix of integers:

```
int matrix[10][20];
```

To use matrix, specify two index values, as in the following statement:

```
cout << matrix[4][5];
```

Multiple-dimensional arrays may have three or more dimensions, but it's hard to imagine any use for a structure with more than three. This creates a three-dimensional array of double values:

```
double cube[4][3][8];
```

> **Note**
> Be careful when creating arrays like that—they can take a lot of memory. In this case, cube occupies 768 bytes ($4 \times 3 \times 8 \times$ sizeof(double)).

INITIALIZING ARRAYS

A common method for assigning values to arrays is to use a for loop as the following code fragment demonstrates:

```
int array[100];
for (int i = 0; i < 100; i++)
  array[i] = i;
```

The first line declares a 100-integer array, named array. The for loop assigns the values 0 through 99 to array[0] through array[99]. (See Chapter 9, "Controlling Program Flow," for more information on for loops.) You can also individually assign values to arrays elements this way:

```
array[3] = 123;
```

That sets the fourth element of array to the value 123. Again, it's the fourth element because array[0] is the first.

> **Tip**
>
> Arrays declared as global variables outside any function are automatically initialized to all zero bytes.

PREINITIALIZING ARRAYS

Another useful method for initializing arrays is to specify initial values in the source code. You've already seen one example of the technique as demonstrated here:

```
char title[] = "My Super Encryption Program";
```

That creates a C-style string variable named `title`. Actually, `title` is a single-dimensional array of `char` values, each initialized to one character from the quoted string. The compiler creates an array exactly big enough to hold the string, plus one byte for its null terminator. You may initialize other types of arrays using a similar declaration. For example, the following creates an array of 10 integers and assigns values to each element:

```
int digits[] = {9, 8, 7, 6, 5, 4, 3, 2, 1, 0};
```

The `digits` array is sized to hold 10 integer values, each initialized to the literal values in braces. Because no size is specified in brackets, the compiler calculates the array's size using the initial values. However, you may specify a different size with a declaration such as

```
int digits[10] = {5, 4, 3, 2, 1};
```

That creates an array of 10 integers but initializes only the first 5. The remaining elements at subscripts 5 through 9 are zeroed if the array is global or set to unpredictable values if the array is local to a function.

INITIALIZING ARRAYS OF STRINGS

A common structure stores an array of C-style strings. For example, Listing 6.15 uses an array to hold the names of the months.

LISTING 6.15   MONTHS.CPP

```cpp
#include <iostream.h>

  char months[12][4] = {
    "Jan", "Feb", "Mar", "Apr",
    "May", "Jun", "Jul", "Aug",
    "Sep", "Oct", "Nov", "Dec"
  };

int main()
{
  for (int month = 0; month < 12; month++)
    cout << months[month] << " ";
  cout << endl;
  return 0;
}
```

Compile and run the program to display the names of the 12 months. Enter these commands:

```
$ g++ months.cpp
$ ./a.out
Jan Feb Mar Apr May Jun Jul Aug Sep Oct Nov Dec
```

To hold the month strings, the program declares months as a multidimensional array with indexes of 12 and 4. It is literally a 12-element array of arrays, each four characters long, room enough for three characters in an abbreviated month name such as Apr plus a null terminator byte for the string. Although used as a single-dimensional array (see the output statement in the program's for loop), months is actually two-dimensional because each string is itself an array of characters.

> **Tip**
>
> Use an array such as months to give string names to enumerated type symbols.

STRUCTURES

A structure, called a struct in C and C++, forms a shell around one or more values of the same or different types. To declare a structure, start with the struct reserved word, and follow with an identifier and a list of declarations (called *structure members)* in braces. End the structure and each member declaration with a semicolon. Structures can be complex data types with many members, or they can be simple, such as this two-member model:

```
struct coordinate {
  int x;
  int y;
};
```

As declared here, the coordinate structure has two integer members, named x and y, which might represent data points for a chart or graph. Unlike an array, a structure declaration is merely a schematic that describes the structure's components. To use a structure, you first have to declare a variable of the structure's type:

```
struct coordinate point;
```

C++, but not C, permits dropping the struct reserved word and writing the preceding declaration more simply as:

```
coordinate point;
```

Either way, the variable point is a single object that contains two integers. Use *dot notation* to refer individually to the structure's members. For example, to assign values to the two integer components of point, you can write the following:

```
point.x = 5;
point.y = 6;
```

Technically, the dot in dot notation is called the *structure-member operator*. It informs the compiler of how and where to find a structure's member. The expression point.x refers to the x int member in the structure point and can therefore be used wherever an int object is allowed.

Note
Member names must be unique within the same structure, but they do not conflict with names used in other contexts. It would not be an error, for instance, if a program declared other variables named x and y.

Structures can store variables of any and all types, including arrays and even other structures. Here's a sample of a complex structure with members of several different types:

```
struct complexStruct {
  double aFloat;
  int anInt;
  char aString[8];
  char aChar;
  long aLong;
};
```

As declared here, complexStruct has five members: a floating point value, an integer, an eight-element char array, a single character, and a long integer. A variable named data declared as

```
complexStruct data;
```

can store member values of these five types in one handy package. As with all structures, you can store values in data's members using dot notation:

```
data.aFloat = 3.14159;
data.aChar = 'X';
```

DEBUGGING DATA OBJECTS

When a program fails to produce expected output, the first place to look for trouble is in any assignments to variables. In this section, you examine some intentionally buggy code in a program that is supposed to convert a temperature in Fahrenheit to Celsius. Unfortunately, the program doesn't seem to work correctly. Using the GNU debugger's data-examination commands, you quickly locate and fix the problem.

Note
The following sections use the console debugger, gdb. You may use a different interface if you prefer—for example, xxgdb for X, or the Emacs editor's debugging commands. For basics on running the GNU debugger using these interfaces, see Chapter 5, "Compiling and Debugging C++ Programs."

IDENTIFYING THE BUG

On the CD-ROM is a file, buggy.cpp, in the src/c06 subdirectory. This is a copy of the celsius.cpp program, also located in the same directory, but with two intentional bugs. To see the problem, compile and run the buggy program using the usual commands:

```
$ g++ buggy.cpp
$ ./a.out
```

Enter a temperature in Fahrenheit such as 75.5. The program is supposed to convert that temperature to Celsius, but as the following output shows, it obviously displays an incorrect result:

```
*** Warning: This program has intentional bugs
Fahrenheit to Celsius conversion
Degrees Fahrenheit? 75.5
Degrees Celsius == -9.44444
```

Apparently, there is something wrong with the program's formula. Let's use the debugger to pinpoint the trouble spot.

LOADING THE CODE

The first step in finding the bug is to compile the program with debugging information. After that, load it into gdb. To follow along, enter these two commands:

```
$ g++ -g -o buggy buggy.cpp
$ gdb -silent buggy
(gdb)
```

The first line selects the default level of debugging information (-g) and specifies the output filename, buggy. The second line loads the compiled code into the debugger. The -silent option skips the debugger's wordy welcoming messages. The final line is gdb's command prompt. We want to examine data values while the program is paused at convenient locations, so first type *L* a couple of times to list the program's source code (to save space, I list only the relevant lines here):

```
(gdb) l
...
22  cin >> input;
23  fdegrees = atol(input);
24  cdegrees = (fdegrees - 32.0 * 5.0) / 9.0;
```

Because the program reports an incorrect result, the obvious place to look is in the calculation at line 24. So, set a breakpoint there and run the program to pause *before* executing that statement:

```
(gdb) break 24
Breakpoint 1 at 0x80487e7: file buggy.cpp, line 24.
(gdb) run
Starting program: /src/c06/buggy
*** Warning: This program has intentional bugs
Fahrenheit to Celsius conversion
Degrees Fahrenheit? 75.5
```

After you type *75.5* and press Enter, the debugger pauses the program at the breakpoint and shows the statement next to be executed:

```
Breakpoint 1, main () at buggy.cpp:24
24          cdegrees = (fdegrees - 32.0 * 5.0) / 9.0;
```

Type *next* and press Enter to execute the suspect statement, and then issue a print command to inspect cdegrees:

```
(gdb) next
25          cout << "Degrees Celsius == " << cdegrees << endl;
(gdb) print cdegrees
$1 = -9.4444444444444446
```

The value of cdegrees definitely shows that the program is not computing the correct result, but it doesn't tell us why. In this case, a look at the expression reveals the problem to be a missing pair of parentheses:

```
(fdegrees - 32.0 * 5.0) / 9.0  //???
```

Because multiplication has higher precedence than subtraction, the first part of this expression multiplies 32.0 times 5.0 and subtracts that result from fdegrees, but the formula calls for subtracting 32.0 from fdegrees before multiplying. Sometimes, however, the problem in an expression is not so obvious. In that case, it's often helpful to divide the expression into pieces and use gdb print commands to inspect the intermediate results. For example, you might comment-out the calculation of cdegrees and replace it with temporary code such as

```
double t1 = fdegrees - 32.0;
double t2 = t1 * 5.0;
doubld t3 = t2 / 9.0;
```

You can then single step these statements and inspect the t1, t2, and t3 temporary variables, and in this way further investigate the cause of a faulty expression. You don't have to perform these steps now, but keep them in mind for future problems.

If you are following along, quit the debugger (type *q* and answer yes when prompted whether you intend to exit the running program). Fix the faulty expression by adding parentheses, changing it to the following:

```
((fdegrees - 32.0) * 5.0) / 9.0
```

Compile the modified buggy.cpp and run. You don't have to load it into the debugger. Again, enter 75.5 when prompted:

```
$ g++ buggy.cpp
$ ./a.out
*** Warning: This program has intentional bugs
Fahrenheit to Celsius conversion
Degrees Fahrenheit? 75.5
Degrees Celsius == 23.8889
```

That looks better. But just to be sure, use a hand calculator to work out the problem and verify the program's result. Enter this expression into your calculator:

```
((75.5 - 32.0) * 5.0) / 9.0
```

Uh oh, that gives 24.167 degrees, not 23.8889. There's another bug in the code, one that's easily missed if we hadn't verified the calculation. Try some other input data—80 and 90.7, for example. Apparently, only fractional values cause the bug to appear. The program correctly converts whole numbers to Celsius without error. *Something is wrong with the program's floating point data.* So, recompile for debugging and load the program into gdb:

```
$ g++ -g -o buggy buggy.cpp
$ gdb -silent buggy
```

Set a breakpoint at the assignment to `fdegrees`, a floating point variable of type `double`, and then run the code up to that point:

```
(gdb) break 23
Breakpoint 1 at 0x80487cb: file buggy.cpp, line 23.
(gdb) run
Starting program: /src/c06/buggy
*** Warning: This program has intentional bugs
Fahrenheit to Celsius conversion
Degrees Fahrenheit? 75.5
```

> **Tip**
>
> You can type **b 23** instead of break 23, and **r** instead of run.

Enter **75.5** when prompted and press Enter. The debugger halts the program at the breakpoint:

```
Breakpoint 1, main () at buggy.cpp:23
23        fdegrees = atol(input);
```

Before executing that statement, be sure that the input variable holds the entered value. To inspect the string, type ***print input***:

```
(gdb) print input
$1 = "75.5", '\000' <repeats 123 times>
```

The debugger assigns a pseudo name, $1, to the expression. From now on, you can print $1 to reexamine this value. Or, simply type ***p$1*** rather than the complete command. You can also use $1 in other expressions—for example, in a display command (more on that in a moment). In this case, the string `"75.5"` looks okay. It is correctly followed by a null (expressed in octal here as `'\000'`). The debugger also tells us that this null repeats 123 times in the string variable. There's no bug here, so let's continue.

The program is currently paused at the statement that assigns a value to `fdegrees`. Issue a next command to execute that statement.

```
23        fdegrees = atol(input);
(gdb) next
```

After the program again pauses, print the value of `fdegrees`:

```
(gdb) print fdegrees
$2 = 75
```

Again, the debugger assigns a pseudo name ($2) that you can use to inspect fdegrees at other times. The variable's value is 75, but it should be 75.5. Something is truncating the floating point value's fractional part. Another look at the offending line reveals the problem:

```
23        fdegrees = atol(input);
```

The program calls atol() (ASCII to long) where it should have called atof() (ASCII to float). Because assignments of long int values to variables of type double are syntactically allowable, the compiler did not report this as an error. To fix the problem, quit the debugger and change atol() to atof(). Now the program correctly converts 75.5 degrees Fahrenheit to a balmy 24.1667 degrees Celsius. Listing 6.16, celsius.cpp, shows the finished program with the intentional bugs repaired.

LISTING 6.16   CELSIUS.CPP

```cpp
#include <iostream.h>
#include <stdlib.h>

double fdegrees, cdegrees;
char input[128];

int main()
{
  cout << "Fahrenheit to Celsius conversion" << endl;
  cout << "Degrees Fahrenheit? ";
  cin >> input;
  fdegrees = atof(input);
  cdegrees = ((fdegrees - 32.0) * 5.0) / 9.0;
  cout << "Degrees Celsius == " << cdegrees << endl;
  return 0;
}
```

Tip

To fix bugs, you first have to find them. In this case, only floating point input caused the bug in celsius.cpp to appear, and a single test run might have missed the problem. The lesson to learn is this: *Always test your programs using a variety of input data.*

OTHER DATA DEBUGGING COMMANDS

Following are some other GNU debugger commands that are useful for examining a program's variables. To follow along, compile the tax.cpp program in this chapter using the -g option and load the result into the debugger with the commands

```
$ g++ -g -o tax tax.cpp
$ gdb -silent tax
```

Set a breakpoint and run the program. When prompted, enter the values shown here:

```
(gdb) break 28
Breakpoint 1 at 0x8048737: file tax.cpp, line 28.
(gdb) run
Starting program: /src/c06/tax
```

```
Price paid? 54.67
Tax rate (ex: .06)? .06
List price = $    51.58
Tax paid   = $     3.09
```

Press Enter and examine the calculated list and tax variables with print commands:

```
(gdb) print list
$3 = 51.575471698113212
(gdb) print tax
$4 = 3.0945283018867897
```

If the values surprise you, remember that floating point binary values are best considered to be approximations. Only integers are perfectly accurate at all times. Floating point values are subject to round-off errors, which though extremely small, might adversely affect program results. For this reason, in accounting and similar software, it might be more appropriate to store monetary values in variables of type long or long long.

AUTOMATICALLY DISPLAYING VARIABLES

To automatically display expressions such as the values of selected variables every time the program pauses, use a display command and specify the variables to inspect. The following commands tell the debugger to display the values of list and tax every time it pauses the program—when a breakpoint is reached, for example, or when you issue a next command:

```
(gdb) display list
1: list = 51.575471698113212
(gdb) display tax
2: tax = 3.0945283018867897
```

As the following screen output shows, running the program to a breakpoint now automatically displays the values of the two variables:

```
Breakpoint 1, main () at tax.cpp:28
28        return 0;
2: tax = 3.0945283018867897
1: list = 51.575471698113212
```

ASSIGNING VALUES

Use the gdb set command to assign values to a program's variables. This is often handier for supplying test data for calculations than rerunning the program from scratch. For example, to set the rate variable in tax.cpp to 0.075, use the following command followed by print to verify the new value:

```
(gdb) set rate = 0.075
(gdb) print rate
$6 = 0.074999999999999997
```

Notice that the internal binary representation of 0.075 is a close approximation.

PART

II

CH

6

SETTING THE RADIX

To set the output radix, use the set-radix command. This command sets the output radix to hexadecimal:

```
(gdb) set output-radix 16
Output radix now set to decimal 16, hex 10, octal 20.
```

The confirmation message is a bit strange, but you can now print integer variables and the debugger displays their values in hexadecimal. For example, to display an int counter equal to 100, type a print command such as the following:

```
(gdb) print counter
$3 = 0x64
```

Note

If you are following along, there is no counter variable in the loaded program. Simply type *print 100* to see the preceding output.

To reset radix to decimal, the default, enter the command with no arguments or specify 10 as follows:

```
(gdb) set output-radix 10
Output radix now set to decimal 10, hex a, octal 12.
```

Again, the confirmation is odd, but ignore it—the command seems to work fine. Use the command set input-radix to alter debugger input values to accept a different radix. Use set radix to alter both the input and output radix.

Note

Changing the radix does not affect the input or output of floating point values, only integers.

FINDING A VARIABLE'S TYPE

To verify the type of an object, use the ptype command. For example, to find the type of the tax variable, enter the command:

```
(gdb) ptype tax
type = double
```

This is useful for verifying that an object is of an expected type—an array element, for example—and avoids having to hunt for a declaration in a lengthy source code file.

DEBUGGING WITH THE assert() MACRO

Anther great way to catch bugs that doesn't require using the GNU debugger is a macro defined in the assert.h standard header file. The macro performs a simple task—halting a program with an error message upon the failed assertion of any expression. To use assert(), add this directive to your program's source file:

```
#include <assert.h>
```

Use assert() to test any true or false condition. For example, suppose that you suspect an int variable named waterLevel is falling below a defined high value. To test for that condition, insert a statement such as

```
assert(waterLevel < 1000);
```

At this place in the program, if waterLevel is less than 1000, the expression is true, and the program continues normally. But if waterLevel is greater than or equal to 1000, assert() halts the program with the following error message:

```
a.out: x.cpp:9: int main(): Assertion 'waterLevel < 1000' failed.
Aborted (core dumped)
```

Warning | If assert() fails, it creates a core dump file. Unless you need that file, remove it as soon as possible to avoid wasting disk space.

The assert() macro expands into an if statement, in this case, something like this:

```
if (!(waterLevel < 1000))
  abort();
```

The reason for using assert() instead of writing statements like that is so that you can easily remove all such tests. To do that, insert the following definition above the #include directive that refers to assert.h:

```
#define NDEBUG
#include <assert.h>
```

Defining the symbol NDEBUG causes the assert.h header to declare assert() as a do-nothing macro. Because the macro now expands to nothing, the compiler effectively removes all assert() statements from the code. If problems develop later, simply comment-out #define NDEBUG and recompile to enable all assertions.

Debugging Variables Roundup

Following is a roundup of suggestions for debugging variables in C++ programs. Also examine the help information in gdb for additional commands you can use (type *help data* at a gdb prompt). When your code shows incorrect results, try these tips:

- Test your code using a wide range of data. In the case of the buggy Celsius converter, testing with only whole numbers such as 80 degrees gave correct results. Only fractional values aggravated the bug. *Just because one test produces no errors does not mean that the code is bug free!*

- Examine input *and* output variables. Often, a problem appears to be in a calculation when the true cause is an error in the input data. That old rule, *garbage in; garbage out*, remains as true today as ever.

- If you can't find the error in a complex expression, break it into pieces with temporary statements and use gdb to inspect the expression's intermediate results.

- Check the results of all expressions using a hand calculator. Keep in mind, however, that the internal binary formats in your system and calculator might differ, as might the algorithms used to display rounded values, so don't expect the results to be exactly the same. For example, my calculator shows 75.5 degrees Fahrenheit equal to 24.166666 degrees Celsius. The celsius.cpp program reports a rounded value of 24.1667.

- Don't use floating point variables in accounting software to store monetary amounts. Use the long or long long values and assume two decimal places in the values. (In other words, store monetary values in cents or the lowest practical denomination in your currency.) Chapter 8, "Controlling Input and Output," in the section "Lucky Pennies" lists a sample program, money.cpp, that shows one way to use long and long long values this way.

- When calling functions—especially those that operate on C-style strings—be sure that you don't mix up the order of any arguments. The statement strcpy(A, B) does not copy A to B, as might seem intuitively correct. It copies string B to A. Check the online info and man-page documentation for standard functions, especially the first time you use one.

SUMMARY

GNU C++ provides seven numeric data types: char, short, int, long, float, double, and long double. An eighth type, long long, can store truly huge integer values but is probably unique to GNU C++. This chapter introduced numeric data types and also explained how to use C-style strings, composed of one or more characters and ending with a terminating null. The chapter also showed how to create arrays and structures, and explained GNU debugging commands to investigate a program's data.

For more information on subjects introduced in this chapter, turn to the following chapters:

- Chapter 5, "Compiling and Debugging C++ Programs"
- Chapter 8, "Controlling Input and Output"
- Chapter 9, "Controlling Program Flow"
- Chapter 10, "Creating and Calling Functions"
- Chapter 11, "Managing Memory with Pointers"

CHAPTER 7

APPLYING FUNDAMENTAL OPERATORS

Operators put the compute in "computing." With operators, programs can manipulate data and calculate the results of mathematical and logical expressions. You've already met some operators. This chapter further explores expressions and the C++ mathematical and logical operators.

EXPRESSIONS

Any construction that C++ evaluates—that is, treats as having a value—is an *expression*. Even a simple variable name such as counter is an "expression." As such, counter equals the value of whatever type of data it holds. Using operators, you create complex expressions, typically involving two or more subexpressions. For example, if valueB and valueC are int variables, the following expression equals the sum of the two variables:

```
valueB + valueC
```

That's not a statement—it is merely an expression that has a computed value—in this case, equal to the sum of valueB and valueC. That value might be used to make a decision as in this code fragment:

```
if (valueB + valueC > 100)
  cout << "Limit reached!" << endl;
```

Only if the sum of valueB and valueC is greater than 100 is the message displayed. (See Chapter 9, "Controlling Program Flow," for more information on if and other flow-control statements.) To save the result of an expression, you can *assign* it to another variable of an appropriate type. For example, if valueA is also an int variable, this statement saves the evaluated expression result in valueA:

```
valueA = valueB + valueC;
```

The single equal sign is the C++ *assignment operator*. It copies into the variable on the left the result of the expression on the right. After the statement executes, valueA equals the sum of valueB plus valueC. The two variables valueB and valueC are unchanged.

C++ uses several kinds of operators, and it's the rare program that doesn't use a healthy mix of them. In the following sections, you meet the C++ arithmetic, relational, logical, negation, increment, decrement, and bitwise operators.

Tip

Be sure to understand the difference between an expression and a statement. An expression has a value. A statement performs an action such as assigning the result of an expression to a variable.

ARITHMETIC OPERATORS

In your early school days, you undoubtedly learned how to use the arithmetic operators + (plus), - (minus), * (times), and / (divide), but probably using the symbols × for times and ÷ for divide. The modulus operator % might be less familiar. It calculates the remainder of an integer division. For example, the expression 24 % 11 ("24 modulo 11") equals 2—the remainder after dividing 24 by 11. The expression 8 % 2 equals 0 because 2 divides evenly into 8. You may use the first four fundamental operators in Table 7.1 on floating point and integer variables. However, the modulus operator works only with integers.

TABLE 7.1   C AND C++ ARITHMETIC OPERATORS

Operator	Description	Example
*	Multiplication	(a * b)
/	Division	(a / b)
+	Addition	(a + b)
-	Subtraction	(a - b)
%	Modulus	(a % b)

In general, an expression's result type equals that of the most complex operand involved. In an expression with all integer variables, for example, the result is an integer value. But if the expression has a double value, the result is double even if all other operands are integers. Expressions may refer to variables, or as Listing 7.1, kilo.cpp, demonstrates, they may also use constants.

LISTING 7.1   KILO.CPP

```cpp
#include <iostream.h>

double miles;        // Miles to convert
double kilometers;   // Result of conversion
char string[128];    // User input

int main()
{
  cout << "How many miles? ";
  cin >> miles;
  kilometers = miles * 1.609344;
  cout << "Kilometers = " << kilometers << endl;
  return 0;
}
```

The simple kilo.cpp listing shows one of the most basic uses for C++ operators—to implement a formula—in this case, one that computes the equivalent distance in kilometers given a number of miles. Compile and run the program with the following commands and enter a value in miles to convert:

```
$ g++ kilo.cpp
$ ./a.out
How many miles? 8
Kilometers = 12.8748
```

ASSOCIATIVITY AND PRECEDENCE

When it evaluates an expression, C++ applies operators to operands in either left-to-right or right-to-left order, a property known as *associativity*. Most expressions evaluate operands in left to right order, but some go the other way—assignments, for example, evaluate from right to left.

Precedence dictates which operators apply before others. In complex expressions, subexpressions with operators of higher precedence evaluate before subexpressions with operators of lower precedence. Appendix B, "C++ Operator Precedence and Associativity," documents these characteristics for all C and C++ operators, many of which you meet in this and other chapters.

From Appendix B, it's evident that multiplication and division have higher precedence than addition and subtraction (see levels 4 and 5 in Appendix B). Always consider such facts. For example, consider this expression:

```
A + B * C - D
```

Because multiplication has higher precedence than addition and subtraction, C++ evaluates the expression by first multiplying B times C. It then adds A to the subexpression's result, after which it subtracts D. The addition is performed before the subtraction in this case because, although operators + and - are equal in precedence, their associativity is left to right. Use parentheses to override the default precedence. For example, C++ evaluates the following expression differently:

```
(A + B) * (C - D)
```

Although the expression employs the same operators and operands as before, because parentheses have the highest precedence over all operators (see level 1 in Appendix B), C++ evaluates the subexpressions (A + B) and (C - D) first. It then multiplies the results of those subexpressions giving, for most input values, very different results than in the absence of parentheses.

In most expressions, common sense and a good helping of parentheses are your best guides to accurate results. You don't need to memorize lots of precedence and associativity rules to understand the evaluation order of expressions such as this:

```
y = ((a * x) + b) / (x + C);
```

Even though the purpose of the formula might not be obvious (it describes a hyperbolic curve, in case you're interested), the parentheses make perfectly clear which subexpressions belong together. Relying on operator precedence to produce a correct answer, you could write the preceding statement as

```
y = (a * x + b) / (x + C);
```

Because multiplication and division associate from left to right, one set of parentheses in the former expression isn't needed. Even so, the extra parentheses make the expression perfectly clear, and they cost nothing in performance.

RELATIONAL OPERATORS

Not all C++ operators are mathematical in nature. Some are *logical*—that is, they evaluate to a true or false result. For example, the less-than operator (<) compares the value of two operands in the expression:

```
(A < B)
```

That expression's value is true only if A is less than B; otherwise, the expression is false. In C and C++, any nonzero value is equivalent to true; zero is false. However, instead of using integer values, in C++, the `bool` data type specifies a true or false value in relational expressions such as:

```
bool result = (A < B);
```

That sets `result` equal to true if A is less than B; otherwise, `result` is set to false. Because the `bool` type is available only in C++, in C, the preceding statement is typically written using type `int`:

```
int result = (A < B);
```

In relational expressions such as (A < B) both operands must be of data types that can be compared. Typically, the operands are of types `int`, `long`, `double`, or other numerical types. A and B cannot be C-style strings because relational operators are not defined for arrays of `char`. However, they can be string objects, as explained in Chapter 22, "Mastering the Standard `string` Class." Table 7.2 lists all C and C++ relational operators.

TABLE 7.2   C AND C++ RELATIONAL OPERATORS

Operator	Description	Example
<	Less than	(a < b)
<=	Less than or equal	(a <= b)
>	Greater than	(a > b)
>=	Greater than or equal	(a >= b)
==	Equal	(a == b)
!=	Not equal	(a != b)

EQUAL OPPORTUNITY OPERATORS

As mentioned in prior chapters, the C and C++ equality operator (==) is a double equal sign (refer to Table 7.2). The operator literally means "is equal to." The C and C++ assignment operator is a single equal sign (=). It assigns the value of an expression on its right to an object on its left. Confusing the two operators is a fertile breeding ground for bugs. Consider, for example, this statement:

```
if (A = B) doSomething();  // ???
```

Unless you are well versed in C and C++ syntax, that might appear to call function doSomething() if A equals B, but that's not what happens! Because all expressions have values—even assignment expressions—C++ evaluates the *expression* (A = B) as being equal to the value assigned from B to A. The result of that expression is, in the foregoing if statement, evaluated as true or false. For example, if B is zero, the statement copies B to A, evaluates (A = B) as zero (false), and therefore does not call doSomething(). Probably, the programmer meant to write the statement like this:

```
if (A == B) doSomething();
```

Now, only if the value of A equals B does the program call doSomething(). The values of A and B are unchanged in the expression (A == B), but the value of B is copied to A in the expression (A = B). Be sure to understand this important difference.

Compile programs with the -Wall option to have GNU C++ check for the common mistake of using the assignment operator (=) where the equality operator (==) is probably intended. In cases where an expression of the form (A = B) is found in an if or other control statement, GNU C++ prints a warning such as

```
$ g++ -Wall atest.cpp
atest.cpp: In function 'int main()':
atest.cpp:10: warning: suggest parentheses around assignment used as truth value
```

There's a reason for the wording of this warning. Some programmers intentionally program an assignment and use its value as a true or false condition. In that case, by tradition, a double set of parentheses indicates that you intend to use the assignment operator and did not accidentally type one equal sign instead of two:

```
if ( (A = B) ) doSomething();
```

GNU C++ does not warn about such statements even for code compiled with the -Wall option. Personally, I regard statements like that as sloppy programming at best, and I suggest steering clear of such trickery. You'll see it in many programs, though. Two ways follow to write the same code with far less potential for trouble. Here's one:

```
if ( (A = B) == 0 ) doSomething();
```

If the assignment of B to A equals zero, then the program calls doSomething(). Even better, write the two actions separately. There is no confusing the intent of this code:

```
A = B;
if (A == 0) doSomething();
```

LOGICAL OPERATORS

Two logical operators, && and ¦¦, combine relational expressions according to the rules for logical AND and logical OR. Use the logical AND operator && in complex relational expressions such as

```
(A < B) && (B < C)
```

The result of that expression is true only if A is less than B *and* B is less than C. Use the logical OR operator ¦¦ similarly. The expression

```
(A < B) ¦¦ (B < C)
```

is true if A is less than B *or* B is less than C. GNU C++ efficiently evaluates complex logical expressions. Given the expression

```
(A <= B) && (B <= C)
```

if A is greater than B, the expression result is known to be false upon evaluating (A <= B); therefore, (B <= C) is not evaluated. This "short-circuiting" of complex logical expressions helps keep programs running quickly. For any relational expression, only the minimum number of evaluations is performed to produce an accurate result.

NEGATION OPERATOR

To negate a logical expression, use the unary NOT operator (!). It is "unary" because it applies to only one operand. Applied to any logical expression, the operator returns the opposite value. For example, consider this expression:

```
!(A < B)
```

The expression is true if A is not less than B. However, it's clearer to write the preceding as follows, using the greater-than-or-equal relational operator:

```
(A >= B)
```

Similarly, the not-equal operator != is related to !. This expression is true if A is equal to B:

```
(A == B)
```

The following statement is true if A is not equal to B:

```
!(A == B)
```

Once again, it is far clearer to use the != (not equal) operator to test for inequality. The following expression is true only if A is not equal to B:

```
(A != B)
```

INCREMENT AND DECREMENT OPERATORS

Two of the handiest, and perhaps most popular, operators are ++ (increment) and -- (decrement). The ++ operator (pronounced "plus plus") adds one to an operand. The -- operator ("minus minus") subtracts one.

> **Note**
>
> C++ gets its name from the ++ operator. Literally, C++ is one up on C.

A few examples clarify how these important operators work. The following two statements are functionally identical:

```
i = i + 1;    // Adds one to i
i++;          // Same as the preceding statement
```

PART

II

CH

7

The expression i++ in the second line is mere shorthand for the longer addition and assignment in the first. The expression i++ adds one to the current value of integer i, and stores the result in i. The following two expressions also have identical effects:

```
i = i - 1;      // Subtracts one from i
i--;            // Same as the preceding statement
```

The expression i-- subtracts one from the value stored in i. You may use the ++ and -- operators only on integers, not on floating point variables. (However, ++ and -- may also be used with pointers. See Chapter 11, "Managing Memory with Pointers.")

In addition to incrementing and decrementing their operands, expressions such as i++ and i-- also have values, as do all expressions. But the value of increment and decrement expressions depends on the position of the operators. This is a subtle, but critical, rule to understand. When ++ or -- follow their operands, the values of the expressions i++ and i-- equal the *unmodified* values. In other words, the statement

```
j = i++;
```

assigns to j the unmodified value of i. If i equals 7, after executing that statement, j equals 7 and i equals 8. C++ increments i *after* assigning the evaluated expression to j. A different result occurs when increment and decrement operators precede their operands. In that case, the expressions equal the *modified* operand values. The statement

```
j = ++i;
```

increments i and then assigns that incremented value to j. If i equals 7, after executing the preceding statement, j and i both equal 8. Another way to visualize these effects is to write increment and decrement expressions in long form. The statement

```
j = i++;
```

operates as though it were the two statements:

```
j = i;
i = i + 1;
```

And the statement

```
j = ++i;
```

operates as though it were written as:

```
i = i + 1;
j = i;
```

Note The same rules for ++ apply to --. The expression i-- equals the value of i before it is decremented by one. The expression --i equals the decremented value of i.

BITWISE OPERATORS

C and C++ provide several bitwise operators that you can use to perform Boolean logic operations on the individual bits of binary values. Table 7.3 summarizes the C and C++ bitwise operators.

TABLE 7.3   BITWISE OPERATORS

Operator	Description	Example
&	Bitwise AND	C = A & B;
¦	Bitwise inclusive OR	C = A ¦ B;
^	Bitwise exclusive OR	C = A ^ B;
<<	Shift bits left	C = A << B;
>>	Shift bits right	C = A >> B;
~	One's complement	C = ~A;

In expressions, the first three bitwise operators in Table 7.3 combine two operands according to the rules for logical AND (&), inclusive OR (¦), and exclusive OR (^). The next two operators, << and >>, shift bits in values left and right. Don't confuse these with the C++ I/O stream operators, which look the same, but are used differently based on their context.

The final operator, ~, flops bits in its operand value, changing all zero bits to ones and all ones to zeros, and creating a result called the *one's complement*. Operator ~ is a unary operator, requiring a single operand. The others are binary operators, which are applied to two operands.

One typical use for bitwise operators is to mask values, applying a Boolean operation to the bits in one value using the bits in another. For example, doing that with the exclusive-OR operator can encrypt text, rendering it unreadable but easily recoverable simply by repeating the masking operation. Listing 7.2, encrypt.cpp, demonstrates this basic idea.

LISTING 7.2   ENCRYPT.CPP

```cpp
#include <iostream.h>
#include <string.h>

char input[128];   // String to encrypt
char mask;         // Exclusive-OR mask
unsigned int i;    // for-loop control variable

main()
{
  cout << "Enter a string to encrypt: ";
  cin.getline(input, sizeof(input));
  cout << "Enter a single-character mask: ";
  cin >> mask;
  cout << "Original string  == " << input << endl;
  for (i = 0; i < strlen(input); i++)
    input[i] = input[i] ^ mask;
  cout << "Encrypted string == " << input << endl;
  for (i = 0; i < strlen(input); i++)
    input[i] = input[i] ^ mask;
  cout << "Decrypted string == " << input << endl;
  return 0;
}
```

Compile the program using the commands:

```
$ g++ encrypt.cpp
$ ./a.out
```

When prompted, enter a string to encrypt, along with a single character mask, as shown in this sample run:

```
Enter a string to encrypt: Social Security #: 123-45-6789
Enter a single-character mask: @
Original string  == Social Security #: 123-45-6789
Encrypted string == r/#)!,'r%#52)49'cz'qrsmtumvwxy
Decrypted string == Social Security #: 123-45-6789
```

The encrypted string is gibberish, but as the final line of output shows, the original text is easily recovered. To encrypt the input string, the program executes this `for` statement:

```
for (i = 0; i < strlen(input); i++)
  input[i] = input[i] ^ mask;
```

(You meet `for` statements in Chapter 9, "Controlling Program Flow.") The loop executes the statement on the second line for every character in the input string. Each character is combined with the `mask` `char` using the bitwise exclusive-OR operator (^). Because the exclusive-OR operator serves as a bit toggle, repeating this loop with the same mask recovers the original data. The assignment can be written more concisely using the shorthand statement:

```
input[i] ^= mask;
```

This performs the identical operation as the former statement—it applies `mask` using the exclusive-OR operator to the character `input[i]` and assigns the result of that operation to `input[i]`. However, using the shorthand operator, only one reference to the array element is needed.

Warning

For several reasons, the encrypt.cpp program in this section is not a secure method for encrypting sensitive data. For one, it is easy to discover the single character mask by simply writing a program to apply the entire ASCII character set to encrypted data. For another, any zero bytes in the data encrypt to the mask's value. However, if all you want is to encrypt text to keep it from curious eyes, a simple exclusive-OR mask can be an effective encryption technique.

OPERATOR TIPS

The following sections contain some tips and shorthand expressions for using the C and C++ operators introduced in this chapter.

MULTIPLE ASSIGNMENTS

When you need to initialize several variables to the same value, you can use statements such as the following:

```
int A, B, C;
A = B = C = 451;
```

That sets A, B, and C to 451. This isn't a special form of syntax, but simply a result of the way C++ evaluates expressions. Because the expression (A = B) equals the value assigned to A, the preceding statement is evaluated as though written using parentheses to group each subexpression:

```
( A = ( B = (C = 451) ) );
```

Note
Unlike most operators, the assignment operator's associativity is right to left. For this reason, expressions such as A = B = C set B and A equal to C's value, in that order.

SHORTHAND ASSIGNMENTS

Assignment statements sometimes do more work than necessary. The following statement refers to A twice:

```
A = A + 45;
```

You can write that same statement more concisely using the shorthand operator += this way:

```
A += 45;
```

Functionally, the two statements are equivalent. However, the second is potentially more efficient, especially if A is a complex expression—a calculated address, for example, or a position in an array returned by a function. (More on such cases in future chapters, especially Chapter 10, "Creating and Calling Functions.") C and C++ provide several other shorthand assignment operators, all of which reduce longhand expressions in this form:

```
i = i op j;
```

to the more concisely written

```
i op= j;
```

The full set of assignment operators is *=, /=, +=, -=, %=, <<=, >>=, &=, ^=, and |=. They are all near the bottom of the precedence order list (see Appendix B), so that any expressions on each side are fully evaluated before the shorthand operators are applied. Following are a few samples of shorthand assignment statements with the equivalent longhand expressions shown in comments:

```
count += 10;    // count = count + 10
count *= 2;     // count = count * 2
count /= 3;     // count = count / 3
count %= 16;    // count = count % 16
```

PART

II

CH

7

THE MIN AND MAX OPERATORS

Newer releases of ANSI C++ compilers, including GNU C++, add two additional operators that many programmers don't even know exist. Use the lesser-of and greater-of operators to compare two values, usually in an assignment. They are also known as the min and max operators. For example, given two integers value1 and value2 (they can be values of other fundamental types), the following statement assigns the lesser value to result:

```
result = value1 <? value2;  // Assign lesser value to result
```

Similarly, the following statement assigns the greater of the two values to result:

```
result = value1 >? value2;  // Assign greater value to result
```

The order of variables in the expressions to the right of the assignment doesn't matter. If value1 equals value2, result is set to that value.

SUMMARY

All expressions have values. Even a simple variable name such as counter is an expression that has a value. With operators, programs create complex expressions that perform calculations and comparisons. Use parentheses to group subexpressions and force a different evaluation order. In the absence of parentheses, C++ evaluates expressions based on operator precedence and associativity, as detailed in Appendix B.

For more information on subjects introduced in this chapter, turn to the following chapters:

- Chapter 9, "Controlling Program Flow"
- Chapter 10, "Creating and Calling Functions"
- Chapter 11, "Managing Memory with Pointers"
- Chapter 22, "Mastering the Standard string Class"
- Appendix B, "C++ Operator Precedence and Associativity"

Controlling Input and Output

It might surprise you that C++ has no native capabilities for input and output (I/O). The same is true of C. In both languages, I/O is provided strictly by library functions. For instance, to read and write data in C++ programs—whether to and from the console, or in a disk file—you must include the iostream.h header file and link the program to the compiled I/O stream library.

Not having I/O facilities built into a programming language might seem to be a drawback, but because I/O in C and C++ is provided by compiled libraries, programmers who develop code for embedded systems or for special-purpose computers are free to devise their own I/O functions and techniques. This fact makes C and C++ well suited to low-level program-ming. However, most software application developers might as well take advantage of the standard libraries. They have been tweaked to the hilt by GNU's authors, and it would be difficult to outdo their efforts.

This chapter explains how to read and write fundamental data objects and strings using C++ I/O streams, and how to format strings to produce good-looking output.

INTRODUCING C++ I/O STREAMS

An I/O stream object behaves much like the standard input and output file streams that are familiar to C programmers. But rather than call a standard library function such as puts(), C++ programs use the "put-to" operator (<<) for output and the "get-from" operator (>>) for input operations. For example, in C++, to write a program's title string to the standard out-put, you can use a statement such as

```
cout << "Fishbowl Screen Saver by Grouper Tom" << endl;
```

You've seen similar statements many times so far in this book. However, the cout object also provides functions you can call to perform many different tasks. To write a single character variable c to the standard output, you can use the statements:

```
char c = 'p';
cout.put(c);
```

The put() function is a *member* of the cout object's class—a new concept that you learn more about in Chapter 12, "Introducing the Class." To call an object's member function, type a period after the object name followed by the function to call. The function is called in reference to its object, in this case, cout.

Similarly, to read a character from the standard input, use the input stream object, cin, along with the get-from operator, >>. This statement reads one character from the standard input into a char variable c:

```
char c;
cin >> c;
```

Notice that the put-to and get-from operators seem to point to their targets. As you can with cout, you can call a member function in reference to cin. For example, the following performs the identical task as the preceding statement:

```
cin.get(c);
```

Listing 8.1, filter.cpp, demonstrates how to use the I/O stream get() and put() member functions to copy the standard input to the standard output. Although for demonstration only (Linux shells already provide filtering capabilities), the program lends useful insights into basic character input and output using C++ I/O streams.

LISTING 8.1   FILTER.CPP

```
#include <iostream.h>

char c;  // Holds characters in transit

int main()
{
  while (cin.get(c) != 0)
    cout.put(c);
  return 0;
}
```

The program calls the member function cin.get() until it returns false (actually a null reference that, because zero is considered "false," is interpreted as such). The while loop states that, as long as cin.get() returns a character in c, cout.put() writes that character to the standard output. (Chapter 9, "Controlling Program Flow," explains while loops and other control statements.) The program ends when the standard input file is closed—for example, when the input stream receives an end-of-file character C-z (Ctrl-Z).

After compiling filter.cpp (specify "filter" as the output filename), you can feed a text file to the program using the shell's input redirection symbol <. To try that, compile and run filter.cpp with the commands

```
$ g++ -o filter filter.cpp
./filter < filter.cpp
```

Note   Filter waits to receive characters from the standard input. If you run the program without specifying an input source, it appears to hang. Press C-c (Ctrl-C) to quit.

In this way, filter operates like the cat command. It copies each character from filter.cpp to the standard output, in this example displaying the program's own text file. To use filter to send a text file to the printer, type a command such as

```
./filter < filter.cpp > lpr
```

It's not really practical to use filter.cpp like that, but with a little extra effort, you can modify the basic code to perform an action on characters as they travel in and out of the program. For instance, Listing 8.2, upper.cpp, adds a statement to filter.cpp to create a utility that converts a text file into all uppercase characters.

LISTING 8.2   UPPER.CPP

```
#include <iostream.h>
#include <ctype.h>      // Need toupper()

char c;  // Holds characters in transit

int main()
{
  while (cin.get(c) != 0) {
    c = toupper(c);
    cout.put(c);
  }
  return 0;
}
```

Tip

Next to an #include directive, I like to write a comment that indicates what function or other declaration the program needs from a header. (See the second line of upper.cpp.) When I revise a program, the comment helps avoid including header files that are no longer needed.

The toupper() function is declared in the standard library's ctype.h header. Actually, toupper() is implemented as a preprocessor macro, but you use it as you do any other callable function. The while loop calls toupper() to convert each character to uppercase. To convert to lowercase, you can instead call tolower(). I wrote the while loop the "long" way for clarity, but you can shorten it to

```
while (cin.get(c) != 0)
  cout.put(toupper(c));
```

READING NATIVE TYPES

I/O stream statements can read and write objects of any C++ data type, not only strings and characters. Listing 8.3, getval.cpp, shows how to use I/O stream statements to read integer and floating point values. The program also demonstrates how to detect input errors if the program's user types an illegal character such as a letter when the program expects numerical input.

LISTING 8.3   GETVAL.CPP

```
#include <iostream.h>
#include <stdlib.h>

void test(void);   // Function prototype

double fp;         // A floating point value
long k;            // A long int value

int main()
{
  cout << "Enter a floating point value: ";
```

```
  cin >> fp;   // Read input into fp
  test();
  cout << "Value entered is: " << fp << endl;
  cout << "Enter an integer value: ";
  cin >> k;    // Read input into k
  test();
  cout << "Value entered is: " << k << endl;
  return 0;
}

void test(void)
{
  if (!cin.good()) {
    cout << "*** Input error detected\n";
    exit(1);
  }
}
```

Compile and run getval.cpp. The program prompts you for a floating point value and then for an integer. It echoes each value you type, as shown in this sample run:

```
$ g++ getval.cpp
$ ./a.out
Enter a floating point value: 3.14159
Value entered is: 3.14159
Enter an integer value: 1234
Value entered is: 1234
```

Run the program again, but this time, enter an illegal character when prompted for a floating point value:

```
./a.out
Enter a floating point value: xyz
*** Input error detected
```

The program detects the error, prints an error message, and halts. In the source code, function test() handles this error condition. (For more about functions, see Chapter 10, "Creating and Calling Functions.") To read a floating point value and test whether an error occurred, the program executes the statements

```
cin >> fp;
test();
```

Function test() checks whether cin.good() returns true. If not, an error occurred during the most recent input to cin. In that case, the program prints the error message and then calls exit():

```
if (!cin.good()) {
  cout << "*** Input error detected\n";
  exit(1);
}
```

Rather than halt the program upon detecting an error, you can clear it and continue. To clear errors reported by cin.good() and allow future I/O to continue normally, execute the statement

```
cin.clear();
```

READING STRINGS

Many sample programs in this book use simple input statements to read strings such as filenames and test values. The following statements, for example, prompt users to enter data into a string variable:

```
char input[32];    // String variable
...
cout << "Enter data: ";
cin >> input;
```

This is adequate for simple programs, but the method doesn't provide for editing or command-line completion features that most Linux users expect from commercial-quality software. Following are two other, and perhaps better, ways to read input strings.

> **Note**
>
> The GNU Readline library provides an extensive set of functions for prompting users for input and providing editing keys, automatic command-line completion, command history, and other features. The sample program rlprompt.cpp (not listed here) in this chapter's directory demonstrates how to incorporate the GNU Readline library into C++ programs.

READING STRINGS WITH `cin.getline()`

Probably the simplest way to input strings safely in C++ programs is to call the `cin` object's `getline()` member function. Listing 8.4, getline.cpp, demonstrates the basic technique for prompting users to enter a line of text.

LISTING 8.4 GETLINE.CPP

```
#include <iostream.h>

#define BUFSIZE 128     // Room for a 127-char string

char buffer[BUFSIZE];   // Character buffer

int main()
{
  cout << "Enter a string: ";
  cin.getline(buffer, BUFSIZE);
  cout << "buffer == " << buffer << endl;
  return 0;
}
```

For safety, it's best to define a constant such as BUFSIZE as shown here, and then use it in declaring the character buffer and in the `cin.getline()` statement. The following statement reads a string no longer than BUFSIZE characters into the program's buffer:

```
cin.getline(buffer, BUFSIZE);
```

The statement specifies buffer as the input destination and BUFSIZE as its size in bytes. The last character inserted by `cin.getline()` into the buffer is a null (ASCII 0). Because one byte is reserved for the terminating null, as programmed here, buffer can hold up to a 127-character string. Compile and run the program, and type a string in response to the prompt. The program echoes your typing and then ends:

```
$ g++ getline.cpp
$ ./a.out
Enter a string: Testing: uno, dos, tres
buffer == Testing: uno, dos, tres
```

Although calling getline() is adequate for many programs, the function's drawbacks soon become apparent. It doesn't recognize editing keys (however, Del seems to work), and if the user enters more characters than specified, they remain in the system input stream. Those characters are then read by subsequent input statements and can lead to confusing interactions. Following is an improved method that avoids these problems and keeps users happy.

READING STRINGS WITH cin.get()

With a special form of the cin.get() member function, you can input character buffers safely, especially when the program's user attempts to type beyond the end of the input buffer. Listing 8.5, getstring.cpp, shows how to use cin.get() this way.

LISTING 8.5   GETSTRING.CPP

```cpp
#include <iostream.h>

#define BUFSIZE 128      // Room for a 127-char string

char buffer[BUFSIZE];    // Character buffer
char c;                  // For checking buffer limit

int main()
{
  cout << "Enter a string: ";
  cin.get(buffer, BUFSIZE, '\n');
  if (cin.get(c) && c != '\n') {
    cout << endl << "*** Buffer length exceeded" << endl;
    while (cin.get(c) && c != '\n') { }  // Throw out excess
  }
  cout << "buffer == " << buffer << endl;
  return 0;
}
```

The getstring.cpp program resembles getline.cpp, but it uses a different method to read a string into the char buffer. Again, a constant BUFSIZE defines the buffer size in bytes. After prompting the user to enter a string, the program calls cin.get() like this:

```cpp
cin.get(buffer, BUFSIZE, '\n');
```

That statement passes to cin.get() the following three arguments:

- The destination name of a char array, in this case, buffer. The resulting string inserted into this array is terminated with a null character (ASCII 0). The maximum length string, then, is one less than BUFSIZE.

- The size of the array in bytes. Lacking a constant, you can use `sizeof(buffer)` in place of `BUFSIZE`.

- The character that, when typed, should end input. If not supplied, this character defaults to `'\n'` (newline).

Using `cin.get()` to input strings requires additional programming because the function leaves the termination character in the input stream. Consequently, when the user presses Enter, that character remains waiting to be read. Therefore, as the sample program demonstrates, if the next call to `cin.get()` reads a newline character, all preceding input must be in the buffer. (This is true even if the user simply presses Enter, in which case the buffer is empty.)

But if `cin.get()` returns a character other than newline, input must have been truncated before the user pressed Enter. In that case, the program displays a warning that the input line length was exceeded, and the following `while` statement throws away the excess characters from the input stream:

```
while (cin.get(c) && c != '\n') { }
```

This states that, while `cin.get(c)` successfully reads a character, and while that character is *not* a newline, simply repeat the loop, doing nothing in the empty statement block. This method is particularly useful in programs that use many small character buffers and that prompt for numerous strings. In other cases, `cin.getline()` is simpler.

CREATING GOOD-LOOKING OUTPUT

Formatting data is like painting. Anyone can slap colors onto a canvas, but creating a good-looking picture takes a good eye and a generous helping of talent. Similarly, a well-written computer program displays data in neatly aligned columns and formats information in ways that make it more usable. A programmer's utility, for example, might display values in decimal, hexadecimal, and octal. An accounting program might display data formatted with a certain number of decimal digits. This section explains some of the ways you can format a program's output by using C++ I/O streams.

FORMATTING OUTPUT WITH I/O STREAMS

An output stream object such as `cout` provides a variety of common output-formatting commands, also called *manipulators*. Listing 8.6, convert.cpp, shows how to use three manipulators to display an entered value in decimal, hexadecimal, and octal.

LISTING 8.6   CONVERT.CPP

```
#include <iostream.h>
#include <stdlib.h>

#define BUFSIZE 128
```

```
char buffer[BUFSIZE];   // Holds user input
int value;              // Holds input converted to an integer

int main()
{
  cout << "Enter an integer value: ";
  cin.getline(buffer, BUFSIZE);  // Read input from user
  value = atoi(buffer);          // Convert to integer
  cout
    << "Decimal=="           << dec << value
    << "  Hexadecimal==0x" << hex << value
    << "  Octal==0"          << oct << value << endl;
  return 0;
}
```

For simplicity, the convert.cpp program calls getline() as described in this chapter to read the user's input. After that statement, the standard library function atoi() (ASCII to integer) declared in stdlib.h converts the contents of the character buffer to an integer value. Near the end of main(), an output stream statement writes the converted value in decimal, hexadecimal, and octal, as shown in this sample run:

```
$ g++ convert.cpp
$ ./a.out
Enter an integer value: 123
Decimal==123  Hexadecimal==0x7b  Octal==0173
```

Output is formatted three ways by using the I/O stream manipulators dec, hex, and oct. Writing these predefined symbols to cout affects the format of subsequent output. Carefully examine the program's output statement:

```
cout
  << "Decimal=="           << dec << value
  << "  Hexadecimal==0x" << hex << value
  << "  Octal==0"          << oct << value << endl;
```

Tip

It might be easier to debug individual output statements than a long, cascaded one as listed here. Consider this when writing your code.

USING I/O STREAM MANIPULATORS

GNU C++ provides several other manipulators in addition to dec, hex, and oct introduced in the preceding section. These are useful for formatting output, and also for reading input in a specific format. Table 8.1 lists the manipulators you can use in I/O stream statements. The middle column indicates whether the manipulator is appropriate in input (I), output (O), or both (I/O) types of statements.

Tip

Include the iomanip.h header file when using manipulators. This isn't required for endl, hex, dec, and oct, but is needed for others such as setprecision() that are implemented as functions.

TABLE 8.1   I/O STREAM MANIPULATORS

Manipulator	I/O	Effect
dec	I/O	Convert to decimal
endl	O	Start new line and flush stream
ends	O	Write null terminator
flush	O	Flush output stream
hex	I/O	Convert to hexadecimal
oct	I/O	Convert to octal
setbase(int n)	I/O	Set radix (number base) to n (0, 8, 10, or 16)
setfill(int c)	O	Set the fill character to c
setprecision(int n)	I/O	Set floating point precision to n
setw(int w)	O	Set column width to w
ws	I	Extract whitespace (input)

You have already used some of the manipulators in Table 8.1. The endl manipulator, as you know, starts a new line on the output in a statement such as

```
cout << "Start a new line" << endl;
```

Similarly, the ends manipulator inserts a null (end of string) character into the output. The following statement writes three strings each terminated by a null character and a new line:

```
cout << "First string"  << ends << endl
     << "Second string" << ends << endl
     << "Third string"  << ends << endl;
```

You wouldn't normally write code like that to display strings, but you might use it to create a file that contains strings in null-terminated format. Use setw() to set the column width for the next object written. This is useful for aligning columns. For example, to set the column width to 10 and write a string right-justified within that column space, use a statement such as

```
cout << setw(10) << s << endl;
```

The width manipulator is short-lived, and it affects only the next output object. Combine setw() with setfill() to fill columns with a character other than a space. The following statement writes an error message in a 40-character column padded with # characters:

```
cout << setfill('#') << setw(40)
     << "Error: very dumb mistake" << endl;
```

Use the flush manipulator to flush the output stream, usually necessary only after detecting an error condition:

```
if (!cout.good())
{
  cout << flush;
  cout.clear();
}
```

You may set the input or output number base, or *radix*, with setbase(n), although it is probably just as well to use hex, dec, and oct. The following two statements set the input radix to octal (base 8) and read a value into an integer variable, n:

```
cin >> setbase(8) >> n;
cout << "n == " << n << endl;
```

If the user types *10*, the program displays n == 8. You may use hex, oct, dec, and setbase() in output and input statements. The following statement reads an integer value n in hexadecimal and then displays the value of n in hexadecimal (base 16) preceded by "0x":

```
cout << "Enter hex value: ";
cin >> hex >> n;
cout << "Value == 0x" << setbase(16) << n << endl;
```

To format floating point values, either for input or output, use the setprecision() manipulator. The value in parentheses indicates how many digits in the input or output to allow. The resulting value is rounded as necessary. If a double variable f equals 3.14159, the following statement displays 3.1416:

```
cout << "f == " << setprecision(5) << f << endl;
```

You may also use setprecision() in an input statement like this:

```
cin >> setprecision(5) >> f;
```

Finally, use the ws (eat whitespace) manipulator to gobble up blanks. This statement ignores any leading spaces in the input:

```
cin >> ws >> s;
```

However, because input statements seem to ignore whitespace anyway, the ws manipulator is rarely used.

FORMATTING WITH THE sprintf() FAMILY

The C++ output-formatting methods described so far in this chapter are adequate for many programs, but the basic techniques don't offer as much control over formatting as sometimes needed. Fortunately, the standard C library provides a set of functions that can handle formatting requirements of any conceivable complexity. To demonstrate, Listing 8.7, convert2.cpp, uses the standard library function sprintf() to prepare a string for an output stream statement.

LISTING 8.7   CONVERT2.CPP

```cpp
#include <iostream.h>
#include <stdio.h>
#include <stdlib.h>

#define BUFSIZE 128

char in_buffer  [BUFSIZE];   // User input
char out_buffer [BUFSIZE];   // Formatted output string
int value;                   // Input buffer converted to int

int main()
{
  cout << "Enter an integer value: ";
  cin.getline(in_buffer, BUFSIZE);  // Get input from user
  value = atoi(in_buffer);          // Convert to integer

  // Format output string in out_buffer using value
  sprintf(out_buffer,
    "Decimal==%d  Hexadecimal==%#x  Octal==%#o",
    value, value, value);

  cout << out_buffer << endl;  // Write formatted string
  return 0;
}
```

The convert2.cpp program runs the same and produces the identical output as convert.cpp (refer to Listing 8.6). In the new program, a call to the standard library function sprintf() (print formatted string) performs the same job as the dec, hex, and oct manipulators in the original code. After formatting, a relatively simple output stream statement prints the formatted buffer (out_buffer) and starts a new line. However, this simple program doesn't reveal the power of sprintf() and related functions. Many C++ programmers use these standard C library functions to format their programs' output, and it's useful to learn how to use them.

The sprintf() function, declared in stdlib.h, prepares a character string with values formatted according to various symbolic rules. To the function, a statement usually passes at least three arguments, separated by commas. These arguments are

- An output char buffer such as out_buffer (see convert2.cpp) sufficiently large to hold the function's result
- A literal string with one or more embedded formatting instructions, each preceded by %
- One object or value for each embedded formatting instruction in the literal string

A simple example demonstrates how to use sprintf(). Consider this statement:

```cpp
sprintf(out_buffer, "Decimal == %d", value);
```

When executed with those arguments, `sprintf()` inserts the value converted into decimal text in place of the formatting instruction %d. The resulting null-terminated string is inserted into out_buffer. If value equals 123, `sprintf()` inserts this string into out_buffer:

```
Decimal == 123
```

Now, take a look again at the more complex `sprintf()` statement in the convert2.cpp program (you may write it all on one line, or divide it as I did here for space reasons):

```
sprintf(out_buffer,
  "Decimal==%d  Hexadecimal==%#x  Octal==%#o",
  value, value, value);
```

This time, value is inserted three times into the literal string, formatted according to the instructions %d, %#x, and %#o. Those formatting instructions convert value into decimal, hexadecimal, and octal, and the function stores the result in out_buffer. If value equals 123, after the preceding statement, out_buffer contains the string

```
Decimal==123  Hexadecimal==0x7b  Octal==0173
```

When using `sprintf()`, you must supply as many values as formatting instructions in the literal string. Following is another sample that uses two variables as arguments declared as

```
int custnum = 123;      // Customer number
double balance = 541.82;  // Customer balance
```

To create an output string containing these values, a program might call `sprintf()` this way:

```
sprintf(out_buffer, "Customer # %d balance : $%8.2f",
  custnum, balance);
```

The `sprintf()` function replaces the formatting instructions %d and %8.2f in the string with the custnum and balance values, and inserts into out_buffer the finished string:

```
Customer # 123 balance : $  541.82
```

The standard C library has related functions such as `fprintf()` (print a formatted string to a file) and `printf()` (print a formatted string to the standard output). They all work the same way, but send their output to different places. However, in C++ programs, I find it best to use `sprintf()` to prepare formatted strings for output and then display them using output stream statements. This avoids mixing I/O methods in the same code. The next section looks more closely at `sprintf()` and explains more about the complexities of formatting instructions.

MORE ABOUT `sprintf()`

Boasting more options than a Mercedes, `sprintf()` is one of the most extensive in the standard library. It is also one of the most confusing to learn how to use. The function is declared as

```
int sprintf(char *buffer, const char *format, ...);
```

Careful readers might spot an inherent danger in `sprintf()`: There is no parameter for specifying the size of the output buffer. If this is a concern, use the alternate `snprintf()` function:

```
int snprintf(char *buffer, int size, const char *format, ...);
```

The alternate function is the same as `sprintf()`, but its second parameter specifies the maximum size of the output buffer. In both functions, buffer is the destination for the function's output. Next is a constant string that usually contains one or more formatting instructions. Finally, the ellipsis indicates that zero or more objects follow, one for each formatting instruction in the preceding string.

> **Tip**
>
> Compile with the GNU C++ `-Wformat` option to have the compiler check that all values in `sprintf()` statements are of the appropriate types. This option works for all `sprintf()` family functions such as `printf()`, `scanf()`, and `fprintf()`. Not many compilers provide this helpful option!

The `sprintf()` function and others in its family return an integer value equal to the number of characters in the final formatted output string, not including the string's terminating null. This value might be useful to fine-tune output—setting a column width, for example.

SYNTAX OF FORMATTING INSTRUCTIONS

Formatting instructions such as `%d` and `%8.2f` follow a complex but highly versatile set of rules. All such instructions begin with a percent sign (%) followed by various digits and symbols selected from a smorgasbord of options. Formatting instructions conform to the syntax

```
% [flags] [width] [.precision] [h¦l¦L] conversion
```

The items in square brackets are optional, but their order is fixed. Items without brackets are required. The following sections explain each of the elements in the preceding formatting instruction syntax. For reference, the syntax is repeated in each section's title, with the discussed element in boldface.

```
% [flags] [width] [.precision] [h¦l¦L] conversion
```

Embedded formatting instructions begin with a required percent sign. To insert a percent-sign character into the output, type the symbol twice like this: `%%`.

```
% [flags] [width] [.precision] [h¦l¦L] conversion
```

Optional flags specify justification rules and state whether to output plus and minus signs, decimal points, trailing zeros, and prefixes in octal or zero-digit characters. If specified, flags can consist of one or more of the characters listed in Table 8.2.

TABLE 8.2   FLAGS FOR THE sprintf() FAMILY

Flag	Description
-	Left-justifies output. Fills any remaining space to the right with blanks. Default output is right-justified.
+	Prefaces numeric values with a plus or minus sign.
' '	A space displays a blank in front of positive numeric values, and a minus sign in front of negative ones. Don't type the quotes—just type a single space.
#	Selects an alternate form for some conversion letters. If the conversion is x or X, this prefaces nonzero arguments with 0x or 0X, respectively. Use it to display hexadecimal values. If the conversion is o, this prefaces the value with 0. If the conversion is e, E, or f, this forces a decimal point to appear in the output (normally, a decimal appears only in nonzero fractions). If the conversion is g or G, a decimal point is forced into the output, and trailing zeros are *not* truncated as they are normally.
0	Specifies zero padding. Except for the conversion letter n, zeros pad the formatted value to the left (normally blanks).

% [flags] **[width]** [.precision] [h¦l¦L] conversion

The optional width value specifies a minimum column width. Normally, any extra space is filled with blanks. But if the width value begins with the digit 0, any extra space is filled with 0 characters. This is useful for aligning integers padded at left with zeros.

The width value also can be an asterisk (*). This causes the *next* int argument to be used as the column width—a rare case in which a formatting command requires two arguments. With this command, you specify two values: an integer that represents the minimum width to use and the value to be formatted within that column width. The width integer comes *before* the value to format. Don't mix them up.

% [flags] [width] **[.precision]** [h¦l¦L] conversion

The optional precision value, which must begin with a period, denotes numeric precision for floating point values or, when used with integer objects, the minimum number of digits. Don't confuse the period with a decimal point! If a period appears at this location in the formatting string, the next value represents the precision to use for the formatted result. The exact meaning of the precision depends on the type of item being formatted.

A positive integer value must follow the period. The default value is 0, so typing .0 is the same as specifying no precision. Default precisions are 1 for conversion characters d, i, o, u, x, and X; 6 for e, E, and f; a variable number of significant digits for g and G; and all characters for conversions s and c (strings and characters).

If the conversion character is g or G, the precision represents the maximum number of significant digits in the formatted result. If the conversion is e, E, or f, the precision equals the number of decimal places to use, and the final digit is rounded. If conversion is s, the precision stands for the maximum number of characters to use from the string. Precision has no effect when using the conversion character c because single characters occupy only one character space in the final output. If the conversion character is d, i, o, u, x, or X, at least the number of digits specified by the precision are output, padded at left as necessary with 0 digits.

`% [flags] [width] [.precision] `**`[h¦l¦L]`**` conversion`

These optional modifiers select among size-related characteristics: h (`short int`), l (`long`), or L (`long double`). You may use only one of the three letters. GNU C++ also recognizes a few nonstandard modifiers such as q, ll, and Z, but these are for compatibility with other systems, and you are best advised not to use them.

`% [flags] [width] [.precision] [h¦l¦L] `**`conversion`**

The required conversion character tells `sprintf()` the type of an argument to be converted according to the formatting instruction. It is your responsibility to ensure that the object is of this type (however, use the GNU C++ `-Wformat` option to check for type mismatches). Table 8.3 lists the conversion characters you may use in formatting strings. Case is significant. A lowercase g is not the same as an uppercase G. See the info `sprintf` pages for more detailed descriptions and some additional quirks and rules.

TABLE 8.3 CONVERSION CHARACTERS FOR `sprintf()`

Conversion	Description
%	A percent sign.
c	A character.
d	A signed decimal.
e	A double value to be formatted using scientific notation (for example, 1.0765e+10).
E	Same as e, but inserts an uppercase E before the exponent.
f	A double value to be formatted in decimal format such as 123.45.
g	A double value to be formatted in either scientific or decimal notation. The format is automatically selected to (we hope) give the most accurate results in the smallest amount of space.
G	Same as g, but if scientific notation is used, an uppercase E is written before the exponent.
i	Same as d; a signed decimal.
n	Treats the argument value as a pointer to an `int` variable in which `sprintf()` (and other functions in this family) stores a count of the number of characters formatted up to this point in the formatting string. Using this conversion character adds no characters to the output. It is valuable for creating variables used as column widths.
o	An unsigned octal.
p	A pointer, formatted in hexadecimal.

Conversion	Description
s	A null-terminated string. You may specify a precision to restrict output to that many characters.
u	An unsigned decimal.
x	An unsigned hexadecimal using the digits 0, ..., 9 and the lowercase letters a, b, c, d, e, and f.
X	Same as x, but uses the uppercase letters A, B, C, D, E, and F.

A `sprintf()` EXAMPLE

Learning to put all the myriad elements together for a `sprintf()` statement might seem to take doctorate-level mental gymnastics. There are so many options, letters, and symbols in a formatting string that it's easy to get hung up trying to format output to look as you want. Following are some sample statements that will help you learn how to use `sprintf()`.

One of the most common uses for `sprintf()` is to format date values. Suppose that your program declares variables to hold the day, month, and year like this:

```
int month = 2;
int day = 16;
int year = 2001;
```

Using `sprintf()`, the program can format and display the date as a string using statements such as

```
sprintf(buffer, "Date: %.2d-%.2d-%.4d", day, month, year);
cout << buffer << endl;
```

That writes the following string to the standard output:

```
Date: 16-02-2001
```

In the `sprintf()` statement, the formatting command `%.2d` specifies a precision of 2 and that the value is decimal (an integer). Using a precision value with the conversion letter *d* pads values with leading zeros within the specified width so that the month value 2 is written as 02. The command `%.4d` writes the full date value 2001. (No Y2K problem here.)

The following sample program in Listing 8.8, sprintfex.cpp, gives additional examples for using `sprintf()` to format integer and floating point values.

LISTING 8.8   SPRINTFEX.CPP

```
#include <iostream.h>
#include <stdio.h>

#define BUFSIZE 128     // Size of formatting buffer

char buffer[BUFSIZE];   // Holds sprintf() output
```

continues

LISTING 8.8   CONTINUED

```cpp
// A few sample variables:

int xint = 123;
long xlong = 12345678L;
char xchar = '@';
char *xstring = "This is pretty cool!";
double xdouble = 3.14159;
long double xlongdouble = xdouble * xdouble;

int main()
{
  cout << "Sample printf() statements" << endl;
  cout << "VARIABLE          RESULT" << endl;
  sprintf(buffer, "xint (decimal) == %d", xint);
  cout << buffer << endl;
  sprintf(buffer, "xint (hex)     == %#x", xint);
  cout << buffer << endl;
  sprintf(buffer, "xint (octal)   == %#o", xint);
  cout << buffer << endl;
  sprintf(buffer, "xlong          == %ld", xlong);
  cout << buffer << endl;
  sprintf(buffer, "xchar          == %c", xchar);
  cout << buffer << endl;
  sprintf(buffer, "xstring        == %s", xstring);
  cout << buffer << endl;
  sprintf(buffer, "xdouble        == %lf", xdouble);
  cout << buffer << endl;
  sprintf(buffer, "xlongdouble(1) == %Le", xlongdouble);
  cout << buffer << endl;
  sprintf(buffer, "xlongdouble(2) == %Lf", xlongdouble);
  cout << buffer << endl;
  return 0;
}
```

Following is the program's output. Compare these lines with each statement's `sprintf()` formatting commands:

```
$ g++ sprintfex.cpp
$ ./a.out
Sample printf() statements
VARIABLE          RESULT
xint (decimal) == 123
xint (hex)     == 0x7b
xint (octal)   == 0173
xlong          == 12345678
xchar          == @
xstring        == This is pretty cool!
xdouble        == 3.141590
xlongdouble(1) == 9.869588e+00
xlongdouble(2) == 9.869588
```

LUCKY PENNIES

Years ago, in my brief career as a computer store sales clerk, I had a raging argument with a customer who insisted his computer didn't work. The fellow had written some accounting software using floating point variables, and he brought his system in repeatedly to demonstrate that it "lost pennies." I was unable to convince him that the trouble was not in his system but in his method. Floating point values in a computer's memory are approximations, I said, and they are not appropriate for storing monetary values. Despite my explanations, the store manager ended up giving the customer his money back, even though his computer worked perfectly well.

Lucky for you and me, GNU C++ provides long and long long (double wide) integers that are perfect for storing monetary values down to the last penny. Simply represent all your monetary amounts as long or long long values and assume two decimal places. In other words, the binary values represent pennies. A long value of 32176 formatted monetarily equals $321.76.

Adding the decimal place is merely a matter of string formatting, not floating point mathematics. To demonstrate one method for inserting a decimal point into integer values, Listing 8.9, money.cpp, prompts for and formats long integer values entered at a program prompt.

LISTING 8.9   MONEY.CPP

```
#include <iostream.h>
#include <stdio.h>      // Need cprintf()
#include <string.h>     // Need memmove()

long value;             // Value in binary
char buffer[32];        // Value in string form

main()
{
  // Prompt for value to convert
  cout << "Value? ";
  cin >> value;

  // Convert value to string form in buffer
  sprintf(buffer, "$ %.3d", value);
  cout << "Unformatted: " << buffer << endl;

  // Move last two characters of buffer down one
  int dest = strlen(buffer) - 1;
  int src  = strlen(buffer) - 2;
  memmove(&buffer[dest], &buffer[src], 3);  // Including null!

  // Insert decimal point and display results
  buffer[src] = '.';
  cout << "Formatted:   " << buffer << endl;

  return 0;
}
```

Compile and run money.cpp, and then enter a value to convert. The program displays the unformatted and formatted strings for comparison, as the following output sample shows:

```
$ g++ money.cpp
$ ./a.out
Value? 87691
Unformatted: $ 87691
Formatted:   $ 876.91
```

Two separate operations are needed to insert the decimal place. First, after obtaining a binary long value, the program uses sprintf() to convert it into string form:

```
sprintf(buffer, "$ %.3d", value);
```

That statement inserts the decimal value into buffer, preceded by a dollar sign (remove that character if you want), in a minimum of three spaces. The 3 in the formatting specification ensures that small values such as -2 come out as $ -0.02, the value 10 comes out as $ 0.10, and zero comes out as $ 0.00.

After preparing the raw formatted string, the program calls a library function to make room for inserting a decimal point character. The memmove() function, declared in the standard string.h header file, moves bytes in a string or other buffer. Before calling memmove(), the program calculates the destination and source locations in the string using its length with the statements:

```
int dest = strlen(buffer) - 1;
int src  = strlen(buffer) - 2;
```

Using those values, memmove() moves the last two characters in the string down by one character, making room for inserting a decimal point:

```
memmove(&buffer[dest], &buffer[src], 3);
```

The memmove() function requires three arguments: a destination, a source, and the number of bytes to move. The reason for moving three characters, and not merely two, is to include the string's null terminator in the operation. The ampersand characters tell the compiler to pass the locations in memory—in other words, the *addresses*—of the source and destination for the move operation. A simple assignment inserts the decimal point and completes the formatting:

```
buffer[src] = '.';
```

Warning

When calling memmove() to shuffle characters in C-style strings, be sure the string buffer is large enough to hold the resulting string.

SUMMARY

This chapter explained how to use C++ I/O streams to read and write data values and strings. The chapter also showed various C and C++ methods to format strings for creating good-looking output.

For more information on subjects introduced in this chapter, turn to the following chapters:

- Chapter 9, "Controlling Program Flow"
- Chapter 10, "Creating and Calling Functions"
- Chapter 12, "Introducing the Class"

PART

II

CH

8

Controlling Program Flow

A computer program runs like a river. Unless diverted, a river's water flows in the shortest path to the sea. Likewise, with no intervention, a C++ program's statements execute one after the other from top to bottom until the program ends. In C and C++ programs, *flow-control statements* operate like dams, channels, water wheels, and aqueducts to direct the program's execution along whatever path you want it to follow.

C and C++ provide two basic types of flow-control statements: those that make decisions based on a conditional true or false argument, and those that create loops for repeatedly executing various operations. This chapter introduces both types of C and C++ flow-control statements.

Conditional Statements

Conditional statements make decisions by examining true or false expressions. Although simple in concept, directing a program's flow through the use of conditional statements is one of the most powerful programming tools at your disposal. The following sections introduce C and C++ conditional `if` and `else` statements, and also explain how to use conditional expressions—a handy shorthand `if-else`.

The `if` Statement

The `if` statement operates just as you might expect. If its stated condition is true, the statement performs an action; otherwise, execution continues with the following statement. A simple `if` statement in outline form looks like this:

```
if (condition)
  statement;
```

The condition can be any expression that evaluates to a true or false value. It must be in parentheses. If the condition is true (nonzero), the statement executes. If condition is false (zero), the statement is skipped. The statement can be any valid C or C++ statement, or it can be a statement block containing one or more statements. For example, this `if` statement performs two statements if its condition is true:

```
if (condition) {
  statement1;
  statement2;
}
```

Note

Indenting statements helps show their relationship in the program's source code. Many C and C++ programmers indent statements by pressing the Tab key. Some also indent the braces around a compound statement block. So that I can fit as much code as possible on the page, however, I use minimal indentation of two spaces in this book's listings.

An `if` statement typically examines a value and performs an associated operation. For example, the following `if` statement displays a message if the variable `value` is greater than 100:

```
if (value > 100)
  cout << "Value is too large" << endl;
```

The condition might also be a C++ `bool` variable, perhaps one named `error`:

```
bool error = false;
```

Elsewhere, a statement can set `error` to true to indicate that an error occurred. Back in function `main()`, an `if` statement inspects `error` and, if true, displays a message and exits the program:

```
if (error) {
  cout << "*** Error detected. Phone home!" << endl;
  exit(1);  // Exit with error code == 1
}
```

You can write the preceding `if` statement's condition like this:

```
if (error == true)...
```

But the simpler form is perfectly acceptable. Remember, even a variable name is an *expression* that has a value. The expression (error) equals true or false, and as such makes a valid `if` statement condition.

C and C++ programmers typically use that fact to test the zero (false) or nonzero (true) value of other types of expressions. Until you become used to the technique, it can be confusing. Consider a program that declares an `int` variable such as

```
int condition = 1;
```

Elsewhere, the program executes this `if` statement:

```
if (condition)
  cout << "Non-zero condition detected" << endl;
```

Because in C and C++ zero is synonymous with false and nonzero with true, this works, but the code is obscure. This is a common technique in C and C++, but it is always better, and costs nothing in performance, to clarify a non-`bool` condition using an explicit expression such as this:

```
if (condition == 0)
  cout << "Condition detected" << endl;
```

COMPLEX CONDITIONS

An `if` statement's condition often uses complex logical expressions to test more than one parameter. To illustrate, Listing 9.1, choice.cpp, prompts you to enter a value from 1 to 10. The program uses an `if` statement to detect an error condition and display a message if you enter a value not in the expected range.

LISTING 9.1   CHOICE.CPP

```
#include <iostream.h>

int number;   // User input

int main()
{
  cout << "Enter a number from 1 to 10: ";
  cin >> number;
  if ( (number < 1) || (number > 10) )
    cout << "Incorrect answer!" << endl;
  return 0;
}
```

Compile and run the program, and enter an integer value. If you enter a value outside the expected range, the program voices its annoyance as the following sample run shows:

```
$ g++ choice.cpp
$ ./a.out
Enter a number from 1 to 10: 11
Incorrect answer!
```

The program uses an `if` statement to test input for validity, probably one of the most common uses for this type of statement. Examine the program's `if` statement closely:

```
if ( (number < 1) || (number > 10) )
  cout << "Incorrect answer!" << endl;
```

The condition tests whether `number` is less than 1 or (||) greater than 10. If either condition is true, the entire expression is true and the program displays an error message. Parentheses group the full expression. Strictly speaking, the inner parentheses aren't needed because the less-than and greater-than operators < and > have higher precedence than the logical OR operator || (see Appendix B, "C++ Operator Precedence and Associativity"). However, the extra parentheses make the statement perfectly clear.

THE `else` STATEMENT

You might think of the `else` statement as the `if` statement's sidekick. It must follow an `if` statement to select an alternative action. In general, use `else` like this:

```
if (condition)
  statement1;
else
  statement2;
```

If the condition is true, `statement1` executes; otherwise, `statement2` goes into action. The statements may be simple or compound. Use parentheses to group related statements as shown here:

```
if (condition) {
  statement1;
  statement2;
} else
  statement3;
```

In that code, if the `condition` is true, statements 1 and 2 execute; otherwise, statement 3 runs. Either or both parts can be compound statement blocks:

```
if (condition) {
  statement1;
  statement2;
} else {
  statement3;
  statement4;
}
```

In that code, statements 1 and 2 execute if the condition is true; otherwise, statements 3 and 4 do their stuff. The placement of the braces is up to you. Some programmers prefer them on separate lines as follows:

```
}
else
{
```

NESTED `if-else` STATEMENTS

You may nest multiple `if-else` statements together, creating a multiway decision maker. The following shows the basic outline for a nested `if-else` statement:

```
if (condition1)
  statement1;
else if (condition2)
  statement2;
else
  statement3;
```

Take that a line at a time, and be sure to understand how it works. If `condition1` is true, then `statement1` executes; otherwise, if `condition2` is true, `statement2` runs. If both `condition1` and `condition2` are false, `statement3` executes. *At least one of the three statements is guaranteed to execute.* You can carry this idea to extremes, writing code such as this:

```
if (condition1)
  statement1;
else if (condition2)
  statement2;
else if (condition3)
  statement3;
else if (conditionN)
  statementN;
else                   // Optional
  defaultStatement;  // Optional
```

Nested `if-else` statements like that are useful for selecting one of several possible actions. The final `else` and associated statement are optional. If you leave out the last two lines in the preceding code, however, it is possible that no statements execute. Be sure that's what you intend.

Each statement in the `if-else` construction may itself be another `if-else`. But such deeply nested `if-else` statements can be confusing. They complicate error handling and are difficult to debug. C++ imposes no limit on the depth of if-else nesting, but in practice, you should limit nesting as much as possible.

As a practical example of nested if-else statements, Listing 9.2, leap.cpp, calculates whether a given year is a leap year. Compile and run the program and then enter a year such as 2001. A new century is a leap year when evenly divisible by 400. Noncentury dates such as 1996 are leap years if evenly divisible by 4.

LISTING 9.2   LEAP.CPP

```cpp
#include <iostream.h>

bool leapYear;
int year;

int main()
{
  cout << "Leap Year Calculator" << endl;
  cout << "Year? ";
  cin >> year;
  if (year <= 0)
    cout << "Year must be greater or equal to 0" << endl;
  else {
    if ( (year % 100) == 0 )
      leapYear = ( (year % 400) == 0 );
    else
      leapYear = ( (year %   4) == 0 );
    if (leapYear)
      cout << year << " is a leap year" << endl;
    else
      cout << year << " is not a leap year" << endl;
  }
  return 0;
}
```

Compile and run leap.cpp using the usual commands:

```
$ g++ leap.cpp
$ ./a.out
```

The program asks for a year and reports whether it's a leap year:

```
Leap Year Calculator
Year? 2000
2000 is a leap year
```

If you enter an invalid year, the program displays an error message:

```
Leap Year Calculator
Year? -50
Year must be greater or equal to 0
```

To perform these actions, leap.cpp uses nested if-else statements. The outermost if-else combo tests whether the input year is greater than or equal to zero. If the input is valid, the following `if-else` statement sets the `bool` flag `leapYear` to true or false according to the algorithm for determining a leap year:

```
if ( (year % 100) == 0 )
  leapYear = ( (year % 400) == 0 );
else
  leapYear = ( (year %   4) == 0 );
```

In the first expression, if the year modulo (%) 100 equals zero, then the year is a century, in which case it's a leap year only if also evenly divisible by 400. If the year is not a century, then `leapYear` is set to true only if the year modulo 4 equals zero—that is, if it is evenly divisible by 4. Following this business, the program checks the value of the `bool` flag and makes its pronouncement:

```
if (leapYear)
  cout << year << " is a leap year" << endl;
```

Note See "The `switch` Statement" later in this chapter for an alternative to nested `if-else` statements.

PART
II
CH
9

THE CONDITIONAL EXPRESSION

A conditional expression is a kind of shorthand `if-else` statement. Conditional expressions follow this general outline:

```
condition ? expression1 : expression2
```

That might look a bit cryptic at first, but it performs a simple job. If the condition is true, the result of the entire expression equals `expression1`. If the condition is false, the result equals `expression2`. Always remember that a conditional expression is just that—it's an expression that has a resulting value; it's not a statement. Usually, a conditional expression is used in an assignment statement, such as the following, that saves the expression's result in a variable:

```
result = condition ? expression1 : expression2;
```

That statement is equivalent to the following `if-else` construction. Both statements set `result` equal to `expression1` if the condition is true or to `expression2` if the condition is false:

```
if (condition)
  result = expression1;
else
  result = expression2;
```

As a practical demonstration of conditional expressions, Listing 9.3, absolute.cpp, converts an entered integer into its absolute value. If you enter a negative value, it's converted to positive. Positive values and zero are left untouched.

LISTING 9.3   ABSOLUTE.CPP

```
#include <iostream.h>

int value, result;

main()
{
  cout << "Value? ";
  cin >> value;
  result = (value >= 0) ? (value) : (value * -1);
  cout << "Result == " << result << endl;
  return 0;
}
```

The program shows a common use for conditional expressions—testing a value for some condition, and then based on the result of that test, performing an action on the value. In this case, if value is greater than or equal to zero, it is assigned unchanged to result; otherwise, the program assigns (value * -1) to result. To operate directly on the input value, you can replace result with value, in which case result isn't needed at all.

Note

Rather than use the technique shown here, to find the absolute value of an integer value, you can more easily include the stdlib.h header file and call the abs() function. Type *info abs* for details.

GNU C++ permits a shortened version of conditional expressions such as the one in absolute.cpp. Often, a program needs to examine whether a variable is true (nonzero), and if so use it as the expression's result; otherwise, a different value is needed. This means referencing the conditional variable twice as in the sample code:

```
result = a ? a : b;
```

Because a nonzero value is considered equivalent to true, in long form, that statement is functionally the same as this:

```
if (a != 0)
  result = a;
else
  result = b;
```

To avoid the double reference to a, GNU C++ permits a third variation that has the identical effect as the preceding two examples:

```
result = a ? : b;
```

In other words, you may omit the duplicate reference to a. In simple code such as the examples here, the shortened expression has no practical value. But in cases where evaluating a conditional expression causes a *side effect*—meaning that the evaluation of one part of the expression causes another value to change or an action to occur—the shorthand version might be useful. This feature might be unique to GNU C and C++.

> **Warning**
>
> Side effects are generally not good programming but are sometimes unavoidable. They can occur, for example, if the evaluation of an expression alters a variable involved in the expression. Try not to write code that exhibits side effects. That might be a bit like telling a legislator not to create laws with loopholes, but with care, it's possible to avoid introducing most kinds of side effects.

REPETITIVE STATEMENTS

Repetitive statements create *loops* that execute statements one or more times. Loops save space by repeating statements, often using altered data on successive executions. Another common use for loops is to *iterate* over a series of values—examining the individual characters in a string, for example.

C and C++ offer three repetitive statements for creating loops: while, do-while, and for. The following sections examine each of these statements and also show how to use the related break and continue statements inside repetitive statement blocks.

THE while STATEMENT

Use a while statement to repeatedly execute a statement *while* a certain condition holds true. A while statement follows this general outline:

```
while (condition)
  statement;
```

While condition is true, the program executes statement over and over with the assumption that the statement performs some action that eventually causes the condition to become false. Usually, the statement changes the value of a variable involved in the controlling condition.

As with other flow-control statements, a while's statement can be a compound block delimited with braces and containing one or more statements:

```
while (condition) {
  statement1;
  statement2;
}
```

Listing 9.4, wcount.cpp, uses a while statement to count from 1 to 10. Although simplistic, the program illustrates elements found in most while loops.

LISTING 9.4   WCOUNT.CPP

```
#include <iostream.h>

int counter;

int main()
{
  cout << "Counting with while" << endl;
  counter = 1;
  while (counter <= 10) {
    cout << "counter == " << counter << endl;
    counter++;
  }
  return 0;
}
```

For a control variable, the program declares an int object named counter. After displaying the program title, an assignment statement initializes counter to 1. After that, a while loop executes two statements *while* counter is less than or equal to 10. The first statement in the while loop's statement block displays counter's value. The second statement is critical—it increments counter by one each time through the loop. In this way, counter eventually reaches 10, causing the expression (counter <= 10) to be false and ending the while loop.

What is the final value of counter after the end of the while statement in wcount.cpp? Prove your guess by inserting this statement before main() returns:

```
cout << "final counter value == " << counter << endl;
```

Does counter's final value (11) make sense? What would counter equal if you changed the while's condition to (counter < 10)? Try also changing counter's starting value. What happens if you initialize counter to 11? Does the loop still execute? Pondering those questions reveals an important property of while loops. A while loop ends immediately if its condition is initially false. Therefore, it's possible for a while loop to execute its statement (or statement block) zero times.

You may use other kinds of control variables in while statements—they don't have to be of type int. For example, Listing 9.5, walpha.cpp, displays the alphabet, using a char variable as the loop's control value.

LISTING 9.5   WALPHA.CPP

```
#include <iostream.h>

char ch;

int main()
{
  cout << "Alphabet courtesy of while" << endl;
  ch = 'a';
  while (ch <= 'z') {
    cout << " " << ch;
```

```
      ch++;
    }
    cout << endl;   // Finish by starting a new line
    return 0;
}
```

Compile and run the program with the following commands. As the output printed here shows, the program displays the alphabet in lowercase:

```
$ g++ walpha.cpp
$ ./a.out
Alphabet courtesy of while
a b c d e f g h i j k l m n o p q r s t u v w x y z
```

Examine the program's while loop closely. It performs two statements while the value of ch is less than or equal to the letter "z." The first statement writes the character to the standard output. The second increments ch to the next character using the ++ operator. As in most loops, that final task is essential to ensure that the loop ends after doing its job.

TRICKS WITH THE CONTROL VARIABLE

One popular trick is to combine the use and increment of the control variable in a while statement with the ++ operator. Recall from Chapter 7, "Applying Fundamental Operators," that the expression i++ equals the value of i *before* the operator increments the variable. Because of that rule, it's often possible to shorten a while loop such as this (taken from Listing 9.5 in the preceding section):

```
char ch = 'a';
while (ch <= 'z') {
  cout << " " << ch;
  ch++;
}
```

Instead of executing two separate statements, only one is needed in the shortened version shown here:

```
char ch = 'a';
while (ch <= 'z')
  cout << " " << ch++;
```

The expression ch++ equals the value of ch *before* that variable is incremented to the next character. Also, because the new loop executes only one statement, braces are not required.

More confusing, but equally common, is a statement that examines and alters the control variable in the conditional expression. However, the programmer's first attempt causes a bug:

```
char ch = 'a';        // ???
while (ch++ < 'z')
  cout << " " << ch;
```

Because the expression ch++ increments ch before the statement that outputs the variable, that loop prints the alphabet from b to z. To start at a, the char ch variable must be initialized to one less than that letter. Here's the bug-free version (chars are just integers, and as such, may be used as shown here in mathematical expressions):

```
char ch = 'a' - 1;  // !!!
while (ch++ < 'z')
  cout << " " << ch;
```

This type of mistake—called an "off-by-one error"—is easy to make, especially in loops that examine and alter the control variable. Even for experienced programmers, off-by-one errors are a common source of bugs. A good way to avoid this trouble is to write your while and other statements the long way, as in preceding examples.

You can similarly use the decrement operator − (two minus signs) in repetitive statements. For example, this while loop counts down from 10 to 1:

```
int i = 11;
while (−i > 0)
  cout << "i == " << i << endl;
```

THE do-while STATEMENT

The do-while (which sounds to me like a '60s pop-group vocal embellishment—do-while diddy dum diddy do) is a sort of upside-down while loop. C's do-while looks like this:

```
do {
  statement;
} while (condition);
```

The statement executes while the condition is true. Compare this with a plain while, which evaluates its condition *before* executing any statements. A plain while loop can never perform any action if the controlling condition is initially false. But a do-while always performs its action at least once because it doesn't get around to evaluating the condition until the end of the loop. This leads to a general two-part rule for choosing between while and do-while:

1. Ask yourself: "Is there at least one condition when the statements in the loop should not execute, not even once?" If the answer is yes, a while loop probably is the correct choice.

2. If the answer to the preceding question is no, a do-while might be appropriate. If the statements in a loop must execute at least once, regardless of the controlling expression's value, use do-while.

A do-while statement can be simple or compound. Technically, braces are needed only if two or more statements are in the loop. However, although you can write do-while statements such as this:

```
do
  statement;
while (condition);
```

it is more common to surround even a single statement in braces:

```
do {
  statement;
} while (condition);
```

Inside the braces, you may insert as many statements as you need:

```
do {
  statement1;
  statement2;
  ...
} while (expression);
```

To demonstrate do-while, Listing 9.6, dwcount.cpp, is similar to the wcount.cpp program but uses a do-while loop to count from 1 to 10.

LISTING 9.6   DWCOUNT.CPP

```
#include <iostream.h>

int counter;

int main()
{
  cout << "Counting with do-while" << endl;
  counter = 1;
  do {
    cout << "counter == " << counter << endl;
    counter++;
  } while (counter <= 10);
  return 0;
}
```

As you can with while loops, it is often possible to combine the use and increment of the control variable. For example, the do-while loop in dwcount.cpp can be shortened to the following:

```
do {
  cout << "counter == " << counter << endl;
} while (++counter <= 10);
```

In this case, however, the ++ operator must be applied *before* counter is evaluated. In other words, the expression ++counter equals the incremented value of the variable; and, therefore, the loop executes one final time when that value is 10. If the statement used counter++ as the condition, the loop would count from 1 to 11. (The expression, however, could also be changed to (counter++ < 10).) Here again, an off-by-one error is easy to make, and the longer version, which costs nothing in performance, is clear and understandable.

THE for STATEMENT

The for statement is one of the most powerful programming tools in C and C++. When you know, or can calculate in advance, the number of times a statement block should execute, a for statement is usually the best choice of repetitive statements. In general outline form, a for statement looks like this:

```
for (expression1; condition; expression2) {
  statements;
}
```

Following the reserved word for are three elements in parentheses. To understand the purpose of each element, it's helpful to examine the equivalent while loop:

```
expression1;
while (condition) {
  statements;
  expression2;
}
```

Compare the for and while loops. Each executes expression1 exactly one time before entering the loop. Usually, this initializes the loop's control variable, but it can be any valid expression. As long as condition is true, one or more statements are executed, followed by expression2. Typically, expression2 modifies the control variable initialized by expression1. For example, the following for loop counts from 1 to 10:

```
int i;
for (i = 1; i <= 10; i++)
  cout << "i == " << i << endl;
```

That initializes the int variable i to 1, and while i is less than or equal to 10, writes its value and executes i++ to increment i so the loop eventually ends. The preceding for loop is functionally equivalent to this while statement:

```
int i = 1;
while (i <= 10) {
  cout << "i == " << i << endl;
  i++;
}
```

C++ permits variables such as i to be declared and initialized inside a for loop. The preceding for loop can be shorted by one line as follows:

```
for (int i = 1; i <= 10; i++)
  cout << "i == " << i << endl;
```

Unfortunately, this leads to a controversial question. Should the integer i belong to the for loop itself, or to the for loop's parent (function main(), for example, if that's where the loop resides)? Current ANSI C++ rules state that the control variable i in this case belongs to the for statement—that is, i's *scope* extends only to its declaring statement block. By this rule, a subsequent statement can define another int i control variable without conflict. However, this isn't true of all C++ compilers, and for more on this controversy, see "for Loop Scoping" in this chapter.

Listing 9.7, ascii.cpp, demonstrates how to use a for loop to display the ASCII character set of char values from 32 to 127, the usual range of common alphanumeric and punctuation characters available on most consoles.

LISTING 9.7   ASCII.CPP

```
#include <iostream.h>

#define NUMCOLS 18    // Number of columns

unsigned char ch;
unsigned int columns;

int main()
{
  for (ch = 32; ch < 128; ch++) {
    if ( (columns++ % NUMCOLS) == 0 )
      cout << endl;      // Start a new line
    cout << " " << ch;
  }
  cout << endl;  // End with a new line
  return 0;
}
```

PART
II

CH
9

Compile and run ascii.cpp using the following commands. As shown here, the program displays the ASCII character set neatly arranged into rows and columns:

```
$ g++ ascii.cpp
$ ./a.out
  ! " # $ % & ' ( ) * + , - . / 0 1
2 3 4 5 6 7 8 9 : ; < = > ? @ A B C
D E F G H I J K L M N O P Q R S T U
V W X Y Z [ \ ] ^ _ ` a b c d e f g
h i j k l m n o p q r s t u v w x y
z { ¦ } ~
```

Take a look at the program's for loop. Minus its statements, the loop is written as follows:

```
for (ch = 32; ch < 128; ch++) {
...
}
```

The first expression in parentheses executes once before the loop begins—it initializes ch to 32, the ASCII value for a blank character. The second expression is the condition that continues or ends the loop. In this case, the expression (ch < 128) is true so long as ch's value is less than 128. When ch equals 128, the loop ends. To ensure that this happens, the third expression increments ch using the ++ operator.

Change the value of the NUMCOLS constant to output a different number of columns. The program's for statement uses the following if statement to start a new row when the columns variable modulo (%) NUMCOLS equals zero:

```
if ( (columns++ % NUMCOLS) == 0 )
  cout << endl;      // Start a new line
```

This code demonstrates a general-purpose method that's useful for performing any action at regular intervals—in this case, starting a new line at a specified column. This is a common task inside for statements and other repetitive loops. Beginners often incorrectly program the job like this:

```
if (columns++ > NUMCOLS) {
  cout << endl;
  columns = 0;  // ???
}
```

That does *not* work because of a subtle logical error. On the first iteration of the for loop, because of the if statement's expression columns++, columns equals 1 before the program reaches the output statement. Setting columns back to zero after starting a new line causes an additional column to be printed on lines two and beyond. Even though columns is initially zero because it is a global variable, it must be reset to 1, not 0, in the preceding if statement:

```
columns = 1;
```

This is another good example of a common off-by-one error. To avoid this sort of trouble, when you need to perform an action at regular intervals, rather than test whether a variable such as columns equals NUMCOLS and then reset that value to zero, it's easier and more intuitive to use the modulo operator as shown in the ascii.cpp listing.

THE break STATEMENT

It's sometimes useful to interrupt a while, do-while, or for loop in progress. To do that, use a break statement—for example, if inside the loop, a statement detects an error. In general, break is typically used as follows to test an additional condition:

```
while (condition1) {
  statement;
  if (condition2)
    break;
}
```

The loop executes the statement normally while condition1 is true. However, if condition2 becomes true, the break statement immediately ends the while loop, and the program continues with the next statement. For example, the statement might set an error flag to true, in which case break ends the loop. Listing 9.8, breaker.cpp, demonstrates the effect of a break statement.

LISTING 9.8   BREAKER.CPP

```
#include <iostream.h>

int count;

int main()
{
  count = 1;
  while (count <= 100)    {
```

```
      if (count > 10)
        break;
      cout << "count == " << count << endl;
      count++;
    }
    return 0;
}
```

Despite the fact that the `while` loop in breaker.cpp tests whether `count` is less than or equal to 100, the program counts only up to 10. This happens because, inside the `while` loop, an `if` statement tests whether `count` is greater than 10. If so, it executes a `break` statement and immediately ends the loop. You may use `break` also in `for` and `do-while` loops. In all cases, executing a `break` statement causes the loop to end immediately.

Note See "The `switch` Statement" later in this chapter for another use for `break`.

THE continue STATEMENT

The C and C++ `continue` statement is similar to `break`, but instead of ending a loop, `continue` forces it to start immediately from its top. The loop doesn't start over—it merely begins its next iteration without executing any more statements in the loop.

Probably the most common use for `continue` statements is to prevent awkward nested `if` statements inside loops. For example, the following code is confusing due to the nesting of the two `if` statements:

```
int i = 1;
while (i++ < 100) {
  if (!condition1) {
    statement1;
    if (!condition2) {
      statement2;
    }
  }
}
```

Using `continue`, the code isn't so messy:

```
int i = 1;
while (i++ < 100) {
  if (condition1) continue;
  statement1;
  if (condition2) continue;
  statement2;
}
```

The two loops are functionally identical. But, in the second, if `condition1` is true, a `continue` statement causes the `while` loop to begin its next iteration without executing `statement1`. Similarly, if `condition2` is true, another `continue` forces the loop to reiterate without executing `statement2`. The loop still ends when `i` reaches 100.

> **Warning**
>
> When using `continue`, especially in `while` and `do-while` loops, be sure that the loop's condition performs an action that eventually ends the loop. In this case, for example, `i++` in the `while` loop's conditional expression ensures that the value of `i` eventually equals 100, ending the loop.

OTHER TYPES OF STATEMENTS

Following are some other types of flow-control statements you might find useful. First is the notorious `goto`, which most experienced programmers rightly avoid using. I also show some interesting variations on `for` loops, and I explain how to use one of the most powerful of C and C++ statements, the `switch`.

THE goto STATEMENT

A `goto` statement directs a program to execute another statement and to continue executing subsequent statements starting from that location. Because a `goto` can "jump" to any place in a program, using `goto` is like exiting a highway through a field rather than at a marked exit. Be prepared for a bumpy ride.

At first glance, `goto` seems tremendously versatile. In practice, however, the statement gives programmers too much freedom to jump from here to there and over yonder. At best, it's difficult to fathom the results of a program that has several `goto` statements. At worst, the code doesn't work at all.

If you must use `goto`, insert a label (an unused identifier and colon) above any statement. Execute `goto LABEL` to direct the program flow to that location. Listing 9.9, gcount.cpp, demonstrates how to use `goto` to count from 1 to 10.

LISTING 9.9   GCOUNT.CPP

```cpp
#include <iostream.h>

int count;

int main()
{
  count = 1;
TOP:
  cout << "count == " << count << endl;
  count++;
  if (count <= 10)
    goto TOP;
  return 0;
}
```

In the sample program, the label `TOP:` marks a target location for a `goto` statement. You may specify any unused identifier as a label. The `if` statement examines an integer variable count.

If count is less than or equal to 10, goto transfers control to TOP:, executing the output and count++ statements until count becomes larger than 10. When that happens, the if statement does not execute the goto, and the program continues to the bitter end.

The program works, but it lacks the intuitive clarity of the while, do-while, and for loops described in this chapter. By all means, learn how to use goto. You might stumble over one in somebody else's code. But avoid using goto in your own programs. This is one statement you can do without.

DO-NOTHING for LOOPS

This is not a new kind of C++ statement (I'm tempted to call it a do-for-nothing loop), but is simply a variation of a common for statement. However, a Do-Nothing for loop is easy to create unintentionally by a misplaced semicolon, as in this faulty code:

```
for (int i = 1; i < 100; i++);  // ???
  cout << " " << i;
```

Because of the semicolon before the comment, C++ "sees" a null statement between the closing parenthesis and semicolon. Although the for loop iterates variable i from 1 to 100, the loop merely executes the phantom null statement, not the output statement as the programmer probably intended. Worse, because the output statement does not belong to the for statement, it executes once after the loop is finished. Fix the code by removing the semicolon before the comment.

> **Tip**
>
> GNU C++ does not warn you about this type of mistake as do some other compilers such as Borland C++. If your code compiles but a for loop doesn't seem to operate correctly, check whether you ended it prematurely with a misplaced semicolon.

On rare occasions, a Do-Nothing for loop can be useful if, for example, the conditional expression calls a function or performs some work of its own. In that case, it is traditional to insert a space between the closing parenthesis and semicolon to indicate that the construction is intentional. It's not a bad idea to add a comment as well:

```
int i;
for (i = 1; f(i); i++) ;  // Semicolon intentional
```

This loop calls function f() as long as that function evaluates to true. Presumably, the function uses the value of i in some way and returns true or false. (See Chapter 10, "Creating and Calling Functions," for more about functions.)

> **Warning**
>
> Beware of side effects in code such as the preceding. If function f() affects the value of i, it might cause unpredictable conflicts with the use of the control variable!

DO-FOREVER for LOOPS

More practical is a Do-Forever for loop, one that never ends—that is, until some external condition occurs. That condition might be a hardware interrupt, or in Linux and UNIX, simply the result of the user pressing C-c (Ctrl-C). The loop is typically written like this:

```
for (;;) ;  // Loop "forever"
```

This for loop initializes no control variable, specifies no controlling condition, and performs no expression. It also has no statements. When executed, the statement hangs the program until an external event occurs that breaks the loop's lock. Again, a blank between the closing parenthesis and semicolon indicates that this is not a mistake, but intentional. If you try this in a test program, press C-c (Ctrl-C) to quit.

Although it might seem frivolous, a Do-Forever for loop can be useful. For example, see "The switch Statement" next for how to use Do-Forever for loops to create program menus. A Do-Forever for loop is also sometimes employed in threaded code that executes multiple tasks, and in X programs to respond to server events as described in Part VI, "X Window Development."

THE switch STATEMENT

A deeply nested if-else statement can look as twisted as the plumbing in an old building. Clearer and more easily maintainable code is possible by replacing the if-else statements with a switch. Consider, for example, the following series of if-else statements, each of which compares an expression with a value:

```
if (expression == value1)
  statement1;
else if (expression == value2)
  statement2;
else if (expression == value3)
  statement3;
else                   // Optional
  defaultStatement;    // Optional
```

Commonly called a *multiway decision tree*, the construction chooses from among various statements based on a series of conditions. There is nothing wrong with nested if-else statements, but using a switch often produces clearer code. Using a switch, you can write the preceding if-else statement this way:

```
switch (expression) {
  case value1:
    statement1;    // Executes if expression == value1
    break;         // Exit the switch statement
  case value2:
    statement2;    // Executes if expression == value2
    break;         // Exit the switch statement
  case value3:
    statement3;    // Executes if expression == value3
    break;         // Exit the switch statement
  default:           // Optional
    defaultStatement;  // Executes if no values match expression
}
```

At first glance, the equivalent `switch` statement might seem equally complex, but after you become familiar with its construction, you'll find `switch` statements easier to manage than deeply nested `if-else` statements. Following the `switch` keyword is an expression to be compared to a set of values. This is often just the name of a variable—for example, one that holds a character typed by the program's user, or an integer value obtained from a calculation. Inside the `switch`'s block, *case selectors* compare the expression to specified values. The expression

```
case value1:
```

compares `value1` for equality with the `switch` statement's expression. If the expression matches this case value, the following statements execute. If the expression does not equal this case's value, the next case is evaluated. The `default:` selector at the end specifies an optional action if no cases match the expression.

> **Tip**
>
> The case and default expressions end with a colon. This is easy to forget, and a common cause of compiler "parse" errors is a missing colon at the end of a `switch` case selector.

Notice that in the preceding sample code each case ends with a `break` statement. As it does in other types of statements, `break` ends the `switch` statement immediately. To understand the purpose of `break` in `switch` cases, examine the first case:

```
case value1;
  statement1;
  break;
```

If the `switch` statement's expression equals `value1`, the program executes `statement1`. After that happens, `break` exits the `switch` statement, and the program continues after the `switch` statement's closing brace. However, if a case does *not* end with `break`, then *the next case's statements are executed.* Known as "falling through a case," the absence of a `break` might be an error but is sometimes intentional. For example, consider this `switch` statement:

```
switch (expression) {
  case value1:
    statement1;  // Fall through to statement2
  case value2:
    statement2;
    break;       // Exit switch statement
  case value3:
    statement3;
    break;       // Not needed but okay
}
```

If `expression` equals `value1`, `statement1` executes. Because no `break` statement follows, the program continues at `statement2`, after which `break` ends the `switch` statement. It's good to add a comment about the intentional "fall-through." On another iteration, if `expression` equals `value2`, then only `statement2` is executed, after which `break` ends the `switch` statement. If `expression` equals `value3`, then only `statement3` is executed. The `break` after `statement3` isn't strictly needed because this is the end of the `switch` statement, but careful programmers add a break after each case so that a newly added case does not accidentally create a fall-through.

Listing 9.10, menu.cpp, demonstrates a good use for a switch statement. The program prompts users to select from a menu of commands. It uses a switch statement to execute different statements based on the character entered. The program also demonstrates a practical use for a Do-Forever for loop.

LISTING 9.10 MENU.CPP

```
#include <iostream.h>
#include <ctype.h>     // Need toupper()
#include <stdlib.h>    // Need exit()

char choice;  // User command character

int main()
{
  for (;;) {     // Do following switch statement "forever"
    cout << "Menu: A(dd D(elete S(ort Q(uit: ";
    cin >> choice;  // Get user command
    switch ( toupper(choice) ) {
      case 'A':
        cout << "You selected Add" << endl;
        break;
      case 'D':
        cout << "You selected Delete" << endl;
        break;
      case 'S':
        cout << "You selected Sort" << endl;
        break;
      case 'Q':
        cout << "You selected Quit. Good bye!" << endl;
        exit(0);  // End program
      default:
        cout << "*** No such command!" << endl;
        break;
    } // switch
  } // for
  return 0;  // Unreachable as currently written
}
```

The main() function in menu.cpp consists mostly of one Do-Forever for loop. Inside that loop, the program first displays a menu of commands. Compile and run the program to see this prompt:

```
$ g++ menu.cpp
$ ./a.out
Menu: A(dd D(elete S(ort Q(uit:
```

Enter a letter in upper- or lowercase to select a command (all are just for show, of course). The program's switch statement confirms your selection:

```
Menu: A(dd D(elete S(ort Q(uit: S
You selected Sort
```

If you enter an unknown command letter, the program displays an error message:

```
Menu: A(dd D(elete S(ort Q(uit: x
*** No such command!
```

To respond to command entries, the program uses a switch statement that begins as follows:

```
switch ( toupper(choice) ) {
```

The toupper() function, declared in the ctype.h standard header, returns the choice char variable converted if necessary to uppercase. Each case in the switch statement compares this value with a literal character to select from among the program's statements. For example, the first case detects the A(dd command:

```
case 'A':
  cout << "You selected Add" << endl;
  break;
```

After displaying the confirming message, break ends the switch. However, because the switch is encased inside a Do-Forever for loop, after the switch statement ends, the program again displays the menu and waits for another command. When you type *q* to quit, the following case ends the program by calling the standard exit() function declared in stdlib.h:

```
case 'Q':
  cout << "You selected Quit. Good bye!" << endl;
  exit(0);  // End program
```

Note   The return statement in menu.cpp never executes. However, it's good form to include it in the event a change causes the program to reach the statement. Some compilers warn about "unreachable" statements such as this, but GNU C++ doesn't notice the condition. In all fairness, unreachable statements are not necessarily errors—they just don't do anything.

for LOOP SCOPING

Finally in this chapter, some further words about declaring control variables in for statements such as this:

```
for (int i = 1; i <= 10; i++)
  cout << "i == " << i << endl;
```

Because the for loop itself declares the int variable i, ANSI C++ rules state that i's *scope*—in other words, its accessibility to statements—is limited to the for statement in which it is declared. Not all C++ compilers follow this rule, and it's a good idea to test how they behave if you plan to rely on this feature. Listing 9.11, forscope.cpp, performs a test that you can use to check how any C++ compiler handles the condition.

LISTING 9.11   FORSCOPE.CPP

```
#include <iostream.h>

int main()
{
  for (int i = 1; i <= 10; i++)
    cout << "i == " << i << endl;
  cout << "Final value of i == " << i << endl;  // ???
  return 0;
}
```

Compiling the forscope.cpp test program with GNU C++ using the following commands produces two warning messages:

```
$ g++ forscope.cpp
forscope.cpp: In function 'int main()':
forscope.cpp:7: warning: name lookup of 'i' changed for new ANSI 'for' scoping
forscope.cpp:5: warning: using obsolete binding at 'i'
```

The compiler issues the warnings because the program's for loop declares int i inside the loop, and the new ANSI C++ rules state that in such cases i is available only to statements inside the loop itself. However, the test program refers to i outside the loop as was permitted in past ANSI C++ drafts. To accommodate older programs that rely on the obsolete specifications, GNU C++ treats the condition as a warning rather than an error, and it completes the compilation. Other C++ compilers might refuse to compile this program at all.

To limit the scope of variables to the for loop that declares them, in GNU C++, compile with the option -ffor-scope. With this option, forscope.cpp does not compile. To use the older specification that places the for loop variable in the outer scope, use the -fno-for-scope option. Do that only if you are compiling older programs that assume the nonstandard rule. With that option, forscope.cpp compiles without any warnings or errors.

SUMMARY

Without intervention, a C or C++ program's statements execute one after the other like water flowing down a river. C and C++ provide conditional and repetitive flow-control statements that alter this normal path. Conditional statements include if, if-else, switch, and conditional expressions. Repetitive statements include while, do-while, and for. In addition, this chapter explained how to use break, continue, and goto statements, and it explained the controversial subject of declaring control variables inside for loops.

For more information on subjects introduced in this chapter, turn to the following chapters:

- Chapter 6, "Creating Data Objects"
- Chapter 7, "Applying Fundamental Operators"
- Chapter 10, "Creating and Calling Functions"

CREATING AND CALLING FUNCTIONS

Writing computer programs is like building bridges. You can't start pouring concrete in midair; you've got to anchor the foundations on land before you can span the water.

Functions are to C and C++ what girders, cable, and stone are to bridge builders. With functions, you can divide a large program into manageable pieces that you can construct one at a time. You can also create functions that calculate formulas and perform other actions needed throughout a program.

This chapter introduces functions and shows some "functional" features available only in C++, such as inline functions and default function parameters. The chapter ends with a look at GNU debugger commands that are useful for debugging function code and data.

INTRODUCING FUNCTIONS

As you know, every C and C++ program has at least one function, main(). Most programs, however, have many other functions, each with a specific task to perform. One of the most common tasks for a function is to calculate the results of a formula. For example, consider how the kilo.cpp program from Chapter 7, "Applying Fundamental Operators," calculates the equivalent distance in kilometers for a given number of miles using this statement:

```
kilometers = miles * 1.609344;
```

By converting that formula into a function named kilos(), as Listing 10.1, fnkilo.cpp, demonstrates, it is available for use not just once, but as many times as needed. In this example, the program calls kilos() several times to display a reference table of miles and kilometers.

LISTING 10.1   FNKILO.CPP

```cpp
#include <iostream.h>
#include <iomanip.h>      // Need setw() manipulator

// Function prototype
double kilos( double miles );

int main()
{
  cout << "Miles     Kilometers" << endl;
  cout << "===================" << endl;
  for (int miles = 10; miles <= 100; miles += 10) {
    cout << setw(5) << miles << " == ";
    cout << kilos( miles ) << endl;
  }
  return 0;
}

// Function implementation (convert miles to kilometers)
double kilos( double miles )
{
  double kilometers = miles * 1.609344;
  return kilometers;  // Function result
}
```

Compile and run the program in the usual way. Enter the following commands, and the program displays a reference table (reduced by a few lines to save space here):

```
$ g++ fnkilo.cpp
$ ./a.out
Miles    Kilometers
   10 == 16.0934
   20 == 32.1869
...
  100 == 160.934
```

PROTOTYPING FUNCTIONS

The fnkilo.cpp program in Listing 10.1 shows the correct way to declare, implement, and use most kinds of functions. In C and C++, because items must be declared before they are used, the first step in creating a function is to declare a *function prototype*. Here's the prototype for the kilos() function in the sample code:

```
double kilos( double miles );
```

The function prototype includes three important elements that the compiler needs to use the function:

1. The function's *return type*—in this case, double. This states that the function returns a value of the indicated type. If the function returns no value but merely performs an action, its return type might be void. Functions can return an object of any valid C or C++ type.

2. The *function name*. This must be a unique identifier formed according to the rules listed in Chapter 6, "Creating Data Objects." Try to pick specifically meaningful names for your functions. The name kilos() suggests what this function does. If I had named it convert(), its specific purpose would be less clear.

3. Any *parameters* that the function needs as input data. In this case, the parameter miles of type double in parentheses indicates that the function requires a number of miles to be converted to kilometers. If the function needs no input data, declare its prototype with an empty pair of parentheses.

> **Tip**
>
> A function prototype always ends with a terminating semicolon.

A program may declare as many function prototypes as it needs. The compiler needs only the functions' prototypes to process statements that call the functions. Because of this, it's common to store function prototypes in a header file and to implement those functions in separate modules (see the section "Functions and Separate Compilation" later in this chapter for an example). However, for simplicity, this book's listings declare and implement most functions in a single source code file.

PART
II

CH
10

Note

Technically, function prototypes are optional. You could, for example, fully implement a function ahead of its use in a program. But doing that is usually impractical, especially in modular programs composed of multiple source and header files. For best results, declare all functions as prototypes and then implement them elsewhere as described next.

IMPLEMENTING FUNCTIONS

Skip to the end of fnkilo.cpp in Listing 10.1. There, you find the `kilos()` function's implementation, reprinted here:

```
double kilos( double miles )
{
  double kilometers = miles * 1.609344;
  return kilometers;  // Function result
}
```

The first important rule to memorize is that the function's declaration—often called its header—must exactly match its prototype. The implementation's header does not, however, end with a semicolon but is followed by a statement block delimited with a pair of curly braces. Inside the braces are the statements that perform the function's actions.

In this case, two statements convert the input parameter `miles` to the equivalent kilometers. The first statement performs the conversion and stores the result in a local variable of type `double` named kilometers. The second statement *returns* that value to the statement that called the function (more on this in a moment).

I purposely wrote the `kilos()` function using two statements for illustration, but a single statement is all that's really needed. Here's a simpler version of `kilos()` that is functionally equivalent to the preceding longer edition:

```
double kilos( double miles )
{
  return miles * 1.609344;
}
```

In the new, improved model, a single statement converts `miles` to kilometers and returns that result to the function's caller. There's no need to perform those actions separately, but there's also no harm in doing so.

CALLING FUNCTIONS

To use a function, a statement *calls* it by name. When a program does this, the function's statements perform their jobs, after which the program continues at the next statement after the one that called the function. In the sample fnkilo.cpp program in Listing 10.1, the following `for` loop calls the `kilos()` function to create a miles-to-kilometers reference table:

```
for (int miles = 10; miles <= 100; miles += 10)
{
  cout << setw(5) << miles << " == ";
  cout << kilos(miles) << endl;
}
```

The second output statement calls the `kilos()` function, passing to it a value in miles to be converted to kilometers. The function *returns* the value that the output statement displays.

A function's return type indicates the manner in which it can be used. In this case, `kilos()` returns a `double` value, and it can therefore be used anywhere a double value is appropriate. You can't assign values to functions—they are not variables. (However, an exception is a reference function, discussed in the section "Returning References" in this chapter and in Chapter 11, "Managing Memory with Pointers.")

FUNCTIONS AND VARIABLES

In performing their actions, functions typically use variables of many different kinds. How you create a variable has important consequences on its use in a function, as the following sections explain.

PART
II
CH
10

GLOBAL VARIABLES AND FUNCTIONS

Variables declared outside function `main()` are available to all statements in a program. For example, if you declare a variable such as this outside any function:

```
double balance;
```

any statement, anywhere, can refer to `balance`, assign it a value, use it in output statements, and affect its value in other ways.

Experienced programmers avoid using global variables, and with good reason. In a complex program, it is simply too easy for the global variable to have conflicting uses among multiple functions. But they are useful for large objects—input buffers, for example.

LOCAL VARIABLES AND FUNCTIONS

Local variables are declared and used inside a function's statement block. In most cases, they are safer than global variables because only their own function's statements may refer to them. To illustrate local variables, Listing 10.2, fncount.cpp, implements a simple function that counts up from minimum to maximum input values.

LISTING 10.2   FNCOUNT.CPP (PARTIAL)

```cpp
void countup( int min, int max)
{
  int counter;  // Local variable

  if (min >= max) return;  // Ignore bad input values
  for (counter = min; counter <= max; counter++)
    cout << counter << " ";
  cout << endl;  // Start new display line
}
```

You met local variables in Chapter 9, "Controlling Program Flow," but now that you know more about functions, consider some further characteristics. A local variable, such as `int counter` in the sample program, exhibits two important features:

- Its *scope* extends only to its declaring function.
- It is created and destroyed automatically each time the function is called and returns.

> **Note**
>
> A local variable is also sometimes called an *automatic variable* because it is automatically created—that is, allocated memory—when its declaring block becomes active.

In the sample code, the local variable `counter` is available only to statements in function `countup()`. Function `main()` cannot refer to `counter`. Only statements in the declaring function may do that. Most important, `counter` is freshly created on the stack when the program calls `countup()`. When the function ends, the local variable is destroyed. For this reason, functions *must* initialize local variables before using them. *Local variables do not retain their values between calls to their declaring functions.*

> **Note**
>
> Local variables are stored in a limited area of memory, called the *stack*, along with function return addresses and parameter values passed to the function. For this reason, it's not a good idea to create large local variables. See Chapter 11, "Managing Memory with Pointers," for advice on creating large objects efficiently.

SCOPE CONFLICTS

When local and global variables have the same name, the compiler decides which variable to use based on its scope. For example, given a global variable named `count`, a function can declare a local variable of the same name. This is not an error, although it can lead to confusing code as the following snippet illustrates:

```
int count;    // Global variable
void any_function()
{
  int count;  // Local variable
  cout << count << endl;  // ???
}
```

Inside the function, the output statement refers to the local variable because its scope takes precedence over the global scope of the outer variable. In another function with no local variable named `count`, that same statement would refer to the global variable. A similar situation can arise within the same function and might cause a bug. For example, consider the following code:

```
void any_function()
{
  int i = 100;
```

```
   for (int i = 1; i < 10; i++)  // ???
      do_something(i);
}
```

The function declares a local variable i initialized to 100. But it also declares an identically named variable inside the for statement. *The two variables are separate and distinct.* The scope of the innermost i extends only to the block in which it is declared. Outside the for loop, any statements refer to the int i set equal to 100. Perhaps this is what the programmer intended, but it's more likely an error.

Note

In technical terms, a variable declared in an inner scope *hides* an identically named variable in an outer scope. Any statement block—a while loop, for example—may define its own local variables, the scope of which extends only to that block.

RESOLVING SCOPE CONFLICTS

Careful programmers never intentionally create scope conflicts as illustrated in the preceding section, but those conflicts can easily arise when incorporating third-party function libraries into existing programs. Suppose that you have written a 5,000-line program with 250 functions, many of which declare and use a local variable named interval. You then add a new function library only to discover that it declares a global variable also named interval. Now what do you do?

Fortunately, in C++, the solution is simple. Use the double-colon *scope resolution operator* (::) to refer to the variable in the outer scope. For example, this statement:

```
cout << ::interval << endl;
```

refers to the interval declared in the outer scope. To refer to the local variable, simply use it normally. Here's a more complete example that shows how to resolve scope ambiguities:

```
int count;          // Global variable
void any_function()
{
  int count;        // Local variable
  count = 1234;     // Assign value to local count
  ::count = 4321;   // Assign value to global count
}
```

The expression count refers to the local variable. The expression ::count refers to the count in the global scope. Problem solved.

Note

C++ offers the concept of a *namespace* that can help prevent scope conflicts. For more information and a practical example, see Chapter 23, "Using the Standard Template Library (STL)."

PARAMETERS AND ARGUMENTS

A function's parameters provide it with input data. For example, the `kilos()` function in this chapter declares a *parameter* named miles of type `double`:

```
double kilos(double miles);
```

A statement such as the following passes a value to `kilos()` for conversion:

```
cout << kilos(100) << " kilometers" << endl;
```

The value 100 is called an *argument*. It is passed to the function's `miles` *parameter*. Inside the function, `miles` equals 100—the value of the argument. A parameter such as `miles` resembles a local variable in that its scope extends only to its declaring function. In this example, the scope of the `miles` parameter extends only to the `kilos()` function. Only statements in the function can refer to `miles`.

There are three types of function parameters: value, reference, and pointer. The following sections explain how to create and use these types of parameters.

Note

Although the following sections explain pointer parameters briefly, their intricacies are best canned up with other worms introduced in Chapter 11, "Managing Memory with Pointers."

VALUE PARAMETERS

A *value parameter* is so called because only a copy of its value is passed to the function. Declare a value parameter the same way you declare a variable, but place the declaration inside the function header's parentheses:

```
void f(int i);
```

The prototype for function `f()` declares a single value parameter, `int i`. Statements that call `f()` pass arguments by value to parameter `i`, as in these samples:

```
f(10);  // Pass 10 to i
f(x);   // Pass value of x to i
```

In the second case, the value of x—in other words, a *copy* of its value—is passed to the `i` parameter. This is important to understand. Because only a copy of x's value is passed to `i`, any changes to `i` inside the function do not affect x's value.

As a practical example of value parameters, consider how you might calculate the cost of running an appliance for a number of hours at a certain number of watts. On your electric bill, you find the cost per kilowatt hour (kwh), perhaps 0.0687. Given the kwh rate, the appliance's power consumption in watts (note that power × 0.001 converts watts to kilowatts), and a length of time in hours, the following formula calculates the cost in dollars of running the appliance:

```
cost = rate * (power * 0.001 * time);
```

To package this formula as a function, a program can prototype it like this:

```
double cost(double time, double power, double rate);
```

The cost() function returns a double value. It declares three value parameters of type double separated by commas—time, power, and rate. The completed function implements the cost formula:

```
double cost(double time, double power, double rate)
{
  return rate * (power * 0.001 * time);
}
```

Elsewhere in the program, statements can pass arguments to the function for processing. A simple statement computes the cost of running a 100-watt appliance for 10 hours at a kwh rate of 0.0687:

```
double result = cost(10.0, 100.0, 0.0687);
```

Listing 10.3, electric.cpp, puts the cost() function into action. In addition to demonstrating value function parameters, the program also shows a general-purpose method for creating a row-and-column reference table.

LISTING 10.3   ELECTRIC.CPP

```cpp
#include <iostream.h>
#include <stdio.h>        // Need sprintf()

#define MAXROW 12        // Number of rows in table
#define MAXCOL 8         // Number of columns in table

// Function prototypes

double cost(double time, double power, double rate);
void printTable(double startHours, double hourlyIncrement,
  double startWatts, double wattsIncrement, double costPerKwh);

int main()
{
  double startHours     = 100;
  double hourlyIncrement = 10;
  double startWatts     = 4;
  double wattsIncrement = 2;
  double costPerKwh     = 0.0687;
  printTable(startHours, hourlyIncrement,
    startWatts, wattsIncrement, costPerKwh);
  return 0;
}

// Return cost of electricity given time, power, and rate
double cost(double time, double power, double rate)
{
  return rate * (power * 0.001 * time);
```

continues

LISTING 10.3   CONTINUED

```
}

// Print table using the cost() function
void printTable(double startHours, double hourlyIncrement,
  double startWatts, double wattsIncrement, double costPerKwh)
{
  int row, col;            // Local variables
  double hours, watts;     // Local variables
  char buffer[24];         // Formatted output buffer

  // Print top line of table
  cout << endl << "Hrs/Watts";
  watts = startWatts;
  for (col = 1; col <= MAXCOL; col++) {
    sprintf(buffer, "%8.0f", watts);
    cout << buffer;
    watts += wattsIncrement;
  }  // for

  // Print table rows
  hours = startHours;
  for (row = 1; row <= MAXROW; row++) {
    sprintf(buffer, "\n%6.1f - ", hours);
    cout << buffer;
    watts = startWatts;
    for (col = 1; col <= MAXCOL; col++) {
      sprintf(buffer, "%8.2f", cost(hours, watts, costPerKwh));
      cout << buffer;
      watts += wattsIncrement;
    }  // for
    hours += hourlyIncrement;
  }  // for
  cout << endl << endl << "Cost of electricity @ ";
  sprintf(buffer, "$%.4f",  costPerKwh);
  cout << buffer << " per KWH" << endl << endl;
}
```

Compile and run the program to display a table that shows the cost of running an appliance of a certain power in watts for a given number of hours. Modify main()'s local variables to display a table with a different range of values. (Alternatively, you might add statements to prompt users for input—I took the easy way out to save space in the printed listing here.) Enter these commands to display the table shown in Figure 10.1.

```
$ g++ electric.cpp
$ ./a.out
```

Figure 10.1
Output of the
electric.cpp program.

```
Hrs/Watts    4    6    8    10   12   14   16   18
100.0 -     0.03 0.04 0.05 0.07 0.08 0.10 0.11 0.12
110.0 -     0.03 0.05 0.06 0.08 0.09 0.11 0.12 0.14
120.0 -     0.03 0.05 0.07 0.08 0.10 0.12 0.13 0.15
130.0 -     0.04 0.05 0.07 0.09 0.11 0.13 0.14 0.16
140.0 -     0.04 0.06 0.08 0.10 0.12 0.13 0.15 0.17
150.0 -     0.04 0.06 0.08 0.10 0.12 0.14 0.16 0.19
160.0 -     0.04 0.07 0.09 0.11 0.13 0.15 0.18 0.20
170.0 -     0.05 0.07 0.09 0.12 0.14 0.16 0.19 0.21
180.0 -     0.05 0.07 0.10 0.12 0.15 0.17 0.20 0.22
190.0 -     0.05 0.08 0.10 0.13 0.16 0.18 0.21 0.23
200.0 -     0.05 0.08 0.11 0.14 0.16 0.19 0.22 0.25
210.0 -     0.06 0.09 0.12 0.14 0.17 0.20 0.23 0.26
Cost of electricity @ $0.0687 per KWH
```

The electric.cpp program makes good use of value parameters in its two functions, cost()
and printTable(). The prototypes for those functions list in parentheses the double para
meters needed as input values. Those same parameters are again listed in the functions'
implementations following main().

Tip

Technically, a function prototype needs to declare only parameter data types—it doesn't
need to name them. Parameters need to have names only in the function's implementation
so that statements can refer to the parameter values. However, it is common and more
sensible to name the parameters in both places.

The program's main() function initializes several local variables, passed by value to the
printTable() function using this statement:

```
printTable(startHours, hourlyIncrement,
  startWatts, wattsIncrement, costPerKwh);
```

Alternatively, the program could pass literal values directly to the function, or it might
define them using #define directives. I used local variables as shown here because you might
want to improve the program by prompting users to enter values to create tables with other
data.

REFERENCE PARAMETERS

A reference parameter looks much the same as a value parameter, but it operates differently.
Declare a reference parameter by prefacing its name with the C++ *reference operator*, &, as
shown here:

```
void any_function(double &value);
```

That declares value as a reference to an object of type double. The parameter is not itself an object of type double—it is a reference to *another* object of that type. To call the function, a statement must pass an object argument of the appropriate type, as in this fragment:

```
double input;
any_function(input);
```

The first line declares a double variable named input. The second passes input *by reference* to any_function(). Inside that function, any statements that change the value of input directly affect the referred-to object. Unlike value parameters, reference parameters refer to their original objects.

Typical uses for reference parameters are functions that initialize multiple variables passed as arguments, and also functions that operate on large input objects such as strings and buffers. Listing 10.4, metrics.cpp, demonstrates how to use reference parameters. The program also shows a good way to implement a selection menu.

LISTING 10.4   METRICS.CPP

```cpp
#include <iostream.h>
#include <stdlib.h>     // Need exit()
#include <ctype.h>      // Need toupper()

// Function prototypes
void displayMenu();
void getCommand(char &command);
void getValue(double &value);
void inchesToCentimeters();

int main()
{
  char choice;  // Menu selection

  displayMenu();
  getCommand(choice);
  switch(toupper(choice)) {
    case 'I':
      inchesToCentimeters();
      break;
    case 'Q':
      cout << "Goodbye!" << endl;
      exit(0);
    default:
      cout << "Error or unimplemented function" << endl;
      exit(1);
  }
  return 0;
}

// Display selection menu
void displayMenu()
{
  cout << "Metrics Converter : Menu"  << endl;
  cout << "==========================" << endl;
  cout << "C : Centimeters to inches" << endl;
```

```
    cout << "E : Meters to feet"        << endl;
    cout << "F : Feet to meters"        << endl;
    cout << "I : Inches to centimeters" << endl;
    cout << "K : Kilometers to miles"   << endl;
    cout << "M : Miles to kilometers"   << endl;
    cout << "Q : Quit"                  << endl;
}

// Prompt for user command
void getCommand(char &command)
{
    cout << "Command? ";
    cin >> command;
}

// Prompt for input value
void getValue(double &value)
{
    cout << "Value to convert? ";
    cin >> value;
}

// Convert inches to centimeters
void inchesToCentimeters()
{
    double value;      // Local variables
    double result;

    cout << "Inches to Centimeters" << endl;
    getValue(value);
    result = value * 2.54;
    cout << value << " inches == ";
    cout << result << " centimeters" << endl;
}
```

Compile and run the program using the usual commands. Select a menu choice and enter a value to convert (to save space here, only the Inches to Centimeters command is finished). Enter the following commands to try the program:

```
$ g++ metrics.cpp
$ ./a.out
Metrics Converter : Menu
I : Inches to centimeters
...
Q : Quit
Command? i
Inches to Centimeters
Value to convert? 12
12 inches == 30.48 centimeters
```

The program's listing shows a common use for reference parameters—prompting for and initializing variables. The program prototypes two such functions:

```
void getCommand(char &command);
void getValue(double &value);
```

Function `getCommand()` declares a reference `char` parameter named `command`. When the function executes the statement

```
cin >> command;
```

your entry in response to the input statement is passed back to the function's caller. In this case, that happens in the `main()` program, at the following statement:

```
getCommand(choice);
```

Because `getCommand()`'s parameter is passed by reference, the function's input statement deposits the entered character into `choice`. Similarly, `getValue()`'s input statement

```
cin >> value:
```

directly affects the object passed by reference to the function.

> **Note**
>
> For another example of value and reference parameters, see Listing 10.6, stopwatch.cpp, in the section "Function Return Values" later in this chapter.

POINTER PARAMETERS

This chapter wouldn't be complete without a mention of pointer parameters. However, you haven't met pointers yet (see Chapter 11, "Managing Memory with Pointers"), so I'll be brief.

A pointer parameter is similar to a reference parameter in that it points to an object of a specified type. However, pointer parameters require *you* to specify the object's address when calling the function. Reference parameters do that automatically.

One common use for pointer parameters is to pass C-style string buffers to and from functions. Listing 10.5, getstr.cpp, demonstrates the basic technique.

LISTING 10.5   GETSTR.CPP

```cpp
#include <iostream.h>

// Function prototype
void getstr(char *s);

// Global string buffer
char input[128];

int main()
{
  cout << "Enter a string: ";
  getstr(input);
  cout << "You entered: " << input << endl;
  return 0;
}

void getstr(char *s)
```

```
{
  cin >> s;
}
```

Compile and run the program with the following commands, and then as shown, enter a string, which is displayed on the last line after you press Enter:

```
$ g++ getstr.cpp
$ ./a.out
Enter a string: abcdefg
You entered: abcdefg
```

The sample program prototypes a function to input a string into a global `char` buffer. The function's prototype shows how to declare a pointer parameter:

```
void getstr(char *s);
```

Parameter `s` is a *pointer to* a `char`. Due to an age-old C specification, pointers and arrays are programmatically equivalent, and therefore, it's common to use a pointer to pass the input `char` array to `getstr()`. To use the function, the program declares `input` as follows and passes it to the function for filling with the user's input:

```
char input[128];
...
getstr(input);
```

FUNCTION RETURN VALUES

As you have seen in this book's listings, functions can return nothing, or they can return a value of any valid C++ type. The following sections explain more about function return values. As a practical example, a sample listing in this section shows how to create an elapsed event timer using the standard GNU C library's time functions.

RETURNING SIMPLE VALUES

As you have seen in many of this book's sample programs, functions might return nothing, or they might return a value of any valid C++ data type such as `int` or `double`. To indicate that a function returns nothing, precede its declaration by `void`:

```
void f();
```

To indicate that a function returns a value of some other type, replace `void` with the type name. This declaration

```
double f();
```

indicates that calling `f()` returns a `double` value. In C and C++, a statement may ignore a function's return value. Given the preceding declaration, the following statement calls `f()` but discards its returned value:

```
f();  // ???
```

PART

II

CH

10

Although allowed, this technique is rarely useful, and you normally save a function's return value in a variable, or use it in a statement as in the following examples:

```
double saved_value = f();
cout << "Value == " << f() << endl;
```

Return values are essential in constructing modular programs. As a practical demonstration, Listing 10.6, stopwatch.cpp, uses the system clock to create a timer, accurate to 1/10 second (depending, of course, on the system clock's accuracy), independent of the computer processor speed.

LISTING 10.6   STOPWATCH.CPP

```cpp
#include <iostream.h>
#include <sys/times.h>   // need times() function
#include <time.h>        // need CLOCKS_PER_SEC
#include <math.h>        // need fabs() function

// Function prototypes
clock_t mark_time();
double elapsed_time(clock_t start_time, clock_t end_time);

// Main program
int main()
{
  clock_t start, stop;  // Variables for mark_time() function

  cout << "Press enter to start timing...";
  cin.get();
  start = mark_time();  // Mark starting time
  cout << "Press enter to stop timing...";
  cin.get();
  stop = mark_time();    // Mark stopping time
  cout << "Elapsed_time == "
       << elapsed_time(start, stop)
       << " seconds" << endl;
  return 0;
}

// Returns current processor time (mark)
clock_t mark_time()
{
  return times(NULL);
}

// Calculate elapsed time in seconds
double elapsed_time(clock_t start_time, clock_t end_time)
{
  double t = fabs(end_time - start_time);  // Processor elapsed time
  return t / (CLOCKS_PER_SEC / 10000);     // Elapsed time in seconds
}
```

Compile and run stopwatch.cpp. When prompted, press Enter to start the elapsed timer, wait a few seconds, and then press Enter again to stop timing and display the results as shown in the following test run:

```
$ g++ stopwatch.cpp
$ ./a.out
Press enter to start timing...
Press enter to stop timing...
Elapsed_time == 6.8 seconds
```

The stopwatch.cpp program uses standard time and math functions, one constant, and two data types declared in three header files included at the beginning of the listing. To mark the beginning of an event, the program prototypes function mark_time() like this:

```
clock_t mark_time(),
```

The standard clock_t type represents the elapsed system time in unspecified units. It is defined by including the time.h header (but in GNU C++ is actually declared in the types.h header file). A second prototype declares a function that returns a double value and uses two clock_t value parameters:

```
double elapsed_time(clock_t start_time, clock_t end_time);
```

Given start_time and end_time parameters, the function calculates the elapsed time interval. Using the two functions, three simple statements create an elapsed event timer:

```
clock_t start = mark time();
...
clock_t stop = mark_time();
cout << elapsed_time(start, stop) << " seconds" << endl;
```

PART
II

CH
10

The mark_time() function calls the standard times() function to obtain the system time:

```
return times(NULL);
```

Another way to use times() is to pass a structure to be filled with time values. Here, NULL simply tells times() to return the current system time as the function return value of type clock_t.

Function elapsed_time() takes advantage of the fact that subtracting two clock_t values equals their elapsed time. These two statements compute the elapsed time using the start_time and end_time value parameters:

```
double t = fabs(end_time - start_time);
return t / (CLOCKS_PER_SEC / 10000);
```

Calling fabs() (floating point absolute value) ensures a positive result in case the two times are accidentally reversed. This is far better than the usual series of if-else statements that reverse pairs of input values. The second statement returns the temporary double result t divided by the standard constant CLOCKS_PER_SEC over 10,000—giving the elapsed time in seconds.

RETURNING REFERENCES

You learned earlier in this chapter how to pass arguments by reference to function parameters. Functions may also return references to objects provided, however, that those objects persist outside the function's scope. In other words, functions may not return references to local variables or parameters. A function declared as

```
double &ref();
```

returns a reference to a `double` object, presumably one that is declared elsewhere. In cases where you don't want to give the function's caller the right to change a referred-to value, declare the function `const` like this:

```
const double &ref();
```

You may use reference functions on each side of an assignment operator. A statement such as the following stores 3.14159 in whatever `double` object to which the `ref()` function refers:

```
ref() = 3.14159;
```

The `ref()` function itself might be written along these lines:

```
double d;
double &ref()
{
  return d;  // Return reference to d
}
```

Because `ref()` merely returns a reference to the global variable d, the reference function is in a sense a *synonym* for that object. If d is hidden away in a library module, all references to it are controlled by forcing the data's users to call `ref()`. This hides the inner nature of the global data and also can aid debugging.

The foregoing sample code is, however, merely for illustration. Similar but more complex programming is invaluable for hiding a data structure's internal representation while providing safe access to its information. For example, a reference function might return a value selected from an array. Reference functions also play a major role in object-oriented programming, the subject of Part III of this book.

RETURNING POINTERS TO DATA

As with pointer parameters, this chapter wouldn't be complete without mentioning also that functions may return pointer values. But see Chapter 11, "Managing Memory with Pointers," for more information on this subject.

OTHER FUNCTIONALITIES

Following are some additional topics about functions, including some features available only in C++.

DEFAULT FUNCTION ARGUMENTS

A useful C++ innovation provides default argument values to function parameters. This can help clean up code when you need to supply only some, but not always all, arguments. For illustration, consider a function that returns the sum of four int values:

```
int sum(int a, int b, int c, int d)
{
  return a + b + c + d;
}
```

To call that function with only two arguments—let's name them v1 and v2—you need to supply zeros to the unused parameters to avoid a compiler error:

```
cout << sum(v1, v2, 0, 0);
```

This is no great imposition, but it does require you to look up sum()'s documentation to determine what values to supply to which unused parameters. Using default arguments, statements like that are unnecessary:

```
int sum(int a, int b, int c = 0, int d = 0);
```

Declared that way, sum() now requires only two arguments, but it can have up to four. The default values must come last in the function's parameter list. In using the new sum() function, if arguments are not specified for c or d, those parameters are given the default values. The following statements are now allowed:

```
cout << sum(1, 2);        // a == 1, b == 2, c == 0, d == 0
cout << sum(1, 2, 3);     // a == 1, b == 2, c == 3, d == 0
cout << sum(1, 2, 3, 4);  // a == 1, b == 2, c == 3, d == 4
```

In some flavors of C++, only the function prototype was permitted to declare default function arguments. GNU C++ permits them in both places. Given sum()'s preceding declaration, implement the function like this:

```
int sum(int a, int b, int c = 0, int d = 0)
{
  return a + b + c + d;
}
```

> **Note**
>
> Any discrepancies between default argument values in the prototype and in the function implementation generate a "default argument..." compilation error.

Listing 10.7, center.cpp, shows a practical example of default function arguments. The program centers an input string by copying it to an output string buffer, surrounded by one or two fill characters—useful for creating error messages and dividing lines. Use the sample program's center() function to prepare strings such as these two examples:

```
**** Error: You goofed big time! ****
<<<<<<< Press any key to continue >>>>>>>
```

LISTING 10.7   CENTER.CPP

```cpp
#include <iostream.h>
#include <string.h>    // Need strlen()

#define SIZE 128        // Character buffer size

// Function prototype
void center(const char *instr, char *outstr,
  int width = 0, char lFill = '-', char rFill = '-');

int main()
{
  char instr[SIZE];    // Input string
  char outstr[SIZE];   // Output string
  int length;          // Length of string in characters

  cout << "Enter a string: ";      // Prompt user for string
  cin.getline(instr, SIZE / 2);    // Read into instr
  length = strlen(instr);          // Get length of entry

  // Prepare output string using some different
  // argument values for illustration
  center(instr, outstr);
  cout << outstr << endl;
  center(instr, outstr, length + 8);
  cout << outstr << endl;
  center(instr, outstr, length + 16, '*', '*');
  cout << outstr << endl;
  center(instr, outstr, 78, '<', '>');
  cout << outstr << endl;
  return 0;
}

// Center a string. Parameters are:
// instr:   Input string pointer
// outstr:  Output string pointer
// width:   Final desired output string width
// fill:    Fill character for output string

/* Older C++ compilers might have to use this implementation:
void center(const char *instr, char *outstr,
  int width, char lFill, char rFill)
*/

void center(const char *instr, char *outstr,
  int width = 0, char lFill = '-', char rFill = '-')
{
  if (outstr == 0)    // The output string must not be null
    return;           // Return immediately if it is null

  if (instr == 0) {   // If input is null
    *outstr = 0;      // Make output into null string,
    return;           // and return.
  }

  // Calculate variables for filling output string
```

```
    int len = strlen(instr);
    if (width < len)
      width = len;
    int wd2 = (width - len) / 2;

    int i;  // String index and for-loop control variable

    for (i = 0; i < wd2; i++)
      outstr[i] = lFill;
    for (/*i = i*/; i < wd2 + len; i++)
      outstr[i] = instr[i - wd2];
    for (/*i = i*/; i < width; i++)
      outstr[i] = rFill;
    outstr[i] = 0;        // Terminate string with null
}
```

When you run the program, it prompts you to enter a string. After you press Enter, the program displays the string centered in four different patterns (shortened here to fit on the page):

```
$ ./a.out
Enter a string:  Test
Test
---- Test ----
******** Test ********
<<<<<<<<<<<<<<<<<<<<<<<<<< Test >>>>>>>>>>>>>>>>>>>>>>>>>>>>
```

The program declares a prototype for function center() with three default argument values:

```
void center(const char *instr, char *outstr,
  int width = 0, char lFill = '-', char rFill = '-');
```

The first two parameters, instr and outstr, address input and output string buffers. The input string is declared const to prevent it from being changed by the function. The last three parameters are given default argument values. This initializes each parameter if it is not supplied in calls to center(). As the first such call in the program demonstrates, you can call center() with as few as two arguments:

```
center(instr, outstr);
```

In this case, the default values for width, lFill, and rFill are used. Because width is zero, the resulting output string is the same as the input—not very useful. The second use of center() supplies a width value:

```
center(instr, outstr, length + 8);
```

The resulting string (stored at outstr) is centered in a space eight characters longer, with hyphens to the left and right of the string. The next statement centers the output string in length plus 16 characters, surrounding it with asterisks:

```
center(instr, outstr, length + 16, '*', '*');
```

Finally, two different fill characters are specified in the last call to center() to bracket a string between < and > characters:

```
center(instr, outstr, 78, '<', '>');
```

INLINE FUNCTIONS

Although calling a function takes place in the barest flutter of an eyelash, numerous function calls can shave points off a program's performance. But avoiding functions is not an acceptable solution to this problem! Functions make programs modular and easier to maintain. Without functions, it is difficult to write even a medium-sized program that runs correctly.

Inline functions give you the best of both worlds. With this technique, you can write a function but have the compiler insert that function's statements directly into the program's source code. One of the best uses for this method is to speed up a `for` statement or other loop. Consider a hypothetical example:

```
for (int i = 0; i < MAX; i++)
  a_function(i);
```

If MAX is very large, the numerous calls to `a_function()` might steal precious time from the program's overall performance. Suppose that `a_function()` executes statements A, B, and C. For better speed, you could insert A, B, and C directly into the loop:

```
for (int i = 0; i < MAX; i++)
{
  A; B; C;
}
```

The amount of time saved should equal the value of MAX times the amount of time it takes to call and return from `a_function()`. However, the program has now lost its modularity. If similar loops appear throughout the program, it is simply impractical to replace `a_function()` with A, B, and C. Worse, if it becomes necessary to modify those statements in some way, you would have to do so everywhere they appeared in the program.

With inline functions, you can retain the program's modularity and tell the compiler to replace calls to `a_function()` with its statements. Simply declare and implement `a_function()` to be `inline` like this:

```
inline void a_function(int i)
{
// ... statements in function
}
```

When you compile the program, C++ replaces every call to `a_function()` with that function's statements. Listing 10.8, inline.cpp, demonstrates how to write and use an inline function.

LISTING 10.8   INLINE.CPP

```
#include <iostream.h>

// Declare and implement inline function before use
inline int max(int a, int b)
{
  if (a >= b)
    return a;
  else
```

```
      return b;
}

// Main program
int main()
{
  int x, y, z;   // Input and result variables

  cout << "X? ";
  cin >> x;
  cout << "Y? ";
  cin >> y;
  z = max(x, y);
  cout << "max(a, b) == " << z << endl;
  return 0;
}
```

The `inline` function `max()` is declared *and implemented* before its use in the program. This tells the compiler to expand any calls to the function by replacing those calls with the function's statements. To compile a program with `inline` functions, and to have the compiler expand them, in GNU C++ you must compile with at least the first level of optimizations using the `-O` option. To compile the sample inline.cpp program and expand its `inline max()` function, use this command:

```
$ g++ -O inline.cpp
```

Running the program produces output such as

```
$ ./a.out
X? 34
Y? 96
max(a, b) == 96
```

Although the program appears to call `max()`, it actually executes that function's statements as though they were written in `main()`. There is nothing special about an `inline` function's statements. Anything that can go in a normal function can go in one declared inline. Usually, `inline` functions are stored in header files, but you can write them in your program's source code files as shown here. Just be sure to implement `inline` functions in full before the program uses them.

FUNCTION OVERLOADING

All programmers face the demandingly creative job of thinking up new function names. Sure, you can invent any old name for a function—the compiler greets a function named `f29q()` with the same enthusiasm as it greets one named `batting_average()`. Humans, however, tend to better comprehend the latter name.

In a large program, coming up with good function names is no joking matter. Consider a graphics program that has to draw umpteen shapes. Each drawing function needs a unique name, leading to programs strewn with functions such as `draw_ellipse()`, `draw_circle()`, `draw_square()`, and `draw_line()`. The code probably also has numerous variables named ellipse, circle, square, and line, and the resulting source code appears to have developed a bad stammer:

```
draw_ellipse(ellipse);
draw_circle(circle);
draw_square(square);
draw_line(line);
```

Wouldn't it be great if you could use the *same* function name—let's call it draw()—to draw all shapes? Then, you could simply write:

```
draw(ellipse);
draw(circle);
draw(square);
draw(line);
```

This is the kind of clarity that function overloading provides. In C++, multiple functions may have the same names as long as they differ in at least one parameter data type. The functions are "overloaded" because, although named the same, they perform distinct actions. The four draw() functions in our hypothetical graphics program are still separate, and they are written just as other nonoverloaded functions. However, the C++ compiler recognizes them *by the way they are used*, not only by their names.

A sample program demonstrates how function overloading can help simplify a program's source code. Listing 10.9, overload.cpp, uses an overloaded function named square() to display the square product of three variables, each of a different data type.

LISTING 10.9 OVERLOAD.CPP

```cpp
#include <iostream.h>

// Overloaded-function prototypes
int square(int a);
double square(double a);
long double square(long double a);

int main()
{
  // Declare and initialize some variables
  int x = 10;
  double y = 20.5;
  long double z = 30.75;

  // Display the variables' square products
  cout << square(x) << endl;
  cout << square(y) << endl;
  cout << square(z) << endl;
  return 0;
}

// Returns the square of an int
int square(int a)
{
  return a * a;
```

```
}

// Returns the square of a double
double square(double a)
{
  return a * a;
}

// Returns the square of a long double
long double square(long double a)
{
  return a * a;
}
```

Running the program displays the square of three different types of variables, showing onscreen the following text:

```
$ g++ overload.cpp
$ ./a.out
100
420.25
945.562
```

The program prototypes three overloaded square() functions. Each function has the same name but declares a different type of parameter. The parameter names don't matter; only their types must be different.

Overloaded functions can clarify a program's meaning. They also help automatically select the correct function to call. In the sample program, this statement calls the correct function for whatever the argument type (y in this case) happens to be:

```
cout << square(y) << endl;
```

Contrast that with the conventional method of creating differently named functions. If, for example, the program has a square_int() function, the following statement may or may not do what the programmer intends:

```
cout << square_int(y) << endl;  // ???
```

Such code makes the programmer responsible for passing objects of the correct type to square_int(). By overloading the square() function, the compiler makes the correct choice for you. Of course, it's up to you to overload functions that perform more or less the same jobs. If you haphazardly give many functions the same name, your program will be as comprehensible as a book written with only one word.

Note

Overloaded functions are essential ingredients in object-oriented programming, introduced in Part III, "Object-Oriented Programming."

Recursive Functions

The concept of *recursion* strikes many as more theoretical than practical, but it is actually a common, everyday event. When you peer into a mirror with another mirror behind, you see an endless series of images infinitely returning themselves. Each image is a recursion of light from the one before.

In programming, recursion occurs when a function calls itself—like dialing your own number, although in C++, you don't get a busy signal. The return addresses of such calls are stacked in memory like reflections in facing mirrors, until some event causes the recursions to unwind. Some algorithms are naturally recursive. For example, the factorial of a value equals that value times the product of its preceding sequential values. The factorial of 5 equals 1 * 2 * 3 * 4 * 5, or 120—equal to 5 times the factorial of 4. From this observation, you can write a recursive factorial function such as in Listing 10.10, fact.cpp.

LISTING 10.10   FACT.CPP

```
#include <iostream.h>

double factorial(int number);

int main()
{
  int input = 8;
  cout << "Factorial of " << input << " == ";
  cout << factorial(input) << endl;
  return 0;
}

double factorial(int number)
{
  if (number > 1)
    return number * factorial(number - 1);
  return 1;
}
```

Compile and run the demonstration program with these commands:

```
$ g++ fact.cpp
$ ./a.out
Factorial of 8 == 40320
```

To understand the `factorial()` function, consider the essential fact that the factorial of n equals n times the factorial of $(n - 1)$. In other words, the factorial of 4 equals 4 * 3 * 2 * 1. The factorial of 3 equals 3 * 2 * 1. So, the factorial of 4 must equal 4 times the factorial of 3. The `factorial()` function uses recursion to implement this self-defining algorithm. The statement

```
d = factorial(8);
```

sets d equal to 40,320 (8 * 7 * ... * 1).

MUTUALLY RECURSIVE FUNCTIONS

Because they call themselves directly, functions such as factorial() in the preceding section are said to be *inclusively recursive*. Another form of recursion occurs when one function calls another, which eventually ends up calling the first function again. If you position three mirrors so that mirror 1 reflects mirror 2, which reflects mirror 3, which again reflects mirror 1, you'd have a graphic illustration of mutual recursion. Kids call them kaleidoscopes.

Mutual recursion is useful for writing *co-routines*. These are functions that depend on one another but don't necessarily require one function to be called before the other. Listing 10.11, onfirst.cpp, demonstrates mutual recursion in a somewhat frivolous way. Named for Abbott and Costello's famous and comically recursive "Who's on First?" routine, onfirst.cpp displays the alphabet. Before continuing, can you figure out how?

LISTING 10.11   ONFIRST.CPP

```
#include <iostream.h>

// Function prototypes
void A(char c);
void B(char c);

int main()
{
  A('Z');
  cout << endl;
  return 0;
}

void A(char c)
{
  if (c > 'A')
    B(c);
  cout << c;
}

void B(char c)
{
  A(--c);
}
```

Compile and run the program using the following commands. As shown here, the program displays the alphabet in uppercase:

```
$ g++ onfirst.cpp
$ ./a.out
ABCDEFGHIJKLMNOPQRSTUVWXYZ
```

PART II CH 10

The main program starts the recursive ball rolling by calling function A() with the argument 'Z'. Function A() examines its parameter c. If c is alphabetically greater than 'A', the function calls B(), which immediately calls A(), passing c-- as an argument. That causes A() to again examine c, equal to one less than its former value, and then again call B(), until c equals 'A'. At this point, the recursion unwinds, executing the output statement 26 times, and displaying the alphabet, one character at a time. Okay, you can laugh now.

Tip

Walk through onfirst.cpp using the GNU debugger's next and step commands to see how it works in slow motion.

FUNCTIONS AND SEPARATE COMPILATION

It's often useful to compile functions in separate modules, an especially valuable technique for creating function libraries that multiple programs can share. To illustrate, the following listings create a modular version of the kilo.cpp program in this chapter. Listing 10.12, kilos.h, is a header file with a single element: the kilos() function prototype.

LISTING 10.12   KILOS.H

```
//================================================================
// kilos.h -- Function kilos() header file
// Copyright (c) 1999 by Tom Swan. All rights reserved.
//================================================================

// Function prototype
double kilos( double miles );
```

In practice, most header files declare several function prototypes along with other items such as constants. They might also declare global variables. But, in this case, the kilos.h header file merely declares a prototype for the kilos() function. Listing 10.13, kilos.cpp, implements the function.

LISTING 10.13   KILOS.CPP

```
//================================================================
// kilos.cpp -- Function kilos() implementation module
// Copyright (c) 1999 by Tom Swan. All rights reserved.
//================================================================

// Convert miles to kilometers
double kilos( double miles )
{
  return miles * 1.609344;
}
```

This is the same function as in the original program. However, kilos.cpp is a separate module that does not have a `main()` function. It is common, and usually wise, to name the header and separate modules files the same—kilos.h and kilos.cpp, in this case. This isn't required, but helps you keep track of modules and their related header files. To finish the program requires writing another module with a `main()` function. Listing 10.14, kilotab.cpp, completes the picture.

LISTING 10.14   KILOTAB.CPP

```
#include <iostream.h>
#include <iomanip.h>      // Need setw() manipulator
#include "kilos.h"        // Need kilos() function

int main()
{
  cout << "Miles      Kilometers" << endl;
  cout << "====================" << endl;
  for (int miles = 0; miles <= 200; miles += 20) {
    cout << setw(5) << miles << " == ";
    cout << kilos( miles ) << endl;
  }
  return 0;
}
```

The finished program includes the separately compiled `kilos()` function with this directive:

```
#include "kilos.h"
```

The quotes tell the compiler that kilos.h is in the current directory, or in one specified by the option `-I` (see Chapter 5, "Compiling and Debugging C++ Programs"). Including the header file declares the `kilos()` prototype, and that's all that's needed for the program to compile. During the final steps of compilation, the GNU linker searches for an object-code module that contains the implementation for the prototyped function. The linker must find implementations for *all* declared functions, or it ends with an error. To compile the separate kilos.cpp module and the kilotab program, and to link their separate object-code files, enter these commands:

```
$ g++ -c kilos.cpp
$ g++ kilotab.cpp kilos.o
$ ./a.out
```

DEBUGGING FUNCTIONS

Finally in this chapter, some words about debugging functions and parameters. As the following sections explain, the GNU debugger offers several commands that are especially valuable for tracing through function statements.

STEPPING OVER FUNCTIONS

When single-stepping code using the GNU debugger, the next command executes one statement. Use this command to execute a function at full speed and pause at the next statement *after* the function returns. To see how this works, enter the following commands to load the electric.cpp program in this chapter into the GNU debugger:

```
$ g++ -g -o electric electric.cpp
$ gdb --silent electric
(gdb)
```

When you see the debugger prompt, (gdb), enter a breakpoint to halt the code just before it calls the printTable() function (the line number refers to the disk file's, not the listing as printed in this chapter):

```
(gdb) b 30
Breakpoint 1 at 0x8048714: file electric.cpp, line 30.
```

Run the program to the breakpoint with a run command:

```
(gdb) run
Starting program: /home/tswan/mgcc/src/c10/electric
Breakpoint 1, main () at electric.cpp:30
30          printTable(startHours, hourlyIncrement,
31            startWatts, wattsIncrement, costPerKwh);
```

You might see only line 31, but no matter. The program is paused before the call to function printTable(). To execute that function at full speed and pause at the next statement, type a next command:

```
(gdb) next
```

This displays the full table. Type *cont* to continue and end the program:

```
(gdb) cont
```

STEPPING INTO FUNCTIONS

When you want to trace the statements inside a function, use the step command. If you are following along, type *run* to again halt the program just before calling printTable(). (If you exited the debugger, repeat the instructions in the preceding section to load the electric program and set a breakpoint.) When you type *step*, the debugger calls the function and immediately pauses execution (I reformatted the lines to fit here, but they should be similar on your screen):

```
(gdb) step
printTable (startHours=100, hourlyIncrement=10,
  startWatts=4, wattsIncrement=2,
  costPerKwh=0.068699999999999997) at electric.cpp:50
50       cout << endl << "Hrs/Watts";
```

Stepping into a function pauses execution before the function's first statement—in this case, the one at line 50. Above this line the debugger shows the values assigned to the function's parameters—useful information that you can inspect to ensure the function's input data is correct. You may now issue additional next and step commands to trace the statements in the function, or type ***cont*** to continue executing at normal speed to the next breakpoint or to the end.

DEBUGGING inline FUNCTIONS

Debugging `inline` functions can be difficult because they are not called and, therefore, are more difficult to trace. You might experience this problem if you compile the program using a command such as this:

```
$ g++ -O -g -o inline inline.cpp
$ gdb inline
```

The -O optimization option enables `inline` function expansion. The -g option adds debugging information to the compiled code file. Although you can issue the preceding commands to load the inline.cpp program into the GNU debugger, you cannot set a breakpoint on any `inline` function calls because they have been replaced by the function's statements. Worse, using the next and step commands to trace `inline` functions doesn't always work as expected. (If you are following along, type *q* to quit.)

To simplify debugging `inline` functions, you can temporarily disable them. The easiest way to do this is to simply compile without optimizations using a command such as

```
$ g++ -g -o inline inline.cpp
$ gdb inline
```

The second line loads the compiled inline.cpp program into the GNU debugger. You can now use the list command to find the line number of the statement that calls max(), set a breakpoint there (type ***break* n** where *n* is the line number), and then type ***run***. When the breakpoint hits, type ***step*** to step inside the max() function. Use next to continue executing max()'s statements. You can do this because the program is not optimized, and max() is therefore treated as a callable function and is not expanded inline. Type *c* to continue; *q* to quit.

To debug optimized code and still allow tracing `inline` functions, you must use a different set of options. For example, the following command compiles inline.cpp with optimizations, but with `inline` function expansion disabled:

```
$ g++ -O -fno-inline -g -o inline inline.cpp
$ gdb inline
```

Repeat the preceding debugger instructions to verify that you can still step inside max(). You must use -O and -fno-inline together. Because `inline` functions are normally not expanded except when optimizing, the following compilation command is pointless:

```
$ g++ -fno-inline -g inline.cpp  // ???
```

PART

II

CH

10

SUMMARY

A typical program contains many functions, each with a specific purpose. Functions modularize a program and make it easier to write and maintain. Functions can declare value, reference, and pointer parameters to which statements pass arguments. Functions may also return values of any valid C++ type. Before using a function, a program must declare it using a prototype that states the function's return type, its name, and any parameters. In addition to introducing functions, this chapter also explained recursive functions and how to use C++ features such as default argument values, inline functions, and overloaded functions. The chapter ended with a look at debugging commands useful for tracing function statements and examining parameter values.

For more information on subjects introduced in this chapter, turn to the following chapters:

- Chapter 5, "Compiling and Debugging C++ Programs"
- Chapter 6, "Creating Data Objects"
- Chapter 11, "Managing Memory with Pointers"
- Chapter 23, "Using the Standard Template Library (STL)"

MANAGING MEMORY WITH POINTERS

Modern software can use a bumper crop of memory, and programmers need reliable techniques for managing this space. In this chapter, you learn how to use C++ memory-management techniques to create *dynamic* objects such as large buffers for holding file data and arrays that expand and contract at runtime. These methods help your programs take advantage of the tremendous amount of memory available on modern PCs and also prepare you for Part III, "Object-Oriented Programming," in which memory management plays an even bigger role in software development.

ALLOCATING MEMORY

Generally, to create an object in memory, you request space from the GNU C++ memory manager. It isn't necessary to know beforehand exactly where the memory exists or its organization. If enough memory is available, the memory manager reserves space for the object and gives you its address. The program uses that address as a *pointer* to the dynamic object's value. The object can be a simple variable, but it is more commonly a complex type such as struct, a string, or an array.

There are two basic ways to create dynamic objects. You can call standard C library functions such as malloc() (memory allocate) and free(). Or, you can use the C++ operators new and delete. I show both methods in the next sections. You need to know how the standard C functions work, if only to understand their use in existing programs. However, in new code, you should use the C++ operators. They are safer and easier to use correctly, and they play a major role in the rest of this book's focus on object-oriented C++ programming.

MEMORY MANAGEMENT WITH new AND delete

C++ adds two operators to the C language, new and delete. These are not functions. They are native operators. Use new to allocate space for a dynamic variable. Use delete to free that space after the program is finished using it. Freeing memory returns it to the memory pool, sometimes called the *heap*. This makes the space available for use in creating other dynamic variables.

Although most dynamic objects are complex types such as structs and arrays, you may use new to allocate memory for an object of any data type. For illustration, it's useful to run through some examples using a simple type such as double. For example, the following statement uses the new operator to reserve space for a dynamic double object. It is called "dynamic" because the object comes and goes under the control of the program:

```
double *dp = new double;
```

That statement actually performs three distinct actions:

- It declares a pointer named dp to a double object.
- It uses new to allocate enough memory to hold one double object.
- It assigns to dp the address of the allocated memory.

Following the statement, dp *points to* a double object in memory. Stored in dp is the address of the first byte of that memory. Like an arrow pointing to an office in a building, a C++ pointer refers, or points, to an object in memory.

You don't have to declare and initialize a pointer in one step. You can declare the pointer ahead of time, and then elsewhere use new to allocate memory and assign its address to the pointer. This is a common technique for creating a dynamic object, demonstrated by this code fragment:

```
double *dp;        // Declare a pointer to a double object
...                // dp is uninitialized here!
dp = new double;   // Allocate space for a double object
```

Merely declaring the pointer in the first statement does *not* allocate memory for a double object. That takes place later in the statement that uses new. Until that second statement executes, the pointer dp is *uninitialized*, analogous to an arrow in an unfinished building that points to a room not yet constructed. Following the arrow to its nonexistent destination could be hazardous to your health. Similarly, using an uninitialized pointer before it is allocated memory is nearly guaranteed to cause a serious bug.

Tip

The phrase "a pointer to a double object" is commonly shortened to "a pointer to double" or "a double pointer."

The new operator reserves exactly enough space in memory to hold one object of the specified type—in this case, 8 bytes, the size of one double variable. Some additional space might be attached to the allocated memory for the memory manager's internal use, and for efficiency reasons, memory might be allocated in certain block sizes. However, as far as the program is concerned, exactly eight bytes are available for holding one double, floating point value. The exact location of those bytes is usually unimportant. The pointer dp always locates the allocated memory, wherever it happens to be.

Note

If enough memory is not available, new *throws an exception*, which if not handled ends the program. Chapter 16, "Handling Exceptions," explains how to trap this exception and deal with such errors. Also see "Dealing with Memory Errors" later in this chapter.

After allocating memory to a pointer such as dp, you can store a value of its declared type in that memory, and then use it as you can any other variable of that type. However, dp alone is *not* a double object. It is a pointer *to* a double object. To use dp as a double object requires *dereferencing* the pointer with the * operator. This statement, for example, assigns a value to the double object to which dp points:

```
*dp = 3.14159;
```

That copies the value 3.14159 into the location in memory addressed by dp. You might think of the dereference operator, *, as a conduit that creates a channel to the addressed memory location. Using the * operator is like following an arrow to its destination. Not using the dereferencing operator causes a compilation error:

```
dp = 3.14159;  // ???
```

That doesn't compile because dp is a pointer. It holds a memory address, and 3.14159 is not a memory address value. Again, using the analogy of an arrow in an office building, the preceding statement is similar to telling a delivery worker to put a chair on a sign that points to an office. But that's ridiculous. You obviously want the worker to put the chair in the office to which the sign refers. This is exactly how pointers work in C++. You use them to find the locations in memory where you want to read and write data.

To retrieve the value of an object addressed by a pointer, again use the dereference operator. This statement writes the value of the addressed double object to the standard output:

```
cout << "Value == " << *dp << endl;
```

Because dp was declared as a double pointer, the expression *dp evaluates to a double object. When you are finished using the dynamic object, delete it like this:

```
delete dp;
```

That deletes the memory addressed by dp and returns that memory to the heap for use in creating other dynamic objects. Deleting a pointer might change the addressed object's contents because of the way the memory manager links together freed blocks. As a firm rule, after deleting a dynamic object, *never use its pointer in any way except to create another object with new.* To help prevent a bug caused by using a deleted pointer, it is a good idea to set deleted pointers to NULL with code such as the following:

```
delete dp;
dp = 0;
```

Or, you can set the pointer to the predefined constant NULL:

```
delete dp;
dp = NULL;
```

Tip

If dp is already NULL, deleting it does no harm, so it is not necessary to test whether dp equals NULL before applying the delete operator.

By resetting a deleted pointer to NULL, other statements can test whether dp addresses an object in memory. For example, the following if statement assigns a value to the dynamic object only if dp is not NULL:

```
if (dp != NULL)
  *dp = 3.14159;
```

You will often see a statement like that shortened to

```
if (dp)
  *dp = 3.14159;
```

The expression (dp) equals the value of dp, so if dp is zero, the expression (dp) is equivalent to false. If dp is nonzero, the expression (dp) evaluates to true. You gain no advantage in using the shorthand expression, but some programmers seem to enjoy, if not relish, being cryptic. Do yourself a big favor: Use clear expressions such as (dp != NULL) and (dp == NULL) and leave shorthand methods to those who actually like to debug code during holiday weekends.

MEMORY LEAKS

After deleting the memory allocated to a pointer, you may reuse that pointer in another allocation statement. For example, following a delete statement, the program may create another dynamic object and assign its address to dp, after which the pointer dp is again initialized and ready for use:

```
dp = new double;
```

Deleting dynamic objects returns their memory to the heap. This is an especially important operation in programs that create many or very large dynamic objects. If you don't religiously delete allocated memory, the heap can become fragmented with formerly allocated objects, a messy condition called a *memory leak*. This is a critical problem to be avoided at all costs. Memory leaks might cause the program to run out of free memory and, in serious cases, can negatively affect the operation of other processes that have their own memory needs. The most common cause of a memory leak is a poorly written function such as

```
void f()
{
  double *dp = new double;
  // ... other statements
  return;  // ??? Memory leak here!
}
```

The function allocates space for a double value using new. Because the function returns without deleting that space, when the function ends, the local variable dp is destroyed, causing the address of the allocated memory to become lost in space. Fix the program by writing the function this way:

```
void f()
{
  double *dp = new double;
  // ... other statements
  delete dp;
  return;
}
```

Now the function properly deletes the allocated memory before returning. When you need a function to allocate memory and not delete it, one solution is to return the pointer as the function result. Here's a sample:

```
double *f()
{
  double *dp = new double;
  *dp = 3.14159;
  return dp;  // Return pointer as function result
}
```

PART

II

CH

11

There is no memory leak here because the function preserves the address of the allocated memory by returning it as the function result. Notice the function's type is `double *` (double pointer). Managing the allocated memory is now the responsibility of the function's caller. Elsewhere in the program, a statement can declare a double pointer and call `f()` like this:

```
double *dynamic_dp = f();
```

The function `f()` allocates space for a `double` value, assigns 3.14159 to that object, and returns the pointer, which the program assigns to `dynamic_dp`. This plugs the leak, but the memory must still be deleted at some point, using the following statement:

```
delete dynamic_dp;
```

MEMORY MANAGEMENT WITH `malloc()` AND `free()`

Many existing C programs use standard library functions to allocate and free memory, and it's good to know how to use the techniques if only so that you can read and understand those programs' source files. In new code, use the C++ `new` and `delete` operators.

To use C memory management functions, include the stdlib.h header file using the directive

```
#include <stdlib.h>
```

This makes the following four functions available to your program:

```
void *malloc(size_t size);
void *calloc(size_t n, size_t size);
void *realloc(void *ptr, size_t size);
void free(void *ptr);
```

Several other memory allocation functions are in the standard C library, but those four are the most commonly used. The first three functions allocate memory. The `free()` function deletes previously allocated memory. Memory allocators return type `void *`, literally a pointer with no type, that can be assigned to any pointer variable. If enough memory is not available, memory allocation functions return `NULL`. The `free()` function returns no value.

> **Note**
>
> I explain here only how to use `malloc()`. For online documentation on using `calloc()`, `realloc()`, and other standard C library memory functions, use the command ***info malloc***. For the full ball of wax on C memory management functions, use the command ***info libc*** and step to the node *Memory Management*. Depending on your Linux version, this might be named *Memory Allocation*.

Calling `malloc()` reserves size bytes of memory. The following statements declare a double pointer dp and then call `malloc()` to allocate space for one `double` value:

```
double *dp;
dp = (double *) malloc( sizeof(double) );
```

Obviously, using the C++ `new` operator is simpler. In plain C, the *type cast* expression isn't needed, and you will find numerous statements such as the following in C source files:

```
dp = malloc( sizeof(double) );
```

However, C++ is much more strict about enforcing type compatibility among objects used in assignment statements. To tell the compiler that you intend to convert `malloc()`'s return value of type `void *` into a `double *`, you must preface the call to `malloc()` with the type cast expression `(double *)`. When converting C programs to C++, this is one change you might have to make. (It is preferable, although possibly more time-consuming, to convert all uses of `malloc()` to use the `new` operator.)

To `malloc()`, pass the size in bytes of the amount of space to reserve. Usually, the safest course is to use `sizeof()` along with the data type of the object. Even so, you might spot an inherent danger here. A simple typing error such as the following allocates an incorrect amount of space:

```
dp = (double *) malloc( sizeof(char) );  // ???
```

Oops. The program just reserved a single byte (the size of a `char` object) and assigned its address to `dp`. Even with all warning levels engaged, the compiler is happy to enable you to make this grave error, one more good reason to use the C++ `new` operator, which obtains the size of an object from its data type. In C++, an obviously incorrect statement such as this

```
double *dp = new char;  // ???
```

results in the following compiler error:

```
test.cpp:9: assignment to 'double *' from 'char *'
```

Getting back to C, if `malloc()` returns a non-NULL pointer, you may use it in the same way as described in the preceding section. When you are finished using the dynamic object, delete that memory by calling `free()`:

```
free(dp);
```

That returns the allocated memory to the heap for use in creating other dynamic objects. If `dp` is `NULL`, deleting it does no harm, so it is not necessary to include a test for a `NULL` pointer before calling `free()`. The same comments from the preceding sections about deleting pointers apply to standard C memory management. Always free the memory your program allocates.

Warning

You may combine C and C++ memory techniques in the same program. However, if you allocate space using `malloc()` or another standard C library function, always use `free()` to delete that space. If you allocate space using `new`, always use `delete`. Although you might discover in the GNU source files that `new` calls `malloc()`, *it is not safe to assume that the two methods are equivalent!* As you learn in Chapter 19, "Overloading Operators," a C++ program can reprogram the `new` operator to use an entirely different memory management system. In such cases, mixing C and C++ memory techniques is begging for disaster. Don't do it.

DEALING WITH MEMORY ERRORS

When creating dynamic objects, a main concern is whether enough memory is available. If a memory allocation error occurs, one of three actions takes place:

- new throws an exception.
- new returns NULL.
- new calls a program function (not recommended).

In GNU C++ and most ANSI C++ compilers, new throws an exception if any memory allocation errors occur. Unless the program itself handles that exception, this causes the program to end. In older versions of C++, new returns NULL, similar to how the standard C library function malloc() works. Using GNU C++ and most ANSI C++ compilers, you can also elect to have new call a program function, although this practice isn't recommended.

Exceptions are the best way to handle out-of-memory and other memory allocation problems. However, ending the program in the event of a memory exception might not be acceptable. Also, many existing programs expect new to return NULL. To reprogram new, include the new.h header using the directive:

```
#include <new.h>
```

Next, insert this statement into the program:

```
set_new_handler(0);
```

The set_new_handler() function assigns the address of the function that new calls to throw a memory exception. Replacing that address with 0 causes new instead to return NULL if any errors occur.

Note

Reprogramming new to return NULL works just fine, but it makes your program incompatible with the ANSI C++ standard.

After calling set_new_handler(), you can write code such as the following to allocate memory and test whether an error occurred:

```
set_new_handler(0);
double *dp = new double;
if (dp == NULL) {
  cerr << "*** Out of memory" << endl;
  exit(1);
}
```

The error message is conventionally written to the standard error output object cerr rather than cout. Alternatively, you may pass the name of a void function to set_new_handler() using code such as

```
void my_handler();
// ...
set_new_handler(my_handler);
```

This works, but exception handling is a much safer approach to dealing with memory allocation problems, so don't waste your time developing a custom error handling function. You learn how to use memory management exceptions in Chapter 16, "Handling Exceptions," under "Exceptions and Memory Management."

Tip

Given the option `-fcheck-new`, GNU C++ adds code that checks `new`'s return value. If `new` returns `NULL`, changes to allocated memory are prohibited. This option isn't needed unless the program uses `set_new_handler(0)` to cause `new` to return `NULL`. The option is probably unique to GNU C++.

POINTERS FOR USING POINTERS

For convenience, many examples in this chapter allocate dynamic memory space for a `double` value. In practice, however, you'll rarely if ever create simple objects this way—it's easier simply to create them as variables. Dynamic objects in real-world software are typically complex types such as strings and arrays. The next sections explain how to use `new` and `delete` to manage these types of dynamic memory objects. (In the coming chapters, you learn how to create dynamic `struct`s as well as their object-oriented cousins, class objects.)

DYNAMIC STRINGS

When created as program variables, character strings are fixed in size and can waste space. For example, code such as the following creates a string buffer of 128 bytes, big enough for a 127-character string plus a null terminator:

```
#define BUF_SIZE 128
// ...
char input_buffer[BUF_SIZE];
```

Storing short strings in the fixed-size buffer wastes memory that could be put to better use. Worse, when declared inside a function, the string is placed on the system stack, which is limited in size and is best kept free of large objects.

A good way to avoid creating large variables that waste memory is to write a function that allocates a dynamic string using just as much memory as needed. Listing 11.1, newstr.cpp, shows one way to write this kind of function.

LISTING 11.1   NEWSTR.CPP

```
#include <iostream.h>
#include <string.h>      // Need strlen(), strcpy()

// Function prototypes
const char *get_string(const char *prompt);
```

continues

LISTING 11.1   CONTINUED

```
size_t mem_block_size(const void *p);

int main()
{
  // Prompt user for and create a dynamic string
  const char *cp = get_string("Enter a string: ");

  // Display some statistics
  cout << "String : " << cp << endl;
  cout << "Length : " << strlen(cp) << " char(s)" << endl;
  cout << "Size   : " << mem_block_size(cp) << " bytes"
       << endl;

  // Delete string when finished
  delete[] cp;   // Notice the brackets!
  return 0;
}

// Prompts user to enter a string. Returns address of a new
// character buffer big enough to hold only that string.
// Be sure to delete the returned pointer!
const char *get_string(const char *prompt)
{
  const int buf_size = 128;            // Size of input buffer
  char *temp = new char[buf_size];     // Create input buffer
  cout << prompt;                      // Prompt user for input
  cin.getline(temp, buf_size);         // Read input from user
  char *result = new char[strlen(temp) + 1];  // Create string
  strcpy(result, temp);                // Copy buffer to result
  delete[] temp;                       // Delete the buffer
  return result;                       // Return entered string
}

// Return size in bytes of an allocated memory block
// addressed by pointer p. Tricky but it works.
size_t mem_block_size(const void *p)
{
  char *cp = (char *) p;          // Convert void * to
                                  //   allow math on p
  return *(size_t *)(cp - 4);     // Size of chunk is
                                  //   four bytes back
}
```

The newstr.cpp program declares two function prototypes, get_string() and mem_block_size(). In the program, this statement prompts the user to enter a string:

```
const char *cp = get_string("Enter a string: ");
```

The const char pointer cp is assigned the result of calling get_string(). The literal string parameter passed to the function is the prompt displayed onscreen. Specifying cp to be const prevents the program from attempting to modify the entered string. This isn't strictly necessary, and you could rewrite the program to use pointers of type char *. However, because the returned string is only as long as necessary, operations that change the string's length might be dangerous, and it is best made const for that reason.

When finished using the string, delete it using a special form of the delete operator:

```
delete[] cp;
```

The empty brackets inform the compiler that cp addresses an array. In this case, the brackets are not strictly needed because the array contains only simple chars. However, as you learn in the next section, other types of arrays might require special handling during deletion, and it's a good idea to get in the practice of using delete[] to delete dynamic arrays.

Now take a look at the get_string() function. It begins by declaring a constant integer, buf_size, equal to 128. This is the maximum size string that the function can return. You might want to change the value to 255 or higher, especially when using this method to read strings from files. Next, the function creates a dynamic buffer of the declared maximum size:

```
char *temp = new char[buf_size];
```

A couple of I/O statements prompt the user to enter a string into the temporary buffer, read by the cin.getline() function. The standard C library string functions, strlen() and strcpy(), are used to create an object just big enough to hold the entered string and to copy the entered string into that location:

```
char *result = new char[strlen(temp) + 1];
strcpy(result, temp);
```

The first statement calls strlen() to obtain the length of the input string stored in the temporary buffer. Because this length does not include the null terminator at the end of the string, the statement adds 1 to the value passed to new. The char * variable result now addresses a string buffer exactly large enough to hold the entered string, transferred by strcpy() into the reserved space. Finally, get_string() calls delete[] to delete the temporary buffer, and it returns the pointer to the reduced-size dynamic string.

Tip

> If get_string() is called frequently, it might be advantageous to create a fixed, global input buffer for use by the function rather than create a temporary buffer each time the function is called.

When you run the program, it prompts you to enter a string. After you press Enter, the program displays your typing and the string's length. It also displays the size of the memory block that new allocated. Here's a sample run:

```
$ ./a.out
Enter a string: Testing, one, two, three
String : Testing, one, two, three
Length : 24 char(s)
Size   : 32 bytes
```

The string's length is simply determined by calling strlen(). However, the size of the memory block might surprise you. In this case, the 24-byte string actually occupies a space in memory of 32 bytes. In the attempt to save memory, the program apparently wastes 8 bytes. That's certainly better than wasting 103 as would be the case with a fixed-length 128-byte buffer, but the results are not perfect. This happens because the GNU C++ memory manager allocates memory only in certain chunk sizes. In cases where maximum efficiency is needed, you might need to take this fact into consideration (see "Other Memory Matters" later in this chapter for more information about how the GNU memory manager works).

POINTER ARITHMETIC

C and C++ permit arithmetic operations on pointer address values. For example, if p is a pointer, p++ increments the pointer to the next object in memory. Similarly, p-- decrements p to the address of a prior object. It's important to understand that an expression such as p++ increments p not to the next address in memory, but to the next object of the type that p addresses. If p addresses a double object of 8 bytes, p++ advances the pointer 8 bytes in memory to point to the next double object. You can also use other arithmetic operators on pointers. For example, the expression (p + 5) equals the address five objects away from p.

Of course, it's your responsibility to ensure that an object exists at the new location. Although it is often just as easy to use arrays to locate successive objects stored together in memory, pointer arithmetic is handy for special circumstances. The next section lists a practical use for the technique.

OBTAINING A MEMORY BLOCK'S SIZE

Obtaining a memory block's size in bytes requires some tricky programming, shown in the newstr.cpp program (refer to Listing 11.1) in function mem_block_size(). Pass a pointer to the function as follows to find a memory allocation's block size in bytes:

```
int k = mem_block_size(cp);
```

That sets k to the size of the block addressed by cp. You may pass any pointer to mem_block_size(). The returned value is not the size of the object in that block—it is the size of the memory allocation itself, including overhead bytes added by the memory manager. In GNU C++ programs, the block's size is stored in its first four bytes. So, to obtain the size value, mem_block_size() looks back four bytes from a given address and returns the integer value located there, using these statements:

```
char *cp = (char *) p;
return *(size_t *)(cp - 4);
```

That might seem a bit cryptic, but is not as involved as it probably looks. The first statement converts the function's void *p parameter to a char * because ANSI C++ forbids arithmetic on void pointers. The second statement performs several operations. It subtracts 4 from cp to address the location that many bytes lower in memory. A type cast expression (size_t *) informs the compiler that an object of type size_t is stored at the calculated location. Finally, a pointer dereference operator at the head of the entire expression obtains the integer value stored there. The function returns this value.

Note

> The size_t data type is defined for all C and C++ programs and, in GNU C++, equates to a long int. It is used in many library declarations. I use it in mem_block_size() because the GNU memory manager defines chunk sizes using size_t.

The mem_block_size() function *probably* works in all GNU C++ implementations, but it might fail with another C++ compiler or operating system. Then again, it might work—many compilers use similar internal representations for memory allocations, and storing the size of a block in its first 4 bytes is fairly standard, at least on small computer systems. If you feel shaky about this assumption, you can revise the second statement as follows to call sizeof():

```
return *(size_t *)(cp - sizeof(size_t));
```

I show this method strictly for your information. Don't rely on it to operate correctly in production code! If you are curious about how the memory manager works, however, this bit of code might help you to poke around.

DYNAMIC ARRAYS

You're not limited to allocating dynamic strings, which, of course, are merely arrays of characters. You may also use new and delete[] to create and dispose of dynamic arrays containing objects of any data type. As Listing 11.2, newarray.cpp, demonstrates, this is a valuable technique for creating arrays of sizes determined at runtime.

PART

II

CH

11

LISTING 11.2   NEWARRAY.CPP

```cpp
#include <iostream.h>
#include <iomanip.h>      // Need setw()

int array_size;  // User-selected array size

int main()
{
  int *array;      // Pointer to array of integers
  int i;           // Array index

  cout << "Array size (1 .. 100) ? ";
  cin >> array_size;
  array_size = 100 <? array_size; // Minimum 100 or array_size
  if (array_size > 0) {
    array = new int[array_size];      // Create dynamic array
 // Fill array with values
    for (i = 0; i < array_size; i++) // Assign values to array
      array[i] = i;
 // Display array contents
    for (i = 0; i < array_size; i++) // Display array contents
      cout << setw(8) << array[i];
    cout << endl;
    delete[] array;               // Notice the brackets!
  } // if (array_size > 0)
  return 0;
}
```

Running the program prompts you to enter an array size from 1 to 100. After reading your response, the program uses the C++ <? (minimum of) operator to restrict this value to the allowed range. This statement, however, might not work with other C++ compilers:

```
array_size = 100 <? array_size;
```

Use the >? (maximum of) operator to return the greater of two values. If `array_size` is zero or less, the sample program ends. Otherwise, it creates an array of integers of the specified size using this statement:

```
int *array;
...
array = new int[array_size];
```

You can use similar code to create arrays of any data type, and of just about any practical size. Use the dynamic array as you do one created as a fixed variable. Because arrays and pointers are functionally equivalent in C and C++, you do not have to dereference the pointer returned by `new`. For example, this fills the array with integer values:

```
for (i = 0; i < array_size; i++)
  array[i] = i;
```

Be sure, as shown in Listing 11.2, to delete the dynamic array using brackets as in this statement:

```
delete[] array;
```

The brackets tell the compiler that `array` is a collection of, probably, two or more objects. Because this array's contents are simple integers, the special form of `delete[]` isn't strictly needed. However, `delete[]` is needed for arrays of objects that each require their own cleanups before the entire array is disposed. Chapter 13, "Creating and Destroying Objects," demonstrates situations where `delete[]` is required to properly dispose of a dynamic array.

MULTIDIMENSIONAL DYNAMIC ARRAYS

To create a two- or three-dimensional dynamic array requires a bit more effort. You may use the following techniques to create arrays of any dimension, but it's difficult to imagine a need for more than two or three. Suppose that you want to allocate space for a 10-by-20 matrix of `double` values. Begin by declaring the pointer to be used for referencing the array:

```
int (*matrix)[20];
```

This states that `matrix` is a pointer to an array of 20 integers. The size may be variable, or literal as shown here. To create the multidimensional array, you actually create an array of those pointers, each of which points to 20 integer values. This works because a multidimensional array is literally an array of arrays—remember, an array and a pointer in C and C++ are one and the same.

The array's declaration must use parentheses in the expression (*matrix) because the array brackets have higher precedence than the pointer symbol *. The array doesn't yet exist; all you've done is tell the compiler that matrix *potentially* addresses an array of a certain size and structure. To allocate memory for an actual 10-by-20 matrix and assign the array's address to matrix, use this statement:

```
matrix = new int[10][20];
```

That allocates space for a 10-element array of 20-element int arrays—that is, a 10-by-20 integer matrix. The resulting address is assigned to the matrix pointer. You may specify constants or variables for the array's dimensions. Listing 11.3, newmatrix.cpp, shows how to create a two-dimensional array sized at runtime.

LISTING 11.3   NEWMATRIX.CPP

```cpp
#include <iostream.h>
#include <iomanip.h>

#define MAX_ROWS 9
#define MAX_COLS 10

int main()
{
  int rows, cols;  // User selectable matrix size
  int r, c;        // Row and column for-loop indexes

  cout << "Rows (1 ... " << MAX_ROWS << ") ? ";
  cin >> rows;
  cout << "Columns (1 ... " << MAX_COLS << ") ? ";
  cin >> cols;

  rows = rows <? MAX_ROWS;    // Minimum of rows and MAX_ROWS
  cols = cols <? MAX_COLS;    // Minimum of cols and MAX_COLS

  if (rows > 0 && cols > 0) {
    int (* matrix)[cols];            // Declare matrix pointer
    matrix = new int[rows][cols]; // Create the dynamic matrix

    // Fill the matrix with integer values
    for (r = 0; r < rows; r++)
      for (c = 0; c < cols; c++)
        matrix[r][c] = (r + 1) * (c + 1);

    // Display matrix in column order
    for (c = 0; c < cols; c++) {
      for (r = 0; r < rows; r++)
        cout << setw(8) << matrix[r][c];
      cout << endl;  // Start new line after each row
    }
    delete[] matrix;    // Notice the brackets!
  }
  return 0;
}
```

Run the program and enter the number of rows and columns you want to create. To declare and create the matrix, the program executes the following statements:

```
int (* matrix)[cols];
matrix = new int[rows][cols];
```

> **Note**
>
> In some versions of C++, cols is required to be a constant; only rows may be variable. However, GNU C++ permits variables in creating arrays of any dimensions.

The expression matrix[r][c] refers to a single element in the matrix at row r and column c. For fun, the sample program uses this expression to fill the matrix with some values, and then writes them to the standard output in column order. Onscreen, you see something like this:

```
$ g++ newmatrix.cpp
$ ./a.out
Rows (1 ... 9) ? 3
Columns (1 ... 10) ? 4
        1       2       3
        2       4       6
        3       6       9
        4       8       12
```

More than two dimensions are rarely useful, but C++ places no restriction on the depth of a multidimensional array. To create an 8-by-8-by-8 cube, you could use these statements:

```
int (* matrix)[8][8];
matrix = new int[8][8][8];
```

Again, in the first line, you are merely declaring matrix as a pointer that potentially addresses a multidimensional array. As declared here, matrix is literally a pointer (an array) of 8 arrays of 8 arrays—conceptually, a three-dimensional cube. It's possible to carry this idea to extremes, adding additional dimensions, but is there a practical use for a four- or higher-dimensional matrix? If there is, I've never seen it!

PASSING ARGUMENTS TO main()

Using pointers, you can access arguments passed to main(). This is an essential technique for obtaining command-line options, filenames, and other data entered by users when they run the program. Listing 11.4, cmdline.cpp, shows one way to pick up command-line arguments.

LISTING 11.4   CMDLINE.CPP

```
#include <iostream.h>

int main(int argc, char *argv[])
{
  cout << "Command line arguments:" << endl;
  for (int i = 1; i < argc; i++)
    cout << argv[i] << endl;
  return 0;
}
```

Compile and run the program specifying command-line arguments. As the following sample run shows, the program echoes each argument on a separate line. Enter these commands:

```
$ g++ cmdline.cpp
$ ./a.out option filename -x
Command line arguments:
option
filename
-x
```

Separate each argument with whitespace, usually just a single blank. In the program, argc equals the number of command-line arguments *plus one*. (The first argument is a copy of the command issued to run the program.) The argv array points to each entered command string. A simple for loop prints each of that array's entries:

```
for (int i = 1; i < argc; i++)
  cout << argv[i] << endl;
```

That's certainly intuitive, but you will often come across less clear code, such as the following, which relies on pointer arithmetic to do the same job:

```
while (--argc > 0)
  cout << *++argv << endl;
```

The while loop decrements argc and uses the cryptic expression *++argv to address each command-line string. This uses pointer arithmetic to advance argv to each char pointer in the argv array. Although this works, it is functionally equivalent to the former for loop. (However, the while loop requires no additional integer index.) You might also come across argv declared in main() like this:

```
int main(int argc, char **argv)  // ???
```

Because pointers and arrays are equivalent in C and C++, the expressions **argv and *argv[] are the same, and you gain nothing with the more cryptic style. In both instances, argv is literally a pointer to an array of other pointers—of type char * in this case. I mention this fact only to counter the notion that the two declarations are functionally different. They aren't. In all cases, to pick up command-line arguments in main(), use the following declaration style from the sample cmdline.cpp (refer to Listing 11.4):

```
int main(int argc, char *argv[])
```

THE getopt() FUNCTION

Responding to program options is a common and essential feature of most Linux programs. Your software probably needs several options to select among the program's features. Writing code to parse option letters and arguments is unnecessary—just use the standard library's getopt() function to do most of the dirty work along with the main() parameters explained in the preceding section.

The first step in using getopt() is to include the unistd.h header file with the directive:

```
#include <unistd.h>
```

That includes various UNIX and Linux standard function prototypes and global variables. In this case, we are interested in the getopt() function declared in unistd.h as

```
int getopt(int argc, char *argv[], const char *opts);
```

The function's options are the same as received by main() (see the preceding section). Simply pass argc and argv directly to getopt(). The third option is a constant string that specifies to getopt() the program's recognized options. To supply this parameter, you might define a constant such as this:

```
#define OPTIONS "xy:z::"
```

Each letter in the OPTIONS string represents a single option. In this case, the program recognizes three option letters: -x, -y, and -z. A colon indicates that an argument must follow the option. So, in this example, the -y option requires an argument as in the command -y filename. A double colon indicates that an option may or may not be followed by an argument. Here, -z might be followed by a string argument as in -z filename, or it may be used alone. However, due to possible ambiguities illustrated in the next listing, optional arguments should have no preceding spaces. In this case, -yfilename and -y filename are both legitimate options. But, because of the double colon in the -z option's definition, only -zfilename is guaranteed to work. The command -z filename with a space before the argument might be ambiguous.

In addition to defining the getopt() function, including unistd.h defines four related global variables. These are

- int opterr—Equals 1 (false) if getopt() detects an error. In that event, getopt() displays an error message.
- int optind—Equals the index of the argv[] array between calls to getopt().
- int optopt—Equals the value of any unrecognized options.
- char *optarg—Equals a pointer to any argument string following a recognized option—for example, a filename.

The getopt() function returns a value equal to a detected option character, a question mark if an unrecognized option is detected, or -1 if the function is done parsing the command line. Some versions of getopt() also return a value of ':' if a parameter is missing.

Although the info pages for libc include an example of how to use getopt(), the sample code is written in C, not C++. Also, the example fails to detect errors properly, and it evades an ambiguity with the double colon specification in an option string. Listing 11.5, options.cpp, fixes these problems and shows how to use getopt() in C++ code.

LISTING 11.5 OPTIONS.CPP

```
#include <iostream.h>
#include <unistd.h>     // Need getopt()
#include <ctype.h>      // Need isprint()

// Constants.
```

```
// - Options must be single letters.
// - A colon means an option requires an argument.
// - A double colon means an option may have an argument.

#define OPTIONS "xy:z::"          // Option letters
bool xoption, yoption, zoption;  // Program flags
char *yarg = NULL;               // yoption argument
char *zarg = NULL;               // Optional zoption argument

// Function prototypes
void instruct();
void results();

int main(int argc, char *argv[])
{
  char c;  // Returned by getopt()

  // Get known options and any arguments
  //
  while ((c = getopt(argc, argv, OPTIONS)) != -1)
    switch (c) {
      case 'x':
        xoption = true;    // option -x
        break;
      case 'y':
        yoption = true;    // option -y arg
        yarg = optarg;     // arg (required)
        break;
      case 'z':
        zoption = true;    // option -z[arg]
        if (optarg)
          zarg = optarg;   // arg (optional)
        break;
      case '?':
        instruct();        // Display instructions
        exit(1);           // End program
      default:
        cerr << "Error in getopt() function" << endl;
        abort();  // ???
    }

  results();  // Display results

  // Get any other non option entries
  //
  if (argc > optind) {
    cout << "Arguments not found by getopt():" << endl;
    for (int i = optind; i < argc; i++)
      cout << " " << argv[i] << endl;
  }
  return 0;
}

// Display usage instructions
```

continues

PART
II

CH
11

LISTING 11.5   CONTINUED

```
void instruct()
{
  cout << "Options" << endl;
  cout << " -x       -- option" << endl;
  cout << " -y arg   -- option and arg" << endl;
  cout << " -z[arg] -- option (no space!)" << endl;
  cout << " ex. ./options -x -y file -z other strings";
  cout << endl;
}

// Display flags and arguments
void results()
{
  cout << " xoption == " << xoption << endl;
  cout << " yoption == " << yoption << endl;
  if (yoption)
    cout << " yarg    == " << yarg << endl;
  cout << " zoption == " << zoption << endl;
  if (zoption && zarg)
    cout << " zarg    == " << zarg << endl;
}
```

> **Note**
>
> You may use the options.cpp program as a shell for any Linux program to be executed on the command line. After reading the following descriptions of the `getop()` function and its use in options.cpp, simply replace the program's option variables with your own.

Compile and run options.cpp in the usual way, but give it an output filename as follows:

```
$ g++ -o options options.cpp
```

Run the program and feed it some options, along with arguments for the -x and -z options. Of course, all options are merely dummies that do nothing. Enter a command such as this:

```
$ ./options -x -zfilename
 xoption == 1
 yoption == 0
 zoption == 1
 zarg    == filename
```

The program displays the values of three bool flags, which indicate that an option was found (1) or not found (0). In this case, the program also displays the optional argument filename after the -z option. No space may precede this name. However, a space may precede the required -y option argument. Try this command:

```
$ ./options -y filename
 xoption == 0
 yoption == 1
 yarg    == filename
 zoption == 0
```

The program correctly sets yoption to true and yarg to the string filename. If you don't supply the required argument, the program displays an error and shows instructions:

```
$ ./options -x -y
./options: option requires an argument -- y
Options
 -x      -- option
 -y arg  -- option and arg
 -z[arg] -- option (no space!)
ex. ./options -x -y file -z other strings
```

The second line is from getopt(). It explains that -y requires an argument. The rest of the text comes from the options.cpp program itself. Usually, it's a good idea to display similar instructions when getopt() returns an error. Similarly, getopt() displays an error for an unrecognized option letter. Try this:

```
$ ./options -b
./options: invalid option -- b
```

Again, in addition to the error message, the program shows instructions not reprinted here. Using getopt(), you can also detect additional string commands—for example, a series of filenames entered after other options. This is a common format used by many UNIX and Linux disk utilities. Here's one more test entry that shows this feature. Enter this command:

```
$ ./options -x -z file1 file2 file3
 xoption == 1
 yoption == 0
 zoption == 1
Arguments not found by getopt():
 file1
 file2
 file3
```

PART
II

CH
11

The program correctly finds the -x and -z options. It also finds the three filenames at the end of the command line—these are not parsed by getopt(), but by the program itself as I explain in a moment. Notice that the expression -z file1 is ambiguous. Because -z is specified as having an *optional* argument ("z::"), it isn't clear whether file1 belongs to -z or is a separate entry. If file1 is supposed to belong to option -z, the entry must be entered with no blanks as -zfile1. Beware of this GNU quirk—optional arguments are unique to GNU and might not work under other UNIX C++ compilers.

Listing 11.5 shows a good way to specify and note options entered by users. Examine these global declarations:

```
#define OPTIONS "xy:z::"        // Option letters
bool xoption, yoption, zoption; // Program flags
char *yarg = NULL;              // yoption argument
char *zarg = NULL;              // Optional zoption argument
```

The OPTIONS constant specifies the recognized commands to getopt(). As mentioned, -x is a loner, -y requires an argument, and -z may have an argument, but it's not required. Each of the three bool flags indicates whether a specific option is entered. For instance, yoption is true if getopt() detects -y on the command line. The two char pointers, yarg and zarg, address any arguments entered after -y and -z.

Flags such as xoption and yoption are best made global variables so that other functions in the program can inspect them and respond appropriately. For example, a help function might display additional text if a flag, voption, is set to true by the user entering -v, usually meaning "verbose."

To parse a command line, a while loop in the sample program calls a long switch statement. Minus its guts, the code looks like this:

```
while ((c = getopt(argc, argv, OPTIONS)) != -1)
  switch (c) {
    ...
  }
```

Technically, getopt() returns an int value, but you may assign it to a char variable as done here. The while loop executes as long as getopt() does not return -1, indicating that it is finished parsing. Simply pass main()'s argc and argv parameters to getopt() along with the program's recognized options. You don't have to use a switch statement to examine getopt()'s results, but it's probably the best choice in most cases. Inside the switch, case statements set the program's flags for detected option letters. For example, the first case in the sample program sets xoption to true if getopt() finds the -x option on the command line:

```
case 'x':
  xoption = true;    // option -x
  break;
```

Similarly, the case for option -y sets its associated flag to true, but it also picks up the required argument that follows -y:

```
case 'y':
  yoption = true;    // option -y arg
  yarg = optarg;     // arg (required)
  break;
```

If the user types -y myfile.txt or -ymyfile.txt, the preceding code sets yoption to true and yarg to the address of the string "myfile.txt". Because an argument is required, the optarg pointer (from unistd.h) is guaranteed to address a string. However, optional arguments are best programmed as follows:

```
case 'z':
zoption = true;    // option -z[arg]
if (optarg)
  zarg = optarg;   // arg (optional) break;
```

The test for a non-NULL optarg might be unnecessary, but it can't hurt. To respond to unrecognized arguments, add a case for a question mark, returned by getopt() if it finds any -x arguments not in the OPTIONS parameter:

```
case '?':
  instruct();    // Display instructions
  exit(1);       // End program
```

It's your choice what to do with unrecognized arguments, but it's usually a good idea to display instructions and bail out as suggested here. If getopt() returns '?', the user is either confused or typed something incorrectly. Proceed with caution.

> **Note**
>
> The info example for getopt() shows some rigmarole for displaying errors depending on whether an unrecognized letter is printable (isprint() from ctype.h returns true). This is unnecessary because GNU's getopt() at that stage has already displayed an error message about the unrecognized option. Perhaps that's not the case in all UNIX systems, but it is in GNU C++ for Linux. If getopt() returns a question mark, all you need to do is display instructions and call exit() as shown here.

A final switch-statement case, although recommended by getopt()'s documentation, is also probably unnecessary. It costs little, however, and is probably wise to include in production code:

```
default:
  cerr << "Error in getopt() function" << endl;
  abort();  // ???
```

If the program gets to this code, something is wrong with getopt(). Careful testing ought to ensure those statements never execute, but it pays to play safe.

Finally, the options.cpp program demonstrates how to recognize any additional nonoption entries such as in the following command:

```
$ ./options -x -z file1 file2 file3
```

The getopt() function does *not* detect the three filenames—it detects only the -x and -z option letters. Following the while and switch statements in options.cpp, if argc is greater than the global variable optind (the current argv[] index as set by getopt()), then there are additional entries still awaiting processing. You can pick them up with a for loop such as this:

```
for (int i = optind; i < argc; i++)
  cout << " " << argv[i] << endl;
```

OTHER MEMORY MATTERS

Internally, the GNU C++ memory manager keeps track of allocated memory blocks, and it performs the actual task of reserving memory when the program uses new. The memory manager links deleted blocks into a list, from which new fulfills allocation requests. Except in programs that reprogram new to use different methods, behind the scenes, the GNU C++ memory manager handles all memory allocations and deletions.

There's no need to understand exactly how the memory manager works, but some of its limitations might be important to you. You might also want to construct code that examines memory blocks, perhaps for debugging purposes. By digging through the compiler sources, I found the following limitations in GNU C++:

- A pointer's size is fixed at 4 bytes regardless of the system's integer or register size.

- Memory blocks are aligned on 8-byte boundaries. This means that a given block's address is evenly divisible by 8. Because a memory block's address is not the same as its associated pointer, this means that pointer address values are *not* similarly aligned.

- The minimum size of an allocated memory block is 16 bytes. Of those bytes, 12 are available to the program, and 4 are reserved for the memory manager's use.

- The maximum size of an allocated memory block is 2,147,483,640 bytes, or $(2^{31} - 8)$ bytes. This restriction apparently exists because of the possibility that size_t could be signed. What a shame that we can create only two billion byte objects and not four billion. (Can you see my straight face?)

- The minimum overhead attached to every memory block is 4 bytes. However, because of block alignment, the actual size of the memory allocation is not equal to four plus the size of the object. It is equal to that value *plus* whatever amount is required to fill the allocation to its minimum alignment.

- The size of a memory block is stored in the 4 reserved bytes just ahead of (at a lower address than) the pointer address value that the program receives from new.

Each allocated memory block has a structure defined by a struct, malloc_chunk, declared as follows:

```
struct malloc_chunk {
  size_t size;              // Size in bytes including overhead
  struct malloc_chunk* fd; // Forward link; start of user data
  struct malloc_chunk* bk; // Backward link
  size_t unused;   // Padding to minimum block size (16 bytes)
};
```

When a program calls new to obtain dynamic memory, the returned pointer actually address-es a location 4 bytes into this structure, at the location of the fd member. While a memory block is in use by the program, only the struct's size member is valid. The program's data fills the rest of the structure starting at fd (except for any unused space at the end of the allocation).

When a program calls delete, the memory manager overwrites the first several bytes of data in the block by creating a record of struct malloc_chunk that links the block into a circular list. The link addresses are stored in the record's fd and bk members, and for this reason, after you delete a dynamic object, the first 8 bytes of its former value are obliterated.

Warning

Never upon pain of serious bugs use a memory allocation after it has been deleted!

DEBUGGING DYNAMIC MEMORY

The GNU debugger has several commands that are useful for examining a program's dynamic memory allocations. The following sections explain these commands and show how to use them to poke around in memory. This operation is not for the faint of heart, but certainly possible. I also explain how to debug a main() function's argc and argv parameters.

DEBUGGING POINTERS

Debugging pointers is similar to debugging other kinds of variables, but you often need to consider whether to examine the pointer value itself or the addressed data. Sometimes you want both. To learn some useful commands for examining pointer data, compile and load this chapter's newstr.cpp program with the commands:

```
$ g++ -g -o newstr newstr.cpp
$ gdb newstr
```

Set a breakpoint on the following statement (it's at line 21 for me)

```
const char *cp = get_string("Enter a string: ");
```

and then run the program:

```
(gdb) b 21
Breakpoint 1 at 0x804881e: file newstr.cpp, line 21.
(gdb) run
```

When the breakpoint hits, the program stops and shows the statement next scheduled to execute.

```
Breakpoint 1, main () at newstr.cpp:21
21          const char *cp = get_string("Enter a string: ");
```

Execute the statement by typing a *next* command, and then enter a string when prompted:

```
(gdb) next
Enter a string: Test string
24          cout << "String : " << cp << endl;
```

Again, the program halts, in this case at line 24. To examine the pointer and addressed string assigned to cp, use a *print* command:

```
(gdb) print cp
$1 = 0x8049da8 "Test string"
```

The debugger assigns a temporary alias $1 to the variable and shows you the address value held in the cp pointer. The debugger also shows you the addressed data—in this case, the string you entered. The debugger knows what type of data to display based on the pointer's type. To see that type, use a *ptyp* command as follows. This tells you that cp is a char pointer (char *):

```
(gdb) ptyp cp
type = char *
```

> **Tip**
>
> To repeatedly display a pointer, use the command *display cp*. Now, every time the program pauses, the debugger shows you the value of cp and the data it addresses. This works for any type of variable, not only pointers.

DEBUGGING ADDRESSED DATA

Another command, tersely named x, inspects data anywhere in memory. The command is particularly useful for looking microscopically at the bytes in buffers and the characters in strings. If you are following along from the preceding section, skip the following commands; otherwise, enter them now:

```
$ g++ -g -o newstr newstr.cpp
$ gdb newstr
(gdb) b 24
(gdb) run
Enter a string: Test string
```

As mentioned, you can type a *print* command to inspect the string assigned to cp at this place in the program:

```
(gdb) print cp
$1 = 0x8049da8 "Test string"
```

Note the address that the debugger reports. To inspect in excruciating detail the bytes at that address, use an x command. For example, to view the addressed string in hexadecimal, enter this command:

```
(gdb) x/12h cp
0x8049da8:      0x6554  0x7473  0x7320  0x7274  0x6e69
                0x0067  0x0251  0x0000
0x8049db8:      0x0000  0x0000  0x0000  0x0000
```

That displays 12 two-byte words in hexadecimal at the address held in cp. If you want, you can enter the address itself. This is usually more tedious than entering a variable name, but is useful for poking around. For example, to examine one byte at the address in cp and display the results in binary, use the following command (instead of the address shown, use the one for cp shown on your screen):

```
(gdb) x /1bt 0x8049da8
0x8049da8:      01110100
```

To display 12 characters at cp, enter the following command:

```
(gdb) x/12c cp
0x8049da8:      84 'T'  101 'e' 115 's' 116 't' 32 ' '
                115 's' 116 't' 114 'r'
0x8049db0:      105 'i' 110 'n' 103 'g' 0 '\000'
```

The x command follows this general format:

```
x /FMT ADDRESS
```

A FMT specification may have up to three parts: a size in bytes, a format letter, and a size letter. Table 11.1 details these elements.

TABLE 11.1 DEBUGGER x COMMAND FMT SPECIFICATIONS

Format Letter	Format	Size Letter	Format
a	address	b	byte (1 byte)
c	char	g	giant (8 bytes)
d	decimal	h	halfword (2 bytes)
f	floating point	w	word (4 bytes)
i	instruction		
o	octal		
s	string		
t	binary		
u	unsigned decimal		
x	hexadecimal		

Use the x command to inspect a number of bytes of memory, in a specific format, and showing each element in a specified size. For example, to examine eight halfword (2-byte) values and show the values in decimal, use a command such as

```
(gdb) x /8dh 0x8049da8
0x8049da8:     25940    29811    29472    29300    28265
               103      593      0
```

> **Note**
> The GNU debugger doesn't permit examining addresses that do not belong to the debugged process. If you enter the preceding address, it almost certainly fails with a "Cannot access memory" error. Load a program such as newstr.cpp and use a variable such as cp as explained in this section to experiment with the x options in Table 11.1.

DEBUGGING PROGRAM OPTIONS

Because the GNU debugger recognizes its own options, as do most Linux programs, attempting to load a program with a command such as the following fails to produce expected results:

```
$ gdb options -x -y filename
```

That causes the debugger to complain with an error message:

```
-y: No such file or directory.
```

To compile the options.cpp program and load it with options into the debugger requires additional steps. First compile and load the program, but do not specify any program options:

```
$ g++ -g -o options options.cpp
$ gdb options
```

To gdb's prompt, enter a ***run*** command along with the options you want the loaded program to recognize. For example, type this command:

```
(gdb) run -x -y filename
Starting program: /src/c11/options -x -y filename
```

The GNU debugger responds with the command used to start the process, along with any options and arguments you specify in the run command. To run the program again, just type ***run***—the debugger reuses the last known set of command-line arguments. To change arguments, you can specify new ones with another run command, or use the ***set args*** command like this:

```
(gdb) set args -f -q
(gdb) run
Starting program: /home/tswan/mgcc/src/c11/options -f -q
/home/tswan/mgcc/src/c11/options: invalid option -- f
...
Program exited with code 01.
```

In this case, I specified unknown arguments -f and -q, causing the program to display an error message and end by calling exit(1).

DEBUGGING main() ARGUMENTS

To inspect main()'s argc and argv options, do *not* set a breakpoint on the main() function's header—the parameters are at that point not yet initialized. Instead, set a breakpoint at the first statement inside main(). For example, using the options.cpp program, set a breakpoint at line 35 and run (or continue) with these commands:

```
(gdb) b 35
Breakpoint 2 at 0x804879f: file options.cpp, line 35.
(gdb) run
```

When the program reaches the specified breakpoint, the GNU debugger halts it and displays something like this:

```
Breakpoint 2, main (argc=3, argv=0xbffffa9c) at options.cpp:35
35          while ((c = getopt(argc, argv, OPTIONS)) != -1)
```

The value of argc equals the number of command-line arguments plus one because the first argument is always the command that started the process. The argv address isn't meaningful, but you can use argv to inspect specific arguments. For example, enter a ***display*** command as follows to inspect the second string addressed by argv:

```
(gdb) display argv[1]
2: argv[1] = 0xbffffb82 "-f"
```

SUMMARY

C++ provides the new and delete operators for allocating and deleting dynamic memory objects. Such objects use memory efficiently and, in general, are preferred over global variables and large local objects in functions. You may use standard C memory management techniques—calling malloc() for example—in C++ programs; however, you should not mix C and C++ memory techniques. This chapter explained how to use new and delete, and also showed methods for creating dynamic arrays and strings that take only as much room as needed. The chapter also explained related techniques for accessing arguments passed to main() and included an example in C++ for sophisticated command-line parsing with the standard C library's getopt() function. The chapter ended with suggestions for debugging pointers and dynamically allocated memory.

For more information on subjects introduced in this chapter, turn to the following chapters:

- Chapter 13, "Creating and Destroying Objects"
- Chapter 16, "Handling Exceptions"
- Chapter 19, "Overloading Operators"
- Chapter 22, "Mastering the Standard string Class"

PART III

OBJECT-ORIENTED PROGRAMMING

## CHAPTER 12

INTRODUCING THE CLASS

You'd have to be living face down in a moon crater not to have heard about object-oriented programming, or OOP, as it is comically known. OOP is the programming paradigm of the future, the model (some say) upon which all the world's software soon will be built. Whether that's true or not, there's no denying the value of OOP in constructing and maintaining complex software applications, and those who ignore OOP risk missing the major contribution of C++ to programming—the *class*.

If this is your initial exposure to OOP, don't be concerned if its advantages elude you at first. C++ lets you learn object-oriented programming techniques at your own speed. Unlike so-called "pure" OOP languages such as Smalltalk, C++ is a hybrid programming language that combines conventional and object-oriented methods. This means that you can use what you already know about conventional C and C++ while you learn how to program with classes and objects. Three concepts distinguish OOP from conventional programming:

- Encapsulation
- Inheritance
- Virtual functions

In this chapter and the next, you learn how to create classes using encapsulation to marry data and functions in objects. You also learn some of the reasons classes and object-oriented programming help you write code that works reliably and is easy to maintain. The rest of the chapters in Part III introduce inheritance and virtual functions along with practical object-oriented programming techniques using GNU C++.

WHY USE OBJECT-ORIENTED PROGRAMMING?

Object-oriented programming and C++ classes help reduce complexity, especially in large software applications. One reason this is true is because OOP encourages programmers to reuse existing code rather than rewrite functions from scratch. Reusing code doesn't mean cutting and pasting source code text. With objects, you build new programming by *inheriting* existing, compiled C++ classes.

Reusing code is far more difficult with conventional programming languages such as C and Pascal. Conventional C programmers, for example, typically rewrite the same functions over and over because *it's too much trouble to reuse existing, tested modules.* C++ classes are easy to reuse and extend, and well-written C++ programs tend to evolve from existing modules the way trees grow by extending their branches. Rather than replant low-level code into every new program, with OOP you write programs that grow naturally from your current crop of tested modules.

INTRODUCING THE CLASS

Simply stated, a class is an object-oriented tool for creating new data types that you can use in much the same way as native C++ types such as char, int, and double. A class *encapsulates* data and functions. It is a special kind of struct that specifies data and the functions that operate on that data.

Comparing a simple struct and a class is a good way to learn the basics of creating classes and objects. Listing 12.1, olddate.cpp, shows the tried-and-true, but older, conventional way of representing date values using a struct and a function.

LISTING 12.1   OLDDATE.CPP

```cpp
#include <iostream.h>

// Conventional struct
struct date {
  int dt_month;
  int dt_day;
  int dt_year;
};

// Function prototype
void display_date(date &dt);

int main()
{
  // Create and display a date struct conventionally
  date dt;
  dt.dt_day   = 4;
  dt.dt_month = 11;
  dt.dt_year  = 2000;
  display_date(dt);
  return 0;
}

// A conventional function that displays dt's members
void display_date(date &dt)
{
  cout << "Date: "
       << dt.dt_month << "/" << dt.dt_day
       << "/" << dt.dt_year << endl;
}
```

PART

III

CH

12

The program declares a struct named date with three integer members for holding the month, day, and year. To display this data, the program also declares a function, display_date(), with a date struct reference parameter. The main() program creates a date struct variable named dt with the following declaration:

```cpp
date dt;
```

It then assigns values to the struct's members and displays the resulting date using statements such as

```cpp
dt.dt_day = 4;
...
display_date(&dt);
```

Passing the initialized dt struct object by reference to the display_date() function writes it to the standard output. Onscreen, after compiling and running the program, you see the following:

```
$ g++ olddate.cpp
$ ./a.out
Date: 11/4/2000
```

There's nothing wrong with conventional programming as demonstrated here. However, the program's code and data are tightly intertwined, and this can be a common source of bugs and maintenance woes. For example, if the internal representation of a date needs changing, every use of the date struct has to be found and fixed. This is one reason the infamous Y2K bug is so difficult to repair in older software.

Now, take a look at the object-oriented way to create a class for representing and displaying dates. Listing 12.2, newdate.cpp, produces the same output as olddate.cpp, but it encapsulates date values and an output function into a C++ class.

LISTING 12.2   NEWDATE.CPP

```cpp
#include <iostream.h>

// A class that encapsulates data and functions
class TDate {
private:
  int dt_month;
  int dt_day;
  int dt_year;
public:
  TDate(int month, int day, int year);
  void Display();
};

int main()
{
  TDate dt_object(11, 4, 2000);  // Construct a class object
  dt_object.Display();           // Tell object to display itself!
  return 0;
}

// The TDate class constructor
TDate::TDate(int month, int day, int year)
{
  dt_month = month;   // Assign values to private data members
  dt_day = day;
  dt_year = year;
}

// The TDate class Display member function
void TDate::Display()
{
  cout << dt_month << "/" << dt_day << "/" << dt_year << endl;
}
```

The class declaration for TDate looks much like a struct, but it contains a few new elements in addition to the three int members, dt_month, dt_day, and dt_year. The reserved word class begins the declaration, followed by the class name, TDate, and a pair of braces that delimit the class's contents. As do all declarations in C and C++, a class declaration ends with a semicolon. Most classes follow a similar design, outlined as follows:

```
class TAnyClass {
private:
  // private class members
public:
  // public class members
};
```

Note

In many of this book's listings, and in my own programs, I capitalize class names such as TDate and TAnyClass, and precede them with capital T, meaning "type." Capitalization is optional, but I like to use it to distinguish object-oriented classes from other elements.

The word private: with a colon is called an *access specifier*. It indicates that the following declarations—the three int members in this case—are private to the class. Only members of this class, and no other statements anywhere else, may read or write the values of these private members. The word public:, another access specifier, declares items to which users of the class have full access. Under either access specifier may appear one or more function prototypes or data declarations. (You meet a third access specifier, protected:, when you learn about inheritance in Chapter 14, "Investing in Inheritance.") The private, protected, and public sections in a class may come in any order, and you can repeat sections of the same type as many times as you want.

Note

If no access specifier is stated, class members are private by default. Members of structs and unions are public by default. You may use access specifiers in C++ structs, but this is rarely of much practical value.

In the sample program, the public: access specifier starts a new section in TDate. In that section, the class prototypes two functions:

```
public:
  TDate(int month, int day, int year);
  void Display();
```

The first function declaration is called a *constructor*. It is named the same as the class, TDate, but has no return type. Optionally, as shown here, a constructor may declare parameters that are used to initialize objects of the class. In this case, the TDate constructor requires values that represent a date's month, day, and year. The next prototype is Display(), a *member function*. Its form is the same as a conventional function prototype. Like all functions, member functions can return values, receive arguments, and declare default parameters, and they may have any legal names. They differ from conventional functions in only one way—they are expected to operate in some fashion on an object of the class. To create such an object, you might use a statement like this:

```
TDate dt_object(11, 4, 2000);
```

That constructs an object named `dt_object` of the `TDate` class. The three integer values are passed to the `TDate()` constructor, which performs whatever steps are necessary for initializing the object. Although the sample `TDate` class has only one constructor, classes may declare multiple constructors for initializing objects in different ways.

> **Note**
>
> As with functions, in this book, empty parentheses after a class name refer to its constructor. `TDate` without parentheses refers to the class declaration as a whole. `TDate()` refers to the `TDate` constructor.

The second statement in the sample program displays the value of a `TDate` object. It uses *dot notation* to specify the class member function to call for a specific object, also sometimes called an *instance* of the class. The following statement calls `Display()` in association with `dt_object`:

```
dt_object.Display();
```

In object-oriented parlance, that statement *commands* `dt_object` to display itself. The object can do that because `Display()` is a function that a `TDate` class object knows how to perform. In the coming chapters, you learn how to use this important OOP concept to create class family trees for building objects that perform actions based on their types, a concept that goes by the fancy name *polymorphism*.

At this point, you might not appreciate the reasons for designating class members private or public and using member functions instead of conventional code. But these are key principles that make object-oriented programming well-suited for managing large software projects. By privatizing data, access to that data is isolated and controlled through the class's public member functions. This makes data-prone bugs less likely while also simplifying debugging. If something goes wrong with a private data member, the cause is almost certainly in a class member function. Even better, changes to internal data representations do not affect the class's users.

PROGRAMMING WITH CLASSES AND OBJECTS

Learning to program with classes and objects requires many programmers to take a mental turn around a logical corner, especially if they are familiar with conventional techniques. For many, the moment of revelation comes with a practical understanding of what a class is and how to use it to design data types for creating objects.

A good way to think about classes and objects is to envision a class as a unit that specifies what an object is and what it does. Classes describe the potential capabilities of objects, just as the native type double describes the nature of a floating point value. A double is not itself a floating point value; a double is a *type* of value. Similarly, a class describes the type of an object. To use a class, the program must construct an object of the class, just as it constructs variables of native types. To handle these construction details, a class implements a *constructor*.

CONSTRUCTORS

Beneath the hood, constructors are class member functions like any others. However, they have the special purpose of initializing new objects of a class. As you have seen, the sample newdate.cpp program declares a prototype for the TDate() constructor in the class's public section:

```
class TDate {
...
public:
  TDate(int month, int day, int year);
};
```

Like any function prototype, this one for TDate() states the constructor's name and any parameters. The constructor code is implemented elsewhere (but see "Inline Constructors" later in this chapter for another method). Because constructors do not return values, their implementations might strike you as odd. For example, newdate.cpp implements TDate's constructor like this:

```
TDate::TDate(int month, int day, int year)
{
  ...
}  // No semicolon here
```

The class name is the first element. It is followed by the C++ scope resolution operator :: and the constructor's function name plus any parameters. Because class and constructor names are always the same, the declaration appears redundant. However, you are not seeing double—the expression TDate::TDate() refers unambiguously to the TDate class constructor named TDate().

The constructor's purpose is to initialize an object of its class. In this case, the TDate() constructor assigns its three integer parameters—month, day, and year—to the class's three private data members using these statements:

```
dt_month = month;
dt_day = day;
dt_year = year;
```

Each constructed object of the class has its own set of those data members, to which the constructor can refer directly as shown here. When the program executes this statement

```
TDate dt_object(11, 4, 2000);
```

the TDate() constructor assigns the three values—11, 4, and 2000—to the dt_object's data members, dt_month, dt_day, and dt_year. The program is free to create as many TDate objects as required using statements such as

```
TDate birthday_paul(5, 18, 1962);
TDate birthday_susan(8, 12, 1970);
```

Each object such as `birthday_paul` and `birthday_susan` has its own separate instances of the `TDate` class data members `dt_month`, `dt_day`, and `dt_year`. In each case, the class constructor initializes the objects by copying the specified arguments to the objects' data members.

Warning

When writing constructors, be careful not to create any objects of the class type in the constructor implementation. If you do, the constructor might end up calling itself over and over in an endless recursion—endless, that is, until the program runs out of memory and aborts with a core dump!

MEMBER FUNCTIONS

A common misconception is that objects *contain* functions such as `Display()`. They don't. Objects contain only data. Constructors and member functions belong to their classes, and only one copy of each member function and constructor exists in the compiled program.

A member function's implementation is similar to that of a conventional function's. For example, the newdate.cpp program implements the `TDate` class's `Display()` member function like this:

```
void TDate::Display()
{
  cout << dt_month << "/" << dt_day << "/" << dt_year << endl;
}
```

The function return type, `void` in this example, comes first. Second is the name of the class that declares the function prototype. The C++ scope resolution operator `::` comes next, followed by the function name and any parameters (there are none in this example). Finally, a pair of braces delimits the function's statement block inside of which are the statements that perform the function's job.

Except for the class name and scope resolution operator, the member function's implementation is the same as a conventional function's. The class name and operator uniquely identify this function as belonging to its class. Together, the expression `TDate::Display()` fully identifies the member function. Consequently, another class may have a `Display()` member function without causing any name conflicts.

Note

To identify a class member function in this book, I use the form `TDate::Display()` only when the name of the function alone is ambiguous.

There's another less obvious difference between a member function and a conventional one. Because member functions are called in conjunction with an object of the class, they can operate on that class's data members without any further qualification. In the `Display()` member function, for instance, this statement displays the object's three integer members:

```
cout << dt_month << "/" << dt_day << "/" << dt_year << endl;
```

The dt_month, dt_day, and dt_year variables are inside the object for which Display() is called. The statement can refer directly to the object's data members because, hidden from view at the source code level, member functions receive a pointer called this that points to the object. To verify that this exists, and to illustrate its purpose, the following statement calls Display() for dt_object in which dt_month, dt_day, and dt_year values reside:

```
dt_object.Display();
```

Less obviously, that statement passes to Display() a this pointer that locates dt_object in memory. It is possible to use this in a member function statement. For example, Display() could execute the following statement:

```
cout << this->dt_month << "/"
     << this->dt_day   << "/"
     << this->dt_year << endl;
```

The this pointer addresses the object for which a member function or constructor is called. You can compile the preceding code—this is a reserved word in C++, and you may use it in member functions to refer to objects. However, most often, you can more simply refer to data members such as dt_month without using this. In a member function, if dt_month is a member of the class, the expression dt_month and this->dt_month are equivalent.

Note

A typical use for this is for an object to pass itself to another function, or to return itself as a function result, but these are advanced techniques to be introduced in Part IV, "Advanced C++ Techniques."

CONSTRUCTING OBJECTS

Beginners to OOP and C++ often fret about how to declare class objects. The different methods are easily remembered by comparing them to the ways for creating variables of native C++ types. Consider these five common methods for creating floating point variables of type double, some of which you might not have seen before:

```
double f1;             // Declare simple variable
double f2 = 3.14159;   // Declare and initialize variable
double f3(3.14159);    // Same as above
double f4(f3);         // Declare f4 and initialize with f3
double f5 = f4;        // Declare f5 as a copy of f4
```

The first declaration declares a variable named f1 of type double. If this declaration is global, f1 is initialized to zero. If the declaration is local to a function, f1 is uninitialized. The second declaration assigns a literal value to another double variable, f2. As you probably know, the first two declarations shown here are the most common ways to create simple variables of native C++ types, and you've seen numerous examples of these techniques in prior chapters.

The third declaration initializes f3 to the literal value 3.14159. The second and third declarations are functionally the same, but the former is more common. The fourth declaration creates f4 and copies to the new variable the value of f3. The fifth declaration declares f5 as a copy of f4. The last two declarations are functionally the same.

You may construct class objects in each of these same ways, using nearly identical statements. Listing 12.3, construct.cpp, demonstrates five ways to construct class objects of a slightly modified TDate class.

LISTING 12.3   CONSTRUCT.CPP

```cpp
#include <iostream.h>

// A class that encapsulates data and functions
class TDate {
private:
  int dt_month;
  int dt_day;
  int dt_year;
public:
  TDate();
  TDate(int month, int day, int year);
  void Display();
};

int main()
{
  TDate t1;                          // Requires default constructor
  TDate t2 = TDate(12, 31, 1999);    // Impractical, but allowed
  TDate t3(1, 1, 2000);              // Uses parameterized constructor
  TDate t4( t3 );                    // Makes t4 a copy of t3
  TDate t5 = t4;                     // Copies t4 into t5

  t1.Display();  // Call member function for each object
  t2.Display();
  t3.Display();
  t4.Display();
  t5.Display();

  return 0;
}

// The TDate class default constructor
TDate::TDate()
{
  dt_month = 0;        // Initialize private data members to zero
  dt_day = 0;
  dt_year = 0;
}

// The TDate class parameterized constructor
TDate::TDate(int month, int day, int year)
{
  dt_month = month;    // Assign values to private data members
  dt_day = day;
  dt_year = year;
}
```

```
// The TDate class Display member function
void TDate::Display()
{
  cout << dt_month << "/" << dt_day << "/" << dt_year << endl;
}
```

The program constructs five TDate objects, t1 through t5, and then calls the Display() member function for each. The following statement constructs an object named t1 of the TDate class:

```
TDate t1;
```

This is one of the most common ways to construct a class object, and the method is exactly the same as declaring an uninitialized object of any other type such as a double variable:

```
double f1;
```

However, when the type is a class, it must have a *default constructor* to handle the creation of objects declared with no argument values. (More on this in the section "The Default Constructor" later in this chapter.)

The sample program demonstrates a second, but impractical, way to construct an object. Although it's unlikely you'll ever use this method, it demonstrates the important concept of a *temporary object*. This statement:

```
TDate t2 = TDate(12, 31, 1999);  // ???
```

is roughly equivalent to the common conventional statement:

```
double f2 = 3.14159;
```

That's a common way to create and initialize objects of simple types such as double, but when using classes, the preceding TDate object construction causes the program to work harder than necessary. This is because the expression to the right of the assignment operator creates a temporary TDate object, which is then copied to a new TDate object t2. The temporary object exists only as long as needed, and it is automatically destroyed after its value is copied to t2. As I explain in Chapter 13, "Creating and Destroying Objects," temporary objects are troublesome and can lead to bugs. It's usually best to avoid creating temporary objects if possible.

A third way to construct a class object, and one of the most common, is to pass arguments to a parameterized constructor. The following statement uses this method to construct a TDate object named t3 initialized to the date 1/1/2000:

```
TDate t3(1, 1, 2000);
```

That calls the TDate class's parameterized constructor, which assigns the three integer arguments to the object's data members—dt_month, dt_day, and dt_year. The statement is exactly equivalent to the native type declaration:

```
double f3(3.14159);
```

As you can with C++ native types, you may also declare and initialize objects using the values of compatible objects. Objects are assignment-compatible if they are of the same class.

(They may also be of related classes, as Chapter 14, "Investing in Inheritance" explains.) The following statement creates a TDate object named t4 using a copy of t3's value:

```
TDate t4( t3 );
```

That creates a new object, t4, and copies to it the value of t3. The statement is equivalent to the following native type declaration, which creates a double variable f4 and assigns to it the value of f3:

```
double f4(f3);
```

The fifth and final method for constructing a class object also copies one object to another:

```
TDate t5 = t4;
```

That creates a new TDate object, t5, equal to the value of t4. This is exactly the same as the preceding method but uses the more intuitive assignment operator. It is exactly equivalent to the native type statement:

```
double f5 = f4;
```

THE DEFAULT CONSTRUCTOR

A default constructor has no parameters and, like all constructors, is named the same as its class. In the sample construct.cpp program, the TDate() default constructor is implemented separately as follows (I moved the individual statements to one line to save space here):

```
TDate::TDate()
{
  dt_month = 0;  dt_day = 0;   dt_year = 0;
}
```

Elsewhere in the program, creating an object with no arguments calls the default constructor, which assigns zero to each data member in the object. The default TDate() constructor makes possible declarations such as

```
TDate t1;
```

That calls the TDate() default constructor to initialize the t1 object. Unlike native type variables, however, this happens whether or not the preceding declaration is inside a function—a subtle but important difference between declarations of class objects and those of native types. Class objects are *always* initialized by a constructor. A native type variable that is local to a function is uninitialized until assigned a value.

THE COPY CONSTRUCTOR

Statements that cause one object to be copied to a newly created object call a special constructor known as the *copy constructor*. This happens when you create objects using statements such as the following (remember, however, the third statement, although allowed, is impractical because it wastefully creates a temporary object):

```
TDate t4(t3);
TDate t5 = t4;
TDate t2 = TDate(12, 31, 1999);  // ???
```

It is the copy constructor's job to copy an object's value to a new object. Usually, all that's needed is to transfer the source object's data members to the target's, and if the class does not explicitly declare a copy constructor, C++ automatically generates one that does the job. This doesn't necessarily mean that the compiler writes code for you, but if the class does not declare a copy constructor, the compiler generates instructions that, in these examples, copy byte for byte the data members from one TDate object to another.

A related operation occurs when assigning one object to another. For example, this statement:

```
t5 = t1;
```

copies t1's data members to t5. To do that, the compiler generates instructions that copy all data bytes from the source object to the target. However, because the two objects were previously constructed, this does *not* call the copy constructor. Constructors are called only the first time a new object comes into being.

> **Note**
>
> For simple classes such as TDate, the automatically generated copy constructor and assignment instructions work just fine. However, when you need more sophisticated copying mechanisms—for example, if the class has any dynamic-memory pointers—you must implement a copy constructor explicitly and provide for assignments of one object to another. See "Copy Constructors" in Chapter 13, "Creating and Destroying Objects," for more on these topics.

INLINE CONSTRUCTORS

A common practice is to declare and implement constructors directly in the class declaration. Rather than prototype constructors in the class and then implement them separately, the class includes both the function prototype and its statements. Listing 12.4, inline.cpp, demonstrates how to declare and implement constructors in a new version of the TDate class.

PART
III
CH
12

LISTING 12.4   INLINE.CPP

```
#include <iostream.h>

// A class that encapsulates data and functions
class TDate {
private:
  int dt_month;
  int dt_day;
  int dt_year;
public:
  TDate() {dt_month = 0; dt_day = 0; dt_year = 0;}
  TDate(int month, int day, int year)
  {
    dt_month = month;   // Assign values to private members
```

continues

Listing 12.4 Continued

```cpp
    dt_day = day;
    dt_year = year;
  }
  void Display();
};

int main()
{
  TDate t1;                         // Requires default ctor
  TDate t2 = TDate(12, 31, 1999);  // Impractical, but allowed
  TDate t3(1, 1, 2000);             // Uses parameterized ctor
  TDate t4( t3 );                   // Makes t4 a copy of t3
  TDate t5 = t4;                    // Copies t4 into t5

  t1.Display();  // Call member function for each object
  t2.Display();
  t3.Display();
  t4.Display();
  t5.Display();

  return 0;
}

// The TDate class Display member function
void TDate::Display()
{
  cout << dt_month << "/" << dt_day << "/" << dt_year << endl;
}
```

The modified TDate class's default constructor is declared and implemented directly in the class:

```cpp
public:
  TDate() {dt_month = 0; dt_day = 0; dt_year = 0;}
```

This format might seem strange at first, but it is merely a shorthand version of C++ source code that you could write in long form like this:

```cpp
public:
  TDate()
  {
    dt_month = 0;
    dt_day = 0;
    dt_year = 0;
  }  // No semicolon here!
```

Compare both versions character for character and you'll see they are identical (except for the comment). Notice especially the placement of semicolons, which as always, terminate statements, and never follow a compound statement block's closing brace.

The parameterized constructor is also declared and implemented directly in the TDate class using the code:

```
public:
...
  TDate(int month, int day, int year)
  {
    dt_month = month;    // Assign values to private members
    dt_day = day;
    dt_year = year;
  }
```

The parameterized constructor implementation assigns its parameter values to the three TDate data members, dt_month, dt_day, and dt_year. The function is written in the conventional style with each statement on a separate line.

You might optionally preface constructors and other member functions with the inline reserved word, but when implementing constructors and functions directly in a class, this isn't necessary. In GNU C++, inline constructors and member functions are expanded in line with the program's code only when compiled with at least the first level of optimization. To enable inline expansion, compile and run the inline.cpp program using the following commands (the option letter is a capital O, not a zero):

```
$ g++ -O inline.cpp
$ ./a.out
```

Warning Inline constructors can produce more efficient code, but it's best to limit the technique to relatively simple constructors. Constructors that perform complex tasks are best prototyped in the class and then implemented separately along with other member functions.

OVERLOADED CONSTRUCTORS

As you can with common functions, you can overload a class's member functions and constructors by giving them the same names but declaring parameters of different types. Because all constructors are named the same as their classes, they are overloaded by default. Most classes have several overloaded constructors that provide different ways to initialize class objects. For example, the TDate class from the preceding section declares two overloaded constructors in the class's public section:

```
public:
  TDate();
  TDate(int month, int day, int year);
```

This is a typical design. The class has a default constructor, in this case named TDate(), and one or more overloaded parameterized constructors also named the same as the class. The default constructor takes care of initializing objects for which the program specifies no arguments. Other constructors handle initializations using argument values. For example, the following statements create two TDate objects:

```
TDate today;
TDate yesterday(4, 5, 2001);
```

The first statement calls the TDate() default constructor. The second calls the class's parameterized constructor. This common class design is perfectly acceptable, but frequently, you can combine the two types of constructors by using default parameters, as Listing 12.5, default.cpp, demonstrates. For illustration, the new TDate class also fully declares and implements its constructor and member function inline.

> **Note**
>
> The word "constructor" is often abbreviated as "ctor." This isn't a reserved word—you can't use it in programs—but you'll often see the abbreviation in references and comments.

LISTING 12.5   DEFAULT.CPP

```
#include <iostream.h>

// A fully implemented class
class TDate {
private:
  int dt_month;
  int dt_day;
  int dt_year;
public:
  TDate(int month = 0, int day = 0, int year = 0)
    {dt_month = month; dt_day = day; dt_year = year;}
  void Display()
    {cout << dt_month << "/"
          << dt_day   << "/"
          << dt_year  << endl;}
};

int main()
{
  TDate default_date;            // Calls default ctor
  default_date.Display();
  TDate tomorrow(4, 5, 2001);    // Calls parameterized ctor
  tomorrow.Display();
  return 0;
}
```

The revised TDate() constructor serves as both the default and parameterized constructor. The class declares and implements the constructor like this:

```
TDate(int month = 0, int day = 0, int year = 0)
  {dt_month = month; dt_day = day; dt_year = year;}
```

If that seems confusing, write the statements out on separate lines. Because the new constructor declares default values for all three parameters—month, day, and year—it serves as both the default and parameterized constructors. When main() constructs this object:

```
TDate default_date;
```

the program calls the constructor as though that statement were written like this:

```
TDate default_date(0, 0, 0);
```

Likewise, the program's second object calls the same constructor, but this time with literal argument values:

```
TDate tomorrow(4, 5, 2001);
```

Using default parameter values to create a default class constructor is a common C++ technique that you will encounter often. When using the method in your own programs, be sure to understand that, when all parameters have default values, the class may not also declare a default constructor with no parameters. The following does not compile:

```
public:
  TDate();
  TDate(int month = 0, int day = 0, int year = 0); // ???
```

This common error confuses the compiler because it cannot decide which constructor should initialize objects declared as

```
TDate today;  // ???
```

That fails because of the rule that overloaded constructors and other functions must differ in at least one parameter type. To resolve the conflict and return to having two separate constructors, one solution is to specify default values for all but one parameter in the alternate constructor. For example, you can fix the preceding declaration by changing it to

```
public:
  TDate();
  TDate(int month, int day = 0, int year = 0);
```

In the parameterized constructor, the month value is now required, but the day and year are optional. The default and parameterized constructors differ in at least one parameter, and constructing TDate objects using the following statements is now possible:

```
TDate t1;              // Calls default TDate() constructor
TDate t2(4);           // Calls parameterized constructor
TDate t3(4, 5);        // Calls parameterized constructor
TDate t4(4, 5, 2000);  // Calls parameterized constructor
```

PART

III

CH

12

DEBUGGING CLASS OBJECTS

The GNU debugger can display the values of class data members, and it can trace member functions, just as well as it can perform those tasks for conventional variables and functions. Following are sample runthroughs of debugging sessions using one of the programs in this chapter. Use the commands described here to examine your own class objects, and also for investigating other object-oriented programs in this book.

Note　Line numbers shown here might differ onscreen if you are following along.

To prepare a sample program for debugging, compile the construct.cpp program from this chapter, and then load it into the GNU debugger using these commands:

```
$ g++ -g -o construct construct.cpp
$ gdb construct
```

Type *L* (list) until you find the declaration of TDate t1, and notice the line number, probably 27. Set a breakpoint at that line to halt the code before the object's construction. Type the command following the (gdb) prompt as shown here:

```
(gdb) break 27
Breakpoint 1 at 0x80486ce: file construct.cpp, line 27.
```

Next, run the program up to the breakpoint. The debugger shows you the statement next to be executed (I deleted some comments to make it fit on this page):

```
(gdb) run
Starting program: /src/c12/construct
Breakpoint 1, main () at construct.cpp:27
27   TDate t1;
```

Examine the value of t1 before it is constructed by using the *print* command:

```
(gdb) print t1
$1 = {dt_month = 1073783640, dt_day = 1, dt_year = 0}
```

You might be surprised to discover that you can examine a class object before it is constructed. This is possible because memory is allocated to the local object t1 before that object is initialized. Until then, the three data members in the TDate class have essentially randomized values that are probably different on your system. To complete the object's construction, issue a *next* command to execute the statement that constructs the object:

```
(gdb) next
28   TDate t2 = TDate(12, 31, 1999);
```

Again, the debugger shows you the next statement to be executed. Before continuing, examine t1 again:

```
(gdb) print t1
$2 = {dt_month = 0, dt_day = 0, dt_year = 0}
```

Now, as you can see, the object's data members are properly initialized. To trace into the constructor for the next object, use the *step* command:

```
(gdb) step
TDate::TDate (this=0xbffffa70, month=12, day=31, year=1999) \
at construct.cpp:53
53   dt_month = month;   // Assign values to private data members
```

Stepping into a constructor is the same as stepping into a conventional function, but you issue the *step* command at an object's creation. The debugger tells you several important pieces of information. It gives the constructor's name TDate::TDate() and shows all its parameter values. The first value is this, equal to the memory address in hexadecimal of the object's location—TDate t2 in this case. The values of the other parameters are also shown.

Continue with the sample program by typing four *next* commands to get out of the constructor and return to the main program (press the up-arrow key to repeat the commands quickly):

```
(gdb) next
54   dt_day = day;
(gdb) next
```

```
55   dt_year = year;
(gdb) next
56   }
(gdb) next
main () at construct.cpp:29
29   TDate t3(1, 1, 2000);
```

Now that object t2 is completely constructed, a *print* command shows its value:

```
(gdb) print t2
$3 = {dt_month = 12, dt_day = 31, dt_year = 1999}
```

Type *cont* to continue the program to its end:

```
(gdb) cont
Continuing.
0/0/0
12/31/1999
1/1/2000
1/1/2000
1/1/2000
Program exited normally.
```

You can then quit the debugger and return to a console prompt:

```
(gdb) quit
$
```

SUMMARY

This chapter introduced some of the basics and advantages of object-oriented programming, or OOP as it is known. In this chapter, you learned how to create and use classes to encapsulate data and code. The chapter also explained several different ways to construct and use class objects, and how to debug their data, constructors, and member functions.

For more information on subjects introduced in this chapter, turn to the following chapters:

- Chapter 10, "Creating and Calling Functions"
- Chapter 13, "Creating and Destroying Objects"
- Chapter 14, "Investing in Inheritance"
- Chapter 21, "Honing Your C++ Skills"

PART

III

CH

12

CREATING AND DESTROYING OBJECTS

The preceding chapter introduced the class and showed several ways to construct class objects. However, the simple classes you have seen so far are not of much practical use. In the real world of programming, classes need more sophisticated devices for safely allocating and destroying dynamic memory, and for passing objects efficiently to and from functions.

This chapter introduces those topics, and ends with a version of the TDate class that encapsulates some of the functions and data types of the standard library's date and time routines. Along the way, the chapter explains techniques for using a *destructor* to clean up objects when they are destroyed, for managing dynamic memory using copy constructors, and for using something called the operator=() member function to copy one object to another. Finally, the chapter ends with advice for declaring and implementing classes in separate modules.

DESTROYING CLASS OBJECTS

As the preceding chapter explained, class constructors initialize newly created class objects. On the flipside of that coin, it is also frequently necessary to destroy objects in a controlled manner. For example, when an object owns a pointer that addresses dynamic memory, the program must delete that memory when the object itself is destroyed. To perform that and other cleanup duties, a class declares a *destructor*.

INTRODUCING THE DESTRUCTOR

Like a constructor, a destructor has the same name as its class but is preceded with the character ~, used in scientific circles and sometimes in programming as a negation symbol. A destructor is, in a sense, the negation of a constructor—what a constructor builds, a destructor destroys. To illustrate destructors, the following code fragment declares a bare-bones class with constructor and destructor prototypes:

```
class TAnyClass {
public:
  TAnyClass();    // Constructor
  ~TAnyClass();   // Destructor
};
```

If the program declares a TAnyClass object, as in the following statement, the class constructor is called to initialize that object:

```
TAnyClass an_object;  // Calls the TAnyClass() constructor
```

When an_object goes out of scope—for example, when its declaring function returns—the object is destroyed. At that time, C++ automatically calls the ~TAnyClass() destructor to give the object the opportunity to perform any cleanup chores before it is tossed away for good. C++ calls the destructor also if the program creates a dynamic TAnyClass object with new operator and then deletes the object:

```
TAnyClass *tp = new TAnyClass;  // Calls TAnyClass() ctor
// ... statements that use the object
delete tp;  // Calls the ~TAnyClass() dtor
```

When the program executes the `delete` statement, C++ calls the `~TAnyClass()` destructor. In that function, statements can perform any cleanup duties needed before the object's memory is returned to the heap.

Note

Like the word constructor (ctor), destructor is often abbreviated "dtor." This isn't a reserved word, but you'll often see it in comments and C++ references.

USING POINTERS TO ADDRESS OBJECTS

Although programs can declare an object as a local or global variable, it is equally if not more common to create an object in dynamic memory and address it with a pointer. For example, this statement declares a pointer to an object of `TAnyClass` from the preceding section:

```
TAnyClass *object_pointer;
```

That declares `object_pointer` as a pointer to an object of the type `TAnyClass`. The object does not yet exist—all the program has done is declare a pointer of a type that *can* address an object of the stated type. Create the object by using the C++ `new` operator:

```
object_pointer = new TAnyClass;
```

Assuming that enough memory is available, `object_pointer` now addresses an initialized object of type `TAnyClass`. It's also common to combine the preceding two steps into one:

```
TAnyClass *object_pointer = new TAnyClass;
```

Either way, the class's constructor initializes the object, after which the object is available for use via the pointer. If `TAnyClass` has a member function named `DoSomething()`, this statement calls the function:

```
object_pointer->DoSomething();
```

The member-dereference operator `->` refers to an item in the object to which `object_pointer` points. Contrast that with a statement that calls `DoSomething()` for a global or local class object:

```
TAnyClass any_object;        // Declare object
any_object.DoSomething();   // Call member function
```

With a dynamic object addressed by a pointer, use the `->` operator to refer to a member of the object's class. With a local or global object, use a period (dot notation). As you must for all dynamic variables, be sure to delete a dynamic class object after you are finished using it. In general, dynamic objects are created, used, and deleted with code such as this:

```
TAnyClass *object_pointer = new TAnyClass;  // Create object
object_pointer->DoSomething();              // Use object
delete object_pointer;                      // Delete object
```

The first statement declares a pointer to a `TAnyClass` dynamic object and uses the `new` operator to create that object by calling its default constructor. The second statement calls a class

PART

III

CH

13

member function using the pointer to address the dynamic object. The last statement deletes the object by using the `delete` operator and specifying the pointer that was earlier assigned the result of `new`. At this time, the class's destructor, if it has one, performs any cleanup operations before the object's memory is sent to that great memory pool in the sky.

Tip

Operator `new` throws an exception if it can't fulfill a request for memory. See Chapter 16, "Handling Exceptions," for advice on how to deal with this condition.

DYNAMIC OBJECTS

You may create dynamic objects of any class. For example, Chapter 12, "Introducing the Class," declared several versions of TDate for representing the date. Listing 13.1, dynadate.cpp, is similar to the construct.cpp program in Chapter 12, but shows two of the most common ways for creating, using, and deleting dynamic class objects addressed by pointers. (To save space here, the listing shows only the class declaration and main() function, not the duplicated code from construct.cpp.)

LISTING 13.1 DYNADATE.CPP (PARTIAL LISTING)

```cpp
#include <iostream.h>

// A class that encapsulates data and functions
class TDate {
private:
  int dt_month;
  int dt_day;
  int dt_year;
public:
  TDate();
  TDate(int month, int day, int year);
  void Display();
};

int main()
{
  // Construct object and call the default constructor
  TDate *tdp1 = new TDate;    // Construct object
  tdp1->Display();            // Call a member function
  delete tdp1;                // Delete the object

  // Construct object and call the parameterized constructor
  TDate *tdp2 = new TDate(8, 12, 1996);  // Construct object
  tdp2->Display();            // Call a member function
  delete tdp2;                // Delete the object

  return 0;
}
```

The `main()` function shows the two most common ways to construct dynamic objects. The first method declares a pointer named `tdp1` and assigns to it the address of a new, dynamic object created by the `new` operator:

```
TDate *tdp1 = new TDate;
```

Because no parameters are specified, that statement calls the `TDate()` default constructor to initialize the object, which in this example, sets the date's data members to zero. Following that, another statement calls the `Display()` member function for the dynamic object:

```
tdp1->Display();
```

Because a pointer addresses the object, the `->` operator is used to access class members. When the program is finished using the dynamic object, it deletes it using the following statement:

```
delete tdp1;
```

Similarly, the sample program creates a second `TDate` object, but this time the following statement calls the parameterized constructor to initialize the object to the date August 12, 1996:

```
TDate *tdp2 = new TDate(8, 12, 1996);
```

Although shown here as one statement, the two actions of declaring and initializing the pointer `tdp2` can be (and often are) divided into separate steps:

```
TDate *tdp2;                       // Declare pointer
tdp2 = new TDate(8, 12, 1996);   // Construct object
```

Merely declaring the pointer does not construct an object. To do that, the program calls `new` as shown and assigns the result to the pointer. The resulting object is used and then deleted in the same way as before:

```
tdp2->Display();  // Call a member function
delete tdp2;      // Delete the object
```

In both instances, the `delete` operator destroys the dynamic object allocated by `new`. If the `TDate` class declares a destructor (the sample class doesn't), it is called at this time to perform any cleanup duties before the object's memory is linked into the available memory pool.

As with all pointers, after deleting a pointer to a dynamic class object, never use that pointer *except* to address a newly constructed object. For example, you can add this code to the sample program's `main()` function just before the `return` statement:

```
tdp1 = new TDate(1, 1, 2001);
tdp1->Display();
delete tdp1;
```

The first line reuses the `tdp1` pointer to address a newly constructed dynamic object of the `TDate` class. Here again, after the program is finished using the dynamic object, it is deleted. Following the `delete` statement, the `tdp1` pointer must not be used in any way except to address another newly constructed object.

USING POINTERS IN CLASSES

Using pointers to address dynamic class objects is only half the story of classes and dynamic memory. A class object may also own other dynamic objects of classes with their own rules of creation and destruction. To illustrate, consider the following hypothetical class, declared and implemented entirely inline:

```
class TAnyClass {
private:
  TDate *tdp;
public:
  TAnyClass() { tdp = new TDate(1, 1, 2000); }
  ~TAnyClass() { delete tdp; }
};
```

The class declares a private pointer, tdp, to a TDate object. Because tdp is private, only statements in the class's member functions may refer to tdp. The object that tdp addresses is created when the TAnyClass object is constructed, a task handled in this case by the TAnyClass() constructor. The constructor's inline statement uses new to construct a TDate object and assign it to the private tdp pointer.

The class destructor deletes the memory that the constructor allocates, and in this way, the memory allocated to tdp is neatly managed. When the program constructs a TAnyClass object, the constructor allocates memory for a TDate object addressed by tdp. When the TAnyClass object goes out of scope or is deleted, the destructor deletes the TDate object addressed by tdp. The class carries out its memory management responsibilities so that the users of the class don't have to attend to these details.

> **Note**
>
> You may question whether the delete statement shown here might mistakenly delete an uninitialized tdp pointer. However, that can't happen because, if new cannot fulfill the request for memory, it throws an exception and the TAnyClass object is *not* constructed. (In general, exceptions thrown in a constructor result in the object not being constructed.) Consequently, because the object is not constructed, its destructor is never called, so even if the use of new fails here, there is no danger of deleting an uninitialized pointer. See Chapter 16, "Handling Exceptions," for details on this topic.

CLASS MEMORY MANAGEMENT

Listing 13.2, prompt.cpp, puts the preceding concepts to work and shows how to manage dynamic memory owned by a class object. The program declares a class that encapsulates the get_string() function from Chapter 11, "Managing Memory with Pointers." The result is a class that you can use to create an object for prompting and storing a line of text entered by the program's user. By encapsulating this code in a class, the constructor and destructor automate memory allocations, whereas in the original code, memory management is the user's responsibility.

Note

Although the TPrompt class in the prompt.cpp program works, it lacks features that provide for safe copying of objects. The next section explains how to fix this problem.

LISTING 13.2   PROMPT.CPP

```cpp
#include <iostream.h>
#include <string.h>        // Need strcpy()

// A class that prompts users to enter a string
class TPrompt {
private:
  char * tp_string;  // Addresses the string input
public:
  TPrompt(const char *prompt);  // Constructor
  ~TPrompt();                   // Destructor
  const char *GetString();      // Returns user's input
};

int main()
{
  // Use the class to construct a local object
  TPrompt prompt1("Prompt #1: ");
  cout << "You entered " << prompt1.GetString() << endl;

  // Use the class to construct a dynamic object
  TPrompt * prompt2 = new TPrompt("Prompt #2: ");
  cout << "You entered " << prompt2->GetString() << endl;
  delete prompt2;

  return 0;
}

// Constructor
TPrompt::TPrompt(const char *prompt)
{
  const int buf_size = 128;        // Size of input buffer
  char *temp = new char[buf_size]; // Create input buffer
  cout << prompt;                  // Prompt user for input
  cin.getline(temp, buf_size);     // Read input from user
  tp_string = new char[strlen(temp) + 1]; // Create string
  strcpy(tp_string, temp);         // Copy buffer to result
  delete[] temp;                   // Delete the buffer
}

// Destructor
TPrompt::~TPrompt()
{
  cout << "Entering destructor for string "
      << tp_string << endl;
  delete[] tp_string;
}
```

PART

III

CH

13

continues

Listing 13.2 Continued

```
// Member function
const char *TPrompt::GetString()
{
  return tp_string;
}
```

In the original code from which I created the TPrompt class, the get_string() function returns a pointer to a dynamic string, allocated in memory by the C++ new operator. Calling the function places the responsibility of deleting that memory on the user. For example, with the original function, you might use statements such as

```
const char *cp = get_string("Enter a string: ");
// ... other statements
delete[] cp;
```

If you forget the delete[] statement, the memory allocated to the string can become lost in space, creating a memory leak that might cause the program to abort with that lovable old friend, a core dump. By encapsulating get_string() in a class, memory management is automatic, and this type of bug can't occur.

To encapsulate the original code, the TPrompt class declares one private data member, a char pointer named tp_string. Because the member is private to the class, only class members may use it. In addition, the class declares a constructor TPrompt() and destructor ~TPrompt(). The constructor code is the same as in the original get_string() function, but instead of returning a char pointer, it saves the user's input string in a memory buffer addressed by the private tp_string pointer. To use the class, the program constructs an object in the usual way with the following statement:

```
TPrompt prompt1("Prompt #1: ");
```

This creates an object, named prompt1, of the TPrompt class, and calls the class constructor to display a message and wait for the user to enter a string. Member function GetString() returns a const pointer to the input string, used here to confirm your typing:

```
cout << "You entered " << prompt1.GetString() << endl;
```

GetString() returns a const char pointer. This copies the address of the privately owned dynamic memory out of the object, but because it is declared const, the class user—that is, the preceding two statements—can't alter that memory.

Warning

> GNU C++ reports the modification of data addressed by a const string pointer as a warning rather than an error. Apparently, this was done to accommodate existing code that uses this questionable technique.

Because the TPrompt class carefully controls the use of its private data, the class assumes all responsibility for managing the object's dynamic memory. To ensure that this memory is properly deleted when an object such as prompt1 goes out of scope or is deleted, C++ calls the class destructor for that object. Take a look at the destructor's programming:

```
TPrompt::~TPrompt()
{
  cout << "Entering destructor for string "
       << tp_string << endl;
  delete[] tp_string;
}
```

As with constructors and member functions, the destructor's header specifies the class name (TPrompt), the C++ scope resolution operator (::), and the function's name, ~TPrompt(). Unlike constructors and member functions, destructors may not declare any parameters. A destructor also has no return value. You may implement destructors inline directly in the class declaration, or you can implement a destructor as shown here independently of its prototype in the class.

Tip

A class may have one and only one destructor. If you need to have different ways to destroy class objects, use flags or values that the destructor's code can inspect and take action accordingly.

For illustration, the ~TPrompt() destructor displays a message so that you can trace when it is called in the sample program, but the second statement is all that's needed. It deletes the memory allocated to tp_string. Because the class destructor is called automatically when a TPrompt object goes out of scope, the destructor ensures that the allocated memory is also deleted. If you haven't done so already, compile and run the program, and observe when the destructor is called for the program's two sample input prompts. Here's a sample run:

```
$ g++ prompt.cpp
$ ./a.out
Prompt #1: aaaa
You entered aaaa
Prompt #2: bbbb
You entered bbbb
Entering destructor for string bbbb
Entering destructor for string aaaa
```

To the first prompt, I typed *aaaa*. To the second, I typed *bbbb*. In both cases, the object's destructors are called to delete the memory allocated to the input strings. The last two lines show that, in both cases, the ~TPrompt() destructor cleans up the objects before they are themselves destroyed.

COPY CONSTRUCTORS

The preceding version of the TPrompt class is not entirely safe for use. To understand why, consider what happens if you create two dynamic TPrompt objects tp1 and tp2 using the following statements (refer back to Listing 13.2, prompt.cpp):

```
TPrompt tp1("Enter first string:  ");
TPrompt tp2("Enter second string: ");
```

So far, so good. The statements construct two TPrompt objects, tp1 and tp2, and prompt the user to enter two strings. But think about what happens if the program copies one of those objects to the other:

```
tp1 = tp2;   // ???
```

That may look innocent enough—it is perfectly acceptable to the compiler—but the assignment causes the tp_string pointer in tp2 to be copied to the tp_string pointer in tp1. Now both pointers address the same memory, causing not one but two bugs. The original tp_string pointer in tp1 is overwritten—its addressed memory is lost in space. Worse, because both pointers now address the same dynamic memory, when the two objects go out of scope, the ~TPrompt() destructor attempts to delete the identical dynamic memory block twice. That leads to a dreaded "segmentation error" by attempting to access memory the program doesn't own, and the process ends abruptly with—you guessed it—a core dump.

To prevent this kind of problem, as a general rule, any objects that own dynamic memory need to provide programming to handle the copying of one object to another. There are two times that this can occur:

- When a new object is constructed using another object
- When one object is assigned to another

To handle these situations, the class needs two new functions. The *copy constructor* creates a new object using the value of another existing object of the same class. (They may also be of related classes, as Chapter 14, "Investing in Inheritance," explains.) The second needed function, named operator=(), handles assignments of one existing object to another that has already been constructed. Both functions use similar code. In general, a copy constructor has the following form:

```
TAnyClass(const TAnyClass &copy);
```

Like all constructors, the copy constructor is named the same as its class, and it has no return value. Its single parameter is a const reference to an object of the same class. C++ calls the copy constructor for objects created using statements such as the second two here:

```
TAnyClass t1;        // Calls default constructor for t1
TAnyClass t2 = t1;   // Calls copy constructor for t2
TAnyClass t3(t2);    // Calls copy constructor for t3
```

The first statement calls the TAnyClass() default constructor to initialize an object, t1. The second statement creates a second object, t2, equal to a copy of t1. This calls the class's copy constructor. The third statement is functionally the same as the second—it, too, calls the copy constructor to create a new object, t3, as a copy of an existing object, t2.

The copy constructor is free to do whatever is necessary to ensure that the copied objects are properly initialized. For example, if the object being copied owns any dynamic memory, the copy constructor might duplicate that memory so that the error of deleting the same memory twice can't occur.

Another related function has an unusual design that you meet again in Chapter 19, "Overloading Operators." It usually looks like this:

```
void operator=(const TAnyClass &copy);
```

The equal sign isn't used as an operator but merely as part of the function's name, `operator=()`. In a class, the function `operator=()` handles assignments that involve objects of the class. The `operator=()` function returns `void`, and it requires a single argument, a const reference to an object of the same class that declares the function. C++ calls the `TAnyClass::operator=()` function for statements such as

```
t1 = t3;   // Calls operator=()
```

Like the copy constructor, the `operator=()` function ensures that copying one object to another is done safely—for example, by duplicating any dynamic memory pointers. Listing 13.3, copyops.cpp, puts the foregoing concepts together in a simple test program that demonstrates when C++ calls a copy constructor and `operator=()` function.

LISTING 13.3   COPYOPS.CPP

```cpp
#include <iostream.h>

// A simple class
class TAnyClass {
public:
  TAnyClass();                          // Default constructor
  TAnyClass(const TAnyClass &copy);   // Copy constructor
  void operator=(const TAnyClass &copy); // Copy function
};

int main()
{
  TAnyClass t1;        // Calls default constructor for t1
  TAnyClass t2 = t1;   // Calls copy constructor for t2
  TAnyClass t3(t2);    // Calls copy constructor for t3
  t1 = t3;             // Calls operator=() member function
  return 0;
}

// Default constructor implementation
TAnyClass::TAnyClass()
{
  cout << "Inside default constructor" << endl;
}

// Copy constructor implementation
TAnyClass::TAnyClass(const TAnyClass &copy)
{
  cout << "Inside copy constructor" << endl;
}

// Overloaded operator=() member function implementation
void TAnyClass::operator=(const TAnyClass &copy)
{
  cout << "Inside operator=() member function" << endl;
}
```

I often write test programs such as copyops.cpp with functions that do nothing more than write a string to the standard output. This provides an informative trace of when each function is called, as in the following sample run. Enter these two commands to see the program's output:

```
$ g++ copyops.cpp
$ ./a.out
Inside default constructor
Inside copy constructor
Inside copy constructor
Inside operator=() member function
```

The program declares a class, TAnyClass, with a default constructor, a copy constructor, and an operator=() member function. The main() function creates and copies objects using these statements:

```
TAnyClass t1;
TAnyClass t2 = t1;
TAnyClass t3(t2);
t1 = t3;
```

Each statement produces one line of text onscreen. The first statement constructs object t1 by calling the TAnyClass() default constructor. The second statement constructs a new object, t2, as a copy of t1. This calls the TAnyClass() copy constructor. The third statement constructs object t3 as a copy of t2, and also calls the copy constructor. The fourth statement assigns an existing object t3 to another, t1. Because the two objects already exist, no constructor is called. However, because TAnyClass implements an operator=() function, C++ calls it to handle the assignment.

The preceding code merely demonstrates the forms of copy constructors and operator=() member functions. Using these tools, it is now possible to create a safe TPrompt class that provides for safely copying class objects. Listing 13.4, prompt2.cpp, shows the resulting program.

LISTING 13.4   PROMPT2.CPP

```
#include <iostream.h>
#include <string.h>      // Need strlen(), strcpy()

// A class that prompts users to enter a string, and also
// provides for safe copying

class TPrompt {
private:
  char * tp_string;  // Addresses the string input
public:
  TPrompt(const char *prompt);          // Constructor
  TPrompt(const TPrompt &copy);         // Copy constructor
  ~TPrompt();                           // Destructor
  void operator=(const TPrompt &copy);  // Assignment operator
  const char *GetString();              // Returns user input
};

int main()
{
```

```
  // Use the class to construct a local object
  TPrompt prompt1("Prompt #1: ");
  cout << "You entered " << prompt1.GetString() << endl;

  // Construct another object
  TPrompt prompt2("Prompt #2: ");
  cout << "You entered " << prompt2.GetString() << endl;

  // Test copy constructor
  TPrompt prompt3(prompt2);
  cout << "Prompt 3    " << prompt3.GetString() << endl;

  // Test operator=() function
  prompt1 = prompt3;
  cout << "Prompt 1    " << prompt1.GetString() << endl;

  return 0;
}

// Constructor
TPrompt::TPrompt(const char *prompt)
{
  const int buf_size = 128;          // Size of input buffer
  char *temp = new char[buf_size];   // Create input buffer
  cout << prompt;                    // Prompt user for input
  cin.getline(temp, buf_size);       // Read input from user
  tp_string = new char[strlen(temp) + 1];  // Create string
  strcpy(tp_string, temp);           // Copy buffer to result
  delete[] temp;                     // Delete the buffer
}

// Copy constructor
TPrompt::TPrompt(const TPrompt &copy)
{
  tp_string = new char[strlen(copy.tp_string) + 1];
  strcpy(tp_string, copy.tp_string);
}

// Destructor
TPrompt::~TPrompt()
{
  delete[] tp_string;   // Delete dynamic memory
}

// Assignment operator
void TPrompt::operator=(const TPrompt &copy)
{
  if (this == &copy) return;     // Avoid copying self to self
  delete[] tp_string;            // Delete old data
  tp_string = new char[strlen(copy.tp_string) + 1];
  strcpy(tp_string, copy.tp_string);
}

// Member function
const char *TPrompt::GetString()
{
  return tp_string;
}
```

The revised TPrompt class declares a copy constructor and operator=() member function that, together, safely handle copying of TPrompt objects. The class's copy constructor uses the new operator, strlen(), and strcpy() functions to create a duplicate of a dynamic string addressed by copy.tp_string:

```
tp_string = new char[strlen(copy.tp_string) + 1];
strcpy(tp_string, copy.tp_string);
```

Inside the copy constructor, the copy parameter refers to the source TPrompt object that is being copied. Each object—the one being copied and the new one being constructed—has a tp_string pointer. Using strlen() and strcpy(), the preceding statements ensure that each object addresses a fresh copy of dynamic memory.

Note

C programmers might use a single strcpy() statement to copy a string, but because that does not use the C++ new operator to allocate memory, it would require calling free() to dispose of the allocated memory. To use new and delete for memory management, I used two statements to perform the string copy.

A statement such as the following calls the copy constructor:

```
TPrompt prompt3(prompt2);   // Calls copy constructor
```

The prompt2 object, the one being copied, is passed by reference to the copy constructor's copy parameter. The copy constructor in turn passes copy.tp_string to strlen() and strcpy() to allocate memory and copy the string. Because there are now two equivalent strings in memory, when prompt3 and prompt2 go out of scope, the TPrompt destructor deletes their pointers. Because those pointers address different memory blocks, no segmentation error occurs.

Likewise, the TPrompt::operator=() function handles assignments of one TPrompt object to another. The function is similar to a copy constructor, but because both objects already exist, the function's statements need to perform some additional tasks:

```
if (this == &copy) return;   // Avoid copying self to self
delete[] tp_string;          // Delete old data
tp_string = new char[strlen(copy.tp_string) + 1];
strcpy(tp_string, copy.tp_string);
```

This is one case when the this pointer is needed. As you might recall, this addresses the object for which a constructor, member function, or destructor is called. In this case, this refers to the object on the left of an assignment operator—in other words, the target object to which the copy is being assigned. In the preceding code fragment, the if statement tests whether the program is assigning the *same* object to itself—a dumb mistake, to be sure, but certainly possible in a complex program with hundreds or more objects whizzing around in memory. In that case, the operator=() function simply returns because, if both objects are the same, there's nothing to copy.

If the two objects are different, the function deletes any existing memory addressed by the target object's tp_string pointer. That pointer is about to be assigned new data from the source object, so its data is no longer needed. The next two statements are the same as in the copy constructor. They call `strlen()` and `strcpy()` to duplicate the copy's string data. Now statements such as the following are safe:

```
prompt1 = prompt3;
```

Given that statement, C++ calls the `TPrompt::operator=()` function to perform the copy. In this case, the `operator=()` function makes a fresh copy of the dynamic memory owned by `prompt3` and saves that copied data's address in `prompt1`. When the two objects go out of scope, C++ calls the `~TPrompt()` destructor for each object. Because the objects' pointers address unique memory blocks, no error occurs.

> **Note**
>
> The preceding discussion shows the most fundamental ways to provide safe construction and copying of objects that own dynamic memory. The techniques work fine, but they can waste memory by needlessly duplicating equivalent data. Other methods are possible that work more efficiently but are more difficult to program. For example, rather than duplicating copied memory blocks, an object can store a reference count of its owners and actually delete the dynamic memory when that count indicates it is the only referenced copy left. Another variation on this theme is known as the "copy on write method." For details on programming both techniques, see Chapter 21, "Honing Your C++ Skills."

INITIALIZING DATA MEMBER OBJECTS

Many classes declare data members that are themselves objects of classes. In general, there are two techniques you can use for this:

- Declare pointers to class objects
- Declare class objects as variables

Which method to use depends on your needs. So far, you have examined sample classes that use the first method, employing pointers to address object data members. You may also declare class objects as variables inside classes. For example, the following hypothetical class declares a `TDate` object as a private data member:

```
class TAnyClass {
private:
  TDate the_date;    // Class object data member
public:
  TAnyClass();       // Default constructor
};
```

As explained, if a class declares a pointer as a data member, it can use the `new` operator in the constructor to initialize the pointer. But a different method is required for initializing a class object declared, not as a pointer, but as a variable such as `the_date`. The technique seems to confuse everyone at first. To clear up the mystery, first take a look at a simple example in Listing 13.5, coords.cpp, that explains the basics of this method, using a demonstration class, `TCoordinate`.

LISTING 13.5   COORDS.CPP

```cpp
#include <iostream.h>

class TCoordinate {
private:
  int tc_x, tc_y;
public:
  // Inline constructors
  TCoordinate(): tc_x(0), tc_y(0) { }
  TCoordinate(int x, int y): tc_x(x), tc_y(y) { }
  // Member function
  void Display();
};

int main()
{
  TCoordinate tc(100, 200);
  tc.Display();
  return 0;
}

void TCoordinate::Display()
{
  cout << "x == " << tc_x << "; y == " << tc_y << endl;
}
```

Examine the two constructors in the sample program's TCoordinate class, which simply stores two integer values in private data members tc_x and tc_y. The constructors are written differently from those you have seen so far in this book. The default constructor is declared and implemented inline as follows:

```cpp
TCoordinate(): tc_x(0), tc_y(0) { }
```

The two *initializing expressions*—tc_x(0) and tc_y(0)—set the two data members to zero. The expressions come between the constructor name and its statement block, preceded by a colon. Separate two or more initializing expressions with commas. In this example, the constructor's statement block is empty, but it may perform other actions. Compare the preceding with a constructor written in the more familiar way:

```cpp
TCoordinate()
{
  tc_x = 0;
  tc_y = 0;
}
```

Functionally, the two constructors are the same. Each sets the two data members—tc_x and tc_y—to zero. Another example shows how the parameterized constructor uses initializing expressions to assign other values to the class's private data members:

```cpp
TCoordinate(int x, int y): tc_x(x), tc_y(y) { }
```

Again, a colon precedes the two initializing expressions, separated by a comma, and followed by the constructor's statement block, empty in this example. The initializing expressions set tc_x to the value of x, and tc_y to the value of y. The statement block is empty because the constructor has no other tasks to perform, but it may execute other statements if needed. The equivalent constructor could be written using the more familiar programming:

```
TCoordinate(int x, int y)
{
  tc_x = x;
  tc_y = y;
}
```

In simple classes like TCoordinate, either method is perfectly acceptable, and both techniques produce the same end results. You may use initializing expressions or statements to initialize data member values. However, consider again our hypothetical class that declares a data member as a TDate object:

```
class TAnyClass {
private:
  TDate the_date;    // Class object data member
public:
  TAnyClass();       // Default constructor
};
```

The question is, how can the class initialize the_date? As you know, all objects must be initialized by calling a class constructor. But, when you try to implement the TAnyClass constructor, you run head-on into a brick wall:

```
public:
  TAnyClass() { the_date //...???
```

To initialize the_date requires calling a TDate class constructor, but it's not possible to call constructors as common functions, and the programmer is stuck. The solution, as you might already suspect, is to use an initializing expression to construct the_date. The completed class follows:

```
class TAnyClass {
private:
  TDate the_date;  // A class object data member
public:
  TAnyClass(): the_date(2, 1, 2001) { }
};
```

The initializing expression (notice the colon) constructs the_date, in this case, by calling the TDate() parameterized constructor. This is, in fact, the *only* way you can initialize data members in a class that are themselves objects of classes.

> **Tip**
>
> You may use initializing expressions for data members of any type; they are required, however, only for initializing data members that are themselves objects of C++ classes.

You may use initializing expressions also when implementing constructors separately from their prototypes. Declare the preceding class as follows:

```
class TAnyClass {
private:
```

```
    TDate the_date;   // A class object data member
public:
    TAnyClass();      // Default constructor prototype
};
```

Elsewhere in the program, implement `TAnyClass()` using initializing expressions, typically indented under the constructor declaration header like this:

```
TAnyClass::TAnyClass(): // A colon means "initializers follow"
  the_date(2, 1, 2001)  // Initialize the_date data member
{
  // ... Other statements to initialize this TAnyClass object
}
```

Here again, the constructor has no other actions to perform, and so its statement block is empty. The second line is all that's needed to initialize `the_date` object. This technique also ensures that objects such as `the_date` are fully constructed before they are used—for example, in a statement inside the constructor's body.

OBJECTS OF MANY FLAVORS

At this point, you should have a good understanding of how to construct objects as global and local variables, and also how to create dynamic objects addressed by pointers. You also know how to declare objects and object pointers as class data members. The following sections introduce a few other ways to construct objects as function parameters and return values, and in arrays—techniques that require some extra care.

PARAMETER CLASS OBJECTS

You may pass class objects to common and class member functions. Suppose that you write a function to which you want to pass a `TDate` object. You might implement the function like this:

```
void any_function(TDate td)
{
  td.Display();
}
```

Function `any_function()` declares a single parameter `td` of the `TDate` class. A statement in the function calls the `TDate` class member function `Display()` for an object passed in `td`. The program might construct a `TDate` object and call `any_function()` with these statements:

```
TDate today(3, 4, 1999);  // Construct object
any_function(today);      // Pass object by value to function
```

However, be careful here. Because the `TDate` object `td` is passed by value to the function, behind the scenes, a *copy* of that object is passed to the function's parameter. Worse, that copy is temporary. It is created automatically, and then deleted when `any_function()` returns. If the `TDate` class declares a destructor, it is called when the temporary object is deleted. All these hidden actions waste many processor cycles merely to pass an object to a function. If the object is very large, precious stack space is also wasted.

Warning

The creation of temporary objects can cause serious bugs if those objects own any dynamic memory pointers and their classes do not provide a copy constructor, a mistake that is easy to make when declaring class objects as function parameters.

Although there is nothing technically wrong with passing copies of objects to functions, it is usually safer and more efficient to pass them as references or pointers. Here's a sample function that declares its parameter as a pointer to a TDate object:

```
void any_function(TDate *tdp)
{
  tdp->Display();
}
```

No matter how large a TDate object is, this function operates efficiently simply because pointers are relatively small. Inside the function, however, statements must use pointer dereferencing to access the object's public class members. The user must also pass an address value, not an object, to any_function(). For example, the following statements construct an object and then pass it by address to the function:

```
TDate today(3, 4, 1999);
any_function(&today);       // Pass object address to function
```

The & operator is required to pass the address of today to the function's TDate pointer parameter. Alternatively, the TDate object could be created dynamically, and its pointer passed directly to any_function() using the following code:

```
TDate *tdp = new TDate(3, 4, 1999);
any_function(tdp);          // Pass object pointer to function
delete tdp;
```

Although passing objects to a function's pointer parameters is common, it is often easier to use a reference parameter. Here's another version of any_function() that works just as efficiently but is more simply programmed:

```
void any_function(TDate &tdr)
{
  tdr.Display();
}
```

This version of any_function() declares its TDate parameter as a reference. Inside the function, that reference is used exactly the same as a TDate object would be without requiring pointer dereferencing. Statements such as the following pass a TDate object by reference to the function:

```
TDate today(3, 4, 1999);
any_function(today);        // Pass object by reference to function
```

The & operator is no longer needed, even though behind the scenes, C++ passes today's address to any_function(). Inside that function, the reference parameter tdr refers to the today object. This technique is the easiest to program, and it does not create a temporary object.

PART

III

CH

13

> **Tip**
>
> In most cases, class objects are best passed by reference to function parameters. If you don't want the function to be able to alter the object, declare it const—for example, `void f(const TDate &tdr)`.

OBJECT FUNCTION RESULTS

It is often necessary to create functions that pass back objects—you might think of them as object-factory functions. A function may return a class object in one of three ways: by value, as a pointer, or as a reference. The first method is probably the least common but is sometimes useful. For example, here's a function that returns a TDate object by value:

```
TDate any_function()
{
  TDate temp(5, 8, 2003);
  return temp;  // Return copy of object ???
}
```

The function constructs a local TDate object named temp and then returns that object as the function's value. Be aware, however, that this type of code actually returns a *copy* of temp, which might be assigned to a variable using this statement elsewhere in the program:

```
TDate new_date = any_function();
```

The function works, but consider all the wasted effort that this code produces. First, any_function() constructs the temp object. Next, it returns that object by value, causing another temporary object to be created. Finally, new_date is constructed using the returned temporary object, which is then finally deleted. That's three constructor calls and two copies of an object where only one is needed! And once again, if the objects own any pointers, their class must have a copy constructor and an operator=() function, or a serious bug could raise its ugly head in even simple code like this.

Often, a better method is to return a pointer to an object. Here's a new version of any_function() that demonstrates the technique:

```
TDate *any_function()
{
  return new TDate(5, 8, 2003);
}
```

The function uses the new operator to construct a new instance of the TDate class and then returns the resulting TDate pointer as the function result. Elsewhere in the program, a statement can call any_function() to obtain a new TDate object:

```
TDate *tdp = any_function();
```

That statement actually performs three actions. It declares tdp as a TDate pointer, it calls any_function() to construct a TDate object, and it assigns the resulting object address to tdp. This is more efficient than returning an object by value because only one object is constructed. However, it's important to understand that the use of new inside any_function() creates an object of global scope. Somewhere, somehow, that object must be deleted. For example, following the preceding code, the program should eventually delete tdp with the following statement:

```
delete tdp;
```

A third way to return an object uses a reference. This combines the advantages of returning pointers—memory addresses being smaller than most objects—and does not result in the creation of a temporary object with all its associated ills. Declare the function as follows:

```
TDate &any_function()
{
  return today;
}
```

The function returns a reference to a TDate object named today that is presumably created elsewhere in the program. It could be any TDate object, perhaps one constructed as a global variable with the statement:

```
TDate today(5, 8, 2003);
```

To obtain a reference to this object, the program calls any_function() using a statement:

```
TDate &date_ref = any_function();
```

All this is just by way of illustration—referring to global objects through a reference function works, but is of no practical value because it is easier just to use the original object. However, by adding another parameter to any_function(), it might return a reference to a *selected* object, perhaps from several stored in an array:

```
TDate &any_function(int selector)
{
  return array[selector];
}
```

A similar function that returns a reference could be used to select objects from another source such as a list or a disk file. The function might also provide a check on the selector's value, ensuring that it is in the proper range. Furthermore, the reference function hides the nature of the objects' data structure. The objects might be stored in an array, on a linked list in memory, or provided by a database server over a network connection.

Another common use for returning objects as references is in writing functions that accept reference parameters. For example, consider a function declared as

```
void second_function(TDate &tdr);
```

A statement could call second_function() by passing an object reference returned from any_function(), using some kind of index value to select a specific object:

```
second_function( any_function(index) );
```

This is highly efficient because only references (address values) are passed to and from the functions. It is also simpler than equivalent code that uses pointers. No object copies result, and no constructors are called. The preceding code is hypothetical, but it demonstrates safe and efficient techniques for passing objects in and out of functions. In a complex program where that happens many times, efficiency is a major concern.

PART

III

CH

13

> **Warning**
>
> Never return a pointer or reference to an object declared as a local variable in a function. All local variables, including those that are class objects, are destroyed when the function ends.

ARRAYS OF CLASS OBJECTS

As you know, you can store values and pointers of any types in arrays. You can also store class objects in arrays, either as variables or as pointers. For example, this creates an array of ten TDate objects:

```
TDate tenDates[10];
```

You may use a similar statement inside a function, but this might waste memory by storing the array on the system stack. In any case, there's only one hard-and-fast rule to remember: *Class objects in arrays must have default constructors.* When the program creates an array such as tenDates, C++ calls the default constructor once for *each* object in the array. In this case, C++ calls TDate() ten times to initialize objects tenDates[0] through tenDates[9].

When the tenDates array goes out of scope (if it's global, this is just before the program ends), C++ calls the ~TDate() destructor, if it has one, for each object in the array. This happens automatically, and you don't need to add any statements to ensure the proper constructor and destructor calls for objects in arrays declared as local and global variables.

DYNAMIC ARRAYS OF CLASS OBJECTS

Rather than allocate arrays of objects as local or global variables, you might consider using new to construct a dynamic object array. For large arrays (or arrays of large objects), this often uses memory more efficiently because many such arrays can be created and deleted. However, you now have some additional responsibilities to initialize and destroy the array.

Because pointers and arrays are equivalent in C and C++, the first step in creating a dynamic array of class objects is to declare a pointer to the type of object for storing in the array. The following declares td_arrayp as a TDate pointer:

```
TDate *td_arrayp;  // Declare pointer to dynamic array
```

That merely declares the pointer. To create the actual array, use new as follows along with an array size in brackets, and assign the resulting address to td_arrayp:

```
td_arrayp = new TDate[6];
```

This statement creates space for six TDate objects in dynamic memory, and it calls the TDate() default constructor to initialize each object. (It might be wiser to #define a constant for the array size, but for simplicity, I use the literal value 6 here.) The pointer td_arrayp addresses the first object in the array, but because a pointer *is* an array, statements may use array-index expressions with the pointer. For example, this for loop calls each object's Display() member function:

```
for (int i = 0; i < 6; i++)
  td_arrayp[i].Display();
```

Although `td_arrayp` is a pointer, references to objects in the array can use array-index expressions and dot notation to call a member function such as `Display()`. As always when using arrays, it is your responsibility to ensure that index values are within the defined array's range. Also, as you must do for all dynamic memory allocated by `new`, when you are finished using the dynamic array, delete it with the following statement:

```
delete[] td_arrayp;
```

The brackets in `delete[]` ensure that C++ calls the `~TDate()` destructor, if it has one, for each object in the array. In past C++ versions, you were required to supply `delete[]` with the number of objects to delete, using a statement such as

```
delete[6] td_arrayp;   // ???
```

This is not an error, but the argument value is no longer required. Compiling a program with such a statement produces the following GNU C++ warning:

```
warning: anachronistic use of array size in vector delete
```

Tip

> If you receive this warning when compiling an existing C++ program, perhaps one downloaded from the Internet, simply hunt for all occurrences of `delete[n]` and change them to `delete[]` with no argument value in brackets.

ARRAYS OF CLASS OBJECT POINTERS

Another highly useful type of array is one that contains not objects but pointers to objects. Each element of the array is a pointer, which requires initializing using `new`. To create this type of class object array, declare a pointer `tdp_array` like this:

```
TDate *tdp_array[10];
```

That creates an array of ten `TDate` pointers, each of type `TDate*`. It does not, however, create any `TDate` objects. To do that, use `new` as in the following `for` loop:

```
for (int j = 0; j < 10; j++)
  tdp_array[j] = new TDate;
```

It's important to understand that, because the array contains pointers to objects, it is your responsibility to construct each one using `new`. After constructing the objects, you can use them by dereferencing the array's pointers. This, for example, calls the `Display()` member function for each object:

```
for (int j = 0; j < 10; j++)
  tdp_array[j]->Display();
```

Finally, delete each object in the array. Again, because the array contains pointers, not the objects themselves, C++ does not delete the objects automatically nor does it call any class destructor. You must do that explicitly by applying `delete` to each array slot, as in the following `for` loop:

```
for (int j = 0; j < 10; j++)
  delete tdp_array[j];
```

PART

III

CH

13

DYNAMIC ARRAYS OF CLASS OBJECT POINTERS

Seeking to use memory as efficiently as possible, and specifically to avoid large global or local variables, programmers are often tempted to combine the foregoing array techniques to create a dynamic array of dynamically addressed objects. In other words, the program has a single pointer that addresses a dynamically allocated array of dynamically allocated objects. There's nothing wrong with this, but it's far easier to accomplish the same results using a class, as the next section demonstrates. I explain the technique here because you might come across it in published programs, but steer clear of this method in your own programs.

Essentially, the technique uses a pointer to address an array of pointers, created in dynamic memory. Each of *those* pointers addresses an object, constructed by new. There are a variety of C and C++ tricks for declaring this kind of dynamic object, but it is all around easiest to use a struct such as

```
struct Tdpp_array {
  TDate *the_array[10];
};
```

That specifies Tdpp_array to be a struct with one member, the_array, an array of ten TDate pointers. Create the struct object using new like this:

```
Tdpp_array *tdp = new Tdpp_array;
```

At this point, tdp addresses a Tdpp_array struct that contains an array of ten TDate pointers. Those pointers are not initialized—only the struct has been created. To create the dynamic TDate objects in the array, you might use new as follows:

```
for (int k = 0; k < 10; k++)
  tdp->the_array[k] = new TDate;
```

Now, tdp addresses the struct, which contains the_array of ten pointers to initialized TDate objects. To access the individual objects requires two uses of the C++ dereference operator ->. For example, this statement calls the Display() member function for each object in the array:

```
for (int k = 0; k < 10; k++)
  tdp->the_array[k]->Display();
```

As always when using pointers to objects, it is your responsibility to delete each memory object allocated by new. In this case, another for loop deletes the dynamic memory occupied by the ten objects:

```
for (int k = 0; k < 10; k++)
  delete tdp->the_array[k];
```

Finally, the array of pointers itself must be deleted by using the following statement:

```
delete tdp;
```

It is not correct here to use delete[] with brackets because tdp is a pointer to a struct; not to an array. As you can see, this technique is messy and takes a lot of thoughtful programming. A better and more object-oriented way to accomplish the same results follows.

OBJECT ARRAYS AS DATA MEMBERS

Structs and classes may declare data members that are arrays of class objects using any of the forms described in this chapter. Not only is this useful in a variety of situations, it is probably the best and most efficient way to construct dynamic arrays of objects allocated memory by new. Rather than fuss with pointers to pointers as in the preceding section, simply declare your array as a member of a class. For example, consider the following hypothetical class that declares a member date_array of ten TDate objects:

```
class TAnyClass {
private:
  TDate date_array[10];
public:
  TAnyClass() { }
};
```

When an object of class TAnyClass is constructed, C++ automatically calls the default TDate() constructor for each object in date_array. Likewise, when a TAnyClass object is destroyed or goes out of scope, C++ calls the ~TDate() destructor (if it has one) for each arrayed object. No extra code is needed to guarantee these constructor and destructor calls, regardless of how the program creates the TAnyClass object. For instance, to create that object as a global variable, declare it in the usual way:

```
TAnyClass an_object;
```

This constructs not only an_object, but also the ten TDate objects in the date_array data member. However, as with all large variables, more efficient memory use is possible using a TAnyClass pointer:

```
TAnyClass *a_pointer;
```

Initialize, use, and delete the pointer as you would any other:

```
a_pointer = new TAnyClass;
// ... use a_pointer here
delete a_pointer;
```

You've seen similar programming many times in this book. Consider, however, that the first statement constructs not only the TAnyClass object, *but also its array of ten TDate objects.* There's no need to use multiple pointers, loops, and delete statements. When new constructs the TAnyClass object, C++ automatically calls the TDate() constructor for each TDate object in date_array. Similarly, when the TAnyClass pointer is deleted, C++ automatically calls the ~TDate() destructor, if there is one, for each arrayed object.

PART

III

CH

13

Tip

In designing your program, try to think in terms of *objects* rather than *function.* For example, if you need an array of ten objects, create a class with such an array. You can then construct the resulting object as you like and let the class handle the memory management details of initialization, storage, and deletion.

OBJECTS AND MODULAR PROGRAMMING

Most of the sample programs in this book are necessarily short and, for simplicity, are implemented entirely in single source code text files. In practice, however, nobody writes real programs that way. Even programs of medium size are best organized into separately compiled modules. You've seen some examples of modular programming in Part II, "C++ Fundamentals." To demonstrate how to use similar techniques for class objects, the following sections present yet another version of the TDate class. The sample program is more than just an illustration. It shows how to *encapsulate* existing functions and data using object-oriented programming. The result is a class, TDate, that you can use in your own code to simplify access to the GNU C library's date and time functions and data types.

THE TDate HEADER FILE

A single module can implement one or more classes for use in other modules. You can write each module apart from other code, and compile it separately. This makes it easy to share the module with many host programs simply by including the class module's header file and linking the host to the module's compiled object code.

The first step in modularizing a class is to write a header file that contains the class declaration. Listing 13.6, tdate.h, demonstrates a typical header file for a new version of the TDate class.

LISTING 13.6   TDATE.H

```
#ifndef _ _TDate_H
#define _ _TDate_H    // Prevent multiple #includes

#include <time.h>    // Need time_t

class TDate {
private:
  time_t tv_time;    // Date and time as a time_t value
public:
  TDate();
  TDate(int month, int day = 0, int year = 0);
  void Update();
  void Display();
  const char *AsString();
};

#endif  // _ _TDate_H
```

The header file declares the TDate class, but it contains no function implementations (however, a header file may contain inline functions). This version of the TDate class is similar to others in this and the preceding chapter. However, the new class stores the date, not as separate month, day, and year values, but using the time_t data type declared in the standard library header time.h. To obtain this data type, the tdate.h header file includes time.h.

The tdate.h header file begins with two directives that prevent its own text from being included more than once. At the end of the file is a third directive that corresponds to the first. Examine the three directives together—minus the class in between—to understand what the directives accomplish:

```
#ifndef _ _TDate_H
#define _ _TDate_H
... items processed only on the first include
#endif
```

The first directive ("if not defined") states to the compiler (actually the preprocessor) that if the symbol _ _TDate_H is not defined, then it should process the following statements. The first of those statements is another directive, which #defines the _ _TDate_H symbol. Subsequently, the *next* time this header is included by another module, the preprocessor recognizes the _ _TDate_H symbol, and it skips directly from #ifndef to the corresponding #endif at the end of the file. In other words, the header file is processed fully the first time it is included. If it is included additional times, the preprocessor ignores the file's contents. As a result, the TDate class is declared only once regardless of how many modules include tdate.h.

> **Note**
>
> A "symbol" such as _ _TDate_H exists only during compilation. The symbol is not part of the program, nor does it need a value. All that matters is whether the symbol has been #defined. It is traditional to precede the symbol's name with two underscores, but this is not a requirement.

Getting back to TDate, notice that its two declared constructors are the same as in most other TDate classes you have seen. Because of that, you can use the new TDate class in most of the sample programming in this and the preceding chapter, *even though its internal data representation has drastically changed.* This principle points out one of the major advantages of restricting access to data members in classes. Because TDate's data is private to the class, that data representation is easily changed by merely updating the class module. Users of the class are unaffected by the change.

> **Tip**
>
> By always making data members private and using member functions to read and write the private data, you greatly simplify future updates to your programs. Follow this advice now, and you will thank yourself many times in the future.

THE TDate MODULE

The second element of the TDate module is its implementation. This is best placed in another file, apart from the class declaration header, and should end with .cpp or another recognized C++ source code filename suffix. Listing 13.7, tdate.cpp, implements the TDate class as a separate module.

Note The tdate.cpp source code file is not a complete program. See the next section for instructions on how to compile and use the separate module.

LISTING 13.7   TDATE.CPP

```cpp
#include <iostream.h>
#include "tdate.h"    // Also includes time.h

// Buffer to hold date string. This buffer is used by all
// TDate objects, and is overwritten by calls to member
// functions.
// String format: Fri 14-May-2004 (15 characters)

#define BUF_SIZE 16
char cbuf[BUF_SIZE];

// Default constructor implementation
TDate::TDate()
{
  Update();  // Initialize object date to today
}

// Parameterize constructor implementation
TDate::TDate(int month, int day = 0, int year = 0)
{
  Update();  // Initialize object date to today

  // Create a tm struct using tv_time data member
  tm t = *localtime(&tv_time);

  // Assign argument values if specified to struct
  t.tm_mon  = month - 1;
  if (day  > 0) t.tm_mday = day;
  if (year > 0) t.tm_year = year - 1900;

  // Convert struct back into tv_time value
  tv_time = mktime(&t);
}

// Update time to "now"
void TDate::Update()
{
  time(&tv_time);  // Calls the standard time() function
}

// Write date and time to the standard output
void TDate::Display()
{
  cout << AsString() << endl;
}

// Return date and time as a formatted string
const char *TDate::AsString()
{
```

```
    tm t = *localtime(&tv_time);  // Convert tv_time to struct
    strftime(cbuf, BUF_SIZE, "%a %d-%b-%Y", &t);  // Create cbuf
    return (const char *)&cbuf;   // Return pointer to buffer
}
```

Together, tdate.h and tdate.cpp, make up a self-contained module for the TDate class. To compile the module, use the -c compiler option as follows:

```
$ g++ -c tdate.cpp
```

That creates the object code file tdate.o in the current directory. It is useful to understand at this point that, should it become necessary to build new code into TDate, a program could *inherit* the TDate class into a new class without having to alter the original module in any way. In fact, only the tdate.h header file is needed—the source code is not required for using and enhancing the modularized TDate class. This is a good example of how, by using classes and objects, you can create truly modular programs that *reuse* code, rather than requiring you to *rewrite* code.

The new TDate class also demonstrates how a class can encapsulate standard functions and data such as those in the GNU C library, a good way to bring conventional programming into the object-oriented fold. For example, the TDate class's Update() member function calls the standard time() function to assign the current date and time to the class's private tv_time data member:

```
time(&tv_time);
```

Because the class's default constructor calls Update(), objects created using this constructor are automatically set to today's date. Using this fact, a host program can create and display the current date with simple statements such as

```
TDate today;
today.Display();
```

How easy! Using a class to encapsulate the often puzzling standard date and time functions has greatly simplified the use of the library.

Note

> The standard library's time_t value equals the number of elapsed seconds from 00:00:00 Universal Coordinated Time (UTC), January 1, 1970. The TDate class shown here can represent dates starting then.

The TDate class's parameterized constructor allows programs to construct a TDate object with an explicit date, using a statement such as

```
TDate future(4, 3, 2005);
```

Only the month is required; the day and year values are optional, and if not specified, default to today's date. In the constructor, after calling Update() to initialize the object to the current date, a statement calls the standard localtime() function. This returns a tm struct with tv_time's value converted into fields representing the day, month, year, and other values:

```
tm t = *localtime(&tv_time);
```

Armed with the initialized struct, the constructor replaces selected fields with month, day, and year parameters (if supplied with values greater than zero):

```
t.tm_mon  = month - 1;
if (day  > 0) t.tm_mday = day;
if (year > 0) t.tm_year = year - 1900;
```

Finally, the constructor converts the modified struct back to a time_t value, storing the result in the object's private tv_time data member:

```
tv_time = mktime(&t);
```

Another interesting member function in the TDate class is AsString(). This function calls the standard library's strftime() function to convert the object's date and time to a formatted string. Because this class concerns itself only with the date, strftime() is given a formatting string that ignores the time information in the tv_time value. The following statements create the string in the module's character buffer cbuf and return it as a const char pointer:

```
tm t = *localtime(&tv_time);  // Convert tv_time to struct
strftime(cbuf, BUF_SIZE, "%a %d-%b-%Y", &t);  // Create string
return (const char *)&cbuf;   // Return pointer to buffer
```

Using this function, a host program can display the time with an output stream statement such as

```
TDate today;
cout << "Today is " << today.AsString() << endl;
```

Tip

The Display() member function in TDate isn't necessarily the best way to write object data to the standard output. A better, and more object-oriented, method is to reprogram the << and >> operators to recognize objects of the TDate class type. Chapter 20, "Customizing I/O Streams," explains how to do this.

A TDate HOST PROGRAM

As mentioned, the TDate class module implemented in the preceding sections is not a complete program. To use the class, a host program with a main() function is needed. The program includes the tdate.h header file and links to the module's compiled object-code file. Listing 13.8, datetest.cpp, tests the TDate class module and shows how to use the separate class module.

LISTING 13.8   DATETEST.CPP

```cpp
#include <iostream.h>
#include "tdate.h"

int main()
{
  // Create default TDate object and display
  TDate today;
  today.Display();

  // Create parameterized TDate object and display as string
  TDate future(5, 14, 2004);
  cout << "Future date: " << future.AsString() << endl;

  // Update future object to today and display as string
  future.Update();
  cout << "Future updated to today: "
      << future.AsString() << endl;

  // Get a pointer to today object as a string
  const char *s = today.AsString();
  cout << "Pointer to today as string: " << s << endl;

  return 0;
}
```

The program includes all the library header files it needs, along with the TDate class header file using the directive

```cpp
#include "tdate.h"
```

Quotation marks indicate that tdate.h is in the current directory, or in a directory specified by an -I option (see Chapter 5, "Compiling and Debugging C++ Programs"). Including the class's header file makes the TDate class declaration available for use in the program, which shows several ways to create and use TDate objects. To compile and run the test, use these commands:

```
$ g++ -c tdate.cpp
$ g++ datetest.cpp tdate.o
$ ./a.out
Mon 08-Mar-1999
Future date: Fri 14-May-2004
Future updated to today: Mon 08-Mar-1999
Pointer to today as string: Mon 08-Mar-1999
```

The first command compiles the tdate.cpp module separately, creating the object-code file tdate.o in the current directory (you might already have completed this step). The second compiles datetest.cpp and links it to the separately compiled tdate.o object code file. The third command runs the resulting executable code file and displays the current date along with some other test results.

CLASSES AND DATA HIDING

Any of the TDate sample listings in this chapter can use the revised TDate class module. For example, copy dynadate.cpp (refer to Listing 13.1) to a new file, perhaps named test.cpp, and add this directive:

```
#include "tdate.h"
```

Delete the TDate class declaration from test.cpp along with all TDate implementation functions, leaving only main(). Compile and run the result with these commands (assuming you have previously compiled tdate.cpp):

```
$g++ test.cpp tdate.o
$./a.out
```

This is a practical demonstration of how, using a class to hide private data, the class's internal structure can change without affecting programs that use the class. It is just one of many powerful aspects of object-oriented programming that can help you write robust, easy-to-maintain software.

SUMMARY

This chapter introduced many techniques for creating objects of C++ classes, including dynamic class objects, destructors, copy constructors, and operator=() member functions. The chapter also showed how to pass objects to functions, return them as function results, and store objects efficiently in arrays. The chapter ended with a revised TDate class that encapsulates some of the functions and data types of standard GNU C library's time and date functions.

For more information on subjects introduced in this chapter, turn to the following chapters:

- Chapter 16, "Handling Exceptions"
- Chapter 19, "Overloading Operators"
- Chapter 20, "Customizing I/O Streams"
- Chapter 21, "Honing Your C++ Skills"

## CHAPTER 14

INVESTING IN INHERITANCE

In the preceding two chapters, you learned how classes encapsulate data and functions into a handy package. As you discover in this chapter, classes can do much more. Using a technique called *inheritance*, you can build new classes from existing ones. With inheritance, you write software based on finished, tested modules, instead of creating every new program from scratch.

CLASSES AS BUILDING BLOCKS

C++ offers two kinds of inheritance: single and multiple. In both cases, a new class *inherits* one or more existing classes to which you want to add new capabilities. The new class is called a *derived class*. For example, you might have a graphics library of classes that draw various shapes. To add a new shape, instead of reprogramming the library, you simply derive a new class from an existing one and add code and data to create the new shape.

Using inheritance, you can also develop hierarchies of related classes that resemble family trees. For instance, a hierarchy of network classes might include high-level classes for downloading specific types of data from a network server, but also provide low-level classes for accessing the operating system's telephony functions.

The following sections describe in general terms the concepts of single and multiple inheritance. Following that I show code examples of both techniques.

SINGLE INHERITANCE

Single inheritance describes the relationship between one class and the class from which it is derived. The *base class* may be any class or struct. The *derived class* inherits the data and function members of the base class. (The derived class, however, does not inherit constructors, but more on that later.) Figure 14.1 illustrates single inheritance.

Figure 14.1
In single inheritance, the derived class inherits the base class.

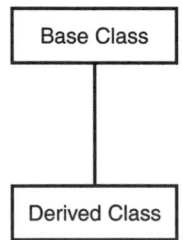

You may derive many classes from a single base class. Even so, as Figure 14.2 illustrates, such relationships are still of the single-inheritance variety because each new class derives from a single base.

Figure 14.2
Many classes may
inherit the same base
class.

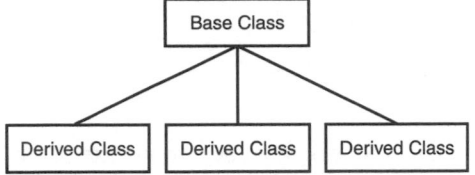

You'll come across many terms that describe derived and base classes. Some programmers call the base class the *ancestor* and the derived class the *descendant*. Others call the base class the *parent* and the derived class the *child*. Classes that share the same base class, as in Figure 14.2, are sometimes called *siblings*. Less common terms include *subclass* for the base, and *superclass* for the derived class.

MULTIPLE INHERITANCE

Multiple inheritance describes the relationship of one class that is derived from two or more other base classes. This resembles the way a child inherits properties from his or her parents. In real life, it takes only two to tango, but in C++, a child class may have as many parents as needed. Figure 14.3 illustrates multiple inheritance.

Figure 14.3
In multiple inheri-
tance, a derived class
inherits the properties
of two or more base
classes.

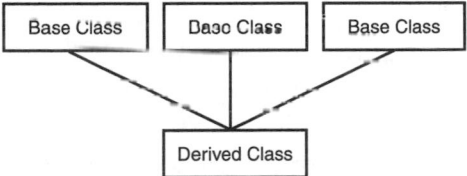

Multiple inheritance seems like a neat idea until it comes time to put it to use. In practice, most tasks can be accomplished using single inheritance. Although it is sometimes useful, multiple inheritance can create troublesome roadblocks (more on that in Chapter 15, "Programming with Virtual Functions").

> **Tip**
> Don't use multiple inheritance unless you have sound reasons for doing so. A reliance on multiple inheritance may indicate a poor design among class relationships, but see Chapter 15 for solutions to problems that multiple inheritance can cause.

CREATING DERIVED CLASSES

A few simple examples explain the mechanics of inheritance. Consider a hypothetical base class, TBase, declared as follows (for simplicity, I implement all functions inline):

```
class TBase {
private:
  int count;
```

```
public:
  TBase(): count(0) {}
  void SetCount(int n) { count = n; }
  int GetCount() { return count; }
};
```

The TBase class declares a single private data member, an integer named count. The class's default constructor initializes count to zero. Two member functions set count to the integer parameter value n, and return count's current value. Statements might use the TBase class like this:

```
TBase base_object;
base_object.SetCount(123);
cout << base_object.GetCount() << endl;
```

The first line constructs a TBase object named base_object. The second line calls the SetCount() member function to assign a value to the class's private data member. The final statement calls GetCount() to obtain the class's count value. Although hypothetical, the design of TBase contains elements found in many real-world classes.

To add new capabilities to TBase, don't rewrite it; inherit it into a new class and add the new capabilities you need. For example, suppose you decide that a function to add a value to the object's count would be useful. To derive a new class from TBase, use a declaration such as

```
class TDerived: public TBase {
public:
  TDerived(): TBase() {}    // constructor
  void AddToCount(int n);   // member function
};
```

The derived class name, TDerived, is followed by a colon and the name of the base class to inherit. The word public states that all members of TBase should retain their current access specifications—private items in TBase remain private, and public items remain public in the derived class. If you change public to private, then all inherited members from TBase become private members of TDerived. To its inheritance, TDerived declares two new items: a constructor and a member function AddToCount(), both in a public section.

The derived class constructor is, like all constructors, named the same as its class. Because a derived class does not inherit constructors, it *must* declare at least one constructor of its own. In this case, the default TDerived() constructor calls the base class constructor TBase() using an initializing expression. The constructor's body is empty, but it could perform other statements if necessary. The design of the TDerived constructor ensures that, when the program constructs an object of the derived class, it calls not only that class's constructor but also the constructor in the ancestor base class. In that way, any inherited items are properly initialized. For example, in this case, the TBase() constructor sets TBase::count to zero.

The derived class member function adds a new capability to the TBase class—function AddToCount(). Given the derived constructor and new member function, the program can create an object and use the new function to add a value to it:

```
TDerived derived_object;
derived_object.SetCount(123);
```

```
derived_object.AddToCount(456);
cout << derived_object.GetCount() << endl;
```

First, the program constructs `derived_object`. This calls the `TDerived()` constructor, and also the `TBase()` constructor, to initialize the object. Next, the program calls the inherited `SetCount()` to assign a value to the object. It then calls the newly added `AddToCount()` function to increment the object's value. Finally, the inherited `GetCount()` function returns the object's value for display. The `TDerived` class *inherits* the `SetCount()` and `GetCount()` functions from `TBase`. Because of that, statements may call those functions for any `TBase` or `TDerived` object. A good way to think about this is to imagine that a `TDerived` object is merely an enhanced or expanded `TBase` object. A `TDerived` object can do anything a `TBase` object can do and more.

The final piece of the inheritance puzzle implements the newly added member function. Although simple, the programming reveals another important aspect about inheritance:

```
void TDerived::AddToCount(int n)
{
  SetCount( GetCount() + n );
}
```

The implementation of `AddToCount()` is the same as for any class member function. First comes the return type (`void`), followed by the class name and the C++ scope resolution operator. The function's name, parameters, and statement block follow. The single statement in that block calls the inherited `SetCount()` and `GetCount()` member functions to add the parameter `int n` to the object's value. It's important to realize that `AddToCount()` cannot simply use a statement such as

```
count += n;  // ???
```

That doesn't compile because `count` is a private member of the `TBase` class. Even though `TDerived` inherits all of `TBase`'s members, only the declaring class can access its private data. `TDerived` must therefore call the `GetCount()` member function to obtain the object's count value, and it must call `SetCount()` to change that value. Although this might seem to be a great imposition—and in this simple example it is admittedly a lot of extra work—in large programs, restricting access to private data as illustrated here greatly increases the security of the program and promotes ease of future maintenance.

THE `TCoordinate` CLASS

Now that you've met some of the basics of classes and inheritance, a practical example illustrates how to create classes that are useful in real-world programming. Representing locations as (x,y) coordinate values is a common programming technique that makes a good example of a usable C++ class. Coordinate objects might represent locations of characters on a text terminal, or the pixels on a graphics display. In this and the next few sections, you investigate a class that stores a coordinate value. You also create derived classes to add a new functions to the basic design.

To make the class easier to use, I wrote it as a separate module. Listing 14.1 shows the header file for the `TCoordinate` class.

PART

III

CH

14

LISTING 14.1   COORDINATE.H

```
class TCoordinate {
private:
  int tc_x, tc_y;
public:
  TCoordinate(): tc_x(0), tc_y(0) { }
  TCoordinate(int x, int y): tc_x(x), tc_y(y) { }
  void Setxy(int x, int y);
  int Getx() const;
  int Gety() const;
};
```

The TCoordinate class contains only one new element you haven't seen before—the use of const in a function prototype—and you should be able to understand most of the programming by reading the class declaration. A private section declares two private data members, tc_x and tc_y, both of type int for storing an X/Y location. Two constructors initialize objects of the TCoordinate class. The default constructor sets tc_x and tc_y to zero. The parameterized constructor sets those two private variables to the values of x and y parameters. The class doesn't need a destructor.

In addition to its constructors, the TCoordinate class declares three member functions. Setxy() changes the object's private data members to new x and y values. Getx() and Gety() return the values of the private data members. The word const following the function declarations informs the compiler that Getx() and Gety() do not change any data members in an object of this class. In general, any member function in a class that makes no changes to an object's data members should be declared const. For reasons that become clear a little later, this is especially important for functions that return the values of private data members.

Tip

Many classes use member functions to set and get the values of private data members in classes. If you are concerned about losing efficiency to many function calls, declare the functions inline and compile with an optimization option such as -O1.

To complete the module, the TCoordinate class needs implementations for its three member functions. Listing 14.2 shows the result. This is not a complete program—you can compile it with the -c (compile only) option, but you can't run the code just yet.

LISTING 14.2   COORDINATE.CPP

```
#include "coordinate.h"
void TCoordinate::Setxy(int x, int y)
{
  tc_x = x;
  tc_y = y;
}

int TCoordinate::Getx() const
{
```

```
    return tc_x;
}

int TCoordinate::Gety() const
{
    return tc_y;
}
```

There's nothing special about the implementation module, except again for the words const following Getx() and Gety(). The module implements the class's three member functions to set and get the values of the private data members tc_x and tc_y. To test the class, we need a host program. A sample is in Listing 14.3, tcoord.cpp (test TCoordinate).

LISTING 14.3   TCOORD.CPP

```
#include <iostream.h>
#include "coordinate.h"

void display(const char *msg, TCoordinate &tc);
int main()
{
    TCoordinate t1;
    display("Default object", t1);
    TCoordinate t2(45, 218);
    display("Parameterized object", t2);
    t1.Setxy(100, 200);
    display("After calling setxy()", t1);
    return 0;
}

void display(const char *msg, TCoordinate &tc)
{
    cout << msg << endl;
    cout << "x == " << tc.Getx() << "; y == " << tc.Gety();
    cout << endl;
}
```

Compile the program using the -c option for the coordinate module, and then link the host program to the module's object code with the following commands:

```
$ g++ -c coordinate.cpp
$ g++ tcoord.cpp coordinate.o
```

Run the program to display the results of three tests using two TCoordinate objects:

```
$ ./a.out
Default object
x == 0; y == 0
Parameterized object
x == 45; y == 218
After calling setxy()
x == 100; y == 200
```

DERIVED CLASS CONSTRUCTORS

Imagine that you are writing a graphics program, in which you represent coordinates using TCoordinate objects. However, in addition to location, you need an object that can store a color value. This illustrates a common problem well-suited to an object-oriented solution. When you discover the need for a new type of data or function, you can often build a new class on an existing one, and in that way reduce your work load while taking advantage of code that's already finished. Listing 14.4, color.h, declares the derived class, TColor.

LISTING 14.4 COLOR.H

```
#include "coordinate.h"  // Need Tcoordinate

// Enumerated color names
typedef enum
{
  UNKNOWN, RED, ORANGE, YELLOW, GREEN, BLUE, INDIGO, VIOLET
} TColors;

// Class declaration
class TColor: public TCoordinate {
private:
  TColors tc_color;  // Private data
  static const char *colornames[];  // Private static data
public:
  TColor(): TCoordinate(), tc_color(UNKNOWN) { }
  TColor(TColors color, int x, int y);
  void SetColor(TColors color) { tc_color = color; }
  TColors GetColor() const { return tc_color; }
  const char *StrColor() const;
};
```

The new TColor class, derived from TCoordinate, inherits the base class's data and member functions. To its inheritance, the new class adds two private data members—variable tc_color of the enumerated TColors type (also declared in the header file), and colornames, a static array of string constants.

A static member refers to data that belongs to a class but that you don't want to duplicate in every class object. In this case, we want to give string names to TColors symbols such as BLUE and RED, but it would be silly to add those identical strings to every TColor class object. Declaring the array *static* indicates that only one copy of colornames exists for all TColor objects. Conversely, because tc_color is not declared static, every TColor object has a distinct copy of that private variable.

Note Static members can also be functions. For an example, see "Static Member Functions" under "Odds and Ends" in Chapter 21, "Honing Your C++ Skills."

In addition to its private data, the TColor derived class declares several constructors and member functions. The default constructor initializes objects created with no argument values as in this statement:

```
TColor color_object;
```

For simplicity, I implemented TColor's default constructor entirely inline. Its statement block performs no actions. To initialize a TColor object, the constructor calls the derived constructor TCoordinate(). It also sets the TColor private data member, tc_color, to the default enumerated value, UNKNOWN.

Two other member functions are also implemented inline. SetColor() changes a TColor object's color to a new value, and GetColor() returns the object's current color. Notice that, as in TCoordinate, member functions that merely return data from a class object but make no internal changes are declared const. The TColor class also declares a parameterized constructor and a member function that are implemented in the separate module, Listing 14.5, color.cpp.

LISTING 14.5   COLOR.CPP

```cpp
#include "color.h"

// Define static array of color strings
const char *TColor::colornames[] = {
  "Unknown", "Red", "Orange", "Yellow", "Green", "Blue",
  "Indigo", "Violet"
};

// TColor member function implementations
// Parameterized constructor
TColor::TColor(TColors color, int x, int y):
  TCoordinate(x, y)     // Initialize base class object
{
  tc_color = color;     // Initialize our private data
}

// Return color name as a string using static array
const char *TColor::StrColor() const
{
  if (tc_color < RED || tc_color > VIOLET)
    return colornames[UNKNOWN];
  else
    return colornames[tc_color];
}
```

The color.cpp module implements the two members of the TColor class that are not implemented inline. However, first in the module is the definition of the colornames static array. Although the class declares this member, it must be implemented in a code module, not in the header file so that other modules can include this same header. This arrangement does not make the colornames array globally available. Because the array is private to the TColor class, it is accessible only to statements in the class's member functions. Creating static objects such as colornames is a great way to limit access to private data on a module level.

PART

III

CH

14

The module also implements the TColor parameterized constructor and a member function. The constructor requires three parameters: a color, and x and y coordinate values. To initialize the base class data, the constructor calls the TCoordinate parameterized constructor, passing the x and y parameters. The constructor also initializes the tc_color private member to the specified color. In this way, statements such as the following fully initialize a TColor object:

```
TColor color_object(RED, 450, 87);
```

The final element in the color.cpp module implements the StrColor() member function. This function returns a constant char* (character pointer) to one of the strings in the static colornames array. Because the function changes no data in the class, it is declared const. Inside the function, for safety, a statement checks that tc_color is in the allowable range before using it to access the colornames array. Listing 14.6, tcolor.cpp, tests the completed module.

LISTING 14.6   TCOLOR.CPP

```
#include <iostream.h>
#include "coordinate.h"  // Need TCoordinate
#include "color.h"       // Need TColor

// Function prototype
void display(const char *msg, TColor &tc);

int main()
{
  TColor color_object(ORANGE, 45, 67);
  display("Original object", color_object);
  color_object.SetColor(GREEN);
  color_object.Setxy(125, 250);
  display("After function calls", color_object);
  return 0;
}

// Display facts about object tc
void display(const char *msg, TColor &tc)
{
  cout << msg << endl;
  cout << "x == " << tc.Getx() << "; y == " << tc.Gety();
  cout << "; color = " << tc.StrColor();
  cout << " (" << tc.GetColor() << ')';
  cout << endl;
}
```

Compile and link the test program with the following commands. You can skip compiling coordinate.cpp if you already did that:

```
$ g++ -c coordinate.cpp
$ g++ -c color.cpp
$ g++ tcolor.cpp coordinate.o color.o
```

These commands demonstrate how a new class such as TColor can be derived from an existing class (TCoordinate) simply by including that class's header file and linking the program to the class's implementation object code file (coordinate.o). This is a good example of how, using inheritance, you can reuse tested code in new programming. Now, run the compiled program:

```
$ ./a.out
Original object
x == 45; y == 67; color = Orange (2)
After function calls
x == 125; y == 250; color = Green (4)
```

The program's output shows the x, y, and color values for a TColor object. Because the TColor class inherits the data and member functions from TCoordinate, it can represent both kinds of data. Furthermore, the TCoordinate class remains usable in its original form, and the new programming has no effect on any other programs that use TCoordinate.

DERIVED CLASS DESTRUCTORS

It's the rare program that derives only one class from another. In most programs, many layers of classes are needed to create the objects you need. As a demonstration, and to show some additional facets about derived classes, let's take the TCoordinate and TColor classes one step further.

Your graphics program is taking shape, but now you discover that not only do you need objects to represent screen locations and colors, but some of those locations need string labels as well. As before, a good solution to the problem is to derive a new class and add the data and functions you need. Listing 14.7, label.h, declares a new class derived from TColor.

LISTING 14.7 LABEL.H

```
#include "color.h"  // Need TColor

class TLabel: public TColor {
private:
  char *tl_label;
public:
  TLabel(): TColor() { tl_label = NULL; }
  TLabel(const char *label, TColors color, int x, int y);
  TLabel(const TLabel &copy);
  ~TLabel() { delete tl_label; }
  const char *GetLabel() const { return tl_label; }
  void SetLabel(const char *label);
  void operator=(const TLabel &copy);
};
```

Because TColor is derived from TCoordinate, the new TLabel class inherits the data and function members from *both* of its ancestors. To its inheritance, the new TLabel class adds a char* variable tl_label for addressing a string in memory.

Three constructors initialize TLabel objects. The default constructor, listed first in the public section, uses an initializing expression to call its ancestor constructor, TColor(). This ensures that all levels of inherited data are properly initialized. The default constructor also sets tl_label to NULL, indicating that this object has no associated label.

The second constructor declares parameters for a string label, a color, and x and y coordinate values. That and the copy constructor that follows are implemented in the class's module, Listing 14.8, label.cpp. Also implemented inline in the class declaration are a destructor, which deletes any string addressed by the private tl_label pointer, and a GetLabel() function that simply returns the value of that pointer. Notice that both the return value of GetLabel() and the function are declared const. This states that the data returned is constant, and that the function makes no changes to a TLabel object's data members.

LISTING 14.8   LABEL.CPP

```
#include <string.h>   // Need strlen(), strcpy()
#include "label.h"    // Need TLabel

// Parameterized constructor
TLabel::TLabel(const char *label, TColors color, int x, int y):
  TColor(color, x, y)      // Initialize base class object
{
  tl_label = NULL;         // So SetLabel can create string
  SetLabel(label);         // Copy label to our object
}

// Copy constructor
TLabel::TLabel(const TLabel &copy):
  TColor(copy)
{
  tl_label = NULL;
  SetLabel(copy.tl_label);
}

// Change label string. Note: label might be NULL.
void TLabel::SetLabel(const char *label)
{
  delete[] tl_label;    // Okay if tl_label == NULL
  tl_label = NULL;      // Set tl_label to NULL
  if (label != NULL)    // If param not NULL...
  {
    tl_label = new char[strlen(label) + 1];
    strcpy(tl_label, label);  // Copy param to tl_label
  }
}

// Copy TLabel objects
void TLabel::operator=(const TLabel &copy)
{
  if (this == &copy) return;         // Don't copy self
  Setxy(copy.Getx(), copy.Gety());   // Copy TCoordinate data
  SetColor(copy.GetColor());         // Copy TColor data
  SetLabel(copy.tl_label);           // Copy TLabel data
}
```

The TLabel implementation module is a little more involved than those you've seen before. But take it one function at a time—the individual statements are fairly simple. First, the parameterized constructor passes to its ancestor TColor class constructor the color, x, and y parameters. This lets the ancestor take care of initializing its portion of the object. All that remains is to use the string parameter label to initialize the object's tl_label data member. Two statements handle the job:

```
tl_label = NULL;
SetLabel(label);
```

The tl_label variable is first set to NULL because of the way SetLabel() works (more on that in a moment). Calling one of the class's own member functions this way is perfectly legitimate in a constructor. However, you must be careful when using this technique not to call any function that uses data not yet initialized.

Next in the module is the class's copy constructor. This is needed because one of the data members is a pointer to dynamically allocated memory, and as you learned in prior chapters, it is especially important for classes to provide safe copying mechanisms to prevent the accidental duplication of a pointer address value. Interestingly, the copy constructor is nearly the same as the parameterized constructor just discussed. However, in this case, the initializing expression TColor(copy) passes copy to the ancestor's automatically generated copy constructor. These statements then finish the job of copying one TLabel object to another:

```
tl_label = NULL;
SetLabel(copy.tl_label);
```

Again, tl_label is set to NULL because of the way SetLabel() works. That function copies the data addressed by the tl_label pointer in the source object (copy) to the current object in construction.

The SetLabel() function itself takes a little more effort to understand. Its job is simple—it assigns the address of a string to the class's private tl_label char pointer—but the programming must carefully deal with any existing data. These statements do the trick:

```
delete[] tl_label;    // Okay if tl_label == NULL
tl_label = NULL;      // Set tl_label to NULL
if (label != NULL)    // If param not NULL...
{
  tl_label = new char[strlen(label) + 1];
  strcpy(tl_label, label);  // Copy param to tl_label
}
```

First, any currently addressed string is deleted. If tl_label is NULL, deleting it does no harm. To ensure that tl_label is NULL at this point, it is next set to that value. In this way, if the function's label parameter is NULL, the object's tl_label pointer also equals NULL. If label is not NULL, two statements create space for the string and copy the label parameter's string to that allocated memory.

Finally in the TLabel class module is the function operator=(). As explained in Chapter 13, "Creating and Destroying Objects," this function is needed to safely copy an object to another that has already been constructed. To do this, the `operator=()` function executes these statements:

```
if (this == &copy) return;
Setxy(copy.Getx(), copy.Gety());
SetColor(copy.GetColor());
SetLabel(copy.tl_label);
```

The first line is typical in all `operator=()` functions—it ignores any attempt to copy the same object into itself. The other three statements initialize the copy by calling the inherited `Setxy()`, `SetColor()`, and `SetLabel()` functions along with `Getx()`, `Gety()`, and `GetColor()`. The calls to `Setxy()` and `SetColor()` illustrate the importance of declaring const member functions. To understand why, take a look at the `operator=()` function header:

```
void TLabel::operator=(const TLabel &copy)
```

The copy parameter, which refers to the source object being copied, is declared as type const `TLabel &`—in other words, a reference to a constant `TLabel` object. If functions such as `Getx()`, `Gety()`, and `GetColor()` were not declared const, statements that pass a const object as an argument would give the compiler a dilemma. For example, this statement:

```
Setxy(copy.Getx(), copy.Gety());
```

passes to `Getx()` and `Gety()` a this pointer for the const object copy. Because the functions are declared as const, there is no danger that they will inadvertently modify the object. Listing 14.9, tlabel.cpp, tests the implemented `TLabel` class. The listing contains nothing new, and you should be able to understand the programming from the source code.

LISTING 14.9   TLABEL.CPP

```cpp
#include <iostream.h>
#include "label.h"      // Need TLabel

void display(const char *msg, TLabel &tl);

int main()
{
  TLabel test("Test Label", RED, 100, 200);
  display("Test object", test);

  TLabel copy_object(test);
  display("Copy constructed object", copy_object);

  TLabel dest_object;
  display("Object before copy", dest_object);
  dest_object = test;
  display("Object after copy", dest_object);

  return 0;
}

// Display facts about object tc
void display(const char *msg, TLabel &tl)
```

```
{
  cout << msg << endl;
  cout << "x == " << tl.Getx() << "; y == " << tl.Gety();
  cout << "; color = " << tl.StrColor();
  cout << " (" << tl.GetColor() << ')';
  cout << "; " << tl.GetLabel();
  cout << endl;
}
```

COPYING DERIVED CLASS OBJECTS

One other wrinkle in copying derived class objects occurs when a class is derived from another with its own copy constructor and operator=() function. This is a common problem that many C++ programmers either ignore or mishandle. Listing 14.10 demonstrates a good way to deal with the situation.

LISTING 14.10   COPY.CPP

```
#include <iostream.h>
#include "label.h"      // Need TLabel

// Test class
class TTest: public TLabel {
private:
  int count;
public:
  TTest(): TLabel(), count(123) { }
  TTest(const TTest &copy);
  void operator=(const TTest &copy);
  int GetCount() const { return count; }
};

// Function prototype
void display(const char *msg, TTest &tx);

int main()
{
  TTest tx, ty;                   // Create two objects
  display("New object (tx)", tx); // Display object values
  display("New object (ty)", ty);

  ty.SetLabel("test string");     // Change ty data
  ty.SetColor(VIOLET);
  ty.Setxy(456, 789);
  display("Modified (ty)", ty);   // Display modified data

  tx = ty;                        // Copy ty to tx !
  display("After (tx = ty)", tx); // Display copied data

  TTest tz(ty);  // Construct tz using copy constructor
  display("Copy constructed tz", tz);  // Display object

  return 0;
```

PART

III

CH

14

continues

LISTING 14.10   CONTINUED

```
}

// Copy constructor
TTest::TTest(const TTest &copy):
  TLabel(copy)                 // Initialize ancestor object
{
  count = copy.count;          // Initialize our own data
}

// Assignment (=) member function
void TTest::operator=(const TTest &copy)
{
  if (this == &copy) return;   // Don't copy self
  *(TLabel *)this = copy;       // Copy ancestor object data
  count = copy.GetCount();      // Copy our own data
}

// Show data in object tx
void display(const char *msg, TTest &tx)
{
  cout << msg << endl;
  cout << "x == " << tx.Getx() << "; y == " << tx.Gety();
  cout << "; color = " << tx.StrColor();
  cout << " (" << tx.GetColor() << ')';
  cout << "; " << tx.GetLabel();
  cout << "; count = " << tx.GetCount();
  cout << endl;
}
```

Compile and run the program using the following commands. You can skip compiling the coordinate.cpp, color.cpp, and label.cpp modules if you have already done so.

```
$ g++ -c coordinate.cpp color.cpp label.cpp
$ g++ copy.cpp coordinate.o color.o label.o
$ ./a.out
```

The sample program derives yet another class from TLabel—in this case, named TTest. As with TLabel, our mission is to create a class with mechanisms for the safe copying of objects—both during construction with statements such as

```
TTest test1;
...
TTest test2(test1);  // Calls copy constructor
```

and for cases where two existing objects are copied in an assignment statement:

```
test1 = test2;  // Calls operator=() member function
```

When writing classes to cover these uses, be sure that all ancestor classes have the chance to copy their own data members. For example, in this case, we want the TCoordinate class to copy its tc_x and tc_y private data members, and TColor to copy its tc_color value. The derived class shouldn't have to do more than copy its own data. Making that happen isn't difficult after you learn the tricks. To handle the copying of objects, the TTest class, derived from TLabel, declares a copy constructor and operator=() function:

```
TTest(const TTest &copy);
void operator=(const TTest &copy);
```

You've already seen several examples of these functions—they are almost always declared as shown except, of course, for the class names. Implementing the copy constructor is the easy part—it merely calls the TLabel() copy constructor passing the copy parameter, which is a reference to the TTest source object:

```
TTest::TTest(const TTest &copy):
  TLabel(copy)  // Initialize ancestor object
{
  count = copy.count;  // Initialize our own data
}
```

The constructor's lone statement is simple—it merely copies the source object's count data member to the target object's data member. The operator=() function, however, is not as simple:

```
void TTest::operator=(const TTest &copy)
{
  if (this == &copy) return;  // Don't copy self
  *(TLabel *)this = copy;      // Copy ancestor object data
  count = copy.GetCount();     // Copy our own data
}
```

As usual, the first statement ignores cases where the program attempts to copy an object onto itself. The second statement is where many programmers get stuck. We want to have the ancestor operator=() function (or one automatically generated by C++) handle base class object copying. To do this, the statement assigns copy (the source object reference) to this (the target object to which we are copying). However, the following statement does *not* work:

```
*this = copy;  // ???
```

That would cause the TTest object to be copied to the object addressed by the this pointer—causing a recursive function call to TTest::operator=() and blowing up the stack. Instead, we want to tell C++ that this addresses an *ancestor* object of type TLabel. Using a type cast does the job:

```
*(TLabel *)this = copy;
```

The type cast expression, (TLabel *), states that this actually addresses a TLabel object. This is perfectly acceptable because a TTest object is, after all, just an enhanced TLabel object (see Figure 14.4). The asterisk outside the expression tells the compiler to dereference the type cast pointer. The result is a call to Tlabel::operator=(), which we can trust to handle the copying of all inherited data members.

Figure 14.4 shows the relationships of the four classes in the TTest hierarchy. The figure also illustrates an important concept—that a pointer to an object may be of that object's class type, or of any derived type. For example, it is perfectly acceptable for a TColor pointer to address a TLabel object because TLabel is derived from TColor. It wouldn't make sense, however, for a TLabel pointer to address a TCoordinate object.

Figure 14.4
Object pointers may be of a class's type, or of an ancestor type from which a class is derived.

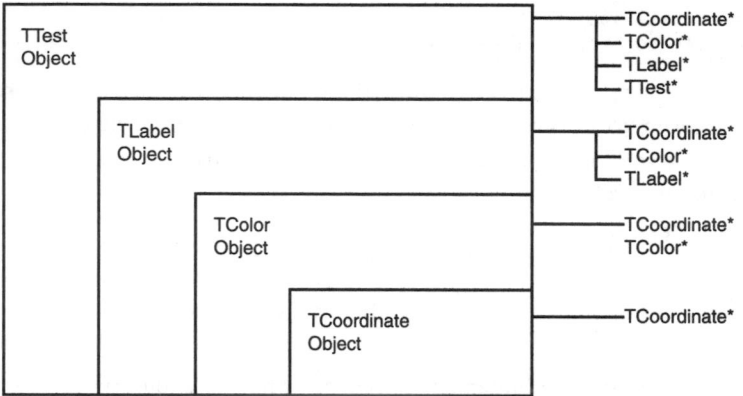

INTRODUCING PROTECTED MEMBERS

A *protected class member* is a cross between a private and a public member. To declare this type of element, use the `protected` reserved word followed by a colon:

```
class TAnyClass {
public:
  // public members
protected:
  // protected members
private:
  // private members
};
```

Declaring a variable or member function *protected* states that other members of this class—*and any classes derived from this class*—may directly use those members. Statements outside the class have no access to proctected members. The following rules describe the effects of private, protected, and public access specifiers:

■ A private member is accessible only to members of the class in which the member is declared.

■ A protected member is accessible to members of its own class and to any members in a derived class.

■ A public member is accessible to all users of the class.

CHANGING ACCESS SPECIFIERS

You can change an inherited item's access rules by declaring the ancestor class public, protected, or private. However, you may only make inherited items more restrictive—you cannot make them less so. For example, you may state that inherited public members are from now on to be private, but you cannot inherit private members and make them public. Usually, you derive classes using the `public` reserved word like this:

```
class TDerived: public TBase {...};
```

Using this declaration, in the TDerived class, all members of TBase retain their present access specifications. Public members from TBase are public members in TDerived. Protected TBase members are protected members of the new class. Private members remain strictly for TBase's own use. Using the protected reserved work creates a different effect:

```
class TDerived: protected TBase {...};
```

That declaration causes public members of TBase to become protected members in TDerived. Protected and private members in TBase remain unaffected. This change means that statements outside TDerived can no longer access the formerly public members TBase. For the utmost in restrictions, inherit a class using the private reserved word:

```
class TDerived: private TBase {...};
```

That kind of declaration is highly unusual because it makes *all* members of TBase private members of TDerived. Statements outside the TDerived class, as well as statements in any further derived classes based on TDerived, cannot call any functions, not even constructors, nor refer to any data members, in TBase.

> **Tip**
>
> Making an inherited class private forevermore hides its contents in the derived class. One possible use for this technique is to help eliminate a class from a complex hierarchy. By hiding the inherited class now, it might be possible to delete it entirely at some point in the future.

QUALIFYING SELECTED MEMBERS

In cases where you need to inherit most of a class normally but selectively change the access rules for individual elements, you can qualify the access rules for selected members. This can be useful, for example, in creating classes that do a better job at protecting and hiding data than their ancestor classes.

To illustrate the technique, imagine you come across a class in which all members are public. This usually indicates a poor design, and you want to upgrade the class to improve its safety. Call the original class A, and its derived improvement B. Listing 14.11, qualify.cpp, shows how to selectively qualify members inherited into B from A.

LISTING 14.11   QUALIFY.CPP

```
#include <iostream.h>
class A {
public:
  int x;
  A(int n): x(n) { }  // Constructor
  void Display() { cout << "x == " << x << endl; }
};

class B: private A {
```

PART **III**

CH **14**

continues

LISTING 14.11 CONTINUED

```
public:
  B(int n): A(n) { }   // Constructor
  A::Display;          // Selectively qualify Display()
};

int main()
{
  B object(123);       // Construct object of type B
  object.Display();    // Call qualified inherited function
  return 0;
}
```

The sample program is simple (you don't even have to run it), but it shows how to change the access rules for selected items inherited from a class. In this case, class A is the poorly designed one. It declares all of its members public, and as such, is no safer than a common C struct. Any statement anywhere in the program can read and write the integer x data member's value in an object of type A.

To improve the class design, class B inherits A using the private reserved word. As mentioned, this completely hides A inside B. The public x variable from A becomes a private member of B, thus protecting it from indiscriminate use. However, the Display() member function also becomes private to B. To retain Display()'s public status so that statements can call it, declare the function as follows:

```
public:
  A::Display;
```

The class name and scope resolution operator :: refer to Display, not as a function prototype, but as a symbol without parentheses. In effect, the declaration states that the symbol Display is to retain its access rules as found in A. The result is that programs can construct objects of the derived class B, and still call the Display() function, as demonstrated in the sample program's statements:

```
B object(123);
object.Display();
```

DEBUGGING DERIVED CLASSES

The GNU debugger helps you investigate the values of class data members, and the actions of member functions, constructors, and destructors. To learn the relevant commands, enter the following commands to compile and load the tlabel.cpp test program into the debugger:

```
$ g++ -g -c coordinate.cpp color.cpp label.cpp
$ g++ -g -o tlabel tlabel.cpp coordinate.o color.o label.o
$ gdb -- silent tlabel (gdb)
```

The first two commands compile tlabel.cpp using the options -g (add debugging information), -c (compile only), and -o (output filename). The third command starts the debugger and skips (-- silent) its wordy welcome. Continue to the next section to explore object creation using debugger commands.

Note

To compile a program or a separate module for debugging, remember to specify the -g compiler option.

INSPECTING OBJECT CONSTRUCTION

At the (gdb) prompt, enter a breakpoint at line 21 to pause the program at the creation of a test TLabel object (see tlabel.cpp, Listing 14.9):

```
(gdb) b 21
Breakpoint 1 at 0x804884e: file tlabel.cpp, line 21.
```

The actual line number might be different for you. Run the program up to the breakpoint, pausing just before the test object's construction:

```
(gdb) run
Starting program: /src/c14/tlabel
Breakpoint 1, main () at tlabel.cpp:21
21 TLabel test("Test Label", RED, 100, 200);
```

To inspect the object's construction, use a *step* command to step inside the class's constructor:

```
(gdb) step
TLabel::TLabel (this=0xbffffa68, label=0x8048e4c "Test Label",
  color=RED, x=100, y=200) at label.cpp:13
13 TLabel::TLabel(const char *label, TColors color,
int x, int y):
```

The debugger's output shows all the parameters passed to the TLabel constructor (notice its name is TLabel::TLabel()). The debugger shows the this pointer address, which is equal to the object's address in memory. It also shows the values of the label, color, x, and y parameters. Strings such as label are shown by address and by value. Enumerated values such as color are shown by name—a most helpful feature.

At this stage, the program is paused at the call to the TLabel parameterized constructor, giving you the chance to review all parameter values. The first task in the constructor is to call its ancestor TColor constructor, although this fact might not be obvious from the debugger's display (again, consult Listing 14.9). Issue a second *step* command to step into the TColor constructor:

```
(gdb) step
TColor::TColor (this=0xbffffa68, color=RED, x=100, y=200)
  at color.cpp:21
21 TColor::TColor(TColors color, int x, int y):
```

Again, the debugger shows the parameter values passed to the constructor. Issue one more *step* command to step further down to the TCoordinate constructor:

```
(gdb) step
TCoordinate::TCoordinate (this=0xbffffa68, x=100, y=200)
  at coordinate.h:15
15 TCoordinate(int x, int y): tc_x(x), tc_y(y) { }
```

This reaches the lowest level in the class hierarchy. You could continue to issue **next** and **step** commands to further trace the code, and inspect each level in the initialization process of this object. When you're finished exploring, type a **continue** command (you can abbreviate it **cont**) to run the program to completion, and then type **q** to quit:

```
(gdb) cont
Continuing.
...
(gdb) q
```

Inspecting Object Data Members

Using the debugger, you can peer inside an object to inspect its data member values. To try this, reload the tlabel.cpp program:

```
$ gdb -- silent tlabel
(gdb)
```

As mentioned in this and prior chapters, providing for safe object copying is a necessary fact of life in C++ object-oriented programming. To inspect how the test program does this, set a breakpoint at the statement that copies one object to another:

```
dest_object = test;
```

Enter the following commands to set the breakpoint (it's at line 29 for me):

```
(gdb) b 29
Breakpoint 1 at 0x80488b7: file tlabel.cpp, line 29.
```

Next, run the program up to the breakpoint. You should see the assignment statement on the last output line:

```
(gdb) run
Starting program: /src/c14/tlabel
Breakpoint 1, main () at tlabel.cpp:29
29 dest_object = test;
```

Use a **print** command to inspect the data members of **dest_object** before the assignment statement executes:

```
(gdb) print dest_object
$1 = {<TColor> = {<TCoordinate> = {tc_x = 0, tc_y = 0},
tc_color = UNKNOWN,
  static colornames = 0x8049f00}, tl_label = 0x0}
```

The debugger assigns a pseudo name $1 to dest_object that you can use in other commands. In the output, braces segment the object according to its class hierarchy, but this style might seem a bit confusing at first. The innermost braces indicate that the tc_x and tc_y data members are set to zero for the TCoordinate portion of the object. At the next higher level, the TColor class's tc_color data member is set to UNKNOWN. Finally, at the dest_object's level, tl_label equals NULL (0x0). This format takes some getting used to, but it shows not only the object's data member values, but also its class organization.

To inspect the value of the object after assigning another to it, and in that way investigate the integrity of the class copy constructors and operator=() functions, issue a **next** command:

```
(gdb) next
30 display("Object after copy", dest_object);
```

Again, **print** the value of dest_object to compare its data members with those listed before:

```
(gdb) print dest_object
$2 = {<TColor> = {<TCoordinate> = {tc_x = 100, tc_y = 200},
   tc_color = RED,
   static colornames = 0x8049f00},
   tl_label = 0x804a538 "Test Label"}
```

I rearranged the lines somewhat to fit on this page. They show that each data member has been assigned a value. To compare those values with the source object, you could enter **print test** (not shown here).

Another useful method for inspecting object data members is to issue a **display** command. This prepares the debugger to display one or more objects each time the program pauses—for example, at a breakpoint or after a next command. If you are following along, enter these commands (if you quit, reload tlabel, set a breakpoint at line 30, run the program, and reissue the **display** command):

```
(gdb) display dest_object.tl_label
1: dest_object.tl_label = 0x804a538 "Test Label"
```

The debugger shows the value of the object's tl_label data member each time the program halts. To see this effect, issue a **next** command:

```
(gdb) next
Object after copy
x == 100; y == 200; color = Red (1); Test Label
32 return 0;
1: dest_object.tl_label = 0x804a538 "Test Label"
```

The first two lines of output after the command line are from the program itself. The last two lines are from the GNU debugger. Line 32 shows the next statement to execute. Last is the value of the tl_label data member, showing the string value and its address in memory. By the way, some other debuggers call display expressions "watches" or "watch expressions."

> **Tip**
>
> Type **display** with no arguments to see a list of all currently displayed expressions. To erase the display list, type **undisplay** and answer **yes** when prompted, "Delete all auto-display expressions?"

CALLING MEMBER FUNCTIONS

When debugging a specific member function, it might be useful to call it out of context. This is especially helpful in large programs when it's inconvenient to step to a statement merely to call a function.

To follow along, reload the tlabel program if necessary, set a breakpoint on line 30, and type *run*. Then issue a *call* command such as this:

```
(gdb) call dest_object.StrColor()
$2 = 0x8048ec7 "Red"
```

The command calls the TColor member function StrColor(), inherited by the TLabel class and therefore available through dest_object. When calling member functions, you must do so in reference to an object of the class. In response to the call command, the debugger displays the function's result.

FINDING THE TYPE OF AN OBJECT

To find the type of an object, use a *ptyp* command as follows:

```
(gdb) ptyp dest_object
type = class TLabel : public TColor {
private:
  char *tl_label;
public:
  TLabel(void);
  TLabel(char const *, TColors, int, int);
  TLabel(TLabel const &);
  ~TLabel(void);
  char * GetLabel(void) const;
  void SetLabel(char const *);
  void operator=(TLabel const &);
}
```

When used with a class object, the ptyp command prints the entire class declaration. Although this is useful for examples such as this one, very large classes display far too much information to be helpful. For that reason, it's probably best to have a copy of the source files handy to look up class and other large structure declarations.

SUMMARY

Using inheritance, you create new classes from existing ones. The new class is called the derived class. Its ancestor is called the base class. In a typical C++ program, many classes are derived from others, creating a hierarchy of classes that resembles a family tree. C++ offers two kinds of inheritance: single and multiple, although in practice, single inheritance is usually adequate. This chapter introduced inheritance along with related topics such as how to provide for the safe copying of derived-class objects. The chapter also introduced the protected: access specifier.

For more information on subjects introduced in this chapter, turn to the following chapters:

- Chapter 15, "Programming with Virtual Functions"
- Chapter 19, "Overloading Operators"
- Chapter 21, "Honing Your C++ Skills"

PROGRAMMING WITH VIRTUAL FUNCTIONS

Simply stated, a virtual function is one that is called based on an object's type. Several related classes, for instance, might declare a virtual function named Display(), each with a different but similar job to perform. For specific class objects, C++ decides which Display() function to call based on the objects' types. In a sense, with virtual functions, different sorts of objects "know" how to display themselves and perform other operations.

You might have heard this feature described as *polymorphism*, a term that weighs higher in exotic appeal than in technical accuracy. Although it's one of the backbones of object-oriented design, polymorphism is much easier to understand and use than many OOP authorities lead programmers to believe. Personally, I try to limit my use of the term. But I have found it useful at social events for getting away from inquisitive bores. "Excuse me, I have to go check my polymorphisms." I imagine they think I'm off to feed the piranhas or something.

POLY WANT A MORPHISM?

The fuel that fires polymorphism is the *pure virtual function*. This is literally a placeholder that a base class expects its derived classes to complete. For example, ignoring other declarations a real class needs, a TShape class might declare a pure virtual function named Draw():

```
class TShape {
public:
  virtual void Draw() = 0;
};
```

The pure virtual function Draw() resembles a common member function, but begins with the reserved word virtual and ends with the expression =0. The presence of one or more pure virtual functions creates what's known as an *abstract class*. This means that it is not possible to create a TShape object because, as an abstraction, the class is incomplete.

To use the abstract class, a derived class is expected to inherit TShape and complete the pure virtual Draw() function. Again ignoring other necessary items such as constructors and data members, you might declare the descendant class like this:

```
class TCircle: public TShape {
public:
  virtual void Draw();
};
```

Because the expression =0 is not specified, Draw() is a normal virtual function that replaces the inherited pure virtual function of the same name. Somewhere, the program must implement the TCircle::Draw() function, in this case, to draw a circle, perhaps by calling a subroutine in a graphics library (this is just for illustration):

```
void TCircle::Draw()
{
  graphicsDrawCircle();  // Or whatever draws a circle
}
```

The word virtual isn't needed in the function's implementation; only in its class prototype. (Virtual functions can also be implemented inline.) Similarly, another class might inherit TShape using the following declaration:

```
class TRectangle: public TShape {
public:
  virtual void Draw();
};
```

As in TCircle, the TRectangle class declares the normal virtual function Draw() without the =0 expression, and the program must implement that function, in this case, to draw a rectangle:

```
void TRectangle::Draw()
{
  graphicsDrawRectangle();  // Or whatever draws a rectangle
}
```

The importance of this code is not in its graphics capabilities but in statements that operate on TShape objects. For example, the program might have a function with a TShape reference parameter:

```
void DoDrawing(TShape &shape)
{
  shape.Draw();  // !!!
}
```

Consider this function carefully. It tells the shape object to Draw() itself. But which Draw() function is called? The answer depends on the object's type. If it's a TCircle object, C++ calls TCircle::Draw(). If it's a TRectangle object, C++ calls TRectangle::Draw().

Instead of writing functions that operate on specific shapes such as TCircle and TRectangle, with virtual functions, you can create a single DoDrawing() function with a reference parameter of the abstract base class TShape. This states that any object of a class derived from TShape may be passed to the function. The program could, for example, create TCircle and TRectangle objects, and pass them to DoDrawing() using statements such as

```
TCircle circle;
TRectangle rect;
DoDrawing(circle);     // !!!
DoDrawing(rectangle);  // !!!
```

Through the magic of inheritance, it is perfectly acceptable to pass the circle and rectangle objects to the function's TShape reference parameter. After all, TCircle and TRectangle objects are specific types of TShapes, in much the same way that oaks and maples are types of trees. Inside the function, however, the statement

```
shape.Draw();
```

calls the Draw() function *based on the type of the shape object*. This is polymorphism. The preceding statement is completely generic. It can draw any shape of a class derived from TShape. What's more, future programming can add another type of TShape object—a TEllipse class, for instance—and the preceding code recognizes the new shape without modification and, especially important, without recompiling. You don't even need the original source code to plug new objects into the program.

Tip
You may declare pointers and references to abstract classes such as TShape, but because you cannot create abstract class objects, it isn't possible to pass TShape objects by value to function parameters.

CREATING A CONTAINER CLASS

A classic and most useful application for virtual functions is the development of *container classes*. A container is a general purpose object that can store other objects. To use a container, you simply construct an object of a container class and stuff your data objects into it. A well-designed container can store, search, sort, and perform other jobs on objects. Because they are designed using C++ object-oriented classes, containers tend to be far more versatile, and much safer, than other common C and C++ storage mechanisms such as arrays and linked lists.

In the coming sections, you develop the TContainer class, which can store and sort data objects. The class is usable, but to keep it within a reasonable size for listing in this book, it is stripped of miscellaneous functions. However, in describing the programming, I suggest some modifications for creating a practical container class based on TContainer.

Note
The TContainer class listings are more lengthy than most in this book. To make the programming more comprehensible, I divided the listings into pieces. The full text is in files container.h, container.cpp, and tcontain.cpp on the CD-ROM.

ABSTRACT CLASSES

Listing 15.1, container.h, shows about half of the container.h header file. This part of the header file declares the TObject abstract class as the basis for data objects to be stored in a container.

LISTING 15.1   CONTAINER.H (PARTIAL)

```
#define DEFAULT_SIZE 100        // Default container capacity

class TObject;                  // Incomplete class declaration
typedef TObject * PTObject;     // Pointer to a TObject object
typedef PTObject * PPTObject;   // Pointer to a TObject pointer

// Abstract class for items to store in a container
//
class TObject {
public:
  virtual ~TObject() { };
  virtual int Compare(PTObject p) = 0;
  virtual void Display() = 0;
};
```

After specifying a DEFAULT_SIZE constant for the default size of a container object, the header declares three items. First is an *incomplete class declaration* in the form

```
class TObject;
```

This states that the symbol TObject is a class with an as-yet-unknown body. It allows the program to use the symbol as though such a class exists. For example, in this case, we need two types of pointers, declared by the next two lines:

```
typedef TObject * PTObject;
typedef PTObject * PPTObject;
```

The first line declares PTObject of type TObject * (pointer to a TObject). The second line declares PPTObject as type PTObject * (pointer to a TObject pointer). I like to include type definitions such as these to make declaring pointers and arrays easier.

VIRTUAL DESTRUCTORS

Next in container.h (refer to Listing 15.1) is TObject's class declaration. It states that TObject has three public virtual member functions. Because no objects are ever created of the TObject abstract class, it has no constructor. However, to provide for the deletion of objects of classes derived from TObject, the class declares a virtual destructor:

```
virtual ~TObject() { };
```

The virtual destructor begins with the virtual reserved word, followed by the function name (always equal to the ~ character and the class name). Destructors may not declare parameters. They may perform statements, but in this case, we want only a placeholder for future destructors in derived classes, so this destructor's body is empty.

Notice that this is not a pure virtual function ending with =0. You may declare pure virtual destructors; however, I wanted to show the difference between pure and normal virtual function declarations. As mentioned, a pure virtual function requires no implementation— it is purely a placeholder that a derived class is expected to supply. A normal virtual function such as the TObject destructor requires an implementation, even if that consists of an empty statement block that does nothing. Both types of virtual functions serve similar purposes— they provide the mechanism that C++ uses to call a specific function based on an object's type.

PURE VIRTUAL FUNCTIONS

The TObject class in Listing 15.1 also declares two pure virtual functions, Compare() and Display():

```
virtual int Compare(PTObject p) = 0;
virtual void Display() = 0;
```

These are typical types of pure virtual functions. The Compare() function returns an integer value as the result of comparing two objects. The first object in that comparison is the one for which Compare() is called. The second is an object addressed by pointer p. You might wonder how TObject can compare two objects of unknown types. It can't. But it can state, using a pure virtual function, that TObject is a class that has the *capability* of comparing two objects of classes derived from TObject. Those classes, as a later example shows, provide actual Compare() functions.

However, before such classes even exist, the compiler allows statements to call the virtual TObject::Compare() function even though it is merely a placeholder and contains no real code. At runtime, an actual Compare() is called based on the type of object involved—an action that goes by the technical term *late binding*. By that process, the actual binding, or linking, of statements to functions such as Compare() occurs at runtime instead of during compilation as is the case for a common C or C++ function.

TObject declares a second pure virtual function, Display(). Here again, a derived class is expected to implement the actual function that C++ calls based on the type of object involved. Later examples show how to derive a class from TObject and complete its pure virtual functions. First, however, let's take a look at the container class.

THE TContainer CLASS

Listing 15.2 shows the rest of the container.h header file and the declaration of the TContainer class.

LISTING 15.2   CONTAINER.H (PARTIAL)

```
class TContainer {
private:
  int size;             // Capacity of objects array
  int count;            // Number of object in array
  PPTObject objects;    // Array of TObject pointers
protected:
  void Quicksort(int left, int right);
public:
  TContainer(int n = DEFAULT_SIZE);  // Constructor
 ~TContainer();                      // Destructor
  //
  // Inline member functions
  //
  bool IsFull() const { return (count >= size); }
  int GetSize() const { return size; }
  int GetCount() const { return count; }
  //
  // Other public member functions
  //
  void PutObject(PTObject pto);
  void ShowAllObjects(const char *msg);
  void Sort();
};
```

Like most well-designed classes, TContainer declares all of its data members private. In this case, there are three variables:

```
int size;
int count;
PPTObject objects;
```

The integer size equals the capacity of the container—how many objects it can hold. The integer count specifies how many objects the container actually holds. The third variable, objects, is of type PPTObject. It is literally a pointer to an array of TObject pointers, the storage mechanism I have chosen for this class.

> **Tip**
>
> Because TContainer's storage mechanism is private to the class, the method used for storing objects in a container can be changed without affecting programs that use the class.

The TContainer class contains one protected declaration—a function Quicksort() that implements the Quicksort algorithm:

```
protected: void Quicksort(int left, int right);
```

Because this function is protected, any classes derived from TContainer may call it. They may also replace the function by redeclaring it and writing new code for the function's implementation. Declaring Quicksort() public seems unwise because program statements are unlikely to need direct access to the container's sorting algorithm. For that, the class provides a public function, Sort(), that calls the protected function.

> **Tip**
>
> It is sometimes difficult to decide whether to make a function public, private, or protected. In general, if a function is called strictly by other member functions, and especially if it depends on the internal nature of the class's private data objects, it is best made private or protected. If a function provides a general operation—such as Display() or Sort()—then it probably should be public.

TContainer declares six public functions. The first three are simple, and for that reason, implemented inline:

```
bool IsFull() const { return (count >= size); }
int GetSize() const { return size; }
int GetCount() const { return count; }
```

Function IsFull() returns true if the container's count equals its size. (The greater-or-equal test is just to cover all base—count should never be greater than size.) GetSize() and GetCount() merely return their associated private variables. In your classes, resist making variables such as size and count public in a misguided attempt to eliminate functions that merely return values. Instead, declare the functions inline and compile with the -O option to have the compiler inject the function statements directly into the code. This costs you nothing in performance but greatly facilitates future maintenance.

Finally in TContainer are three public member functions that are implemented in a separate module:

```
void PutObject(PTObject pto);
void ShowAllObjects(const char *msg);
void Sort();
```

Function PutObject() inserts a new object into the container. Its parameter pto is of type PTObject (pointer to a TObject). The actual type of object is determined at runtime, but it must be one of a class derived from TObject. Except for that restriction, PutObject can insert *any* type of data into the container. The other two functions have obvious purposes. ShowAllObjects() provides a simple way to display the container's contents. Sort() arranges the contained objects. The next section explains more about how it is possible to write functions such as these before even considering what objects the container actually holds.

> **Note**
>
> The preceding listings describe all aspects of a container class without knowledge of the types of data it may contain. Such generality is one of the main benefits that object-oriented programming provides.

CALLING VIRTUAL FUNCTIONS

Listing 15.3 shows part of the TContainer class's implementation module and demonstrates how a program can call virtual functions that are not yet completed.

LISTING 15.3   CONTAINER.CPP

```
#include <iostream.h>
#include <stdlib.h>      // Need exit()
#include "container.h"   // Need TContainer

// Constructor
TContainer::TContainer(int n)
{
  if (n <= 0) n = 1;  // Must have at least one element
  size = n;              // Remember capacity
  count = 0;            // Container is empty
  //
  // Create array of object pointers and set to NULL
  //
  objects = new PTObject[size];
  for (int i = 0; i < size; i++)
    objects[i] = NULL;
}

// Destructor
// Define DEBUG to display trace
TContainer::~TContainer()
{
  for (int i = 0; i < count; i++)
    delete objects[i];  // Delete contained objects
#ifdef DEBUG
  cout << "Deleting container" << endl;
#endif
  delete objects;        // Delete array of TObject pointers
}

// Insert new object into container
void TContainer::PutObject(PTObject pto)
```

```
{
  if (IsFull()) {
    cout << "*** Error: Container is full" << endl;
    exit(1);
  }
  objects[count] = pto;
  count++;
}
```

The first function implemented in container.cpp is the `TContainer()` constructor. After initializing the `size` and `count` private data members, the constructor creates the storage mechanism used to hold objects. Examine these statements carefully:

```
objects = new PTObject[size];
for (int i = 0; i < size; i++)
  objects[i] = NULL;
```

The first line creates an array of `PTObject` pointers and assigns the result to the private `objects` pointer. Other storage mechanisms are certainly possible, but this one is general enough to handle any type of object of a class derived from `TObject`. The program can address such objects using a `TObject` pointer because, at runtime, C++ calls that class's virtual functions based on the object's *actual* type. The second statement uses a `for` loop to initialize each `TObject` pointer in the `objects` array to `NULL`. No real objects exist at this point until the program calls `PutObject()` to insert them. But the container is constructed and ready to go. In the program, a statement can construct a container and insert an object using statements such as

```
TContainer box;
box.PutObject(new TMyClass(data));
```

Or, the container could also be created using `new`:

```
TContainer * pbox = new TContainer(10);
pbox->PutObject(new TMyClass(data));
```

This hypothetical code assumes that `TMyClass` is derived from `TObject`. Specifying a count for the container such as 10 is optional—the container's size defaults to 100 if no size is given.

Next in container.cpp is the `TContainer` destructor. This shows an obscure use for virtual functions that might not be obvious from the source code, but it is a vital technique to learn for creating general-purpose containers:

```
for (int i = 0; i < count; i++)
  delete objects[i];   // Delete contained objects
delete objects;        // Delete array of TObject pointers
```

The `for` loop deletes each object in the array. It can do this because `TObject` declares a virtual destructor. Because of that, at runtime, C++ calls the *actual* destructor for the objects in the array. The only rule is that those objects must be of classes derived from `TObject`. After deleting the individual objects, the program deletes the `objects` pointer itself. This completely frees all allocated memory when the container itself is destroyed.

> **Note**
>
> The TContainer destructor includes an output statement that you can enable to trace
> destructor calls at runtime. To enable the trace, specify the -DDEBUG (define DEBUG) option
> when compiling the module.

Finally in this portion of the TContainer implementation module is the function
PutObject(), which inserts a new object into the container. The function begins by checking
whether the container is full:

```
if (IsFull()) {
  cout << "*** Error: Container is full" << endl;
  exit(1);
}
```

This points out a major deficiency in the TContainer class. Ideally, if the container is full, it
would take steps to expand itself to accommodate new data. Failing that, it would throw an
exception to report any errors instead of exiting the program with an error message. However, the code to improve the class would expand this chapter to unwieldy lengths, and
exceptions are for Chapter 16, "Handling Exceptions."

If the container is not full, two simple statements insert the new object:

```
objects[count] = pto;
count++;
```

At this point, TContainer has no specific knowledge of the type of object it holds. All it
knows, and all it needs to know, is that pto of type PTObject addresses an object of a class
derived from TObject. The function also increments count to keep track of how many
objects are in the container.

Listing 15.4, container.cpp, completes the TContainer implementation module and shows
additional uses of virtual TObject member functions.

LISTING 15.4   CONTAINER.CPP (PARTIAL)

```
// Call Display() for all objects in container
void TContainer::ShowAllObjects(const char *msg)
{
  cout << msg << endl;
  cout << "Number of objects == " << count << endl;
  for (int i = 0; i < count; i++)
    objects[i]->Display();  // Calls virtual function!
  cout << endl << endl;
}

void TContainer::Quicksort(int left, int right)
{
  int i = left;
  int j = right;
  PTObject test = objects[(left + right) / 2];
  PTObject swap;
  do {
    while (objects[i]->Compare(test) < 0) i++;
```

```
      while (test->Compare(objects[j]) < 0) j--;
      if (i <= j) {
        swap = objects[i];
        objects[i] = objects[j];
        objects[j] = swap;
        i++;
        j--;
      }
  } while (i <= j);
  if (left < j) Quicksort(left, j);
  if (i < right) Quicksort(i, right);
}

// Sort objects in container
void TContainer::Sort()
{
  if (count > 1) Quicksort(0, count - 1);
}
```

Function ShowAllObjects() calls the Display() member function for each object in the container using a for loop:

```
for (int i = 0; i < count; i++)
  objects[i]->Display();
```

Although apparently simple, this for loop shows the power of a virtual function. The code for TObject::Display() doesn't even exist at this point, but C++ allows statements to call it as shown here. It can do that because the pointers in the objects array address objects of types descended from TObject. Those types implement the *actual* Display() function that C++ calls. In other words, at runtime, C++ decides which actual Display() function to call based on the type of object that objects[i] addresses. Even better, if another module creates an entirely new class based on TObject (or another derivative), the preceding code recognizes the new type of object *without* modification and *without* recompiling!

In a similar way, the class's protected Quicksort() member function calls the Compare() pure virtual member function declared in TObject. It does that in the following two while loops:

```
while (objects[i]->Compare(test) < 0) i++;
while (test->Compare(objects[j]) < 0) j--;
```

As with the calls to Display(), the calls to actual Compare() functions are routed at runtime. The container possesses no knowledge of the types of objects it contains. All it knows is that they are of types descended from TObject, and that this class has the capability of comparing two objects. It is up to the derived classes to define what Compare() really does, but because the function is virtual, the program can call it in advance of the function's implementation.

Finally in the TContainer implementation module, function Sort() calls Quicksort() to sort the container's contents:

```
if (count > 1) Quicksort(0, count - 1);
```

As implemented here, the Quicksort algorithm works only for two or more objects, and it is therefore more convenient to call it using what you might call a utility function. However, I included this code to show how, by way of a public member function such as Sort(), the module controls access to its actual sorting mechanism in the protected Quicksort() function. Any changes to the sorting algorithm do not affect statements that call the public Sort() function.

Note

> The Quicksort() function in TContainer moves only TObject pointers, and it is therefore very fast and efficient. Its speed depends entirely on the efficiency of the Compare() virtual function in classes derived from TObject. The size of objects in the container otherwise have no direct effect on sorting speed.

DERIVING FROM ABSTRACT CLASSES

The preceding sections fully implement the TContainer class. To compile the class's module, container.cpp, with tracing enabled, use the command

```
$ g++ -c -DDEBUG container.cpp
```

You now have two files, container.h and container.o, containing the compiled code for the TContainer class. Most important is to realize that you may now derive new classes from TObject and insert objects of your classes into the container. To do this requires only those two files. The original source code in container.cpp isn't needed, and unless you revise the module, it never needs recompiling. Virtual functions and object-oriented inheritance make it possible to use and expand the TObject and TContainer classes to accommodate new data types and operations.

As an example of how this works, Listing 15.5 shows part of a test program that puts TContainer to work. The program demonstrates how to inherit and complete an abstract class such as TObject that contains one or more pure virtual member functions. Because of the listing's length, I discuss it in pieces here.

LISTING 15.5 TCONTAIN.CPP (PARTIAL)

```cpp
#include <iostream.h>
#include <string.h>      // Need strlen(), strcpy()
#include <stdlib.h>      // Need free()
#include "container.h"   // Need TContainer

class TMyObject: public TObject {
private:
  char *sp;  // Pointer to a string
public:
  TMyObject(const char *s) {
    sp = new char[strlen(s) + 1];
    strcpy(sp, s);
  }
  virtual ~TMyObject();
  virtual int Compare(PTObject p);
  virtual void Display();
};
```

Because TContainer stores objects of classes descended from TObject, and because TObject is an abstract class with three virtual functions, the first step in using the container is to derive a new class from TObject. Any name will do—I call my class TMyObject. Its lone private data member is a pointer to a string—this might be any object or pointer to whatever type of data you want to store in the container.

As usual, a constructor initializes objects of the TMyObject class. In this case, the inline constructor calls the standard library functions strlen() and strcpy() to copy the string passed to the constructor's parameter. The other three functions are implemented separately, as shown in Listing 15.6.

LISTING 15.6   TCONTAIN.CPP (PARTIAL)

```
// Destructor
// Define DEBUG to trace
TMyObject::~TMyObject()
{
#ifdef DEBUG
  cout << "Inside destructor for " << sp << endl;
#endif
  delete[] sp;
}

// Compare two TMyObject objects
int TMyObject::Compare(PTObject p)
{
  return strcmp(sp, ((TMyObject *)p)->sp);
}

// Display contents of this object
void TMyObject::Display()
{
  cout << sp << "  ";
}
```

These three TMyObject functions are declared exactly the same as the pure virtual member functions in TObject, minus the =0 suffix. First implemented here is the virtual destructor. It begins by displaying a trace if the DEBUG symbol is defined during compilation. You can remove this code if you want—I include it only to demonstrate how virtual destructors operate. The destructor uses delete[] to dispose of the memory the constructor allocates.

The virtual function Compare() calls another standard function, strcmp(), to compare two strings in TMyObject objects. Carefully examine this code:

```
return strcmp(sp, ((TMyObject *)p)->sp);
```

Variable sp belongs to the object for which Compare() is called. The other string is in the object addressed by the pointer p passed to Compare(). The function merely returns the result of the standard comparison function. Recall from earlier that the Quicksort() function calls Compare(), but consider that the preceding code is written *after* the TContainer class and its sorting functions were compiled. At runtime, C++ calls TMyObject::Compare()

to compare two TMyObject objects in the container, and in that way, can sort objects of which it has no prior knowledge.

The final virtual function in TMyObject, Display(), finishes the completion of the abstract TObject class. Now that all three virtual member functions are implemented, it is possible to compile a program that creates a container and stores objects inside. Listing 15.7 lists the rest of the program.

LISTING 15.7   TCONTAIN.CPP (PARTIAL)

```
int main()
{
  cout << endl << "Test TContainer class" << endl << endl;

  TContainer * container = new TContainer(100);

  container->PutObject(new TMyObject("Peach"));
  container->PutObject(new TMyObject("Mango"));
  container->PutObject(new TMyObject("Lime"));
  container->PutObject(new TMyObject("Banana"));
  container->PutObject(new TMyObject("Kiwi"));
  container->PutObject(new TMyObject("Grapefruit"));
  container->PutObject(new TMyObject("Orange"));
  container->PutObject(new TMyObject("Lemon"));
  container->PutObject(new TMyObject("Apple"));

  container->ShowAllObjects("Before sorting");
  container->Sort();
  container->ShowAllObjects("After sorting");

  delete container;

  return 0;
}
```

The program's main() function creates a TContainer object in dynamic memory using new. It doesn't have to create the container this way. It could define it as a global variable:

```
TContainer container;
```

If you don't supply a size value, the container defaults to a maximum size of 100 objects. Statements such as the following insert new objects into the container:

```
container->PutObject(new TMyObject("Peach"));
container->PutObject(new TMyObject("Mango"));
```

Because PutObject() simply stores a pointer to a TObject-derived object, this code is highly efficient. It uses new to construct a data object of the TMyObject class. Simply passing the result to PutObject() inserts the object's pointer into the container. No temporary objects result from this code. After inserting a bunch of objects, the program displays them by calling the TContainer member function ShowAllObjects(), and sorts them alphabetically by calling Sort(). The statements are easily understood:

```
container->ShowAllObjects("Before sorting");
container->Sort();
container->ShowAllObjects("After sorting");
```

Finally, the program deletes the container with the statement:

```
delete container;
```

That line is deceptively simple, as a trace of the program at runtime reveals. Not only does this single statement delete the container object, it also deletes all objects held in the container by calling the virtual ~TMyObject() destructor. To verify that this is indeed the case, compile the container.cpp module and tcontain.cpp program with the -D option to specify a symbol named DEBUG. Enter these commands to compile and run the test:

```
$ g++ -c -DDEBUG container.cpp
$ g++ -DDEBUG tcontain.cpp container.o
$ ./a.out
```

The DEBUG symbol enables tracing of the TContainer and TMyObject destructors, producing the following output onscreen (I deleted a few lines for brevity). As the output shows, deleting the container also deletes all objects stored in the container:

```
Before sorting
Number of objects == 9
Peach  Mango  Lime  Banana  Kiwi  Grapefruit  Orange  Lemon  Apple
After sorting
Number of objects == 9
Apple  Banana  Grapefruit  Kiwi  Lemon  Lime  Mango  Orange  Peach
Inside destructor for Apple
Inside destructor for Banana
...
Inside destructor for Orange
Inside destructor for Peach
Deleting container
```

Note See also Chapter 17, "Creating Class Templates," for another approach you might use for developing generic classes such as containers that can store objects of various types.

MULTIPLE INHERITANCE

As mentioned, multiple inheritance seems like a grand idea until it comes time to use the technique. The topic is appropriate in this chapter because of a common trouble that arises in using multiple inheritance that resembles a kind of recursion caused by a class appearing multiple times in the hierarchy. The solution uses something called a *virtual base class*—but first, let's take a look at the basics of multiple inheritance.

LOADING THE BASES

Deriving a class from multiple base classes is easy. As many C++ books show, simply inherit two or more base classes using a declaration such as

```
class D: public A, public B, private C {
// ... class contents
};
```

In this example, the new, derived class D inherits three classes, A, B, and C. It specifies that members in A and B retain their private, protected, and public access status in the new class, but that all members of C are to become private members of D.

The trouble with the foregoing example is that, although technically correct, it doesn't take reality into consideration. Chances are, unless you are the lucky type, some names in A, B, and C will conflict. For instance, suppose that classes A and B each have a public Display() member function. To decide which function to call requires using the class name and C++ scope resolution operator in statements such as these:

```
Display();      // ??? Ambiguous. Won't compile.
A::Display();   // Call A's Display() function
B::Display();   // Call B's Display() function
```

Unless class D declares its own Display() function, the first line doesn't compile. As shown, to resolve the name conflict among multiple Display() functions, you must use designations such as A:: and B::. This works, but is messy, and it places the responsibility of calling the correct function on the programmer—a requirement that object-oriented programming is supposed to help you avoid.

USING MULTIPLE BASE CLASS CONSTRUCTORS

When inheriting from multiple base classes, you must be careful to create constructors that initialize all inherited elements. In general, you might declare the derived class and its constructor like this:

```
class D: public A, public B, private C {
public:
  D(): A(), B(), C() { }
};
```

The constructor D() calls the constructors for the three inherited classes, but in this case, it performs no other actions so its statement block is empty. Again, the code seems simple enough at first. However, C++ specifies that the constructors are called in the order listed. If one class object depends on one of the others, the resulting conflict can cause impossibly confusing results. This can happen particularly when classes declare themselves to be friends of other classes, a topic for Chapter 18, "Overloading Your Friends" in Part IV, "Advanced C++ Techniques." To avoid this type of trouble, try to create classes that operate as independently as possible—good advice whether or not you intend to use multiple inheritance.

> **Note**
>
> In many cases, instead of fussing with multiple inheritance, a class can declare objects of other classes as private data members and in that way incorporate more than one class into the design of a new one. This technique also gives the class total control over the order in which the contained objects are initialized.

USING VIRTUAL BASE CLASSES

Derived classes and their bases form a class hierarchy that can grow tremendously complex even in relatively simple programs. A base class can be inherited by one or more other classes that in turn can become base classes for still more classes. All these classes are consequently related by single or multiple inheritance as though they were biblical characters begetting one another until no one can tell who is related to whom.

It's easy to understand how conflicts arise in such a complex class family tree, especially when multiple inheritance is involved. One of the most common conflicts occurs when a derived class inherits too many copies of a particular base—like lottery winners, for example, who suddenly acquire more "cousins" than they previously knew existed.

To demonstrate how derived classes can get into inheritance trouble, examine the classes from the following program in Listing 15.8, franch.cpp. The program uses familiar relationships between fictitious companies and three fictitious franchisees: Bob, Ted, and Alice. The program might seem a bit silly, but borrowing familiar relationships from the real world helps to explain a typical and often exasperating problem with multiple inheritance.

LISTING 15.8   FRANCH.CPP

```
#include <iostream.h>
#include <string.h>    // Need strlen(), strcpy()
#include <stdlib.h>    // Need free()

class Company {
private:
  char *name;
public:
  Company(const char *s) {
    name = new char[strlen(s) + 1];
    strcpy(name, s);
    cout << " In constructor for ";
    Display();
  }
  virtual ~Company() {
    cout << " In destructor for ";
    Display();
    delete[] name;
  }
  void Display() { cout << name << endl; }
};
```

continues

LISTING 15.8   CONTINUED

```cpp
class Jennys: public Company {
public:
  Jennys(): Company("Jenny's") { }
};

class McDougles: public Company {
public:
  McDougles(): Company("McDougles") { }
};

class BurgerQueen: public Company {
public:
  BurgerQueen(): Company("BurgerQueen") { }
};

class Bob:
  public Jennys,
  public McDougles {
};

class Ted:
  public McDougles,
  public BurgerQueen {
};

class Alice:
  public Jennys,
  public McDougles,
  public BurgerQueen {
};

int main()
{
  Bob *bobp;
  Ted *tedp;
  Alice *alicep;

  cout << endl << "Initializing Bob's restaurant" << endl;
  bobp = new Bob;
  cout << "Initializing Ted's restaurant" << endl;
  tedp = new Ted;
  cout << "Initializing Alice's restaurant" << endl;
  alicep = new Alice;

  cout << endl << "Deleting Bob's restaurant" << endl;
  delete bobp;
  cout << "Deleting Ted's restaurant" << endl;
  delete tedp;
  cout << "Deleting Alice's restaurant" << endl;
  delete alicep;
  return 0;
}
```

Figure 15.1 shows the relationships among the classes in Franch.cpp. At the root of the hierarchy is the Company class, which serves as a base class for three derived classes: Jennys,

McDougles, and BurgerQueen. Each of these "company" classes is derived from Company, and each class therefore inherits a name data member and a Display() member function.

Figure 15.1
The three classes Bob, Ted, and Alice are derived using multiple inheritance.

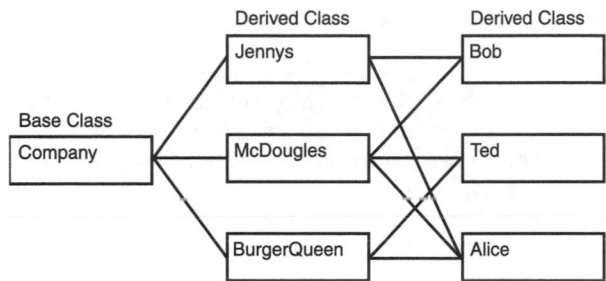

Our three adventurous investors, Bob, Ted, and Alice, are derived using multiple inheritance (refer to Listing 15.8). Class Bob derives his culinary empire from two Company classes, Jennys and McDougles. Class Ted derives his fortunes from McDougles and BurgerQueen. Alice, the most enterprising soul in the group, takes on the three Company classes: Jennys, McDougles, and BurgerQueen. When you compile and run the program with the following commands, you see a report that indicates when the constructors and destructors are called for objects created of the highest level classes, Bob, Ted, and Alice:

```
$ g++ franch.cpp
$ ./a.out
```

Although I don't show the program's lengthy output here, onscreen you see the results of creating objects with a statement such as

```
bobp = new Bob;
...
delete Bob;
```

As you see onscreen when you run the program, all the proper constructors and destructors for the complex class hierarchy are called. So far, so good. But a subtle problem with the class relationships arises if another class is derived from the group of companies and investors. Suppose that a corporation purchases some of the parent companies and selected franchisees. As in the real world of corporate finance, the complex relationships among companies and people can easily get out of hand. Consider a Corporation class that attempts with multiple inheritance to inherit the McDougles company along with franchisees Ted and Alice:

```
class Corporation:
  public McDougles,     // ???
  public Ted,
  public Alice {
...
};
```

Refer to Figure 15.1 and you can see why this Corporation can never get off the ground. This is because Ted and Alice already derive in part from McDougles. When Corporation attempts to do the same, it ends up with multiple McDougles base classes. At this point, the compiler warns you about the ambiguous and inaccessible base class:

```
atest.cpp:59: warning: direct base 'McDougles' inaccessible
in 'Corporation' due to ambiguity
```

> **Note**
>
> Some compilers report the foregoing condition as an error and do not compile the program. GNU C++ merely issues a warning. However, if you receive this warning in code that uses multiple inheritance, ignoring it could lead to serious bugs. The following section explains how to fix the problem.

FIXING AMBIGUOUS BASE CLASSES

When you receive a warning about an ambiguous base class in a hierarchy of classes related through multiple inheritance, try to identify those base classes that require only a single object. In the case of Corporation, it makes sense to have only one McDougles company. Even though Ted is derived from McDougles, it is the same McDougles that Corporation is attempting to inherit. In the process of acquiring Ted's assets, the Corporation does not end up with two separate McDougles parent companies. There's only one such parent that is related to Corporation directly and indirectly through Ted.

In similar, but less frivolous, situations, in which a multiple-derived class requires only one copy of a multiple-inherited base class, you can reduce those bases to one instance by declaring them all to be *virtual base classes*. In a class hierarchy, there is only one copy of a virtual base class object, even when that object's class is inherited more than once. Listing 15.9, conglom.cpp, demonstrates how to form a Corporation class that uses virtual base classes and solves the problem of a proliferation of McDougles bases. Compile the program and run it using the commands:

```
$ g++ conglom.cpp
$ ./a.out
```

LISTING 15.9   CONGLOM.CPP

```cpp
#include <iostream.h>
#include <string.h>    // Need strlen(), strcpy()
#include <stdlib.h>    // Need free()

class Company {
private:
  char *name;
public:
  Company(const char *s) {
    name = new char[strlen(s) + 1];
    strcpy(name, s);
    cout << " In constructor for ";
    Display();
  }
  virtual ~Company() {
    cout << " In destructor for ";
    Display();
```

```
     delete[] name;
   }
   void Display() { cout << name << '\n'; }
};

class Jennys: public Company {
public:
   Jennys(): Company("Jenny's") { }
};

class McDougles: public Company {
public:
   McDougles(): Company("McDougles") { }
};

class BurgerQueen: public Company {
public:
   BurgerQueen(): Company("BurgerQueen") { }
};

class Bob:
   virtual public Jennys,
   virtual public McDougles {
};

class Ted:
   virtual public McDougles,
   virtual public BurgerQueen {
};

class Alice:
   virtual public Jennys,
   virtual public McDougles,
   virtual public BurgerQueen {
};

class Corporation:
   virtual public McDougles,
   public Ted,
   public Alice {
private:
   char *name;
public:
   Corporation(): McDougles(), Ted(), Alice()
     { name = "Conglomerate Industries"; }
   void Display() { cout << name << endl; }
};

int main()
{
   cout << endl << "Forming a corporation" << endl;
   Corporation *cp;
   cp = new Corporation;
   cp->Display();
   delete cp;
   return 0;
}
```

In the new program, class Company is unchanged, as are Jennys, McDougles, and BurgerQueen. However, Bob, Ted, and Alice are modified to prevent future derivations from ending up with too many copies of their parent base classes. For example, Bob is now declared as

```
class Bob:
  virtual public Jennys,
  virtual public McDougles {
};
```

Adding the reserved word virtual to the listed base classes tells the compiler that, in a subsequent derivation, there should be only one instance of those two base classes. Similarly, Ted and Alice declare their base classes virtual. The revised code now permits the Corporation class to be declared with no ambiguous references to base classes:

```
class Corporation:
  virtual public McDougles,
  virtual public Ted,
  virtual public Alice {
...
};
```

The Corporation class inherits McDougles, Ted, and Alice. By specifying McDougles as a virtual base class, only one copy of that Company class exists in the final result, despite the fact that Ted and Alice are also derived from McDougles. Ted and Alice don't strictly need to be virtual in this case, unless another class is derived from Corporation.

Note

Don't be too concerned if the preceding discussion takes a reading or two to understand—as I mentioned, multiple inheritance can be more trouble than it first seems. If you need to use multiple inheritance, be prepared for the warning mentioned here, and if this happens, try making inherited classes virtual bases to fix the problem.

DEBUGGING CLASSES WITH VIRTUAL FUNCTIONS

The GNU debugger has no special support for debugging class objects that have virtual functions. However, when classes are implemented in separate modules, setting breakpoints and tracing code takes a few extra tricks as explained next.

DEBUGGING CLASSES IN SEPARATE MODULES

To follow along, compile the container.cpp module and tcontain.cpp test program for the TContainer, TObject, and TMyObject classes. Use these commands:

```
$ g++ -g -c -DDEBUG container.cpp
$ g++ -g -DDEBUG -o tcontain tcontain.cpp container.o
```

The commands create the executable code file tcontain with debugging information attached. Load the result into the GNU debugger:

```
$ gdb --silent tcontain
```

To demonstrate a problem when debugging separate modules, type *list* until you find the line that constructs a new TContainer object and set a breakpoint there (it's line 31 for me):

```
(gdb) list
...
31 TContainer * container = new TContainer(100);
(gdb) b 31
Breakpoint 1 at 0x80489e5: file tcontain.cpp, line 31.
```

Next, run the program up to the breakpoint:

```
(gdb) run
Starting program: /src/c15/tcontain
...
Breakpoint 1, main () at tcontain.cpp:31
31 TContainer * container = new TContainer(100);
```

The program is now paused just before it constructs the TContainer object. Unfortunately, attempting to trace into the operation produces unexpected results. Try a *step* command:

```
(gdb) step
strcmp (p1=0x80485ff "_ _environ", p2=0x8048516
  "_ _builtin_new") at ../sysdeps/generic/strcmp.c:30
../sysdeps/generic/strcmp.c:30: No such file or directory.
Current language:  auto; currently c
```

This fails to produce the expected results because, apparently, the debugger attempts to trace into the code for the C++ new operator rather than the TContainer() constructor. So, try again. First, delete all breakpoints:

```
(gdb) delete
Delete all breakpoints? (y or n) y
```

Then, list the module that implements the TContainer class. For unexplained reasons, it is apparently necessary to give a starting line number along with the filename:

```
(gdb) list container.cpp:1
```

After specifying a line number the first time, you can simply type *list* again to display more of the file. Enter list commands until you find the following lines:

```
(gdb) list
...
13 // Constructor
14 TContainer::TContainer(int n)
15 {
16   if (n <= 0) n = 1;
```

Set a breakpoint on the first statement in the constructor, and then run the program (if the debugger asks whether to restart the program from the beginning, answer yes):

```
(gdb) b 16
Breakpoint 2 at 0x8048ec0: file container.cpp, line 16.
(gdb) run
Starting program: /src/c15/tcontain
...
Breakpoint 2, TContainer::TContainer (this=0x804abf0, n=100)
at container.cpp:16
16  if (n <= 0) n = 1;  // Must have at least one element
```

Now the program correctly halts inside the TContainer constructor. The debugger shows the parameter values passed to the constructor: this (the address of the object being constructed), and the value of n, equal in this case to the requested container size.

Tip

Type **ptyp this** to find out the type of object addressed by a this pointer.

DEBUGGING VIRTUAL FUNCTION CALLS

To debug a virtual function call, set a breakpoint in the base class that calls, for example, a pure virtual function in an abstract class. To demonstrate, load the tcontain program into the debugger if necessary (or type **delete** to erase all breakpoints if the program is currently loaded). Then, **list** the module containing a virtual function call—in this case, container.cpp. Again, supply a starting line number the first time you type **list**:

```
(gdb) list container.cpp:1
...
56 for (int i = 0; i < count; i++)
57   objects[i]->Display();  // Calls virtual function!
```

Line 57 calls the pure virtual function Display(). The goal is to find out, using the debugger, which actual Display() the program calls at runtime. To do that, set a breakpoint on the statement that calls the function:

```
(gdb) b 57
Breakpoint 3 at 0x80490b8: file container.cpp, line 57.
```

When you run the program, it halts at the breakpoint location:

```
(gdb) run
Starting program: /src/c15/tcontain
...
Breakpoint 3, TContainer::ShowAllObjects (this=0x804abf0,
msg=0x80493fd "Before sorting") at container.cpp:57
57   objects[i]->Display();  // Calls virtual function!
```

To trace the virtual function call and discover what object's Display() function is bound to the statement, type a **step** command:

```
(gdb) step
TMyObject::Display (this=0x804ad98) at tcontain.cpp:71
71 cout << sp << "   ";
```

The resulting output shows that TMyObject::Display() is bound at runtime to the statement that calls the pure virtual function TObject::Display(). Notice that the only argument passed to Display() is the address of the object. At this point, you can type **cont** to continue the program to its end (type **cont** again if this hits any breakpoints), and then type **q** to quit the debugger.

SUMMARY

This chapter introduced virtual functions, a feature that is sometimes called *polymorphism*. Using this technique, you can create abstract classes that declare pure virtual functions. Derived classes inherit one or more abstract classes and provide actual code for the inherited virtual functions. This enables C++ to call the actual functions depending on the objects' types. This chapter also illustrated a common problem caused by multiple inheritance when a class ends up with multiple inherited copies of a base class, and explained how to fix the problem using virtual base classes.

For more information on subjects introduced in this chapter, turn to the following chapters:

- Chapter 16, "Handling Exceptions"
- Chapter 17, "Creating Class Templates"
- Chapter 18, "Overloading Your Friends"

HANDLING EXCEPTIONS

Writing functions that handle errors reliably is always difficult because, for one reason, errors are by nature unpredictable. Worse, as programs become more complex, and therefore invite more intricate error conditions, functions that handle those errors are even more difficult to write and maintain.

Recognizing these problems, C++ designers added the concept of an *exception*. As you learn in this chapter, an exception is an object that operates with the independence of a satellite in orbit around the earth. It enables a function to report exceptional conditions apart from the function's normal operation. By incorporating exception handling into C++ programs, it's easy to manage even the most complex error condition in the most deeply nested chain of function calls.

A FEW GOOD TERMS

Exceptions come with their own terminology and concepts. Following are some overviews that help you to read and understand the information in this chapter:

- An *exception* is just that—it's an object that describes an *exceptional condition* requiring special handling. Exceptions are best used for a program's error handling, but they are not limited to that use.

- To create an exception, a function *throws* an object that describes the nature of the exception. The object can be a string, an object of a class, or any other object. An *exception object* is not necessarily a *class* object, but in practice, it usually is.

- To handle an exception, a function *catches* the object thrown as an exception by another function. Statements that catch exceptions are called *exception handlers*.

- Programs prepare to catch exceptions by *trying* one or more statements that might throw exceptions. In general, to use exceptions, you *try* one or more statements, and you *catch* any exceptions those statements *throw*.

Note

Because exceptions are available only in C++, the standard C function library does not report errors using exceptions. However, C++ libraries use exceptions extensively. For more examples of exception handling, see Chapter 25, "Applying Standard Algorithms."

INTRODUCING EXCEPTIONS

Now, let's see what exceptions look like in C++. Upon detecting an error condition, a function can *throw an exception*. For example, it might throw a string that describes an error condition:

```
throw "overflow";
```

Elsewhere in the program, a string exception handler can catch and display the thrown object. The handler specifies the object's type (const char * in this case) in a catch expression like this:

```
catch (const char * message) {
  cout << "***Error! " << message << endl;
  // ... other error response actions
}
```

The catch statement traps the thrown string exception object and displays it using an output stream statement. What happens next is up to you. If you take no further action, the program continues normally. Or, the catch statement might call another function, set a flag, or cause the program to repeat the function call that led to the error. In any case, after the exception is handled, it is destroyed. An exception is a mechanism for reporting and dealing with exceptional conditions—it does not dictate a course of action. That's still your job.

When a statement throws an exception, three important actions take place that affect the program's operation:

- The function containing the statement that throws the exception immediately returns to its caller.

- The exception object overrides any value that the function normally returns.

- The exception causes C++ to search for an exception handler (a catch statement). *No other program statements are allowed to execute until the exception is handled.*

The last effect is critical. If the program itself doesn't handle an exception, it eventually arrives in a C++ default exception handler. In most cases, the *unhandled exception* ends the program. This is advantageous in small programs and tests because it helps prevent damage that might be caused by an error such as a memory leak or a disk space shortage. When writing small, noncritical programs, you can simply ignore error conditions, knowing that any serious exceptions simply cause the program to end. For example, if the C++ new operator cannot fulfill a request for a dynamic memory allocation, it throws an exception that halts the program. Of course, in production software, all exceptions must be handled to prevent the program from halting unexpectedly.

THROWING EXCEPTION OBJECTS

Although any object such as a string or an integer value can be an exception object, an exception is usually an object of a class. In its simplest form, such a class can be merely a name with no contents declared like this:

```
class Overflow { };
```

That's not just an illustration—it is a complete C++ class. To use it to report an error, throw an instance of the class using the following statement:

```
throw Overflow();
```

PART III CH 16

That statement constructs an object of the `Overflow` class, and it throws that object back to the function's caller. In that function, the program can trap the exception with code such as

```
catch (Overflow) {
  cout << "Overflow detected" << endl;
}
```

THE STANDARD exception CLASS

Usually, exception classes derive from a base class that provides information about a problem. So that your exception handling is compatible with the C++ default handlers, for best results, base your own exception handlers on the standard C++ `exception` class, declared as

```
class exception {
public:
  exception () { }
  virtual ~exception () { }
  virtual const char* what () const;
};
```

To make the class available in your program, include the standard exception header file, which in this case, does not end in .h. Also include the standard string header for use in storing descriptive messages in exception objects:

```
#include <exception>
#include <string>
```

The `exception` class declares three public members: a do-nothing default constructor, a virtual destructor, and a virtual function `what()` that returns type `const char *`, and because of the `const` suffix, states that calling the function makes no changes to the object. To use the exception class, derive another class, something like this:

```
class TMyException: public exception {
private:
  string what_str;
public:
  TMyException(const string &what_arg):
    what_str(what_arg) { }
  virtual const char *what() const {
    return what_str.c_str();
  }
};
```

The derived class publicly inherits the standard `exception` class, adding a private string object named `what_str`. The new class's constructor specifies a reference parameter to a C++ string object, and it uses an initializing expression to assign `what_arg` to `what_str`. The constructor has no other duties to perform, so its statement block is empty. The virtual `what()` function returns a `const char *` to a C-style string by calling the `what_str` object's `c_str()` function. Function `what()` is traditional in exception objects for obtaining a description of the problem that caused the exception to be thrown.

To use the derived class, a function statement throws an object of the derived class with a string description as an argument. The function might be written something like this:

```
int AnyFunction()
{
  if (errorCondition)
    throw TMyException("Underflow");
  else
    return aValue;
}
```

If an error condition is detected, the function throws an object of the TMyException class; otherwise, it returns a value normally.

> **Note**
>
> For more information on C++ string objects, see Chapter 22, "Mastering the Standard string Class."

PART

III

CH

16

INTRODUCING try BLOCKS

Now it's time to toss in another wrinkle—*try blocks*, which seem to confuse everybody the first time they use them. To prepare for trapping an exception in a catch statement, using the TMyException class and sample AnyFunction() from the preceding section, a program enables exception handling with code such as this:

```
int x;
try {
  x = AnyFunction();  // Might throw an exception
  cout << "x == " << x << endl;  // May not execute
}
catch (TMyException except) {
  cout << except.what() << endl;
  exit(1);
}
```

A try block executes one or more statements, some of which might throw an exception. In this case, the sample AnyFunction() throws an exception of type TMyException if it detects an error. If that happens, no assignment is made to x, and the output statement does not execute. Instead, the program hops immediately to the first catch statement that matches the exception's type. In this case, the sample catch statement traps the exception object, displays its message by calling what(), and then ends the program by calling exit().

One or more catch statements *must* follow a try block. You cannot have a try block in one place and its catch statements in another. That would be like having a ball game's pitcher on the mound and the catcher in the parking lot. In all cases, you must follow a try block with one or more catch statements that catch any exceptions thrown by the tried statements.

MULTIPLE catch STATEMENTS

A single try block may be followed by multiple catch statements to trap different sorts of errors. For example, to handle a TMyException object and also exceptions thrown as character strings, the program could use code such as

```
try {
  // .. call functions that might throw exceptions
}
catch (TMyException except) {
  cout << except.what() << endl;
}
catch (const char* message) {
  cout << message << endl;
}
```

Any exceptions not trapped explicitly in a catch statement remain alive and are passed upward in the function call chain. *The presence of a live exception disables the program's normal execution until the exception is handled.* In this case, if an exception of an unknown type is thrown in the try block, the unhandled exception is passed to the function that called this one. This process continues until the exception is handled or the exception object reaches a default C++ exception handler, in which case the program most likely ends with a rude error message and a core dump.

Don't attempt to catch all exceptions to prevent such unexpected events. Code such as the following is extremely dangerous to the health of your program:

```
try {
  // .. Call functions that might throw exceptions
}
catch (exception e) {  // ???
}
```

That code might appear to trap all possible errors, but in practice, it does an end run around critical error handlers that are expected to respond to memory faults, disk problems, and other unforeseen difficulties.

> **Tip**
> To use exceptions properly, trap only those exceptions you know a function might throw.

NESTING try BLOCKS

Multiple try blocks and catch statements can be nested, although the resulting program is often messy. A try block, for example, can have a nested try block and catch statement as in the following hypothetical example. Assume that TOverflow and TUnderflow are classes derived from the standard exception class. In this case, if functionA() throws an exception, the program skips the nested try block entirely:

```
try {
  functionA();    // Try function (outer block)
  try {
    functionB();  // Try function (inner block)
```

```
    }
    catch (TOverflow except) {
      // handle overflow condition
    }
}
catch (TUnderflow except) {
  // handle underflow condition
}
```

You can usually avoid such unwieldy programming by placing the calls to various functions inside another function, typically written inline to avoid an extra function call:

```
inline void f()
{
  functionA();
  functionB();
}
```

This allows the program to use a single try block followed by catch statements to trap any exceptions thrown by functionA() or functionB():

```
try {
  f();
}
catch (TOverflow except) {
  // handle overflow condition}
catch (TUnderflow except) {
  // handle underflow condition
}
```

USING try BLOCKS

Some additional examples help clarify what try blocks are and how to use them. A try block may execute multiple statements as in this code fragment:

```
int x;
try {
  cout << "Here we go!" << endl;
  x = AnyFunction();
  cout << "x == " << x << endl;
}
catch (TMyException except) {
  cout << except.what() << endl;
}
```

The sample try block first displays a message. This is unlikely to cause any exceptions to be thrown, and so it doesn't strictly need to be inside a try block—but there's no harm in placing it there. Next, the program calls AnyFunction(), assigning the function's return value to integer x. However, if AnyFunction() throws an exception, the try block immediately ends and no value is assigned to x. The output statement following AnyFunction() is also skipped. Because of the exception, the program jumps directly to the catch statement that lists the type of exception object.

The preceding code also illustrates another subtle aspect of exceptions that helps make error handling easier than in conventional programming. In C, for example, it is typical to reserve a special value as an error indicator. Using standard error handling methods, AnyFunction() might return –1 to indicate a problem, detected conventionally with an if statement:

```
int x = AnyFunction();
if (x == -1)
  ErrorHandler(x);
```

This technique has many problems. For one, the reserved value –1 contains no information about the problem. Also, it isn't always convenient to reserve a value as an error indicator. Furthermore, it's too easy for programmers to ignore an error value returned from a function. All these troubles are eliminated by using exceptions in C++.

PROGRAMMING WITH EXCEPTIONS

Now that you've met the basics of exception handling, examine the program in this section for a practical example of how to use exceptions for reporting errors. The program implements a function, power(), that raises a double floating point value to an exponent, which may be fractional. An illegal input value, such as a negative base raised to a fractional exponent ($-4^{1.5}$, for example), throws an exception. So that you can use the function in other programs, I wrote it as a separate module. Listing 16.1, power.h, declares the power() function and exception class used to report errors.

LISTING 16.1   POWER.H

```
#include <exception>  // Need exception class
#include <string>     // Need string class

class TPowExcept: public exception {
  double b;           // Base value
  double e;           // Exponent value
  string what_str;    // Error description
public:
  TPowExcept(double b_arg, double e_arg,
    const string &what_arg):
    b(b_arg), e(e_arg), what_str(what_arg) { }
  virtual const char *what() const {
    return what_str.c_str();
  }
  void Report();
};

double power(double b, double e) throw(TPowExcept);
```

Take a look first at the end of the header file where the power() function is prototyped. The declaration ends with throw(TPowExcept), an optional indicator of what kinds of exceptions this function might throw. This is called a *declared exception*. Even though it is optional to declare a function's exceptions, you should almost always do so. This makes perfectly clear the types of exceptions you need to trap in catch statements after calling the function in a try block.

Also in the power.h header file is the declaration for the TPowExcept class, derived from the standard exception class. Three private data members hold values that describe the nature of a problem. Doubles b and e are the input values to power() that were found to be illegal, and what_str further describes the problem. The TPowExcept constructor is written inline. It assigns its three arguments to the three private data members but performs no other chores. The virtual what() function returns the string value of the what_str private object. Function Report() is implemented in Listing 16.2, power.cpp.

LISTING 16.2   POWER.CPP

```cpp
#include <iostream.h>
#include <math.h>        // Need modf(), fmod()
#include "power.h"       // Need TPowExcept, power()

// Display error message in exception object
void TPowExcept::Report()
{
  cout << "Domain error: base == " << b
       << ", exponent == " << e << endl;
  cout << what() << endl;
}

// Subfunction called by power()
double fpower(double b, double e)
{
  return exp(o * log(b));
}

// Returns b raised to the e power
// Throws TPowExcept exception for illegal input values
double power(double b, double e) throw(TPowExcept)
{
  if (b > 0.0) return fpower(b, e);
  if (b < 0.0) {
    double ipart;
    double fpart = modf(e, &ipart);
    if (fpart == 0) {
      if (fmod(ipart, 2) != 0)  // i.e. ipart is odd
        return -fpower(-b, e);
      else
        return fpower(-b, e);
    } else
      throw TPowExcept(b, e, "Result is a complex number");
  } else {
    if (e == 0.0) return 1.0;
    if (e < 1.0)
      throw TPowExcept(b, e, "Exponent must be zero or >= 1.0");
    return 0.0;
  }
  throw TPowExcept(0, 0, "Error in power() function");
}
```

The exception class's `Report()` function displays the values of the object's `b` and `e` `double` variables, and also writes an additional message held in `what_str`. The `TPowExcept` class not only contains all values that fully describe a problem with the `power()` function, but also the means for displaying an error message.

Function `power()` uses the `TPowExcept` class to report errors. For example, if you attempt to raise a negative value to a fractional exponent, the program throws the following exception:

```
throw TPowExcept(b, e, "Result is a complex number");
```

This is all that `power()` needs to do to report this type of error. In throwing the exception, the function passes the faulty base and exponent values and a string message to the `TPowExcept()` constructor.

> **Note**
>
> The last statement in the `power()` function is unreachable—it should never execute. I included it, however, to demonstrate how you can insert internal error-reporting code that might be useful during debugging. To see how this works, comment-out the `return 0.0;` statement. I sometimes like to use similar programming to make sure that I've covered all the bases, especially in a function that uses nested `if-else` statements. However, some C++ compilers complain about the final `throw` statement—if that happens on your system, you can delete that line.

Listing 16.3, tpower.cpp, tests the power module and demonstrates how to use `try` and `catch` statements to trap a function's exceptions.

LISTING 16.3   TPOWER.CPP

```cpp
#include <iostream.h>
#include "power.h"    // Need TPowExcept, power()

int main()
{
  double base, exponent, result;  // Input and result variables
  try {
    cout << "base? ";
    cin >> base;
    cout << "exponent? ";
    cin >> exponent;
    result = power(base, exponent);  // Exception possible here
    cout << "result == " << result << endl;
  }
  catch (TPowExcept &except) {
    except.Report();  // Display error message
    return 1;         // Exit with error
  }
  return 0;  // Exit with no error
}
```

Compile the power.cpp module and the test program with the following commands:

```
$ g++ -c power.cpp
$ g++ tpower.cpp power.o
```

Run the program and enter base and exponent values to test the power() function:

```
$ ./a.out
base? 2
exponent? 2.8
result == 6.9644
```

Try other values to force the function to throw an exception. For example, run the program again and enter these values:

```
$ ./a.out
base? -4
exponent? 1.5
Domain error: base == -4, exponent == 1.5
Result is a complex number
```

This time, the test program responds to the exception object that power() throws. To make that happen, the main() function's try block prompts you for base and exponent values (these statements could also precede the try block). After that, the program calls power() with the following statement:

```
result = power(base, exponent);
```

If power() throws an exception, the assignment to result and the next output statement are skipped. In that event, the program hops to the catch statement that declares an exception object matching the one that power() throws. There is only one such type of exception in this example, but there might be others. Handling the error is simple. The program merely calls the exception object's Report() function and ends the program by returning from main():

```
except.Report();
return 1;
```

> **Tip**
>
> After handling an exception in a catch statement, the exception object is automatically destroyed. You don't need to take any additional actions to delete exception objects.

UNHANDLED EXCEPTIONS

Usually, an unhandled exception is bad news. If a function throws an exception, but no catch statement traps it, the exception object ends up in a default exception handler. As mentioned, this usually halts the program, and worse, dumps memory to a core file. The exact action depends on the type of exception, and whether the program itself has replaced any of the default handlers. For an unhandled exception, C++ calls one of three functions:

- Exceptions that are not handled by a catch statement cause the program to call unexpected(). An *unexpected exception* is defined as any exception that isn't handled by a catch statement. By default, unexpected() calls terminate(), explained next.

- Unexpected exceptions for which C++ detects a corrupted stack or that result from a class destructor that throws an exception (a dangerous practice to be reserved only for the most critical of problems) cause the program to call the terminate() function. By default, terminate() calls abort(), explained next.

- The abort() function is the lowest on the totem pole. If the program reaches this stage in its exception handling, it ends immediately and writes memory to a core dump file. To prevent this, you can rewrite the unexpected() and terminate() functions, and in that way, trap any exceptions that aren't handled in catch statements.

Replacing unexpected() and terminate()

You can replace unexpected() and terminate() with new code to deal with unhandled exceptions in whatever way you want. For example, it might make sense during the program's development to replace unexpected() to simply notify you of any unhandled exceptions. You can then add appropriate catch statements to trap the exceptions before they become terminal. You might also replace terminate() with diagnostics for debugging the cause of a corrupted stack or exceptions thrown during the disposal of objects (which might indicate a problem with memory management).

Usually, however, replacing unexpected() is enough to ensure that the program never halts unexpectedly due to an unhandled exception. The terminate() function is best used to shut down critical services, save open files, and perform other disaster recovery before ending the program. If the program ever ends up in terminate(), you should assume the worst, clean up as much as possible, and end gracefully. You can never replace abort().

Including the exception header file provides two functions you can call to replace the default exception handlers. The functions are declared as

```
terminate_handler set_terminate (terminate_handler func);
unexpected_handler set_unexpected (unexpected_handler func);
```

In each case, pass a function that returns void and declares no parameters to the set_terminate() and set_unexpected() functions. For example, write your own handler like this:

```
void MyHandler()
{
  // ... statements in your handler
}
```

To use the handler for trapping unexpected exceptions, pass the function name as an argument to set_unexpected():

```
set_unexpected(MyHandler);
```

Alternatively, you can save the address of the original handler with code such as

```
unexpected_handler saved_handle;  // Variable
saved_handle = set_unexpected(MyHandler);
```

You might then restore the original handler's address—a good technique to use if several modules install their own custom handlers. Similarly, set the default terminate() function by calling the following:

```
set_terminate(MyHandler);
```

TRAPPING ALL EXCEPTIONS

Writing custom exception handlers that safely handle all possible exceptions is not as easy as the basic techniques suggest. This section shows an example that simulates several types of errors and uses custom handlers to trap them safely. Listing 16.4, unexpect.cpp, demonstrates how to replace the default exception handlers with custom functions that trap all possible program errors. It deals with exceptions of unknown types, and it demonstrates how to obtain one last chance to perform critical measures before ending the program.

PART

III

CH

16

LISTING 16.4   UNEXPECT.CPP

```
#include <iostream.h>
#include <exception>

#define MAXERR 10

// Exception class used when errors exceed limit
class MaxError { };

// Normal error exception class
class Error {
private:
  static int count;  // Count of Error objects
public:
  Error();         // Constructor
  void Say();      // Report static error count
};

// Prototype for function that throws an exception
void run() throw(Error);

// Prototypes for custom exception handlers
void custom_unexpected();
void custom_terminate();

// Global static counter for Error class objects
int Error::count;

void main()
{
  set_unexpected( custom_unexpected );
  set_terminate( custom_terminate );
  for (;;) {
    try {
      run();  // Throws an exception
    }
    catch (Error e) {
      e.Say();
    }
  }
  return 0;
}
```

continues

LISTING 16.4 CONTINUED

```cpp
// Function that throws an exception
void run() throw(Error)
{
  throw Error();
  //  throw "An unknown exception object";
}

// Our unexpected exception handler
void custom_unexpected()
{
  cout << "Inside custom_unexpected function" << endl;
  throw Error();  // Continues program
}

// Our terminate exception handler
void custom_terminate()
{
  cout << "Inside terminate function" << endl;
  cout << "Exiting program" << endl;
  exit(1);  // Exits program
}

// Error class constructor
Error::Error()
{
  count++;
  if (count > MAXERR)
    throw MaxError();  // Abort object construction!
}

// Error class reporting function
void Error::Say()
{
  cout << "Error: count = " << count << endl;
}
```

The unexpect.cpp program lists all the elements needed to trap all possible exceptions. The program doesn't prevent abnormal termination, but it does take over from the default action of calling abort() with its inevitable core dump. By using similar code, you can trap every type of exception and, at the very least, have the opportunity to shut down the program in an orderly fashion if it becomes necessary to end it prematurely. Compile and run the program using these commands:

```
$ g++ unexpect.cpp
$ ./a.out
Error: count = 1
Error: count = 2
...
Error: count = 10
Inside custom_unexpected function
Inside terminate function
Exiting program
```

As the program's output shows, it forces ten exceptions to occur, all of which are handled normally. After the tenth instance, however, the program generates a more serious error that results in custom handlers receiving the problem. Finally, the program ends gracefully with an error message—and despite the unexpected exceptions, no core dump. These actions simulate a typical situation where one error leads to another, which leads to another, and eventually causes a variety of ills.

To keep track of how many errors have occurred, the program's Error class constructor near the end of the listing increments the class's static count variable. Because count is static, only one copy of its value exists for all Error objects. Also in Error is a function, Say(), that displays count's value.

In the course of constructing an Error object, if count equals or exceeds constant MAXERR, the constructor throws an exception of type MaxError. Because the program doesn't catch this type of error, this action kicks in the custom handlers. This simulates what can happen when calling functions in a third-party library that might throw an exception of an unknown type. It could also happen in your own code if you neglect to catch a specific type of exception.

> **Note**
>
> When a constructor throws an exception, the object is not constructed. See "Exceptions and Constructors" later in this chapter for more on this topic.

Function main() in the unexpect.cpp program (refer to Listing 16.4) installs handlers that replace the default unexpected() and terminate() functions. The program then executes a Do-Forever for loop in which a try block calls a local function, run(). That function intentionally throws an exception of type Error, trapped back in main() by a catch statement. The first ten times this happens, the program displays a message by calling the Error object's Say() member function. After the tenth error, however, the Error class's constructor gives up the good fight and throws an exception of type MaxError by executing these statements:

```
count++;
if (count > MAXERR)
  throw MaxError();
```

This simulates a serious condition in which an object cannot be constructed. In this case, the problem is even more serious than normal because it occurs in the constructor of the Error class object. Because main()'s try-catch statements do not recognize errors of type MaxError, this action causes main() to end, and control to pass to our custom unexpected exception handler. In that function, two statements execute:

```
cout << "Inside custom_unexpected function" << endl;
throw Error();  // Continues program
```

The first statement is just so that you can observe when the custom handler is called. The second shows how you can continue the program at this stage. In a real-life situation, the unexpected handler might examine the state of the program and take steps to allow the user to close files or reestablish network communication—whatever it takes to get back to normal. The custom handler now has two options:

- It can call `terminate()`, in which case the program enters its critical shutdown phase, or
- It can throw an exception of a known type.

The second measure is your first line of defense against an unexpected exception. Throwing an exception from within an unexpected exception handler in effect *translates* unknown exceptions to a known type. Typically, a loop in `main()` catches an exception of that type so that the program can continue running after performing its recovery logic.

In this case, however, throwing the `Error` object causes *another* unknown exception to be launched into orbit. This simulates the serious condition when, even after attempting to recover from a problem, the program is unable to continue. The result is a call to the custom `terminate()` function, which displays an error message and ends by calling the `exit()`:

```
cout << "Inside terminate function" << endl;
cout << "Exiting program" << endl;
exit(1);  // Exits program
```

Although simple, the demonstration program simulates extreme conditions that cause the program to be unable to continue. But at least it ends as gracefully as possible.

A simple change to the program also demonstrates how to handle unexpected exceptions and still allow the program to continue. Only when the program is no longer able to construct `Error` objects does our terminate function end the show. To make this change, rewrite the `run()` function to throw a string object:

```
void run() throw(Error)
{
   throw "An unknown exception object";
}
```

Compile and run the modified unexpect.cpp program using the same commands as before:

```
$ g++ unexpect.cpp
$ ./a.out
Inside custom_unexpected function
Error: count = 1
...
Inside custom_unexpected function
Error: count = 10
Inside custom_unexpected function
Inside terminate function
Exiting program
```

This time, because `main()` doesn't recognize exceptions of type `const char *`, each `Error` exception causes our custom unexpected exception handler to be called. In effect, the handler translates the unexpected exception into a known type, an object of the `Error` class. This allows the program to continue operating despite the presence of the unexpected condition. Eventually, however, the `Error` class exceeds its maximum count, and its constructor throws an error of type `MaxError`. The unexpected handler doesn't receive this type of exception—instead, the terminate function is called, and the program ends.

EXCEPTIONS AND LOCAL OBJECTS

When a function throws an exception, C++ automatically destroys any local variables created in that function. Be sure that you understand this effect. It can cause unforeseen consequences when the local variables are themselves objects of classes.

> **Note**
>
> Some compilers have a special option to enable the destruction of local objects in the event their declaring block throws an exception. GNU does this by default.

PART

III

CH

16

A simple example, localexcept.cpp in Listing 16.5, demonstrates how GNU C++ destroys objects in functions that throw exceptions. You might use the program as a test of how other C++ compilers deal with this critical situation.

LISTING 16.5   LOCALEXCEPT.CPP

```
#include <iostream.h>
#include <exception>

class A {
public:
  A() { cout << "A constructor" << endl; }
  ~A() { cout << "A destructor" << endl; }
};

void f();

int main()
{
  try {
    f();
  }
  catch (const char *s) {
    cout << s << endl;
  }
  return 0;
}

void f()
{
  A a;  // Construct object of class A
  throw ("Error condition");
}
```

The program declares a class, A, with only two members: a constructor and a destructor. Each of these functions displays a message as a trace of when they are called. Function f() constructs an object of type A and then throws an exception using a string to keep things simple. When you compile and run the program, it shows that the object is properly destroyed *before* the catch statement in main() receives the thrown exception:

```
$ g++ localexcept.cpp
$ ./a.out
```

```
A constructor
A destructor
Error condition
```

So far, so good. But if the function constructs an object dynamically addressed by a pointer, a very different effect results. Suppose, for example, that function f() constructs the object like this:

```
void f()
{
  A *p = new A;
  throw ("Error condition");  // ???
}
```

Because the dynamic object has global scope, as do all objects created with new, the object's destructor is *not* called when the function ends with an exception. Worse, the pointer p is destroyed, leaving the object floating in space and causing a memory leak. To avoid this problem, before throwing an exception, you must delete any dynamic objects. You might, for example, use a flag to indicate an error inside the function, and if the flag is set, delete any dynamic objects before throwing the exception:

```
bool error_flag;
...
if (error_flag) {
  delete p;
  throw ("Error condition");
}
```

This type of mistake can easily happen in functions that return pointers to objects constructed with new. Remember that, if the function throws an exception, it does not return a value as it does normally.

EXCEPTIONS AND CONSTRUCTORS

Class constructors may throw exceptions to indicate that they cannot successfully construct an object. This is a relatively new specification in C++ that some older compilers might not recognize, but GNU C++ is up-to-date in this department. You already saw one example of the technique in this chapter's Error class. To throw an exception in a constructor, simply use a statement as in the following class:

```
class AnyClass {
public:
  AnyClass() {
    if (condition) throw Error(); }
  ~AnyClass();  // Destructor
};
```

The key concept here is that if a constructor throws an exception—causing the constructor to end abnormally—the object is not constructed, and, most important, any class destructor is not called. Only fully constructed objects are destroyed by calling their destructors, a fact that has especially important consequences in classes that own objects of other classes. Consider this version of AnyClass:

```
class AnyClass {
  OtherClass x;
public:
  AnyClass(): x() {
    if (condition) throw Error(); }
 ~AnyClass();  // Destructor
};
```

Object x of type OtherClass (not shown) is initialized by AnyClass's constructor using the expression x(). If the OtherClass object's constructor throws an exception, then the AnyClass object's constructor is aborted and the destructor is not called. This effect can be even more crucial in classes that own multiple class objects:

```
class AnyClass {
  OtherClass a, b, c;
public:
  AnyClass(): a(), b(), c() { }
 ~AnyClass();  // Destructor
};
```

If object b's constructor throws an exception, object c is not constructed, and neither is the AnyClass object. However, object a's destructor is called because that object was fully constructed before the construction of b caused a problem. In cases where objects have pointers to dynamic memory, it might take a little thought to be sure that, in the event of a constructor throwing an exception, all objects are properly disposed. In rare cases, it might be necessary to rearrange the initialization order of class-object data members (a, b, and c in the example) so that everything works as intended.

CLASSES THAT THROW THEMSELVES AROUND

A class can also throw an exception object of its own class type. Usually, this is done in an exception class by a member function, often called Raise(). You might, for example, design the exception class like this:

```
class Error {
public:
  void Raise() { throw Error(); }
};
```

The class might also declare other functions, constructors, a destructor, and data members. If e is an object of type Error, the following statement throws another object of the Error class:

```
e.Raise();  // Throws fresh Error object
```

Depending on other services in the Error class, this might be a good way to throw an exception after it is initially handled. Doing this keeps the exception alive, causing C++ to continue searching upward in the function call chain for a matching exception handler. In many cases, you can do this simply by throwing the same object received by a catch statement:

```
catch (TError e) {
  // .. initially handle this type of error
  throw e;  // rethrow exception to this function's caller
}
```

EXCEPTIONS AND MEMORY MANAGEMENT

As mentioned in prior chapters, operator new throws an exception if it can't fulfill a memory allocation request. In GNU C++, the exception is an object of the class bad_alloc. Suppose that the program has a function f() that uses new to create a dynamic object of type TAnyClass:

```
TAnyClass * f()
{
  return new TAnyClass();
}
```

To trap the exception that new throws if the memory allocation fails, use try and catch statements such as

```
try {
  TAnyClass * p = f();  // Might throw exception
}
catch (bad_alloc error) {
  cout << error.what() << endl;
  exit(1);
}
```

Although the preceding code works, it is inconvenient to trap bad_alloc exceptions at every use of new. Because an out-of-memory condition usually indicates a serious problem, it's more common to trap the error at a higher level—for instance, in main(), using code such as this:

```
int main()
{
  for (;;) {
    try {
      run();   // Main program loop
    }
    catch (bad_alloc error) {
      cout << "Out of memory" << endl;  // ???
      cout << error.what() << endl;  // ???
      exit(1);
    }
  }
}
```

The basic idea is to use a Do-Forever for loop that repeatedly calls a function—run() in this example—that you might refer to as the main program engine. The catch statement traps all bad_alloc exceptions thrown by run(), or by any other functions that run() calls. However, the output statements are questionable because, if the system is out of memory, there might not be enough free bytes left to execute the output statements themselves. If an exception occurs during the output statements, the program calls terminate() and ends abruptly with a core dump.

A useful trick that can alleviate this kind of trouble is to allocate a pool of memory at the start of the program to be deleted in the event of a memory allocation failure. For example, you might reserve a block of 2,048 bytes:

```
char *reserve = new char[2048];
```

That might also be in a try block, but there's usually some memory available when the program begins running. In the event of a bad_alloc exception, delete the reserved memory:

```
delete reserve;
reserve = NULL;
```

You can then repeat the operation that led to the error in hopes that the use of new will succeed. If not, another bad_alloc exception is thrown, and you might have to abort the program. One way to do that is to handle and then *rethrow* the exception:

```
catch (bad_alloc error) {
  if (reserve = NULL)
    throw (error);
}
```

PART III CH 16

That causes the exception object to remain alive outside the exception handler, and unless there's another handler higher up in the function-call chain, the program eventually calls the current unexpected exception handler. In that handler, you could perform an orderly shutdown, close files, and do whatever else is necessary before ending the program.

DEBUGGING EXCEPTIONS

The GNU debugger offers one command for trapping exceptions, but it seems not to work in the release I'm using. However, you might try it with a newer compiler—perhaps it will work for you. First, compile a program such as unexpect.cpp in this chapter (refer to Listing 16.4) and load it into the debugger using these commands:

```
$ g++ -g -o unexpect unexpect.cpp
$ gdb --silent unexpect
(gdb)
```

Set a breakpoint on function main() by specifying its name to the break command (abbreviated simply as b), and then run the program:

```
(gdb) b main
Breakpoint 1 at 0x80489ee: file unexpect.cpp, line 40.
(gdb) run
Starting program: /src/c16/unexpect
Breakpoint 1, main () at unexpect.cpp:40
40 set_unexpected( custom_unexpected );
```

The debugger's catch command is supposed to set a breakpoint on every catch expression in the current context. Type *catch* to see whether it works for you. If not, you can search for the words "catch" and "throw," and then set breakpoints individually on the reported line numbers. At least this is easier than hunting through a long listing. Repeat the search command until it reports "Expression not found" (press the up-arrow key to repeat the command without retyping):

```
(gdb) search catch
47   catch (Error e) {
(gdb) search catch
Expression not found
```

Do the same for "throw," and then set the breakpoints on all reported line numbers.

SUMMARY

As this chapter explained, C++ exceptions are objects that functions can throw to report exceptional conditions. To provide exception handling, programs call functions in `try` blocks, followed by `catch` statements for the types of exception objects those functions might throw. Any unhandled exceptions call low-level `unexpected()` and `terminate()` functions that you can replace with custom versions to trap all possible errors and prevent programs from shutting down unexpectedly. This chapter also explained related topics such as rethrowing an exception, deriving classes from the standard exception class, and writing exception handlers for out-of-memory errors reported by the C++ `new` operator.

For more information on subjects introduced in this chapter, turn to the following chapters:

- Chapter 22, "Mastering the Standard `string` Class"
- Chapter 25, "Applying Standard Algorithms"

## CHAPTER 17

CREATING CLASS TEMPLATES

Just as a class is a kind of schematic for building objects, a *template* is a schematic for building functions and classes. Also called *parameterized types*, templates provide specifications for general-purpose classes and functions that automatically mold themselves to new uses.

> **Note**
>
> For more information about using templates, see Chapter 23, "Using the Standard Template Library (STL)."

INTRODUCING CLASS TEMPLATES

Templates are typically used to create general-purpose functions and classes that are not tied to any specific data types. For example, a sorting function makes a good template because sorting algorithms do not depend directly on the type of data on which they operate. Implementing the function as a template reduces it to its most general form. When you compile the program, C++ uses the template to generate, or *instantiate*, an actual function that works with a specific type of data.

Template classes are similarly generic. One excellent example is a container class that provides searching and other functions but can work with any data type from the lowliest integers to complex class objects.

TEMPLATE FUNCTIONS

A template function describes the generic properties of a function. Most often, you declare template functions in separate header files and include them in various modules. A template function generally looks like this:

```
template <class T>
void f(T param)
{
  // ... function body
}
```

The reserved word `template` begins the show and is always followed by angle brackets with one or more expressions. Each of those expressions—there's only one in this example—begins with the word `class` and is followed by any identifier of your choosing. In this case, I use `T` to indicate "type." The word `class` here does not necessarily refer to a C++ class, but to any "class" of data type.

Following the template's preface is the item being declared in template form. In this example, it's a function named `f()` that returns `void` and receives a single parameter of type `T`. The actual data type is specified later when the program uses the template—here, `T` is just a placeholder that refers to an as-yet undefined type. A function might also return a value of a placeholder type:

```
template <class FutureType>
FutureType AnyFunction(FutureType param)
{
  // ... function body
}
```

That declares a template function named AnyFunction() that returns a value of type FutureType and receives a parameter of that same type. Again, the exact nature of FutureType isn't known. A template can also declare multiple parameters of different placeholder types (or the same types):

```
template <class T1, class T2>
T1 NewFunction(T1 param1, T2 param2, T1 param3)
{
  // ... function body
}
```

The NewFunction() template declares two placeholder types, T1 and T2. The function returns a value of type T1 and declares three parameters: two of type T1 and one of type T2. You may specify value parameters and return values as shown here, and also pointers and references to placeholder type objects. For example, here's how you might declare a Copy() template function that accepts a reference to an object and returns a pointer to an object of the same type:

```
template <class T>
T * Copy(const T &param)
```

Again, the template is completely generic. It states only its name and that it returns a pointer of some type and accepts a const parameter reference of that same type. The actual data types are determined later when the function is used. This means that the same template can be used to create a variety of Copy() functions that operate on many different types of data. To use the template function, simply declare it in a prototype like this:

```
template TMyClass * Copy(const TMyClass &param);
```

When the compiler processes that function prototype, it uses the template to construct an actual function for the specified data type TMyClass. In this example, C++ replaces the templates placeholder T with TMyClass, and it creates an actual function that works with data of that type. Alternatively, you can simply use the function and let the compiler create the actual function based on its context in the program. However, it's best to declare a function prototype before its first use in a program.

> **Tip**
>
> GNU C++ seems to require template function prototypes to be prefaced with the keyword template. Some other C++ compilers do not require this. If the function is implemented in another module—that is, if it is declared in a prototype or used in a statement—you might also need to preface the prototype with the word extern to prevent C++ from instantiating multiple instances of the same function.

A complete sample program demonstrates how to create template functions and instantiate them in different ways. Although the example is simple, I divided it into header and program files because, in most cases, this is how you will write most templates. Listing 17.1, minmax.h, shows the header file for two template functions, min() and max().

LISTING 17.1   MINMAX.H

```
#pragma interface

template <class T>
 T max(T a, T b)
{
  if (a > b)
    return a;
  else
    return b;
}

template <class T>
 T min(T a, T b)
{
  if (a < b)
    return a;
  else
    return b;
}
```

Note

The #pragma interface directive in minmax.h might no longer be needed. Some versions of GNU C++ require it to help the linker resolve uses of template functions and classes.

Take a close look at the declaration of the template function, max():

```
template <class T>
 T max(T a, T b)
```

The template reserved word comes first, followed by angle brackets containing the place-holder type-name T. The second line declares max() as a function that returns a value of type T and receives two parameters, a and b, also of type T. The body of the function is common C++ code:

```
if (a > b)
  return a;
else
  return b;
```

The actual types of a and b aren't yet known, and we assume only that objects of those types can be compared in the expression (a < b)—if not, the program simply doesn't compile. Template function min() is written similarly but, of course, returns the lesser value of its two parameters.

We now have two functions, min() and max(), that are completely generic in nature. They can operate on any data type provided that objects of that type can be compared. Listing 17.2, tminmax.cpp, tests the functions and shows how to instantiate templates for use with different types of data.

LISTING 17.2   TMINMAX.CPP

```
#include <iostream.h>

#pragma implementation "minmax.h"
#include "minmax.h"

// Instantiate template functions
//
template int min(int, int);
template double min(double, double);
template char min(char, char);

template int max(int, int);
template double max(double, double);
template char max(char, char);

int main()
{
  int i1 = 100, i2 = 200;
  double d1 = 3.14159, d2 = 9.87654;
  char c1 = 'A', c2 = 'z';

  cout << "max(i1, i2) == " << max(i1, i2) << endl;
  cout << "max(d1, d2) == " << max(d1, d2) << endl;
  cout << "max(c1, c2) == " << max(c1, c2) << endl;

  cout << "min(i1, i2) == " << min(i1, i2) << endl;
  cout << "min(d1, d2) == " << min(d1, d2) << endl;
  cout << "min(c1, c2) == " << min(c1, c2) << endl;

  return 0;
}
```

PART
III

CH
17

Note

The #pragma implementation directive in tminmax.cpp might no longer be needed. It corresponds to the #pragma interface directive in the template-function header file, minmax.h, included in the module. Although not strictly required in this small example, the directives help ensure that only one instance of a function from a template is created. Neither directive is needed with newer versions of GNU C++.

The test program includes the minmax.h header file. Using the template functions in that file, the compiler explicitly instantiates actual functions using template prototypes such as

```
template int min(int, int);
```

This causes the compiler to implement a function named min() with type int at every place that class T appears in the template function. The result is an actual function that returns the minimum of two integer arguments, as though you had written that function like this:

```
int max(int a, int b)
{
  if (a > b)
    return a;
```

```
   else
      return b;
}
```

The great thing about templates is that C++ writes this code for you. All you need to do is create the template, declare the function prototype with actual data types, and then use the function.

TEMPLATE CLASSES

Template classes are even more powerful than template functions. A template class provides the skeleton for a generic class that is later instantiated with user-specified data types. A template class's declaration is similar to that of a template function's. It begins with the template reserved word followed by one or more placeholder types in angle brackets. In general, template classes are in this form:

```
template <class T>
class TAnyClass {
  // ... class members
};
```

Don't confuse the two uses of the word class—they have different meanings. The first line states that class T is a placeholder for a type to be determined later. The rest of the declaration is a C++ class declaration just like any other, except that members may use the placeholder type as though it were a real data type. For example, the template class might declare a private data member of type T:

```
template <class T>
class TAnyClass {
private:
   T var;
public:
   TAnyClass(T arg): var(arg) { }
};
```

The template class is completely generic. It stores a private variable named an_object of type T. Its constructor assigns to var an argument value also of type T when an object of TAnyClass is constructed. This *same* class template might store any type of data. To use the template, simply create an object of the template class type and specify an actual data type to use:

```
TAnyClass< int > int_object(123);
```

That creates a TAnyClass object named int_object, using the data type int in every place where the placeholder T appears in the template. The object stores the value 123 in its private var data member. The data type might also be another class:

```
TAnyClass< TOtherClass > class_object( other_object );
```

That creates an object named class_object from the TAnyClass template, using TOtherClass as the data type where T appears in the template. The value of other_object is copied to the private var data member.

As with template functions, template classes are typically declared in header files. For example, Listing 17.3, db.h, demonstrates how to create a template class that can store a small database of records. The actual type of those records comes later when the program creates an object of the template class. At that time, C++ generates an actual class to handle the object's creation.

LISTING 17.3   DB.H

```
#include <string>

class DBError {
private:
  string msg;
public:
  DBError(const string &msg_arg): msg(msg_arg) { }
  const string & what() const { return msg; }
};

template<class T>
class TDatabase {
private:
  T *rp;        // Records pointer
  int num;      // Number of records
public:
  TDatabase(int n): num(n)
    { rp = new T[num]; }
  ~TDatabase()
    { delete[] rp; }
  T &GetRecord(int recnum) throw (DBError);
};

template<class T>
T &TDatabase<T>::GetRecord(int recnum) throw (DBError)
{
  if (0 <= recnum && recnum < num)
    return rp[recnum];
  else
    throw DBError("Bad record number");
}
```

The header file declares two classes. DBError is a normal C++ class that the template class TDatabase uses to report errors. The template class TDatabase is declared using a single placeholder data type:

```
template<class T>
class TDatabase {...
```

That creates the template, TDatabase, as a template class for an as-yet-unknown type of data, T. The template's private section declares a pointer rp to an object of the unknown type, and also an integer variable that counts how many records the database holds:

```
private:
  T *rp;        // Records pointer
  int num;      // Number of records
```

As this shows, template classes (and template functions) may declare and use specific types of data such as int num—all data in a template doesn't have to be generic. The template's constructor initializes the private variables, again using the placeholder type T to create an array for holding records:

```
TDatabase(int n): num(n)
  { rp = new T[num]; }
```

We still haven't specified what T really is, but even so, C++ allows statements to use the type. Here, operator new creates an array of T objects, and it saves the number of records in num. In this case, the TDatabase() constructor is implemented inline. You can also declare and implement member functions in template classes separately. For example, TDatabase declares a public reference function GetRecord():

```
T &GetRecord(int recnum) throw (DBError);
```

This states that GetRecord() returns a reference to an object of the unknown placeholder type T. To GetRecord(), the program passes an integer equal to the record's number. The function reports errors by throwing an exception object of type DBError. The function's implementation shows how versatile a class template can be. Its declaration, however, can be a bit daunting at first:

```
template<class T>
T &TDatabase<T>::GetRecord(int recnum) throw (DBError)
```

The function implementation begins with template <class T>, which as you've seen in other examples, states that this is a template and that T is a placeholder for a data type to be specified later. Line two states that GetRecord() is a member of the template class TDatabase<T> and that the function returns a reference to an object of type T&. As in all member function implementations, the C++ scope resolution operator denotes the class that declares the function. Errors are reported by throwing an exception of type DBError. The GetRecord() function uses the object of type T in a completely generic way:

```
if (0 <= recnum && recnum < num)
  return rp[recnum];
else
  throw DBError("Bad record number");
```

If the requested record number is in range, the function returns a reference to the record in the array at rp[recnum]; otherwise, it throws an exception of type DBError. This works the same for data of any type—from common C++ types, to strings, structs, and class objects. The template class is a completely generic container.

Tip

> Template class containers mold themselves to accommodate objects of any type. Contrast this with the TContainer class in Chapter 15, "Programming with Virtual Functions," that can store only objects derived from an abstract base class, TObject. Template class containers eliminate the need to specify a base class type. However, the *entire* template class is instantiated anew for every type of data specified.

Listing 17.4, tdb.cpp, puts the TDatabase template class into action. The sample program declares a class, TRecord, for storing record objects in the database.

LISTING 17.4   TDB.CPP

```cpp
#include <iostream.h>
#include <string>        // Need string class
#include "db.h"          // Need TDatabase template

// Type of objects to store in database
class TRecord {
private:
  string name;  // Record data
public:
  TRecord(): name() { }
  TRecord(const string &s): name(s) { }
  void Assign(const string &s) { name = s; }
  const string & GetName() const { return name; }
};

int main()
{
  int rn;                      // Record number index
  TDatabase<TRecord> *pdb;     // Pointer to db of TRecords

  pdb = new TDatabase<TRecord>(3);  // Create 3-record database

  // Assign record data
  //
  pdb->GetRecord(0).Assign("George Washington");
  pdb->GetRecord(1).Assign("John Adams");
  pdb->GetRecord(2).Assign("Thomas Jefferson");

  // Display database contents
  //
  for (rn = 0; rn <= 2; rn++)  {
    cout << rn << ": ";
    cout << pdb->GetRecord(rn).GetName() << endl;
  }

  // Prompt user for record numbers
  //
  for (;;)  {
    cout << "Record number? (q to quit) ";
    cin >> rn;                 // Get requested record number
    if (!cin.good()) break;   // Bad character entered
    try {
      TRecord &tr = pdb->GetRecord(rn);
      cout << rn << ": " << tr.GetName() << endl;
    }
    catch (DBError error) {
      cout << "***Error: " << error.what() << endl;
    }
  }
  return 0;
}
```

To understand how the sample program uses the TDatabase template class, first examine the TRecord class. This is not a template, but a normal C++ class. The class has a private string object representing the record's data. It also declares two constructors: a default constructor with no parameters and one that receives a reference to a string object for copying to the object's private name member. In addition, TRecord declares a function, GetName(), that returns a constant reference to the private string object.

For the database object, created using the TDatabase template class, the program creates a pointer pdb using the declaration:

```
TDatabase<TRecord> *pdb;      // Pointer to db of TRecords
```

At this point, when C++ compiles the program, it constructs an actual class from the TDatabase<T> template. C++ inserts TRecord wherever the placeholder type T appears in the template, and in that way creates a database class that can store objects of type TRecord. To create the database object, the program calls new like this:

```
pdb = new TDatabase<TRecord>(3);   // Create 3-record database
```

The name of the instantiated class is TDatabase<TRecord>, not simply TDatabase. To the instantiated class constructor, TDatabase<TRecord>(), the statement passes a requested database size, 3 in this example. If you declared a database of integers, its name would be TDatabase<int>, instantiated as a completely new class using the template. The beauty of template classes is that they can mold to just about any type. The prime disadvantage is that every such use creates an entirely new instantiation.

After creating the database object, the program assigns strings to records using statements such as

```
pdb->GetRecord(0).Assign("George Washington");
```

Function GetRecord(), a member of the TDatabase<T> template class, returns a reference of type T&. Because the class is instantiated using the TRecord class, the actual GetRecord() function returns a reference to a TRecord object. Even though the template class has no knowledge of TRecord, the preceding statement can call TRecord::Assign() because the actual database object has been molded by the compiler to accommodate objects of type TRecord.

Reference functions such as TDatabase<T>::GetRecord() are particularly handy in template classes for efficiently returning objects of placeholder types. However, reference functions also bring into play the question of what to do if the function cannot return an object. What if, for example, the database is empty, or the user specifies an out-of-range record number?

This is where exceptions prove their value. Because exceptions effectively override a function's normal return value, they are ideal in reporting errors from functions that cannot reserve a particular value as an error indicator. For example, a pointer-function can return NULL to indicate an error, but there is no such animal as a NULL reference, and a reference function is best programmed to throw an exception to indicate a problem. Take a look at how this mechanism works in the sample database program. After creating a few sample records, the program prompts you to enter a record number. If you enter an illegal number, the program's exception handler reports the problem:

```
try {
  TRecord &tr = pdb->GetRecord(rn);
  cout << rn << ": " << tr.GetName() << endl;
}
catch (DBError error) {
  cout << "***Error: " << error.what() << endl;
}
```

The try block calls reference function GetRecord() for record number rn. If that record number is out of range, the function throws an exception of type DBError. This causes the assignment to the TRecord reference variable tr *not* to take place, and the program also skips the output statement. In the event of an error, the exception handler displays a message, and there's no need to include extra programming to test the function's return value.

TEMPLATE INSTANTIATION

An important issue in any program that uses templates is how and where those templates are instantiated. When the C++ compiler reads a template's declaration—usually in a header file—it acquires the information it needs to create actual instances of the template class or function for specific data types. In programs composed of many modules, it's important to consider where the compiler stores the code it generates for a template instantiation.

To deal with this issue, compiler writers have come up with a number of schemes, some of which are experimental in some versions of GNU C++. The following sections explain the two most common models of template instantiation, and also explain how to resolve some problems you might encounter in programs that use templates. First, however, to understand the resolution, you need to understand the problem that templates pose to the C++ compiler.

TROUBLE WITH TEMPLATES

When the C++ compiler encounters the use of a template, it generates the actual code for the template class or function based on the data type at that location. For example, consider a template function f() declared as

```
template <class T>
  void f(T data);
```

This probably appears in a header file, included in a module, call it moduleA, that needs to call f() for a specific data type. To instantiate the template, the module declares a function prototype using an actual data type:

```
template void f(int data);
```

The word template might not be needed. In fact, the prototype itself is possibly unnecessary, and the program can simply use the function in a statement such as

```
int count = 100;
f(count);
```

This is called *automatic template instantiation*, and depending on your version of GNU C++, might or might not require a preceding function prototype. In any case, using f()'s template declaration, C++ performs two actions:

1. It instantiates the template, meaning that it writes the symbolic code for an actual function based on the data type (int here) for the placeholder type (T) in the function.

2. It compiles the generated function and stores its code in the current module.

Action number two is where the problem with templates comes into play. Consider now that the program expands into two modules, moduleA and moduleB. The second module also needs to call f() using an integer argument. So, on compiling moduleB, which also includes the template's header file, the compiler generates another instance of f(int) and stores its code in moduleB's object code file.

Now there are two identical instances of f(int). Obviously, this is wasteful, and it complicates debugging. We want the compiler to recognize that it has already instantiated the function and to use that instantiation in all modules. But granting that wish isn't half as easy as making it. The following sections discuss some of the solutions currently making the rounds in C++ compiler design.

THE BORLAND MODEL

The Borland C++ model offers a simple solution to the proliferation of template instantiations. In this model, the compiler instantiates a template in each module. Using the example from the preceding section, after compiling, the object-code files modulea.o and moduleb.o (or any temporary files named similarly) contain identical instances of function f(int). In other words, under this model, the compiler simply ignores the problem.

However, during linking, the Borland linker recognizes that the same function exists in multiple modules, and it collapses all such instances into one. This solves the problem but comes with a troublesome disadvantage. In a program with dozens of modules using the same template classes and functions, the compiler has to generate instances of all of them. This makes the compiler work harder than necessary, and as a consequence, programs that extensively use templates take longer to compile.

THE CFRONT MODEL

The AT&T C++ to C translator, CFront, handles template instantiation differently. In this approach, a *template repository* is created during compilation of statements that use template classes and functions. The repository doesn't contain code, but symbolic linker names and other information that enable the compiler to create the template instances that the linker needs. In other words, this is a two-pass system. On pass one, the compiler creates a repository that tells the linker where to find and, if necessary, how to create any template instances needed to complete the final code file.

There are two main advantages with this approach. One is a decrease in compilation time because template instantiation doesn't occur until the program's modules are linked together. Two is that the operating system's own linker can handle template instantiations. The so-called Borland model requires a specially programmed linker. The downside of the CFront model is a large increase in compiler complexity. It's not easy for the compiler to generate all the information needed to build the final program when many of its pieces are missing and require creation during the link stage.

THE GNU C++ MODEL

Depending on your version of GNU C++, template instantiation might take a variety of forms, none of which exactly matches the preceding descriptions. Your first option is simply to live with multiple template instantiations, especially if you are using a version of GNU C++ 2.7.2 or earlier. Each module that uses a template gets its own instantiation of the class or template. This works, but at a cost of efficiency, compiler speed, and obviously, a waste of memory and disk space.

Your second option is to obtain a patched linker, known as the collect2 program (but renamed via a directory link to ld) that knows about object repositories. Your system might already use collect2 because of this linker's capability to call global class constructors at the start of a program (before main() is called), and also to call global destructors after main() returns. Normal UNIX linkers cannot do this, and on those systems, collect2 is inserted into the link process to handle these special chores. The *patched* version of collect2 also knows about object repositories for linking to template instantiations.

If you have the patched linker, you can compile a module with the -frepo g++ option to generate a repository file ending in .rpo. Later on, the linker uses this file to generate the template instantiations it needs. Although the stock GNU C++ compiler can generate .rpo files, they are useless unless you have the patched linker.

> **Note**   Object repositories are experimental in GNU C++ 2.7.2 and earlier. If you are using an older compiler, check out the following Web site for updates to GNU C++:
> `http://egcs.cygnus.com.`

Frankly, neither solution is all that attractive. Following is another approach that works with all GNU C++ implementations, and although it takes some additional programming, is the simplest solution of all.

DEALING WITH LINKER PROBLEMS

If you try using templates, you might receive linker errors about unresolved functions. This happens because the linker cannot find the template instantiations that the compiler creates for a particular module. The following listings illustrate the problem.

Listing 17.5, template.h, shows typical declarations for a template class and a template function in a header file that one or more modules might include.

LISTING 17.5   TEMPLATE.H

```
// A template class
//
template <class T>
class TAnyClass {
private:
  T data;
public:
  TAnyClass(const T arg): data(arg) { }
  const T & GetData() const;
};

// A template function prototype
//
template <class T>
TAnyClass<T> * MakeObject(const T param);
```

The template.h header file declares TAnyClass as a template with a private data member of type T, a constructor to initialize that data, and a function that returns a constant reference to data's value. As with all templates, type T is but a placeholder—the real type is determined later during the template's instantiation.

The header file also declares a template function MakeObject(). This function receives a constant parameter of type T and returns a pointer to a new object of type TAnyClass<T>. So far, so good. Listing 17.6, template.cpp, implements the template module.

LISTING 17.6   TEMPLATE.CPP

```
#include "template.h"
#include <string>

// A template class member function
//
template <class T>
const T & TAnyClass<T>::GetData() const
{
  return data;
}

// A template function
//
template <class T>
TAnyClass<T> * MakeObject(const T param)
{
  return new TAnyClass<T>(param);
}

// ======== Cut Here =======
// Explicit template instantiations for TAnyClass
//
template class TAnyClass<int>;
template class TAnyClass<double>;
template class TAnyClass<string>;
```

```
// Explicit template instantiation for function MakeObject()
//
template TAnyClass<string> * MakeObject(const string param);
```

The implementation module provides the contents for the member function GetData() in the TAnyClass template. The member function is still in template form—it uses placeholder type T—but its statement block provides what the function does—in this case, simply returning the object's private data, whatever that happens to be.

Similarly, the template function's statement uses the C++ new operator to construct an object of type TAnyClass<T>, and it returns a pointer to this object as the function's result. Again, this is still a template. The actual instantiation of the function happens later when a data type is supplied for T.

Unfortunately, this is where the trouble begins. Listing 17.7, usetemplate.cpp, attempts to use the template class and template function by including the header file. The result, however, is a series of confusing linker errors.

LISTING 17.7   USETEMPLATE.CPP

```
#include <iostream.h>
#include <string>
#include "template.h"

int main()
{
  TAnyClass<int> int_object(123);
  cout << "int_object    == " << int_object.GetData() << endl;

  TAnyClass<double> double_object(3.14159);
cout << "double_object == " << double_object.GetData() << endl;

  TAnyClass<string> string_object("String object");
  cout << "string_object == " << string_object.GetData() << endl;

  string s("Dynamic string object");
  TAnyClass<string> *p = MakeObject(s);
  cout << "*p == " << p->GetData() << endl;
  delete p;

  return 0;
}
```

To see the errors caused by the linker not finding the template instantiations, comment-out or delete the lines in the template.cpp file (refer to Listing 17.6) from the comment that reads "Cut Here" to the end. Then type the following commands:

```
$ g++ -c template.cpp
$ g++ usetemplate.cpp template.o
/tmp/cca011931.o: In function 'main':
/tmp/cca011931.o(.text+0x1e): undefined reference to
'TAnyClass<int>::GetData(void) const'
```

The template module (template.cpp) compiles, but attempting to link the main program and module produces *undefined reference* errors. Although I show only one such error here, if you are following along, several others appear onscreen. The problem occurs because GNU C++ doesn't provide automatic template instantiation, and therefore, although the compiler is happy with the use of templates, it doesn't generate the actual class and functions. When the linker looks for these items, it doesn't find them, and the compilation fails in the final act. The solution requires two steps:

1. Explicitly instantiate each instance of the template you need.
2. Declare `extern` prototypes for each function in every module that uses the template.

The lines you cut from template.cpp earlier perform the first step. The second might may not be needed, but if you still receive linker errors, try adding `extern` declarations such as the following in any module that uses a template class or function:

```
extern template class TAnyClass<int>;
extern template class TAnyClass<double>;
extern template class TAnyClass<string>;
extern template TAnyClass<string> * MakeObject(string param);
```

These declarations tell the linker to hunt for the template instantiations in all the modules linked to the program.

KNOWN TEMPLATE BUG

Template friend functions and inline member functions might not compile correctly. For example, the following declaration in a template class produces an "internal compiler error 163":

```
template <class T>
friend ostream & operator<< (ostream & ofs, const T &param) {
  cout << data;
  return ofs;
}
```

Perhaps a later version of GNU C++ will fix this problem. Until then, a plausible workaround is to derive a new class from `ostream` and overload `operator<<()` as a member function instead of as a friend. Chapter 20, "Customizing I/O Streams," shows several examples of this method.

DEBUGGING TEMPLATES

Template instantiation occurs behind the curtains during compilation—a tremendous disadvantage when a template function or class doesn't work as expected. It's difficult enough to find errors in programs. It's doubly hard when the cause is hidden from view. Fortunately, the GNU debugger can show exactly how the compiler instantiates a template function or class, and in that way, help you pinpoint problems with the template's design.

VIEWING TEMPLATE CLASS INSTANTIATIONS

To follow along and view the instantiation of a C++ template class, compile the tdb.cpp program in this chapter and load it into the GNU debugger by using these commands:

```
$ g++ -g -o tdb tdb.cpp
$ gdb --silent tdb
(gdb)
```

We want to investigate the construction of a template class object and also trace the use of that object. So, the first task is to find some good places to set breakpoints in the code. Type a few *list* commands until you find the statement that constructs a TDatabase object (it's line 31 for me). Set a breakpoint at the statement and then run the program:

```
(gdb) b 31
Breakpoint 1 at 0x80492a1: file tdb.cpp, line 31.
(gdb) run
Starting program: /src/c17/tdb
...
Breakpoint 1, main () at tdb.cpp:31
31 pdb = new TDatabase<TRecord>(3);
```

At this point, the pdb pointer has been declared as type TDatabase<TRecord>*. This causes the compiler to instantiate the class template using the specified TRecord data type. To see the results of the template expansion, use a *ptyp* command:

```
(gdb) ptyp pdb
type = class TDatabase<TRecord> {
private:
  TRecord *rp;
  int num;
public:
  TDatabase<TRecord> & operator=(TDatabase<TRecord> const &);
  TDatabase(TDatabase<TRecord> const &);
  TDatabase(int);
  ~TDatabase(void);
  TRecord & GetRecord(int);
} *
```

The results are most interesting, especially when compared with the original template (refer to Listing 17.3, db.h). The name of the instantiated class is now shown as TDatabase<TRecord>. Its pointer data member rp is declared of type TRecord *, and there are a few new items in the class's public section. The first two member functions show how C++ automatically generates an operator=() function and copy constructor unless these are explicitly provided in the class. In addition to these newcomers, the instantiated class fleshes out the template's destructor and GetRecord() function. The lone asterisk at the end of the debugger's output indicates that pdb is a pointer to the listed class.

TRACING TEMPLATE CLASS FUNCTIONS

To trace how the class is used, you can set breakpoints in class template member functions—even though those functions are actually constructed by C++ during compilation. In some cases, you might run into oddities because support for C++ templates in the debugger is not yet operating at full power. However, the necessary commands seem to work well enough to track down most kinds of template errors. One way to find potential breakpoint locations is to list the template's header file. For example, if you are following along, enter the following command to delete all current breakpoints (reload tdb if you quit the debugger):

```
(gdb) delete
Delete all breakpoints? (y or n) y
```

Next, type a *list* command followed by the filename and line number of the TDatabase template class's header file. Type *L* alone a few more times until you find the line shown here (the line number might be different for you):

```
(gdb) l db.h:1
...
26 TDatabase(int n): num(n)
```

Set a breakpoint on this line to halt the program when it calls the TDatabase constructor and then run the program to the breakpoint (if the program is already running and you are asked whether to restart it, answer yes):

```
(gdb) b 26
Breakpoint 2 at 0x804991c: file db.h, line 26.
(gdb) run
Starting program: /src/c17/tdb
Breakpoint 2, TDatabase<TRecord>::TDatabase (this=0x1,
n=-1073743212)
at db.h:26
26 TDatabase(int n): num(n)
```

The debugger's output shows a problem: The values for parameters this and n are obviously incorrect. Perhaps your version of gdb is repaired. Despite this trouble, it's still possible to view the correct values. Type *next* to enter the constructor, and then use *ptyp* to find out the type of member rp (record pointer):

```
(gdb) next
27 { rp = new T[num]; }
(gdb) ptyp rp
type = class TRecord {
...
public:
TRecord & operator=(TRecord const &);
TRecord(TRecord const &);
...
TRecord(basic_string<char, string_char_traits<char>,
_ _default_alloc_template<true, 0> > const &);
} *
```

I deleted several lines of the output, which might surprise you. The TDatabase template class's rp variable is actually of type TRecord * (pointer to a TRecord object). In addition to the explicitly declared members of this class (refer to Listing 17.4, tdb.cpp), C++ has added an operator=() function and a copy constructor. Also, the template's declaration of its constructor

```
TRecord(const string &s)
```

is replaced with an elongated declaration that indicates class string is itself a complex nested template. Chapter 22, "Mastering the Standard string Class" covers C++ string objects, so I won't go into the declaration here. But it is highly interesting that you can use the GNU debugger to find out exactly how C++ instantiates template and other classes in the compiled program.

SETTING BREAKPOINTS IN TEMPLATE CLASSES

Another useful method for setting breakpoints in template classes is to use the name of an instantiated class function instead of a source code line number. Reload the tdb program into the debugger, if necessary, and enter the following command to set a breakpoint in the GetRecord() member function (again, the line number might be different for you):

```
(gdb) b 'TDatabase<TRecord>::GetRecord(int)'
Breakpoint 3 at 0x80496e4: file db.h, line 36.
(gdb)
```

Actually, you don't have to type all that. Just type *b' TD* (including the apostrophe), press Tab, type *::Get*, press Tab again, and you're finished. In general, you can use command-line completion this way to enter lengthy identifiers—after all, the debugger knows all the symbols in the program and can easily search for matches using partial input.

> **Note**
>
> I wonder why other debuggers don't have handy features such as command-line symbol completion. Probably because you have to pay for the products!

After setting the breakpoint in GetRecord(), run or continue the program until it halts:

```
(gdb) cont
Continuing.
Breakpoint 3, TDatabase<TRecord>::GetRecord (this=0x804b680,
  recnum=0) at db.h:36
36 if (0 <= recnum && recnum < num)
```

This time, the parameters to GetRecord() seem to be correct. You can now proceed to step through the instantiated function and examine the program's exception handling. Type *q* when you're finished.

> **Tip**
>
> When the program is paused in a member function, the command *ptyp this* displays the type of object for which the function was called.

SUMMARY

Templates are schematics for creating actual functions and classes. A template specifies one or more placeholder types that C++ replaces with actual types during compilation. This makes it possible to write completely generic functions and classes that mold during compilation to accommodate actual types of data. Templates are typically written in header files included into modules. Some useful examples of templates are sorting functions and container classes.

For more information on subjects introduced in this chapter, turn to the following chapters:

- Chapter 15, "Programming with Virtual Functions"
- Chapter 16, "Handling Exceptions"
- Chapter 22, "Mastering the Standard string Class"
- Chapter 23, "Using the Standard Template Library (STL)"

PART IV

ADVANCED C++ TECHNIQUES

## CHAPTER 18

OVERLOADING YOUR FRIENDS

We all need a little help from our friends, and C++ friends help solve some tricky problems in object-oriented programming. This chapter introduces the subjects of friend classes and friend functions, and it sets the stage for Chapter 19, "Overloading Operators," in which you learn how to use friends to create *overloaded operators*. These are special functions that provide for the evaluation of expressions such as A + B, where A and B are class objects. But first, you need to learn the basics of C++ friends.

WHAT ARE FRIENDS FOR?

One of the main gifts of C++ object-oriented programming is the encapsulation of data and functions in classes. As many of this book's sample programs demonstrate, a typical class provides public functions that access private data. This helps prevent common errors caused by misuse of data, and it also facilitates maintenance and debugging.

But rules are made to be broken, and in C++, you can break the rules of encapsulation by using friends, although you do so at some risk to your program's welfare. Declaring a friend of a class is like giving a pal a copy of your house key. If you go away for the weekend, don't be surprised on your return to discover your buddy asleep on the couch and the refrigerator seriously depleted.

Even so, friends are useful in certain circumstances, and with care, can be put to work safely. C++ classes can declare two kinds of friends. An entire class might be a friend of another class, or a single function might be declared as a friend. In general, friends have special access to the class's members, even though the friend might not be a member of the class's own family.

> **Note**
>
> If friends have a counterpart in conventional C programming, it's the `goto` statement. Like `goto`, a friend enables you to break the very rules intended to help you write reliable code. Don't interpret this chapter as a blanket endorsement of friends. Experienced C++ programmers use friends only when absolutely necessary.

FRIEND CLASSES

A class might declare another class as a friend. The first class (the one that declares the friend) gives another class (the friend) permission to access all private and protected members of the first class. Public members are always accessible, so you don't need to declare a class as a friend to give it access to public members. You declare a friend so that it can access another class's private and protected declarations.

Typically, a friend class is used when one of two unrelated classes requires access to the other class's inner secrets. For example, you might declare a class such as

```
class AClass {
private:
  double value;
public:
```

```
  AClass(double arg): value(arg) { }
};
```

Class `AClass` declares a private data member, `value`, of type `double`. To that member, the class constructor assigns an argument value. However, as written here, `AClass` provides no access to its private data. After `value` is initialized, the private data member is as safe from harm as a bear cub by its mother's side.

Next, suppose you declare another class that contains an object of `AClass` as a data member. This is a typical design in which friends come into play:

```
class BClass {
private:
  AClass anObject;  // AClass object data member
public:
  BClass(double arg): anObject(arg) { }
  double GetValue() { return anObject.value; } // ???
};
```

The class does not compile because its member function `GetValue()` attempts to access the private `value` data member in `anObject`. Because `value` is private to `AClass`, only members of that class can access the data member.

In cases like this, programmers are sorely tempted to "fix" the problem by changing the original access specifier in `AClass` from `private` to `public`. This works, but it's like swatting a fly with a sledgehammer because it makes `value` available to *all* users of `AClass`. What's needed is special access to `AClass`'s private data from inside `BClass`.

The solution is to make `BClass` a friend of `AClass`. This states that `BClass` objects have special permission to access the private and protected members inside `AClass`, without making those members available to statements outside either class. To make this change, use the `friend` reserved word inside the class to which the other class needs access. In this example, `BClass` needs to use the private `value` data member inside `AClass`. So, to give `BClass` permission to do that, `AClass` declares `BClass` as a friend. Here's the new `AClass` declaration:

```
class AClass {
  friend class BClass;  // BClass is a friend of AClass
private:
  double value;  // AClass and BClass may use this member
  ...
};
```

The only difference from the previous `AClass` declaration is the addition of `friend class BClass` just after `AClass`'s opening line. This tells the compiler to grant `BClass` access to `AClass`'s private and protected members. Other statements in other classes and in the program are still prevented from using `AClass`'s restricted members. You may declare any number of classes as friends. The only restriction is that the `friend` reserved word must appear inside a class declaration. A few other facts about friends are worth remembering:

■ A class must name all its friends in advance. You cannot create friends at runtime.

- The class containing the private and protected data is the one that declares another class to be a friend, thus giving that friend special access to the normally hidden members of the declaring class. A class can never declare itself to be a friend of another class—that would be like inviting yourself to dinner at a stranger's house.

- A friend class might be declared before or after the class that declares the friend. The order of declarations is unimportant, but the friend class is typically declared last so that any member functions in the friend class can refer to the other class's private and protected elements.

- Derived classes of the friend do not inherit special access to the original class's private and protected members. Only the specifically named friend class has that permission.

- A derived class might be a friend of its base class, although in such cases, using protected members in the base accomplishes the same goal of giving the derived class (the friend) access to restricted members in the base class.

Listing 18.1, friend.cpp, demonstrates how a friend class can access another class's private and protected members.

LISTING 18.1   FRIEND.CPP

```cpp
#include <iostream.h>
#include <string>        // Need string class

class Pal {
  friend class Buddy;   // Buddy is a friend of Pal
private:
  string label;
protected:
  void PutLabel(string arg) { label = arg; }
public:
  Pal(string arg): label(arg) { }
};

class Buddy {
private:
  Pal palObject;
public:
  Buddy(string arg): palObject(arg) { }
  void FriendDemo();
};

int main()
{
  Buddy aBuddy("First Message");
  aBuddy.FriendDemo();
  return 0;
}

// Demonstrate how Buddy object can access Pal private
// and protected members
void Buddy::FriendDemo()
{
```

```
  cout << "Reading private Pal::message from Buddy" << endl;
  cout << palObject.label << endl;
  cout << "Calling protected Pal:PutLabel function" << endl;
  palObject.PutLabel("Second Message");
  cout << palObject.label << endl;
  cout << "Writing private Pal::message from Buddy" << endl;
  palObject.label = "Third Message";
  cout << palObject.label << endl;
}
```

Compile and run the program in the usual way. Its output shows how a friend class can access a private string label in another class:

```
$ g++ friend.cpp
$ ./a.out
Reading private Pal::message from Buddy
First Message
Calling protected Pal:PutLabel function
Second Message
Writing private Pal::message from Buddy
Third Message
```

In the friend.cpp program, class Pal declares Buddy as a friend. This gives Buddy access to Pal's private string label data member and also its PutLabel() protected member function. The Pal class also declares a constructor, but it provides no other access to its private and protected members. A program statement could construct a Pal object like this:

```
Pal palObject("A String");
```

But that's all it could do. Because Pal provides no functions to read and write its data, the only possible operation is to construct an object of type Pal. However, because Buddy is a friend of Pal, it can access Pal's normally hidden declarations. To demonstrate, the sample program creates an object of type Buddy and calls its FriendDemo() member function:

```
Buddy aBuddy("First Message");
aBuddy.FriendDemo();
```

Inside FriendDemo(), various statements show how Buddy takes advantage of its friendship with Pal. The following statement, for example, calls Pal's protected member function PutLabel():

```
palObject.PutLabel("Second Message");
```

Buddy can go even further, writing new values to Pal's private string data. The following statement stores a new label in the Pal object:

```
palObject.label = "Third Message";
```

Although the sample listing is hypothetical, it demonstrates a practical use for friend classes. In this case, class Pal provides for the storage of some data, represented by its string object, label. Another class, the friend of Pal, provides access to Pal's private data, which remains protected from abuse by other program statements. A similar design might make sense in other cases to divide the storage of data from its access functions among two separate classes—for instance, if two programming teams need to develop the individual classes.

MUTUAL FRIEND CLASSES

Two classes can declare each other as friends, giving each class access to the other's private and protected members. This is the object-oriented equivalent of two people staying in adjacent hotel rooms and keeping the inner door open. Outsiders can't see what's going on inside, but the two guests are free to visit each other's rooms.

Using mutual friend classes destroys the barriers that normally prohibit access to a class's restricted members, and it's rare that you'll use this technique. It is occasionally useful, however, to provide mutual access to static data members among two classes. Listing 18.2, mutual.cpp, demonstrates the basic technique.

LISTING 18.2   MUTUAL.CPP

```cpp
#include <iostream.h>

class BClass;

class AClass {
  friend BClass;
private:
  static int x;
public:
  AClass(int arg) { x = arg; }
  void AFunction();
};

class BClass {
  friend AClass;
private:
  static int y;
public:
  BClass(int arg) { y = arg; }
  void BFunction();
};

int AClass::x;
int BClass::y;

int main()
{
  AClass a(123);
  BClass b(456);
  a.AFunction();
  b.BFunction();
  return 0;
}

void AClass::AFunction()
{
  cout << "Inside AClass::AFunction()" << endl;
  cout << "x == " << x << "; y == " << BClass::y << endl;
}

void BClass::BFunction()
```

```
{
  cout << "Inside BClass::BFunction()" << endl;
  cout << "x == " << AClass::x << "; y == " << y << endl;
}
```

Compile and run the program, which displays the values of the x and y private static members of two mutually friendly classes:

```
$ g++ mutual.cpp
$ ./a.out
Inside AClass::AFunction()
x == 123; y == 456
Inside BClass::BFunction()
x == 123; y == 456
```

An incomplete class declaration is the key to making mutual friend classes cooperate. The sample listing begins by declaring that symbol BClass is a class:

```
class BClass;
```

This permits AClass to declare BClass as a friend. BClass in turn declares AClass as a friend. This gives each class access to the other's private and protected members. As mentioned, a typical application is to access static data members in two different classes. Here, two integer variables, AClass::x and BClass::y, are declared static in their respective classes. Because they are static, only one copy of each integer variable exists for all objects created of the two classes. Because they are private, the variables are normally accessible only from within their declaring classes.

However, because of the close mutual relationship between AClass and BClass, the member functions in those classes can access the other's private static data. To do this requires telling the compiler exactly what object to use. For example, in AFunction, the static variable BClass::y must be referenced using that fully qualified name. Similarly, BFunction() references AClass's x variable using the fully qualified name AClass::x.

> **Note**
>
> The sample program in this section proves that mutual friend classes are possible using GNU C++, but if you find you need this capability often, it might be an indicator of a poorly designed class hierarchy. Most classes are better off as complete strangers to one another.

FUNCTIONS AND FRIENDS

A friend function is similar to, but less onerous than, a friend class. Declaring a function as a friend of a class gives that function access to private and protected members in class objects. The friend function might be a common C++ function, or a class member function. The following sections discuss both types.

> **Note**
>
> Friend functions are typically used to implement overloaded operators, the topic for the next chapter.

Friend Functions

In a typical design, a friend function declares parameters of classes to which the function owes its friendship. Inside the friend function, statements can access normally hidden members in class object arguments that are passed to the function. Listing 18.3, friendfn.cpp, demonstrates how to declare and use a friend function for two classes.

Listing 18.3   FRIENDFN.CPP

```cpp
#include <iostream.h>
#include <string>        // Need string class

class Two;  // Incomplete class declaration

class One {
  friend void Show(One &c1, Two &c2);
private:
  string s1;  // Accessible to One and Show()
public:
  One() { s1 = "Testing "; }
};

class Two {
  friend void Show(One &c1, Two &c2);
private:
  string s2;  // Accessible to Two and Show()
public:
  Two() { s2 = "one, two, three"; }
};

int main()
{
  One obj1;
  Two obj2;
  Show(obj1, obj2);
  return 0;
}

// Implement the friend function
void Show(One &obj1, Two &obj2)
{
  cout << obj1.s1 << obj2.s2 << endl;
}
```

When you compile and run the program with the following commands, it calls a friend function that writes the values of two private `string` data members in two separate classes:

```
$ g++ friendfn.cpp
$ ./a.out
Testing one, two, three
```

The friendfn.cpp program declares two classes, One and Two. An incomplete class declaration allows One's members to refer to Two before the Two class is declared. Both classes identically declare a friend function named Show() as

```
friend void Show(One &c1, Two &c2);
```

Because the friend function prototype appears inside the classes, statements in Show() are granted access to the private and protected members in One and Two. Function Show() declares reference parameters obj1 and obj2 of the two class types. Because Show() is a friend of those classes, statements inside Show() can access the private and protected members in its two parameters. For example, Show() writes the values of the private string variables s1 and s2 using the statement

```
cout << obj1.s1 << obj2.s2 << endl;
```

Other functions that are not friends of One and Two cannot use similar expressions because s1 and s2 are private members of their respective classes.

FRIEND MEMBER FUNCTIONS

A friend function can also be a class member. In a typical case, a class declares a member function of another class as a friend. The friend member function can access the declaring class's private and protected members. Listing 18.4, friendmf.cpp (that's *mf* for *member function*), shows the basic strategy for using friend member functions.

PART
IV

CH
18

LISTING 18.4 FRIENDMF.CPP

```cpp
#include <iostream.h>
#include <string>        // Need string class

class One;  // Incomplete class declaration

class Two {
private:
  string s2;  // Accessible to Two's members
public:
  Two() { s2 = "one, two, three"; }
  void Show(One &c1);
};

class One {
  friend void Two::Show(One &c1);
private:
  string s1;  // Accessible to One and Two::Show()
public:
  One() { s1 = "Testing "; }
};

void main()
{
  One obj1;
```

continues

LISTING 18.4   CONTINUED

```
  Two obj2;
  obj2.Show(obj1);
}

void Two::Show(One &obj1)
{
  cout << obj1.s1 << s2 << endl;
}
```

The program's output is the same as friendfn.cpp, but it uses a different technique to provide access to private data. Compile and run the program with the commands:

```
$ g++ friendmf.cpp
$ ./a.out
Testing one, two, three
```

The new program, friendmf.cpp, is similar to friendfn.cpp but uses a friend member function to access the private members of two classes. As in the other program, the new code declares two classes—One and Two. In this case, however, class Two declares Show() as a common public member function. Class One declares that *same* member function as a friend, using the class name Two and C++ scope resolution operator to tell the compiler where to find this function:

```
friend void Two::Show(One &c1);
```

Given that declaration, function Two::Show() is a friend of class One and can therefore access One's private and protected members. The order of the two classes is reversed from the earlier listing because the class that prototypes the member function must be declared before the class that specifies the member function as a friend. For One to declare Two::Show() as a friend of the class, the compiler must already have seen Two's declaration.

Another difference is the way Show() refers to private data in the two classes. (Refer to the function implementation at the end of Listing 18.4.) The function now declares only one reference parameter, &obj1, of the One class. Because Show() is a member of class Two, it can access all members of Two directly. However, the expression obj1.s1 in the output statement is allowed because Show() is a friend of class One, of which s1 is a private data member.

SUMMARY

A class may declare another class or function as a friend. This gives the friend access to the declaring class's normally private and protected members. Because friends break the very rules that help authors write robust C++ programs, experienced programmers use them only when absolutely necessary. However, friends are useful in some cases—for example, in creating overloaded operators, the subject of the next chapter.

For more information on subjects introduced in this chapter, turn to the following chapters:

- Chapter 13, "Creating and Destroying Objects"
- Chapter 19, "Overloading Operators"

OVERLOADING OPERATORS

One goal of object-oriented programming is to make it possible for programmers to create new data types that work exactly the same as native types. C++ comes very close to achieving this Holy Grail through the use of *overloaded operators*, introduced in this chapter.

WHAT IS OPERATOR OVERLOADING?

In a nutshell, an overloaded operator is a function that provides for the evaluation of expressions involving class objects. For example, the expression A + B, as you know, equals the sum of two objects that might be of types such as int or double. With operator overloading, A and B can be objects of any C++ class. Most operators can be overloaded so that expressions such as A++ and statements like C += B; work for class objects as they do for values of native C and C++ types.

> **Note**
>
> As you are about to discover, friends and operator overloading cooperate fully with one another—as should all good friends. If you haven't read Chapter 18, "Overloading Your Friends," you might want to do so before continuing.

INTRODUCING OVERLOADED OPERATORS

Operator overloading can greatly contribute to a program's organization and clarity. for example, with appropriately overloaded operators, you can declare a class such as TAnyClass and define some objects of that class type:

```
TAnyClass c1, c2, c3;
```

You can then use these objects in statements such as

```
c3 = c1 + c2;
```

In many cases, a statement like that is more understandable, and potentially easier to write, than the equivalent function call. Using conventional code, for instance, a statement roughly equivalent to the preceding might be:

```
c3 = ObjectSum(c1, c2);
```

Another great use for operator overloading is in providing for the input and output of class objects. Instead of writing a function that displays an object in a statement like this:

```
anObject.Display();
```

using operator overloading, you can add anObject's class to the types of data that the << operator recognizes. By doing that, to display anObject's value, you simply write the following:

```
cout << anObject << endl;
```

Operator overloading doesn't always improve the program's clarity, but when it does, it is a highly useful tool. To understand how to use operator overloading, it helps to first review what you know about operators in general. The common plus-sign operator (+), of course, sums two values. The minus sign (-) subtracts two values. These and other symbols are called *binary operators* because they require two arguments. Others, such as the not operator (!), are *unary operators* because they require only one argument. Unary minus is an example of an operator with both binary and unary forms. The expression -count negates count's value the same as if you called a function Negate():

```
Negate(count);  // Conceptually equivalent to -count
```

Operator overloading uses functions like that to add new data types to those C++ normally recognizes in expressions. You have already seen one example of operator overloading in the class copy function, operator=(). This *overloads* the assignment operator (=) to provide for the copying of two objects in statements such as

```
objA = objB;
```

Assuming that the two objects are of the same class—let's call it TAnyClass—the preceding statement calls the operator=() function to perform the actual copying. So that the involved objects can access private data members easily, the overloaded operator functions are typically declared as friends. The following sections explain how this works for overloaded binary and unary operator member functions.

OVERLOADED FRIEND OPERATORS

A simple example illustrates operator overloading for a hypothetical class named ZZ:

```
class ZZ {
public:
  friend ZZ operator+(ZZ a, ZZ b);
  friend ZZ operator-(ZZ a, ZZ b);
  friend ZZ operator*(ZZ a, ZZ b);
  friend ZZ operator/(ZZ a, ZZ b);
  // ... other class declarations
};
```

This is not a complete class, but it demonstrates one way to declare overloaded operators as friend functions. It isn't strictly necessary to declare the functions as friends unless the class needs to give the operators permission to access protected and private data—but overloaded operators are typically declared as shown here. The function names are operator+(), operator-(), operator*(), and operator/(). Normally, you can't use symbols such as +, -, *, and / in function names, but for the purpose of overloading operators, C++ allows a function name to consist of the reserved word operator and one of the symbols from Table 19.1.

PART
IV
CH
19

TABLE 19.1 OPERATORS THAT MAY BE OVERLOADED

*	/	+	-	%	^	&	¦
~	!	,	=	<	>	<=	>=
++	--	<<	>>	==	!=	&&	¦¦
*=	/=	%=	^=	&=	¦=	+=	-=
<<=	>>=	->	->*	[]	new	delete	
<?	>?						

> **Note**
>
> Operators +, -, *, and & may be overloaded for binary and unary expressions. Operators not in the table—such as the comma operator, scope resolution operator : :, and the ? : conditional expression operator—may not be overloaded.

The hypothetical ZZ class declares operator functions for the first four operators in the table. Each function has the following general form:

```
friend ZZ operator+(ZZ a, ZZ b);
```

The function is declared as a friend of the class to give the function access to the class's private and protected members (the sample class here has no such data, however). The function returns type ZZ so that its result may be assigned to another ZZ object. (However, the function might return a different type.) Most important, the function's name operator+() identifies the function as the method by which expressions that use the plus operator can handle objects of this class. For example, the program can construct three ZZ objects and use the following statement to add two of them and assign the results to the third:

```
ZZ a, b, c;
...
c = a + b;
```

> **Note**
>
> In most cases, classes that overload operators must provide operator=() functions and copy constructors. See Chapter 13, "Creating and Destroying Objects," for help in writing these functions.

When overloading operators, keep in mind that the compiler does not enforce mathematical concepts for class objects. It's a good idea to write functions such as operator+() that perform addition-like actions. Similarly, the code for operator*() should perform an operation that at least resembles mathematical multiplication. The actions of overloaded operators are up to you, but if you sidestep tradition—for example, defining a plus sign that multiplies instead of adds—the results are likely to be confusing at best.

EXAMPLE OF OVERLOADED OPERATORS

A working example of overloaded operators helps illustrate the preceding concepts. Listing 19.1, strops.cpp, shows the beginnings of a class that can store integer values in string form. By using overloaded operators, the program evaluates mathematical expressions for string objects—not something that C++ ordinarily can do.

LISTING 19.1   STROPS.CPP

```
#include <iostream.h>
#include <stdlib.h>    // Need atol()
#include <string>       // Need string class

class TStrOp {
private:
```

```
      string value;
public:
  TStrOp(): value("0") { }
  TStrOp(string arg): value(arg) { }
  long GetValue() { return atol( value.c_str() ); }
  friend long operator+(TStrOp a, TStrOp b);
  friend long operator-(TStrOp a, TStrOp b);
};

int main()
{
  TStrOp a("1234");
  TStrOp b("4321");

  cout << "Value of a == " << a.GetValue() << endl;
  cout << "Value of b == " << b.GetValue() << endl;
  cout << "a + b +  6 == " << (a + b + 6)  << endl;
  cout << "a - b + 10 == " << (a - b + 10) << endl;
  return 0;
}

// Implement operator+() friend function
long operator+(TStrOp a, TStrOp b)
{
  return (atol(a.value.c_str()) + atol(b.value.c_str())));
}

// Implement operator-() friend function
long operator-(TStrOp a, TStrOp b)
{
  return (atol(a.value.c_str()) - atol(b.value.c_str())));
}
```

Before examining the program's class and overloaded functions, take a look at main(). There, you find two objects created of type TStrOp:

```
TStrOp a("1234");
TStrOp b("4321");
```

Each object stores a string value. Even so, the program can add and subtract them using expressions such as the following, extracted from the program's output statements:

```
(a + b + 6);
(a - b + 10);
```

Now, compile and run the program to see the results of these expressions. Enter these commands:

```
$ g++ strops.cpp
$ ./a.out
Value of a == 1234
Value of b == 4321
a + b +  6 == 5561
a - b + 10 == -3077
```

Operator overloading makes it possible to add and subtract objects that store integer values in string form. To make this happen, two friend functions in the TStrOp class overload the plus and minus operators. The two functions are declared as the public members:

```
friend long operator+(TStrOp a, TStrOp b);
friend long operator-(TStrOp a, TStrOp b);
```

So that TStrOp objects can participate in expressions involving other integer values, each operator returns type long. Each is a binary operator, so it receives two argument values, both objects of the TStrOp class. Examine the overloaded operator implementations following main(). Because the functions are friends, they do not require prefacing with their class names but are implemented as other common C++ functions. Also, because they are friends, they can directly access the private data member string in the TStrOp class. For example, to convert object a's value to a long integer, the function uses the following expression:

```
atol(a.value.c_str());
```

That passes the C-style string of the string-class object value in object a to the standard atol() function, resulting in the string's equivalent integer value. Because the overloaded operator functions are friends of the class, they can access the private data members a.value and b.value.

> **Note**
>
> The technique for overloading operators in this section is just one of several possible variations. Other methods are introduced throughout this chapter.

OVERLOADED CLASS MEMBER OPERATORS

Overloaded functions also can be members of a class, as Listing 19.2, strops2.cpp, demonstrates. The program is similar to the strops.cpp demonstration in the preceding section, but illustrates how to overload operators using class member functions instead of friends.

LISTING 19.2 STROPS2.CPP

```cpp
#include <iostream.h>
#include <stdlib.h>    // Need atol()
#include <string>       // Need string class

class TStrOp {
private:
  string value;
public:
  TStrOp(): value("0") { }
  TStrOp(string arg): value(arg) { }
  long GetValue() { return atol( value.c_str() ); }
  long operator+(TStrOp b);
  long operator-(TStrOp b);
};

int main()
{
```

```
    TStrOp a("1234");
    TStrOp b("4321");

    cout << "Value of a == " << a.GetValue() << endl;
    cout << "Value of b == " << b.GetValue() << endl;
    cout << "a + b +  6 == " << (a + b + 6)  << endl;
    cout << "a - b + 10 == " << (a - b + 10) << endl;
    return 0;
}

// Implement operator+() member function
long TStrOp::operator+(TStrOp b)
{
    return (atol(value.c_str()) + atol(b.value.c_str()));
}

// Implement operator-() member function
long TStrOp::operator-(TStrOp b)
{
    return (atol(value.c_str()) - atol(b.value.c_str()));
}
```

Because the overloaded operator functions in the revised program are members of the TStrOp class, they already have access to the class's private members (and any protected members, although there aren't any in this case). For that reason, the operator functions do not need to be friends of the class. In addition, the overloaded operator member functions receive a hidden this pointer to the object for which the functions are called. The functions therefore need only single parameters, not two as before. They are still binary operator functions because they still receive two parameters—but the this parameter is not explicitly declared.

Compile and run the program as you did the preceding one, using these commands:

```
$ g++ strops2.cpp
$ ./a.out
Value of a == 1234
Value of b == 4321
a + b +  6 == 5561
a - b + 10 == -3077
```

Using overloaded operator member functions, the program can add and subtract objects of the TStrOp class using values in string form.

TYPES OF OVERLOADED OPERATORS

Now that you've met the basics of operator overloading, you are ready to explore examples that show how to write functions for specific operators. Each of the following sections covers a category of operators that you might implement for a C++ class.

UNARY OPERATORS

Unary operators such as unary plus and unary minus require only one argument. For example, the expression -A equals the negative value of +A. You can overload these and other unary operators with techniques similar to those illustrated in the preceding sections. As with binary operators, you may declare an overloaded unary operator function as a friend or as a member of a class. An overloaded unary operator friend function declares only one parameter of the class type because it needs only one value on which to operate. For example, copy file strops2.cpp to test.cpp, and add to the copy the following declaration in the public section of class TStrOp:

```
friend long operator-(TStrOp a);
```

Even though the class already overloads the minus operator, because the new declaration specifies only one parameter, there is no conflict. This is not a special rule—C++ permits overloading of any member function as long as all such functions differ by at least one parameter data type. Implement the new friend function by adding the following code after main():

```
long operator-(TStrOp a)
{
  return -atol(a.value.c_str());
}
```

As a friend, the unary operator friend function has access to the private value data member in object a. To negate that string as an integer, the function calls the standard library's atol() function and returns its negative result. To test out the new overloaded operator, add this statement to main():

```
cout << "-a == " << -a << endl;
```

Compile and run the program. As its output shows, it is now possible to evaluate the negative value of a string with the simple expression -a:

```
$ g++ test.cpp
$ ./a.out
Value of a == 1234
...
-a == -1234
```

As with overloaded binary operators, you can also declare overloaded unary operators as member functions. Start with a fresh copy of strops2.cpp, and add the following declaration to the TStrOp class's public section:

```
long operator-();
```

The declaration is similar to the friend but requires no parameters. This is because, as a class member function, it receives a this pointer to the object for which it is called, and it already has access to the class's private data. Implement the function by inserting the following after main():

```
long TStrOp::operator-()
{
  return -atol(value.c_str());
}
```

That's simpler than the friend function because it can refer directly to value. Again, to return the negative integer value of the object's string data, the overloaded operator calls the standard library's atol() function, passing the C-style string of the value object and returning the negative result. The member function is used identically to the friend. To test it, add this statement to main():

```
cout << "-a == " << -a << endl;
```

TYPE CONVERSION OPERATOR

Using operator overloading, you can supply your own type conversion rules for class objects. The results are similar to the way C++ automatically converts values of some types in expressions. For instance, if A is type double and B is an int, the result of the expression A + B is a value of type double. To evaluate the expression, C++ converts the int B to a double and then adds it to A.

It is frequently advantageous to define similar conversion rules for C++ classes. Conversion operators take the following general form:

```
operator type();
```

where *type* is the data type to which you want to convert objects of the class. This might be any type such as long:

```
operator long();
```

The function should return a value of the specified type, using whatever means are necessary to perform the conversion. For example, using the TStrOp class from the preceding section, instead of repeatedly passing the string data member value to atol(), you might define an overloaded type conversion operator that automatically translates the object's string to a value of type long. To do that, add this inline member function to the TStrOp class's public section:

```
operator long() { return atol(value.c_str()); }
```

With a type conversion rule in place, C++ conversions of TStrOp objects to long values are automatic. The program can create an object of type TStrOp and assign it to a long integer variable:

```
TStrOp myValue("9876");
long x = myValue;   // !!!
```

When the compiler encounters the second statement, it calls the overloaded type conversion operator function for the TStrOp class to convert myValue to a long integer. C++ already knows how to assign long integers, so when the conversion is finished, the rest of the job is intrinsic.

Even better, the conversion operator greatly simplifies the implementation of other member functions. Function operator+(), for example, is now much simpler:

```
long TStrOp::operator+(TStrOp b)
{
  return (long)*this + (long)b;
}
```

The type cast expression (long) converts the objects involved in addition expressions to long integer values via the type conversion operator function. Because this is a member function, the expression (long)*this converts the object for which the operator+() function was called. The expression (long)b does the same for the function's TStrOp parameter. The class's GetValue() member function along with other overloaded functions, operator-() and unary operator-(), are similarly simplified by the new type conversion rule. Listing 19.3, strops3.cpp, shows the finished program, minus function main(), which is unchanged. Compile and run it as you have the preceding two sample programs.

LISTING 19.3 STROPS3.CPP (PARTIAL)

```
#include <iostream.h>
#include <stdlib.h>     // Need atol()
#include <string>       // Need string class

class TStrOp {
private:
  string value;
public:
  TStrOp(): value("0") { }
  TStrOp(string arg): value(arg) { }
  long GetValue() { return (long)(*this); }
  long operator+(TStrOp b);
  long operator-(TStrOp b);
  long operator-();
  operator long() { return atol(value.c_str()); }
};

int main()
{
...
}

// Implement operator+() member function
long TStrOp::operator+(TStrOp b)
{
  return (long)*this + (long)b;
}

// Implement operator-() member function
long TStrOp::operator-(TStrOp b)
{
  return (long)*this - (long)b;
}

// Implement unary operator-() member function
long TStrOp::operator-()
{
  return -(long)(*this);
}
```

Array Subscript Operator

You can overload the array subscript operator [] to provide array-like access to a class's data members, even though that data might be stored as individual members or in a linked list. The technique is particularly useful in creating container classes that operate like common arrays and are therefore easily used even by relatively inexperienced programmers. A simple example, Listing 19.4, ssop.cpp, demonstrates how to overload [] for a class that stores four integer values as separate data members.

LISTING 19.4   SSOP.CPP

```
#include <iostream.h>

class TError { };

class PseudoArray {
private:
  int value0;
  int value1;
  int value2;
  int value3;
public:
  PseudoArray(int v0, int v1, int v2, int v3):
    value0(v0), value1(v1), value2(v2), value3(v3) { }
  int &operator[](unsigned i) throw(TError);
};

int main()
{
  PseudoArray pa(10, 20, 30, 40);

  try {
    for (int i = 0; i <= 3; i++)
      cout << "pa[" << i << "] == " << pa[i] << endl;
    pa[2] = 123;
    cout << "pa[2] == " << pa[2] << endl;
    //    pa[10] = 0;   // ???
  }
  catch (TError) {
    cout << "*** Error detected" << endl;
  }

  return 0;
}

// Implement overloaded operator[] member function
int &PseudoArray::operator[](unsigned i) throw(TError)
{
  switch (i) {
    case 0: return value0;   // Note: breaks not needed
    case 1: return value1;
    case 2: return value2;
    case 3: return value3;
    default: throw TError();
  }
}
```

The key to implementing an `operator[]` function is providing safe read and write access to data using array-like expressions. We want to be able to write statements such as these:

```
PseudoArray pa;
pa[2] = 123;
cout << "pa[2] == " << pa[2] << endl;
```

We also want the program to respond reasonably if users specify an out-of-bounds index. Probably the best way to achieve these ends is to declare the `operator[]` function as returning a reference to a value instead of merely a copy of a value stored in the class. The function also reports errors by throwing an exception. The sample program shows the basic techniques for creating a class with a reference `operator[]` function. Compile and run the program using these commands:

```
$ g++ ssop.cpp
$ ./a.out
pa[0] == 10
pa[1] == 20
pa[2] == 30
pa[3] == 40
pa[2] == 123
```

The Listing 19.4 demonstrates also how the overloaded `operator[]` function reports errors by throwing an exception. To see this effect, remove the comment delimiters from the following statement in `main()`:

```
pa[10] = 0;   // ???
```

This attempts to assign zero using an out-of-bounds array index. Compile and run the modified program, which now displays an error message:

```
*** Error detected
```

In the sample program, class `PseudoArray` declares four private integer values. To provide array-like access to this data, the class overloads the `[]` operator using the member function prototype:

```
int &operator[](unsigned i) throw(TError);
```

This states that function `operator[]()` returns a reference to an `int` object, using an `unsigned int` index, `i`. The function reports errors by throwing an object of class `TError`. (That class is bare-bones simple to keep the listing reasonably short.) The overloaded operator function's implementation uses a `switch` statement to return one of the class's private integer variables, or the function throws an exception if the requested index is out of range. Because the overloaded operator returns a reference to an `int` object, the program can read and write values using array-like expressions. For example, `main()` assigns a value to `pa[2]` and displays that value using these statements:

```
pa[2] = 123;
cout << "pa[2] == " << pa[2] << endl;
```

Although it appears the program is using a simple array, `pa` is actually an object of the `PseudoArray` class. This makes `pa` as easy to use as a common array but safer because access to the object's data is carefully controlled. Interestingly, the program has, in effect, added C++ exception handling to the common C-language array data structure!

FUNCTION CALL OPERATOR

Overloading the function call operator—represented by a pair of parentheses ()—effectively makes a class object appear to be a callable function. The overloaded operator()() function may return a typed value, or void, and it may optionally declare parameters. It must be a nonstatic class member. Here's a sample class with an overloaded function call operator that returns an int value:

```
class TAnyClass {
private:
  int x;
public:
  TAnyClass(int arg): x(arg) { }
  int operator()();
};
```

This example of the overloaded operator()() function declares no parameters. Implement it separately using code such as this:

```
int TAnyClass::operator()()
{
  return x;
}
```

Or, you can more simply create an inline function directly in the class:

```
int operator()() { return x; }
```

Either way, a program can use an object of the class as though it were a callable function. Statements such as the following are possible:

```
TAnyClass object(100);
int q = object();  // Call object as a function
```

The second statement appears to call a function named object(), but it actually calls the operator()() function of TAnyClass for object. This technique might be useful to hide the fact that object() is not really a function, or more likely, to upgrade existing code that calls a function in need of extensive repairs. By converting the original function to a class, and providing it with an overloaded function-call operator()(), the existing programming can be compiled to take advantage of other features available only with object-oriented C++ classes.

CLASS MEMBER ACCESS OPERATOR

Overloading the unary struct- and class member access operator, ->, provides pointer-like access to members. There may be few if any practical uses for this technique, but it might serve as a debugging device to trace member function calls. Listing 19.5, access.cpp, demonstrates the basic method.

PART
IV
CH
19

LISTING 19.5   ACCESS.CPP

```cpp
#include <iostream.h>

class TAnyClass {
private:
  int x, y;
public:
  TAnyClass(int xarg, int yarg): x(xarg), y(yarg) { }
  TAnyClass * operator->();
  int Getx() const { return x; }
  int Gety() const { return y; }
};

int main()
{
  TAnyClass test(123, 456);
  cout << test->Getx() << endl;
  cout << test->Gety() << endl;
  return 0;
}

TAnyClass * TAnyClass::operator->()
{
  cout << "Accessing member: ";
  return this;
}
```

To overload the `->` operator, insert a prototype such as the following into a class's public section:

```cpp
TAnyClass * operator->();
```

This states that the `operator->()` function returns a pointer to an object of its class. Technically, it should be possible to return a reference or an object value, but GNU C++ seems to recognize only the pointer variety. (There's no real benefit in using the other forms, and no need for concern about this minor problem.)

Implement the overloaded operator as shown at the end of Listing 19.5. The function may perform any actions—here it displays a string that indicates when the function is called. The final statement should always be as shown. Returning `this` returns a pointer to the object for which the function is called.

To demonstrate how the overloaded operator works, the sample program constructs a test object of type `TAnyClass` and then executes two output statements:

```cpp
TAnyClass test(123, 456);
cout << test->Getx() << endl;
cout << test->Gety() << endl;
```

Even though `test` is constructed as a local variable, because of the overloaded `operator->()` function, statements may use `test` as though it were a pointer to a `TAnyClass` object. When you compile and run the program using the following commands, its output shows that the overloaded operator is called before `Getx()` and `Gety()` in the expressions `test->Getx()` and `test->Gety()`:

```
$ g++ access.cpp
$ ./a.out
Accessing member: 123
Accessing member: 456
```

INCREMENT AND DECREMENT OPERATORS

Overloading the ++ and -- operators is particularly intriguing. You might use this method to create operators for advancing a container from record to record, or for other operations that are sequential in nature. Both prefix (++x and --x) and postfix (x++ and x--) operators can be overloaded, as demonstrated in Listing 19.6, incdec.cpp.

LISTING 19.6   INCDEC.CPP

```cpp
#include <iostream.h>

class TAnyClass {
private:
  int x;
public:
  TAnyClass(int xarg): x(xarg) { }
  int operator++()    { return ++x; }  // Prefix ++
  int operator++(int) { return x++; }  // Postfix ++
  int operator--()    { return --x; }  // Prefix --
  int operator--(int) { return x--; }  // Postfix --
  int Getx() const { return x; }
};

int main()
{
  TAnyClass t(100);

  /*
  //
  // Demonstrates bug in GNU C++ also found in Borland C++ 4.5
  // Following should produce same output as code at end
  // of main(), but due to evaluation order of the output
  // stream statement, ++t in the first line for example is
  // evaluated before t.Getx(). Should be the other way
  // around.
  //
  cout << "t == " << t.Getx() << "; ++t == " << ++t << endl;
  cout << "t == " << t.Getx() << "; t++ == " << t++ << endl;
  cout << "t == " << t.Getx() << "; --t == " << --t << endl;
  cout << "t == " << t.Getx() << "; t-- == " << t-- << endl;
  */

  cout << "t == " << t.Getx();
  cout << "; ++t == " << ++t << endl;
```

PART
IV

CH

19

continues

LISTING 19.6   CONTINUED

```
  cout << "t == " << t.Getx();
  cout << "; t++ == " << t++ << endl;
  cout << "t == " << t.Getx();
  cout << "; --t == " << --t << endl;
  cout << "t == " << t.Getx();
  cout << "; t-- == " << t-- << endl;

  return 0;
}
```

The overloaded function `operator++()` defines a prefix increment operator for a class object—in this case, for `TAnyClass`. To define a postfix increment operator, declare an `int` parameter in the function. Usually, you define both operators as follows:

```
int operator++()    { return ++x; }  // Prefix ++
int operator++(int) { return x++; }  // Postfix ++
```

The `int` parameter needs no name, and its value is unimportant. This merely takes advantage of the C++ overloading rule that states any function may be overloaded (have the same name) as long as all such functions differ in at least one parameter type. This is how it's possible to define different ++ operators for the same class. Define decrement operators similarly:

```
int operator--()    { return --x; }  // Prefix --
int operator--(int) { return x--; }  // Postfix --
```

What the operators do is up to you. Here, they simply operate on the class's private x integer variable. In another situation, they might advance or retard a pointer to objects linked together in a list, or move forward and back through a database. It's totally up to you what the operators do. However, be sure to respect the general nature of prefix and postfix operations. A prefix expression such as `++object` should return `object`'s value *and then* perform the increment. A postfix expression such as `object++` should return the incremented value of `object`, whatever that means.

To demonstrate the overloaded operators, the program writes the current value of a test object and then applies each operator in turn. Compile and run the program with the following commands to see the results as printed here:

```
$ g++ incdec.cpp
$ ./a.out
t == 100; ++t == 101
t == 101; t++ == 101
t == 102; --t == 101
t == 101; t-- == 101
```

Each operator expression such as `++t` applies to the value shown at its left. Study each line to verify that prefix and postfix operations are evaluated correctly. For example, the value of `t++` equals the value of `t` *before* its value is incremented.

In practice, writing `operator++()` and `operator--()` functions might not be as simple as the incdec.cpp program in Listing 19.6 implies. Later in this chapter, Listing 19.9 shows a more realistic example of how to program these operators for objects other than simple integer values. See "Increment and Decrement Operators Revisited" for more on this topic.

Note

Listing 19.6, incdec.cpp, demonstrates a subtle bug in GNU C++ that I discovered also in Borland C++ 4.5 (fixed in 5.0). The output stream statements are written as shown in the listing to force the correct evaluation order of statements such as t.Getx() and ++t. If these are written in a single cascaded output statement:

```
cout << "t == " << t.Getx() << "; ++t == " << ++t << endl;
```

the statement ++t is incorrectly evaluated *before* t.Getx(), and the results are very different. This unintended side effect in output statements is a serious matter. Until it is fixed, beware of this bug—it is easily missed. Both forms of output statements are in the incdec.cpp file on the CD-ROM.

OVERLOADED OUTPUT STREAMS

The default output stream operator << recognizes all native C and C++ data types such as int, double, char, and char *. By overloading the output stream operator, you can add your own class data types that output statements can write. Instead of writing a Display() or similar output function, by overloading the << operator, your program can use code such as the following to write the values of any type of object:

```
TYourClass object;

cout << "object == " << object << endl;
```

Listing 19.7, pointout.cpp, demonstrates how to overload the << operator for a version of the TCoordinate class from Chapter 14, "Investing in Inheritance."

PART
IV

CH
19

LISTING 19.7   POINTOUT.CPP

```
#include <iostream.h>

class TCoordinate {
private:
  int tc_x, tc_y;
public:
  TCoordinate(): tc_x(0), tc_y(0) { }
  TCoordinate(int x, int y): tc_x(x), tc_y(y) { }
  void Setxy(int x, int y);
  int Getx() const;
  int Gety() const;
  friend ostream &
    operator<<(ostream & os, const TCoordinate &t);
};

int main()
{
  TCoordinate p(10, 20);
```

continues

LISTING 19.7   CONTINUED

```
  cout << p << endl;
  return 0;
}

// Implement the overloaded << operator friend function
//
ostream &
operator<<(ostream & os, const TCoordinate &t)
{
  os << "x == " << t.tc_x << "; y == " << t.tc_y;
  return os;
}
```

In the sample program, the operator<<() function is declared as a friend of its class so that it can access the private data members tc_x and tc_y. The function returns type ostream &—a reference to an ostream object. The function also declares two parameters: an ostream reference object os and a const reference to an object of the class for which the operator is being overloaded (TCoordinate in this example). The TCoordinate reference parameter must be const in GNU C++ (some other compilers do not require this), which is just as well because writing an object in an output stream statement certainly should not change its value.

Because the overloaded operator function returns an ostream reference, objects of the class may be used in cascaded output statements. For instance, if p1 and p2 are TCoordinate objects, this simple statement displays their values:

```
cout << p1 << endl
     << p2 << endl;
```

You can provide the same output capabilities for any class. In the operator<<() function's implementation, write whatever you want to the os parameter, as the sample program does in the following statement:

```
os << "x == " << t.tc_x << "; y == " << t.tc_y;
```

The target of the output statement is os, not cout, as you might assume. By writing to the ostream reference object os passed to the overloaded function, TCoordinate objects can be written to any destination such as a disk file. More on that, however, in Chapter 20, "Customizing I/O Streams."

Listing 19.7 demonstrates how the overloaded output operator works. The program constructs a TCoordinate object and writes it to cout with these statements:

```
TCoordinate p(10, 20);
cout << p << endl;
```

Compile and run the program using the following commands to see the text that the second statement produces:

```
$ g++ pointout.cpp
$ ./a.out
x == 10; y == 20
```

OVERLOADED INPUT STREAMS

Overloading the input stream operator >> effectively teaches C++ how to input objects of a class. Listing 19.8, pointin.cpp, is similar to pointout.cpp, but adds both input and output operators for TCoordinate objects.

LISTING 19.8   POINTIN.CPP

```cpp
#include <iostream.h>

class TCoordinate {
private:
  int tc_x, tc_y;
public:
  TCoordinate(): tc_x(0), tc_y(0) { }
  TCoordinate(int x, int y): tc_x(x), tc_y(y) { }
  void Setxy(int x, int y);
  int Getx() const;
  int Gety() const;
  friend ostream &
    operator<<(ostream & os, const TCoordinate &t);
  friend istream &
    operator>>(istream & is, TCoordinate &t);
};

int main()
{
  TCoordinate p;

  cout << "Before: " << p << endl;
  cout << "Enter x and y values (ex. 10 20): ";
  cin >> p;
  if (!cin.good())
    cout << "*** Input error" << endl;
  else
    cout << "After:  " << p << endl;

  return 0;
}

// Implement the overloaded << operator friend function
//
ostream &
operator<<(ostream & os, const TCoordinate &t)
{
  os << "x == " << t.tc_x << "; y == " << t.tc_y;
  return os;
}

// Implement the overloaded >> operator friend function
//
istream &
operator>>(istream & is, TCoordinate &t)
{
  is >> t.tc_x >> t.tc_y;
  return is;
}
```

PART

IV

CH

19

The overloaded input stream operator >> function is declared similarly to the output function as a friend of the following class:

```
friend istream &
  operator>>(istream & is, TCoordinate &t);
```

The operator>>() function returns a reference to an istream (input stream) object so that it can be used in cascaded input statements. It declares two parameters: an istream reference named is and a reference to a TCoordinate object. In this case, the input object cannot be constant because the input operator presumably changes its value in some way. In this case, the function's implementation simply reads from the input stream parameter is into the TCoordinate object's tc_x and tc_y private data members using the following statement:

```
is >> t.tc_x >> t.tc_y;
```

Following this, the function returns the same input stream reference (is). All operator>>() functions should end the same.

The main() program demonstrates how to use the TCoordinate class's new input capability. The program first constructs a default object and then prompts you to enter values into it:

```
TCoordinate p;
cin >> p;
```

To try this, enter the following commands to compile and run the program, and then type two integer values separated by a blank as shown here:

```
$ g++ pointin.cpp
$ ./a.out
Before: x == 0; y == 0
Enter x and y values (ex. 10 20): 45 62
After:  x == 45; y == 62
```

Note

Chapter 20, "Customizing I/O Streams," explains more about overloading input and output stream operators, and shows how to use them to read and write objects in disk files.

INCREMENT AND DECREMENT OPERATORS REVISITED

As mentioned, successfully overloading the operator++() and operator--() functions is not as simple as demonstrated earlier in this chapter in the incdec.cpp program (refer to Listing 19.6). This is so primarily because, to distinguish between prefix and postfix operations, often requires special care.

For example, in a container class that stores class objects instead of integer values, careful programming is needed to correctly implement prefix and postfix increment and decrement operations. For readers who are struggling with this, Listing 19.9, refincdec.cpp, shows how to use temporary objects to provide these operators for two hypothetical classes.

LISTING 19.9   REFINCDEC.CPP (PARTIAL)

```cpp
#include <iostream.h>

// Sample class for object upon which increment and
// decrement operations are defined. Can be anything
// that defines public Increment() and Decrement()
// functions. The output stream operator is just for
// this demonstration and is not required.
//
class TObject {
private:
  int x;
public:
  TObject(int arg): x(arg) { }
  //  int Getx() const { return x; }
  //  int Putx(int arg) { x = arg; }
  void Increment() { x += 1; }
  void Decrement() { x -= 1; }
  friend ostream & operator<<(ostream & os, const TObject &t) {
    os << t.x;
    return os;
  }
};

// Represents the class that overloads ++ and -- operators
// for an object of type TObject. Only that class name needs
// to be changed to use this class. The overloaded output
// stream operator is for this demonstration only.
//
class TAnyClass {
private:
  TObject object;
  TObject temp;
public:
  TAnyClass(int arg): object(arg), temp(arg) { }
  const TObject & operator++() {      // Prefix ++object
    object.Increment();
    return object;
  }
  const TObject & operator++(int) {  // Postfix object++
    temp = object;
    object.Increment();
    return temp;
  }
  const TObject & operator--() {      // Prefix --object
    object.Decrement();
    return object;
  }
  const TObject & operator--(int) {  // Postfix object++
    temp = object;
    object.Decrement();
    return temp;
  }
```

PART

IV

CH

19

continues

LISTING 19.9   CONTINUED

```
  friend ostream & operator<<(ostream & os, const TAnyClass &t) {
    os << t.object;
    return os;
  }
};

int main()
{
  TAnyClass t(100);

  cout << "t == " << t;
  cout << "; ++t == " << ++t << endl;
  cout << "t == " << t;
  cout << "; t++ == " << t++ << endl;
  cout << "t == " << t;
  cout << "; --t == " << --t << endl;
  cout << "t == " << t;
  cout << "; t-- == " << t-- << endl;

  return 0;
}
```

Running and compiling refincdec.cpp produces the same output as the original program. Enter the following commands to run the test:

```
$ g++ refincdec.cpp
$ ./a.out
t == 100; ++t == 101
t == 101; t++ == 101
t == 102; --t == 101
t == 101; t-- == 101
```

That's the same output as the original program, but because the output stream operator is overloaded for the class, main() can more simply write object t instead of calling the Getx() function.

Internally, the program's classes handle the expressions such as ++t and t++ differently. To represent the class of object requiring the overloaded operations, TObject provides two member functions:

```
void Increment();
void Decrement();
```

To use the method described here, your own class needs to provide only these two functions. It may provide others, and what happens when the functions are called is up to you. For the demonstration, the functions simply increment and decrement an integer value. Most important, however, is that there is no need to distinguish between prefix (++x) and postfix (x++) operations.

That job is handled by a second class, represented in Listing 19.9 as TAnyClass. The class declares two objects of type TObject:

```
private:
  TObject object;
  TObject temp;
```

The `temp` object makes it possible for the overloaded operators to return the correct prefix and postfix values regardless of the nature of the actual data. For example, the overloaded postfix `operator++()` function is implemented inline using this code:

```
const TObject & operator++(int) {  // Postfix object++
  temp = object;
  object.Increment();
  return temp;
}
```

It is necessary to assign the current `object` value to `temp` so that `object` can be incremented but still permit the function to return the unincremented value. There might be other ways to achieve this same result (pushing the original object onto a stack container, for example, and then popping it off as the return value). However, the method shown here should be adequate for most purposes. Simply replace `TObject` with your own class and provide `Increment()` and `Decrement()` member functions. If your class addresses any dynamic memory, be sure to provide a copy constructor and `operator=()` function as well (see Chapter 13, "Creating and Destroying Objects").

OTHER OPERATOR OVERLOADING CONCERNS

When overloading operators for your own classes, keep the following restrictions in mind:

- C++ does not "understand" the meaning of an overloaded operator. It's your responsibility to define meaningful operations for specific operators.

- C++ is unable to derive complex operators from simple ones. For example, in a class with overloaded operator functions `operator*()` and `operator=()`, C++ cannot combine those functions to evaluate expressions in statements such as `a *= b`. To handle the shorthand operator, the class must additionally overload the `operator*=()` function.

- You cannot change the syntax of an overloaded operator. Binary operators must remain binary. Unary operators must remain unary. It is not possible to create a unary division operator because no such capability exists for C++.

- You cannot invent new operators. You may overload only the operators listed in Table 19.1.

- You cannot overload preprocessing symbols such as `#define`.

OVERLOADING AND MEMORY MANAGEMENT

C programs use standard library functions such as `malloc()` and `free()` to allocate and deallocate memory. By contrast, C++ programs use operators `new` and `delete`. Below the hatch, many C++ compilers implement `new` and `delete` by calling `malloc()` and `free()`. It is a mistake, however, to conclude that no significant differences exist between C and C++ memory management.

One reason that's so is because new and delete are *operators*, not functions. As operators, new and delete may be overloaded just as others such as + and <<. By overloading new and delete, you provide custom memory management for objects of specific classes. This gives you total control over how objects are allocated memory in a way that malloc() and free() cannot duplicate.

The following sections explain how to overload new and delete and take control over memory management duties. This does not change the way the operators work for other data types. It changes the storage details only for objects of specific classes.

OVERLOADING THE new OPERATOR

To overload the new operator, insert the following function prototype into any class:

```
void * operator new(size_t size);
```

Regardless of the class type, the new operator is always declared the same. It must return a void pointer, and its lone parameter equals the size in bytes of the requested memory space. The operator has no access to the class's data members. Its only purpose is to allocate space for an object of the class, but other than possibly setting that space to zero bytes or another preset value, the overloaded operator should do nothing more than allocate some memory.

How it does that is up to you. You could allocate disk space, use a container object, or simply stuff objects into a global buffer. Listing 19.10 demonstrates how to overload new and store objects of a class type in a simple C++ array.

LISTING 19.10   OVERNEW.CPP

```cpp
#include <iostream.h>
#include <stddef.h>      // Need size_t

#define BUFSIZE 512

class BrandNew {
private:
  int value;       // Represents object's data
  int mylocation;  // Objects index in storage buffer
public:
  BrandNew(int arg);
  int GetValue() const { return value; }
  int GetLocation() const { return mylocation; }
  void * operator new(size_t size);
};

char buf[BUFSIZE];   // Our own memory storage array
int index;           // Index into global buf[]

int main()
{
  cout << "Creating local instance" << endl;
  BrandNew b1(10);
  cout << " b1 == " << b1.GetValue() << endl;
```

```
  cout << "Allocating space via new" << endl;
  BrandNew *b2 = new BrandNew(20);
  BrandNew *b3 = new BrandNew(30);
  BrandNew *b4 = new BrandNew(40);
  BrandNew *b5 = new BrandNew(50);

  cout << "*b2 == " << b2->GetValue() << endl;
  cout << "*b3 == " << b3->GetValue() << endl;
  cout << "*b4 == " << b4->GetValue() << endl;
  cout << "*b5 == " << b5->GetValue() << endl;

  int b4index = b4->GetLocation();
  cout << "Location of object b4 == buf["
       << b4index << ']' << endl;

  return 0;
}

// Class constructor
BrandNew::BrandNew(int arg):
  value(arg)
{
  cout << "Inside constructor" << endl;
  mylocation = index;  // Save global index in object
}

// Implement overloaded new operator function
void * BrandNew::operator new(size_t size)
{
  cout << "Inside overloaded new. Size == " << size << endl;
  if (index >= BUFSIZE - sizeof(BrandNew))
    return 0;    // Or throw an exception here
  else {
    int k = index;                // Save global index
    index += sizeof(BrandNew);    // Increment index
    return &buf[k];               // Return reference to object
  }
}
```

The sample program implements an extremely simple memory-management scheme by defining two variables—a buffer of size BUFSIZE and an index into that buffer:

```
char buf[BUFSIZE];
int index;
```

By overloading the new operator, class objects can be stored in the program's buffer but accessed using pointers. To represent objects, the program declares class BrandNew and overloads the new operator with the following declaration:

```
void * operator new(size_t size);
```

Any uses of new to allocate storage for BrandNew objects are now directed to the overloaded operator. In the sample program, the operator is implemented by these statements:

```
int k = index;
index += sizeof(BrandNew);
return &buf[k];
```

The first statement saves the global buffer index in a temporary variable. Next, index is incremented by the size of a BrandNew object—this is where the next object will be stored. Finally, the overloaded operator function returns the address of the buffer where memory has been set aside for one BrandNew object. At this point, C++ calls that object's class constructor to initialize the memory space.

The main program demonstrates how the overloaded new operator works. This statement, for example, constructs a BrandNew object:

```
BrandNew *b4 = new BrandNew(40);
```

Because BrandNew overloads the new operator, the resulting object is placed in the program's own buffer. Even so, it is used as though it had been allocated dynamic memory by the C++ memory manager. This statement, for example, displays the object's value:

```
cout << "*b4 == " << b4->GetValue() << endl;
```

To demonstrate a related and possibly useful technique, the BrandNew class saves its own location in a private variable named mylocation. With this method, not only do BrandNew pointers locate class objects, but the objects themselves "know" their locations. Compiling and running the program shows this by displaying the index in the global buffer where object *b4 is stored:

```
$ g++ overnew.cpp
$ ./a.out
...
*b2 == 20
*b3 == 30
*b4 == 40
*b5 == 50
Location of object b4 == buf[24]
```

OVERLOADING THE delete OPERATOR

In most cases, when a class overloads the new operator, it should also overload delete. The example in the preceding section doesn't bother to do this because all objects are stored in a simple buffer, and therefore no harm comes from simply ending the program. However, it's easy to add the delete operator to that program's class. Although not listed here, the CD-ROM contains the finished program in file overnew2.cpp.

The revised BrandNew class overloads operator delete using the function prototype

```
void operator delete(void *p);
```

The operator returns no value, and it receives a single parameter—a void pointer equal to the address of the object being deleted. Alternatively, you can add a size parameter to the following declaration:

```
void operator delete(void *, size_t size);
```

In this case, size equals the size in bytes of the object that is being deleted. This is rarely necessary, however, because the expression sizeof(T) where T is the class name gives the same value. Either way, the program can now delete the objects it created using the overloaded new operator:

```
delete b2;
delete b3;
delete b4;
delete b5;
```

Compiling and running the revised program with the following commands shows the results of those four deletions:

```
$ g++ overnew2.cpp
$ ./a.out
...
Deleting object at 0x804a160
Deleting object at 0x804a168
Deleting object at 0x804a170
Deleting object at 0x804a178
```

The reported addresses are inside the program's global buffer. The overnew2.cpp program implements the overloaded delete operator as follows:

```
void BrandNew::operator delete(void *p)
{
  cout << "Deleting object at " << p << endl;
}
```

All this does is display a message and the object's address as a confirmation that the overloaded operator is indeed called. In a real setting, the program would have to perform some operation to reserve the deleted memory. For example, you might call a container class's deletion function, link the object's memory into a list of disposed memory blocks, or do whatever else is necessary to free the space allocated by the class's overloaded new operator. In addition, your overloaded new and delete operators can throw exceptions to indicate any problems. See Chapter 16, "Handling Exceptions."

> **Tip**
>
> Saving the object's location inside the object itself, as demonstrated in overnew.cpp and overnew2.cpp, can in some cases help the overloaded delete operator dispose of an object's memory.

SUMMARY

With overloaded operators, expressions such as (A + B) can be made to work for objects of classes as well as native C and C++ data types. Most operators can be overloaded. For example, to overload the plus operator for a class, simply provide an overloaded operator function named operator+(). Overloaded operators can make programs clearer by allowing programmers to use common expressions that involve class objects. However, it's up to you to provide operations that make sense.

PART

IV

CH

19

For more information on subjects introduced in this chapter, turn to the following chapters:

- Chapter 13, "Creating and Destroying Objects"
- Chapter 16, "Handling Exceptions"
- Chapter 18, "Overloading Your Friends"
- Chapter 20, "Customizing I/O Streams"

CUSTOMIZING I/O STREAMS

In the preceding chapter, you learned how to overload the I/O (input and output) stream operators << and >> for C++ classes. As you discover in this chapter, there's much more to that story. Using operator overloading, you can tap into the C++ I/O stream library for reading and writing objects of all kinds, not only with the keyboard and console, but also in text and binary files on disk.

This chapter explains how to create, read, and write files containing any type of data. The chapter also includes my classes, `bifstream`, `bofstream`, and `bfstream`, that you can use to read and write data in native binary form in disk files. I also explain related topics such as opening and closing files, detecting a file's presence, creating temporary files, and searching files for specific records.

FILE STREAMS

C++ file streams provide an object-oriented way to read and write information in disk and other types of files. The trouble is, the file-stream library is designed to work only with text files. But don't let this limitation turn you off from using streams for file handling. Later in this chapter, I explain how to build new classes for reading and writing data of all types in binary form. First, however, let's take a look at the I/O services that C++ file streams provide.

FILE STREAM CLASS

To use file streams, include the fstream.h header file, usually along with iostream.h if your program also does any console I/O. Insert these directives into the program:

```
#include <iostream.h>
#include <fstream.h>
```

The following overviews explain some essential facts about C++ file streams:

- All file stream classes except `filebuf` are ultimately derived from class `ios` (I/O stream). Because of their heritage, file streams can use `iostream` member functions, manipulators, state flags, and other stream-handling techniques.

- Use the `ifstream` class (input file stream) for reading data from files. The `ifstream` class is derived from `istream`. It is literally an input-stream class expanded to work with files.

- Use the `ofstream` class (output file stream) for writing to files. The `ofstream` class is derived from `ostream`. Similar to `ifstream`, `ofstream` is literally an output-stream class expanded to work with files.

- Use the `fstream` class for reading and writing data in the *same* file.

- The `filebuf` class provides buffered I/O services to the `ifstream`, `ofstream`, and `fstream` classes. You'll rarely, if ever, need to use the `filebuf` class. To keep programs portable, it's best to use the file I/O services provided by higher-level classes `ifstream`, `ofstream`, and `fstream`.

TEXT FILE STREAMS

Text file streams are simple and easy to use. They also make a great introduction to file stream techniques. There are four main areas to cover:

- Creating new text files
- Opening existing text files
- Reading from text files
- Writing to text files

The following sections explain these techniques both for single-character operations and for strings. In most cases, you should use the `ifstream` and `ofstream` classes to carry out text-file I/O. Because text files are usually formatted in variable-length lines, it's best not to attempt simultaneous reading and writing in the same file using the `fstream` class.

CREATING TEXT FILES

To create a new text file, define an object of the `ofstream` class. Pass two arguments to the class constructor—a filename and an *open mode* value:

```
ofstream ofs("newfile.txt", ios::out);
```

Merely constructing the object, named `ofs` here, creates the named file with a length of zero. If the file already exists, it is overwritten. This method differs greatly from conventional file handling in C where you need to define a file handle and then call a function to create the file. With file streams, you simply create a file object and use it.

The actual format, number of characters, and other characteristics of the filename string might differ among various operating systems. To keep your programs portable, you might want to use a variable instead of a literal string as shown in many of this chapter's examples. The second argument, `ios::out`, selects an access mode for the file. The `ios` class declares the `out` mode along with other `out_mode` enumerated constants as listed in Table 20.1.

TABLE 20.1   THE ios CLASS'S open_mode CONSTANTS

Constant	Standard	Effect
app	no	The next write operation appends new information to the end of the file.
ate	yes	Seeks to the end of the file when opened. The word "ate" stands for "at end." It has nothing to do with "eating" data as is often assumed.
bin	yes	Replaced by `binary` in newer ANSI C++ and in GNU C++ implementations.
binary	yes	Opens file in `binary` (nontext) mode.
in	yes	Opens the file for input (reading).

continues

Constant	Standard	Effect
nocreate	no	If the file does not already exist, does *not* create a new file. Useful for checking whether a file exists.
noreplace	no	If the file already exists, does *not* overwrite the file.
out	yes	Opens the file for output (writing).
trunc	no	Opens and truncates an existing file. New information written to the file replaces the file's current contents.

TABLE 20.1 CONTINUED

Unfortunately, the constants in Table 20.1 are not the same in all implementations of the ios class. The open_mode enumerated type identifier might even be named openmode with no underscore. GNU C++ defines all the open_mode constants listed in the table, as do most modern ANSI C++ compilers. However, if you are writing code to support other systems, don't be surprised to find differences among open_mode (or openmode) types.

> **Tip**
>
> GNU C++ defines open_mode in file streambuf.h as a member of class ios.

Specify multiple options by combining constants in logical-OR expressions. For example, you might define a symbolic constant such as OFSMODE like this:

```
#define OFSMODE ios::out | ios::app
```

Or, even better, you can define a const value of type open_mode using a statement such as

```
const ios::open_mode OFSMODE = ios::out | ios::app;
```

Whichever method you choose, pass the OFSMODE constant to the ofstream class constructor's second parameter as in this sample:

```
ofstream ofs("newfile.txt", OFSMODE);
```

You can, of course, pass multiple options directly to the constructor by using a statement such as

```
ofstream ofs("newfile.txt", ios::out | ios::app);
```

In this chapter, for simplicity, examples use this form. However, for better portability, because of the discrepancies among open_mode constants, it's probably best to define a constant listing the modes you want to use.

After creating or overwriting a file, always check that the ofstream object is ready for use. You can perform this check using an if statement as follows:

```
#include <iostream.h>
#include <fstream.h>
#include <stdlib.h>
...
ofstream ofs("newfile.txt", ios::out);
if (!ofs) {
```

```
    cerr << "Error: unable to create file" << endl;
    exit(1);
}
```

The first three lines include the necessary library header files. To avoid duplication, future examples in this chapter don't show these same lines. Constructing the ofstream object, ofs (it can be another name if you want), opens newfile.txt for output, creating that file if it doesn't already exist. The if statement tests whether the file was properly attached to the ofs object. If not, the program writes an error message to cerr and exits by calling the standard library's exit() function.

Object Validity Checks

Many programmers question the if statement's expression (!ofs). If ofs is an object of the ofstream class, you might wonder how that expression can make any sense. C programmers especially are used to this type of expression used with a pointer, but ofs is a variable—an object—not a pointer, so how can (!ofs) check its validity?

The answer is buried in the ios class, which overloads the C++ *not* operator!() function using the following inline declaration:

```
    int operator!() const { return fail(); }
```

Because the operator is overloaded, statements such as the following call the operator!() function, which returns the value of the I/O stream fail() function, as shown here:

```
    if (!ofs) {
    ...
    }
```

This is a good example of how, using operator overloading, programs can be more understandable. The preceding is equivalent to the somewhat less clear expression

```
    if (ofs.fail()) {
    ...
    }
```

OPENING TEXT FILES

Opening a file for input is similar to creating or overwriting a new file. Use the ifstream class as in the following sample code to open a file named oldfile.txt:

```
ifstream ifs("oldfile.txt", ios:in);
if (!ifs) {
    cerr << "Error: unable to open file" << endl;
    exit(1);
}
```

Object ifs is constructed from the ifstream class and initialized with a filename and an open_mode constant. The if statement uses the ios class's overloaded operator!() function on the object to test whether the operation was a success. If so, the object—and attached file—are ready for reading; otherwise, the program halts with an error message.

> **Note**
>
> Instead of halting programs on detecting a file error, it is far better to throw an exception. See Chapter 16, "Handling Exceptions," for help with this topic.

The preceding sections cover all the basics of creating and opening files. If you are familiar with conventional methods that call functions to perform these operations, you might think some critical factors are missing. Remember, however, that *file streams are object-oriented*. To open a file, simply create an input file stream object, and then as explained in the next sections, use I/O stream statements to read data. To write to or create a new file, construct an output file stream object and use stream statements to write data. When the file stream object is deleted or goes out of scope, the file is automatically closed. Trust the C++ classes to do their jobs so that you gain time for more important concerns.

Now, let's examine some sample programs that read and write text files using the techniques described so far. There are four important methods to master:

- Reading text a character at a time
- Writing text a character at a time
- Reading text a line at a time
- Writing text a line at a time

Reading Text a Character at a Time

Listing 20.1, rchar.cpp, demonstrates how to use a file stream object to read a text file one character at a time. Just to keep things interesting, the program also counts the number of characters and lines in the file. Such requirements always come with built-in ambiguities—for example, should the definition of a "character" include the newline symbol at the end of a line? I decided not to count end-of-line characters; therefore, the total character count that rchar.cpp reports probably doesn't match the file's directory size.

Listing 20.1 RCHAR.CPP

```cpp
#include <iostream.h>
#include <fstream.h>
#include <stdlib.h>

int main(int argc, char *argv[])
{
  if (argc <= 1) {
    cerr << "Error: filename missing" << endl;
    exit(1);
  }
  ifstream ifs(argv[1], ios::in);
  if (!ifs) {
    cerr << "Error: unable to open " << argv[1] << endl;
    exit(2);
  }
  char c;
```

```
    long nc = 0, nl = 0;
    while (ifs.get(c)) {
      if (c == '\n')
        nl++;   // Count number of lines
      else
        nc++;   // Count number of characters
      cout.put(c);
    }
    cout << endl << endl << "Total characters : " << nc;
    cout << endl << "Number of lines   : " << nl << endl;
    return 0;
}
```

Compile and run rchar.cpp using the following two commands. The program can read and display any text file, but here, the second command tells it to read and display its own source code:

```
$ g++ -o rchar rchar.cpp
$ ./rchar rchar.cpp
```

Note

> Because some of the programs in this chapter are dependent on one another, all compilation commands use the -o option to give the compiled code file a name other than the usual a.out.

The main() function in rchar.cpp begins by checking whether you supplied a filename on the command line. If not (argc is less than or equal to 1), the program displays an error message and exits. The following statement attempts to open the specified file:

```
ifstream ifs(argv[1], ios::in);
```

If this succeeds, the ifs object is available for use as a source in an input stream statement. A simple while loop, for example, reads all characters from the file and displays them using an output-stream statement:

```
while (ifs.get(c))
  cout.put(c);
```

WRITING TEXT A CHARACTER AT A TIME

Creating and writing a text file is equally simple, as Listing 20.2, wchar.cpp, demonstrates.

LISTING 20.2   WCHAR.CPP

```
#include <iostream.h>
#include <fstream.h>
#include <stdlib.h>

int main(int argc, char *argv[])
{
  if (argc <= 1) {
```

PART

IV

CH

20

continues

LISTING 20.2   CONTINUED

```
      cerr << "Error: filename missing" << endl;
      exit(1);
   }
   ifstream ifs(argv[1], ios::in);
   if (ifs) {
     cerr << "Error: " << argv[1] << " already exists" << endl;
     cerr << "         Specify a different filename" << endl;
     exit(2);
   }
   ofstream ofs(argv[1], ios::out);
   if (!ofs) {
     cerr << "Error: unable to write to " << argv[1] << endl;
     exit(3);
   }
   ofs << "1: A string" << endl;
   ofs.put('2');
   ofs.put(':');
   ofs.put(' ');
   ofs.put('C').put('h').put('a').put('r').put('s');
   ofs << endl;
   return 0;
}
```

Compile and run the program by issuing the following commands. The program will not overwrite an existing file:

```
$ g++ -o wchar wchar.cpp
$ ./wchar test.txt
```

Assuming test.txt did not previously exist, wchar.cpp writes text to the file. Examine the file's contents with the following command:

```
$ cat test.txt
1: A string
2: Chars
```

If you again try to run the program, it detects the presence of test.txt and exits with an error message:

```
$ ./wchar test.txt
Error: test.txt already exists
        Specify a different filename
```

If the specified file does not exist, The program creates a new file using an object of the ofstream class:

```
ofstream ofs(argv[1], ios::out);
if (!ofs) {
...
}
```

If the expression (!ofs) is true, then an error occurred and the program exits. Otherwise, the program continues on to use output statements to write text to the file. This statement writes a string and newline character to the file:

```
ofs << "1: A string" << endl;
```

And this writes a single character:

```
ofs.put('2');
```

Or, you could use the following statement to do the same:

```
ofs << '2';  // Same as preceding
```

By the way, because the put() member function returns ostream & (a reference to an object of the ostream class, an ancestor of ios), you can string together multiple put() function calls in an odd-looking construction such as this:

```
ofs.put('A').put('B').put('C');
```

I dislike cryptic and tricky statements such as that, but I mention it here because I've seen this technique in C++ programs. The following is clearer, produces the same results, and is not so unusual-looking:

```
cout << 'A' << 'B' << 'C';
```

READING TEXT A LINE AT A TIME

Many if not most text files are organized into variable-length lines, punctuated by newline control characters. Use the technique in this section to read text files a line at a time. As a bonus, this is usually faster than reading files one character at a time, although a disadvantage is the need to assume a maximum line length from the start. Listing 20.3, rline.cpp, is similar to rchar.cpp, but it reads a specified text file a line at a time and reports the number of characters and lines in the file:

LISTING 20.3   RLINE.CPP

```cpp
#include <iostream.h>
#include <fstream.h>
#include <stdlib.h>
#include <string.h>

#define BUFLEN 128

int main(int argc, char *argv[])
{
  if (argc <= 1) {
    cerr << "Error: filename missing" << endl;
    exit(1);
  }
  ifstream ifs(argv[1], ios::in);
  if (!ifs) {
    cerr << "Error: unable to open " << argv[1] << endl;
    exit(2);
  }
  char buffer[BUFLEN];
  long nc = 0, nl = 0;
  while (!ifs.eof()) {
```

PART

IV

CH

20

continues

LISTING 20.3   CONTINUED

```
    ifs.getline(buffer, sizeof(buffer), '\n');
    if (!(ifs.eof() && strlen(buffer) == 0)) {
      nc += strlen(buffer);
      nl++;
      cout << buffer << endl;
    }
  }
  cout << endl << endl << "Total characters : " << nc;
  cout << endl << "Number of lines  : " << nl << endl;
  return 0;
}
```

Compile and run the program using the following commands. You can specify the name of any text file to read and display—here, the second command displays the program's own source code file:

```
$ g++ -o rline rline.cpp
$ ./rline rline.cpp
```

The program opens a file using the same technique as for reading text a character at a time. To read lines of text, the program calls the `getline()` member function using the following statement:

```
ifs.getline(buffer, sizeof(buffer, '\n');
```

The `buffer` is an array of `char`. Calling `getline()` and specifying the destination, buffer size, and line-ending character ensures that the entire line is read. The following statement reads only the next word (text separated by whitespace):

```
ifs >> buffer;  // ???
```

Instead of that, it's a good idea to preset the buffer size with the `setw()` manipulator. For example, to read a file a word at a time, include the iomanip.h header file and use a statement such as in the following fragment:

```
#include <iomanip.h>
...
ifs >> setw(BUFLEN) >> buffer;
```

This also ensures that the statement does not overwrite the end of the buffer, although GNU C++ apparently won't do that, anyway.

The sample rline.cpp program also demonstrates one way to detect the end of a file by calling the `eof()` member function in reference to a file stream object. This function makes it easy to write a simple `while` loop that ends after processing every last smidgen of data in the file:

```
while (!ifs.eof()) {
  ifs.getline(buffer, sizeof(buffer), '\n');
  // Process line in buffer
}
```

WRITING TEXT A LINE AT A TIME

The last of the four fundamental text-file techniques in this section explains how to write a text file a line at a time. Listing 20.4, wline.cpp, demonstrates the method.

LISTING 20.4   WLINE.CPP

```cpp
#include <iostream.h>
#include <fstream.h>
#include <stdlib.h>
#include <string.h>
#include <string>

#define STR "2: Another literal string"

int main(int argc, char *argv[])
{
  if (argc <= 1) {
    cerr << "Error: filename missing" << endl;
    exit(1);
  }
  ifstream ifs(argv[1], ios::in);
  if (ifs) {
    cerr << "Error: " << argv[1] << " already exists" << endl;
    cerr << "       Specify a different filename" << endl;
    exit(2);
  }
  ofstream ofs(argv[1], ios::out);
  if (!ofs) {
    cerr << "Error: unable to write to " << argv[1] << endl;
    exit(3);
  }
  ofs << "1: A literal string" << endl;
  ofs.write(STR, strlen(STR));
  ofs << endl;
  char *c = "String addressed by pointer";
  ofs << "3: " << c << endl;
  string string_object("4: A string object");
  ofs << string_object << endl;
  return 0;
}
```

Compile and run the program with these commands:

```
$ g++ -o wline wline.cpp
$ ./wline newfile.txt
```

Check the contents of the new file by typing the following:

```
$ cat newfile.txt
1: A literal string
2: Another literal string
3: String addressed by pointer
4: A string object
```

As in wchar.cpp, if the specified file exists, the program displays an error message and exits. Test this by entering the same filename again:

```
$ ./wline newfile.txt
Error: newfile.txt already exists
       Specify a different filename
```

The code for detecting an existing file and opening a file for output is the same as in wchar.cpp. The program differs in how it writes lines of text to the output. Basically, there are two choices. You can write a string using an output stream statement such as this:

```
ofs << "Write me to disk!" << endl;
```

Or, you can call the write() member function with two arguments: a pointer to a string and the number of characters to write. For example, this writes a string addressed by char pointer s and uses the strlen() function declared in the standard string.h header file:

```
#include <string.h>
...
ofs.write(s, strlen(s));
```

That does not write a newline character, however, and is for that reason typically useful only for writing a portion of a string.

The last two statements in the wline.cpp program demonstrate how to construct and write a C++ string object to an output file:

```
string string_object("4: A string object");
ofs << string_object << endl;
```

Note

Chapter 22, "Mastering the Standard string Class," explains more about using string objects.

BINARY FILE STREAMS

Don't look for binary file operations in the GNU C++ file stream library. There aren't any. Although you can open a file for binary access—a capability provided by most disk operating systems, including Linux—reading and writing binary data such as floating point values in their native form is a summit left for programmers to conquer.

The required steps are rarely covered in books on C++ programming, and to accomplish the task, I developed three new classes described in this section. The classes provide binary file I/O for all native C++ data types—and you can easily add new types such as your own classes. Sample programs in the following sections explain how to use the classes. We need four basic capabilities:

- Write one or more bytes of any object to a file.
- Read one or more bytes of any value from a file to an object.
- Translate an object of any size into bytes.
- Translate a collection of bytes into any object.

INTRODUCING BINARY FILE STREAMS

Construct a binary file stream object in almost the same way as you construct other file objects—a text file, for example. However, specify the ios::binary open_mode constant. For example, to create a new binary file, construct an ofstream object using code such as

```
ofstream ofs("newfile.dat", ios::out | ios::binary);
if (!ofs) {
  cerr << "Error: unable to create or write file" << endl;
  exit(1);
}
```

> **Note**
>
> Older C++ compilers might recognize ios::bin in place of the newer ANSI C++ and GNU C++ constant ios::binary.

To open an existing binary file for reading, construct an ifstream object using similar programming:

```
ifstream("oldfile.dat", ios::in | ios::binary);
if (!ifs) {
  cerr << "Error: unable to open file" << endl;
  exit(1);
}
```

Unfortunately, although the preceding code opens files for binary input and output, the ofs and ifs objects have no provisions for reading and writing binary data. To examine this problem, and to understand the solution described in this section, it's helpful first to look at the wrong way to proceed.

THE WRONG SOLUTION

> **Note**
>
> The programming in this section is on the CD-ROM in file src/c20/wrong.cpp. Because the program demonstrates incorrect techniques, it isn't listed here. However, you can run it with the commands *g++ wrong.cpp* followed by *./a.out*.

Constructing input and output file streams as in the preceding section might seem to work—until, that is, you attempt to use the file objects to read and write binary values in files. Consider what happens, for example, if you create a new file like this:

```
ofstream ofs("test.dat", ios::out | ios::binary);
```

Thinking that this creates a new file, test.dat, ready for writing data in binary format, you then attempt to output some double floating point values using statements such as

```
if (ofs) {
  double d = 3.14159;
  ofs << d;        // ???
  ofs << d * d;    // ???
}
ofs.close();
```

After closing the input file, you then attempt to read the file's contents by constructing an input stream object and using statements such as

```
ifstream ifs("test.dat", ios::in | ios::binary);
if (ifs) {
  double d;
  ifs >> d;     // ???
  cout << "d == " << d << endl;
  ifs >> d;     // ???
  cout << "d * d == " << d << endl;
}
```

The program seems to run smoothly, but the reported results are obviously wrong. Here's what the program displays:

```
$ ./a.out
d == 3.1416
d * d == 0.86959
```

What's wrong? The first value seems okay, but pi squared is hardly equal to 0.86959. Examining the file's data using the Linux hexdump utility provides a clue to solving this mysterious bug. If you compiled and ran the wrong.cpp program, enter the following command to examine the contents of test.dat:

```
$ hexdump -bc test.dat
0000000 063 056 061 064 061 065 071 071 056 070 066 071 065 071
0000000   3   .   1   4   1   5   9   9   .   8   6   9   5   9
```

The file's contents reveals that the data has been stored as text despite the fact that the file was opened for binary I/O. This is because C++ I/O streams are designed to convert binary values to text, and they do not alter that action in any way based on how a file is opened. When the program reads the file, the standard input statements perform the reverse task: in this case, reading the first value as 3.141599 and the second as 0.86959. Because the two values were written one after the other, there is no indication in the file that the second value should actually be 9.86959, and the input stream incorrectly "assumes" that the decimal point separates the two values.

This is an interesting problem, but fortunately, as the next section explains, it is not too difficult to solve.

THE RIGHT SOLUTION

To read and write binary data requires deriving new classes from `ifstream` and `ofstream`. Because a `char` in C++ is the same as a byte, an array of `char` values can be used as a buffer for holding a series of bytes representing any value in binary form. To write a value in binary, the program copies the value's bytes to the output buffer and then writes that buffer as a series of bytes to disk. Similarly, to read a binary value, the program reads bytes into a `char` array and then copies those bytes to a variable of an appropriate type.

Actually, the buffer array isn't needed if we simply *pretend* that a binary value is a collection of bytes—which, of course, describes the nature of all data objects. Listing 20.5, wdouble.cpp, demonstrates the basic method of writing some `double` values in binary to a disk file.

Note

When using the binary-file methods in this and the next sections, be aware that other C++ compilers may use different formats for representing binary data. You should not expect to be able to write a file of binary `double` values and read them correctly on another operating system.

LISTING 20.5   WDOUBLE.CPP

```cpp
#include <iostream.h>
#include <fstream.h>
#include <stdlib.h>

#define FILENAME "test.dat"

class bofstream: public ofstream {
public:
  bofstream(const char *fn)
    : ofstream(fn, ios::out | ios::binary) { }
  void writeBytes(const void *, int);
  bofstream & operator<< (double);
};

bofstream & bofstream::operator<< (double d)
{
  writeBytes(&d, sizeof(d));
  return *this;
}

int main()
{
  bofstream bofs(FILENAME);
  if (!bofs) {
    cerr << "Error: unable to write to " << FILENAME << endl;
    exit(1);
  }
  cout << "Writing to " << FILENAME << endl;
  double d = 3.14159;
  bofs << d;
  bofs << d * d;
  bofs << 9.9999999;
  d = 4.7E-8;
  bofs << d;
  return 0;
}

void bofstream::writeBytes(const void *p, int len)
{
  if (!p) return;
  if (len <= 0) return;
  write((char *)p, len);
}
```

Compile and run the wdouble.cpp program using the following commands. Except for a confirmation message, the program displays no other output:

```
$ g++ -o wdouble wdouble.cpp
$ ./wdouble
Writing to test.dat
```

To provide for writing double values in binary, the program derives a new class, bofstream (binary-output-file-stream), from ofstream. The new class provides three member functions. First is a constructor declared and implemented inline as

```
bofstream(const char *fn):
  ofstream(fn, ios::out | ios::binary) { }
```

The constructor merely calls the ancestor ofstream class constructor with a filename and with the two open_mode constants shown. To use the constructor, a program simply constructs an object of the bofstream class:

```
bofstream bofs(FILENAME);
```

Member function writeBytes() writes a number of bytes to the open file. The function is declared in bofstream as the following:

```
void writeBytes(const void *, int);
```

Function writeBytes() returns no value. Its first parameter is a constant void pointer that addresses the object to write to disk. The second int parameter equals the size of the object in bytes. Examine the function's implementation closely:

```
if (!p) return;
if (len <= 0) return;
write((char *)p, len);
```

If the pointer is NULL, the function merely returns and takes no further action. Similarly, if the specified length is less than or equal to zero, nothing happens. The third statement calls the inherited write() function to write len bytes of data starting at the address held in pointer p as a series of char values—that is, as a stream of bytes.

To provide for writing a *specific* type of data, the bofstream class declares a third member function:

```
bofstream & operator<< (double);
```

That overloads the output stream operator << for values of type double written to an object of the bofstream class. To carry out that job, the overloaded operator function executes these statements:

```
writeBytes(&d, sizeof(d));
return *this;
```

The parameter d is the double object to write to disk. First, writeBytes() writes to the file sizeof(d) bytes located at the address in d. Finally, the function returns its own object so that cascaded output statements such as the following write to this same destination (assume all variables are doubles):

```
bofs << d1 << d2 << d3;
```

Listing 20.6, rdouble.cpp, completes the picture by reading the binary double values written to test.dat by wdouble.cpp. The program shows how to derive a new class from ifstream to read values of specific types in binary.

LISTING 20.6 RDOUBLE.CPP

```cpp
#include <iostream.h>
#include <fstream.h>
#include <stdlib.h>

#define FILENAME "test.dat"

class bifstream: public ifstream {
public:
  bifstream(const char *fn)
    : ifstream(fn, ios::in | ios::binary) { }
  void readBytes(void *, int);
  bifstream & operator>> (double &);
};

bifstream & bifstream::operator>> (double &d)
{
  readBytes(&d, sizeof(d));
  return *this;
}

int main()
{
  bifstream bifs(FILENAME);
  if (!bifs) {
    cerr << "Error: unable to open " << FILENAME << endl;
    cerr << "        compile wdouble.cpp and run first\n";
    exit(1);
  }
  double d;
  long count = 0;
  cout.precision(8);
  bifs >> d;
  while (!bifs.eof()) {
    cout << ++count << ": " << d << endl;
    bifs >> d;
  }
  return 0;
}

void bifstream::readBytes(void *p, int len)
{
  if (!p) return;
  if (len <= 0) return;
  read((char *)p, len);
}
```

To run the full test, compile both wdouble.cpp and rdouble.cpp, and then run the two programs together. Following is the full set of commands and output lines:

```
$ g++ -o wdouble wdouble.cpp
$ g++ -o rdouble rdouble.cpp
$ ./wdouble
Writing to test.dat
$ ./rdouble
1: 3.14159
2: 9.8695877
3: 9.9999999
4: 4.7e-08
```

Compare the output from rdouble.cpp with the statements in wdouble.cpp that write binary values to disk. They are consistent with the expected results. This indicates that, instead of writing and reading data in text form, the derived bofstream and bifstream classes now handle data in native, binary format. The new bifstream (binary-input-file-stream) class is derived from ifstream. Its constructor is declared and implemented inline as follows:

```
bifstream(const char *fn):
  ifstream(fn, ios::in | ios::binary) { }
```

As in the bofstream constructor, this code merely calls its ancestor class constructor, passing a filename string and the two open_mode constants that open the file for binary input. The bifstream class also declares a function, readBytes(), as follows:

```
void readBytes(void *, int);
```

This is the counterpart to the bofstream::writeBytes() function, and it declares the same parameters—a pointer to the data object to write and its size in bytes. The readBytes() function executes three statements to read a value in binary:

```
if (!p) return;
if (len <= 0) return;
read((char *)p, len);
```

If the pointer is NULL, or the requested size is less than or equal to zero, the function does nothing. Otherwise, it calls the inherited read() function to input len bytes from the open file into the address at pointer p.

Finally, the bifstream class overloads the C++ input stream operator >> with the following declaration:

```
bifstream & operator>> (double &);
```

Because of this declaration, any statements that write a double variable to a bifstream object call the overloaded function. Its implementation calls the readBytes() function to perform the actual input duty:

```
readBytes(&d, sizeof(d));
return *this;
```

As before, d is the double object to be loaded from the file. First, readBytes() reads sizeof(d) bytes into memory at the address of d. Then, the function returns its own bifstream object so that cascaded input statements such as the following work properly:

bifs >> d1 >> d2 >> d3;

CLASSES FOR BINARY FILE I/O

Expanding the concepts in the preceding two sections leads to versatile versions of the bofstream and bifstream classes. With the revised classes that follow, you can read and write all native C++ data types in binary form. Listing 20.7, bstream.h, declares the two classes

LISTING 20.7   BSTREAM.H

```
#include <iostream.h>
#include <fstream.h>

// Binary output file stream

class bofstream: public ofstream {
public:
  bofstream(const char *fn)
    : ofstream(fn, ios::out | ios::binary) { }
  void writeBytes(const void *, int);
  template <class T>
    bofstream & operator<< (const T & data);
};

template <class T>
bofstream & bofstream::operator<< (const T & data)
{
  writeBytes(&data, sizeof(data));
  return *this;
}

// Binary input file stream

class bifstream: public ifstream {
public:
  bifstream(const char *fn)
    : ifstream(fn, ios::in | ios::binary) { }
  void readBytes(void *, int);
  template <class T>
    bifstream & operator>> (T & data);
};

template <class T>
bifstream & bifstream::operator>> (T & data)
{
  readBytes(&data, sizeof(data));
  return *this;
}
```

The new `bofstream` and `bifstream` classes are similar to the ones listed earlier but are designed using templates to accommodate any C++ data type, including your own classes. In fact, the only significant differences in the two classes are the declarations and implementations of the overloaded input and output operators as templates. To understand the programming, examine the declaration for the `bofstream` class's overloaded output operator:

```
template <class T>
  bofstream & operator<< (const T & data);
```

This states that `T` is a placeholder type to be defined later. The overloaded `operator<<()` function returns a reference to a `bofstream` object (the same one for which it is called), and it accepts a parameter of type `const T &`—in other words, a constant reference to an object of an unspecified type. The template's implementation writes the object using these statements:

```
writeBytes(&data, sizeof(data));
return *this;
```

These are the same statements you examined earlier—but because the type of data is not yet known, they now appear in the header file. No code is generated until C++ instantiates the template.

The overloaded input operator for the `bifstream` class is written similarly as a template. Listing 20.8, bstream.cpp, implements the `bofstream` and `bifstream` class member functions, `writeBytes()` and `readBytes()`. Again, these are the same functions presented earlier.

LISTING 20.8   BSTREAM.CPP

```
#include "bstream.h"

void bofstream::writeBytes(const void *p, int len)
{
  if (!p) return;
  if (len <= 0) return;
  write((char *)p, len);
}

void bifstream::readBytes(void *p, int len)
{
  if (!p) return;
  if (len <= 0) return;
  read((char *)p, len);
}
```

We now have two general-purpose classes, `bofstream` and `bifstream`, with overloaded operators that, through the use of templates, can adapt to any data type. To use the classes, compile the module using the command

```
$ g++ -c bstream.cpp
```

That creates object code file bstream.o in the current directory. The next section lists a test program that includes bstream.h header file to read and write binary values in a file.

READING AND WRITING BINARY VALUES

Listing 20.9 demonstrates how to use the `bofstream` and `bifstream` classes to read and write values of type `double` in a file.

LISTING 20.9   TBDOUBLE.CPP

```
#include <iostream.h>
#include <stdlib.h>      // Need exit()
#include "bstream.h"

#define FILENAME "tbdouble.dat"

int main()
{

// Construct binary output file
  bofstream bofs(FILENAME);
  if (!bofs) {
    cerr << "Error: unable to write to " << FILENAME << endl;
    exit(1);
  }

// Write values and close file
  double d = 3.14159;
  bofs << d << d * d << d * d * d;
  bofs.close();

// Construct binary input file
  bifstream bifs(FILENAME);
  if (!bifs) {
    cerr << "Error: unable to open " << FILENAME << endl;
    exit(2);
  }

// Read and display values from file
  int count = 0;
  cout.precision(8);
  bifs >> d;
  while (!bifs.eof()) {
    cout << ++count << ": " << d << endl;
    bifs >> d;
  }

  return 0;
}
```

Compile and run the sample program with the following commands (skip the first command if you already compiled bstream.cpp):

```
$ g++ -c bstream.cpp
$ g++ -o tbdouble tbdouble.cpp bstream.o
$ ./tbdouble
1: 3.14159
2: 9.8695877
3: 31.006198
```

To construct a binary output file, the program creates an object of type `bofstream` using the statement

```
bofstream bofs(FILENAME);
```

If this succeeds, the program simply writes values to disk using statements such as

```
bofs << d << d * d << d * d * d;
bofs.close();
```

The last statement closes the file. Although the program doesn't show it, you may write *any* type of data to the `bofs` object. However, it's your responsibility to read that data in the same order as written. The objects in the file are simply binary values with no indicators of their types.

To read the values just written, the program constructs an object of the other bstream.cpp class, `bifstream`:

```
bifstream bifs(FILENAME);
```

It then uses input stream statements such as the following along with a `while` loop to read and display all values previously stored on disk:

```
bifs >> d;
```

READING AND WRITING BINARY CLASS OBJECTS

The preceding demonstration only hints at the power of the `bofstream` and `bifstream` classes. For example, you can also use these classes to read and write class objects in binary. First, we need a sample class with some private data members to represent any kind of object data. Listing 20.10, tanyclass.h, declares the test class.

LISTING 20.10   TANYCLASS.H

```
#include <iostream.h>

class TAnyClass {
private:
  int x;   // Private class data members
  int y;
public:
  friend ostream & operator<< (ostream &, const TAnyClass &);
  friend istream & operator>> (istream &, TAnyClass &);
public:
  TAnyClass(): x(0), y(0) { }
  TAnyClass(int X, int Y): x(X), y(Y) { }
};
```

The test class, `TAnyClass`, declares two private integer values. A public section declares two friend functions that overload the I/O stream operators `<<` and `>>`. These functions must be friends of the class because we don't want them to receive a `this` pointer, but rather, a reference to the stream object—not the TAnyClass object—for which they are called. As declared here, to write a TAnyClass object to the standard output, the program can use simple statements such as the following:

```
TAnyClass object(1, 2);
cout << object;
```

It can similarly read new values into a TAnyClass object by using an equally simple statement:

```
cin >> object;
```

In addition to its two friends, TAnyClass declares two constructors—a default that sets the two private variables to zero, and a parameterized version that accepts integer arguments to initialize x and y. Listing 20.11, tanyclass.cpp, implements the two friend functions:

LISTING 20.11   TANYCLASS.CPP

```
#include <iostream.h>
#include "tanyclass.h"

// Implements overloaded ostream output operator
ostream & operator<< (ostream &os, const TAnyClass &c)
{
  os << "-- TAnyClass object --" << endl;
  os << "x == " << c.x << "; ";
  os << "y == " << c.y << endl;
  return os;
}

// Implements overloaded istream input operator
istream & operator>> (istream &is, TAnyClass &c)
{
  cout << "Enter value for X: ";
  is >> c.x;
  cout << "Enter value for Y: ";
  is >> c.y;
  return is;
}
```

The sample listing is just a suggestion. You can implement the overloaded operators using any method to read and write class objects. You can now compile the TAnyClass module with the following command:

```
$ g++ -c tanyclass.cpp
```

Listing 20.12, tbobj.cpp (test binary object) demonstrates how to use the binary file classes, bofstream and bifstream, to read and write a TAnyClass object in a disk file.

PART

IV

CH

20

LISTING 20.12   TBOBJ.CPP

```cpp
#include <iostream.h>
#include <stdlib.h>       // Need exit()
#include "tanyclass.h"
#include "bstream.h"

#define FILENAME "tbobj.dat"

int main()
{
  bofstream bofs(FILENAME);
  if (!bofs) {
    cerr << "Error: unable to write to " << FILENAME << endl;
    exit(1);
  }

  TAnyClass obj;  // Default object

  // Prompt user to enter object values
  cin >> obj;

  // Write object to disk and close file
  cout << "Writing object to disk" << endl;
  bofs << obj;
  bofs.close();

  // Construct binary input file
  cout << "Opening file" << endl;
  bifstream bifs(FILENAME);
  if (!bifs) {
    cerr << "Error: unable to open " << FILENAME << endl;
    exit(2);
  }

  // Read object from file. Use a new TAnyClass
  // object to be sure values are new.
  cout << "Reading object from disk" << endl;
  TAnyClass newObject;
  bifs >> newObject;

  cout << "Object from disk:" << endl;
  cout << newObject;

  bifs.close();
  return 0;
}
```

Before examining the test program, compile and run it using the following commands. Enter values when prompted. The program writes the TAnyClass object to disk, reads it back, and displays its value to confirm the I/O operations (skip the first two commands if you already compiled the bstream.cpp and tanyclass.cpp modules):

```
$ g++ -c bstream.cpp
$ g++ -c tanyclass.cpp
$ g++ -o tbobj tbobj.cpp bstream.o tanyclass.o
```

```
$ ./tbobj
Enter value for X: 135
Enter value for Y: 791
Writing object to disk
Opening file
Reading object from disk
Object from disk:
-- TAnyClass object --
x == 135; y == 791
```

The demonstration program shows how easy it is to read and write even complex class objects. For example, these statements create an object and prompt the user to enter values:

```
TAnyClass obj;  // Default object
cin >> obj;
```

Equally simple statements create a new file (or overwrite an existing one) and then write the object to disk:

```
bofstream bofs(FILENAME);
...
bofs << obj;
bofs.close();
```

Closing the file is optional, but this prepares for reopening it to read its data. Again, the programming is simple. Three statements open the input file, read a TAnyClass object (constructed beforehand), and display its value:

```
bifstream bifs(FILENAME);
bifs >> newObject;
cout << newObject;
```

> **Note**
>
> To limit this chapter's length, I have purposely avoided mentioning some issues concerning file I/O and class objects that you may need to consider. For example, if the class declares any dynamic pointers, the addressed data must be written to disk and then reallocated memory on reading. Likewise, any object data members of classes will need default constructors and the means to read their data from disk. Also, objects must be read in the same order written unless you construct a way to identify the classes of stored objects.

COMBINING THE INPUT AND OUTPUT CLASSES

By creating yet one more class, it's possible to combine the bofstream and bifstream classes into one class that can read and write values in the same file without first closing it between operations. This new class, bfstream, completes the binary file I/O classes described in this chapter. Like its counterparts, bfstream can read and write objects of any types, including all C and C++ native types and classes of your own design (remember, however, that pointers and class object data members may require special handling). Listing 20.13, bfstream.h, declares the bfstream class.

LISTING 20.13 BFSTREAM.H

```cpp
#include <iostream.h>
#include <fstream.h>

// Binary input and output file stream

class bfstream: public fstream {
public:
  bfstream(const char *fn)
    : fstream(fn, ios::in | ios::out | ios::binary) { }
  void writeBytes(const void *, int);
  void readBytes(void *, int);
  template <class T>
    bfstream & operator<< (const T & data);
  template <class T>
    bfstream & operator>> (T & data);
};

template <class T>
bfstream & bfstream::operator<< (const T & data)
{
  writeBytes(&data, sizeof(data));
  return *this;
}

template <class T>
bfstream & bfstream::operator>> (T & data)
{
  readBytes(&data, sizeof(data));
  return *this;
}
```

The bfstream class is derived from fstream, which provides low-level file stream operations. The bfstream constructor merely calls its ancestor constructor, passing a filename string and three open_mode constants as arguments:

```cpp
bfstream(const char *fn):
  fstream(fn, ios::in | ios::out | ios::binary) { }
```

Constructing a bfstream object opens the file if it exists, or creates a new file if not, for input and output in binary mode. It is still necessary, however, to provide overloaded input and output operator functions that perform the actual binary I/O. As in the bofstream and bifstream classes, the overloaded operators are written as templates. That way, the compiler generates actual functions based on the type of data involved, and in that way, the bfstream class can handle data of any type. Its readBytes() and writeBytes() member functions are the same as already described and are not listed here (see file src/c20/bfstream.cpp on the CD-ROM). Compile the module with the following command:

```
$ g++ -c bfstream.cpp
```

You now have a class that can read and write binary data of any type in the same file. Program bfstest.cpp in Listing 20.14 demonstrates how to use the new class.

LISTING 20.14   BFSTEST.CPP

```cpp
#include <iostream.h>
#include <stdlib.h>      // Need exit()
#include "tanyclass.h"
#include "bfstream.h"

#define FILENAME "abcde.dat"

int main()
{
  TAnyClass a(0,1), b(2,3), c(4,5), d(6,7), e(8,9);
  TAnyClass aa, bb, cc, dd, ee;

  // Construct output file stream object bfs
  bfstream bfs(FILENAME);
  if (!bfs) {
    cerr << "Error: unable to create " << FILENAME << endl;
    exit(1);
  }

  // Write records to file
  cout << "Writing five records to file" << endl;
  bfs << a << b << c << d << e;

  // Reset file to beginning, read and display records
  cout << "Reading five records from file" << endl;
  bfs.seekg(0);
  bfs >> aa >> bb >> cc >> dd >> ee;
  cout << aa << bb << cc << dd << ee;

  // Seek record number 3 and change it
  TAnyClass x(123,456);                 // Construct new object
  long rn = 3;                          // Define record number
  bfs.seekp(sizeof(TAnyClass) * rn);    // Seek to record #3
  bfs << x;                             // Write object to file

  // Seek to record number 3 again and read it
  TAnyClass y;                          // Construct empty object
  bfs.seekg(sizeof(TAnyClass) * rn);    // Seek to record #3
  bfs >> y;                             // Read object from file

  cout << endl << "Changed record #3 (4th record) to" << endl;
  cout << y;

  // Make sure other records are undisturbed;
  cout << endl << "Re-reading five records" << endl;
  bfs.seekg(0);
  bfs >> aa >> bb >> cc >> dd >> ee;
  cout << aa << bb << cc << dd << ee;

  // Close file object
  bfs.close();

  return 0;
}
```

The following commands compile and run the test. If you already compiled the tanyclass.cpp and bfstream.cpp modules, you can skip the first two commands:

```
$ g++ -c tanyclass.cpp
$ g++ -c bfstream.cpp
$ g++ -o bfstest bfstest.cpp tanyclass.o bfstream.o
$ ./bfstest
```

The program's output, which is a bit lengthy to list here, displays five TAnyClass objects in this format:

```
-- TAnyClass object --
x == 0; y == 1
```

It writes the five objects to a disk file and then alters one of them by seeking to the middle of the file and writing a new record there. This simulates how you might use the bfstream class to create database files of records, and read and write specific records. (See also "Seeking in Streams" later in this chapter.)

To create and open a new file for binary input and output, use the bfstream class like this:

```
bfstream bfs(FILENAME);
if (!bfs) {
  cerr << "Error: unable to create " << FILENAME << endl;
  exit(1);
}
```

Instead of exiting, however, you might throw an exception to report an error. After opening the file, you may read and write data of any type. To provide some objects, the sample program constructs a few TAnyClass objects:

```
TAnyClass a(0,1), b(2,3), c(4,5), d(6,7), e(8,9);
TAnyClass aa, bb, cc, dd, ee;
```

I used different objects only to prove that the program indeed reads them after writing to disk. A single statement writes the first five objects:

```
bfs << a << b << c << d << e;
```

An equally simple statement reads the objects from disk into the other set of TAnyClass objects:

```
bfs >> aa >> bb >> cc >> dd >> ee;
```

To write a specific object anywhere inside the file, the program uses the following code:

```
TAnyClass x(123,456);
long rn = 3;
bfs.seekp(sizeof(TAnyClass) * rn);
bfs << x;
```

First, a new TAnyClass object is constructed. Then, after assigning a record number to a long variable, the inherited seekp() function seeks to that record's position (more on that in a moment). Finally, using the output stream operator, the new object is written to disk, replacing whatever object is already at that location. Similar code reads a record at any location:

```
TAnyClass y;
bfs.seekg(sizeof(TAnyClass) * rn);
bfs >> y;
```

Again, I defined a new TAnyClass object, y, just for test purposes. After seeking to a file position, an input stream statement reads the object from disk. To read all objects, seek to position zero and use an input stream statement:

```
bfs.seekg(0);
bfs >> aa >> bb >> cc >> dd >> ee;
```

FILE STREAM TECHNIQUES

Following are some additional techniques and tips for using file streams in C++ programs.

DETECTING A FILE'S PRESENCE

Detecting the existence of a file is a common operation that many programs need to perform. One way to do this is to attempt to open the file using code such as

```
ifstream ifs("test.txt", ios::in);
if (ifs)
  return true;
else
  return false;
```

The if statement in effect states that, if the ifs object is properly constructed, then the file exists. You might use this code in a bool function that returns true if a file exists. (When the ifs object goes out of scope, the file closes automatically.) Although this programming is intuitive, you might wonder how an expression such as (ifs) can serve as a test for an object's validity. Recall from earlier in this chapter how the opposite test calls the overloaded operator!() function:

```
if (!ifs) {
...
}
```

Similarly, the expression (ifs) calls another overloaded operator, declared as operator void *() for the ifstream class using the following inline declaration:

```
operator void*() const {
...
}
```

The expression (x), where x is an object of the class for which the overloaded operator is declared, calls the operator function. You can use this overloaded operator to return a pointer to an object, or as in this case, as a test of the object's validity. GNU C++ defines operator void *() for stream classes such as ifstream using code such as

```
operator void*() const {
  return fail() ? (void*)0 : (void*)(-1);
}
```

In the overloaded operator's conditional statement, if the call to function `fail()` is true, the returned result equals a NULL-pointer to zero, meaning false; otherwise, the result is true (a NULL-pointer to –1, the "most nonfalse" value possible). However, at least one other ANSI C++ compiler defines this function differently using the following statement:

```
return fail() ? 0 : this;
```

In that case, the overloaded `operator void *()` function returns zero for false, or the object's address in memory for true. I bring these examples up to show contrasting views on how to code this type of overloaded operator but also to point out the inherent danger of assuming any particular encoding. The latter example might result in a security breach by returning a nonconstant address to an object considered `const`—and for that reason, the GNU C++ statement is superior.

SEEKING IN STREAMS

For database work, programs need to pick and choose specific records in files, a process called *seeking*. You already saw some examples of seeking in bfstest.cpp, Listing 20.14, that tests this chapter's `bfstream` class. This section explains various seeking functions available for C++ streams.

Input file-streams define two overloaded member functions for seeking in input streams. These are inherited from the `istream` class:

```
istream & seekg(streampos);
istream & seekg(streamoff, ios::seek_dir);
```

Each function is named the same—`seekg()`, the "g" meaning "get." In other words, `seekg()` sets the internal file position for subsequent "get" or "read" operations. The `streampos` and `streamoff` parameters are system-dependent integers, equivalent to type `long` in GNU C++ for Linux.

> **Tip**
>
> For portability, don't pass variables of type `long` to `seekg()`. Instead, use the type names `streampos` and `streamoff`.

The first overloaded form of `seekg()` positions an input stream to a specific byte. The second form positions the stream to an offset from one of three positions defined by `ios::seek_dir` as listed in Table 20.2.

TABLE 20.2   THE `ios::seek_dir` CONSTANTS

Constant	Value	Description
beg	0	Seek from beginning of file
cur	1	Seek from current position
end	2	Seek from end of file

Always supply positive offsets for `ios::beg`. Supply positive offsets for `ios::cur` to seek forward toward the end of the file, or use negative offsets to seek backward toward the beginning of the file. Always supply negative offsets for `ios::end`.

To position the internal file pointer for output streams, use the following two overloaded output file stream functions, inherited from the `ostream` class:

```
ostream & seekp(streampos);
ostream & seekp(streamoff, ios::seek_dir);
```

These functions are similar to `seekg()`, but the "p" in their names means "put." Use them to seek in output files for subsequent "put" or "write" operations. As in the `seekg()` functions, parameters `streampos` and `streamoff` are equivalent to type `long` in GNU C++ for Linux, but might be defined as another type on a different operating system.

The following code fragments, taken from file seekdemo.cpp on the CD-ROM located in path src/c20, demonstrate how to use `seekg()` and `seekp()` to locate records in a file. The sample program is similar to the bfstest.cpp program in this chapter, so it's not listed in full here. It uses the bfstream.cpp and tanyclass.cpp modules, also in this chapter.

The program begins by constructing some objects to store in a file. Records a, b, c, d, and e are initialized to the values in parentheses. Records aa, bb, cc, dd, and ee are given default values (0, 0) to better test the program's I/O:

```
TAnyClass a(0,1), b(2,3), c(4,5), d(6,7), e(8,9);
TAnyClass aa, bb, cc, dd, ee;
```

Using the `bfstream` class in this chapter, the program creates or overwrites a file named seekdemo.dat, defined as the constant `FILENAME`:

```
bfstream bfs(FILENAME);
if (!bfs) {
  cerr << "Error: unable to create " << FILENAME << endl;
  exit(1);
}
```

Some input and output statements write the five `TAnyClass` objects to disk and then read them back into memory:

```
bfs << a << b << c << d << e;
bfs.seekg(0);
bfs >> aa >> bb >> cc >> dd >> ee;
cout << "Records stored in " << FILENAME << endl;
cout << aa << bb << cc << dd << ee;
```

The second statement shows how to position the file's internal pointer to the first record. After that, a cascaded input statement reads the file's records into objects aa, bb, cc, dd, and ee, which are then displayed by writing them to `cout`. All this is made possible by the `bfstream` class's overloaded file stream operator, and the `TAnyClass` output operator friend functions. To seek and read a specific record, use code such as the following:

```
streampos rn = 3;   // Record number
bfs.seekg(sizeof(TAnyClass) * rn);
bfs >> aa;
cout << aa;
```

Notice that the record number `rn` variable is of type `streampos`, not `long`, even though these types are equivalent in GNU C++ for Linux. The second statement positions the internal file pointer to the byte at the calculated position. Remember always that `seekg()` and `seekp()` position to bytes in the file, not to records. To find a record, then, requires multiplying the record number by the size in bytes of one record. The final two statements read the record from the binary file stream object `bfs` and display it on the standard output. Use the second overloaded form of `seekg()` to seek to a *relative* position as in this code fragment:

```
rn = 2;  // Number of records to seek backwards
bfs.seekg(-(sizeof(TAnyClass) * rn), ios::cur);
bfs >> bb;
cout << bb;
```

The second statement, in this case, seeks 16 bytes backward (a negative value) from the current position. Because the preceding operation leaves the internal file pointer addressing the *next* record, the code repositions the file pointer to the record just before that one. You can also seek backward from the end of the file, as this code demonstrates:

```
rn = 1;  // Number of records to seek from end of file
bfs.seekg(-(sizeof(TAnyClass) * rn), ios::end);
bfs >> cc;
cout << cc;
```

That shows a handy way to locate the last record in the file. It works the same for any type of records, as long as they are all of the same size. You can similarly search for a particular record from the beginning of the file without first seeking to position zero—simply specify `ios::beg` as the second argument to `seekg()`:

```
rn = 4;  // Number of records to seek from beginning of file
bfs.seekg((sizeof(TAnyClass) * rn), ios::beg);
bfs >> dd;
cout << dd;
```

Finally, use `seekp()` to position the file pointer before a write operation. The following fragment prompts the user for a new record and then stores it at record number 2 (the third in the file; the first is number 0):

```
TAnyClass newObject;
cin >> newObject;  // Prompt user for value
rn = 2;  // Record to overwrite
bfs.seekp(sizeof(TAnyClass) * rn, ios::beg);
bfs << newObject;
```

Check for success by rereading the same record into a new `TAnyClass` object:

```
TAnyClass oldObject;  // Use a new object for the test
rn = 2;
bfs.seekg(sizeof(TAnyClass) * rn, ios::beg);
bfs >> oldObject;
cout << oldObject;
```

Finally, close the file before ending the program:

```
bfs.close();
```

This step isn't strictly necessary because, when the `bfs` object (of this chapter's `bfstream` class) goes out of scope, C++ automatically calls the class destructor, which closes the open file. However, it's good programming to close files when you are finished using them.

> **Tip**
>
> In the foregoing examples, `seekp()` and `seekg()` work the same because the `bfstream` class is designed to read and write in the same file. However, when using input files of the `bifstream` or `ifstream` classes, you must use `seekg()`. Similarly, use `seekp()` along with output files of the `bofstream` or `ofstream` classes.

SUMMARY

By overloading the C++ input and output stream operators, you provide the means for reading and writing objects of class types using I/O stream statements. Using the file stream classes described in this chapter, you can provide disk-file I/O. This chapter also explained how to read and write native data objects and class objects in binary files.

For more information on subjects introduced in this chapter, turn to the following chapters:

- Chapter 16, "Handling Exceptions"
- Chapter 19, "Overloading Operators"
- Chapter 22, "Mastering the Standard `string` Class"

## CHAPTER 21

HONING YOUR C++ SKILLS

Learning to program is like learning to walk. When you can stand without toppling over, the real work begins—figuring out how to get from point A to point B.

Now that you have learned most of what C++ has to offer, you might be wondering about your next step. In this chapter, you meet some additional, but vital, tools for mastering C++. You won't use these features all the time, but you might find the information in this chapter invaluable for solving special problems.

COPYING CLASS OBJECTS

As mentioned in Chapter 13, "Creating and Destroying Objects," it is important to provide for the safe copying of class objects. This is especially so in objects that have pointers to dynamically allocated memory. In such cases, a copy constructor and assignment function (in the form of an overloaded operator=() function) provide the necessary programming to guard against the duplication of pointers, a state that can lead to serious errors such as segmentation memory faults.

Although those solutions are adequate for many purposes, the techniques described so far do not provide the efficiency needed in practical software development. In this section, after a quick review of copy constructors and assignment functions, I explain two approaches to safe and efficient object copying: reference counting and the copy-on-write method. Full examples of these techniques provide useful guides for adding these features to your own classes.

COPY CONSTRUCTOR AND ASSIGNMENT REVIEW

Most classes need two types of functions that provide for the safe copying of class objects. Several examples in this book have shown samples of the two types:

- A *copy constructor* provides the means to create a new object as a copy of an existing one.
- An *overloaded* operator=() assignment function provides the means to copy one object to another of the same or related type.

It's important to understand that a copy constructor is called *only* when a new class object is created using the value of an existing object. Conversely, the operator=() function is called to assign the value of an existing object to another one that has already been constructed. The two functions perform similar jobs, but only the constructor has the additional task of initializing a brand new object.

It's also important to understand that a copy constructor and operator=() function might be called as a secondary result of an operation, not necessarily from an explicit program statement. For example, this statement:

```
TAnyClass A(B);
```

obviously constructs a new object A using the value of B, and calls the TAnyClass copy constructor to carry out that chore. Likewise, this statement:

```
A = B;
```

obviously assigns object B to A and, because both objects already exist, calls the `TAnyClass` `operator=()` function to perform the copy. However, other situations lead to calling these two functions. Two less obvious but common ones are

- Passing an object to a function parameter
- Returning an object as a function result

Always carefully consider whether your program causes any temporary objects to be created as a result of these and similar actions. To guard against problems such as duplicated class data member pointers, provide a copy constructor and `operator=()` function as described in this chapter.

MEMBERWISE INITIALIZATION

In the absence of a copy constructor or `operator=()` function, C++ performs copying of one object to another using a technique officially known as *memberwise initialization*. This is merely a fancy way of saying that, unless you provide alternate programming, C++ copies data members byte-for-byte from one object to another. In other words, if `fA` and `fB` are floating point variables of type `double`, the following assignment copies the bytes from `fB` to `fA`:

```
fA = fB;    // Copy fB to fA
```

Likewise, if A and B are class objects, this statement does the same for their data members:

```
A = B;
```

This works fine for simple objects, but if their class declares any pointers to dynamic memory, the assignment causes those pointers to address the same allocated memory blocks. When those blocks are deleted, the program fails when the memory manager attempts to dispose of the same memory more than once.

> **Note**
>
> This same error can happen in subtle ways. For example, if a class declares an object of another class, and *that* class has any pointers, the duplication of a pointer as a result of an object copy might not be obvious from the source code.

COPY CONSTRUCTOR

A class copy constructor is typically declared and implemented as follows (T represents any type):

```
class TAnyClass {
private:
  T *p;    // Pointer to object of type T
public:
  TAnyClass(const TAnyClass &copy);
...
};
```

The class normally declares other members, constructors, and a destructor. The copy constructor, however, is always declared as shown here. Its single parameter is a constant reference to an object (named copy here) of the class type. The body of the constructor is usually written along these lines:

```
TAnyClass::TAnyClass(const TAnyClass &copy):
  p(NULL)
{
  if (copy.p != NULL)
    p = TDuplicate(copy.p);
}
```

That's hypothetical, but it shows the basic steps in a typical copy constructor. First, an initializing expression sets p to NULL. Then, in the function's body, if the object copy's p pointer is not NULL, a statement calls a function to copy the data addressed by copy.p to the new object's p pointer. The TDuplicate() function is for illustration only. In a real setting, if the data is a C-string, this statement might call strcpy() to make a fresh copy of the characters.

OVERLOADED operator=() FUNCTION

An overloaded operator=() function resembles a copy constructor but does not have the responsibility of initializing a new object. Using the same class as in the preceding section, TAnyClass might overload operator=() like this:

```
class TAnyClass {
private:
  T *p;
public:
  void operator=(const TAnyClass &copy);
...
};
```

Here again, I don't show other members that the class probably needs. The operator=() function returns no value, and its single parameter is the same as the copy constructor's. Its body, however, needs some special handling as shown here:

```
void TAnyClass::operator=(const TAnyClass &copy)
{
  if (this == &copy) return;
  delete p;
  p = NULL;
  if (copy.p != NULL)
    p = TDuplicate(copy.p);
}
```

The first statement, often left out by C++ programmers, checks whether a statement has ordered an object to be copied to itself. This is a rare occurrence, but it's essential to guard against. The this pointer addresses the object for which the operator=() function was called. If that pointer equals the *address* of the copy, then they are the same object and the function returns without taking any action.

If the objects are different, as they usually are, the first step is to delete the data addressed by this object. Even if p is NULL, the second and third statements are allowed because deleting a NULL pointer does no harm. It's important to set p to NULL in case copy.p is NULL, in which case both objects address no data. This step is also frequently forgotten. Finally, if the copy object's p pointer is not NULL, the function performs whatever action is necessary to copy the data addressed by copy.p to the target object's p pointer. Again, as with the copy constructor, both objects now address unique memory allocations, avoiding the problems caused by duplicated pointers.

CALLING operator=() FROM A COPY CONSTRUCTOR

You can usually avoid wasteful duplications in a copy constructor and overloaded operator=() function by combining their programming. The technique, however, might seem magical until you understand how it works. Inside the copy constructor, instead of statements that copy data, use code such as the following:

```
TAnyClass::TAnyClass(const TAnyClass &copy):
  p(NULL)
{
  *this = copy;  // !!!
}
```

As before, the constructor carries out its initialization responsibility of setting p to NULL. After that, the single assignment statement copies the copy parameter to *this. Because this points to the object being constructed, the statement calls the class's overloaded operator=() function to carry out the actual copying.

> **Tip**
>
> Be sure that the copy constructor initializes *all* class data members before executing the assignment statement shown here.

REFERENCE COUNT OWNERSHIP

The preceding methods have the distinct disadvantage of leading to multiple copies of the same data in memory. For example, if TData addresses a string using a pointer, copying one TData object to another results in two identical strings in memory. Although we have prevented segmentation memory errors by not duplicating pointers, the result is highly inefficient. In cases where the program stores large strings, database records, and buffers, needlessly copying those objects might use up available memory. Also, if two objects address duplicate copies of the same data, if that data needs to be changed, how can the other object know to make the same change to its data?

One answer to these dilemmas is to design a class that keeps track of how many owners it has. This is called *reference counting*. Many programmers attempt to write this code by creating a class that somehow keeps track of duplicate objects. But the object-oriented approach attacks the problem from the other side of the fence—it makes the data object *itself* responsible for counting how many other objects own it.

Figure 21.1 shows the relationship between a class that, through reference counting, keeps tracks of its owners. Objects A through F own data objects Data1, Data2, and Data3. Those objects track their ownership counts, shown in parentheses.

Figure 21.1
Using reference counting, a data object keeps track of the number of its owners.

Data objects such as Data1, Data2, and Data3 in Figure 21.1 provide a function that returns a copy of themselves. Instead of constructing an entirely new object, however, the function merely increments its object's ownership counter and returns that same object. For example, from Figure 21.1, if a new object G is constructed using Data3, that object's function increments Data3's ownership counter to indicate that three objects own that data. In this way, only one copy of the unique data exists in memory.

Deleting objects also takes special handling. Again, using Figure 21.1, if the program deletes object B, it must not also delete Data2 because two other objects, C and D, still own that data. To handle the deletion of B, Data2's destructor simply decrements its ownership count, changing 3 to 2. Likewise, if object D is deleted, Data2's ownership counter is again decremented from 2 to 1, indicating that only one object owns it. If C is then deleted, Data2 is also disposed of because its ownership counter now equals 1, signaling that this is the only copy of the data, and it therefore may be safely deleted.

COPY-ON-WRITE METHOD

Reference counting alone is only half the game in providing for safe, efficient, object copying. Another required piece of the puzzle is what happens when a change is made to a duplicated object. For example, from Figure 21.1, if the program assigns new data to object D, the program must take three actions:

1. Make a copy of Data2 and assign it to D.
2. Decrement Data2's ownership count.
3. Change the original data.

Those are the essential steps in the *copy-on-write* method—an object is copied only when its data changes. Figure 21.2 shows the resulting organization among objects. The original Data2's ownership counter indicates that it is now owned by two objects, B and C. The modified Data2 value, labeled Data2.1, is uniquely addressed by object D.

Figure 21.2
In the copy-on-write method, objects are copied only when their data changes.

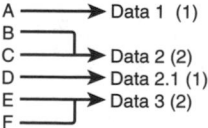

To program reference counting and the copy-on-write method takes some careful thought. Following are three listings that provide a shell you can use to add these features to your own classes. File cow.h (that's "cow" for copy-on-write) declares two classes, TData and TContain, that create objects as illustrated in Figures 21.1 and 21.2. Listing 21.1 shows the first class in the cow.h header file.

LISTING 21.1   COW.H (PARTIAL)

```
#include <string.h>    // Need strcmp(), strcpy(), strlen()

// A class that manages a pointer to data and keeps track
// of the number of owners of this object. This class is
// implemented entirely inline.

class TData {

  friend class TContain;  // Only this class may use TData

private:         // All members are private!

  char *cp;      // Pointer to string
  int owners;    // Number of owners of this TData object

  // Parameterized constructor
  //
  TData(const char *cp_arg): cp(0), owners(1)
  {
    if (cp_arg) {
      cp = new char[strlen(cp_arg) + 1];
      strcpy(cp, cp_arg);
    }
  }

  // Destructor
  //
  ~TData()
  {
    delete[] cp;
  }

  // Return pointer to this object as a copy
  // and increment ownership counter
  //
  TData *GetCopy()
  {
    owners++;
    return this;
  }

  // Put new data into object (copy on write)
  //
  TData *PutData(const char *s)
  {
    /*
```

continues

PART
IV

CH
21

LISTING 21.1 CONTINUED

```
     if this is the only copy
        delete old data
        insert new data
        return this object
     else
        decrease ownership count
        return new object
   */

   if (owners <= 1) {
     delete[] cp;
     cp == NULL;
     if (s) {
       cp = new char[strlen(s) + 1];
       strcpy(cp, s);
     }
     return this;
   } else {
     owners--;
     return new TData(s);
   }
 }

 // Delete this copy of a TData object
 //
 int DeleteCopy()
 {
   return owners--;
 }

 // Return pointer to object data
 //
 const char *GetString() const
 {
   return cp;
 }

 // Return number of owners
 // For testing only; can be deleted
 //
 int NumberOfOwners()
 {
   return owners;
 }

};
```

The TData class provides the basis for objects that are copied only when their data changes. Duplicate copies of TData objects are counted by the objects themselves. The class, which is implemented here entirely inline, differs significantly in two ways from most classes in this book:

- TData declares another class as a friend.
- All TData members are private to the class.

Although it's possible to use a single class, the methods are conceptually easier to understand using separate classes. The TData class is the one that stores the actual data such as the Data1, Data2, and Data3 objects in Figures 21.1 and 21.2. This could be any type of data, but for the sample program, I used a C-style string addressed by a pointer cp of type char*.

The program itself is not permitted to make objects of the TData class, and for that reason, *all* its members including its constructors and destructor are private to the class. Only TData's friend TContain may create TData objects and call TData member functions. It is highly unusual to make all members in a class private, but this is one case where the technique is essential.

To refer to the data in question (in this case a string), and to account for its ownership, the class declares two private data members:

```
char *cp;
int owners;
```

The cp pointer could address an object of any type. Here, as mentioned, it addresses a C-style string of type char*. The integer owners keeps count of how many TContain objects own this TData object. Because TData is totally private, only its friend class TContain (presented later) may construct TData objects.

At a minimum, the TData class requires a constructor and destructor. The constructor initializes a new TData object by setting cp (the data pointer) to NULL and owners to 1:

```
TData(const char *cp_arg): cp(0), owners(1)
```

Because this is a brand new TData object, it is the only such copy that exists, and therefore it has exactly one owner.

Inside the constructor, statements copy the parameter data (cp_arg here) by calling the standard library strlen() and strcpy() functions:

```
if (cp_arg) {
  cp = new char[strlen(cp_arg) + 1];
  strcpy(cp, cp_arg);
}
```

In your own class, do whatever is necessary to copy the object data. Because copying of TData objects is strictly controlled, the class doesn't need an overloaded operator=() function. The TData destructor simply deletes its addressed data:

```
~TData()
{
  delete[] cp;
}
```

There is no need to check this TData object's ownership count because, as explained later, the TData object's owner deletes this object only if the ownership count equals 1. However, if the owners variable is not 1, you can treat this as an internal error:

```
if (owners != 1)
  throw TError("Internal error in ~TData()");
```

PART

IV

CH

21

You might add that to your TData destructor for testing purposes, but this should not be necessary in production code.

One key method in reference counting and the copy-on-write method is a function that returns a copy of a TData object. Regardless of the type of data, the function is implemented as follows:

```
TData *GetCopy()
{
  owners++;
  return this;
}
```

Instead of constructing a new object of type TData, when another class (the friend TContain here) requests a new copy of an object, it calls GetCopy(). This function merely increments the object's owners variable *and returns its own address*. In this way, the TData object keeps a count of how may other objects own this one.

Similarly, when an owning object (such as object C in Figure 21.1) wants to delete a TData object, it calls DeleteCopy() implemented simply as follows:

```
int DeleteCopy()
{
  return owners--;
}
```

Only if the result of DeleteCopy() indicates this is the only such copy, does the owner actually delete the TData object. Together, GetCopy() and DeleteCopy() implement the reference-counting side of the equation. To implement the copy-on-write code requires a bit more effort. In pseudo code, the steps are something like this (printed as a comment in the cow.h header file):

```
if this is the only copy
  delete old data
  insert new data
  return this object
else
  decrease ownership count
  return new object
```

When the program changes the value of a data object, one of two actions occurs. If the data is the only copy, it is first deleted and then the new data is inserted into the TData object. However, if the object has more than one owner, the original data must not be deleted. Instead, its ownership count is decreased, and a new TData object for the new data is created. In C++, the preceding steps are programmed in the TData class's PutData() function:

```
if (owners <= 1) {
  delete[] cp;
  cp == NULL;
  if (s) {
    cp = new char[strlen(s) + 1];
    strcpy(cp, s);
  }
  return this;
```

```
} else {
  owners--;
  return new TData(s);
}
```

You can use this same programming for other types of data with only minor changes. Remove the brackets from delete[] if the addressed data is not an array. Also, do whatever is necessary to copy the addressed information. Here, the program calls strlen() and strcpy() to copy the string addressed by cp. The rest of the code should require no changes to handle any sort of data. In the else clause, owners is decreased and a clone of this TData object is constructed using the new data addressed by parameter s.

Two other TData member functions are optional and are provided here only for test purposes. You probably need some way to get to the data in the TData class. GetString() in this case simply returns the private cp pointer. Both the return value and the function must be const because *all* changes to the addressed data must go through TData's PutData() function to preserve the integrity of the copied objects:

```
const char *GetString() const
{
  return cp;
}
```

Also provided is a function that you may remove. It returns the number of owners for a later test program that shows onscreen the object relationships as illustrated in Figures 21.1 and 21.2:

```
int NumberOfOwners()
{
  return owners;
}
```

Next in the cow.h header file is the TContain class that puts the finishing touches on the reference counting and copy-on-write methods provided by the TData class. Because all members of TData are private, only TContain can create and use TData objects, and in that way, all copies of TData objects are safely encapsulated in a TContain object. Listing 21.2 shows the rest of the cow.h file.

LISTING 21.2   COW.H (PARTIAL)

```
// A class that stores a pointer to a TData object and
// provides for safe copying of TContain objects. This
// class is implemented in cow.cpp.

class TContain {
private:
  TData * tp_data;
public:
  TContain(const char *arg);        // Constructor
  TContain(const TContain &copy);   // Copy constructor
  ~TContain();                      // Destructor
```

continues

LISTING 21.2   CONTINUED

```
  void operator=(const TContain &copy); // Assignment operator
  const char *GetString() const;        // Returns object data
  void PutNewData(const char *s);       // Member function

  // For test puposes only
  //
  int NumTDataOwners() {
    return tp_data->NumberOfOwners();
  }

};
```

TContain is a more normal-looking class. At the program level, to store reference-counted data, statements create TContain objects. Inside TContain, functions use TData members to implement reference counting and the copy-on-write method. Private to the class is a pointer to a TData object declared as

TData * tp_data;

In addition to its data member, the TContain class declares a constructor for the type of data in question (a C-style string in this case), a copy constructor, a destructor, an overloaded assignment operator=() function, and two functions—GetString() and PutNewData()—for retrieving and changing an object's data. You can name these two functions as you like. Finally, strictly for test purposes, TContain has a single inline function, NumTDataOwners(), that you may delete in production code. The other members represent the minimum requirements for implementing reference counting and the copy-on-write method. Listing 21.3, cow.cpp, shows the implementations of the TContain members.

LISTING 21.3   COW.CPP

```
#include "cow.h"        // Need TData and TContain classes

// Constructor
//
TContain::TContain(const char *arg)
{
  tp_data = new TData(arg);
}

// Copy constructor
//
TContain::TContain(const TContain &copy)
{
  tp_data = copy.tp_data->GetCopy();
}

// Destructor
//
TContain::~TContain()
{
  if (tp_data->DeleteCopy() <= 1)
```

```
      delete tp_data;
}

// Assignment operator
//
void TContain::operator=(const TContain &copy)
{
  if (this == &copy) return;         // Can't copy self
  if (tp_data->DeleteCopy() <= 1)    // Delete TData object if
    delete tp_data;                  // any and if unique
  tp_data = copy.tp_data->GetCopy(); // Get TData copy
}

// Return pointer to object's data
//
const char *TContain::GetString() const
{
  return tp_data->GetString();
}

// Assign new data to TContain object
//
void TContain::PutNewData(const char *s)
{
  tp_data = tp_data->PutData(s);
}
```

In your own program, you should be able to use the member functions in the TContain class as listed with few if any changes. The class constructor creates a new TData object, assigning its address to the TContain class's tp_data pointer:

```
tp_data = new TData(arg);
```

The copy constructor is specially written to call the TData class's GetCopy() member function:

```
tp_data = copy.tp_data->GetCopy();
```

Internally, this assigns copy.tp_data to tp_data in the target object, causing both pointers in two TContain objects to address the *same* TData object. However, that object's owners variable is incremented by GetCopy() (see for example objects E and F in Figure 21.1).

When the program destroys a TContain object, it must check whether the TData object it owns is owned by any other TContain objects. If so, that TData object must not be disturbed. This is the reference-counting side of the equation, implemented by the TContain destructor:

```
if (tp_data->DeleteCopy() <= 1)
  delete tp_data;
```

Only if calling TData::DeleteCopy() returns a value less than or equal to 1 is tp_data actually deleted. This preserves the TData object if it is owned by other TContain objects.

The overloaded `operator=()` assignment function requires a bit more programming. `TContain` implements this function using these statements:

```
if (this == &copy) return;
if (tp_data->DeleteCopy() <= 1)
  delete tp_data;
tp_data = copy.tp_data->GetCopy();
```

You've seen the first step many times in this book. It ignores any requests to copy an object to itself. The second statement uses the same code as in the `TContain` destructor. This deletes the addressed `TData` object only if calling `DeleteCopy()` indicates that it is owned by no other `TContain` objects. Finally, `GetCopy()` creates a copy of the `TData` object being copied. However, as explained, calling `GetCopy()` merely increments the `TData` object's owners count, and as a consequence, no data is duplicated.

Function `PutData()` implements the copy-on-write method simply by calling `TData`'s `PutData()` member function:

```
tp_data = tp_data->PutData(s);
```

This causes the `TData` object to be copied, and the new data inserted in that copy. If the original copy had only one owner, it is deleted. Finally in the `TContain` class, function `GetString()` provides a way to get to the data in the `TData` object. Your own program needs a similar function, but you can name it differently.

With the cow.cpp module and header file, all the elements to implement reference counting and the copy-on-write method are in place. Listing 21.4, cowdemo.cpp, tests the `TData` and `TContain` classes. To save space here, I deleted all but a few of the tests in the program. I also deleted the local functions that merely pause for you to press Enter and display object data for viewing the results of the tests. The complete source file is, of course, in the file on the CD-ROM.

LISTING 21.4   COWDEMO.CPP

```
#include <iostream.h>
#include "cow.h"          // Copy-on-write classes

#define BUFSIZE 256
char buffer[BUFSIZE];     // Temporary input buffer

// Local function prototypes
//
void pause(const char *s);
void show(const char *s, TContain *tp);
void show_objects();

// Pointers to test TContain objects
//
TContain *A, *B, *C, *D, *E, *F;

int main()
{
  pause("1: Construct object A");
```

```
    A = new TContain("aaaa");
    show_objects();

    pause("2: Construct object B from existing object A");
    B = new TContain(*A);
    show_objects();

    pause("3: Construct object C from existing object B");
    C = new TContain(*B);
    show_objects();

    pause("4: Change data in object B");
    B->PutNewData("DDDD");
    show_objects();

    pause("9: Create new object F from B");
    F = new TContain(*B);
    show_objects();
...
    pause("99: Delete object C");
    delete C; C = NULL;
    show_objects();

    return 0;
}
```

Enter the following commands to compile and run the cow.cpp module and cowdemo.cpp test program:

```
$ g++ -c cow.cpp
$ g++ cowdemo.cpp cow.o
$ ./a.out
```

Press Enter to run each test, and observe the results. (You might want to simultaneously view a copy of the program's source code to see the statements executed to produce each test.) The first four tests demonstrate reference counting and the copy-on-write method. The first two tests construct two TContain objects, A and B, with the same TData objects. Test 3 then executes the following statement:

```
C = new TContain(*B);
```

That calls the TContain copy constructor to replicate B. Onscreen, you see the results of the test:

```
3: Construct object C from existing object B
object A
 string ............: aaaa
 num data owners....: 3
object B
 string ............: aaaa
 num data owners....: 3
object C
 string ............: aaaa
 num data owners....: 3
```

There are now three TContain objects, A, B, and C. Each owns the *same* TData object. That object's reference counter equals 3, indicating that three objects own the string "aaaa," but only one copy of that string exists in memory. The test indicates that the reference-counting side of the technique is working. To test the copy-on-write method, test 4 changes the data in object B, using this statement:

```
B->PutNewData("bbbb");
```

Test 4's results show what happens when the data in one of the three objects is changed:

```
4: Change data in object B
object A
 string ............: aaaa
 num data owners....: 2
object B
 string ............: bbbb
 num data owners....: 1
object C
 string ............: aaaa
 num data owners....: 2
```

Now, objects A and C own the TData object with the string "aaaa," and therefore that TData object's owners counter now equals 2. Object B's data was changed, and therefore a unique copy of it exists in memory.

Other tests in the program put the TContain copy constructor and assignment operator=() function through some additional paces. Finally, the program deletes each object. As it does that, observe onscreen how the reference counts are decremented. Only when the TData objects' counts equal 1 are those objects actually deleted.

NAMESPACES

As of this writing, namespaces and the using reserved word are not yet implemented in GNU C++. However, in the path src/c21 on the CD-ROM is a test program, namespace.cpp, that you can try to compile and run. At present, the compiler chokes on this program, so it isn't listed or discussed here.

ODDS AND ENDS

Even in a book this size, some subjects don't seem to fit into any specific categories. Following are some topics and techniques that you might not need often, but then again, perhaps you'll find one of the following odds and ends essential to your project.

EXPLICIT CONSTRUCTORS

Use the explicit reserved word to force calls to a required class constructor. This can solve a problem that occurs when C++ implicitly converts objects into a class type. For example, consider the common class in Listing 21.5, implicit.cpp.

LISTING 21.5   IMPLICIT.CPP

```cpp
#include <iostream.h>
#include <stdlib.h>      // Need atoi()

class TAnyClass {
private:
  int value;
public:
  TAnyClass(int n) { value = n; }
  TAnyClass(const char *ns) { value = atoi(ns); }
  int GetValue() { return value; }
};

int main()
{
  TAnyClass v1 = 123;
  TAnyClass v2 = "96";
  cout << "v1 == " << v1.GetValue() << endl;
  cout << "v2 == " << v2.GetValue() << endl;
  return 0;
}
```

TAnyClass declares two constructors, one that requires an int argument and another that requires a char pointer to a NULL-terminated string. Each constructor assigns its parameter to the private value data member. (For simplicity, the class is implemented entirely inline.) The alternate constructor calls the standard atoi() function declared in stdlib.h to convert its string parameter to an integer. The main program declares two variables of type TAnyClass and then displays their values by calling the class's GetValue() member function.

In the two statements in main() that construct variables v1 and v2, the values 123 and "96" are *implicitly* converted into objects of their class types so that the assignment statements compile. To *explicitly* state that such values must only be class objects, and thus prevent the implicit conversions, preface the constructors with the reserved word explicit. Listing 21.6, explicit.cpp, shows the revised class and gives examples of allowable declarations of TAnyClass objects.

LISTING 21.6   EXPLICIT.CPP

```cpp
#include <iostream.h>
#include <stdlib.h>      // Need atoi()

class TAnyClass {
private:
  int value;
public:
  explicit TAnyClass(int n) { value = n; }
  explicit TAnyClass(const char *ns) { value = atoi(ns); }
  int GetValue() { return value; }
};
```

PART

IV

CH

21

continues

LISTING 21.6   CONTINUED

```
int main()
{
  TAnyClass v1 = TAnyClass(123);
  TAnyClass v2 = TAnyClass("987");
  TAnyClass v3(456);
  TAnyClass v4("654");
  cout << "v1 == " << v1.GetValue() << endl;
  cout << "v2 == " << v2.GetValue() << endl;
  cout << "v3 == " << v3.GetValue() << endl;
  cout << "v4 == " << v4.GetValue() << endl;
  return 0;
}
```

Using the revised class, because of the explicit constructors, any attempts you make to create objects using statements such as these (taken from Listing 21.5, implicit.cpp) now produce errors:

```
TAnyClass v1 = 123;   // ???
TAnyClass v2 = "96";  // ???
```

Compiling the program with statements such as those causes GNU C++ to issue these error messages:

```
explicit.cpp: In function 'int main()':
explicit.cpp:25: conversion from 'int' to
➡ non-scalar type 'TAnyClass' requested
explicit.cpp:26: conversion from 'char[3]'
➡ to non-scalar type 'TAnyClass' requested
```

Because the TAnyClass constructors are explicit, C++ no longer allows values such as 123 and "96" to be implicitly converted to TAnyClass objects for assigning to other TAnyClass objects or for use in constructing new objects.

> **Tip**
>
> In practice, classes with explicit constructors such as those in this section probably also need copy constructors and operator=() functions.

MUTABLE DATA MEMBERS

To prevent a class member function from modifying the value of a data member in that class (or one inherited from an ancestor class), declare the function const like this:

```
class TAnyClass {
...
  int x;
  int GetValue() const { return x; }
};
```

If any statement in GetValue() attempts to change x, the compiler issues an error message. However, the const designation makes *all* data members in the class unchangeable. This can be troublesome in designing functions that need to change some data but designate other values as hands off. Listing 21.7, constant.cpp, demonstrates the basic problem.

LISTING 21.7   CONSTANT.CPP

```cpp
#include <iostream.h>

class TAnyClass {
private:
  int value;
  long counter;
public:
  TAnyClass(int arg): value(arg), counter(0) { }
  int GetValue() /*const*/ {
    counter++;  // ???
    return value;
  }
  int GetCounter() const { return counter; }
};

int main()
{
  TAnyClass v1(123);
  cout << "v1 value   == " << v1.GetValue() << endl;
  cout << "v1 counter == " << v1.GetCounter() << endl;
  return 0;
}
```

Class TAnyClass declares two data members, an integer value, and a long counter. We want member function GetValue() to return the integer and guarantee that its value isn't changed by calling that function. However, to keep track of how many times GetValue() is called, we want the function also to increment counter. If you remove the comment delimiters from const in the GetValue() declaration, compiling the program causes GNU C++ to complain with the following error message:

```
$ g++ constant.cpp constant.cpp:
In method 'int TAnyClass::GetValue() const':
constant.cpp:21: increment of read-only member 'TAnyClass::counter'
```

Listing 21.8, mutable.cpp, makes counter *mutable* to allow changes to it even in const functions such as GetValue().

LISTING 21.8   MUTABLE.CPP

```cpp
#include <iostream.h>

class TAnyClass {
private:
  int value;
  mutable long counter;
public:
  TAnyClass(int arg): value(arg), counter(0) { }
  int GetValue() const {
    counter++;
    return value;
```

PART
IV

CH
21

continues

LISTING 21.8 CONTINUED

```
  }
  int GetCounter() const { return counter; }
};

int main()
{
  TAnyClass v1(123);
  cout << "v1 value   == " << v1.GetValue() << endl;
  cout << "v1 counter == " << v1.GetCounter() << endl;
  return 0;
}
```

Now that counter is mutable, GetValue() can be declared const but still be permitted to change the value of counter. This can be important in cases where you need to pass a const class object to another function that calls GetValue()—a copy constructor, for example. In such cases, stating that counter is mutable overrides the compiler's objections even for const objects. Be sure to understand, however, that the misuse of mutable effectively defeats the purpose of using constant objects in the first place—to guard against unexpected changes to objects as a result of a function call.

USING typename

Use the typename reserved word in a template to define a placeholder for a data type. For example, Listing 21.9, typename.cpp, declares a template function that returns the maximum of two values of any type.

LISTING 21.9 TYPENAME.CPP

```
#include <iostream.h>

//template <class T> T max(T a, T b)

template <typename T> T max(T a, T b)
{
  if (a > b)
    return a;
  else
    return b;
}

int main()
{
  int v1 = 123;
  int v2 = 321;
  cout << "max(123, 321) == " << max(v1, v2) << endl;
  return 0;
}
```

Above the template declaration is a comment that shows the more common way to create a data type placeholder. Normally, templates are declared like this:

```
template <class T> T max(T a, T b)
```

If like many programmers you find the use of the word class here disconcerting, you can use typename instead:

```
template <typename T> T max(T a, T b)
```

However, except for being a little clearer, there seems to be no advantage of using typename in place of class. Use

POINTERS TO MEMBER FUNCTIONS

You can address class member functions with pointers, but not in the same way as conventional functions. This is because a member function is called in reference to an object, for which the function receives a this pointer. To address a member function with a pointer therefore requires new techniques.

Note

A static function is an exception to this rule—it does not refer to an object of its class, and therefore, it does not receive a this pointer.

Because a member function is bound to its class name, declaring the pointer requires using the function type *and* class name. For example, for a class TAnyClass, you can declare a pointer to one of its member functions by using the following declaration:

```
double (TAnyClass::*myfnptr)();
```

This states that myfnptr addresses a TAnyClass member function that declares no parameters and returns a value of type double. It doesn't specify which function exactly, only that the function must have these characteristics. To declare myfnptr as a pointer to a class member function that returns void and declares an int parameter, use a declaration such as this:

```
void (TAnyClass::*myfnptr)(int);
```

Again, which member function isn't specified, only that it must conform to the stated design. It is still necessary to create an object of the class and to assign the address of a class member of the appropriate form to the pointer. Listing 21.10, mfnptr.cpp, shows the basic steps required to define and use pointers to member functions.

LISTING 21.10   MFNPTR.CPP

```
#include <iostream.h>
#include <iomanip.h>    // Need output stream manipulators

class TAnyClass {
private:
  int value;
```

continues

LISTING 21.10   CONTINUED

```
public:
  TAnyClass(): value(0) { }
  int GetValue() { return ++value; }
};

// Declare pointer to member function

int (TAnyClass::*myfnptr)();

void main()
{
  int i;
  TAnyClass object;

  cout << "Call GetValue the normal way:" << endl;
  for (i = 0; i < 9; i++)
    cout << setw(8) << dec << object.GetValue();
  cout << endl;
  cout << "Call GetValue using a pointer" << endl;
  myfnptr = &TAnyClass::GetValue;
  for (i = 0; i < 9; i++)
    cout << setw(8) << dec << (object.*myfnptr)();
  cout << endl;
  cout << "Use dynamic instance and pointer" << endl;
  TAnyClass *fp = new TAnyClass(object);
  for (i = 0; i < 9; i++)
    cout << setw(8) << dec << (fp->*myfnptr)();
  cout << endl;
}
```

The single-line declaration following TAnyClass states that myfnptr is a pointer to a TAnyClass member function that returns no value and declares one int parameter. The program may assign the address of any such matching function to the pointer, and then use it to call that function. For example, the test programming in main() constructs an object of type TAnyClass and then calls the GetValue() member function by using the following expression:

```
object.GetValue()
```

To call that same function using a pointer, the program assigns to myfnptr the address of the GetValue() member function in TAnyClass:

```
myfnptr = &TAnyClass::GetValue;
```

Alternatively, you may declare and initialize a member function pointer by using a single statement such as

```
int (TAnyClass::*myfnptr)() = &TAnyClass::GetValue;
```

Be sure not to follow the function name with parentheses. You merely want to refer to the function by name, not to call it. Either way, to use the pointer, follow these two rules:

1. Refer to an object of the class (unless the function is static).

2. Surround the function call with parentheses.

If `data` is an `int` variable, and `object` is a `TAnyClass` object, the following statement copies to `data` the result returned by `GetValue()` using a member function pointer:

```
int data = (object.*myfnptr)();
```

The period and asterisk is one C++ symbol, called the *pointer-to-member operator*. It is used to dereference a member function pointer for a class object. The parentheses in the expression `(object.*myfnptr)` are necessary because the function-call operator—a set of empty parentheses—has higher precedence than the pointer-to-member operator. The preceding statement is equivalent to the following:

```
int data = object.GetValue();
```

You can also call member functions by using a pointer for objects themselves addressed by pointers. For example, in the sample program, a statement assigns to pointer `fp` the address of a `TAnyClass` object created by the `new` operator:

```
TAnyClass *fp = new TAnyClass(object);
```

Following this, the next expression calls `GetValue()` by using the member function pointer:

```
(fp->*myfnptr)();
```

The triple-character symbol `->*` is a variation of the pointer-to-member operator. Again, extra parentheses are needed because `()` has higher precedence than `->*`. The preceding statement is equivalent to this:

```
fp->GetValue();
```

STATIC MEMBER FUNCTIONS

Chapter 14, "Investing in Inheritance," introduces static members. In brief, a static data member exists for all objects of a class, as compared to a nonstatic member that is allocated space in every class object. Member functions may also be static. Unlike a nonstatic member function, a static function is not called in reference to an object but solely in reference to the class. This can be useful for designing functions that initialize a value or perform some other action that affects all subsequently constructed objects. To declare a static member function, precede its prototype with the reserved word `static`:

```
class TAnyClass {
public:
  static void GlobalInit();
...
};
```

Note	Static member functions may not be virtual.

Implement the static member function as you do others, but do not repeat the static designation:

```
void TAnyClass::GlobalInit()
{
// ... statements to perform
}
```

The static member function may perform any actions, but because it is not called in reference to a class object, statements in the function may not refer to nonstatic data members. Such members exist only in class objects, and therefore, they simply aren't available to the static function. However, the function may use static data members, and in fact, it is typical for a static member function to initialize static data members for a class. Listing 21.11, static.cpp, demonstrates one common way to use static data and function members.

LISTING 21.11   STATIC.CPP

```cpp
#include <iostream.h>
#include <iomanip.h>  // Need setw()

#define BUFSIZE 64

// A class with static data and function members
//
class TAnyClass {
private:
  static char buffer[BUFSIZE];
public:
  TAnyClass() { }
  static void InitBuffer();
  void DisplayBuffer(const char *msg);
  void FillBuffer(char byte);
};

// Actual buffer definition. This would usually appear
// in another module linked to the program.
//
char TAnyClass::buffer[BUFSIZE];

int main()
{
  TAnyClass objectA, objectB, objectC;
  TAnyClass::InitBuffer();
  objectA.DisplayBuffer("Object A buffer");
  objectA.FillBuffer(2);
  objectB.DisplayBuffer("Object B buffer");
  objectB.FillBuffer(3);
  objectC.DisplayBuffer("Object C buffer");
  return 0;
}
```

```
// Static function initializes the buffer
void TAnyClass::InitBuffer()
{
  for (int i = 0; i < BUFSIZE; i++)
    buffer[i] = i;
}

// Non static function called in reference to object
void TAnyClass::DisplayBuffer(const char *msg)
{
  cout << msg << endl;
  for (int i = 0; i < BUFSIZE; i++)
    cout << setw(4) << (int)buffer[i];
  cout << endl;
}

// Fill buffer with indicated value
void TAnyClass::FillBuffer(char byte)
{
  for (int i = 0; i < BUFSIZE; i++)
    buffer[i] = byte;
}
```

The test program shows how to create a static buffer for use in all objects of a specific class. The program's class, TAnyClass, declares two static members:

```
static char buffer[BUFSIZE];
static void InitBuffer();
```

Because buffer is private to the class, only class member functions may refer to it. Function InitBuffer(), also declared static, fills the buffer with sequential values. Function FillBuffer() fills the buffer with a value passed as an argument. We don't want the large buffer to be inside every object—instead, we want all objects of TAnyClass to refer to the *same* buffer. This is the prime purpose of using static members. To demonstrate how this works, the test program constructs three TAnyClass objects:

```
AnyClass objectA, objectB, objectC;
```

Next, the static InitBuffer() function is called. Because it is static, it is called in reference to the class, not to any specific object of the class:

```
TAnyClass::InitBuffer();
```

That statement could appear in another location—it doesn't have to follow the construction of the three objects. To demonstrate that all three objects use the same buffer, the program displays the buffer's initial contents and then fills it with the value 2:

```
objectA.DisplayBuffer("Object A buffer");
objectA.FillBuffer(2);
```

Even though FillBuffer() is called in reference to objectA, calling DisplayBuffer() for a different object displays all 2s:

```
objectB.DisplayBuffer("Object B buffer");
```

PART

IV

CH

21

Likewise, filling the buffer by calling `FillBuffer()` for `objectB`, but then calling `DisplayBuffer()` for `objectC`, proves that the objects are all sharing the same buffer:

```
objectB.FillBuffer(3);
objectC.DisplayBuffer("Object C buffer");
```

Because the buffer itself is static, it must be defined somewhere in the program where the linker can find it. In this case, the following statement creates the actual buffer:

```
char TAnyClass::buffer[BUFSIZE];
```

This definition must match the static declaration in the class. Typically, the preceding definition and static member function `InitBuffer()` are in a separate module linked to the program. Because the buffer is a private member of the class, even though it is declared as a global variable, its use is strictly controlled through the class. This is a good way to share data among class objects without giving the rest of the program free access to that data.

> **Tip**
>
> Static member functions cannot be declared `const` because they are not called in reference to class objects.

PERSISTENT OBJECTS

You might occasionally need to store an object at a specific location, perhaps in a global buffer. Such objects are said to *persist* beyond the scope of their declarations, and for that reason they are sometimes called *persistent objects*. The technique for creating persistent objects relies on overloading the `new` operator.

Listing 21.12, persist.cpp, demonstrates how to store an object at a specific address—in this case, inside a global array. The program also shows how a statement can call a destructor—a special allowance that C++ makes because, when taking over an object's construction, it might be necessary to destroy an object through its destructor but not call `delete` to actually dispose of that object's memory.

LISTING 21.12   PERSIST.CPP

```cpp
#include <iostream.h>

class TPersist {
private:
  int x, y;
public:
  TPersist(int a, int b): x(a), y(b) { } // Constructor
  ~TPersist() { x = 0; y = 0; }  // Destructor
  void *operator new(size_t, void *p) { return p; }
  friend ostream& operator<< (ostream &os, TPersist &p);
};

// Create storage for TPersist buffers
//
```

```
char buffer[sizeof(TPersist)];

int main()
{
  TPersist *p = new(buffer) TPersist(10, 20);
  cout << *p << endl;
  cout << "Address of buffer == " << &buffer << endl;
  cout << "Address of *p      == " << &(*p) << endl;
  p->~TPersist();  // Explicit call to destructor
  // p->TPersist::~TPersist();  // For older compilers
  cout << "After calling destructor:" << endl;
  cout << *p << endl;
  return 0;
}

ostream& operator<< (ostream& os, TPersist &p)
{
  os << "x == " << p.x << ", y == " << p.y;
  return os;
}
```

Class TPersist overloads the new operator in an unusual way. Rather than allocate memory to an object pointer, the overloaded operator simply returns its void pointer parameter p. To construct an object using new, and store that object in a known location, the main program executes the following statement:

```
TPersist *p = new(buffer) TPersist(10, 20);
```

The expression new(buffer) calls the overloaded new operator for TPersist and passes the address of buffer (an array of char) as an argument. Because the overloaded operator simply returns that address, this strange-looking statement in effect assigns buffer's address to p and also calls the TPersist constructor to initialize the newly allocated object stored inside the buffer.

When you compile and run the program, it displays the address of the object in two ways and also shows the object's x and y values before and after its class destructor is called:

```
$ g++ persist.cpp
$ ./a.out
x == 10, y == 20
Address of buffer == 0x8049c68
Address of *p      == 0x8049c68
After calling destructor:
x == 0, y == 0
```

The two addresses are the same, proving that the TPersist object is indeed inside the program's own buffer. Because of that, it would be a mistake to delete the object. However, some means must be provided to call a destructor to clean up objects no longer needed. To do this, C++ permits the program to execute a statement such as

```
p->~TPersist();
```

An explicit destructor call is unusual and should be employed only when it isn't possible to delete an object. Older compilers may require you to specify the class name as follows (this also works with newer GNU C++ releases). Use this form for the best portability:

```
p->TPersist::~TPersist();
```

NESTED CLASS DECLARATIONS

By nesting certain kinds of declarations in classes, you can provide a class with data types that are determined solely by the class. A class can nest a typedef symbol, a struct, or even another class. Such declarations are sometimes useful for providing items that are intimately tied to the class's internal design. For example, using a nested typedef declaration, you can create a class that keeps track of how many objects of its type exist at any one time in a program—a device that might be useful for debugging.

Listing 21.13, objcount.cpp, demonstrates how to create an automatic object counter by exporting a data type from the class.

LISTING 21.13   OBJCOUNT.CPP

```cpp
#include <iostream.h>

class TAnyClass {
private:
  typedef int CLASS_COUNTER;
  static CLASS_COUNTER ClassCount;
  static int GetCount() { return ClassCount; }
public:
  TAnyClass() { ClassCount++; }   // Constructor
 ~TAnyClass() { ClassCount--; }   // Destructor
  static void ShowCount();
};

// Define static member
//
TAnyClass::CLASS_COUNTER TAnyClass::ClassCount;

TAnyClass globalObject;

int main()
{
  cout << "On entry to program" << endl;
  TAnyClass::ShowCount();

  TAnyClass localObject;
  cout << "After constructing one object" << endl;
  TAnyClass::ShowCount();

  TAnyClass objectA, objectB, objectC;
  cout << "After constructing three objects" << endl;
  TAnyClass::ShowCount();

  TAnyClass * pointer = new TAnyClass;
  cout << "After creating a dynamic object" << endl;
```

```
    TAnyClass::ShowCount();
    delete pointer;
    cout << "After deleting the dynamic object" << endl;
    TAnyClass::ShowCount();

    return 0;
}

void TAnyClass::ShowCount()
{
    cout << "Number of objects == " << TAnyClass::GetCount();
    cout << endl;
}
```

The sample program uses static members to store a count of the objects of type TAnyClass in existence at any one time. To keep track of this count, the class constructor increments the static ClassCount variable. The class destructor decreases this value. To export the counter's type, the class nests the typedef declaration:

```
typedef int CLASS_COUNTER;
static CLASS_COUNTER ClassCount;
```

In this way, the class itself determines the type of the static ClassCounter variable. Although this is a simple example, it might be used to change the type from int to long—or even to a class object—without requiring any changes except to the preceding declaration. Because the ClassCounter is static, it must be defined somewhere in the program. The test program defines the variable like this:

```
TAnyClass::CLASS_COUNTER TAnyClass::ClassCount;
```

The importance of this programming is that ClassCount's type is hidden inside TAnyClass. Thus, this variable can be declared without the program having any specific knowledge of its type. When you compile and run the program, the rest of the test statements show how many TAnyClass objects exist at various stages.

Complex nested declarations are also possible. A class can declare an inner struct like this:

```
class TAnyClass {
public:
  struct ClassStruct {
    int x, y;
  };
};
```

The struct is exported by the class and must therefore be used in reference to the class. For example, the program could define an object of type ClassStruct by using a statement such as

```
TAnyClass:ClassStruct structure;
```

Statements as follows refer to the struct's x and y members:

```
structure.x = 1;
cout << "y == " << structure.y << endl;
```

It's common to use this technique to provide the design of an object from inside a class. Listing 21.14, nest.cpp, demonstrates the basic technique of a class that exports the type of another class for use in the program.

LISTING 21.14   NEST.CPP

```
#include <iostream.h>

class TAnyClass {
public:
  class TOtherClass {
  private:
    int x, y;
  public:
    TOtherClass(int x_arg, int y_arg): x(x_arg), y(y_arg) { }
    int Getx() { return x; }
    int Gety() { return y; }
  };
};

int main()
{
  TAnyClass::TOtherClass object(10, 20);
  cout << "x == " << object.Getx() << endl;
  cout << "y == " << object.Gety() << endl;
  return 0;
}
```

The sample program declares TAnyClass with only a single member—an exported class of type TOtherClass. (In practice, TAnyClass would probably declare its own constructors, destructor, data members, and member functions.) The nested TOtherClass has two private integer variables, a constructor that initializes those data members, and two member functions that return the private data values.

The nested class is a public member of TAnyClass so that statements in the program can refer to both classes. It's also possible to nest classes in protected and private sections, and, in fact, this is useful in complex class hierarchies that export class declarations for use only in that class and in derived classes.

To create an object of type TOtherClass, the program uses the following statement:

```
TAnyClass::TOtherClass object(10, 20);
```

The object is of type TOtherClass, not TAnyClass. Although it's possible to construct an object of the outer class as follows, it's important to realize that this does *not* create an object of TOtherClass:

```
TAnyClass value;
```

TAnyClass exports the TOtherClass *class declaration*; it does not contain an object of that type. Although the preceding statement compiles, there's nothing in this case to do with the resulting object because TAnyClass declares no other members.

SUMMARY

This chapter explained how to create classes that efficiently provide for duplicated data by using reference counting and the copy-on-write method. The chapter also detailed a number of C++ odds and ends such as explicit constructors, mutable data members, pointers to member functions, static member functions, persistent objects, and nested class declarations.

For more information on subjects introduced in this chapter, turn to the following chapters:

- Chapter 13, "Creating and Destroying Objects"
- Chapter 14, "Investing in Inheritance"

PART

IV

CH

21

PART V

C++ CLASS LIBRARIES

## CHAPTER 22

MASTERING THE STANDARD string CLASS

It seems that everybody and their uncles' brothers (plus a certain computer-book author) have written their own string class at one time or another. But finally, GNU C++ and other ANSI C++ compilers provide a standard string class template that does away with the many different versions of the string class that have floated around the networks.

This chapter introduces the standard string class, provided as a template so that it can use characters of different types and sizes. Standard strings are safer and easier to use than common C-style null-terminated strings addressed with pointers. Because you can easily convert between null-terminated strings and string objects, there's no reason not to use this newer type of string in C++ programs.

INTRODUCING string TEMPLATES

To use standard strings, simply include the string header file without the .h suffix:

```
#include <string>
```

That directive also includes standard C-style string functions such as strcpy() defined in string.h. To use string-class *objects* it's important not to type the .h suffix—you may, however, include both headers if you want. After including the string header file, create string objects as follows:

```
string mystring;  // Empty string
string anystring = "Program Title";
```

There are many other ways to construct string objects—I show numerous examples throughout this chapter. Memory for a string's characters is allocated internally using new, so you don't have to create string objects using pointers. However, you certainly may do so using a statement such as

```
string *sp = new string("Dynamic duo");
cout << *sp << endl;
delete sp;
```

The first statement allocates dynamic memory to a string object addressed by pointer sp and stores the quoted text also in memory. After displaying the string, the final statement deletes the object. If you simply create strings as variables, however, the string class takes care of deleting the string's character data.

Like common C-style strings, a C++ string object is a sequence of characters, individually accessible using the indexing operator. To display a single character from a string, you can use statements such as

```
string s = "abcdefghijklmnopqrstuvwxyz";
cout << "10th character == " << s[9] << endl;
```

Likewise, you can assign individual characters to a string by using a statement such as this:

```
s[12] = 'M';
cout << s << endl;
```

If you are following along, the second statement shows that the assignment changes lower-case m to M in the alphabet string object stored in s. This is an excellent example of how operator overloading can simplify complex programming. Although the assignment to s[12] appears to access a simple array of characters, it actually calls the string class's overloaded operator[]() function to perform the assignment. Consequently, this and other statements can be made to work with strings of any type regardless of the nature of their internal characters and memory storage details.

So, why not just use arrays of char? That's a good question, and many C++ programmers continue to use C-style null-terminated strings along with standard string-library functions. However, the C++ string class provides several advantages:

- The string class throws exceptions for many kinds of errors such as attempting to access characters beyond the length of the string.

- string objects automatically resize themselves as needed to accommodate longer or shorter string assignments.

- string objects can use any size characters, including so-called *wide characters*. Operations on string objects are independent of the size and type of characters in a string. (As of this writing, however, wide strings of type wstring are not defined in GNU C++.)

- string objects use reference counting and the copy-on-write method to help prevent duplicate strings from wasting memory.

- Searching for substrings, replacing portions of strings, inserting text into strings, and performing many other common string operations are easily done by calling string-class member functions.

Note

Internally, the string class is merely a typedef declaration of the basic_string template class. For details on this class, hunt for the bastring.h header file, and if you have installed the libg++ source files, the class's implementation in bastring.cc. See the Web and FTP sites listed in Appendix C for where to find this and other source files. On my system, I found these files in the path:

```
/usr/src/redhat/SOURCES/libg++-2.7.2/libstdc++/std.
```

DECLARING string OBJECTS

One advantage of using the string class is that it provides many ways to construct string objects. I show most of the common methods in this section. But feel free to try others. The string class provides numerous constructors for creating strings in various ways. You've already seen one of the simplest methods. Here are some more:

```
#include <string>
...
string s1("Stringing in the rain");
string s2 = "Any string of yours is a string of mine.";
string s3(s1);
```

These examples show three of the most common methods for constructing string objects. String s1 is created using a literal string in parentheses. String s2 uses an assignment, but is otherwise created in the same way. String s3 is created using a copy of s1. However, because the string class uses reference counting, only one copy of the string data is stored in memory for both string objects s1 and s3. Listing 22.1, sdeclare.cpp, demonstrates some other ways to construct string objects.

LISTING 22.1 SDECLARE.CPP

```
#include <iostream>
#include <string>
#include <vector>

void ShowString(const char* s, const string& sr);

string sEmpty;
string sFromLiteral("Stringing in the rain");
string sFromString(sFromLiteral);
string sFromAssign = "A string in time saves mine";
string sFilled(40, '#');
string sPartial(sFromAssign, 9, 7);
char buffer[5] = { 'a', 'b', 'c', 'd', 'e' };
string sFromPointers(buffer + 1, buffer + 5);

vector<char> cVector(buffer, buffer + 5);
string sFromIterators(cVector.begin(), cVector.end());

int main()
{
  ShowString("sEmpty", sEmpty);
  ShowString("sFromConst", sFromLiteral);
  ShowString("sFromString", sFromString);
  ShowString("sFromAssign", sFromAssign);
  ShowString("sFilled", sFilled);
  ShowString("sPartial", sPartial);
  ShowString("sFromPointers", sFromPointers);
  ShowString("sFromIterators", sFromIterators);
  return 0;
}

void ShowString(const char* s, const string& sr)
{
  cout << s << " : " << sr << endl;
  cout << " length:"   << sr.length();
  cout << " size:"     << sr.size();
  cout << " capacity:" << sr.capacity();
  cout << endl;
}
```

Compile and run the test program to see the results of several test strings (to save space, I show only some of the output statements here):

```
$ g++ sdeclare.cpp
$ ./a.out
sEmpty :
```

```
length:0 size:0 capacity:0
sFromConst : Stringing in the rain
length:21 size:21 capacity:32
...
sFilled : ######################################
length:40 size:40 capacity:64
sPartial : in time
length:7 size:7 capacity:16
```

To fill a string with a specific character, use a statement such as

```
string sFilled(40, '#');
```

That creates a 40-character string filled with hatch mark characters. (Some people call them *pound signs*. Savvy Linux gurus know them as Klingon warships.) The string's *capacity* is 64 (see the preceding output). This is because the string class attempts to allocate space efficiently without waste. The resulting string in this example could grow by another 24 characters before a new memory allocation is required.

To explicitly reserve extra space in a string, you are supposed to be able to supply a length argument as in this statement:

```
string sReserve("Short and Sweet", 64);
```

Although this works, the leftover space in the string has whatever byte values happen to be at this location in memory. In other words, the preceding statement sets the string's length, size, and capacity to 64. Probably, this is not the effect you want. As a workaround, you can assign null characters to a string object of the desired capacity:

```
string sReserve(64, '\0');
```

You can also specify a range of characters to use for initializing a new string object created with a statement such as the following:

```
string sFromAssign = "A string in time saves mine";
...
string sPartial(sFromAssign, 9, 7);
```

That creates sPartial using seven characters beginning with the character at sFromAssign[9]. The result in this example is a string equal to "in time."

You can also use iterators to create string objects. (Chapter 23, "Using the Standard Template Library (STL)," explains more about iterators.) There are two basic forms of this kind of string object. The first constructs a string from a character buffer, or from a portion of a buffer:

```
char buffer[5] = { 'a', 'b', 'c', 'd', 'e' };
string sFromPointers(buffer + 1, buffer + 5);
```

The expressions buffer + 1 and buffer + 5 are known as *iterators* (here in the form of char* pointers). The two expressions define the range of characters to use in the original buffer for initializing the string object. This provides one way to convert arrays of characters to string objects. In this case, the resulting string, "bcde," begins with the second character in buffer. Note that buffer + 5 is one *plus* the last index position in buffer. This is called the *past-the-end* value.

You can also use iterator functions such as provided by a standard template library container class. For example, the following constructs a string object using a vector of characters, initialized from the preceding buffer:

```
vector<char> cVector(buffer, buffer + 5);
string sFromIterators(cVector.begin(), cVector.end());
```

This is an excruciatingly complex method for constructing a simple string object, but it demonstrates the wide variety of methods available. Whatever your source of character data, you can probably pass it to the string class and receive a properly constructed object in return. (See Chapter 24, "Building Standard Containers," for information about iterators and standard template container classes such as vector.)

READING AND WRITING string OBJECTS

Most well-designed C++ classes provide input and output services, and the string class is no exception. Use I/O stream statements to read and write string objects. For example, the following statements write a string to the standard output:

```
string s("Write me right out");
cout << s << endl;
```

Similar statements prompt users to input strings:

```
cout << "Enter a string: ";
cin >> s;
```

However, the second statement reads only the first word entered because whitespace (blanks and tabs, for example) terminate the input. To read an entire string including blanks and other whitespace, use the getline() function provided by including the string header. Just call the function directly—it is not a class member function. For example, these statements read one string from the standard input into a string object:

```
string s;
getline(cin, s, '\n');
```

Specify three arguments to getline(): an istream object reference (cin in this example), a string object such as s, and the character that should terminate input (a newline control here). Listing 22.2, rstrings.cpp, shows how to use this technique to read a text file using a string object.

LISTING 22.2   RSTRINGS.CPP

```
#include <iostream.h>
#include <fstream.h>
#include <string>

int main(int argc, char *argv[])
{
  string s;  // String object

  if (argc <= 1) {
    cerr << "Error: filename missing" << endl;
```

```
    exit(1);
  }
  ifstream ifs(argv[1], ios::in);
  if (!ifs) {
    cerr << "Error: unable to open " << argv[1] << endl;
    exit(2);
  }

  while (ifs.good()) {
    getline(ifs, s, '\n');
    cout << s << endl;
  }

  ifs.close();
  return 0;
}
```

Compile the program to the output file rstrings, and then run it as follows to read and display the program's own source text:

```
$ g++ -o rstrings rstrings.cpp
$ ./rstrings rstrings.cpp
```

To read from a file, the program creates an object, ifs, of the ifstream class. While that class's good() member function returns true, there is more input waiting to be read. To do that, the program calls getline() passing ifs as an argument:

```
getline(ifs, s, '\n');
```

GETTING string FACTS

The string class provides several member functions that report various aspects about a string object such as its length and capacity. Table 22.1 lists the string member functions you can call to obtain facts about any string object.

TABLE 22.1   THE string CLASS FACT-FINDING FUNCTIONS

Function	Returns	Description
capacity()	size_type	Capacity of string in bytes
empty()	bool	True if string has no characters
length()	size_type	Length of string in characters
max_size()	size_type	Capacity of string in characters
size()	size_type	Same as length()

Most functions in Table 22.1 return a value of type size_type, equated in the string class to size_t, and in GNU C++, equivalent to type long. The size() and length() functions return the same value, equal to the number of characters in a string object. A string's capacity() indicates how much memory is reserved for the string. This differs from max_size(), which takes into account the size of an individual character. For this reason, it's best to call `max_size()` for determining whether a string of a certain size can be assigned to a `string` object without requiring a new memory allocation. A string's `length()`, `size()`, and `capacity()` can never exceed its `max_size()`. Call the `empty()` function to determine whether a string has no characters. This is simply easier than checking whether `length()` equals zero.

string SIZE OPERATIONS

Two `string` class member functions, `resize()` and `reserve()`, provide some measure of control over how much memory is allocated to a `string` object. Call `resize()` to expand or contract a string's length. For example, the following statement changes a string's length to 64 characters without disturbing the string's contents, as long as the new size is greater than its current value:

```
s.resize(64);
```

> **Note**
>
> This statement and others in this section are taken from file sizes.cpp in the src/c22 path on the CD-ROM.

If the specified value is smaller than the string's current length, the string is downsized and its characters are potentially truncated:

```
s.resize(10);
```

When resizing a string to a larger length, its capacity is also changed if necessary by allocating new memory to the object. Also, any bytes in that memory might have any values. To resize a string and insert a specific character into the newly allocated space, use this form of `resize()`:

```
s.resize(32, '=');
```

That changes the length of the `string` object s to 32 and fills any new space in the string with equal signs. Call `reserve()` to expand a `string` object's capacity *without* altering its current length:

```
s.reserve(128);
```

That does not change the string's length in characters, but it reallocates the string's memory to the new capacity.

> **Note**
>
> As of this writing, the `string`-class `reserve()` function in GNU C++ does nothing.

string EXCEPTIONS

The `string` class throws two types of exceptions for various errors. The exceptions are objects of classes derived from class `exception` defined in the stdexcept header file. The two `string` exception classes are as follows:

■ length_error—This exception is thrown on an attempt to increase a string's length beyond its maximum capacity.

■ out_of_range—This exception is thrown if an index or other position or length value is out of range given this string object's size.

You probably can ignore length_error exceptions (but production code should trap them). In GNU C++ and Linux, a string object's maximum size is near the maximum value of a signed long integer and is, for all practical purposes, unlimited. If you want to trap this error, use programming such as this:

```
try {
  string s;
  s.reserve(length);  // Assume length is defined elsewhere
  // .. continue program here
} catch (length_error err) {
  cout << "*** Error " << err.what() << endl;
  exit(1);  // Or retry failed operation
}
```

Note

A string object's maximum size is not determined by how much memory is available but only by how large an object the string class can *potentially* handle. Any errors allocating memory to string objects throw exceptions as explained in Chapter 16, "Handling Exceptions."

Listing 22.3, sexcept.cpp, demonstrates a more practical use for string exceptions. (Some of my readers have suggested that my books could be more romantic, hence this program's racy title.)

LISTING 22.3 SEXCEPT.CPP

```
#include <iostream.h>
#include <string>      // Need string class
#include <stdexcept>   // Need out_of_range
#include <stdlib.h>    // Need exit()

int main()
{
  cout << "This program intentionally ends with an" << endl;
  cout << "error message." << endl;

  string s("abcdefghijklmnopqrstuvwxyz");
  try {
    int pos = 0;
    // Following uses <= to force exception (should be <).
    while (pos <= s.length()) {
      cout << "Char " << pos << " == " << s.at(pos) << endl;
      pos++;
    }
```

continues

LISTING 22.3 CONTINUED

```
  }
  catch (out_of_range err) {
    cout << "*** Error: " << err.what() << endl;
    exit(1);
  }
  return 0;
}
```

To trap string exceptions, include the stdexcept header file as shown in the listing. Catch errors of type out_of_range after trying operations that assume a specific character index in a string object. In this case, the program's try block executes a while statement that, due to the careless programmer's sloppy work, incorrectly uses operator <= instead of < to peruse the characters in a string object. To return each character *at* a specified index, the loop calls the string class at() function using the expression

```
s.at(pos)
```

When pos equals the length of the string, because the first character's position is zero, the function throws an exception of type out_of_range. The sample program's catch statement traps this error and gives it a name (err). After an output statement displays the nature of the error, the program ends by calling exit(). Compile and run the test program with the following commands:

```
$ g++ sexcept.cpp
$ ./a.out
This program intentionally ends with an
error message.
Char 0 == a
Char 1 == b
...
Char 25 == z
*** Error: pos >= length ()
```

The last line shows the error message. Notice that it tells you the statement in the string class function that threw this exception. In production code, you probably should display something more meaningful to users, but the default description is useful for debugging.

USING string OPERATORS

The usual assignment, comparison, and some mathematical operators are overloaded in the string class. These functions allow using statements such as the following to assign one string to another:

```
string newString;
string oldString = "Old";
newString = oldString;
```

The third statement calls the string class's overloaded operator=() function to carry out the assignment. Because the string class uses reference counting and the copy-on-write method, assignments such as these are handled as efficiently as possible and do not result in duplicated data in memory. You can also assign a literal string to a string object using the following programming:

```
string stringObject;
...
stringObject = "Literal string";
```

It's also possible to assign a character to a string object. The character is converted into a string object with a length equal to one:

```
string charString;
...
charString = 'Q';
```

However, don't try the following—you cannot declare and initialize a string object using a character:

```
string charString = 'q';   // ???
```

That fails to compile because, apparently, C++ evaluates the literal character as an integer value, and there is no string constructor for creating strings using integers.

Use the overloaded mathematical operators + and += to concatenate (join) two strings. For example, the following statements append text to the end of an existing string object named colors, leaving one space between the words:

```
string colors = "red";
colors += " white";
colors += " blue";
```

The resulting string is "red white blue." Use the + operator to concatenate two strings and create a temporary string object that you can assign to another string or use to construct a new one:

```
string first = "First", second = " Second";
string third = (first + second);
```

That sets string third equal to the concatenation of strings first and second. In addition to + and +=, the string class overloads the subscript operator [], which you can use to access a string's individual characters. The following statement displays the fifth character in a string object:

```
cout << aString[4] << endl;
```

This is the same as calling the at() function introduced earlier:

```
cout << aString.at(4) << endl;
```

Tip

Because the overloaded operator[] function calls at(), indexing a string out of its current range throws an exception of type out_of_range.

CALLING string MEMBER FUNCTIONS

Various string member functions perform operations such as appending new text to string objects and finding patterns embedded in strings. Some functions such as find() duplicate standard algorithms described in the next three chapters, but the native string functions described here are generally faster and easier to use, especially for character strings.

Table 22.2 lists the functions described in this and the next sections. All functions except swap(), which returns void, return a reference of type basic_string&. Because this is just another name for the string class, this means that you can use these functions alone or in stream statements, assignments, and other places where a reference to a string object is appropriate.

TABLE 22.2	string MEMBER FUNCTIONS
Function	**Description**
append()	Appends text from one string to another
assign()	Assigns text from one string to another
insert()	Inserts text from one string to another
remove()	Removes text from a string
replace()	Replaces text in a string
substr()	Returns a substring of a string
swap()	Swaps two strings

Note

The programming described next is taken from the file strfn1.cpp on the CD-ROM, which is not listed here.

To try some of these functions, the test program defines two global string objects as follows:

```
#include <string>
...
string aString;
string alphabet = "abcdefghijklmnopqrstuvwxyz";
```

All programming samples that follow in this section use these two

strings. Call append() to add text to the end of an existing string—useful for adding a label. For example, these statements append the alphabet onto the end of aString:

```
aString = "Alphabet: ";
aString.append(alphabet);
```

You can also pass a literal string to append():

```
aString.append("== The End! ==");
```

To append only a portion of a string, specify a starting index and the number of characters to copy. The following statement appends up to six characters from alphabet to aString starting with the fifth character:

```
aString.append(alphabet, 4, 6);
```

Use the assign() function to assign a new string, or portions of a string, to any string object. Call the function for the object to which you want to make the assignment. Using the two strings from the beginning of this section, call assign() using any of the following styles. Comments show the resulting strings assigned to aString:

```
aString.assign(alphabet);        // "abc...xyz"
aString.assign(alphabet, 2, 6);  // "cdefgh"
aString.assign(alphabet, 20);    // "uvwxyz"
aString.assign(8, '*');          // "********"
```

The first statement assigns one string object to another and is equivalent to the following:

```
aString = alphabet;
```

The second statement assigns six characters to aString starting from alphabet[2]. The third statement assigns characters to aString starting from alphabet[20] and continuing to the end of the source string. The last statement assigns a string of eight asterisk characters to aString. Some versions of ANSI C++ also permit assigning characters to strings, but GNU C++ issues an error message for statements such as this:

```
aString.assign('@');  // ???
```

If your program fails to compile because of this kind of statement, replace it with the following:

```
aString.assign(1, '@');
```

Tip

One disadvantage of using the string class template is that even a simple mistake tends to cause GNU C++ to display many lines of confusing error messages listing possible "candidate" function arguments. To find your mistake in the midst of the compiler's wordy output, hunt for the line number first and then check your typing before attempting to decipher the error message's text.

You can also pass a pair of *iterators* to assign() (see Chapter 23, "Using the Standard Template Library (STL)" for information about iterators). For example, the following statements assign a portion of a character array to a string object:

```
char buffer[26];
strcpy(buffer, alphabet.c_str());
aString.assign(buffer + 5, buffer + 10);  // aString == "fghij"
```

The second statement shows how to access a string-class object as a null-terminated, C-style string (an array of char). The string class's c_str() member function returns a const char* to the string object's text in this format. Because the pointer is const, only read operations are possible—you cannot use c_str()'s returned pointer to make changes to a string object.

You may also pass a pair of iterators from any structure that contains character data, not only a C-style array of char. The following sample statements, for example, copy characters from a standard template vector object to a string:

```
vector<char> v(buffer, buffer + 26);
aString.assign(v.begin(), v.end());  // aString == "abc...xyz"
```

To swap two strings, which you might do in a sorting or randomizing operation, use the swap() function like this:

```
aString.swap(alphabet);
```

That swaps the values of the two string objects aString and alphabet. Interestingly, it doesn't matter which string object does the swapping—the following statement produces the same results as the preceding:

```
alphabet.swap(aString);
```

Be aware that the functions described here throw out_of_range and length_error exceptions to report errors. Use try and catch blocks to trap these errors as follows:

```
try {
  cout << "Intentional error follows..." << endl;
  aString.assign(alphabet, 100);  // Force exception
  show("After assign with bad index");
}
catch (out_of_range err) {
  cout << "*** Range error: " << err.what() << endl;
}
catch (length_error err) {
  cout << "*** Length error: " << err.what() << endl;
}
```

The use of a bad index value (100) in calling assign() causes that function to throw an out_of_range exception.

INSERTING AND DELETING strings

To insert characters into strings, and to delete portions of strings, call the insert() and remove() string-class member functions. Combine the two functions by calling replace(), which performs an insertion followed by a removal.

> **Note**
>
> The sample statements in this section are taken from file strfn2.cpp on the CD-ROM.

Use insert() as follows to insert text anywhere in a string. For example, the third statement sets string object s1 to the string "It's a beautiful life":

```
string s1 = "It's a life";
string s2 = "It's a beautiful day";
s1.insert(7, s2, 7, 10);
```

Pass to insert() the index (7 here) where the insertion is to be made in the object (s1 in this case). Next, specify the source string (s2), an index into that string (7 again), and the number of characters (10) to copy.

Tip

> The insert() function calls replace(), and therefore, it reports any errors by throwing out_of_range and length_error exceptions.

To remove text from a string, call the remove() function. Unfortunately, GNU C++ (as of version 2.7.2) fails to instantiate the remove() template properly, leading to errors. Here's how the function is supposed to work:

```
string myName = "Tom Swan";
size_t blank_pos = myName.find(' ');
myName.remove(0, blank_pos + 1);  // Fails to compile
cout << "Last name == " << myName << endl;
```

After creating a string initialized to my name, the find() function (see "Searching string Objects" later in this chapter) locates the index position of the first blank in the string. The third statement calls remove() to delete this many characters plus one starting at the beginning of the string (index 0). The resulting string equals my last name. However, as mentioned, GNU C++ doesn't accept the call to remove() shown here. As a workaround until this bug is fixed, call replace() instead of remove() and pass a null string as a third argument:

```
myName.replace(0, blank_pos + 1, "");  // remove() work-around
```

The replace() function is useful for inserting text into strings with placeholder characters. For example, you might create a set of error message string objects with at signs (or another unused character) representing where you want to insert some text—a filename for example:

```
string errString = "Error: @ not found";
```

To insert an actual filename in place of the @ character, call the find() function to locate that character's position and then pass the result to replace() like this:

```
int k = errString.find('@');
string temp(errString);
temp.replace(k, 1, "filename.xxx");
```

That sets the temp string object to the string "Error: filename.xxx not found". To replace(), pass a starting index (k), a count of the number of characters to replace in the target string, and the text to insert at that position. This text can be a literal string as shown here, or another string object. It can also be any string function such as append() and assign() that returns a reference to a string object.

Tip

> The replace() function throws an out_of_range exception if given an index value greater than the string object's length. For best results, call replace() inside a try block.

You can also pass iterators to insert(), remove(), and replace() string functions. (The next chapter explains more about iterators.) The iterators can be generated by a standard template container's begin() and end() functions (or rbegin() and rend() reverse iterators), or they can be the string class's own begin(), end(), rbegin(), or rend() functions. Iterators can also be simple char pointers into a C-style null-terminated array of characters. Following are some sample statements that use iterators with string objects. Comments show the resulting strings:

```
string alphabet = "abcdefghijklmnopqrstuvwxyz";
vector<char> alphaVect(alphabet.begin(), alphabet.end());
string s = "========";           // ========
s.insert(s.begin() + 4, '@');     // ====@====
s.insert(s.begin() + 4, 3, '$');  // ====$$$@====
s.insert(s.begin(),               // defgh====$$$@====
  alphaVect.begin() + 3, alphaVect.begin() + 8);
```

Using the alphabet string constructed by the first statement, the next line creates a vector container of characters using the alphabet object's begin() and end() iterators to define the range of characters to use (in this case, the entire string). The third statement creates a test string, s, with eight equal signs. This makes the insertions easy to see as shown in the comments after each call to the insert() function.

Note

See the next three chapters for more information about the standard template library's iterators, containers, and algorithms.

COPYING strings

Using the copy() string-class member function, you can copy all or a portion of a string object to an array of characters. This is a good way to extract the characters in a string object for use as a C-style null-terminated string—in a call to a standard string library function, for example.

Note

The sample programming in this section is taken from file strfn3.cpp on the CD-ROM.

For test purposes, we need a string object and a character buffer, defined in the sample program as follows:

```
string alphabet = "abcdefghijklmnopqrstuvwxyz";
char buffer[40];
```

Given those variables, the following statements insert the first three characters from the alphabet string object into the char buffer:

```
alphabet.copy(buffer, 3);
buffer[3] = 0;  // Insert null
```

That sets `buffer` equal to `"abc"`. It's important to remember that `copy()` transfers only the number of characters requested. If you intend to use the results as a null-terminated string—in an output statement for instance or as an argument to a standard string function such as `strcmp()`—you must insert a null terminator into the buffer as shown here.

An overloaded form of the `string copy()` function copies a specified number of characters from a starting index. The following statement copies into `buffer` six characters from alphabet starting with the character at index position 3:

```
alphabet.copy(buffer, 6, 3);
buffer[6] = 0;  // Insert null
```

Again, it's your responsibility to insert a null terminator if you intend to use the results as a C-style string. The preceding code sets `buffer` to the string `"defghi"`. Because `copy()` doesn't insert a null terminator, the function is generally usable for replacing portions of strings while leaving other characters undisturbed. For example, the following statement copies into buffer three characters from the `alphabet string` object starting at index position 4:

```
alphabet.copy(buffer, 3, 4);
```

Given the code that preceded that statement, this replaces the first three characters of the text in `buffer`, changing it to the string `"efgghi"`.

Another way to copy portions of strings is to call the `substr()` function. Unlike `copy()`, however, `substr()` returns a newly constructed `string` *object*, not a reference. Usually, you'll use `substr()` in calls to other functions, or you might assign its result to a string variable. You can also use `substr()` in output stream statements such as the following:

```
cout << alphabet.substr(20) << endl;
cout << alphabet.substr(6, 8) << endl;
```

The first statement displays a substring of `alphabet` starting with the twenty-first character and continuing to the end of the string. The second statement displays eight characters starting with `alphabet[6]`. Onscreen, the statements display as follows:

```
uvwxyz
ghijklmn
```

You can also assign `substr()` to another `string` object. For example, this statement sets string s to `"klmno"`:

```
string s = alphabet.substr(10, 5);
```

CONVERTING TO NULL-TERMINATED STRINGS

Despite the existence of the C++ standard `string` class, C-style strings continue to be popular. Although most string operations are easily handled by `string`-class objects, you will probably need to convert `string` objects into null-terminated arrays of characters and vice versa. Listing 22.4, cstring.cpp, demonstrates ways to convert between these two types of strings.

LISTING 22.4   CSTRING.CPP

```cpp
#include <iostream.h>
#include <string>     // Need string class
#include <string.h>   // Need C-style string functions

#define BUFSIZE 64
char cstring[BUFSIZE];

int main()
{
  // Initialize C-style string
  //
  strcpy(cstring, "Test string");
  cout << "cstring == " << cstring << endl;

  // Convert a C-style string to a string object
  //
  string sobject1(cstring);
  cout << "sobject1 == " << sobject1 << endl;

  // Convert a string object to a C-style string
  //
  string sobject2("Test string object");
  int index = sobject2.length();
  sobject2.copy(cstring, index);
  cstring[index] = 0;
  cout << "cstring == " << cstring << endl;

  // Convert to constant C-style string pointer
  //
  string sobject3("String object as const char *");
  const char *sp = sobject3.c_str();
  cout << "sp == " << sp << endl;
  // sp[4] = '#';   // ??? not permitted

  // Convert to C-style string without using copy()
  //
  char buffer[BUFSIZE];
  string sobject4("String object copied to buffer");
  strcpy(buffer, sobject4.c_str());
  cout << "buffer == " << buffer << endl;

  buffer[4] = '#';   // permitted
  sobject4.assign(buffer);
  cout << "buffer == " << buffer << endl;

  return 0;
}
```

For test purposes, the program creates a global C-style string variable and initializes it by calling the strcpy() function:

```cpp
#define BUFSIZE 64
char cstring[BUFSIZE];
...
strcpy(cstring, "Test string");
```

Converting the null-terminated string in the cstring buffer to a string-class object is the simplest of the demonstrated tasks. Just construct an object using the original array:

```
string sobject1(cstring);
```

That creates sobject1 using the characters in cstring. The method to use for converting in the other direction—from a string object to a null-terminated C-style string—depends on how you intend to use the resulting string. Most important is whether you want a copy of the original characters or merely want to use the string object as an array of char. You've already seen one way to copy the characters out of a string object into an array of char using code such as this:

```
string sobject2("Test string object");
int index = sobject2.length();
sobject2.copy(cstring, index);
cstring[index] = 0;
```

That copies the entire sobject2's text to the cstring array of char. As mentioned, you must insert a null terminator into the resulting string. But if all you want to do is use the string object in C-style string format, it's easier to call the string class's c_str() function. You may assign the function's result to a const char pointer as in this fragment:

```
string sobject3("String object as const char *");
const char *sp = sobject3.c_str();
cout << "sp == " << sp << endl;
```

The second statement assigns to sp a pointer to the string in sobject3 in C-style, null-terminated format. However, because c_str() returns a const pointer, any attempts to change the characters in the resulting string cause the compiler to issue an error message. For example, this statement, commented-out in the listing

```
sp[4] = '#';  // ??? not permitted
```

results in the following error messages:

```
cstring.cpp: In function 'int main()':
cstring.cpp:44: assignment of read-only location
```

To use a string object as a C-style string and be able to modify the results requires copying the characters out of the object. You can then make your change and insert the results back into the object—for example, by calling assign() as described earlier in this chapter. Instead of calling the string class copy() function as described, you can use the c_str() function along with a standard library function (include the string.h header file) to make a copy of a string object using statements such as the following:

```
char buffer[BUFSIZE];
string sobject4("String object copied to buffer");
strcpy(buffer, sobject4.c_str());
```

The third statement calls the standard string library function strcpy() to transfer the characters in sobject4 as a C-style string to buffer. Because buffer now holds a copy of the object's text, the compiler permits changes to it:

```
buffer[4] = '#';  // permitted
```

After making whatever changes you want to the string, assign the modified buffer to the object using a statement such as this:

```
sobject4.assign(buffer);
```

COMPARING AND SEARCHING string OBJECTS

Two of the most common operations performed on string data are comparing and searching. With C-style strings, these jobs usually require revisiting the online documentation for functions such as strcmp() and strstr()—at least that's true for me because I can never remember which arguments to use in what order. With string class objects, as the following sections explain, comparing and searching is intuitive and less likely to lead to hard-to-find bugs.

COMPARING string OBJECTS

Compare string objects using the same logical operators that you use in mathematical expressions. For example, if s1 and s2 are string class objects, you can compare them in if statements such as these:

```
if (s1 == s2) ...  // Do if s1 equals s2
if (s1 <  s2) ...  // Do if s1 is less than s2
if (s1 >= s2) ...  // Do if s1 is greater than or equal to s2
if (s1 != s2) ...  // Do if s1 is not equal to s2
```

Those and similar expressions are possible because the string class overloads C++ logical operators. The string class doesn't overload all C++ operators; only those that are sensibly used with string objects. You can't, for example, apply the increment operator to string objects. These statements do not compile:

```
s1++;  // ???
s2++;  // ???
```

If you prefer to call a function to compare string objects, use the string class's compare() member function. This function is useful also for comparing portions of strings. To try compare(), define some variables such as these:

```
int result, pos, count;
string s1, s2;
```

> **Note**
>
> The programming in this section is taken from file scompare.cpp on the CD-ROM in the src/c22 directory.

There are three basic forms of compare(), all of which return an integer result:

```
result = s1.compare(s2, pos, count);
result = s1.compare("Literal string", pos);
result = s1.compare("Literal string", pos, count);
```

The first form requires a string object (s2 here) to compare against the object for which compare() is called (s1 in these samples). Also pass position and count integer values to use in the first object (s1). To compare an entire string, set pos to zero and count to the s1's length. All of s2 is used in the comparison. The second form shows how to compare a string object (s1) with a literal string. Because only the position index is given, all of s1 is compared starting at s1[pos]. The third form specifies a position and count of characters to use from the string object.

The result of a comparison is less than zero if s1 < s2, and greater than zero if s1 > s2. If the result is zero, the two strings are identical. To try compare(), assign some test values to the program's variables:

```
s1 = "ABCDEFG";
s2 = "ABCDEFGHIJKLMNOP";
pos = 2;
count = 8;
```

Next, call compare() using each of the three forms. The results are shown as comments:

```
result = s1.compare(s2, pos, count);      // result>0 (s1>s2)
result = s1.compare("CDEFG", pos);        // result=0 (s1==s2)
result = s1.compare("CDEFG", pos,count);  // result<0 (s1<s2)
```

> **Tip**
>
> Ignore the exact value returned by compare(). Only the sign of the result matters.

SEARCHING string OBJECTS

The string class provides two fundamental search functions. Use find() to search for a substring starting at the beginning of a string. Use rfind() to search for a substring starting at the end of a string and searching back toward its beginning. Each function returns the index in the source string where a substring is found, or if no match is found, a value greater than the length of the string. Tests indicate that the "no-match" value equals a string's maximum capacity, or 4,294,967,295, although it would be a mistake to rely on this exact value.

> **Note**
>
> The sample statements in this section are from the file strsrch.cpp on the CD-ROM.

The following statements demonstrate how to use find() and rfind():

```
string alphabet = "abcdefghijklmnopqrstuvwxyz";
...
cout << alphabet.find("klmnop") << endl;
cout << alphabet.rfind("def") << endl;
cout << alphabet.find("White Elephant") << endl;
cout << alphabet.rfind("White Elephant") << endl;
```

After creating a string object initialized to the lowercase alphabet, the first output statement displays 10, the index of the string "klmnop". The next statement displays 3, the index of "def". In this case, however, rfind() searches the string from back to front. The final two statements display a value greater than the length of alphabet, indicating that there are no *White Elephants* in the alphabet.

Instead of literal strings, you can pass string objects to find() and rfind() to perform searches. These statements display 12, the index of the search string object in the alphabet:

```
string search = "mnop";
cout << alphabet.find(search) << endl;
```

As you can with compare(), you can also specify a starting position to begin the search somewhere other than its beginning or end:

```
cout << alphabet.find(search, 4) << endl;
```

That also displays 12, but change 4 to 15 and find()'s return value indicates that it can't find the substring. To search backward from a starting position, specify an index value to rfind(). The following does not find xyz in the alphabet because it searches from index 10 to the beginning:

```
cout << alphabet.rfind("xyz", 10) << endl;
```

The find() and rfind() functions can also search for characters in a string object:

```
cout << alphabet.find('z') << endl;
cout << alphabet.rfind('a') << endl;
```

Other string-search functions locate the first character from a character set, represented by a string object. Given the alphabet string defined at the beginning of this section, the following statements show how to use these functions, find_first_of() and find_last_of():

```
string vowels("aeiou");
cout << alphabet.find_first_of(vowels) << endl;   // 0
cout << alphabet.find_last_of(vowels) << endl;    // 20
```

Use find_first_of() to locate the index of the first occurrence of any characters in the argument string (vowels in this example). Use find_last_of() to locate the last such index. The preceding statements report 0 and 20 as shown in the comments.

Use these functions' "not" counterparts, find_first_not_of() and find_last_not_of(), to locate the first nonmatching characters of a set. The following statements find the first and last nonvowel indexes in the alphabet string (the function results are shown as comments):

```
cout << alphabet.find_first_not_of( vowels ) << endl;   // 1
cout << alphabet.find_last_not_of( vowels ) << endl;    // 25
```

Specify a starting index to search for character sets in a string at a position other than the beginning or end. This is useful for continuing a search for characters as demonstrated by the following while loop that finds all vowels in the alphabet:

```
int p = alphabet.find_first_of( vowels );
while (p < alphabet.length()) {
  cout << "a[" << setw(2) << p << "] == '";
  cout << alphabet[p] << '\'' << endl;
  p = alphabet.find_first_of( vowels, p + 1 );
}
```

The first call to find_first_of() locates the first of the characters in the vowels string. To continue the search at the next character, the last statement in the loop searches at the former position plus one. Compiling and running this code displays the index and character values:

```
a[ 0] == 'a'
a[ 4] == 'e'
a[ 8] == 'i'
a[14] == 'o'
a[20] == 'u'
```

DEBUGGING string OBJECTS

There are no special debugging commands that affect string objects, but in displaying strings, the GNU debugger shows some values that might seem strange at first. To follow along, compile sdeclare.cpp, Listing 22.1, for debugging and load it into gdb using these commands:

```
$ g++ -g -o sdeclare sdeclare.cpp
$ gdb --silent sdeclare
```

Type *list 1* followed by *list* (or just *l*) to list some lines until you find the line that constructs sFromString (the line numbers might be different for you):

```
(gdb) list
...
18 string sFromLiteral("Stringing in the rain");
19 string sFromString(sFromLiteral);
```

Set a breakpoint on line 19 and run the program up to that statement:

```
(gdb) b 19
Breakpoint 1 at 0x804a2de: file sdeclare.cpp, line 19.
(gdb) run
Starting program: /home/tswan/gpl/src/c22/sdeclare
Breakpoint 1, global constructors keyed to buffer () at sdeclare.cpp:19
19 string sFromString(sFromLiteral);
```

Notice that the breakpoint is in a global constructor, called *before* main() executes. The program is paused before the construction of sFromString. Execute that statement by typing a *next* command and then print the string to investigate its value:

```
(gdb) next
...
(gdb) print sFromString
$2 = {static npos = <optimized out>,
static nilRep = <optimized out>,
dat = 0x804d7b8 "Stringing in the rain"}
```

I broke the lines to fit here, but they should look similar on your screen. The reported string is labeled "dat" along with its address in memory. The other two items, npos and nilRep, are static global variables defined by the string class library modules. Because these values aren't used in the finished code (they merely represent a string's maximum capacity and nil value in the basic_string class template), the compiler optimizes them out of existence. It is a credit to the GNU debugger and compiler authors that the debugger doesn't report these values simply as not found but *knows* that they have been deleted purposefully. However, this wasn't the case for this book's technical editor, so maybe the values are now used in some fashion.

If you are following along, type *c* and then *q* to continue the program to its end and quit the debugger.

SUMMARY

The standard string class provides a new way to create and use character strings in C++ programs. Although you may continue to use C-style null-terminated arrays of char as strings, the ANSI C++ string class described in this chapter is superior for many reasons. For example, string objects report errors by throwing exceptions, and because the string class is designed as a template, it can use characters of any type and size. This chapter introduced the string class and showed several examples of how to create string objects and call string-class member functions.

For more information on subjects introduced in this chapter, turn to the following chapters:

- Chapter 16, "Handling Exceptions"
- Chapter 23, "Using the Standard Template Library (STL)"
- Chapter 24, "Building Standard Containers"
- Chapter 25, "Applying Standard Algorithms"

USING THE STANDARD TEMPLATE LIBRARY (STL)

Although many programmers continue to use standard C functions, relying on these old standards in C++ is like hitching a donkey to a Mercedes. You may eventually arrive at your destination, but you're wasting the true power of a finely constructed vehicle.

Although there are times when standard C functions come in handy (using the `sprintf()` function to format strings and calling `random()` to create random sequences, for example), the standard functions do not use exceptions to report errors, and they are not adaptable to handle new data types. Standard functions also use memory allocation techniques and data structures that are prone to causing bugs especially in code written by less experienced programmers.

The C++ standard template library, or STL, offers an alternative in the form of a collection of data structures and algorithms that perform many of the tasks found among the standard functions but are safer and more versatile. The STL was originally conceived and developed by Alexander Stepanov and Meng Lee at HP Labs. Recently, the ANSI C++ standards committee formally adopted the STL, although some implementation details still differ among vendors and compiler versions due largely to differences in template compilation and linking.

This chapter introduces some of the concepts you need to understand before you use the STL's containers and algorithms, explained in detail in Chapter 24, "Building Standard Containers," and Chapter 25, "Applying Standard Algorithms." This chapter also gives a general overview of the STL's components.

INTRODUCING THE STANDARD TEMPLATE LIBRARY

A core feature of the STL is the separation of data structures from algorithms that operate on data. Although a simple idea on its face, this separation of powers makes the STL truly versatile. For example, because the STL's `sort()` algorithm is completely generic, you can use it with virtually any collection of data, including lists, vectors, and arrays.

Note

STL algorithms are provided as template functions. To distinguish them from other components, in this book STL algorithms such as `sort()` are followed by a pair of empty parentheses.

Another key STL feature is that it is *not* object-oriented. To achieve its versatility, the STL relies more heavily on templates than on encapsulation, inheritance, and virtual functions (polymorphism)—OOP's three main anchors—and you won't find any significant class hierarchies in the STL. At first, this lack of object orientation might seem to be a drawback, but it is the library's low-level nature that gives its components wide generality. Also, because the STL is based on templates, it tends to produce smaller code files that run fast due to the heavy use of inline code.

PART

V

CH

23

> **Tip**
>
> Be sure to compile with at least one level of optimization (-O) to enable inline expansion in programs that use the STL.

STL COMPONENTS

The STL provides a large number of template classes and functions that you may use in OOP and conventional programming. All of the STL's approximately 50 algorithms are completely generic, and they are not wed to any specific data types. The following paragraphs describe the three essential STL components:

- *Iterators* provide access to objects in a container. For example, a pair of iterators defines a range of objects in an `list` or `vector`. Iterators resemble pointers, and in fact, a C++ pointer is a type of iterator. However, iterators can also be class objects for which the pointer-access `operator*()` function and other pointer-like operators are defined.

- *Containers* are data structures such as lists, vectors, and deques (double-ended queues) provided in the STL as template classes. To access the data in an STL container, a program uses iterators of a type exported by the container class.

- *Algorithms* are template functions that operate on data in a container. For example, the STL provides algorithms such as `sort()` to sort data in a `vector`, and `find()` to search a `list` of objects. The functions possess no special knowledge of the types and structures of data on which they operate, and they are therefore usable on just about any structure from simple arrays to highly complex containers.

HEADER FILES

To avoid conflict with other header files, the STL's headers drop the usual .h extension. To include standard `strings`, iterators, and algorithms, use directives such as the following:

```
#include <string>
#include <iterator>
#include <algorithm>
```

If you browse these and other STL files, you might come across headers such as iterator.h and stl_iterator.h. Avoid referring to such files by these names, which might differ among various STL implementations. For best results, and to ensure portability, use the plain filenames without the .h suffixes. Table 23.1 lists many of the more commonly used STL headers for various container classes. This is not a complete list, and I introduce other headers at the appropriate times in this and the next two chapters.

Table 23.1	**STL Header Files and Container Classes**
#include	**Container Class**
<deque>	deque
<list>	list
<map>	map, multimap
<queue>	queue, priority_queue
<set>	set, multiset
<stack>	stack
<vector>	vector, vector<bool>

Namespaces

Depending on your version of GNU C++ for Linux, namespaces might or might not be recognized. A namespace works like an envelope that encompasses identifiers under another name. The identifiers exist within that name's space, and in that way, avoid conflicts with other identifiers. For example, it's common for libraries and program modules to define a sort() function. To prevent conflicts with the STL's sort() algorithm, this and other STL identifiers are encased in the namespace std. Uses of the STL's sort() algorithm are compiled as std::sort(), helping to prevent a name conflict.

Although namespaces might not be implemented for your compiler, you can still use them. To indicate that you want to recognize the namespace std, insert this directive in a source file, typically after all #include directives:

```
using namespace std;
```

Iterators

An *iterator* provides access to object values and can also define ranges of objects in a container. Iterators resemble pointers, and, in fact, a C++ pointer *is* an iterator. However, iterators are not necessarily pointers, and you shouldn't expect them to hold address values. An array index, for example, is also a type of iterator.

Iterators come from a variety of sources. A program might create an iterator as a variable. In other cases, an STL container class generates an iterator for use with a specific type of data. As with pointers, you must dereference an iterator by using the * operator to "get to" its data. You may also apply mathematical operators such as ++ to iterators. Typically, the ++ operator increments an iterator to address the next object in a container. If this advances the iterator beyond the last value in a container, the iterator becomes equal to the *past-the-end* value. Dereferencing an iterator equal to the *past-the-end* value is never allowed and is equivalent to using a NULL or uninitialized pointer.

TYPES OF ITERATORS

You can use five types of iterators with STL data structures and algorithms. The following paragraphs briefly describe these five types:

- *Input iterators* provide read-only access to data.
- *Output iterators* provide write-only access to data.
- *Forward iterators* provide read and write, forward (incrementing) access to data.
- *Bidirectional iterators* provide read and write, forward and backward (incrementing and decrementing) access to data.
- *Random access iterators* provide read and write, random movement through data.

Although STL implementation details differ among vendors and compiler releases, it's helpful to think of the preceding iterators as a class hierarchy. In this sense, iterators lower in the preceding list are of classes derived from iterators higher up. Because of these derivations, you may, for example, use a forward iterator where an algorithm calls for an output or an input iterator. However, if an algorithm specifies a bidirectional iterator, then only that type of iterator and its descendant random access iterator are permitted.

POINTER ITERATORS

A pointer is one type of iterator, as the simple program in this section demonstrates. This program also points out a major feature of the STL—its capability to work with data structures, not only of its own class types, but of *any* C or C++ type. Listing 23.1, iterdemo.cpp, shows how to use pointers as iterators for searching a common array using the STL's find() algorithm.

LISTING 23.1 ITERDEMO.CPP

```
#include <iostream.h>
#include <algorithm>

using namespace std;

#define SIZE 100
int iarray[SIZE];

int main()
{
```

continues

LISTING 23.1   CONTINUED

```
  iarray[20] = 50;
  int* ip = find(iarray, iarray + SIZE, 50);
  if (ip == iarray + SIZE)
    cout << "50 not found in array" << endl;
  else
    cout << *ip << " found in array" << endl;
  return 0;
}
```

After including the headers for I/O streams and STL algorithms (notice that algorithm lacks the usual .h suffix), the sample program tells the compiler to use the std namespace. This is optional, and you may delete this line because name conflicts are unlikely in such a small program.

To provide a data structure, the program defines a global array of integers using constant SIZE. Because it's a global variable, the array is automatically initialized to all zero values at runtime. The following statement uses the STL find() algorithm to search for the value 50, inserted at index 20:

```
iarray[20] = 50;
int* ip = find(iarray, iarray + SIZE, 50);
```

To find(), the program passes three arguments of values typical in many STL algorithms. The first two arguments are iterators that define the range of values to search. Because C and C++ arrays are equivalent to pointers, the expression iarray *points to* the first value in the array. Likewise, the second iterator, iarray + SIZE, equals the *past-the-end* value—in this case, one element beyond the last object in the array. The third argument is the value to locate, 50 in this example. The find() algorithm returns an iterator of the same type as its first two arguments, in this case an integer pointer assigned in the test program to ip.

Tip

Keep in mind that the STL uses templates. As such, STL algorithms automatically mold themselves according to the types of data they use.

To determine whether find() is successful, the sample program tests ip against the *past-the-end* value using the following statement:

```
if (ip == iarray + SIZE) ...
```

If the expression is true, then the iterator equals the *past-the-end* value. Because that value addresses no valid object, this means that the search argument is not in the specified range. But if ip does not equal the *past-the-end* value, then it addresses a valid object, and it is safe to dereference the pointer using the expression *ip as shown in the output statement:

```
cout << *ip << " found in array" << endl;
```

Remember always that it is *not* correct to test whether an algorithm's returned iterator equals NULL. Do not use code such as this:

```
int* ip = find(iarray, iarray + SIZE, 50);
if (ip != NULL) ...   // ??? incorrect
```

When using STL algorithms, it is necessary only to test whether ip equals the *past-the-end* value, whatever that happens to be for a particular container. Although ip is in this case a C++ pointer, its use must conform to the rules for STL iterators. Other sample listings in this and the next two chapters show concrete examples that illustrate the proper ways to use many different types of iterators.

CONTAINER ITERATORS

Although, as the preceding section demonstrates, C++ pointers are iterators, it is more common to use iterators exported by a container class. These types of iterators are used in *exactly* the same way as in iterdemo.cpp, but instead of declaring iterators as pointer variables, you can call a container function to obtain an iterator object for use with algorithms such as find(). Two typical container functions are begin() and end(). They represent the full range of objects in most types of containers. Some containers also provide *reverse iterators* by way of functions rbegin() and rend() for specifying a range of objects in reverse order.

To demonstrate container iterators, Listing 23.2, vectdemo.cpp, creates a *vector*—the STL's equivalent of a C++ array—and uses an iterator to search for a value in the container. The program is the STL equivalent of the conventional C++ iterdemo.cpp program in the preceding section.

LISTING 23.2 VECTDEMO.CPP

```
#include <iostream.h>
#include <algorithm>
#include <vector>

using namespace std;

vector<int> intVector(100);

void main()
{
  intVector[20] = 50;
  vector<int>::iterator intIter =
    find(intVector.begin(), intVector.end(), 50);
  if (intIter != intVector.end())
    cout << "Vector contains value " << *intIter << endl;
  else
    cout << "Vector does not contain 50" << endl;
}
```

The program defines a vector of 100 int values using the standard vector container class template. This statement instantiates the vector template for data elements of type int:

```
vector<int> intVector(100);
```

The statement also calls the vector class's constructor to reserve space for 100 objects of the indicated type. (Chapter 24, "Building Standard Containers," explains in detail methods for constructing container objects.)

For the demonstration, the first statement in `main()` assigns the value 50 to the `vector` at the indexed position 20. Notice that the following statement appears to use a simple array, even though it is accessing an STL `vector` container:

```
intVector[20] = 50;
```

After that, the program searches the container for a value, using a pair of iterators that define the range of values to search. The statement might look daunting at first:

```
vector<int>::iterator intIter =
  find(intVector.begin(), intVector.end(), 50);
```

Take that a piece at a time, and be sure to understand each part before continuing. Many statements that call STL algorithms are in this form. The first line defines an iterator named `intIter` of the type `iterator` exported from the `vector<int>` class. This name, `vector<int>`, is the full name of the *instantiated* `vector` template class, and its `iterator` data type is molded to suit the type of data (`int` here) stored in the container. The second line calls the STL's `find()` algorithm to search the `intVector` container. This is similar to the way `find()` searches an array of integers in the iterdemo.cpp program, but in this case, to obtain iterators for the container, the program calls the container class's `begin()` and `end()` functions. Function `begin()` always returns an iterator to the first object in a container. Function `end()` always returns the *past-the-end* value. The third argument is the search argument.

Following the call to `find()`, the value assigned to `intIter` indicates whether the search was successful. As mentioned in the preceding section, if the result of `find()` equals the *past-the-end* value, then the search argument isn't in the container. An `if` statement in the sample program detects this condition as follows:

```
if (intIter != intVector.end()) ...
```

The container's `end()` function returns the *past-the-end* value. If `intIter` does not equal that value, then it points to a valid object in the container—in this case, displayed with the statement

```
cout << "Vector contains value " << *intIter << endl;
```

Even though the program has no special knowledge of `intIter`'s type, it is dereferenced as shown to get to its addressed value. Although in this example the `vector` container stores simple integer values, this programming works the same for *any* data type, including containers that store complex class objects.

CONSTANT ITERATORS

As you can with pointers, you can assign new values to objects referenced by iterators. First define the iterator for the container class you are using:

```
vector<int>::iterator first;
```

That creates the iterator `first` for the `vector<int>` class, which exports the `iterator` data type. Initialize `first` to point to an object in the container. The following statement sets `first` to the first object in intVector, a container of the vector<int> class, and assigns to that object the value 123:

```
first = intVector.begin();
*first = 123;
```

This works for most types of containers and all iterators except the output-only variety. To prevent such assignments, declare the iterator const like this:

```
const vector<int>::iterator result;
result = find(intVector.begin(), intVector.end(), value);
if (result != intVector.end())
  *result = 123;  // ???
```

The first statement defines result as an iterator for use with a vector<int> container. The second statement calls find() to search for value and assigns the algorithm's return value to result. If result is a valid pointer to an object in the container, the last statement attempts to change the object's value. However, this statement does not compile because result is declared const. Use this method to protect data in containers from inadvertent changes.

Warning   Another way to protect data from change is to declare the container const.

PROGRAMMING WITH ITERATORS

Now that you have seen some examples of iterators, you're ready to dig deeper into how specific types of iterators work. The following sections explore each type of iterator in the STL. Because using iterators requires a good knowledge of the STL's container classes and algorithms (which also require knowing how to use iterators), you might want to mark this section for rereading after you finish the next two chapters.

INPUT ITERATORS

An input iterator is the most general type. Input iterators at a minimum can be compared with == for equality and != for inequality, dereferenced with * to access data values, and incremented with ++ to advance the iterator to the next object in a container or to the *past-the-end* value.

To understand more about iterators and how algorithms use them, it's useful to take a close look at a specific algorithm such as find(). The STL declares and implements the find() template function as follows:

```
template <class InputIterator, class T>
InputIterator find(
  InputIterator first, InputIterator last, const T& value) {
    while (first != last && *first != value) ++first;
    return first;
  }
```

As a template, the find() algorithm refers to no specific type of data but uses placeholders to represent actual data types provided when the template is used. One of these placeholders is named InputIterator. This type of iterator could be any type of object that has certain capabilities, such as being comparable using the != operator and being incremented with ++. The other type of placeholder is named T. It represents the type of data in the container.

> **Tip**
>
> Don't go hunting for InputIterator's type declaration in the STL's source files. This is just an arbitrary name, not a defined type, that *becomes* a real type when the find() template function is instantiated.

The find() algorithm declares three parameters. First are two iterators of type InputIterator, named first and last. The third parameter is a constant reference to an object, named value here, of type T&. The find() algorithm's statements show how, using template placeholders instead of real data types, a completely general search function is written with absolutely no knowledge of the type of data searched. Examine the algorithm's while statement closely:

```
while (first != last && *first != value) ++first;
```

The statement executes while the first iterator is not equal to the last, and while the value addressed by first does not equal the search argument. As long as this condition is false, the loop increments first. The algorithm is completely general, and it can search any type of container such as a list, a vector, or an array.

After the search, first either points to the object equal to the search argument, or first equals last, in which case the search has failed. The find() algorithm simply returns this value.

> **Note**
>
> In the preceding find() algorithm, notice that if the search argument is not located, incrementing first *must* eventually cause it to equal last. If first and last refer to values in different containers, this algorithm potentially never ends. Although the compiler does not prevent this situation, with reasonable care, this shouldn't cause any problems.

OUTPUT ITERATORS

An output iterator is write-only by default and is typically used to copy data from one location to another. Because output iterators cannot be used to read objects, you never use them in search and other types of algorithms. For example, the copy() algorithm can transfer objects from one data structure to another using an output iterator to specify the destination. However, that iterator cannot be used to read the copied values. For that, another input iterator (or descendant) is needed.

To demonstrate how to use an output iterator, Listing 23.3, outiter.cpp, uses the copy() algorithm to transfer an array of double values to a vector container. You might use a similar technique to upgrade a conventional C program that uses arrays to one that uses STL container classes. (The demonstrated technique is also useful for initializing containers for test programs such as those in this and the next two chapters.)

LISTING 23.3   OUTITER.CPP

```cpp
#include <iostream.h>
#include <algorithm>    // Need copy()
#include <vector>       // Need vector

using namespace std;

double darray[10] =
  {1.0, 1.1, 1.2, 1.3, 1.4, 1.5, 1.6, 1.7, 1.8, 1.9};

vector<double> vdouble(10);

int main()
{
  vector<double>::iterator outputIterator = vdouble.begin();
  copy(darray, darray + 10, outputIterator);
  while (outputIterator != vdouble.end()) {
    cout << *outputIterator << endl;
    outputIterator++;
  }
  return 0;
}
```

Compile and run the program, which uses the copy() algorithm to display the resulting vector of double values:

```
$ g++ outiter.cpp
$ ./a.out
1
1.1
...
1.9
```

The program defines a common array of 10 double values, initialized to 1.0, 1.1, ..., 1.9. It also defines a vector<double> container large enough to hold 10 values. The first statement in main() declares and initializes an iterator named outputIterator for the vector. So that it points to the container's first object, this statement assigns to outputIterator the result of the begin() function for the container vdouble. Passing the iterator to the copy() algorithm transfers the values from the common array to the vector container:

```
copy(darray, darray + 10, outputIterator);
```

The first two arguments are input iterators that define the range of source values to copy. In this case, the iterators are pointers to the global darray. The third argument is an output iterator that defines the beginning of the destination to which objects are to be transferred. You might wonder how this statement "knows" what types of objects are being copied, but this information is implicit in the types of iterators involved. A pointer such as darray and a pointer expression such as darray + 10 are not simply address values—they are *typed* pointers, in this case, to values of type double. Similarly, outputIterator "knows" the type of container to which it belongs.

FORWARD ITERATORS

A forward iterator can read and write data values, and it can be incremented to the next value in a sequence. As its name implies, however, a forward iterator cannot be decremented. The `replace()` algorithm shows a typical use for forward iterators. It is declared as follows:

```
template <class ForwardIterator, class T>
void replace (ForwardIterator first,
              ForwardIterator last,
              const T& old_value,
              const T& new_value);
```

Use `replace()` to change to `new_value` all objects equal to `old_value` in the range `first` to `last`. For example, given the `vdouble` vector in the outiter.cpp program (refer to Listing 23.3), the following statement replaces all values equal to 1.5 with the value of *pi:*

```
replace(vdouble.begin(), vdouble.end(), 1.5, 3.14159);
```

BIDIRECTIONAL ITERATORS

Bidirectional iterators can be incremented and decremented, a requirement of some algorithms in the STL. The `reverse()` algorithm, for example, requires two bidirectional iterator arguments. The algorithm is declared as follows:

```
template <class BidirectionalIterator>
void reverse (BidirectionalIterator first,
              BidirectionalIterator last);
```

Use `reverse()` to reverse the objects in a container. For example, after sorting a container in low to high order, you can reverse its objects for a high-to-low ordering. In some circumstances, this might be faster than resorting the container the other way around. To reverse the values in the `vdouble` vector from outiter.cpp (refer to Listing 23.3), use the following statement:

```
reverse(vdouble.begin(), vdouble.end());
```

RANDOM ACCESS ITERATORS

Random access iterators can access data in any order, and they can be used to read and write data values. (Non-const C++ pointers are random access iterators.) The STL's sorting and searching algorithms use random access iterators, which also have the capability of being compared using relational operators.

The `random_shuffle()` algorithm demonstrates random access iterators. The algorithm specifies two of these iterators that define a range of values in a sequence to be shuffled—to prepare test data for a program, for instance, or as part of an encryption method. The `random_shuffle()` algorithm is declared as follows:

```
template <class RandomAccessIterator>
void random_shuffle (RandomAccessIterator first,
                     RandomAccessIterator last);
```

Using the `vdouble` vector from outiter.cpp (refer to Listing 23.3), the following statement scrambles all values in the container:

```
random_shuffle(vdouble.begin(), vdouble.end());
```

ITERATOR TECHNIQUES

Learning to use iterators along with STL containers and algorithms requires learning a few new techniques described in the following sections.

IOSTREAMS AND ITERATORS

Many of this book's sample programs use I/O stream statements to read and write values. For example, the following statements prompt for, read, and display a value entered by the program's user:

```
int value;
cout << "Enter value: ";
cin >> value;
cout << "You entered " << value << endl;
```

With iterators, there's another way to use streams and standard algorithms. The key to understanding the method, which can help you write functions adaptable to different types of objects, is that an input or output stream can be accessed using iterators as though the stream were a container. In this way, any algorithm that can accept an iterator argument (most do) can work with streams in the same way as they do with other data structures. Listing 23.4, outstrm.cpp, demonstrates the technique by using an output stream iterator and the `copy()` algorithm to display a container's objects.

LISTING 23.4   OUTSTRM.CPP

```
#include <iostream.h>
#include <stdlib.h>    // Need random(), srandom()
#include <time.h>      // Need time()
#include <algorithm>   // Need sort(), copy()
#include <vector>      // Need vector

using namespace std;
```

continues

LISTING 23.4 CONTINUED

```cpp
void Display(vector<int>& v, const char* s);

int main()
{
  // Seed the random number generator
  srandom( time(NULL) );

  // Construct vector and fill with random integer values
  vector<int> collection(10);
  for (int i = 0; i < 10; i++)
    collection[i] = random() % 10000;;

  // Display, sort, and redisplay
  Display(collection, "Before sorting");
  sort(collection.begin(), collection.end());
  Display(collection, "After sorting");
  return 0;
}

// Display label s and contents of integer vector v
void Display(vector<int>& v, const char* s)
{
  cout << endl << s << endl;
  copy(v.begin(), v.end(),
    ostream_iterator<int>(cout, "\t"));
  cout << endl;
}
```

The test program uses the standard C library's random() function to fill a vector of 100 integers with values selected at random. A local Display() function in the test program shows the vector's contents before and after sorting, using the standard sort() algorithm. Function Display() demonstrates how to use an output stream iterator. The following statement in the function calls the copy() algorithm to transfer the values from the container to the standard output by way of the cout output stream object:

```cpp
copy(v.begin(), v.end(),
  ostream_iterator<int>(cout, "\t"));
```

As usual, v.begin() and v.end() define the range of objects in the container. The third argument (second line) is where the magic begins. It instantiates the ostream_iterator template for type int, creating an output iterator object for passing to copy() as the destination for the copied data. The small string argument is used as a separator between objects—in this case, a tab character. Compile and run the program to display a vector of randomized values, which are sorted and redisplayed:

```
$ g++ outstrm.cpp
$ ./a.out
Before sorting
```

```
677    722    686    238    964    397    251    118    11    312
After sorting
11     118    238    251    312    397    677    686    722   964
```

This is a marvelous demonstration of the versatility of algorithms in the STL, even more interesting when you consider that streams predated the STL's invention. To define an output stream iterator, the STL provides the template class `ostream_iterator`. This class provides a constructor with two arguments: an `ostream` object and a string value. From this template, an iterator object is easily created using an expression such as this:

```
ostream_iterator<int>(cout, "\n")
```

The resulting iterator is ready for use with any STL algorithm for any type of container that holds `int` values and that can accept an output iterator.

INSERTION ITERATORS

To insert values into a container, as you might suppose, you can use an *insertion iterator*. These are also called *adapters* because they adapt or convert a container into an iterator that you can pass to an algorithm such as `copy()`. Consider a program that defines a `list` and a `vector` each containing `double` values:

```
list<double> dList;
vector<double> dVector;
```

A single `copy()` statement can insert the values from the `vector` into the front of the `list` by using a `front_inserter` iterator object:

```
copy(dVector.begin(), dVector.end(), front_inserter(dList));
```

The three types of insertion iterators are as follows:

- *Plain inserters* insert objects in front of any other object in a container.

- *Front inserters* insert objects into the front of a data collection—for example, at the head of a list.

- *Back inserters* insert objects at the tail of a collection—for example, at the end of a vector, an operation that might cause the vector to grow in size.

Using an inserter might cause other objects in a container to move in position, thus invalidating any existing iterators for those values. Inserting a value into a vector, for example, causes other values to move aside to make room. However, insertions in structures such as linked lists are more efficient because they do not cause other objects to move.

Typically, a plain inserter is used following a search of a container. The insertion is then made ahead of that location. Listing 23.5, insert.cpp, demonstrates how to use all three types of insertion iterators.

LISTING 23.5   INSERT.CPP

```cpp
#include <iostream.h>
#include <algorithm>
#include <list>

using namespace std;

int iArray[5] = { 1, 2, 3, 4, 5 };

void Display(list<int>& v, const char* s);

int main()
{
  list<int> iList;

  // Copy iArray backwards into iList
  copy(iArray, iArray + 5, front_inserter(iList));
  Display(iList, "Before find and copy");

  // Locate value 3 in iList
  list<int>::iterator p =
    find(iList.begin(), iList.end(), 3);

  // Copy first two iArray values to iList ahead of p
  copy(iArray, iArray + 2, inserter(iList, p));
  Display(iList, "After find and copy");

  return 0;
}

void Display(list<int>& a, const char* s)
{
  cout << s << endl;
  copy(a.begin(), a.end(),
    ostream_iterator<int>(cout, " "));
  cout << endl;
}
```

Compile and run the test program to display the before and after results of the find() and copy() algorithms on a list of integers. Enter these commands:

```
$ g++ insert.cpp
$ ./a.out
Before find and copy
5 4 3 2 1
After find and copy
5 4 1 2 3 2 1
```

The program defines a global integer array containing the sequence 1, 2, 3, 4, 5. The STL copy() algorithm transfers those values into a list container using a front_inserter object:

```
copy(iArray, iArray + 5, front_inserter(iList));
```

This causes the original data to be inserted at the head of the list, thus reversing the value order and creating the list 5, 4, 3, 2, 1. Change front_inserter to back_inserter, compile, and run to insert the values in their original order.

Next, the program uses the find() algorithm to search the list for the value 3. The following statement constructs an iterator p for a list<int> container, to which the program assigns the result of find():

```
list<int>::iterator p =
  find(iList.begin(), iList.end(), 3);
```

After this statement, p refers to the value 3 in iList, or if that value does not exist in the defined range, p equals the *past-the-end* value. Finally, the program calls copy() using a plain insertion iterator, obtained from iList:

```
copy(iArray, iArray + 2, inserter(iList, p));
```

This inserts the range of values from iArray to iArray + 1 into iList at p, the result of the preceding call to find(). Remember that a range always specifies one *plus* the last object in that range; therefore, iArray to iArray + 2 is a range of two, not three, objects.

Try changing the search argument to find() to a value not in the list such as 99. Because this sets p to the *past-the-end* value, the final copy() statement appends the first two values from iArray onto the end of the list rather than in the middle.

MISCELLANEOUS ITERATOR FUNCTIONS

Two other iterator functions are useful for operations involving containers and STL algorithms. These are

- advance() increments or decrements an iterator a specified number of times.
- distance() returns the number of operations required to increment or decrement an iterator by a certain amount.

Some simple examples show how to use these two functions. Suppose that you define a list of integers by using the list template class:

```
list<int> iList;
```

Assume that the list is filled with values. As demonstrated in this chapter, you can use the find() algorithm to locate a specific value in the list. The following statement searches iList for the value 2:

```
list<int>::iterator p =
  find(iList.begin(), iList.end(), 2);
```

Following this search, use advance() to increment the list<int> iterator ahead two values. If you are following along, also use output statements to display the before and after value of *p (the value addressed by the iterator):

```
cout << "before: p == " << *p << endl;
advance(p, 2);  // same as p = p + 2;
cout << "after : p == " << *p << endl;
```

Pass to advance() an iterator and positive integer equal to the number of increment operations to perform. This value must be positive for forward-moving iterators; it can be negative for bidirectional and random access iterators.

Use the distance() function to determine the number of increment or decrement operations required to move an iterator from one value to another, or to the *past-the-end* value. For example, the following statements set k to the number of elements from p to the end of iList (usually following a search):

```
int k = 0;
distance(p, iList.end(), k);
cout << "k == " << k << endl;
```

> **Warning**
>
> The distance() function is iterative—that is, it *accumulates* a value in its third argument, k in this example. Because of this, you must initialize k to zero before calling distance(). *Failing to initialize this variable is almost certain to produce incorrect results.*

FUNCTIONS AND FUNCTION OBJECTS

In the STL, functions are known as *algorithms*, implying that they have a more general purpose than other functions such as those in the standard C library. STL algorithms are implemented as template functions or template classes with overloaded operator()() function-call operators. These classes are used to create *function objects* for use with a wide variety of actions on data in containers. The following sections explain how to use STL algorithms along with functions and function objects.

FUNCTIONS AND PREDICATES

It's often necessary to perform user-defined actions on data held in containers. For example, you might need to instruct an STL algorithm to call a function for all objects in a container. In that way, you can plug your own code into the algorithm and teach it a new trick.

As an example, Listing 23.6, foreach.cpp, teaches the STL for_each() algorithm how to perform three different functions on double values stored in a vector container.

LISTING 23.6   FOREACH.CPP

```
#include <iostream.h>
#include <stdlib.h>      // Need random(), srandom()
#include <time.h>        // Need time()
#include <vector>        // Need vector
#include <algorithm>     // Need for_each()

vector<double> v(5);     // Vector object

// Program functions to pass to for_each()
//
void initialize(double & rd);
void show(const double &rd);
void multiply(double & rd);

int main()
{
```

```
    srandom( time(NULL) );   // Seed random generator
    for_each(v.begin(), v.end(), initialize);
    cout << "Vector before multiply" << endl;
    for_each(v.begin(), v.end(), show);
    for_each(v.begin(), v.end(), multiply);
    cout << endl;
    cout << "Vector after multiplying * 10" << endl;
    for_each(v.begin(), v.end(), show);
    cout << endl;
    return 0;
}

// Set rd to a floating point value between 0 and 1.0
void initialize(double &rd)
{
  rd = ( 1.0 * random() / RAND_MAX);
}

// Display the value of rd
void show(const double &rd)
{
   cout << rd << "   ";
}

// Multiply rd by 10
void multiply(double & rd)
{
   rd *= 10;
}
```

Compile and run the program to display a small vector of floating point `double` values between 0 and 1.0 selected at random. Enter these commands:

```
$ g++ foreach.cpp
$ ./a.out
Vector before multiply
0.5629   0.197134   0.484129   0.00931074   0.237529
Vector after multiplying * 10
5.629   1.97134   4.84129   0.0931074   2.37529
```

The program uses functions instead of explicit loops to initialize the `vector`, display its values, multiply them by 10, and display the final results. This demonstrates how, using functions and algorithms, you can perform any actions you want on all or some objects in a container. The program constructs a `vector<double>` container, simply named `v`, as a global variable:

```
vector<double> v(5);
```

To perform operations on the container's values, the program prototypes three functions: `initialize()`, `show()`, and `multiply()`. Each function declares one parameter of the same type as the objects in the container. Although that type is `double` in this example, it can be any type of object including a class. To perform the function on all contained objects, the program calls the STL `for_each()` algorithm using the following statement:

```
for_each(v.begin(), v.end(), initialize);
```

The first two arguments are iterators that define the range of objects for which the algorithm calls `initialize()`. Notice that you supply only the *name* of the function, with no arguments or parentheses. The `for_each()` algorithm passes to the function a reference to each object in the container. To display the values in the container, and to multiply them by 10, the program uses similar statements:

```
for_each(v.begin(), v.end(), show);
for_each(v.begin(), v.end(), multiply);
```

In the case of `show()`, the `double` reference parameter is `const`. The other functions, `initialize()` and `multiply()`, declare a non-const `double` reference, indicating that the functions assign a value to the referenced object. Each function operates on one object. To set an object to a random value, for instance, the `initialize()` function assigns a value to its reference parameter `rd`:

```
void initialize(double &rd)
{
  rd = ( 1.0 * random() / RAND_MAX);
}
```

The `for_each()` algorithm calls this function for a defined range of objects in a container. The function uses the standard C library `random()` function to obtain an integer value at random, converted here to a value between 0 and 1.0. This keeps the code neat and simple, and avoids having to write `for` and `while` loops to operate on container objects.

Another type of function is called a *predicate*. This is a function that returns a `bool` or an `int` true or false value. Use predicate functions with algorithms such as `find_if()`, which returns an iterator to a value for which a predicate function returns true. Listing 23.7, findif.cpp, demonstrates how to use `find_if()` to search objects in a container.

LISTING 23.7 FINDIF.CPP

```
#include <iostream.h>
#include <stdlib.h>      // Need random(), srandom()
#include <time.h>        // Need time()
#include <vector>        // Need vector
#include <algorithm>     // Need for_each()

#define VSIZE 24         // Size of vector
vector<long> v(VSIZE);   // Vector object

// Function prototypes
void initialize(long &ri);
void show(const long &ri);
bool isMinus(const long &ri);   // Predicate function

int main()
{
  srandom( time(NULL) );   // Seed random generator

  for_each(v.begin(), v.end(), initialize);
  cout << "Vector of signed long integers" << endl;
  for_each(v.begin(), v.end(), show);
```

```
    cout << endl;

    // Use predicate function to count negative values
    //
    int count = 0;
    vector<long>::iterator p;
    p = find_if(v.begin(), v.end(), isMinus);
    while (p != v.end()) {
      count++;
      p = find_if(p + 1, v.end(), isMinus);
    }
    cout << "Number of values: " << VSIZE << endl;
    cout << "Negative values : " << count << endl;

    return 0;
}

// Set ri to a signed integer value
void initialize(long &ri)
{
  ri = ( random() - (RAND_MAX / 2) );
  //  ri = random();
}

// Display value of ri
void show(const long &ri)
{
  cout << ri << "   ";
}

// Returns true if ri is less than 0
bool isMinus(const long &ri)
{
  return (ri < 0);
}
```

Compile and run the test program to display a series of signed integer values selected at random and then count the number of negative values. Although this is an arbitrary action, it might be part of a test for a random number generator's distribution. Enter these commands (the program's output is shortened to save room here):

```
$ g++ findif.cpp
$ ./a.out
Vector of signed long integers
-242686306   -674155175   267974268   -447339946   438491145
...
Number of values: 24
Negative values : 15
```

The program defines a vector of long integers using the following directive and statement:

```
#define VSIZE 24         // Size of vector
vector<long> v(VSIZE);   // Vector object
```

Two functions, `initialize()` and `show()`, initialize the `vector` and display its contents (this is similar to how those functions work in the foreach.cpp program—refer to Listing 23.6). In addition, the program declares the predicate function prototype:

```
bool isMinus(const long &ri);  // Predicate function
```

The function `isMinus()` returns type `bool`, and it receives as an argument one `const` reference to the type of objects in the container. This parameter is usually `const` because a predicate function returns a true or false value based on its examination of the object's value. However, it might be non-`const` if the predicate needs to change a value in the course of this examination.

To prepare for using the predicate function, the program creates two variables, an integer `count` and an iterator `p` for the type of container:

```
int count = 0;
vector<long>::iterator p;
```

Using `p`, the `find_if()` algorithm, and the `isMinus()` predicate function, the following statements count the number of negative values in the container:

```
p = find_if(v.begin(), v.end(), isMinus);
while (p != v.end()) {
  count++;
  p = find_if(p + 1, v.end(), isMinus);
}
```

This isn't the only possible solution, but it demonstrates how algorithms use functions to examine the values of objects in containers. The first statement begins the search, setting iterator `p` to the first value in the defined range for which `isMinus()` returns true. While `p` addresses a valid object, the local `count` variable is increased by one, and the search continues with the next object at `p + 1`. When `p` equals the *past-the-end* value, the search is done.

Always test similar programming for outside cases. In this example, it's a good idea to verify that the code works if the container has no negative values. To do that, change the statement in function `initialize()` from this:

```
ri = (random() - (RAND_MAX / 2));
```

to return the always-positive value of the standard `random()` function:

```
ri = random();
```

FUNCTION OBJECTS

Instead of passing a function to an STL algorithm, you might need to pass an object of a class that performs a more complex service than demonstrated in the preceding sections. Such an object is called a *function object* because, although it's a class object, it behaves like a callable function. For example, a function object can retain information collected on each use—keeping statistical data about objects in a container searched, for instance, by the `for_each()` or `find_if()` algorithms.

Technically, a function object is an instance of any struct or class that overloads the function-call operator function, operator()(). By overloading this operator, an object of type TAnyClass may be constructed and used as a function this way:

```
TAnyClass object;   // Construct object
object();           // Calls TAnyClass::operator()() function
```

You probably won't write code like that, but the importance of being able to "call" objects as though they were functions is realized when using a standard algorithm. For example, a program can pass object to for_each() as follows for a vector v:

```
for_each(v.begin(), v.end(), object);
```

That performs the TAnyClass::operator()() function for the defined object on each value in the container. The object might define static variables, count the number of times it is called, or perform a variety of other tasks based on the values it is fed from the container by for_each().

The STL defines several function objects that perform mathematical operations on values. Because they are templates, they work on values of *any* types, including old standards such as long and double, but also on classes of your own making that overload mathematical operators. Some of these functions have obvious names, such as plus() and multiplies(). Similarly, comparison function objects such as greater() and less-equal() compare two values.

PART

V

CH

23

> **Note**
>
> Some versions of ANSI C++ define a times() function object. GNU C++ names this multiplies(); however, you might find one or the other function object in a GNU source file. For the names of other function objects, examine the function.h header file, which is probably in usr/include/g++, and is included by the directive #include<functional>.

A useful demonstration of function objects is the accumulate() algorithm. By default, accumulate() sums the values in a container. Remember that such values do not have to be simple—by overloading the operator+() function, the values could be class objects. For demonstration, however, Listing 23.8, accum.cpp, uses accumulate() to sum a set of long integers. The program also demonstrates how to teach accumulate() to use a function object to find the product of a container's values.

LISTING 23.8   ACCUM.CPP

```
#include <iostream.h>
#include <numeric>       // Need accumulate()
#include <vector>        // Need vector
#include <function.h>    // Need multiplies() (or times())

#define MAX 10
vector<long> v(MAX);     // Vector object
```

continues

LISTING 23.8 CONTINUED

```cpp
int main()
{
  // Fill vector using conventional loop
  //
  for (int i = 0; i < MAX; i++)
    v[i] = i + 1;

  // Accumulate the sum of contained values
  //
  long sum =
    accumulate(v.begin(), v.end(), 0);
  cout << "Sum of values == " << sum << endl;

  // Accumulate the product of contained values
  //
  long product =
    accumulate(v.begin(), v.end(), 1, multiplies<long>());
  cout << "Product of values == " << product << endl;

  return 0;
}
```

When you compile and run the program, it creates a small vector of long integers, initialized to the values 1 through 10, and then displays the sum and product of those values. Enter these commands to see the program's output:

```
$ g++ accum.cpp
$ ./a.out
Sum of values == 55
Product of values == 3628800
```

The program defines a vector of 10 long integers using this directive and statement:

```cpp
#define MAX 10
vector<long> v(MAX);
```

Then, just for the sake of being different, main() uses a conventional for loop to initialize the vector's values:

```cpp
for (int i = 0; i < MAX; i++)
  v[i] = i + 1;
```

To sum the values in vector v, the program calls accumulate() as follows and assigns its result to a long integer variable, sum:

```cpp
long sum =
  accumulate(v.begin(), v.end(), 0);
```

As usual, begin() and end() define the full range of values in the vector. The third argument provides an initial value for the accumulation. When summing values, this is usually zero as in the listing. However, it could be another value. For example, a subsequent statement could pass sum to accumulate() to compute a running total of two or more containers.

By telling `accumulate()` to use a different function object, this algorithm can do other sorts of mathematical operations on a container's objects. To demonstrate, the sample program finds the product of all contained values—in this case, equal to the factorial of 10. The arguments to the `accumulate()` algorithm are a little different:

```
long product =
  accumulate(v.begin(), v.end(), 1, multiplies<long>());
```

Again, `begin()` and `end()` define the range of values in the container, and the result is assigned to a program variable (`product`). The other two arguments provide a starting value (1) and a function object (`multiplies`). The starting value must be 1 in this case because we are multiplying the objects in the container against that value.

> **Note**
>
> As mentioned, depending on your version of ANSI C++, `multiplies()` might be named `times()`.

Examine the form of the function object passed to `accumulate()`. In this example, the statement constructs the function object for type `long` (using the STL `multiplies` template) and also calls that object's `operator()()` function.

GENERATOR FUNCTION OBJECTS

One particularly useful type of function object is called a *generator*. This kind of function has a memory—that is, it "remembers" a value from previous calls. A good example of a generator function is a random number generator that uses its previous value to compute the next value in a random sequence.

Conventional C programmers write a generator typically by using a static or global variable to retain a value between function calls. The problem with this method is the separation of the data from the function that relies on it. Encapsulating a function's "memory" using a class is a cleaner, and less bug-prone, way to create generator functions. By using a template class, it's also possible to apply the generator to an STL algorithm.

Before inspecting a full example, examine a simple demonstration that shows the basic technique for using a function generator object. Listing 23.9, randfunc.cpp, calls the `random_shuffle()` algorithm, which you met earlier in this chapter in the section "Random Access Iterators." A variation of this algorithm can call a function for the next number in a random sequence. Using a function generator object, this makes it possible to replace the algorithm's default random number generator with a custom subroutine.

LISTING 23.9   RANDFUNC.CPP

```
#include <iostream.h>
#include <stdlib.h>     // Need random(), srandom()
#include <time.h>       // Need time()
#include <algorithm>    // Need random_shuffle()
```

continues

LISTING 23.9   CONTINUED

```
#include <vector>       // Need vector
#include <functional>  // Need ptr_fun()

using namespace std;

// Data to randomize
int iarray[10] = {1, 2, 3, 4, 5, 6, 7, 8, 9, 10};
vector<int> v(iarray, iarray + 10);

// Function prototypes
void Display(vector<int>& vr, const char *s);
unsigned int RandInt(const unsigned int n);

int main()
{
  srandom( time(NULL) );  // Seed random generator
  Display(v, "Before shuffle:");

  pointer_to_unary_function<unsigned int, unsigned int>
    ptr_RandInt = ptr_fun(RandInt);  // Pointer to RandInt()
  random_shuffle(v.begin(), v.end(), ptr_RandInt);

  Display(v, "After shuffle:");
  return 0;
}

// Display contents of vector vr
void Display(vector<int>& vr, const char *s)
{
  cout << endl << s << endl;
  copy(vr.begin(), vr.end(), ostream_iterator<int>(cout, " "));
  cout << endl;
}


// Return next random value in sequence modulo n
unsigned int RandInt(const unsigned int n)
{
  return random() % n;
}
```

Compile and run the program, which displays the before and after effects of the random_shuffle() algorithm applied to a small array of integer values. Enter these commands:

```
$ g++ randfunc.cpp
$ ./a.out
Before shuffle:
1 2 3 4 5 6 7 8 9 10
After shuffle:
6 7 2 8 3 5 10 1 9 4
```

For its random number generator, the test program declares a prototype for a function that returns an unsigned int value:

```
unsigned int RandInt(unsigned int n);
```

As programmed here, RandInt() returns a value from 0 to n–1 selected at random. The program defines an array of integers and uses them to initialize a vector, v:

```
int iarray[10] = {1, 2, 3, 4, 5, 6, 7, 8, 9, 10};
vector<int> v(iarray, iarray + 10);
```

Scrambling the values in the vector is now a simple matter of calling the random_shuffle() algorithm. Due to a quirk in the STL, however, it isn't possible to pass the RandInt() function directly to random_shuffle() without receiving a compiler warning. To prevent the warning, first define a pointer to the function using the following statement:

```
pointer_to_unary_function<unsigned int, unsigned int>
  ptr_RandInt = ptr_fun(RandInt);
```

This somewhat verbose statement uses the STL's pointer_to_unary_function template to define a variable, here named ptr_RandInt, initialized to the address of our program's RandInt() function. A unary function declares a single parameter and returns a value, in this case both of type unsigned int as indicated in brackets. Armed with the pointer to the function, the program can now call random_shuffle() using this statement:

```
random_shuffle(v.begin(), v.end(), ptr_RandInt);
```

As usual, begin() and end() define the range of values on which to operate. Passing the function pointer to the algorithm causes it to call that function for a random value used to scramble the container's contents. In this simple example, the generator merely calls the standard C library's random() function:

```
unsigned int RandInt(unsigned int n)
{
  return random() % n;
}
```

Troubles with Constant References

In randfunc.cpp, Listing 23.9, it should be possible to pass the STL's ptr_fun object directly to random_shuffle() and similar algorithms that require a pointer to a unary function (one argument and a return value) or binary function (two arguments and a return value). However, ptr_fun() generates a constant reference to one of these types of functions, but random_shuffle() is written to receive a non-const argument. The following code should work, but it produces a compiler warning:

```
random_shuffle(v.begin(), v.end(), ptr_fun(RandInt));
```

The expression ptr_fun(RandInt) should produce a reference to the RandInt() function that is acceptable to random_shuffle(). However, this statement causes the compiler to issue a lengthy warning that reads, in part, "initialization of non-const reference ... from rvalue" ... plus a mess of confusing template instantiations. Despite appearances, this is actually a simple problem—it is caused by ptr_fun() generating a const reference (identified as an "rvalue," meaning an object that might be on the right side of the equal sign in an assignment statement).

continues

continued

If the preceding statement compiles with your version of GNU C++, then use this easier method of calling `random_shuffle()` with a replacement generator function. If the preceding produces the warning, you have two choices. One is to define a `const` version of the algorithm. Locate the original in file stl_algo.h in the /usr/include/g++ directory (version 2.7.2) and add `const` to the third parameter (`RandomNumberGenerator& rand`) as shown here in bold:

```
template <class RandomAccessIterator,class RandomNumberGenerator>
void random_shuffle(
  RandomAccessIterator first,
  RandomAccessIterator last,
  const RandomNumberGenerator& rand) {  // <-- add const
  ...
}
```

I edited the template to fit on this page—it probably looks a little different in your editor. For your information, the full template is in file template.h on the CD-ROM in directory src/c23. Include the header in a copy of randfunc.cpp, and the preceding statement that uses `ptr_fun()` should work.

Another solution is demonstrated in the sample randfunc.cpp program in Listing 23.9. Instead of passing `ptr_fun(RandInt)` directly to `random_shuffle()`, define a non-`const` pointer to the function and pass the pointer variable. This is the simpler solution, although it isn't as clean.

GENERATOR FUNCTION CLASS OBJECTS

Listing 23.10, fiborand.cpp, demonstrates a more sophisticated use for function objects created from a class template. This is a powerful concept, and the sample program is a good example of how a function object can define entirely fresh actions for STL algorithms. In this case, the program teaches `random_shuffle()` how to use a Fibonacci random number generator.

> **Note**
>
> For more information about how the Fibonacci random number generator works, see my article "Algorithm Alley," in *Dr. Dobb's Journal*, January 1994.

LISTING 23.10   FIBORAND.CPP

```
#include <iostream.h>
#include <algorithm>    // Need random_shuffle()
#include <vector>       // Need vector
#include <functional>   // Need unary_function

using namespace std;

// Data to randomize
int iarray[10] = {1, 2, 3, 4, 5, 6, 7, 8, 9, 10};
vector<int> v(iarray, iarray + 10);

// Function prototype
```

```
void Display(vector<int>& vr, const char *s);

// The FiboRand template function-object class
template <class Arg>
class FiboRand : public unary_function<Arg, Arg> {
  int i, j;
  Arg sequence[18];
public:
  FiboRand();
  Arg operator()(const Arg& arg);
};

void main()
{
  FiboRand<int> fibogen;   // Construct generator object
  cout << "Fibonacci random number generator" << endl;
  cout << "using random_shuffle and a function object" << endl;
  Display(v, "Before shuffle:");
  random_shuffle(v.begin(), v.end(), fibogen);
  Display(v, "After shuffle:");
}

// Display contents of vector vr
void Display(vector<int>& vr, const char *s)
{
  cout << endl << s << endl;
  copy(vr.begin(), vr.end(),
    ostream_iterator<int>(cout, " "));
  cout << endl;
}

// FiboRand class constructor
template<class Arg>
FiboRand<Arg>::FiboRand()
{
  sequence[17] = 1;
  sequence[16] = 2;
  for (int n = 15; n > 0; n--)
    sequence[n] = sequence[n + 1] + sequence[n + 2];
  i = 17;
  j = 5;
}

// FiboRand class function operator
template<class Arg>
Arg FiboRand<Arg>::operator()(const Arg& arg)
{
  Arg k = sequence[i] + sequence[j];
  sequence[i] = k;
  i--;
  j--;
  if (i == 0) i = 17;
  if (j == 0) j = 17;
  return k % arg;
}
```

Compile and run the program in the usual way. As the following lines show, the fiborand.cpp program displays similar results as randfunc.cpp (refer to Listing 23.9). Enter these commands to see the program's output:

```
$ g++ fiborand.cpp
$ ./a.out
Fibonacci random number generator
using random_shuffle and a function object
Before shuffle:
1 2 3 4 5 6 7 8 9 10
After shuffle:
6 8 5 2 4 3 7 10 1 9
```

The program performs its actions using an entirely different method of generating numbers at random. The algorithm for the Fibonacci generator is encapsulated in a class—providing a good example of how a function object can be made to "remember" values from previous uses. In this case, class FiboRand maintains a sequence of 18 values (index[0] is ignored) and two index variables, i and j, that retain their values between calls to the generator. Using a class avoids having to make these values static variables—and thus, the program could define as many FiboRand generator objects as it needs without conflict. The resulting generator is completely modular and is ready for use in other programs.

The FiboRand class is derived from the unary_function() template, using the following declaration:

```
template <class Arg>
class FiboRand : public unary_function<Arg, Arg> {...
```

Arg is the user-defined data type. The class also declares two member functions—a constructor that initializes a FiboRand function (and seeds the random generator), and an overloaded operator()() function. This function permits the random_shuffle() algorithm to "call" a FiboRand object as though it were a function. The only requirement is that values of type Arg can be added.

Passing an instance of the FiboRand class template creates a function object that random_shuffle() can use. Although it might take a little effort to program the function object class, given the finished FiboRand, a simple statement passes the new generator to the STL random_shuffle() algorithm:

```
FiboRand<int> fibogen;
random_shuffle(v.begin(), v.end(), fibogen);
```

Here again, it is apparently necessary to create an object using the FiboRand template and then pass the *object*—not the *generator function reference*—to random_shuffle(). This avoids the compiler warning mentioned earlier about the initialization of "a non-const reference."

BINDER FUNCTION OBJECTS

A *binder* creates a function object from another function object f() and an argument value v. The function object must be binary—that is, it must accept two arguments, A and B. Two binder objects are in the STL (Standard Template Library):

- bind1st() creates a function object that applies value V to the first function argument A.

- bind2nd() creates a function object that applies value V to the second function argument B.

The purpose of these two binders is clearer by examining how they are used. Listing 23.11, binder.cpp, demonstrates how to search a list of values using bind1st().

LISTING 23.11   BINDER.CPP

```
#include <iostream.h>
#include <algorithm>
#include <functional>
#include <list>

using namespace std;

// Data
int iarray[10] = {1, 2, 3, 4, 5, 6, 7, 8, 9, 10};
list<int> aList(iarray, iarray + 10);

int main()
{
  int k = 0;
  count_if(aList.begin(), aList.end(),
    bind1st(greater<int>(), 8), k);
  cout << "Number elements < 8 == " << k << endl;
  return 0;
}
```

The program defines an array of 10 integers, which are used to initialize a linked list container. Algorithm count_if() counts the number of elements in the list that satisfy a certain condition. This is done by *binding* a function object with an argument and passing the resulting object to the algorithm's third parameter. The algorithm used here returns its resulting count in the fourth argument, k. This value must be initialized to zero as shown in the listing. Carefully examine the binder expression:

```
bind1st(greater<int>(), 8)
```

This constructs an object of the binary_function template that combines the function object greater<int>() with an argument value, 8. Because the program uses bind1st(), that value is applied to the function's first argument, thus creating an object that computes the result of the expression:

```
8 > q
```

where q is one of the container's values. Despite appearances, then, the full statement

```
count_if(aList.begin(), aList.end(),
  bind1st(greater<int>(), 8), k);
```

actually counts the number of values in aList that are *less than or equal to* 8 (or, more strictly speaking, the number of values for which 8 is greater). To make the statement count the number of values greater than 8, replace the count_if() statement with the following:

```
count_if(aList.begin(), aList.end(),
  bind2nd(greater<int>(), 8), k);
cout << "Number elements > 8 == " << k << endl;
```

This code is written as a comment at the end of the listing file. Because bind2nd() is now used, the resulting function object performs the expression:

```
q > 8
```

where q is again a value from the container. Thus, the modified statement counts the number of elements greater than 8.

NEGATOR FUNCTION OBJECTS

A *negator* creates a function object from another function object, but it has the opposite effect. Where the original function returns true, the negator object returns false. There are two negators in the STL (Standard Template Library): not1() and not2(). Pass any unary function object to not1(). Pass any binary function object to not2(). Negators are often used in conjunction with binders to create function objects with a negated logic.

For example, you might use a negator to search a list of values. Using a copy of the program binder.cpp (refer to Listing 23.11), construct an iterator named start for the list<int> class and assign to the iterator the result of the find_if() algorithm. The following code demonstrates this process by searching the list for a matching condition:

```
list<int>::iterator start;
start = find_if(aList.begin(), aList.end(),
  bind2nd(greater<int>(), 6));
if (start != aList.end())
  cout << "start == " << *start << endl;
```

The condition for the search is specified by the binder bind2nd(). After the search, if start is not equal to the *past-the-end* value, the iterator addresses the first listed value greater than 6. To perform the opposite search and look for the first value that is *not* greater than 6, pass the binder expression to not1() as follows:

```
start = find_if(aList.begin(), aList.end(),
  not1(bind2nd(greater<int>(), 6)));
```

You must use not1() in this case because bind2nd() returns a unary_function object. Use not2() similarly to create a function object for any binary_function object.

SUMMARY

The C++ standard template library (STL) is a comprehensive collection of data structures and algorithms. Two features characterize the STL (Standard Template Library): the separation of data structures from algorithms and its non-object-oriented nature. Access to objects is provided by iterators, which in use resemble pointers. Containers are data structures such as lists and vectors and are provided as class templates. Algorithms are function templates that operate on data in containers. Because the STL is template-based, its components work with just about any data type and structure.

For more information on subjects introduced in this chapter, turn to the following chapters:

- Chapter 17, "Creating Class Templates"
- Chapter 19, "Overloading Operators"
- Chapter 24, "Building Standard Containers"
- Chapter 25, "Applying Standard Algorithms"

PART

V

CH

23

BUILDING STANDARD CONTAINERS

The Standard Template Library (STL) provides 10 container data structures in the form of class templates. Because they are templates, the containers mold themselves to accommodate any type of object. As introduced in the preceding chapter, access to objects in a container is through the use of iterators. This makes containers completely general in nature, and you can use them to store simple values, structures, class objects, or pointers to objects. To create multilevel structures, a container can even store other containers. The possibilities for data storage using STL container templates are limitless.

This chapter explores the STL's container templates and shows examples of how to create and use each type.

INTRODUCING STANDARD CONTAINERS

Table 24.1 lists the STL's 10 container class templates arranged roughly in order of complexity.

TABLE 24.1 STANDARD C++ CONTAINER CLASS TEMPLATES

Class Template	Description
vector	Linear sequence, similar to an array
list	Double-linked list
deque	Double-ended queue
set	Associative array of unique keys
multiset	Associative array of nonunique keys
map	Associative array of unique keys and values
multimap	Associative array of nonunique keys and values
stack	Last-in-first-out (LIFO) data structure
queue	First-in-first-out (FIFO) data structure
priority_queue	Critical-event-ordered queue or vector

Following are some rules, regulations, and definitions that help explain some important aspects of STL containers:

- A container may store any type of object, including fundamental values of types int and double, strings, structures, class objects, and pointers. However, a container may not store references to objects.

- A class copy constructor handles an object's insertion into a container. By overloading the assignment operator=() function and providing a copy constructor, you gain total control over container insertions—especially valuable in managing the effects of operations such as copying one container to another. See Chapter 12, "Introducing the Class," and Chapter 21, "Honing Your C++ Skills," for more information about copy constructors.

- Containers automatically allocate and release memory as needed for object storage. A container may be a global or local variable, or it may be created by new and disposed of by delete.

- A vector can grow to accommodate new data, but it doesn't automatically shrink in size. Other containers such as lists, deques, and sets grow and shrink as needed to use memory efficiently.

- When a program destroys a container, it first calls any destructor for its owned objects. This means that you can safely destroy a container without first removing its contents.

- However, the preceding rule does not apply when a container stores pointers to objects. In that case, as with C++ arrays, it is your responsibility to destroy the addressed objects and to free any allocated memory before destroying the container.

Tip

See "Pointers in Containers" near the end of Chapter 25, "Applying Standard Algorithms," for details on the safe destruction of objects addressed by pointers.

VECTORS

A vector is like a smart array that maintains size information and can grow to make room for storing more data. A vector provides random access to data through the C++ subscript operator[]() function. The vector template class also provides a number of useful member functions that you can call to operate on object values.

Because a vector provides immediate, random access to data, it takes no longer to access the last element in a vector container than it does the first. However, because elements in a vector are stored physically together, insertions into the middle of a vector cause other elements to move, an action that takes time proportional to the number of moved objects. Insertions at the end of a vector are efficient, unless the insertion requires the vector to expand. When that happens, a vector expands, meaning that its data might have to be copied to another memory block. Thus vector expansions may temporarily require more than twice the amount of occupied memory. If your program does a lot of insertions, you may want to use a list or another more memory-efficient data structure described in this chapter.

Note

The programming in the following sections is taken from the file vector.cpp on the CD-ROM in the src/c24 directory.

DECLARING VECTORS

The following statements demonstrate several different ways to construct vector containers. First include the vector header file along with any others needed:

```
#include <vector>
#include <string>
```

Then use statements such as the following to construct `vector` containers for specific types of data:

```
vector<int> vint;
vector<string> vstring(10);
vector<double> vdouble(100);
```

The first statement constructs an empty `vector` that can hold values of type `int`. However, it's rarely useful to construct empty vectors, and you'll normally specify an initial size as the other two statements demonstrate. The first of these constructs a `vector` container, `vstring`, big enough to hold 10 `string` objects. The second statement constructs a `vector` named `vdouble` big enough for 100 values.

Warning

Attempting to insert an object into an empty `vector` may cause a memory segmentation fault. To prevent this unhappy event, always specify a size for `vector` containers.

Because the containers are `vector`s, the most common way to insert data into them is to use array index expressions such as the following:

```
vstring[1] = "Value == ";
vdouble[2] = 3.14159;
```

You can also access elements in a `vector`, for example, to display their values in an output statement:

```
cout << vstring[1] << vdouble[2] << endl;
```

You may store other types of data in `vector` containers. However, any structures, including class objects, require the following elements:

- A default constructor
- A copy constructor
- A destructor
- An overloaded `operator*()` (address of) function
- An overloaded `operator=()` (assignment) function

You need to implement those elements only if C++ cannot generate them automatically. For example, if your class declares any pointers to allocated memory, the class must have an explicit copy constructor and `operator=()` function to prevent memory leaks.

Listing 24.1, coordinate.h, provides a test class with the kinds of elements needed in designing classes of objects to be stored in a `vector` container. The class, `TCoordinate`, stores an (x,y) coordinate value. To use the class, simply include its header file—all member functions are written inline, and there is no corresponding module to compile. For space reasons, Listing 24.1 is taken from coordinate.txt, which lists the class's members but does not show their implementations. Load coordinate.h into your editor if you want to inspect the programming, all of which has been fully described in other chapters.

LISTING 24.1   COORDINATE.H (CLASS MEMBERS)

```
class TCoordinate {
private:
  int tc_x, tc_y;
public:
  TCoordinate();
  TCoordinate(int x, int y);
  TCoordinate(const TCoordinate& arg);
  ~TCoordinate();
  void operator=(const TCoordinate &copy);
  bool operator== (const TCoordinate& arg) const;
  bool operator< (const TCoordinate& arg);
  inline friend ostream &
    operator<<(ostream & os, const TCoordinate& q);
  inline friend istream &
    operator>>(istream & is, TCoordinate& q);
  void Setxy(int x, int y);
  int Getx() const;
  int Gety() const;
};
```

Given the TCoordinate class, you can create a vector of class objects and a pointer to those objects using statements such as these:

```
vector<TCoordinate> vobject(10);
vector<TCoordinate *> vpointer(10);
```

The first statement constructs a vector of 10 TCoordinate objects. The second statement constructs a similar vector but stores *pointers* to TCoordinate objects. To insert a class object into a vector, construct it and assign the result using an array index expression:

```
vobject[0] = TCoordinate(10, 20);
vpointer[0] = new TCoordinate(30, 40);
```

Because TCoordinate provides overloaded << and >> operators, you can display the object values with output statements such as the following:

```
cout << "vobject[0]  : " << vobject[0] << endl;
cout << "vpointer[0] : " << *vpointer[0] << endl;
```

As mentioned, when storing pointers in containers, it is your responsibility to delete any objects created using new:

```
delete vpointer[0];
```

You may also construct a vector using iterators. For example, these statements copy an array of int values into a vector:

```
int iarray[24];
vector<int> v1(iarray, iarray + 24);
```

This statement copies the values from vector v1 to a new vector v2:

```
vector<int> v2(v1.begin(), v1.end());
```

In addition to these methods for constructing vector containers, a second argument passed to the constructor is supposed to initialize the values in a container:

```
vector<int> vinit(32, -1);  // ???
```

That should set all 32 elements in vinit to –1, but at this writing, the statement does not compile. Work around this problem by passing a variable instead of a literal initial value:

```
int x = -1;
vector<int> vinit(32, x);
```

USING VECTORS

The *size* of a vector container equals how many elements it stores. If vdouble is a vector of 100 double values, the following statement displays 100:

```
cout << "Size of vdouble == " << vdouble.size() << endl;
```

A vector's *capacity* indicates how large the vector may become before a memory allocation is needed for holding more objects:

```
cout << "Capacity == " << vdouble.capacity() << endl;
```

A vector's size may be the same or less than its capacity. A vector's maximum size returns the upper limit on how many objects a vector can hold:

```
cout << "Max size == " << vdouble.max_size() << endl;
```

The maximum size does not, however, indicate how much memory is available to the vector. You can alter a vector's capacity without affecting its current size by calling the reserve() function. This is a memory-efficient way to avoid frequent allocations in cases where you can determine in advance how many values the program ultimately stores in the container. For example, the following statement changes the vdouble container's capacity to 250, but its size remains at 100:

```
vdouble.reserve(250);
```

BOOLEAN VECTORS

The STL treats a Boolean vector container as a special superset of the vector class template. Define a Boolean vector using the C++ bool data type like this:

```
vector<bool> vbool(16);
```

That creates a vector named vbool of 16 true and false values. Use subscript expressions to assign values to vector elements:

```
vbool[0] = true;
vbool[1] = false;
```

You can also specify an initial value. For example, this constructs an eight-element Boolean vector with all values initialized to true:

```
vector<bool> vbinit(8, true);
```

As with all `vector` containers, a Boolean `vector`'s size equals the number of values it contains. This is not necessarily the same as the container's size in bytes, as the following statements suggest:

```
cout << "vbool size  == " << vbool.size() << endl;
cout << "vbool bytes == " << sizeof(vbool) << endl;
```

The first statement reports `vbool`'s size as 16 elements. The second shows that the container's size in bytes is twice that value, or 32, indicating that each `bool` object takes two bytes.

> **Note**
> The `bit_vector` class is a synonym for the `vector<bool>` class. Neither class is a packed array of bits.

A `vector`'s values are interpreted as 1 for `true` and 0 for `false`. This means that the following statement displays 1 0, not the words "true" and "false," as might be expected:

```
cout << vbool[0] << " " << vbool[1] << endl;
```

Calling Vector Functions

The `vector` template provides a number of useful member functions that you can call. I already explained one of these functions, `reserve()`. Another two, `front()` and `back()`, return the first and last elements in a `vector`:

```
cout << "First == " << vdouble.front() << endl;
cout << "Last  == " << vdouble.back() << endl;
```

Three more highly useful functions are `erase()`, `resize()`, and `insert()`. To demonstrate these functions, define a `vector` of six integers as follows:

```
int ia[6] = { 1, 2, 3, 4, 5, 6 };
vector<int> sixints(ia, ia + 6);
```

Erasing a `vector` object moves any others upward in the container. For example, after calling `find()` to locate a specific element, pass the resulting iterator to `erase()` to remove that object:

```
vector<int>::iterator p =
  find(sixints.begin(), sixints.end(), 3);
sixints.erase(p);
```

In the not-too-recent past, `erase()` didn't alter the size of the `vector`; as a result, values at the end of the moved objects become duplicated. For that reason, `erase()` is often followed by `resize()`, as follows:

```
sixints.resize(5);
```

This does no harm but is no longer necessary. You can also use `resize()` to increase the number of elements in a `vector`. Using the empty `vint` object from the preceding section, the following increases its size to 10 and assigns a value to a `vector` slot:

```
if (vint.empty())
  vint.resize(10);
vint[3] = 123;
```

The call to empty() is true if the vector's size equals zero.

Call insert() to insert a new value into a vector and move any other values down. The following statement inserts the value 99 into the sixints vector at the third position (the second position past the first):

```
sixints.insert(sixints.begin() + 2, 99);
```

Use the pop_back() and push_back() functions to use a vector as a stack. This statement pushes the value 123 onto the end of the vector:

```
sixints.push_back(123);
```

Remove the last element by calling pop_back() with no arguments:

```
sixints.pop_back();
```

Because that doesn't return the pushed value but merely removes it, to save the value requires an extra step before calling pop_back(). This sets top to the value on the top of the stack:

```
int top = sixints[ sixints.size() - 1];
```

Note See "Stacks" later in this chapter for a more rigorous stack container class template.

Exchange two vectors by calling swap() for one of the containers, and pass the other as an argument. This swaps vector v and sixints:

```
vector<int> v(6);
sixints.swap(v);
```

LISTS

A list is a linear collection of double-linked objects. Each object in a list contains two pointers that can address another object. This organization makes a list a highly efficient data structure. Regardless of object order, a list takes only as much space as necessary, plus a smidgen extra for the links and perhaps a few bytes to fill each memory block to its minimum allocation size. This makes a list an excellent choice for storing data in fragmented memory and in that way potentially squeeze more information into limited memory than a vector, in which objects are stored physically together.

Insertions and deletions of list objects are absolutely efficient. It takes no more time to delete the first item in a list than it does the last. Also, deleting objects from the middle of a list doesn't cause other objects to move but merely requires the container to adjust a few links. There are no holes in a list.

On the other hand, lists are poor choices when you need rapid access to data—during a search for matching values, for example. Searches in a list are linear by nature and therefore take time proportional to the number of examined objects. For fast, random access to data, a vector may be more appropriate than a list. However, if you need the benefits of a list and random access (you want to eat your cake and have it, too), all is not lost: Consider using a set, a map, or a priority_queue as described later in this chapter.

Note

The sample programming in the following sections is taken from the file list.cpp in the src/c24 directory on the CD-ROM.

DECLARING LISTS

The following statements show a few ways to construct different kinds of list containers:

```
list<int> ilist(10);
list<double> fplist(10, 1.0);
list<string> strlist(24);
```

The first line creates an empty list that can store int values. The second creates a list of 10 double values, each initialized to 1.0. The third creates a list of 24 strings. You may store other types of data in a list container. However, struct and class objects require the following members:

- Default constructor
- Copy constructor
- Destructor
- Assignment operator=() function
- Equality operator==() function (must be const)
- Less-than operator<() function (must be const)
- Address-of operator*() function

You must explicitly declare the constructors and destructor, but the operator functions are optional. Unless the class declares a pointer to allocated memory, for example, you don't have to overload the operator=() assignment function. Using the TCoordinate class in file coordinate.h (refer to Listing 24.1), the following statements construct lists of class objects:

```
list<TCoordinate> coords(10);
list<TCoordinate *> coordPtrs(10);
```

The first statement creates a list of 10 TCoordinate objects. The second creates a list of pointers to TCoordinate objects. Insert an object into the first list using a statement such as this:

```
coords.insert(coords.begin(), TCoordinate(4, 5));
```

When the list is destroyed, it calls the TCoordinate destructor for each object in the list. To insert a pointer to an object created dynamically with new, use a statement such as the following:

```
coordPtrs.insert(coordPtrs.begin(), new TCoordinate(6, 7));
```

In this case, because the container stores pointers, it is your responsibility to call any required destructor. For example, to remove a listed object from `coordPtrs` requires two statements:

```
delete coordPtrs.front();
coordPtrs.remove(coordPtrs.front());
```

The first statement deletes the memory allocated to the first object in the `list`. The second statement removes the now invalid pointer to that object.

USING LISTS

To determine the number of objects in a `list`, call the `size()` function. Try this. First define a `list` container and fill it with some values:

```
list<int> anyList;
for (int i = 0; i < 10; i++)
  anyList.insert(anyList.end(), i);
```

Call `empty()` and `size()` to determine whether the `list` is empty, or if not, to display the number of elements it contains:

```
if (anyList.empty())
  cout << "List is empty" << endl;
else
  cout << "List has " << anyList.size() << " elements" << endl;
```

There are several other ways to insert objects into a `list` container. You can use the `insert()` function as shown in the preceding samples, or you can call `push_front()` and `push_back()` to insert objects at the beginning or end of the `list`. Given the `anyList` container, add objects to its head and tail with code such as this:

```
anyList.push_back(1234);
anyList.push_front(4321);
```

> **Tip**
>
> To display the contents of the `list` examples in this section, the sample list.cpp program on the CD-ROM uses the following output statement:
>
> ```
> copy(c.begin(), c.end(),
>   ostream_iterator<int>(cout, " "));
> ```

To insert multiple objects initialized to a certain value, the following is supposed to work but fails to compile:

```
anyList.insert(anyList.begin(), 4, -1);  // ???
```

GNU C++ seems not to like the literal initializing value, and the following uses a variable as a reasonable workaround to the problem:

```
int value = -1;
anyList.insert(anyList.begin(), 4, value);
```

That inserts four integer objects equal to –1 into the `list` container. Another way to insert an object is to use an iterator. It's common to do this following a search of a `list` for a specific value, perhaps using the `find()` algorithm. First, define an iterator for the container's class:

```
list<int>::iterator p;
```

Then call `find()` or another search algorithm, followed by an insertion:

```
p = find(anyList.begin(), anyList.end(), 8);
if (p != anyList.end())
  anyList.insert(p, -2);
```

To `find()`, pass two iterators that define the search range of objects in the container. Also pass the value to find, 8 in this case. After the search, if the iterator p is not equal to the *past-the-end* value, it addresses a listed object. Pass the iterator and a new object value to insert in the `list`. Actually, you don't have to test p's value because, even if the `list` is empty, `find()` sets p to the *past-the-end* value, and the insertion is made at the end of the `list`, or a new `list` is begun.

To remove objects from a `list` container, you have several options. Call `erase()` to remove a specific element, usually following a search statement as in this sample code:

```
p = find(anyList.begin(), anyList.end(), 7);
if (p != anyList.end())
  anyList.erase(p);
```

That searches for the value 7 in the `list` of integers and, if found, calls `erase()` to remove that value from the `list`. The `list` container automatically deletes any allocated memory and calls the object's class destructor. However, if the `list` contains pointers, it's your responsibility to delete any allocated memory.

To remove all equal values in a `list`, call `remove()` and specify the value that you want to locate:

```
anyList.remove(-1);
```

That removes all integer values equal to –1 from `anyList`. Use an alternate form of `erase()` to remove all objects in a defined range. Often, you'll do this after searching for a specific element, as in this code:

```
p = find(anyList.begin(), anyList.end(), 3);
anyList.erase(p, anyList.end());
```

Using the iterator p defined earlier, the first statement calls `find()` to locate the value 3 in the `list`. The second statement calls `erase()` to remove all objects from that point to the end of the `list`. Even if the searched-for object isn't found, this code works correctly because if p equals the *past-the-end* value, the second statement does nothing. (You might, however, test the value of p as described earlier.)

Lists are often used as stacks and queues where objects are pushed and popped from the front and back of a `list` container. Remove the first object of a `list` by calling `pop_front()`. Remove the last by calling `pop_back()`. For example, this loop displays and removes all objects from `anyList`:

```
while (!anyList.empty()) {
  cout << anyList.front() << endl;
  anyList.pop_front();
}
```

Replace front() with back() and pop_front() with pop_back() to delete objects in reverse order. In either case, the list reduces itself one object at a time, like a snake eating itself by the tail until it disappears.

Finally, here's a unique function—in fact, its name is unique(). Call it to remove all but one of every duplicated value in a list. For example, create a list and insert a series of duplicate adjacent values:

```
for (int i = 0; i < 10; i++) {
  anyList.insert(anyList.end(), i);
  anyList.insert(anyList.end(), i);
}
```

That inserts into anyList (emptied by prior statements) the sequence 0, 0, 1, 1, ..., 9, 9. Remove the duplicated values by calling unique():

```
anyList.unique();
```

After that, anyList contains the sequence 0, 1, ..., 9. The list does not have to be sorted, but the duplicated values must be adjacent.

CALLING LIST FUNCTIONS

As with all container data structures, the list template class provides several member functions that perform highly specialized jobs using iterators to refer to objects. You can use iterators to assign values to list elements, and this might be faster than deleting old items and inserting new ones. For example, the following assigns values selected at random (using the standard C library's random() function) to all integer values in anyList, using an iterator named here iter:

```
list<int>::iterator iter;
for (iter = anyList.begin(); iter != anyList.end(); iter++)
  *iter = (int)random() % 1000;
```

The for loop sets iter to each object in the list, and the single associated statement assigns to the dereferenced *iter a value at random modulo 1000 (just to save display room). It's interesting to note that all the mechanics of traversing the list's links are hidden inside the overloaded ++ operator. Because the iterator "knows" it is exported from a list container, the expression iter++ follows the list's links to the next object—even though iter is used as a pointer, which in this case it is.

Call reverse() to reorder a list from front to back. If anyList contains the values 10, 20, 30, 40, this statement changes the list to 40, 30, 20, 10:

```
anyList.reverse();
```

This is one way to convert a last-in, first-out stack into a first-in, first-out queue. Call sort() to order listed objects in ascending value:

```
anyList.sort();
```

Perform comparisons by calling the object's class operator<() function. To sort in descending order, pass a binary function template such as greater_equal() to sort():

```
anyList.sort(greater_equal<int>());
```

You cannot pass `list` containers to the standard `sort()` algorithm because it requires random access iterators. Lists provide only bidirectional iterators, and, therefore, the `list` class template provides its own specialized `sort()` member function. The sorting function is stable—that is, objects with equal sorting key values retain their original relative order after sorting.

You can merge two `list`s. For example, define a couple of `list` containers and initialize them by using common C++ arrays:

```
int buf1[4] = { 10, 20, 30, 40 };
list<int> list1(buf1, buf1 + 4);
int buf2[4] = { 15, 25, 35, 45 };
list<int> list2(buf2, buf2 + 4);
```

Merge the two lists, `list1` and `list2`, using this statement:

```
list1.merge(list2);
```

That merges `list2`'s objects into `list1` and also removes the objects from the source `list2`. The resulting `list1` now contains the sequence 10, 15, 20, 25, 30, 35, 40, 45. As a beneficial side effect, the automatic removal of source objects prevents more than one `list` from addressing the same dynamic objects in memory, which would cause a serious bug when those objects are deleted.

Another kind of insertion function is called a *splice*. Like merging, splicing takes the objects from one `list` and inserts them into another. However, as when splicing an audiotape, the entire splice is inserted at a specific location. Call `splice()` with two arguments as shown here:

```
list2.splice(list2.begin(), list1);
```

The first argument is the iterator in the target `list` at which to make the insertions. In this case, `begin()` provides that location, but because `list2` is empty, any iterator value would do. The second argument is the source of the splice. In effect, the preceding statement swaps the two `list`s.

To splice a single value from one `list` to another, use code such as this:

```
list1.splice(list1.begin(), list2,
  find(list2.begin(), list2.end(), 35));
```

If `list1` is initially empty, and `list2` contains the values 10, ..., 35, 40, 45, after the statement executes, `list1` equals 35, and that value is deleted from `list2`. Notice how the result of `find()`, an iterator, is passed directly to `splice()` to specify the location of an object from the source `list`. Here's a third variation that splices a portion of one `list` onto another:

```
list1.splice(list1.end(), list2,
  find(list2.begin(), list2.end(), 25),
      list2.end());
```

The target `list` (`list1`) calls `splice()` with four arguments. First is the iterator into the target `list` at which to make the splice. Second is the source of the splice, `list2`. Following those arguments are two iterators that define the range of objects to use from the source. The first iterator is the result of a find() search for the value 25 in list2. The second iterator is the end of that list. As a result, all objects from 25 to the end of list2 are spliced onto the end of list1. The spliced objects are removed from the source list2.

Deques

The STL's deque container, or "double-ended queue," is not exactly the same as the classic deque data structure. A deque container combines the features of a vector with a list. In this sense, a deque is a type of list for which vector-like indexing operations are allowed along with the capability to use list-like push and pop operations.

A deque is advantageous for algorithms requiring access to the front and rear of lists. This makes a deque resemble a stack with queue- and list-like features that allow pushing and popping objects at either end of the queue. The STL's deque class also permits insertions anywhere in the container, although middle insertions are not as efficiently handled as with plain lists. Insertions and deletions at a deque's beginning or end are done as efficiently as possible.

> **Note**
>
> The programming samples in the following sections are taken from file deque.cpp in the src/c24 directory on the CD-ROM.

Declaring Deques

Declare deque containers in much the same way as you do other STL data structures. For example, after including the deque and string header files

```
#include <deque>
#include <string>
```

you can define deque containers using statements such as the following:

```
deque<string> d1;
deque<double> d2(10);
```

The first statement creates an empty deque of string objects. The second creates a 10-element deque of double values. You should be able to initialize a deque's values with a statement such as this:

```
deque<int> d3(12, -1);   // ???
```

However, this doesn't compile with GNU C++. Instead of a literal value, passing a variable works around this minor problem:

```
int value = -1;
deque<int> d3(12, value);
```

That creates a deque container, d3, with 12 double values initialized to –1.

USING DEQUES

The most common way to insert and remove objects in `deque` containers is through calls to `push_front()`, `push_back()`, `pop_front()`, and `pop_back()` member functions. The following statements create a `deque` container named `fruits` of `string` objects and then call `push_front()` and `push_back()` to insert strings onto the deque's front and rear:

```
deque<string> fruits;
fruits.push_front("Apple");
fruits.push_back("Banana");
fruits.push_front("Pear");
fruits.push_back("Orange");
```

The resulting `list` is Pear, Apple, Banana, Orange. Display and remove the `string` objects using a loop such as the following:

```
cout << "Deleting the fruits deque" << endl;
while (!fruits.empty()) {
  cout << fruits.front() << endl;
  fruits.pop_front();
}
```

Replace `pop_front()` with `pop_back()` to remove objects from the rear of a `deque` container.

PART

V

CH

24

CALLING DEQUE FUNCTIONS

The `deque` class's member functions, such as `insert()`, `erase()`, `size()`, and `swap()`, are the same as for the STL `vector` and `list` template classes. However, `deque` containers possess one unique characteristic over a `list`—indexing. The STL `deque` permits random access to its elements through the C++ array indexing operator [ ]. For example, a common `for` loop displays all values in a `deque` container:

```
for (int i = 0; i < fruits.size(); i++)
  cout << "fruits[" << i << "]: " << fruits[i] << endl;
```

SETS AND MULTISETS

A `set` is a collection of unique values. A `multiset` is a collection of possibly nonunique values. Sets of either type are automatically maintained in order, as defined by a default or explicit function object. Insertions and deletions in a `set` container are optimized, and searches for values in `sets` are fast. A `set` container is practically unlimited in size. The objects in a `set` are called *keys*.

The `set` and `multiset` containers resemble bags in some other container class libraries. In this sense, a `set` is like a sack that you can rummage through to look for values. You can also perform logical set operations on two `sets`—for example, finding the union of two sets of objects. (More on this in Chapter 25, "Applying Standard Algorithms.")

DECLARING SETS

A `set` container is a bit more complex to create than others. In addition to specifying the type of data to store in a `set`, you also must define a function object for maintaining values in order. First, include the set header file for the set class template, along with the functional or other header file that declares the function objects you want to use, such as less and less_equal:

```
#include <set>
#include <functional>
```

Next, to make it easier to create set container objects, use typedef to define the instantiated set class. For example, the following declares TIntSet as the name of a set container that can hold integer values and that uses the less function object to maintain those values in order:

```
typedef set<int, less<int> > TIntSet;
```

You can then define objects of type TIntSet. This creates an empty set of integers named intSet:

```
TIntSet intSet;
```

Create other types of sets using similar statements. Here are two more typedefs that declare names for set classes of types double and string:

```
typedef set<double, greater<double> > TDoubleSet;
typedef set<string, less<string> > TStringSet;
```

Use the typedefs to construct container objects:

```
TDoubleSet doubleSet;
TStringSet stringSet;
```

To insert values into a set container, call the insert() member function. These statements, for example, insert floating point constants from the standard C library math.h header file into the doubleSet container:

```
doubleSet.insert(M_E);
doubleSet.insert(M_LOG2E);
doubleSet.insert(M_PI);
```

And these statements insert strings into the stringSet object:

```
stringSet.insert("Lemon");
stringSet.insert("Papaya");
stringSet.insert("Mango");
```

Another way to insert values into a set is to use iterators. Using the TIntSet typedef from before, the following statements transfer values from a common int array to a new set container, evenSet:

```
int evenBuf[4] = { 2, 4, 6, 8 };
TIntSet evenSet(evenBuf, evenBuf + 4);
```

You can also copy one set to another by passing iterators from the source set to the set class constructor. The following statement, for instance, copies the values from doubleSet to a new set named setCopy of the type TDoubleSet:

```
TDoubleSet setCopy(doubleSet.begin(), doubleSet.end());
```

USING SETS

There's only one way to insert values into a set container—by calling the insert() member function. Because sets are always maintained in order, there are no methods for inserting values into specific positions. You simply toss values into set containers and let them determine their own locations. Use the find() algorithm to locate a specific value in a set:

```
TDoubleSet::iterator double_iter =
  find(doubleSet.begin(), doubleSet.end(), M_PI);
```

The statement creates an iterator, double_iter, of the iterator type exported by TDoubleSet. Calling find() for the range of values in the set returns an iterator if the search argument, M_PI here, is found. If so, double_iter is used as a pointer to retrieve the value from the set container:

```
if (double_iter != doubleSet.end())
  cout << *double_iter << " is in the doubleSet" << endl;
```

To make it easier to display the values in a set, you might want to overload the << operator for a specific set type. For example, to provide output for the TDoubleSet type, declare the function prototype:

```
ostream & operator<< (ostream & os, const TDoubleSet & c);
```

The only difference for another type of set is the typedef name. Implement the overloaded operator<<() function as follows:

```
ostream & operator<< (ostream & os, const TDoubleSet & c)
{
  copy(c.begin(), c.end(),
    ostream_iterator<TDoubleSet::value_type>(os, " "));
  return os;
}
```

This programming is a bit different from other output functions described so far. It uses the copy() algorithm to transfer a defined range of values from a container—from begin() to end()—to an *output stream iterator*, a template named ostream_iterator in the iterator header file. The set template class exports an object named value_type, which is used to construct a destination iterator for the output stream. To the result of this the program passes the output stream object (os) and a separator—a space in this case (use "\n" for a new line). Finally, the overloaded operator function returns os to enable cascaded output statements. As a result, it takes only relatively simple statements to display the values in set objects:

```
cout << "intSet    == " << intSet    << endl;
cout << "doubleSet == " << doubleSet << endl;
cout << "stringSet == " << stringSet << endl;
```

PART

V

CH

24

Tip

You can use similar programming to overload the output stream operator for *any* STL container template. Remember to include the iterator header file.

As mentioned, sets are ordered by the function object used to instantiate the set template. Normally, you will use greater or less in creating sets. Try changing the typedefs for the TIntSet, TDoubleSet, and TStringSet to use greater or less and observe the results of the preceding output statements.

To erase a value from a set, pass that value to the erase() member function:

```
doubleSet.erase(M_LOG2E);
```

Or, to erase a range of objects, you can pass a pair of iterators to erase(). The following statement erases the entire stringSet container:

```
stringSet.erase(stringSet.begin(), stringSet.end());
```

The two iterators could address any values in the set. For instance, you might call find() to locate two values and erase them plus all others between. However, when specifying the range of values, be careful to include all those you intend to erase. First define two iterators:

```
TIntSet::iterator p1, p2;
```

Then, call the set class's find() member function to initialize the iterators to address specific values in the set:

```
p1 = intSet.find(20);
p2 = intSet.find(40);
```

In this case, I elected to call the set class find() member function instead of using the STL find() algorithm, which is not a member of a class. The reason for using a member function is that sets are automatically ordered, and, therefore, the internal find() is potentially faster than the standalone algorithm. Either would work, however. After finding the values, erase them by passing the two iterators to erase():

```
if (p1 != intSet.end())
  intSet.erase(p1, p2);
```

If the first search fails, then there's nothing to erase. If the second fails, the preceding statement erases from p1 to the end of the set. This, however, is where the potential for trouble arises. If the search for 40 succeeds, the preceding statement deletes from 20 up to *but not including* 40. If the original set of values equals {10 20 30 40}, the resulting set equals {10 40}. To also erase the value 40, increment p2 to the *next* value. Because 40 might be (and in this case is) the last in the set, this requires p2 to be tested:

```
if (p2 != intSet.end()) p2++;
if (p1 != intSet.end())
  intSet.erase(p1, p2);
```

Now the program correctly erases from p1 to p2 including the value at p2, or if p2 equals the *past-the-end* value, to the end of the set.

As you can with other containers, you can also insert class objects into sets. Using the TCoordinate class from the coordinate.h header file on the CD-ROM, instantiate a set class for the container:

```
typedef set<TCoordinate, less<TCoordinate> > TCoordSet;
```

That specifies `TCoordSet` as a set class that can store `TCoordinate` objects using the `less` function object to maintain object order. Given the `typedef`, a simple statement constructs a set container:

```
TCoordSet coords;
```

Insert `TCoordinate` objects into the set as you do other types:

```
coords.insert(TCoordinate(1,2));
coords.insert(TCoordinate(3,4));
coords.insert(TCoordinate(5,6));
coords.insert(TCoordinate(7,8));
```

On the CD-ROM in the set.cpp file (located in src/c24), you find an overloaded output operator function similar to the one described before but for the `TCoordSet` typedef. This function is prototyped as

```
ostream & operator<< (ostream & os, const TCoordSet & c);
```

The operator's implementation is identical to the one shown earlier but simply uses the `TCoordSet` typedef and specifies a newline character as the value separator. Because the `TCoordinate` class also overloads the output stream operator, a simple statement displays all `TCoordinate` object values in the set container:

```
cout << coords << endl;
```

Onscreen, that displays all values in the `set`, an excellent example of how, using overloaded operators and class templates, a program's source code can be greatly simplified:

```
x == 1; y == 2
x == 3; y == 4
x == 5; y == 6
x == 7; y == 8
```

> **Note**
>
> The preceding output is the same regardless of the order objects are inserted into the `set`. To order the objects from high to low, change the function object from `less` to `greater` in the `TCoordSet` typedef. The ordering is made possible in this case because `TCoordinate` overloads the less-than `operator<()` function. Regardless of the selected order, however, the class does not have to overload the greater-than operator.

CALLING SET FUNCTIONS

The set class's member functions are far and few between. The next chapter covers traditional operators such as union and intersection for `set` containers, so I won't go into those operations here. You can't sort a `set` container (nor would you want to). Also, `set` iterators are constant, so you can't assign new values to dereferenced set iterators.

A `multiset`, also declared in the set header file, is the same as a set but permits duplicate values. Again, it's clearer to create a `typedef` name for the set type:

```
typedef multiset<int, less<int> > TIntMultiSet;
```

That makes `TIntMultiSet` a `multiset` container type that can store `int` values ordered by the `less` function object. Create a `multiset` container in the same way you do a `set`. The following creates a buffer of integers (just to provide a source of values) and transfers the buffer into a new `multiset` named `intMultiSet`:

```
int buffer[6] = { 2, 4, 6, 4, 8, 4 };
TIntMultiSet intMultiSet(buffer, buffer + 6);
```

Displaying the resulting `set` shows that the values are kept in sorted order regardless of their original order. The program displays this line of output:

```
intMultiSet  == 2 4 4 4 6 8
```

One useful function, `count()`, determines how many objects of a particular value are in a `set` or `multiset`. If the container is a `set`, `count()` reports either 1 or 0. If the container is a `multiset`, `count()` reports the number of duplicated values. For example, this statement:

```
cout << "Number of 4s == " << intMultiSet.count(4) << endl;
```

displays the number of values equal to 4 in `intMultiSet`:

```
Number of 4s == 3
```

MAPS AND MULTIMAPS

The `map` and `multimap` templates create *associative containers* that store keys and associated values of any type. The two templates are identical in all respects but one: keys in a `map` must be unique; keys in a `multimap` may be duplicated. In use, `map` and `multimap` containers are similar to `vectors`, which provide the subscript operator `[ ]`. However, unlike a `vector`, indexing a `map` or `multimap` structure performs a lookup operation on that key value. Also, you may use any data object as the indexing key, including strings, integers, floating point values, and others. This differs from the `vector` class, which does not permit defining the data type of an index.

A `map` or `multimap` is ideal for applications that require dictionaries or other associative databases. The structures automatically maintain their elements in key order, making searches fast regardless of the key type. It must be possible to compare key values using the less-than operator. Except for that requirement, any type of key is permitted.

Note

The programming in the following sections is taken from file map.cpp on the CD-ROM in the directory src/c24.

DECLARING MAPS AND MULTIMAPS

Although this and the next two sections show examples of `map` containers, the programming is the same for a `multimap` except that duplicated keys are allowed. Declaring a `map` or `multimap` container takes a bit more effort than other types of STL container templates. A `map` or `multimap` requires three elements:

- A key type
- A value type
- A comparison function object

To create an associative array of strings and integer values, include the map and string header files and then construct a map container as follows:

```
#include <map>
#include <string>
...
map<string, int, less<string> > relation;
```

That creates the object relation as a map data structure. The key is a string, the associated value is type int, and the less function object is used to maintain key order in the container. This works, but it complicates the process of inserting objects into the container. Instead of using the preceding method, then, it's usually best to define two data types—one for the map container and one for the type of value to insert:

```
typedef map<string, int, less<string> > TRelation;
typedef TRelation::value_type TValue;
```

The first declaration states that TRelation is a map class with a string key associated with an int value and ordered using the less function object. The second declaration states that TValue is the type of object to be inserted in a TRelation container. This type is exported as value_type by the map template. With these typedefs, it's now possible to construct the container and insert a few objects using statements such as the following:

```
TRelation relation;
relation.insert(TValue("Label1: ", 1));
relation.insert(TValue("Label2: ", 2));
relation.insert(TValue("Label3: ", 3));
```

Each TValue object consists of a string and an associated integer value. To access the stored objects, remember that each association is of the TValue type, exported by the map container class. This type provides two variables, first and second, that refer to the key and value of each object. Using an iterator for the map container, the following while statement displays the keys and values in the relation map:

```
TRelation::iterator p = relation.begin();
while (p != relation.end()) {
  cout << p->first << " " << p->second << endl;
  p++;
}
```

Compiling and running the test program displays the labels and associated values:

```
$ g++ map.cpp
$ ./a.out
Label1:  1
Label2:  2
Label3:  3
```

PART

V

Ch

24

USING MAPS AND MULTIMAPS

As a practical demonstration of map containers, Listing 24.2, scores.cpp, creates a database of people's names and their bowling scores (or those from another type of game). The program also demonstrates how to simplify displaying association objects by overloading the output stream operator. (Only the essential parts of the program are listed here—other statements in the file are discussed after the listing.)

LISTING 24.2   SCORES.CPP

```cpp
#include <iostream.h>
#include <string>
#include <map>

typedef map<string, double, less<string> > TScores;
typedef TScores::value_type TValue;
ostream& operator<< (ostream& os, const TValue& r);
void show_scores();

TScores scores;

int main()
{
  scores.insert( TValue("Barbara", 85.5) );
  scores.insert( TValue("Peter",   78.9) );
  scores.insert( TValue("Flo",     98.0) );
  scores.insert( TValue("Xavier",  87.3) );
  show_scores();
  cout << endl;
...
  return 0;
}

ostream& operator<< (ostream& os, const TValue& r)
{
  cout << r.first << "\t== " << r.second;
  return os;
}

void show_scores()
{
  cout << "Scores:" << endl;
  TScores::iterator it = scores.begin();
  while (it != scores.end()) {
    cout << *it << endl;
    it++;
  }
}
```

Compiling and running the test program displays the database of names and score averages:

```
$ g++ scores.cpp
$ ./a.out
Scores:
Barbara == 85.5
```

```
Flo     == 98
Peter   == 78.9
Xavier  == 87.3
```

As in the map.cpp program, scores.cpp declares two typedefs, TScores and TValue, to simplify the creation of a map container and association objects. To create the scores container, the program simply declares it like this:

```
TScores scores;
```

And then, to insert association objects into the container, the program executes statements such as

```
scores.insert( TValue("Barbara", 85.5) );
```

The primary difference between map.cpp and scores.cpp is the way the new program displays association objects. To simplify this process, the program overloads the C++ output stream operator using the following function prototype:

```
ostream& operator<< (ostream& os, const TValue& r);
```

This teaches C++ how to write one association object of the typedef name TValue. The overloaded operator's body writes the object's first and last values using this statement:

```
cout << r.first << "\t== " << r.second;
```

With the overloaded operator, the program can now simply write each association object using an iterator and while loop:

```
TScores::iterator it = scores.begin();
while (it != scores.end()) {
  cout << *it << endl;
  it++;
}
```

Another way to access objects in a map container is to use subscript expressions with key indexes. For example, the following statement displays Peter's score:

```
cout << "Peter's score == " << scores["Peter"] << endl;
```

Unlike a common vector, a map or multimap's index value is of its key type, here a string. Hidden from view is the internal programming that searches the associative container for a matching key value. If that search fails, however, a new association object is added to the database. For example, because "Tom" is not in the scores map, this statement adds a new entry for "Tom" with the associated value initialized to its default (zero in this case):

```
cout << "Tom's score   == " << scores["Tom"] << endl;
```

If you don't want to add a new association object automatically, call the map's find() function to search for a key and display the associated value only if found. For example, you might search for "George" (who isn't in the database) using the following statement:

```
TScores::iterator p = scores.find("George");
```

If p equals the *past-the-end* value, then "George" isn't in the database, and the program can avoid automatically adding a new entry:

```
if (p == scores.end())
  cout << "(not found)" << endl;
```

There are two basic ways to display the results of a search. For instance, you can search for Flo's entry using find():

```
TScores::iterator result = scores.find("Flo");
```

If result does not equal the *past-the-end* value, use the iterator that find() returns to access the key and value parts of the association object:

```
cout << "result->first  == " << result->first << endl;
cout << "result->second == " << result->second << endl;
```

Because the scores.cpp program overloads the C++ output stream operator for TValue objects (the type of association objects in the scores map), you can also use the following statement to display the results of a search (or for any other valid iterator):

```
cout << "*result == " << *result << endl;
```

Keys are constant, but their associated values are modifiable. It seems that Flo had a bad day at the lanes. Lower her score by simply assigning it to the scores container:

```
scores["Flo"] = 76.7;
```

That changes the value associated with the key "Flo". Although simple-looking, that statement could perform an entire database search by using appropriate classes to instantiate the map template. Call the erase() function to remove an association object. Flo's scores have been in the cellar too long, so let's remove her from the team:

```
scores.erase("Flo");
```

Erase any association object simply by passing a key value to the erase() function. If the object isn't in the database, nothing happens. Although more complicated, you can also search for a key and pass the resulting iterator to erase() using code such as this:

```
TScores::iterator piter = scores.find("Peter");
if (piter != scores.end())
  scores.erase(piter);
```

That erases Peter's entry if it's in the scores map. To erase more than one object at a time, define two iterators as the range of objects to delete:

```
TScores::iterator p1 = scores.find("Tom");
TScores::iterator p2 = scores.find("Xavier");
if (p1 != scores.end() && p2 != scores.end())
  scores.erase(p1, ++p2);
```

That erases all association objects from Tom through Xavier, assuming that they are stored alphabetically in low-to-high order. That's so in this example because the less function object is defined as the ordering mechanism for the container. Notice that p2 is incremented to one object beyond the end of the range. To erase an entire container, pass its begin() and end() iterators to erase():

```
scores.erase(scores.begin(), scores.end());
```

CALLING MAP AND MULTIMAP FUNCTIONS

Like all containers, map and multimap provide useful member functions. Two are standard issue:

- size() returns the number of objects in the container.
- empty() returns true if the container has no objects.

A useful trick is to call the map or multimap count() function to determine whether a specific key value is in the container. This is particularly useful in multimaps that can hold duplicate keys, but it also works for plain maps such as scores. This sets n equal to the number of records for the key "Peter":

```
int n = scores.count("Peter");
```

If n equals zero, then Peter isn't in the container.

MULTIMAP BOUNDS

With multimap containers, use the lower_bound() and upper_bound() functions to search for ranges of association objects. For example, using typedefs, define names for multimap containers and association objects:

```
typedef multimap<string, int, less<string> > TMulti;
typedef TMulti::value_type TMultiValue;
```

That makes TMulti a multimap class that can store string keys along with associated int values, arranged by key using the less function object. TMultiValue is a name for the type of objects in the container. Using the type definitions, create a container and insert some objects:

```
TMulti multi;
multi.insert( TMultiValue("Label1", 100) );
multi.insert( TMultiValue("Label2", 200) );  // Duplicate keys
multi.insert( TMultiValue("Label2", 300) );
multi.insert( TMultiValue("Label2", 400) );
multi.insert( TMultiValue("Label5", 500) );
```

Notice that there are three different entries keyed to the string "Label2". To count how many objects there are for a particular key, call the count() function:

```
cout << "Label2 count == " << multi.count("Label2") << endl;
```

For performing operations on all objects that possess the same key, define two iterators of the iterator type exported by the multimap container:

```
TMulti::iterator p1 = multi.lower_bound("Label2");
TMulti::iterator p2 = multi.upper_bound("Label2");
```

Calling lower_bound() for a specific key returns the first such object. Calling upper_bound() for the same key returns the last such object *plus one*. Use the iterators in calls to erase()

PART

V

CH

24

and other functions that accept a pair of iterators. You can also use them in loops such as the following, which displays all association objects keyed to `"Label2"`:

```
while (p1 != p2) {
  cout << p1->first << " : " << p1->second << endl;
  p1++;
}
```

Stacks

The STL offers three types of `stack` containers. One is constructed using a `vector`; another is made from a `deque`; a third is a `list`. A `vector` `stack` stores all objects together in memory. A `deque` or `list` `stack` stores objects using a double-linked `list`. Except for these internal storage details, all three `stack` types recognize the same operations and are functionally interchangeable.

> **Tip**
>
> The use of a `stack` should determine its type. If you plan on storing large objects in a `stack` container, a more memory-efficient `list` or `deque` might be appropriate; otherwise, you might want to use a `vector`.

Stacks are useful in many algorithms. They are especially good for storing and retrieving information in a certain processing order—the results of subexpression evaluations in an electronic calculator, for example. As mentioned earlier in the chapter, a `stack` is a last-in, first-out (LIFO) data structure. Objects in a `stack` must support less-than and equality operators. Except for that requirement, you may store any type of data in a `stack` container.

Although you can use a `vector` or a `list` container as a `stack`, operations on values in the container are not restricted. For example, all `vector` objects are accessible using array indexing. Because the `stack` container imposes classic data-access restrictions, only the top object is accessible, and the only way to insert and remove objects is to push and pop them at the "business end" of the `stack`. These restrictions are important for ensuring that `stack`-based algorithms work properly, and so it is probably best to use a `stack` container instead of forcing a less-restrictive `vector` or `list` into the role of a `stack`.

> **Note**
>
> The programming samples in the following sections are taken from file stack.cpp in the src/c24 directory on the CD-ROM.

Declaring Stacks

Include at least two header files to use `stack` containers. The first is named stack; the second is the underlying structure to use in implementing a `stack` container. For example, to create a `vector`-based `stack`, include both headers:

```
#include <stack>
#include <vector>
```

For list- or deque-based stacks, include those headers as well. To create a stack container, specify the type of data to store and type of structure to use for maintaining the stack:

```
stack<int, vector<int> > int_stack;
```

That works just fine, but a typedef declaration helps clarify the programming:

```
typedef stack<int, vector<int> > TIntStack;
```

That makes TIntStack a stack class that can store int values and that uses an integer vector as its storage mechanism. You can now construct the actual container with a simple statement such as this:

```
TIntStack int_stack;
```

USING STACKS

To insert values into a stack, call the push() function as in this loop:

```
for (int i = 1; i < 10; i++)
  int_stack.push(i);
```

Call top() to refer to the top object on the stack—the only object available for use. (In its classic form, a stack prevents access to any other objects.) Call pop() to remove the top object. Call empty() to determine whether the stack is empty. Together, the three functions can pop and display all values pushed onto the int_stack container:

```
while (!int_stack.empty()) {
  cout << int_stack.top() << " ";
  int_stack.pop();
}
```

A stack may store any kind of object. For example, include the coordinate.h header file listed in this chapter and then use a typedef declaration to create a type name for a stack of TCoordinate class objects:

```
typedef stack<TCoordinate, deque<TCoordinate> > TCoordStack;
```

Construct the stack container and fill it with TCoordinate objects using statements such as

```
TCoordStack coord_stack;
coord_stack.push(TCoordinate(10, 20));
```

The preceding while loop, along with the empty(), top(), and pop() functions, works the same for stacks of objects as it does for simple integer values. Just change the stack object name to display and remove all TCoordinate objects.

QUEUES

There are two types of queue containers in the STL. One is based on a list. The other is based on a deque. Both types of queues provide the same operations; only their underlying data structure is selectable. For the most part, a list is the better choice for storing large objects and large numbers of objects; otherwise, a deque is potentially faster. A queue is a first-in, first-out (FIFO) data structure that works like a line at the post office. Unless the program cheats, objects enter only at the back of the line and exit at the front.

> **Note**
>
> It may seem backward that a `queue` is based on a `deque` (a double-ended queue) and not the other way around, but this is a classic setup. A `queue` is constructed internally the same as a `deque` but has more restrictive insertion and deletion operations.

Queues are often used for scheduling applications—for example, a phone-messaging system that routes callers in the order received, or a work scheduler that assigns jobs as they come in. Objects stored in queues must support less-than and equality comparison operators. Except for meeting those requirements, you may store any type of data in an STL `queue`.

> **Note**
>
> The programming samples in the following sections are taken from the queue.cpp file on the CD-ROM in the src/c24 directory.

DECLARING QUEUES

Declare `queues` similar to the way you declare `stacks`. Include the queue header file plus either the `list` or `deque` header files depending on how you want to implement the `queue` container:

```
#include <queue>
#include <list>
#include <deque>
```

> **Tip**
>
> Include all three headers and try both types of underlying data structures to see which works best.

To create a queue container, specify the type of data object to store along with the type of container (`list` or `deque`) to use as the underlying data structure:

```
queue<TCoordinate, list<TCoordinate> > suzyQueue;
```

That creates the container `suzyQueue` for `TCoordinate` objects (declared in the coordinate.h header described earlier in this chapter), and using the `list` template as the underlying data structure. For a clearer program, it's best to create a `typedef` name for this data structure:

```
typedef queue<TCoordinate, list<TCoordinate> > TQueue;
```

To use a `deque` instead, just change `list` to `deque`. Using the `TQueue` `typedef` name, it's a simple matter to create a queue container, in this case named `suzyQueue`:

```
TQueue suzyQueue;
```

USING QUEUES

Call the `push()` member function to insert an object into a `queue`. Because all objects must enter at the rear of a `queue`, this is the only way you can insert data into this type of container:

```
for (int i = 1; i < 10; i++)
  suzyQueue.push(TCoordinate(i, i * 10));
```

The `for` loop pushes nine `TCoordinate` objects initialized using the value of index `i` and `i` times 10. As you can with most containers, call `size()` to count the number of queued objects:

```
cout << "Number of objects == " << suzyQueue.size() << endl;
```

Call the `front()` function to examine the topmost object. This is the object that will be removed the next time the program calls `pop()`:

```
cout << "First object inserted: " << suzyQueue.front() << endl;
```

Note   Some early versions of the STL called the `front()` function `top()`.

Although not allowed in a strictly classic `queue`, the STL data structure permits examining the entry-end of the `queue` using the `back()` function. The following statement shows the object most recently inserted:

```
cout << "Last object inserted : " << suzyQueue.back() << endl;
```

Call `empty()` to determine whether the queue has no objects. Combine the `empty()`, `front()`, and `pop()` functions to display and pop all objects in a queue, as in the following `while` loop, which also calls `size()` to number each displayed object:

```
while (!suzyQueue.empty()) {
  cout << suzyQueue.size() << " : ";
  cout << suzyQueue.front() << endl;
  suzyQueue.pop();
}
```

The loop completely empties the `queue`. Compiling and running the test program shows the loop's output (reduced to save room here):

```
$ g++ queue.cpp
$ ./a.out
Creating queue of TCoordinate objects
Number of objects == 9
...
9 : x == 1; y == 10
8 : x == 2; y == 20
...
1 : x == 9; y == 90
Number of objects == 0
Queue is empty
```

PRIORITY QUEUES

A *priority queue* is similar to a `stack` or a `queue`, but it always maintains objects in a critical order. Also, regardless of insertion order, the most critical objects are removed from the container before less critical ones. This type of container is good for scheduling and critical-path programs that need to ensure that critical tasks get priority.

Criticality is determined by applying the less-than operator to element pairs, or by a user-supplied comparison function object. Every insertion or deletion from a priority queue causes the critical objects (the ones found by the comparison) to move to the front of the queue.

There are two kinds of priority queues. One is based on a vector. the other is constructed from a deque. A vector priority queue is generally faster but less memory-efficient than a deque.

Priority queues are useful in any application that prioritizes data. A good example is a to-do list in which items with low priorities (1-Clean oven, 2-Sweep garage) are less critical than those with higher values (8-Cash paycheck, 9-Call mother). You insert objects into a priority queue in no particular order. The objects come out of the queue based on their priority. An example of a to-do list program follows (see "Creating a To-Do List Priority Queue"), but first, let's examine the basics of this useful STL container.

Note | The sample programming in the following sections comes from the pqueue.cpp file on the CD-ROM in the src/c24 directory.

DECLARING PRIORITY QUEUES

To create a priority queue, include the queue and vector or deque header files:

```
#include <queue>
#include <vector>
```

As with other relatively complex data structures, it's usually best to define a name for the instantiated priority queue class. For example, the following statement specifies that TPQueue is the name of a priority_queue class that can store integer values:

```
typedef priority_queue<int, vector<int>, less<int> > TPQueue;
```

The priority_queue's underlying data structure is a vector, and it uses the less function object to maintain objects in order. Using less causes entries with *higher* values to be given higher priority. To give entries with *lower* values priority, change less to greater. Using the typedef name, the following constructs a priority_queue container named pQueue:

```
TPQueue pQueue;
```

USING PRIORITY QUEUES

Use priority queues in the same way as common queues. For example, the following loop inserts integer values selected at random into the pQueue container using the standard C library's random() function:

```
for (int i = 0; i < 10; i++)
  pQueue.push(random() % 1000);
```

As with most containers, size() reports the number of objects in the priority_queue:

```
cout << "Number of insertions == " << pQueue.size() << endl;
```

Even though the objects are inserted at random, popping them removes objects with higher priority—in this case, those that have higher values. The following loop displays all objects as they are removed from the priority_queue:

```
while (!pQueue.empty()) {
  cout << pQueue.top() << " ";
  pQueue.pop();
}
```

Note

The top() function is defined for priority queues, but this is called front() for plain queues, a small but annoying discrepancy in the STL.

Compiling and running the test program shows that it regurgitates its random integer values in high to low order:

```
$ g++ pqueue.cpp
$ ./a.out
Pushing random integers into priority queue
Number of insertions == 10
Displaying and popping objects
975 974 642 624 584 368 317 238 113 73
```

CREATING A TO-DO LIST PRIORITY QUEUE

For a practical demonstration of a priority queue, Listing 24.3, todo.cpp, creates a prioritized to-do list.

LISTING 24.3 TODO.CPP

```
#include <iostream.h>
#include <string>
#include <queue>
#include <deque>

// Items to store in priority queue
class Item {
  int weight;      // Priority
  string item;     // Description
public:
  Item(): weight(0), item("") { }
  Item(int w, string s): weight(w), item(s) { }
  int GetWeight() const { return weight; }
  const string & GetItem() const { return item; }
  bool operator< (const Item& arg) const
    { return weight < arg.weight; }
};

ostream& operator<< (ostream& os, const Item& r);

// Enable one of the following typedefs. The less function object
// gives higher-numbered objects priority. Use the greater function
```

continues

LISTING 24.3   CONTINUED

```
// object to give lower-numbered objects priority.

typedef priority_queue<Item, deque<Item>,
➥ less<Item> > TItemQueue;
//typedef priority_queue<Item, deque<Item>,
➥ greater<Item> > TItemQueue;

int main()
{

  TItemQueue todo;   // Construct container

  // Insert some Item objects into the queue
  //
  todo.push(Item(1, "Clean oven"));
  todo.push(Item(8, "Cash paycheck"));
  todo.push(Item(2, "Sweep garage"));
  todo.push(Item(9, "Call mother"));

  // Display most critical object
  //
  cout << "The most critical item is:" << endl;
  cout << todo.top() << endl;

  // Display and remove objects in critical order
  //
  cout << "Removing items in critical order:" << endl;
  while (!todo.empty()) {
    cout << todo.top() << endl;
    todo.pop();
  }

  return 0;
}

// Display an Item object
ostream& operator<< (ostream& os, const Item& r)
{
  cout << "(" << r.GetWeight() << ") " << r.GetItem();
  return os;
}
```

Compile and run the todo.cpp program to display a list of chores, prioritized by number with higher-numbered items given priority. The program displays the most critical item, followed by all objects in priority order. Enter these commands:

```
$ g++ todo.cpp
$ ./a.out
The most critical item is:
(9) Call mother
Removing items in critical order:
(9) Call mother
(8) Cash paycheck
(2) Sweep garage
(1) Clean oven
```

The program bases its `priority_queue` container on the STL `deque` template. A `typedef` name makes creating the actual container clearer:

```
typedef priority_queue<
  Item, deque<Item>, less<Item> > TItemQueue;
```

To the `priority_queue` template, specify three items: The type of data to store in the container (`Item`), the underlying data structure (`deque<Item>`), and a function object (`less<Item>`) used to maintain the order of objects in the queue. Change `less` to `greater` to order entries from low to high.

The `Item` class represents the data to store in the `queue`. The class declares a weight and a string that describes the job to be done. The most important member of the `Item` class is its overloaded `operator<()` function. When designing your own `priority_queue` data objects, your class needs an operator similar to this one:

```
bool operator< (const Item& arg) const
  { return weight < arg.weight; }
```

The overloaded operator's parameter is a constant reference to an object of the class type. The operator itself is `const` because it makes no changes to `Item`'s data members. Return a true value if the priority of the current object—the one for which the operator function is called—is less than the priority of the parameter (`arg` in this example).

Tip

> You do *not* need to overload the greater-than operator even if you change the ordering. Only the less-than operator is needed in the class of object to be stored in the queue.

Given the `TItemQueue` typedef name, creating the container is easy:

```
TItemQueue todo;
```

To insert objects into the `todo` container, call the `push()` member function like this:

```
todo.push(Item(1, "Clean oven"));
...
todo.push(Item(9, "Call mother"));
```

The integer values represent the weights, and the strings of course describe each entry. You can use any type of data for either element simply by changing the `Item` class's members. No changes to the `priority_queue` template are needed to accommodate other types of data.

Call the `top()` function to examine the most-critical object in the `queue`:

```
cout << todo.top() << endl;
```

To remove the most critical object, call `pop()`. The following `while` loop calls that function plus `empty()` and `top()` to display all objects and empty the queue:

```
while (!todo.empty()) {
  cout << todo.top() << endl;
  todo.pop();
}
```

SUMMARY

The STL provides 10 container template classes for creating fundamental data structures such as lists, vectors, and queues. Because they are template-based, the classes can store any types of objects or pointers (but not references). The 10 standard classes are `vector`, `list`, `deque`, `set`, `multiset`, `map`, `multimap`, `stack`, `queue`, and `priority_queue`. In most cases, you access objects in a container by using one or more iterators. For this purpose, container classes export the type name `iterator`. Container template classes also provide several member functions you can call to sort, search, insert, and delete objects. You can also use standard algorithms to perform various actions on objects in containers as the next chapter explains.

For more information on subjects introduced in this chapter, turn to the following chapters:

- Chapter 12, "Introducing the Class"
- Chapter 17, "Creating Class Templates"
- Chapter 21, "Honing Your C++ Skills"
- Chapter 23, "Using the Standard Template Library (STL)"
- Chapter 25, "Applying Standard Algorithms"

APPLYING STANDARD ALGORITHMS

Using standard algorithms, you can sort, merge, search, copy, and perform other magic on objects in STL containers. The standard algorithms work with all types of data structures, and they simplify common programming tasks. For example, the sort() algorithm can operate on a list or a vector regardless of the type of data the container holds. Also, because standard algorithms are not object-oriented, they carry out their duties equally well in OOP and in conventional applications.

The Standard Template Library (STL) provides every algorithm as a generalized template function that defines the algorithm's name, a return type or void, and any parameters. Extensive use of inline code keeps algorithms running fast without sacrificing versatility. To use most algorithms, you simply define any required data types and provide one or more iterators that define a range of objects or values on which to operate. Using this information, GNU C++ constructs a function that performs the required task.

Tip

Remember to compile using at least one level of optimization (for example, -O1) to enable inline function expansion.

INTRODUCING STANDARD ALGORITHMS

In GNU C++, the algo.h and algobase.h header files define all standard algorithm template functions. To use one or more standard algorithms from these files, include the standard algorithm header using the following directive:

```
#include <algorithm>
```

Don't include algo.h or algobase.h—they might be named something else in another ANSI C++ compiler system, or their declarations might be combined into one file. Always include algorithm as shown here to ensure portability. Also include any other STL headers such as vector, deque, and list, that define the container you want to use. You may use standard algorithms with simple C++ arrays and other structures of your own making; you can even invent your own containers if you want. In most cases, however, you will use a standard container along with a standard algorithm described in this chapter.

The following sections explain how to use most STL algorithms in categories sorted alphabetically. Because of this arrangement, in some cases topics are mentioned before they are introduced, so you might need to read this chapter a couple of times to fully understand all the algorithms. Also read Chapter 23, "Using the Standard Template Library (STL)," and Chapter 24, "Building Standard Containers," for information on using the STL and standard container class templates.

Note

Because of the large number of sample programs in this chapter, many of which contain duplicate statements, the following sections do not list the sample programs in full. Of course, all files mentioned in this chapter are on the CD-ROM in the src/c25 directory. Each section begins with references to the algorithms discussed and to the relevant source file. To compile the sample programs, use the following commands where *name-ex.cpp* is the name of the program's source code file:

```
$ g++ name-ex.cpp
$ ./a.out
```

ACCUMULATION ALGORITHM

Algorithm:

```
accumulate()
```

Sample program:

```
accum-ex.cpp
```

An accumulation is an arbitrary operation that combines a collection of objects in some specified fashion. For example, a simple accumulation sums a list or an array of integers, or calculates a combined product or factorial. The accumulate algorithm is defined as follows:

```
DataType accumulate(
   InputIterator first, InputIterator last,
   DataType initial [, BinaryFunction ] )
```

Note

In this and other algorithm definitions, bracketed items such as `BinaryFunction` are optional. I also changed a few identifiers for clarity—replacing T with `DataType` for instance.

Two iterators, `first` and `last`, define a range of data objects in a container. The initial argument provides a starting value for the type of data objects. This value should be 0 for addition operations, and 1 for multiplication. By default, `accumulate()` sums the specified range of data objects. To perform a different operation, you can optionally specify a binary function object such as `multiplies`.

To demonstrate how to use `accumulate()`, the sample program defines a container with a few floating point values:

```
double data[5] = { 1.2, 3.4, 5.6, 7.8, 9.10 };
vector<double> array(data, data + 5);
```

To sum the values in the array, the program calls `accumulate()` with three arguments:

```
double sum = accumulate(
  array.begin(), array.end(), 0.0);
```

The first two arguments are iterators that define the range of objects on which to operate (double values in this case). The third argument is the starting value for the accumulation, set to 0.0 here. To keep a running total—summing multiple containers, for example—define a variable of the appropriate type and pass it to accumulate()'s third parameter. By default, accumulate() applies the plus operator (+) to the starting value and all others in the defined range, one after the other. The function returns the resulting value, assigned here to the double variable, sum.

To perform a different type of accumulation, specify a function object as the fourth argument. For example, the following statement multiplies all values in the container:

```
double product = accumulate(
  array.begin(), array.end(), 1.0, multiplies<double>());
```

The multiplies function object is declared in the functional header file. Specify a data type (such as double) to the template and append an empty pair of parentheses to indicate that the program is to call the object as a function—an operation performed by calling operator()() for this function object. Because the operation is a multiplication, the starting value passed to accumulate()'s third parameter is 1.0.

> **Note**
>
> Some C++ compilers name the multiplies function template *times*.

COPYING ALGORITHMS

Algorithms:

```
copy()
copy_backward()
```

Sample program:

```
copy-ex.cpp
```

There are two copy() algorithms. The first, copy(), copies a range of data objects from an input source container to a destination, in a forward direction. The algorithm is declared as follows:

```
OutputIterator copy(
  InputIterator first, InputIterator last,
  OutputIterator result)
```

> **Note**
>
> The OutputIterator and InputIterator identifiers are template placeholders, not defined types. The actual types of iterators are defined when you use the function—for example, when operating on a container of double values, the OutputIterator type becomes double*, and the InputIterator is const double*.

Two iterators specify the range of source data objects to copy. A third iterator specifies the starting location of the destination container. The copy() algorithm returns an output iterator equal to the final object in the destination plus one. Thus, the original result argument and the function's return value define the range of copied objects in the destination.

The second copy() algorithm, copy_backward(), works the same as copy() but copies objects from the end of a range in a backward direction. The algorithm is defined as follows:

```
BidirectionalIterator2 copy_backward(
  BidirectionalIterator1 first,
  BidirectionalIterator1 last,
  BidirectionalIterator2 result)
```

The parameters are essentially the same as for copy(), but they are specified as bidirectional iterators because input and output iterators move only in a forward direction. The first and last iterators define the input range of objects to be copied. The result iterator is the starting location in the destination. The algorithm returns the final object's location *minus one*.

For sample data, the sample program defines an array of integers used to initialize two vector containers:

```
int data[10] = { 1, 2, 3, 4, 5, 6, 7, 8, 9, 10 };
vector<int> a(data, data + 10);
vector<int> b(10);
```

The vector a contains the 10 integer values. The vector b is defined as a container with 10 possible values. A simple statement copies the objects from container a to b:

```
copy(a.begin(), a.end(), b.begin());
```

You might also save the final iterator in a variable of the iterator type exported by the container class:

```
vector<int>::iterator end =
  copy(a.begin(), a.end(), b.begin());
```

Following that statement, b.begin() and end define the range of copied data in the destination container. To copy objects in the reverse direction, use copy_backward() as follows:

```
copy_backward(a.begin(), a.end(), b.end());
```

Take care to specify the iterators in the correct order. The first and last iterators define the range of source values *in forward order*, but the starting iterator is at the end of the destination container (b). Again, you might save the resulting iterator in a variable:

```
vector<int>::iterator start =
  copy_backward(a.begin(), a.end(), b.end());
```

Following that, start and b.end() define the range of copied objects.

Tip

In most cases, use copy() unless you are copying objects in the *same* container, in which case copy_backward() might be necessary to prevent overwriting objects during the copy.

You can also use copy() to transfer objects to an output stream object. This isn't a special case, but a demonstration of the STL's versatility in defining the nature of a container. An output object such as cout, for example, is a "container" to which you can copy objects. All that's needed is an appropriate iterator such as ostream_iterator defined in the STL. The following statement uses the copy() algorithm to transfer all values from the vector container b to the standard output object cout, separating each value with a blank:

```
copy(b.begin(), b.end(),
  ostream_iterator<int>(cout, " "));
```

Tip

To define your own class for an input or output stream iterator, examine the STL source file iterator.h and use the ostream_iterator or istream_iterator template classes as the basis for your designs.

Counting Algorithms

Algorithms:

```
count()
count_if()
```

Sample program:

```
count-ex.cpp
```

Use the count() and count_if() algorithms to determine how many objects of a specified value or that satisfy some other condition are in a container. The count() algorithm requires two input iterators: a constant value to search for and an integer variable to hold the resulting count. The algorithm is defined as follows:

```
void count(
  InputIterator first, InputIterator last,
  const DataType& value, Size& n)
```

The first two parameters, as in many algorithms, are iterators that define the range of objects to inspect. The DataType reference value is the value to compare with each object. For each matching value found, count() increments the Size reference n. (I don't know why this variable's type is named "Size." Calling it CounterType or something similar would be closer to its purpose.)

The sample program defines a vector of integers, set to values selected at random with these following statements:

```
vector<int> a(100);
...
srandom( time(NULL) );  // Seed random generator
for (int i = 0; i < 100; i++)
  a[i] = random() % 1000;
```

Following that, a `for` loop calls `count()` to find the value in the array with the most duplicates:

```
for (int i = 0; i < 100; i++) {
  int v = *(a.begin() + i);
  int k = 0;
  count(a.begin(), a.end(), v, k);
  if (k > sum) {
    sum = k;          // Save current maximum sum
    value = v;        // Save associated search value
  }
}
```

The first statement in the loop assigns to `v` each successive value in the `vector` array. Variable `k`, which `copy()` increments for each matching value, is initialized to zero. Calling `count()` for all values in the `vector` array, and passing the search argument `v` and counter variable `k`, locates all duplicate values. The two arguments are saved in variables `sum` and `value`, declared elsewhere, for later display.

The other counting algorithms, `count_if()`, counts a number of specified values that satisfy a Boolean predicate function. This more general counting algorithm can count values of any type matching any conceivable condition. The `count_if()` algorithm is defined as follows:

```
void count_if(
  InputIterator first, InputIterator last,
  Predicate pred, Size& n)
```

As with `count()`, the first two parameters are iterators that define the range of objects to search. The Predicate (`pred`) parameter is a Boolean predicate function (see Chapter 23, "Using the Standard Template Library (STL)," in the section titled "Functions and Function Objects"). In most cases, you will create a predicate function along these lines:

```
#include <functional>
...
template<class Arg>
class is_even : public unary_function<Arg, bool>
{
  public:
    bool operator()(const Arg& arg1) {
      return (arg1 % 2) == 0; }
};
```

Include the functional header file and then create a template class derived from the STL `unary_function` template. `Arg` is a placeholder for a data type of the same kind as in the container to be searched. The predicate function needs only one overloaded operator— `operator()()`, which permits objects of the class to be called as though they are function names. The function's lone parameter is a constant reference to the type of objects in the container. The function returns a `true` or `false` `bool` value based on an evaluation of the parameter `arg1`. In this case, the function returns `true` if the value is even. The class name, `is_even`, reflects the function's purpose.

PART

V

CH

25

Use the predicate function as demonstrated in the sample program statement that counts how many even values are in the vector array:

```
count_if(a.begin(), a.end(), is_even<int>(), numEvens);
```

After the two iterators, the function object is created and called. The count_if() algorithm applies the function object to each value in the specified range and for each match increments the final argument, numEvens. Be sure to initialize this variable before calling count_if().

FILLING ALGORITHMS

Algorithms:

```
fill()
fill_n()
```

Sample program:

```
fill-ex.cpp
```

Use the fill() and fill_n() algorithms to stuff values into containers, or to initialize a non-empty data structure. The fill() algorithm requires two iterators and a value to copy to each object in the defined range. The algorithm is defined as follows:

```
void fill(
  ForwardIterator first, ForwardIterator last,
  const T& value)
```

The other algorithm, fill_n(), works the same as fill() but requires only a single iterator that specifies where filling is to begin. Other parameters specify the count (n) of values to fill from that location and a value to copy to each value in that range. The algorithm is defined as follows:

```
OutputIterator fill_n(
  OutputIterator first,
  Size n, const T& value)
```

Unlike fill(), which returns void, fill_n() returns an output iterator equal to the last object's location plus one. Thus, following a call to fill_n(), the first iterator and the function result define the range of objects filled with the specified value.

To demonstrate how to use fill() and fill_n(), the sample program defines and initializes a vector with these statements:

```
int data[10] = { 1, 2, 3, 4, 5, 6, 7, 8, 9, 10 };
vector<int> a(data, data + 10);
```

To replace the values 2 through 9 with 99, the program executes the following statement:

```
fill(a.begin() + 1, a.end() - 1, 99);
```

The first two arguments provide the starting and ending iterators for the range of objects to fill. Remember that the second iterator is one *past* the last target value. In this case, the statement assigns 99 to all but the first and last values in the vector array. Use fill_n() as follows to fill a specified number of objects in a container:

```
fill_n(a.begin() + 2, 6, 0);
```

That statement assigns zero to the six values starting with the third element in the vector array. You can also use an insertion iterator to insert new values into a structure with fill_n(). For example, the following statement inserts into the backside of the vector three values equal to 22:

```
fill_n(back_inserter(a), 3, 22);
```

This has the effect of appending the three new values onto the end of the vector array. For more information on this topic, see Chapter 23, "Using the Standard Template Library (STL)," under the section titled "Insertion Iterators."

FINDING ALGORITHMS

Algorithms:

```
min()
max()
min_element()
max_element()
```

Sample program:

```
minmax-ex.cpp
```

There are several algorithms in the STL that you can use to find objects that match certain criteria. (See also "Searching Algorithms" later in this chapter for related functions.) Of the finding algorithms, min() and max() are the simplest. They are defined as follows:

```
inline const T& min(const T& a, const T& b [, Compare comp ])
inline const T& max(const T& a, const T& b [, Compare comp ])
```

Unlike most STL algorithms, min() and max() do not use iterators to access objects in a container. Instead, the functions declare two constant reference parameters to the values, a and b, to be compared. The functions return a reference to the maximum or minimum of the two arguments. You may optionally provide a comparison function object as a third argument. In that case, the result of min() and max() depends on what the comparison function does. For example, the comparison function might ignore digits in string arguments, or it could perform an alphabetic comparison that differs in some way from normal.

To demonstrate min() and max(), the sample program defines two variables of type double:

```
double v1 = 123.45;
double v2 = 543.21;
```

The program assigns to a third variable, v3, the lesser of the two test values, and to a fourth variable, v4, the greater:

```
double v3 = min(v1, v2);
double v4 = max(v1, v2);
```

Although these statements are simplistic, they demonstrate how the function templates mold themselves to whatever type of data you are using. The same statements could compare objects of complex classes just as easily as they compare simple values as shown here.

To alter the nature of the comparison itself, supply a function object as a third argument to min() or max(). The following statement demonstrates this technique:

```
v4 = max(v1, v2, less<double>());  // ???
```

This is questionable because, in this case, the effect is to cause max() to find the minimum value. In practice, you will use this alternate method along with a function object of a class template derived from the STL's binary_function class in the functional header file.

> **Tip**
>
> To compare objects using min() and max(), their class needs only to overload the operator<() less-than function. In that case, you can use the simpler algorithms, and you do not need to supply a function object.

The min() and max() algorithms operate on two values. To find the maximum and minimum among a range of values stored in a container, call the max_element() and min_element() algorithms. These are defined as follows:

```
ForwardIterator max_element(
  ForwardIterator first, ForwardIterator last
  [, Compare comp ])
ForwardIterator min_element(
  ForwardIterator first, ForwardIterator last
  [, Compare comp ])
```

Each algorithm requires a pair of iterators that define the range of objects to search. The functions return an iterator to the located value. Keep in mind that this iterator might equal the *past-the-end* value if, for example, the container is empty. To demonstrate how to use the algorithms, the sample program defines a vector array of 10 integer values:

```
int data[10] = { 1, 2, 3, 4, 5, 6, 7, 8, 9, 10 };
vector<int> a(data, data + 10);
```

To store the function results, the program also defines an iterator of a type exported by the container's class:

```
vector<int>::iterator result;
```

The following statement assigns to result the location of the maximum value in the vector array:

```
result = max_element(a.begin(), a.end());
```

Similarly, this statement locates the minimum value:

```
result = min_element(a.begin(), a.end());
```

In either case, because the result is an iterator, it must be dereferenced to access the located value. However, be sure to test whether the result equals the *past-the-end* value before using it:

```
if (result != a.end())
  cout << "min_element(a.begin(), a.end()) = "
       << *result << endl;
```

FINDING DUPLICATES

Algorithm:

```
adjacent_find()
```

Sample program:

```
dup-ex.cpp
```

To find consecutive duplicate values among the objects in a container, call the `adjacent_find()` algorithm. The algorithm is defined as follows:

```
ForwardIterator adjacent_find(
  ForwardIterator first, ForwardIterator last
  [, BinaryPredicate binary_pred ])
```

The function requires two iterators that define the range of objects to search. You can optionally pass it a binary predicate function object that returns a bool true or false value based on a comparison of two objects (usually true only if the two objects are equal). The algorithm can be useful for creating unique data sets. For instance, the sample program defines a vector array with some purposely duplicated values:

```
int data[14] = { 1, 2, 3, 3, 3, 4, 5, 6, 6, 6, 7, 8, 9, 10 };
vector<int> a(data, data + 14);
```

The program calls `adjacent_find()` to locate the first element among the duplicated values—the 3s and 6s in the sample data. The algorithm returns an iterator, equal to the *past-the-end* value if the sequence has no adjacent duplications. A simple while loop calls the vector's `erase()` function to remove the located duplicates, leaving the unique sequence 1, 2, ..., 10 in the container:

```
vector<int>::iterator iter =
  adjacent_find(a.begin(), a.end());
  while (iter != a.end()) {
    a.erase(iter);
    iter = adjacent_find(a.begin(), a.end());
  }
```

Two calls to `adjacent_find()` are needed to locate every duplicate value in the vector array. The first such call locates the initial duplicate. The second call inside the loop repeatedly finds duplicates until none remains.

Lexically Comparing

Algorithm:

```
lexicographical_compare()
```

Sample program:

```
lex-ex.cpp
```

This one's a tongue twister. Call `lexicographical_compare()` to compare object values in two containers. The function is most useful with character data, but it is fully generalized and you can use it with any structure containing values that can be compared with the less-than operator. The function returns `true` if one structure is less than another based on a comparison of its held values. It returns `false` if the structure is greater than or equal to another. The algorithm is defined as follows:

```
bool lexicographical_compare(
  InputIterator1 first1, InputIterator1 last1,
  InputIterator2 first2, InputIterator2 last2
  [, Compare comp ])
```

Pass two pairs of iterators that define the range of objects in two containers (or two different ranges in the same container) to be compared. Optionally, provide a function object that returns true if one value is less than another.

The sample program demonstrates how to use the algorithm to compare two lists of characters—a somewhat impractical type of string but useful here for showing the form of the statements involved. The program defines the list structures `name1` and `name2` as follows and initializes them using common C-style null-terminated string arrays:

```
char s1[] = "George Washington";
char s2[] = "Abraham Lincoln";
list<char> name1(s1, s1 + sizeof s1 - 1);
list<char> name2(s2, s2 + sizeof s2 - 1);
```

Each character in the lists is a separate, double-linked object. To compare the lists alphabetically, the sample program executes the following statement:

```
bool result = lexicographical_compare(
  name1.begin(), name1.end(),
  name2.begin(), name2.end());
```

That sets `result` to `true` if `name1` is less than `name2`. The four iterators specify the range of values to compare in each list.

Merging Algorithms

Algorithms:

```
merge()
inplace_merge()
```

Sample program:

```
merge-ex.cpp
```

There are two forms of merging algorithms. One merges the objects in one data structure with another and deposits the results in a third container. Another merges objects within the same container. Let's take a look at the second and easier-to-use inplace_merge() algorithm defined as follows:

```
void inplace_merge(
  BidirectionalIterator first,
  BidirectionalIterator middle,
  BidirectionalIterator last [, Compare comp ])
```

The first and last iterators refer to the range of objects into which the merged objects are combined. The middle iterator specifies the start of the source objects for the merge. You may optionally pass a binary (two-parameter) function that returns true if one object value is less than another.

To demonstrate in-place merging, the sample program defines a container using the following statements:

```
int d1[9] = { 2, 4, 6, 8, 1, 3, 5, 7, 9 };
list<int> list1(d1, d1 + 9);
```

That sets list1 to the sequence shown—four even numbers followed by five odd ones in the range of 1 to 9. Calling find() locates the first odd value (1) in the list:

```
list<int>::iterator middle = find(
  list1.begin(), list1.end(), 1);
```

The program passes the resulting middle iterator plus the target range of the merge (the entire container) using the following statement:

```
inplace_merge(list1.begin(), middle, list1.end());
```

The result is a merge of the values in the same list, producing the sequence 1, 2, ..., 9.

To merge two sequences into a third, use the somewhat more complex merge() algorithm defined as follows:

```
OutputIterator merge(
  InputIterator1 first1, InputIterator1 last1,
  InputIterator2 first2, InputIterator2 last2,
  OutputIterator result [, Compare comp ])
```

The first four iterators define the range of objects in the two containers to be merged. The result iterator is the starting location in the destination container. To demonstrate the algorithm's use, the sample program defines two lists, one with even and another with odd values:

```
int d2[4] = { 2, 4, 6, 8 };
int d3[5] = { 1, 3, 5, 7, 9 };
list<int> list2(d2, d2 + 4);
list<int> list3(d3, d3 + 5);
```

The program also defines a third list to hold the merged data. Be sure to create a data structure that is large enough to contain the results, or that can be automatically expanded. In this case, the sample program creates an integer list container equal to the combined sizes of the two source lists and initializes all values in the new list to zero:

```
list<int> list4(list2.size() + list3.size(), 0);
```

Following that, the program calls `merge()` as follows to merge `list2` into `list3` and save the results in `list4`:

```
merge(list2.begin(), list2.end(),
  list3.begin(), list3.end(), list4.begin());
```

The first two iterators define the range of elements in `list2`. Similarly, the next two iterators define the range of elements in `list3`. The last argument specifies the starting location in the destination container, here the beginning of `list4`. After this statement, `list4` contains the sequence 1, 2, ..., 9. The containers `list2` and `list3` are unchanged.

> **Note**
>
> Merging is a stable operation. This means that, after merging, any duplicated objects retain their original relative order in the container.

SET ALGORITHMS

Algorithms:

```
set_union()
set_intersection()
set_difference()
set_symmetric_difference()
includes()
```

Sample program:

```
set-ex.cpp
```

As described in Chapter 24, "Building Standard Containers," under "Sets and Multisets," the set container does not provide operators such as union, intersection, and others. This is because sets are merely ordered containers of objects—they are not sets in a mathematical sense. To provide for the logical operations commonly applied to such sets of data, the STL provides general-purpose algorithms that work on any ordered data collection. You may use these algorithms with set containers, but you may also use them with vectors, lists, and any other containers whose data objects can be maintained in some logical order.

The four basic set algorithms are `set_union()`, `set_intersection()`, `set_difference()`, and `set_symmetric_difference()`. These all take the same general form shown here for `set_union()`, defined as follows:

```
OutputIterator set_union(
  InputIterator1 first1, InputIterator1 last1,
  InputIterator2 first2, InputIterator2 last2,
  OutputIterator result [, Compare comp ])
```

The first two pairs of iterators define the range of objects in one or two containers for which the algorithm is to be applied. The fifth iterator, result, specifies the starting location in a container to hold the result of the logical set operation. The source objects are unchanged. You may optionally supply a binary function object as a final argument. The function object should return true if one object value is less than another.

A related algorithm, named includes(), returns true if one set of objects is a subset of another. The algorithm is defined as follows:

```
bool includes(
  InputIterator1 first1, InputIterator1 last1,
  InputIterator2 first2, InputIterator2 last2
  [, Compare comp ] )
```

The iterators define the range of objects to be examined. As with the set algorithms, you may optionally pass a binary function object that compares two values. To demonstrate these algorithms, the sample program defines a string list using the typedef declaration:

```
typedef list<string> TSet;
```

That declares TSet as the name of a list container that can hold string objects. The program uses the type definition name to create and then sort lists of test strings using statements such as this:

```
TSet colors1;
colors1.push_back("Red");
colors1.push_back("Orange");
colors1.sort();
```

Two other sets of string lists, colors2 and colors3, are created, initialized, and sorted using similar statements (see the set-ex.cpp listing on disk). To determine whether one list is a subset of another, the program calls includes() as follows:

```
if (includes(
  colors2.begin(), colors2.end(),
  colors1.begin(), colors1.end()))
    cout << "colors1 is a subset of colors2" << endl;
```

The output statement displays a message if colors1 is a subset of colors2. Notice the order of the iterators. The set to be tested comes first, followed by the potential subset. Call set_union() to form the union of two sets. This and other set algorithms deposit their results in another container, created in the sample program using the following statement:

```
TSet colors4(colors1.size() + colors3.size());
```

That makes colors4 large enough to hold all values from colors1 and colors3. To form the union of those two containers and save the result in colors4, the sample program calls set_union():

```
set_union(
  colors1.begin(), colors1.end(),
  colors3.begin(), colors3.end(), colors4.begin());
```

PART

V

CH

25

In this case, the two pairs of iterators could be reversed with the same results placed in colors4. If colors1 equals the set {Orange, Red} and colors3 equals {Blue, Indigo, Violet}, their union in colors4 equals {Blue, Indigo, Orange, Red, Violet}. The source sets must be ordered (by sorting, for example). However, the result is automatically maintained in order.

> **Tip**
>
> Use the set container to automatically maintain objects in a specified order. When using a list or other container as a set, it is your responsibility to maintain object order.

To form the intersection of two sets, call the set_intersection() algorithm. For the demonstration, the sample program creates another set to hold the results of the operation:

```
TSet colors5(max(colors1.size(), colors2.size()));
```

Just for the sake of being different, I used the max() algorithm to create a new container of a size equal to colors1 or colors2, whichever is larger. To find the intersection of the two sets—all values in the one set that are also members of the other—the program calls set_intersection():

```
set_intersection(
  colors1.begin(), colors1.end(),
  colors2.begin(), colors2.end(), colors5.begin());
```

Given that colors1 equals the set {Orange, Red} and that colors2 equals {Green, Orange, Red, Yellow}, their intersection in colors5 is the set of common values {Orange, Red}. To find the difference between two sets, the program defines one more container as

```
TSet colors6(colors2.size());
```

The results can be no larger than the second set, so we simply use its size to create the new container. The program finds the difference between colors1 and colors2 using the following statement:

```
set_difference(
  colors2.begin(), colors2.end(),
  colors1.begin(), colors1.end(), colors6.begin());
```

Given the preceding color sets, that statement assigns to colors6 the values {Green, Yellow}—all the values in colors2 that are not members of colors1. When calling set_difference(), the order of the first two pairs of iterators is critical—the algorithm finds the elements in the first range that are not members of the second. Use set_symmetric_difference() to find the dissimilar elements in two sets regardless of order. To demonstrate symmetric difference, the sample program defines a new set, colors7, and then calls set_symmetric_difference() as follows:

```
TSet colors7(colors4.size());
set_symmetric_difference(
  colors1.begin(), colors1.end(),
  colors4.begin(), colors4.end(), colors7.begin());
```

Given that `colors1` equals the set {Orange, Red} and that `colors4` equals {Blue, Indigo, Orange, Red, Violet}, the program inserts into `colors7` the set {Blue, Indigo, Violet}. In this case, the same set results regardless of the order of the source set iterators.

When it isn't convenient to predetermine the size of a resulting set, you can use an insertion iterator along with any of the set algorithms. For example, define an empty set of strings and an insertion object using statements such as:

```
TSet colorsX;
insert_iterator<TSet> ins(colorsX, colorsX.begin());
```

That makes `colorsX` an empty list of strings. Use the STL `insert_iterator` template instantiated for the same class as the container. The object, named `ins` here, is constructed using the name of the container (`colorsX`) and the place where insertions are to begin—here the beginning of the empty container. If the destination container is not empty, this could be another iterator that, for example, is defined to begin insertions in the middle or at the end. Use the `ins` insertion iterator object as demonstrated in the sample program:

```
set_union(
  colors1.begin(), colors1.end(),
  colors3.begin(), colors3.end(), ins);
```

That finds the union of the two sets `colors1` and `colors3`, and deposits the results into wherever the insertion iterator object `ins` dictates.

ITERATIVE ALGORITHMS

Algorithm:

```
for_each()
```

Sample program:

```
for-ex.cpp
```

The `for_each()` algorithm performs an arbitrary operation on objects in a defined range. Use this algorithm to call a function of your own making for the values in a container. The `for_each()` algorithm is defined as follows:

```
Function for_each(
  InputIterator first, InputIterator last, Function f)
```

As usual, two iterators define the range of objects for which you want the algorithm to call a function, `f()`. The word *Function* here is a template placeholder that defines the type of function you want to call. This means that `for_each()` returns whatever value your function returns—void, a reference, a pointer, or an object—whatever value is appropriate.

> **Note**
>
> Past versions of the STL defined `for_each()` as returning `void`. The newer version is more versatile and, because it can also return `void`, is compatible with the earlier form.

The only firm rule is that the specified function must not alter the container by adding or deleting objects, which would change the meaning of the iterator arguments. Although you can use for_each() with common functions, it's more likely you'll create a class that overrides operator()()—the function-call operator. This permits an expression to "call" an object as though it were a function, and in that way provide the means to program highly complex operations. To demonstrate how to use for_each() this way, the sample program creates a vector of integer data named array:

```
int data[5] = { 2, 4, 6, 9, 10 };
vector<int> array(data, data + 5);
```

We want to perform some operation on all values in the array container. To show how to use a class template for this, the sample program derives class Times from the STL's unary_function class:

```
template <class T>
class Times: private unary_function<T, void>
{
  T multiplier;
public:
  Times(const T& m): multiplier(m) { }
  void operator()(const T& arg)
    { cout << setw(4) << arg * multiplier << endl; }
};
```

You may inherit the unary_function class privately as shown here, or using the protected or public access specifiers. Only two items are needed: a parameterized constructor for an as-yet unspecified type T and an overloaded operator()() function. Here, the sample program multiplies an argument against a multiplier value saved in a Times object and also displays that value.

To use the Times class, construct it using a value that is, in this example, multiplied to each value in the array container:

```
Times<int> t10(10);
```

To perform the operation on every value, call for_each(), passing the range of objects for which to call the Times object's overloaded operator()() function:

```
for_each(array.begin(), array.end(), t10);
```

Because the overloaded class operator displays each value as it is multiplied, this simple statement also shows the resulting values, as you see when you compile and run the program with these commands:

```
$ g++ for-ex.cpp
$ ./a.out
...
array * 10
  20
  40
  60
  90
 100
```

RANDOMIZING ALGORITHMS

Algorithm:

```
random_shuffle()
```

Sample programs:

```
rand-ex.cpp
```

It always interests me that, in such an orderly and methodical business as computer programming, randomness intrigues programmers like no other subject. Although sorting is one of the topics all programmers learn early on, the methods for shuffling values into random order are equally appealing if not more so. For scrambling your container's eggs, the STL provides an algorithm, `random_shuffle()`, defined as follows:

```
void random_shuffle(
  RandomAccessIterator first, RandomAccessIterator last
  [, RandomNumberGenerator& rand ])
```

As with most algorithms, two iterators define the range of objects on which to operate. An optional third parameter is a reference to a random-number generator. By default, this generator is similar to the Fibonacci generator described in Chapter 23, "Using the Standard Template Library (STL)," under the section titled "Generator Function Class Objects."

The sample program demonstrates how to use `random_shuffle()` both ways. To demonstrate the default random-number generator, the program creates a vector of integers and fills it with values from 0 to 99:

```
vector<int> array;
...
for (int i = 0; i < 100; i++)
  array.push_back(i);
```

Calling `random_shuffle()` as follows scrambles the values in the original array:

```
random_shuffle(array.begin(), array.end());
```

You might use this algorithm to prepare test data, to investigate the effectiveness of sorting programs, or simply to provide random sequences of known values—as indexes into another container, for example, to be accessed randomly.

To teach `random_shuffle()` how to use another random-number generator, include the `functional` header file, and derive a class from the STL's `unary_function` template. Listing 25.1, from rand-ex.cpp, shows the class's design.

LISTING 25.1   RAND-EX.CPP (PARTIAL)

```
// A random-number generator class
class TRandom : public unary_function<long, long> {
public:
  TRandom(bool seed = true)
```

continues

LISTING 25.1   CONTINUED

```
    { if (seed) NewSequence(); }
  long operator()(const long& arg)
    { return random() % arg; }
  void NewSequence()
    { srandom( time(NULL) ); }
};
```

The class could also be a template, but because I intend to use it to generate long values at random, I made it a plain class derived from the unary_function template, instantiated using a long function return value and a long argument value.

The TRandom class has three public member functions. First is a constructor that, depending on whether its parameter seed is true, calls NewSequence() for a new sequence. That function calls the standard C library's srandom() function with a time value as the seed—resulting in a new sequence, provided that at least one second elapses between such calls. The overloaded operator()() function is required by the random_shuffle() algorithm. It returns long and declares a single parameter, applied with the modulus operator to the standard C library's random() function.

To use the generator, simply define an object of the following class type:

```
TRandom generator;
```

Alternatively, pass true or false to TRandom's constructor to select whether to seed a new sequence. Replace the preceding object with either of these two statements:

```
TRandom generator(true);    // Default: seed new sequence
TRandom generator(false);   // Repeat same sequence
```

Pass the random-number generator object to random_shuffle(), which calls the TRandom class's overloaded operator()() function to scramble the values in the array (sorted beforehand in the sample program):

```
random_shuffle(array.begin(), array.end(), generator);
```

This also shows how, using an appropriate class, it's possible to plug in new code into STL algorithms.

REMOVAL ALGORITHMS

Algorithm:

    remove()

Sample programs:

    remov-ex.cpp

The STL's removal algorithms provide several different ways to remove and erase objects in containers, the simplest and most basic of which is remove(). The algorithm is defined as follows:

```
ForwardIterator remove(
  ForwardIterator first, ForwardIterator last,
  const T& value)
```

Two iterators specify the range of objects to be searched for a specified value—the one to remove from the container. To demonstrate how to use remove(), the sample program creates an array container of 10 integer values, using a vector template:

```
int data[10] = { 1, 2, 3, 4, 5, 6, 7, 8, 9, 10 };
vector<int> array(data, data + 10);
```

The program demonstrates one idiosyncrasy with remove(). Calling remove() with a search argument of 6

```
remove(array.begin(), array.end(), 6);
```

removes that value but doesn't adjust the resulting array. Because of that, the container now has the values

```
1 2 3 4 5 7 8 9 10 10
```

The duplicated 10 at the end of the container is the result of remove() deleting the value 6 and moving other values up one notch. However, the final value also needs erasing. Do that by instead calling remove() as follows and save the result, an iterator, in a variable:

```
vector<int>::iterator start =
  remove(array.begin(), array.end(), 6);
```

The iterator, start, is of the iterator type exported by the container class. To clean up the final container, pass the iterator returned by remove(), along with a second iterator that defines the end of the range (usually the end of the container), to the container's erase() function:

```
array.erase(start, array.end());
```

Now the array correctly holds nine values. On the other hand, perhaps you don't want to erase the leftover value. In that case, you could set it to zero:

```
*start = 0;
```

PART

V

CH

25

Tip

Keep in mind that remove() affects *only* the target value, not any others in a container. Removing an object from a container then usually requires a follow-up operation on the remaining values. This is, however, always optional.

REMOVING ON CONDITION

Algorithms:

```
remove_if()
remove_copy()
remove_copy_if()
```

Sample programs:

```
remov-ex.cpp
```

The STL provides three variations on the remove() algorithm. The remove_if() algorithm removes values that satisfy a condition. This algorithm is defined as follows:

```
ForwardIterator remove_if(
  ForwardIterator first, ForwardIterator last
  [, Predicate pred ])
```

The arguments are the same as for remove(), but the predicate function object determines whether the operation should be performed on a specific value. Usually, the predicate is a class derived from the STL's unary_function template. Include the functional header and then design your class as demonstrated in the sample program:

```
template<class T>
class is_even: public unary_function<T, bool>
{
  public:
    bool operator()(const T& x){
      return (x % 2) == 0; }
};
```

The class doesn't have to be a template. If you know the type of data in the container, change T to that type. For example, you could change T to int in this case. The new class, is_even, requires only one element—an overloaded operator()() function. this function returns a bool true or false value, based on some condition applied to the constant reference argument, x. In this case, I programmed the function to return true if x is even.

To apply the predicate class to the values in a container, pass an object of the class to the remove_if() algorithm. For example, the following statement removes all even values from the array container:

```
start = remove_if(array.begin(), array.end(), is_even<int>());
```

Here, again, the resulting iterator is saved, so a follow-up operation can erase leftover values now in the container. Using the values in array (1 through 10, not including 6), the preceding statement leaves these values in array:

```
1 3 5 7 9 7 8 9 10
```

The last four values are left over from the removal of the four even values in the original array. To clean up the results, call the container's erase() function using the saved iterator:

```
array.erase(start, array.end());
```

Now the array contains only the odd values:

```
1 3 5 7 9
```

Tip

It isn't necessary to test whether the iterator returned by `remove_if()` equals the *past-the-end* value. Passing that value to `erase()` does no harm, and in effect, does nothing.

Two other removal algorithms, `remove_copy()` and `remove_copy_if()`, work the same as `remove()` and `remove_if()` but deposit their results in a destination container. The objects in the original container are unaffected. The `remove_copy()` algorithm is defined as follows:

```
OutputIterator remove_copy(
  InputIterator first, InputIterator last,
  OutputIterator result, const T& value)
```

Two iterators define the range of objects to search for a value, a constant reference to the object type T. The third iterator, result, specifies a starting location in a container to which the algorithm copies the removed values. The `remove_copy_if()` algorithm is defined similarly as follows:

```
OutputIterator remove_copy_if(
  InputIterator first, InputIterator last,
  OutputIterator result, Predicate pred)
```

The only difference is that a predicate object determines which objects match the criteria for removal. The predicate object is usually of a class such as `is_even`, derived from the STL's `unary_function` template, as described in the preceding section.

To demonstrate how to use `remove_copy()`, the sample program defines two `vector` containers:

```
vector<int> invec(data, data + 10);
vector<int> outvec(invec.size(), 0);
```

The invec vector is initialized to the sequence of values 1, 2, ..., 10. The outvec vector is the same size as invec, but its values are initialized to zero. To create a new vector minus the value 8, call `remove_if()` as follows:

```
start = remove_copy(
  invec.begin(), invec.end(), outvec.begin(), 8);
```

The resulting outvec container now contains the sequence of values minus 8:

```
1 2 3 4 5 6 7 9 10 0
```

The trailing zero, however, again requires a follow-up erasure:

```
outvec.erase(start, outvec.end());
```

Call `remove_copy_if()` along with a predicate function object that determines whether a value should be removed. To demonstrate, the sample program constructs a vector of integers, oddballs, of the same size as invec (still holding the sequence 1, 2, ..., 10), initialized to zero.

```
vector<int> oddballs(invec.size(), 0);;
```

PART
V
CH
25

Calling `remove_copy_if()` with the following arguments removes all odd values into odd-balls, without disturbing `invec` in any way:

```
start = remove_copy_if(invec.begin(), invec.end(),
  oddballs.begin(), is_even<int>());
```

To additionally erase the unused values in the destination `vector`, the program calls `erase()`, passing the iterator returned by the algorithm and the container's `end()` value:

```
oddballs.erase(start, oddballs.end());
```

After that, the `oddballs` vector contains the sequence

```
1 3 5 7 9
```

REMOVING UNIQUE VALUES

Algorithms:

```
unique()
unique_copy()
```

Sample programs:

```
uniq-ex.cpp
```

Call the `unique()` algorithm to remove all duplicated values from a container. The algorithm is similar to `remove()` in that it does not clean up values left over by others moved during the removal. You normally call `erase()` to throw away these leftovers, but this is always optional. The `unique()` algorithm is defined as follows:

```
ForwardIterator unique(
  ForwardIterator first, ForwardIterator last)
```

Simply pass two iterators to `unique()`, and the algorithm removes all duplicate values. To demonstrate, the sample program defines a vector of integers and fills it with duplicated values:

```
vector<int> array;
...
for (int i = 1; i < 9; i++)
  for (int j = 1; j <= i; j++)
    array.push_back(i);
```

The resulting `vector` contains these values:

```
1 2 2 3 3 3 4 4 4 4 5 5 5 5 5 6 6 6 6 6 6
7 7 7 7 7 7 7 8 8 8 8 8 8 8 8
```

To remove the duplicates, the program calls `unique()`. This must be followed by `erase()` to clean up the resulting `vector` of values left over by the algorithm's moving values upward at each removal:

```
vector<int>::iterator start =
  unique(array.begin(), array.end());
    array.erase(start, array.end());
```

A variation of unique() copies its results to a destination container. The unique_copy() algorithm is defined as follows:

```
inline OutputIterator unique_copy(
  InputIterator first, InputIterator last,
  OutputIterator result
  [, BinaryPredicate binary_pred ])
```

Pass first and last iterators that define the range of objects on which to apply the algorithm. Pass in result an iterator that defines the starting location in a destination container. The algorithm copies a unique set of values from the source container to the destination. The source container objects are not altered in any way. You can optionally pass a binary predicate function object that compares two values and returns true via an overloaded operator()() function if those values are equal. To demonstrate how to do that, the sample program derives a class from the STL's binary_function template (defined in the functional header file):

```
class are_equal: public binary_function<int, int, int>
{
  public:
    bool operator()(const int& arg1, const int& arg2)
      { return (arg1 == arg2); }
};
```

That's just for demonstration purposes—the new class merely returns true if two integer arguments are the same. But it demonstrates the form to use for creating a more complex predicate function object—one that compares objects based on a variety of criteria. For instance, a predicate could ignore case in strings, or it might consider two objects to be equal only if some of their data members are the same.

To use the predicate class, construct an object and pass it to unique_copy() as follows (this code is commented-out in the sample program):

```
are_equal pred;  // Construct binary predicate object
start = unique_copy(source.begin(), source.end(),
  destination.begin(), pred);
```

PART

V

CH

25

REPLACEMENT ALGORITHMS

Algorithms:

```
replace()
replace_if()
replace_copy()
replace_copy_if()
```

Sample program:

```
rep-ex.cpp
```

You can replace values in a container using these four algorithms. The simplest, `replace()`, is defined as follows:

```
void replace(
  ForwardIterator first, ForwardIterator last,
  const T& old_value, const T& new_value)
```

The two iterators define the range of objects to be scanned. T represents the type of data in the container. The algorithm replaces all values equal to `old_value` with `new_value`. Use `replace_if()` to provide a predicate function that determines matching values to replace. This variation is defined as follows:

```
void replace_if(
  ForwardIterator first, ForwardIterator last,
  Predicate pred, const T& new_value)
```

The only difference is the predicate object. The other parameters are the same as for `replace()`. To demonstrate how to use these algorithms, the sample program defines a vector of integers initialized to the values shown here:

```
int data[10] = { 2, 4, 6, 2, 8, 2, 1, 2, 2, 9 };
vector<int> array(data, data + 10);
```

A call to `replace()` sets to zero every value equal to 2:

```
replace(array.begin(), array.end(), 2, 0);
```

Use the `replace_if()` algorithm to replace values that satisfy a condition programmed as a predicate function object. For example, create a class such as `is_even` (see "Counting Algorithms" earlier in this chapter and also the count-ex.cpp sample program on the CD-ROM). Construct an object of the class for the type of data in your container and pass the object to `replace_if()`:

```
replace_if(array.begin(), array.end(), is_even<int>(), 0);
```

That replaces every even value in the array with zero. Two other replacement algorithms work exactly the same as `replace()` and `replace_if()` but copy the resulting objects to another container. These are `replace_copy()` and `replace_copy_if()`, defined as follows:

```
OutputIterator replace_copy(
  InputIterator first, InputIterator last,
  OutputIterator result,
  const T& old_value, const T& new_value)

OutputIterator replace_copy_if(
  Iterator first, Iterator last,
  OutputIterator result,
  Predicate pred, const T& new_value)
```

The only difference is the addition of a third iterator, `result`, which locates the starting place for copying the function results. For examples of similar functions, see "Removing on Condition" earlier in this chapter and the discussions of the `remove_copy()` and `remove_copy_if()` algorithms.

SEARCHING ALGORITHMS

Algorithms:

```
find()
find_if()
```

Sample program:

```
find-ex.cpp
```

The find() and find_if() algorithms search a container for a specified value. See also "Finding Algorithms" earlier in this chapter for related algorithms. The STL defines find() as follows:

```
InputIterator find(
  InputIterator first, InputIterator last, const T& value)
```

As usual, two iterators define the range of objects to scan. The algorithm returns an iterator to the first value it finds of type T, representing the type of data in the container. The find_if() algorithm is defined similarly as follows:

```
InputIterator find_if(
  InputIterator first, InputIterator last, Predicate pred)
```

Instead of a value reference, find_if() uses a predicate function object that determines whether a value matches. For an example, see "Counting Algorithms" earlier in this chapter and also the is_even class in the count-ex.cpp sample program.

To demonstrate the find() and find_if() algorithms, the sample program creates a vector with the integer values shown here:

```
int data[10] = { 1, 2, 3, 4, 5, 6, 7, 8, 9, 10 };
vector<int> array(data, data + 10);
```

To locate the value 6, the program creates an iterator and calls find() like this:

```
vector<int>::iterator start =
  find(array.begin(), array.end(), 6);
```

That sets start to the location of the value 6 in the vector array. If this value equals the *past-the-end* value, then the search failed. Otherwise, start might be passed to another algorithm. For example, this statement erases all values from the vector from 6 to the end:

```
array.erase(start, array.end());
```

Call find_if() to search a container for a value that matches another kind of specification defined by a predicate function object. For example, using the is_even class, the following statements locate the first even value in the vector and then erase values from there to the end:

```
start = find_if(array.begin(), array.end(), is_even<int>());
array.erase(start, array.end());
```

SORTING ALGORITHMS

Algorithms:

```
sort()
stable_sort()
```

Sample program:

```
sort-ex.cpp
```

I'd be surprised to discover a subject in computer programming that has occupied more time and discussion than sorting. Finally, there's a completely general way to create sorting functions for any type of data in any structure. You can use the sorting algorithms described here with any container holding objects accessible by random access iterators. The simplest variation, sort(), is defined as follows:

```
void sort(
  RandomAccessIterator first, RandomAccessIterator last)
```

Simply pass iterators for the range of objects to sort. The algorithm uses the Quicksort method, generally considered to be the fastest for most kinds of data. A variation allows you to specify a comparison function object:

```
void sort(
  RandomAccessIterator first, RandomAccessIterator last,
  Compare comp)
```

The only difference is a third parameter that specifies a comparison function object. Usually, this is a class derived from the STL's `binary_function` template. Overload the `operator<()` function to return `true` if a value of your container's data type is less than another value, both passed as arguments to the operator function.

Another way to customize the `sort()` algorithm is to provide for comparisons in the object's class itself. This is typical in cases where objects are to be sorted based on a portion of their values. For example, a class might define several fields. To sort the objects based on the values of selected fields, create a class as demonstrated in Listing 25.2, from the sort-ex.cpp sample program on the CD-ROM.

LISTING 25.2   SORT-EX.CPP (PARTIAL)

```
class TData
{
  string s;  // String data
  int n;     // Associated integer data
  friend ostream& operator <<(ostream &os, const TData& d);
public:
  TData(): s(""), n(0) { }
  TData(const char* S, const int N): s(S), n(N) { }
  bool operator< (const TData& d) const
// { return n < d.n; }    // For sorting on the integer data
  { return s < d.s; }  // For sorting on the string data
};
```

```
// Output a TData object
ostream& operator <<(ostream &os, const TData& d)
{
  os << "(" << d.n << "): " << d.s;
  return os;
}
```

The TData class defines private string and int variables, and it also provides two overloaded operators. The first, operator<<(), is a friend function that displays the contents of a TData object. The second overloaded function, operator<(), compares two TData objects, returning true if one is less than another passed as an argument of type const TData&. For sorting on the TData objects' string data, the function compares the string objects. A commented-out statement compares the objects' integer data. This demonstrates how a class can determine the nature of a comparison on objects. You might also create a class that sets a flag to determine which of several possible fields are involved in the comparison, thus producing differing sorts by simply throwing a switch one way or the other.

To demonstrate how to use the TData class along with the sort() algorithm, the example program defines an associative array of TData objects as a vector container:

```
vector<TData> array;
```

Several statements push TData objects into the vector:

```
array.push_back(TData("Loretta", 85));
...
array.push_back(TData("Betty",   94));
```

The integers have no real purpose here, but they represent data for any kind of object that has more than one internal value. Sorting the vector is a simple matter of calling the sort() algorithm with iterators for the vector's beginning and end:

```
sort(array.begin(), array.end());
```

Because the TData class compares strings in its operator<() function, the objects are sorted by name. To sort by integer value, enable the commented-out statement in the TData class and add comment brackets to the other comparison.

Tip

You can more quickly sort a list container by calling that class's sort() member function. However, for sorting vectors, deques, and even ordinary arrays, the STL sort() algorithm is fast and easy to use.

The sort() algorithm does not maintain the relative order of duplicate objects in containers. If you need to do that, call the alternate stable_sort() algorithm, which is defined the same as sort(). For example, to sort the sample vector described here, call stable_sort() as follows:

```
stable_sort(array.begin(), array.end());
```

This algorithm is generally slower than sort(), so don't use it unless absolutely necessary. However, one good use for stable_sort() is to sort the same container of objects on different fields. For example, the objects' class could represent database records to be sorted first by state and then by last name, or age, or other fields.

OTHER STL TOPICS

The following sections contain information about two additional topics that apply generally to programs that use the STL. As you will learn, exception handling is almost nonexistent in the STL's algorithms, except for a few string class member functions. You also take a look at some problems and solutions caused by storing object pointers in containers.

EXCEPTION HANDLING IN THE STL

Exception handling in the STL is virtually nonexistent. In all fairness to its designers, this is understandably necessary to preserve the completely general nature and, more importantly, the speed of the containers and algorithms. For this reason, algorithms do not check whether iterators are valid, nor do they prevent common mistakes such as reversing iterators. Only the standard string class throws exceptions, and then only for some obvious problems such as specifying an index beyond the length of a string.

Listing 25.3, excpt-ex.cpp, demonstrates how to trap one kind of common string exception. It also shows a workaround for a minor bug in the string class.

LISTING 25.3   EXCPT-EX.CPP

```
#include <iostream.h>
#include <string>
#include <stdexcept>

int main()
{
  string s("Never-never land");
  try {
    //     s.remove(100, 10);  // Doesn't compile
    s.replace(100, 10, "");    // Work-around
  }
  catch (out_of_range e) {
    cout << "*** Range error: " << e.what() << endl;
    return 1;
  }
  return 0;
}
```

To recognize standard exceptions, include the stdexcept header file. Using a try block, call a string function such as remove() that throws an exception of type out_of_range and use a catch statement to trap that type of error. The error object's what() function describes the nature of the problem. Catch another type of exception, length_error, using similar code.

Note

For more information on exceptions, see Chapter 16, "Handling Exceptions." For information on strings and exceptions, see Chapter 22, "Mastering the Standard string Class."

POINTERS IN CONTAINERS

Finally, a few words about storing pointers in containers and the trouble this can cause (and what to do about it). Until now, most examples have shown objects stored directly in containers. However, you may certainly construct objects using new and store the resulting pointers in STL containers.

However, doing that means you assume responsibility for memory allocation and deletions. One common error is to erase pointers from containers without first deleting the objects addressed by those pointers. To demonstrate one way to handle this situation, Listing 25.4, point-ex.cpp, creates a vector of string-object pointers.

LISTING 25.4   POINT-EX.CPP

```cpp
#include <iostream.h>
#include <string>
#include <vector>

// Define vector of string pointers
vector<string*> array;

int main()
{
// Insert some dynamic string objects into the array
  array.push_back(new string("The point of this"));
  array.push_back(new string("code is to store"));
  array.push_back(new string("pointers to string objects"));
  array.push_back(new string("in a container."));

// Display the data in the vector
  for (int i = 0; i < array.size(); i++)
    cout << *array[i] << endl;

// Delete and erase the string objects and pointers
  for (int j = 0; j < array.size(); j++)
    delete array[j];
  array.erase(array.begin(), array.end());

  return 0;
}
```

PART

V

CH

25

The program defines a vector of string pointers, and it uses statements such as the following to create string objects dynamically and store their pointers in the container:

```cpp
array.push_back(new string("The point of this"));
array.push_back(new string("code is to store"));
array.push_back(new string("pointers to string objects"));
array.push_back(new string("in a container."));
```

Notice how `new` creates each `string` object dynamically. This isn't really necessary because the `string` class stores character data dynamically in the first place, but it demonstrates the basic techniques for keeping pointers in containers.

To access the stored objects, dereference the values in the container. For example, the following statement displays a *string* at index `i`:

```
cout << *array[i] << endl;
```

Never erase any pointers from a container without first deleting their addressed memory. The example program shows how to do that using a `for` loop to delete all memory allocations. Only *after* this is done does the program call `erase()` to remove the pointers from the container:

```
for (int j = 0; j < array.size(); j++)
  delete array[j];
array.erase(array.begin(), array.end());
```

SUMMARY

The STL provides numerous algorithms in the form of template functions. Algorithms are completely generalized, and most can work with any type of data and containers. Most algorithms declare iterator parameters for accessing a range of objects in an STL container. Algorithms are not object-oriented, but they may be used in both OOP and conventional programming.

For more information on subjects introduced in this chapter, turn to the following chapters:

- Chapter 16, "Handling Exceptions"
- Chapter 22, "Mastering the Standard `string` Class"
- Chapter 23, "Using the Standard Template Library (STL)"
- Chapter 24, "Building Standard Containers"

## CHAPTER 26

INTRODUCING X PROGRAMMING

It's probably fair to assume that most Linux users run X and a window manager on a color graphics display. Under Linux, XFree86 is a freely distributed collection of X servers optimized for PC hardware, but for all practical purposes, X and XFree86 are the same. (Although sometimes called "X Window," the correct name for this bitmapped windowing software is just plain X.)

Writing software that takes advantage of X capabilities means learning many new concepts. To develop even a simple program, programmers must choose from a bewildering collection of tools such as Motif and Athena Widgets, Sun's Open Look, the General Drawing Kit (GDK), Xlib (the X function library), the GIMP toolkit (GTK), Gnome window manager, and other X add-ons. All this goes to show that X is a deceptively simple name for a highly complex programming environment. Programmers who dive headlong into all this complexity might easily drown in the details. Just to display a single dot in an X application requires an understanding, among other topics, of network communication, virtual color maps, and event-driven asynchronous logic. If you have sampled X programming and become confused, at least know that you are in good company.

This and the next two chapters help ease you into X and C++ programming on their most fundamental level—the Xlib function library. Because all window managers and toolkits ultimately call Xlib functions, learning how to use the library provides basic knowledge that makes it easier to use X add-ons and extensions. In the last chapters of this part, you build on these fundamentals with the help of an object-oriented C++ class library, V, that simplifies many graphical design problems such as how to create a pull-down menu, a toolbar of buttons, and dialog boxes. The V library is also an excellent example of how C++ object-oriented programming can simplify highly complex jobs and also provide cross compatibility for X and Microsoft Windows software development.

> **Note**
>
> This and the next chapters in this part assume that you have X configured and running on your system. If you haven't done that, follow the suggestions in Chapter 2, "Installing Linux," before continuing.

THE WORLD ACCORDING TO X

Many programmers are tempted to jump right into X programming the way they learn other topics—by reading a few sample source code files and then building code using the sample files as shells. But when their programs fail to work properly, these are the souls who carry armloads of X tutorials back from the bookstore and spend all night searching for solutions to their problems. These unfortunates also swamp the networks with email messages expressing their many frustrations with X architecture.

A better way to learn X programming is to start at the very beginning. X is methodically designed, and its underlying philosophies are not difficult to master for those who are willing to spend a little time studying some new concepts.

To help you begin on the right track, the following sections provide overviews of key X principles. After that, I explain each step of a sample program that demonstrates common X programming techniques. Learn these basics, and you'll find it much easier to absorb and understand the examples in the coming chapters. Knowing Xlib fundamentals also makes it relatively easy to learn how to use higher-level X toolkits.

> **Note**
>
> Readers with some X experience can skip the rest of this section and go directly to "Introducing Xlib Programming." However, I urge all to read through the following overviews for a better understanding of the example programs that follow.

A FEW GOOD TERMS

Following are some critical X terms and phrases used in this and the other chapters in this part. While learning about X programming, you might want to mark this section for future reference.

API An Application Programming Interface, or API, provides functions, and often structures and other data declarations, for operating system software. For example, Xlib is the API for X development. Xlib provides functions that X applications can call to perform various actions such as displaying text and graphics in a window.

Child window A child window is one that another parent window owns. Except for the root window, every X window is a child of a parent window. See also *Parent window*, *Root window*, and *Window*.

Client In general terms, under the client/server model, a client requests data or services from server software. Typically, the client and server are separate tasks that might run at different locations on a network, an arrangement otherwise known as *distributed processing*. In X, however, the client/server model works a little differently. An X client is another name for an application—for example, a game or a word processor. The X client might run locally on the user's system, or it might run on another system over a network. A client might be shared by multiple users, and it might communicate with more than one X server. The window manager is itself a client application. See also *Client/server*, *Server*, and *X server*.

Client/server This term describes the relationship between the X server and one or more client applications. All X installations, whether operating on a standalone workstation or across a network, are based on the X client/server model. See also *Client*, *Server*, and *X server*.

Colormap X uses one or more colormaps to relate hardware display capabilities with the values that programs can use to specify visual colors. By using colormaps instead of directly specifying colors—for example, as red, green, and blue values or as grayscale intensities—X clients can display information correctly regardless of the display's characteristics. As a data structure, a colormap's internal format depends on the nature of the

PART
V

CH

26

display. A grayscale colormap, for example, is an entirely different structure internally from one used on a 24-bit-plane true color system. See also *Display*, *Screen*, and *X server*.

Display   In X programming, a display encompasses the graphics terminal (which might be composed of multiple screens, physical or virtual), and at least two input devices—a keyboard and mouse with one or more buttons. The X server's primary job is to manage the display for client applications. See also *Client*, *Screen*, and *Window*.

Event   An event is a message sent from the X server to a client that describes an occurrence needing the client's attention. For example, a mouse click inside a window is sent as a ButtonPress event. Another example is a "notify" event that tells the client something has changed concerning a window. An Expose event, for instance, tells the client that a portion of a window has been uncovered, and therefore, needs to be redrawn. Events are queued in Xlib and occur asynchronously among other activities. A major part of the programming of an X client application involves getting and responding to X server events. See also *Event loop*, *Request*, and *Xlib*.

Event loop   The heart of an X client application is its event loop. In this loop, the client plucks events from the Xlib event queue and calls Xlib functions to perform operations in response to user actions such as resizing a window or clicking a mouse button. See also *Event* and *Request*.

Focus   The focus indicates which window receives keyboard and mouse input events. Only one window at a time can have the focus. It identifies the window to which the X server sends events. See also *Event* and *Window*.

Graphics context   Xlib graphics functions, also called graphics primitives, use a graphics context to specify visual characteristics such as line width, colors, and fill patterns. Using a graphics context reduces the number of parameters passed to Xlib functions and also limits network traffic by centralizing characteristics that remain the same between Xlib function calls. See also *Colormap* and *Xlib*.

GUI   This is an acronym for Graphical User Interface, pronounced *gooey*. (You might say it's a sticky subject.) Many pieces go into the making of a GUI, and X is only one part of the interface familiar to Linux and UNIX users. In addition to X, a window manager and one or more toolkits are responsible for creating the actual objects such as buttons and pull-down menus that many users associate with a GUI. This fact distinguishes X from other GUIs such as Microsoft Windows that lock users into a specific look and feel and also make it difficult to extend the interface's capabilities. X is far more flexible, highly extensible, and designed specifically to work on a wide variety of hardware.

Keyboard focus   See *Focus*.

Motif   The Open Software Foundation's (OSF) Motif toolkit implements a look and feel for X clients through the use of widgets such as buttons and pull-down menus. Linux installations extend Motif widgets using the Xaw3d library (Three-D Athena Widgets). See also *Widget*.

Parent window   Any window may be the parent to a child window. In addition to providing a logical connection among related windows, a parent provides many of the attributes of its children. For example, unless the client specifies a different background, a child window inherits the background color from its parent. In most cases, a client's main window (also called a top-level window) is a child of the X root window. But a client window may itself be a parent for another child window such as a dialog box. See also *Root window*, *Window*, and *Screen*.

Request   In the X client/server model, calls to Xlib functions do not perform actions directly but generate *requests* to the X server. Such requests carry out operations such as changing colormap values, drawing lines, and filling shapes with patterns. To reduce network traffic, Xlib queues requests and then sends them en masse to the X server. Typically, this happens when the client application's event queue becomes empty and the program is blocked waiting for the next event to arrive. However, a client can explicitly empty the request queue by calling XFlush(), XSynch(), and similar functions. See also *Event*, *X server*, and *Xlib*.

Root window   All windows are ultimately children of the root window, which provides the background color and other characteristics of the user's screen (or screens). The X server creates the root window when X is first initialized—for example, when the user types **startx**. See also *Child window*, *Window*, and *Window manager*.

Screen   A screen is one component of a display. In many X installations, users have access to multiple screens, which can be physical terminals or virtual screens selected with function keys or by clicking the mouse button. See also *Display* and *Window*.

Server   In general terms, under the client/server model, a server is a task that provides data or services to one or more clients. The client and server may run on the same hardware or at different locations in a network environment. In X, the server manages the display for one or more client applications. See also *Client* and *X server*.

Widget   This is an informal term that refers to an object such as a button or a check box implemented by one or more Xlib function calls. Toolkits such as Motif and the Athena Xaw3d library provide numerous widgets that simplify X programming and provide a consistent look and feel for applications.

Window   A window is not only the familiar bordered kind. An X window is also a structure that defines the attributes of framed windows plus other visual components such as buttons and scrollbars. In this sense, these and other GUI components are all windows. See also *Child window* and *Parent window*.

Window manager   A window manager is an X client application responsible for the placement and relative *stacking order* of graphical windows. A window manager provides access to display screens, and it might also provide menu bars or other features for starting applications, performing file operations, and carrying out system chores. One key difference between X and other GUIs such as Microsoft Windows is that X window managers are not intrinsic to X and Xlib. They are just client applications with a special

PART

V

CH

26

role to play. Ideally, all client applications should operate correctly regardless of the specific window manager that is running, and as a result, users have much more control over their virtual desktop than with other GUIs such as Microsoft Windows. If you don't like the looks or other capabilities of your window manager, you are free to load a different one, or even create your own. See also *Client*, *Display*, *Server*, and *X server*.

X   X is a bitmapped graphical windowing system that provides a hardware-independent user interface through a client/server model. Xlib is the programming API for X. An X installation is composed of many parts and pieces that produce a graphical user interface, or GUI. See also *X server*.

X server   The X server manages the user's display, which consists of all input and output devices, including one or more screens, a keyboard, and a mouse. Unlike other types of servers typically found on a network, an X server typically operates locally on the user's machine, and it communicates with one or more clients that may operate locally or at some other location on a network. An X server is essentially a collection of network protocols for communicating with X clients through requests and events. In this sense, an X server provides a hardware-independent programming language for creating graphical user interfaces. See also *Client*, *Display*, *Event*, *GUI*, *Request*, and *Xlib*.

XFree86   Distributed with every Linux release, XFree86 provides several X servers tweaked specifically for Linux and PC (Intel 80x86) hardware. XFree86 runs under more than a dozen types of UNIX flavors, including Linux. It is capable of establishing communications between itself and client applications using the most efficient means—directly through bitstreams in a standalone workstation or over a network connection. See also *Display* and *Window*.

Xlib   The X API is known as Xlib, the X function library. It forms the core of X capabilities that all client applications and window managers use. Programming with Xlib takes place at the lowest level and requires defining every aspect of an application's visual appearance. For example, using Xlib to create a button in a window means developing every aspect of the button's appearance, including any animation or shadowing effects. Although programming with Xlib can be difficult, its fundamentals introduced in this and the next two chapters are essential for successfully using toolkits such as Motif and Xaw3d that provide higher-level graphical objects. Regardless of the toolkit you use, you can always drop into Xlib to send requests to the X server. See also *Client*, *Server*, *Window*, and *X server*.

A VERY BRIEF HISTORY OF X

X dates back to around 1987 when the first release appeared from the Massachusetts Institute of Technology (MIT). Most of what remains from this early release is the concept of the client/server model and associated network protocols that enable X to run successfully on widely differing hardware platforms.

The current release, X11R6 (version 11, revision 6) is fairly stable, and any changes are not expected to break existing code. Because X is highly extensible, this is a promise that may very well be kept. As mentioned, X is the proper name for this bitmapped windowing system, although many authors incorrectly call it "X Windows." Xlib provides a programming interface (API) of C and C++ functions for writing X client applications. This and the next two chapters introduce you to Xlib programming on its most fundamental levels.

X INSTALLATIONS

Depending on your installation, the X programming libraries might be located in a variety of paths. In most cases, the directories /usr/X11/include and /usr/X11/lib provide all the necessary files to compile and link X client applications. These might be named /usr/X11R6/include and /usr/X11R6/lib, respectively. However, the pathnames might be implemented as links to other directories. For example, X11 may actually be a link to the X11R6 directory.

Note

See "Introducing Xlib Programming" later in this chapter for suggestions on specifying include and library pathname options to compile and link X client applications using GNU C++.

TOOLKITS

An X toolkit provides visual and other utilities for client applications to share. Many toolkits are available, including the OSF Motif widget library and Sun's Open Look. These and other toolkits are further enhanced by extensions such as the Athena Xaw3d library, which provides a pseudo three-dimensional look to visual objects such as buttons and window borders. On top of all this is the relatively new visual object and container library known as Gnome, based on the Gtk+ library. Gnome utilities such as a file manager provide visual alternatives to entering shell commands in a character-based terminal window.

Some programmers learn X programming by basing their projects on one or more of these toolkits, but this approach avoids certain issues that can cause much head-scratching down the road. Although it is tempting to jump right in and start developing an application's menus and buttons using widgets, you'll do yourself a favor by first learning the Xlib fundamentals introduced in this and the next two chapters.

However, few developers would consider writing an entire application using only Xlib. This approach, although not impossible, requires the application to handle every aspect of its visual interface. Programming directly in Xlib also invites programmers to design incompatible components. Anyone who has used X over the last few years knows that clients can differ greatly in appearance, placement of buttons, and responses to scrollbars. Such differences can erode the advantages that a GUI offers. To avoid this type of problem, use what you learn in this chapter about Xlib programming as a stepping stone to a higher-level toolkit that provides the look and feel you want. (The last two chapters in this book present the widget-based C++ class library V that additionally helps smooth the transition from Xlib fundamentals to real-world software development.)

Network Protocols

Most X tutorials begin with a diagram such as the one in Figure 26.1, which shows the relationship between the X server, the window manager, the display, and a client application. As the figure suggests, X uses a client/server model to manage the user's display and to implement the bare-bones elements of a graphical user interface.

Figure 26.1
X uses the client/server model to manage the user's display and communicate with client applications, possibly over a network.

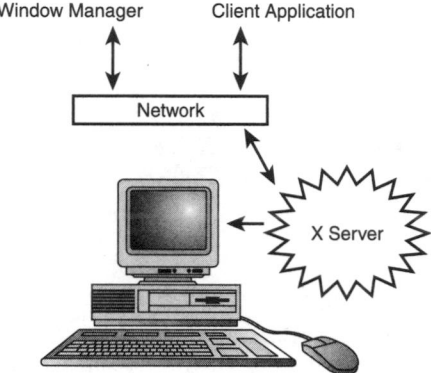

At one end of the client/server model, the *X server* manages the user's local display, which includes one or more screens, a keyboard, a mouse, and possibly other input devices. The display's screens might be physical terminals or virtual screens. In a network environment, many X servers can be operating on a variety of hardware configurations.

At the other end of the model is a *client application*. A client is any program that communicates with the X server to carry out its input and output interfacing. One important client application is the *window manager*. This software has the responsibility for positioning windows, for enforcing a stacking order among overlapping windows, and for enacting illusions such as showing a window in an iconic state.

Together, the X server, window manager, and client applications create a virtual desktop on the user's display screens. Because the X server and one or more clients might run at different locations on a network, they communicate using network protocols that form the very core of X. This occurs even when the X server and clients run on the same workstation, although in that case, the server and clients correspond directly using interprocess communications instead of through network messages. To perform X activities, clients make *requests* to the X server. The server in turn sends *events* to clients, which can include error messages. Both requests and events are queued in Xlib, a fact that leads to critical performance concerns. For instance, limiting network traffic by reducing the number of requests sent to the X server is an important goal in X client software development.

To request a service from the X server, a client calls an Xlib function. Often, this is done in reference to a *graphics context* (GC) that specifies visual features such as line width and shape-fill patterns. In a typical case, a client prepares a graphics context and then calls an Xlib function such as XDrawLine() to request that the server draw one or more lines using the GC's values.

It isn't essential to know every last detail about how X network protocols manage requests and events. However, it's important to understand that simply calling an Xlib function doesn't necessarily produce the desired results, at least not right away. Frequently, the visual effects of calling an Xlib function might take place after many other function calls. Also, because Xlib queues the client's requests, they are sent en masse to the X server only when the request queue is flushed, not necessarily when the program calls the function. This type of event-driven, asynchronous logic poses new hurdles to programmers who are more familiar with conventional input and output techniques.

Even more vexing is that not all window managers are alike, and virtually no actual effect can be safely assumed. For instance, a client application might pass a window title string to the X server, but there is no guarantee that the window manager will display that string at any specific location. It might not even display a window title at all. Another good example concerns graphics and color. X clients can assume only that the display is bitmapped, and thus can support multiple graphical windows. However, it's up to the window manager whether those windows should overlap or simply be tiled side by side. Also, although most modern PC computer displays support color graphics, a well-written client should assume that only two contrasting colors are available. Even assuming that those colors are black and white is not entirely safe.

EVENT-DRIVEN PROGRAMMING

Event-driven programming isn't difficult to master as long as you keep in mind that an X client application responds to events in the order they arrive, not always in the order you expect them to occur. When an action takes place such as the user clicking a mouse button, the X server posts an event message to the client for the focused window. This event is stored in Xlib along with other events in the order received. To respond to events, your program retrieves them one by one and branches to an appropriate statement.

The code that retrieves and handles events is known as the *event loop*. All clients have one such loop for handling events for all of the client's windows. Each event arrives as a structure that provides information specific to the event—the X and Y coordinate values, for example, of the mouse pointer when the user clicks a mouse button.

An event loop doesn't have to process every type of event—only those it needs. When creating a window, the program specifies an *event mask* that tells the X server which events to send. Unless you specifically request a certain type of event—key presses, for example—they are not sent to your program. Events not handled by a client generally propagate to the child's parent window.

PART
V

CH
26

Note

Error messages are also sent from the X server as events. However, they are queued differently and require separate programming from the client's event loop.

X WINDOWS

There are two types of X windows—input and output, and input only. Input and output windows are the most common because most windows display at least some type of visual response to user input. A button, for example, typically indicates visually that it has recognized a mouse click.

As a structure, a window possesses *attributes* that determine visual aspects such as the window's border patterns, background color, size, and position. It's important always to remember that these and other specifications are only "hints" to the X server about how a window should be displayed. The actual appearance, location, size, and other visual features of a window depend on the rules and regulations enforced by the window manager.

There are two ways to create windows. A simple window specifies only minimal attributes such as position, size, foreground, and background colors. Other attributes are inherited from the parent window. You can also create windows the "hard way" by specifying a structure and bit mask that provides any attributes you want to override from the parent. (Chapter 27, "Controlling Xlib Input and Output," explains this technique.) However, regardless of how you create a window, depending on the window manager and the hardware's limitations, the actual output might appear very differently from one display to another.

Using toolkits and widgets helps minimize those types of differences by providing useful standards for common components such as menu items, buttons, check boxes, dialogs, scrollbars, and other types of visual objects. Although such standards have been extremely lax in the history of X, the current Gnome project promises to provide better and more visually consistent components for creating and customizing a virtual desktop.

THE GRAPHICS CONTEXT

All output requests take place in reference to a graphics context, or GC. The GC specifies parameters such as line width, a colormap, fill patterns, and other characteristics for many Xlib functions such as XDrawLine() and XFillRectangle(). The GC minimizes the number of arguments passed to Xlib functions, and thus has a positive effect on network traffic between the client application and X server. The GC also helps you maintain multiple configurations. For example, a program can create multiple GCs for a specific window and easily switch between them. The actual GC for a particular window resides in the X server and is referenced by a simple ID value provided to the client. This keeps GC references fast.

Tip

Some X servers can maintain only a limited number of GCs, and most X experts recommend creating as few as possible in client applications.

In most all cases, a client creates a GC *after* it creates an associated window. Every GC is tied specifically to a window, and it uses whatever attributes are assigned during the window's creation (or reassigned later). There are numerous ways to create and initialize GCs, but in most cases, the easiest method is to first create the window and then create a GC for use in graphics requests for that window.

COLORMAPS

One of the more difficult subjects to understand in X programming is the concept of a colormap. Actually, the concept itself is relatively easy to comprehend, but following the many rules for using colormaps can be an intricate and difficult process to learn. Because video hardware varies widely in the world of X programming for Linux and UNIX, a colormap might be a very different animal from one display to another. Chapter 28, "Breaking Out of Xlib Fundamentals," explains how to use colormaps.

A colormap assumes only that the display is bitmapped—that is, each pixel (picture element) on a screen displays one distinct dot. The X server cannot work with other types of video hardware such as vector displays, but those are rarely used for computer terminals, anyway. Usually, virtual colormaps can be swapped with the hardware's default colormap, and in that way, provide instant color configurations for multiple applications, or even for multiple windows within the same client. Depending on the number of available colors, however, this technique can cause color changes among inactive windows, especially when a color-intensive application receives the focus. For example, bringing up a true-color application such as a photographic editor might cause background windows to blush suddenly in shocking pink. Despite such quirks, however, colormaps do more than just provide a programming interface to video hardware. In most cases, they also permit clients to define the colors they need with no concern for how many or what types of colors are actually available.

A key element of a colormap is the concept of a *bit plane*. Typically, video display hardware provides memory that stores color values using one or more bits per pixel. Each bit is a member of one bit plane for all of the display's pixels. Although plenty of 8- and 16-bit-plane displays still are in use, 24-bit-plane color displays are fast becoming as common as toasters.

The number of bits in the video display's circuitry determines the *depth* of the display and, indirectly, the number of possible colors it can display. Each pixel on a screen is associated with the bits in one or more planes. On a 24-bit-plane video system, each pixel is represented by a 24-bit integer, with one bit on each plane. Figure 26.2 shows conceptually how bit planes represent a pixel's value in video memory.

PART

V

CH

26

Figure 26.2
In many systems, one pixel value is represented as a number of bits, each a member of a bit plane.

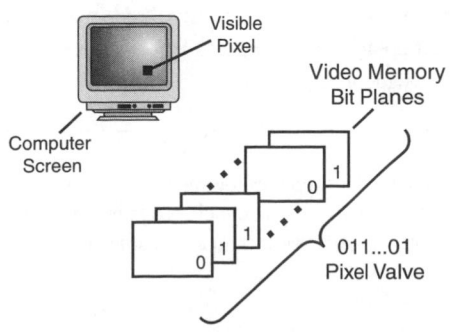

Tricks with video bit planes can produce interesting graphical illusions. For example, by drawing into one or more planes, images appear to float on top (or within) other images without affecting the bits in other planes.

Monochrome displays differ in the way their color values are interpreted. Simple monochrome displays might even be one-dimensional, using a single bit (one plane) for each screen pixel. Such displays have only two colors, known in X programming as "white" and "black" even though the actual colors can be any contrasting hues (green and light green, for example). More common, however, especially in desktop publishing applications, are monochrome grayscale graphical displays. In these types of displays, bit planes provide index values into a colormap's grayscale intensity levels.

Regardless of the type of hardware on your system, it's important to realize that bit-plane values in video memory do not directly represent colors. (However, some true-color displays might be an exception to that rule.) Instead, the bits in video memory are used in one way or another as indexes into arrays of other values such as red, green, and blue levels that determine the actual colors you see onscreen. This permits programs to work on a variety of hardware and also enables users and system administrators to fine-tune colormap values so that, for instance, blue really looks blue.

Using colormaps may be difficult, but the end results are highly advantageous because they result in X client software that works correctly on all types of video hardware. You don't have to understand exactly how bit-plane values are translated to actual color values or grayscale intensities. Ideally, even if the screen supports only one-dimensional black-and-white pixels, the user should be able to see all the application's output.

INTRODUCING XLIB PROGRAMMING

That's enough background. Now, let's take a look at an X client and the basic steps needed to get a window to appear onscreen. Because even that simple task takes many lines of code, the following sample program, xwelcome.cpp, is discussed in pieces here. For reference, the complete listing follows at the end of the section. Also see the sidebar, "Compiling X Clients," for how to compile and run the xwelcome.cpp program and other X client applications listed in this and the next two chapters.

In most cases, about six basic steps are involved in a typical X client application. The following sections describe each of these steps in reference to the xwindow.cpp listing on the CD-ROM (in the c26/xwelcome path).

Compiling X Clients

Because compiling X applications requires several compiler and linker options, it's impractical to type the necessary commands. For this reason, each example program in this and the following chapters is stored in a named directory such as src/c26/xwelcome. In each named directory is a file named Makefile that specifies the necessary compiling and linking commands. Before using this Makefile, you might have to modify some of the settings in a related file, Config.mk. Locate that file in the outer directory (src/c26 for this chapter), and load it into your editor. Listing 26.1 shows the Config.mk file's default settings.

LISTING 26.1 C26/CONFIG.MK

```
# Edit the following for your installation
CC       =    g++
X11INC   =    /usr/X11R6/include
X11LIB   =    /usr/X11R6/lib
LIBS     =    -lX11


#================================================================
# Compiler and linker flags
CFLAGS   =    -O -I$(X11INC)
LFLAGS   =    -O -L$(X11LIB)
```

Edit the first four variables in Config.mk to select the compiler name (CC), X include directory (X11INC), and X compiled library directory (X11LIB). Also specify the Xlib pathname (LIBS) for the GNU linker. The default settings should work for most readers, but if you have trouble compiling, it's likely the compiler can't find the files it needs. In that case, search for your X11 installation directories and make the appropriate adjustments to Config.mk. To compile all programs for loading into the GNU debugger, add -g to CFLAGS.

If you are using Red Hat Linux 5.1 or earlier, you might have to change X11R6 to X11 in the pathnames listed in Config.mk. If so, make this same change to the Config.mk files located in the src/C26, src/C27, src/C28, and src/C29 directories.

After configuring your system, change to a named directory and run the make utility to compile and link a sample program. For example, to compile the xwelcome demonstration, enter commands such as these:

```
$ cd src/c26/xwelcome
$ make
g++ -c -O -I/usr/X11/include -o xwelcome.o xwelcome.cpp
g++ -o xwelcome -O -L/usr/X11/lib xwelcome.o -lX11
```

The last two lines show the compilation and linking commands issued by make using the commands in Makefile. To run the program, enter its compiled executable filename as follows, prefaced with ./ to tell the shell to look in the current directory:

```
$ ./xwelcome
```

If all goes well, that should display the sample window in Figure 26.3. To quit the program, press any key when the program's window is active (that is, when it has the input focus). Most sample programs in this and the next chapters end on sensing a keypress, or they provide a menu command or a button named Exit. You can also click the window's close button, shown by most window managers as a small lowercase x. Another way to end X clients, although unusual, is to switch to the shell window from which you started the program and type C-c (Ctrl-C). However, this might not work with all X applications.

You can also use make and the supplied Makefiles to clean up a directory after you are finished trying out the sample program. To use this feature, enter **_make clean_**. Notice that this also removes the compiled executable file:

```
$ make clean
rm -f xwelcome.o
rm -f *~
rm -f xwelcome
```

Figure 26.3
The xwelcome
program's window.

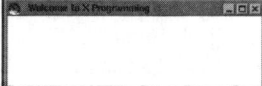

INCLUDING XLIB HEADERS

All X client applications include the Xlib.h header file, usually along with one or two other X declaration files. The xwelcome.cpp sample program includes the following three headers:

```
#include <X11/Xlib.h>
#include <X11/Xutil.h>
#include <X11/Xos.h>
```

Including Xlib.h also includes X.h, and as a result, this declares most data types and structures needed by Xlib programs. The Xutil.h header includes many common X function declarations and is also needed by most X clients. Including Xos.h is optional, but it can help reduce problems caused by system dependencies and differences among declarations in other headers—such as, for instance, the names of various string.h functions and the size of a word data type.

You might find other hardware- or operating-system-dependent include files on a specific installation. For best results, avoid including these files into X clients. There should be no reason to include any header files other than those located in your include/X11 (or X11R6) system directory.

CONNECTING TO THE X SERVER

The first programming step in every X client is to connect to the X server. If this can't be done, either there is a serious network problem or X simply isn't running. First, declare a global display pointer as follows:

```
Display *display;
```

Because almost all Xlib functions require a reference to a Display structure, the pointer to it is usually made global to avoid having to pass it to the program's subroutines. The first step inside main() initializes the display pointer using statements such as the following:

```
display = XOpenDisplay(NULL);
if (display == NULL) {
  cerr << "Failure connecting to X Server";
  exit(1);
}
```

If XOpenDisplay() fails, it returns NULL. Always check for this condition, and exit the program with an error message if the connection can't be established. There are other ways to call XOpenDisplay(). You can, for example, pass the name of a host and a display number separated by a colon as a string, but these and other possibilities are system-dependent. (The environment variables HOSTDISPLAY and DISPLAY typically specify the correct values.) Passing NULL for Linux XFree86 installations is usually the best choice. Depending on the argument passed to XOpenDisplay(), the connection to the X server may be established locally or across a network.

Keep in mind that a "display" comprises at least one or more screens, a keyboard, and a mouse. On Linux XFree86 installations, the window manager may provide multiple screens selectable using the mouse or by pressing keys such as M-Tab (Alt-Tab). In the client program, however, only one `Display`-structure pointer is needed to access all the user's input and output devices.

PREPARING WINDOW ATTRIBUTES

Before creating and displaying a window, most X clients need some information about the state of the display such as its dimensions and color values. Most such values are easily obtained by using Xlib macros to extract members of the `Display` data structure. For example, xwelcome.cpp uses the following three macros to find out some information about the display maintained by the X server:

```
int intScreenNum = DefaultScreen(display);
int intDisplayWidth = DisplayWidth(display, intScreenNum);
int intDisplayHeight = DisplayHeight(display, intScreenNum);
```

The first statement assigns to integer `intScreenNum` the number of the display's default screen. This screen number is then used in two more macro calls to find the width and height of the screen in pixels. The reason for using macros such as `DefaultScreen()` and `DisplayWidth()` is because the contents of the `Display` data structure are intended to remain "opaque." Not referencing these members directly allows Xlib's programmers to change the members' names without affecting X client programs. Always use macros as shown here to access `Display`-structure members. This helps protect your code from future changes to Xlib.

> **Tip**
>
> It's a good idea to adopt useful naming conventions for your program's variables. For example, xwelcome.cpp prefaces its integer variables with `int`. Xlib contains an overwhelming number of declarations, function names, structures, and other elements, and it's a good idea to choose program identifiers that describe both their type and purpose. All Xlib functions, by the way, begin with a capital `X`, so you probably should *not* do the same with your program's functions.

Using the display parameters determined so far, the xwelcome program calculates the approximate width, height, and position of its window with these statements:

```
int intWidth = intDisplayWidth / 3;
int intHeight = intDisplayHeight / 8;
int intXPos = 0;
int intYPos = 0;
```

These steps prepare for creating a window one-third the width of the screen, and one-eighth its height. The window's initial position is determined by the window manager, so the two position variables are simply zeroed. Always keep in mind that, due to differences among X installations, all specifications such as window sizes and positions are mere hints to the window manager, which is free to arrange windows in any way it sees fit.

GETTING COLOR VALUES

Another important set of values concerns the background and foreground colors used for painting the window's display surface (sometimes called its *canvas*), and for displaying graphics and text. As mentioned, because X installations use a wide variety of output devices, a properly written X client can assume only that two contrasting colors are available. At a minimum, then, the following statements initialize two integer variables to the only two colors you can count on:

```
int intBlackColor, intWhiteColor;
intBlackColor = BlackPixel(display, intScreenNum);
intWhiteColor = WhitePixel(display, intScreenNum);
```

Despite the macro names BlackPixel() and WhitePixel(), the actual visible colors might not actually be black and white. In any case, however, they are guaranteed to be colors that the user can distinguish.

CREATING AN X WINDOW

We now have enough information to create an X window. The simplest method for doing that is to call XCreateSimpleWindow() with the following arguments:

```
Window win =
XCreateSimpleWindow(
  display,                      // X server display struct
  DefaultRootWindow(display),   // Parent window
  intXPos, intYPos,             // Position
  intWidth, intHeight,          // Window width & height
  0,                            // Border width (default)
  intBlackColor, intWhiteColor); // Background, foreground
```

Assign the function result to a variable of type Window. This represents the window's ID number (probably as an unsigned long integer value) for future references to the window structure maintained by the X server. The first argument is the display pointer returned by XOpenDisplay(). Next comes the ancestor window, and because every window except the root must have a parent window, a valid parent-window ID is required by all new windows. In most cases, a client's main window lists the root window as its ancestor by calling the DefaultRootWindow() macro as shown, but this argument can be another Window ID value. After this information comes the position, width, and height of the window. As mentioned, these are merely hints to the window manager about where you want the window shown. Finally, specify the background and foreground colors obtained earlier. Optionally, reverse the two colors to produce a light-on-dark window interior.

Tip

Creating a window by calling XCreateSimpleWindow() or its more complex sister function XCreateWindow() does not display the window onscreen. This step merely prepares a Window structure in the X server. Several more statements, explained in the next sections, are required before the window becomes visible.

ASSIGNING A WINDOW TITLE

Despite this section's title, it isn't strictly possible to assign a title to an X window. However, you can provide a title string in the hopes that the window manager will use it to identify the newly constructed window. There's no guarantee that the string will appear in any particular location, although most window managers display it in a title bar atop the window's frame. To specify the title string, call the Xlib function XStoreName() as follows:

```
XStoreName(display, win, "Welcome to X Programming");
```

Pass the display pointer (from XOpenDisplay()) and the window ID (from XCreateSimpleWindow() or XCreateWindow()) as the first two arguments. Also specify the string that you want to use for the window's title. If the window manager supports window title bars, the string ought to appear on top of the window.

> **Tip**
>
> It's generally not a good idea to display messages as window titles because there is no guarantee that users will see the text. I have broken this rule in xwelcome.cpp because we haven't yet covered window output techniques.

DISPLAYING A WINDOW

Like a zombie stalking its victim, xwelcome.cpp is trudging along toward the point where its window actually appears. But don't start screaming yet. Given an initialized display pointer and window ID value, the following statement requests that the X server take the necessary steps to make the window visible:

```
XMapWindow(display, win);
```

Mapping a window makes it visible and available for input and output. The two arguments pass the global display pointer and win ID to XMapWindow(). Conversely, *unmapping* a window makes it invisible. You can map and unmap any window as often as you want to make it appear and disappear. This technique is especially useful for displaying dialog and other child windows quickly without having to repeat the steps to create the windows.

But even though the program has requested that a window be mapped to the display, it *still* might not become visible, at least not right away. Other intervening processes must take place between the X server, window manager, and client application before the user sees the effect of the preceding statement. (Okay, now you can scream.) The window is guaranteed to be visible, and therefore ready for input and output, only after the client receives an Expose event for this window. Prior to that event, a ConfigureNotify event usually arrives because the window manager might have altered the requested window size and position hints. Never attempt to draw into a window immediately after calling XMapWindow(). Before doing that, two more steps are required, explained next.

PART

V

CH

26

Masking Events

An X client operates asynchronously from the activities of user interventions and the requirements of the X server and window manager. This differs greatly from the usual relationship between input and output in a conventional program that prompts users to enter data, waits for a response, and then performs an action based on that input.

Events are messages that the X server sends to the client application. For example, if the user clicks a mouse button when the mouse pointer is inside a window, the X server posts a ButtonPress event to that window's Xlib event queue. During the course of even a simple X client application, many such events are queued simultaneously.

The next section describes how to retrieve and respond to X server events, but before getting even the first event, the client application must tell the X server the types of events it expects to receive. This reduces network traffic, and also simplifies the program's source code. For example, a drawing program might request mouse movement events while another type of program might need only mouse button-click events. Other events are allowed to propagate to the window's parent, where they are either handled or allowed to suffer an obscure end.

All events are known as *input events*, even those not directly related to user-input activity. Specify the events to receive for a window by calling XSelectInput() like this:

```
XSelectInput(display, win,
  ExposureMask | KeyPressMask | StructureNotifyMask);
```

The first two arguments specify the global display pointer and window ID value obtained earlier. The third argument is the *event mask*. Except when specifying only one type of event, this mask is typically a logical-OR expression of two or more event types defined in Xlib. In this example, ExposureMask tells the server that we want to be informed when the window becomes exposed. This happens the first time the window appears and also whenever it is partially or wholly uncovered perhaps by the user moving aside another window. The second event type, KeyPressMask, indicates that we want to be informed when the user presses a key. The StructureNotifyMask tells the X server to send an event message when the user modifies the size or location of the window. The order of event types in the event mask is not important. Table 26.1 shows the event types declared in Xlib. The symbols are actually implemented as unsigned long int bit-shift macros, but that fact is safely tucked away and forgotten.

Table 26.1   Xlib Event Masks

Button1MotionMask	EnterWindowMask	PointerMotionHintMask
Button2MotionMask	ExposureMask	PointerMotionMask
Button3MotionMask	FocusChangeMask	PropertyChangeMask
Button4MotionMask	KeymapStateMask	ResizeRedirectMask
Button5MotionMask	KeyPressMask	StructureNotifyMask

ButtonMotionMask	KeyReleaseMask	SubstructureNotifyMask
ButtonPressMask	LeaveWindowMask	SubstructureRedirectMask
ButtonReleaseMask	OwnerGrabButtonMask	VisibilityChangeMask
ColormapChangeMask		

The names of the event-mask bits in Table 26.1 are generally, but not always, the same as the names of the event messages minus the suffix "Mask." The KeyPress event, for example, is associated with the KeyPressMask bit mask. However, the Expose event is associated with ExposureMask. You just have to memorize these discrepant relationships. Table 26.2 shows all Xlib event types.

TABLE 26.2   XLIB EVENT TYPES

ButtonPress	Expose	MapRequest
ButtonRelease	FocusIn	MotionNotify
CirculateNotify	FocusOut	NoExpose
CirculateRequest	GraphicsExpose	PropertyNotify
ClientMessage	GravityNotify	ReparentNotify
ColormapNotify	KeymapNotify	ResizeRequest
ConfigureNotify	KeyPress	SelectionClear
ConfigureRequest	KeyRelease	SelectionNotify
CreateNotify	LeaveNotify	SelectionRequest
DestroyNotify	MapNotify	UnmapNotify
EnterNotify	MappingNotify	VisibilityNotify

Each event message is transmitted as a structure that contains information specific to that event. For instance, a mouse movement event carries with it the relative coordinate values of the mouse cursor's "hot spot." Other events carry different types of information such as a window's position, or a keypress code. All event messages are declared in Xlib using C++ unions so that an event's associated information is readily available. But this also implies that it is your responsibility to refer to the correct information for a specific event type. More on this subject in the next sections.

WRITING THE EVENT LOOP

Finally, the client application is ready to enter the section of code where it spends the rest of its runtime life—the event loop. Before explaining this important programming, it's useful to review the steps that led to this critical juncture. So far, the xwelcome.cpp program has

- Connected to the X server by calling XOpenDisplay()
- Initialized window variables using macros such as XDisplayWidth()

PART
V

CH
26

- Obtained at least two contrasting color values through the `BlackPixel()` and `WhitePixel()` macros

- Created a window structure by calling `XCreateSimpleWindow()` and saving the function result in a `Window` ID variable

- Optionally specified a possible window title by calling `XStoreName()`

- Mapped the window by calling `XMapWindow()`, making the window potentially visible

- Specified the types of events the client wants to receive for this window by calling `XSelectInput()` with an appropriate event mask expression.

Every X client application performs most of the preceding steps in one fashion or another. After these steps, the program is ready to enter the infamous *event loop*, shown in Listing 26.2.

LISTING 26.2   XWELCOME.CPP (EVENT LOOP)

```
bool done = false;
XEvent event;
while (!done) {
  XNextEvent(display, &event);
  switch (event.type) {
  case Expose:
    cout << "Expose event received" << endl;
    break;
  case ConfigureNotify:
    cout << "ConfigureNotify event received" << endl;
    break;
  case KeyPress:
    cout << "Keypress detected" << endl;
    done = true;   // Exit on any keypress
    break;
  }
}
```

To provide a holding pen for each event as it arrives, the program declares a variable, here named `event`, of Xlib's `XEvent` structure data type. For a loop-control value, the program also declares a C++ `bool` variable, `done`, initialized to false. While this variable remains false, the event loop continues looping. There are other ways to write an event loop. Some programmers use a so-called "do-forever" `for` or `while` statement that repeats an indeterminate number of times. Regardless of how it's programmed, the event loop begins by obtaining the next event with the following statement:

`XNextEvent(display, &event);`

Pass the global `display` pointer and a reference to the `event` structure as arguments. This deceptively simple statement performs three crucial activities:

- It retrieves the next event from the Xlib queue for the focused window of the indicated display.

- If the event queue is empty, XNextEvent() flushes the Xlib request queue, sending all pending requests such as drawing commands to the X server.

- If the event queue is empty, after flushing the request queue, XNextEvent() *blocks*, meaning that it does not return until a new event arrives from the X server.

After obtaining each event, most client applications use a switch statement to branch to one or more statements for handling specific events. (Refer to Table 26.2 for a list of X event type names.) In this case, the program responds to three event types, and it displays a message for each one. To see the effects of these statements, view the terminal window you used to start xwelcome while you move and resize the program's window.

In this example, the only event that does anything useful is KeyPress. To end the event loop, the switch statement's case for this event executes these statements:

```
case KeyPress:
  cout << "Keypress detected" << endl;
  done = true;    // Exit on any keypress
  break;
```

That sets done to true and ends the while loop. Following that, the program shuts down its connection with the X server by calling another Xlib function and returning from main():

```
XCloseDisplay(display);
return 0;
```

Calling XCloseDisplay() disconnects the client/server connection, unmaps all client windows (causing them to become invisible), and destroys all associated data structures held in the server for this client. However, although calling XCloseDisplay() is a proper way to terminate an X client, there is no guarantee that the program ever reaches the preceding statements. Another event passed to the window manager might terminate the client/server connection, shutting down the program's task before XNextEvent() returns. For example, if the window has a default close button in a title bar, and if the user clicks that button, the window manager itself receives the associated event and terminates the client, resulting in a message such as this onscreen:

```
X connection to :0.0 broken (explicit kill or server shutdown).
```

Tip

One way to prevent this common message is to encase the entire client in a C++ class with a destructor that calls XCloseDisplay(). Declaring a global object of the class ensures that the destructor is called during the program's termination sequence.

THE XWELCOME.CPP LISTING

For reference, Listing 26.3 shows the complete xwelcome.cpp listing described in the preceding sections. This file is in the c26/xwelcome directory on the CD-ROM.

LISTING 26.3   XWELCOME.CPP

```cpp
#include <iostream.h>
#include <stdlib.h>     // Need exit()

#include <X11/Xlib.h>   // Most X programs need these headers
#include <X11/Xutil.h>
#include <X11/Xos.h>

Display *display;        // X server display structure

int main()
{
  // Attempt to establish communications with the X Server
  //
  display = XOpenDisplay(NULL);
  if (display == NULL) {
    cerr << "Failure connecting to X Server";
    exit(1);
  }

  // Calculate window's dimensions and position
  //
  int intScreenNum = DefaultScreen(display);
  int intDisplayWidth = DisplayWidth(display, intScreenNum);
  int intDisplayHeight = DisplayHeight(display, intScreenNum);
  int intWidth = intDisplayWidth / 3;
  int intHeight = intDisplayHeight / 8;
  int intXPos = 0;
  int intYPos = 0;

  // Get the most basic of colors (black and white)
  //
  int intBlackColor, intWhiteColor;
  intBlackColor = BlackPixel(display, intScreenNum);
  intWhiteColor = WhitePixel(display, intScreenNum);

  // Create window (this does not make it visible)
  Window win =
  XCreateSimpleWindow(
    display,                        // X server display struct
    DefaultRootWindow(display),     // Parent window
    intXPos, intYPos,               // Position
    intWidth, intHeight,            // Window width & height
    0,                              // Border width (default)
    intBlackColor, intWhiteColor);  // Background, foreground

  // Assign a name for the window title bar (probably)
  //
  XStoreName(display, win, "Welcome to X Programming");

  // Map the window to the display
  // Window is visible when first Expose event is received
  //
  XMapWindow(display, win);

  // Specify the types of events we want to receive
```

```
    //
    XSelectInput(display, win,
      ExposureMask | KeyPressMask | StructureNotifyMask);

    // The infamous event loop
    //
    bool done = false;
    XEvent event;
    while (!done) {
      XNextEvent(display, &event);
      switch (event.type) {
      case Expose:
        cout << "Expose event received" << endl;
        break;
      case ConfigureNotify:
        cout << "ConfigureNotify event received" << endl;
        break;
      case KeyPress:
        cout << "Keypress detected" << endl;
        done = true;   // Exit on any keypress
        break;
      }
    }

    // Disconnect X server connection and exit.
    // (Program may never get to here)
    //
    XCloseDisplay(display);
    return 0;
}
```

DEBUGGING X CLIENTS

Debugging an X client application is particularly difficult largely due to its asynchronous, event-driven nature. In conventional programs, even object-oriented ones, setting a breakpoint at a specific statement is a great way to investigate the state of a program at a strategic location. But doing the same in an X client often provides few clues about a program's operation because the events that cause trouble might be the result of Xlib function calls that occurred long before the event is received.

You may certainly compile and run X client applications using the GNU debugger—the last section in this chapter explains how. First, however, let's look at some other ways to obtain information useful for debugging X clients.

DEBUGGING WITH X UTILITIES

Most X installations come with several useful utility programs mixed in with a gaggle of screen savers and addicting games. (If I hadn't played so many rounds of Spider, I might have finished this book a month early.) Following are descriptions of utilities that are useful for investigating system parameters and for debugging X client applications. Run all the utilities listed in this section by typing their names in a terminal window. Many are text-based, but some also display a graphical window.

PART

V

CH

26

> **Tip**
>
> Check out the source code files for the utilities mentioned here, available via FTP from numerous online sources (see Appendix C, "Web and FTP Sites") and also on a variety of Linux CDs. The files provide details on how to obtain useful system parameters in your own programs.

XDPYINFO

Run this X display information utility to find out various display and screen facts such as the name of the display and the current X version number. This program also provides the dimension, resolution, and depth of the display. The dimension indicates the display's screen size such as 1024 by 768 pixels. The resolution indicates the display's density (75×75 dots per inch for me). The depth tells you how many bit planes are available. You can also find out the class of the display. In my case, and probably for most Linux users, this is set to TrueColor.

XEV

This "X Event Tester" is a great utility for investigating what events the X server posts for various actions such as clicking the mouse pointer in a window. You can also use it to find out the codes returned when you press certain keys. Position a terminal window so that you can view the effects of actions on this program's small graphical window.

XLSATOMS

Run this program for a complete list of *atoms*—symbolic names for string data stored in the X server. This program is particularly useful for debugging clients that create and use their own atoms. You can also find the names of loaded fonts among the reported information.

XLSCLIENTS

This utility simply reports the names of all client applications currently known to the X server. It also reports the command line options passed to a particular program. For example, here are some of the clients reported by xlsclients to be running on my system while I wrote these words:

```
$ xlsclients
localhost.localdomain   /bin/sh /home/ts/Office51/bin/soffice
...
localhost.localdomain   nxterm +ut -geometry +153+115
localhost.localdomain   spider
localhost.localdomain   nxterm
```

As you can tell from the next-to-last entry, I paused for another session with my favorite solitaire game. (If this goes on, I might need professional counseling.)

XLSFONTS

For a complete, and probably overwhelming, list of available fonts on your X installation, run this program. It is useful for finding specific fonts, and because the list is sorted for locating types of installed fonts such as all styles of Courier. (Chapter 27, "Controlling Xlib Input and Output," lists the source code for a similar program, xfont.cpp.)

XPROP

This is one of those utilities, found on every development system, that displays an encyclopedia of information, some of which is useful and some having a purpose known only to the original author. However, you might want to play with this program. It appears to require a command-line argument, so don't type its name alone. To view properties for a particular window by name (obtained, perhaps, from the program's window title bar), enter a command using the -name option such as

```
$ xprop -name nxterm
```

That displays various properties for a window named "nxterm." To examine facts about the root window, enter the command:

```
$ xprop -root
CUT_BUFFER0(STRING) = "\n"
```

Among other information, this command shows the current contents of the "cut" buffer, otherwise known as the Clipboard. It makes sense that the root window owns this information, identified by the atom CUT_BUFFER0. (On my system, and probably others, there are eight cut buffers named by atoms CUT_BUFFER0 through CUT_BUFFER7.) To find out more about xprop, use the -help option as follows:

```
$ xprop -help
```

XSYSINFO

This is a cute little program that displays some facts about memory use and CPU loads. It might be helpful in identifying memory hogs and processor pigs, although it could be improved if its window-stacking order were changed to make it stay on top of other windows.

This utility may or may not be installed automatically. If you can't find it, look for its package file named something like xsysinfo.rpm (minus any version information in the filename). See Chapter 3, "Installing GNU C++," for information about installing packages using the Red Hat Package Manager (RPM).

XWININFO

One of the most useful utilities, xwininfo lets you click on any window and see a list of its parameters, position, size, gravity (the relation of a child window to its parent during resize and move operations), plus other useful information. If you are having trouble getting your

PART

V

CH

26

windows to look the way you want, use this utility to inspect the information that the X
server knows about that window. Here's a sample run for a program running on my system:

```
$ xwininfo
...
xwininfo: Window id: 0x30000d6 "spider"
  Absolute upper-left X:  21
  Absolute upper-left Y:  124
  Relative upper-left X:  0
  Relative upper-left Y:  0
  Width: 910
  Height: 449
  Depth: 24
  Visual Class: TrueColor
  Border width: 0
  Class: InputOutput
  Colormap: 0x23 (installed)
  Bit Gravity State: NorthWestGravity
Window Gravity State: NorthWestGravity
  Backing Store State: NotUseful
  Save Under State: no
  Map State: IsViewable
  Override Redirect State: no
Corners:  +21+124  -93+124  -93-195  +21-195
  -geometry 910x449+16+101
```

DEBUGGING WITH OUTPUT STATEMENTS

Tracing an X client's events is probably one of the most useful techniques for investigating
the cause of a bug. If you build this logic into your programs from the start, you can produce a complete history of the events the client receives from the X server. Often, it is the
order of events that causes a problem (such as multiple drawings in response to Expose events
that can cause a window to develop a bad case of the jitters).

To trace events, use #ifdef and #ifndef directives along with a symbol such as DEBUG to
enable output statements in the client's event loop. For example, using xwelcome.cpp (refer
to Listing 26.3), following is a portion of a modified switch case with an output statement
enabled by the DEBUG symbol:

```
bool done = false;
XEvent event;
while (!done) {
  XNextEvent(display, &event);
  switch (event.type) {
  case Expose:
#ifdef DEBUG
    cout << "Expose event received" << endl;
#endif
    break;
  ...
  }
}
```

Compile the program with the option -DDEBUG to enable the output statement. Compile
without that option to ignore the output statement. On the CD-ROM, in the c26/xwelcome

path, file Makefile.dbg compiles a copy of xwelcome.cpp as xdebug.cpp with debugging enabled. Compile and run the program with these commands:

```
$ make -f Makefile.dbg
$ ./xdebug
ConfigureNotify event received
Expose event received
ConfigureNotify event received
Keypress detected
```

Tip

Notice that `ConfigureNotify` and `Expose` events are received for the new window. This is always true for a newly created and mapped window. The X server sends the first event to indicate the current size and position of the window because the window manager might have altered those values before showing the client window for the first time. After this, the `Expose` event tells the client to display the window's contents.

Also remember the time-tested C and C++ technique for making "assertions" about function results. To use this method in X clients, include the assert.h header file with the following directive:

```
#include <assert.h>
```

Next, use the `assert()` macro to test any true or false condition. Typically, `assert()` is applied to the result of a function that returns a pointer to a structure. If that pointer is NULL, we want the program to halt with an error that identifies where the problem occurred. Here's how to use `assert()` to test the result of connecting to the X server:

```
Display *display;        // X server display structure
...
display = XOpenDisplay(NULL);
assert(display);
```

If `XOpenDisplay()` returns NULL, `assert()` halts the program and displays an error message such as

```
xdebug: xdebug.cpp:28: int main(): Assertion 'display' failed.
Aborted (core dumped)
```

This also dumps memory and the stack to a core file, which you can remove. To disable all assertions, compile the program with the option -DNDEBUG (defining NDEBUG).

DEBUGGING WITH THE GNU DEBUGGER

Although debugging X clients using the GNU debugger can be difficult, this is still a good way to investigate the cause of a bug. It is especially helpful for inspecting the values of complex X structures. One useful trick is to set a breakpoint inside the client's event loop, and then use debugger commands to inspect event structure members. Although this produces a virtual ream of data, you may find the technique helpful for pinpointing the cause of a bug caused by the misuse of event data.

PART
V

CH
26

To demonstrate this, the xdebug.cpp program (a copy of xwelcome.cpp located in the c26/xwelcome directory on the CD-ROM) is prepared for debugging using the -g option. Specify this by using the make utility's -f option to select an alternate Makefile, in this case Makefile.dbg. Compile the program with the following command:

```
$ make -f Makefile.dbg
```

Next, load the resulting code file into the debugger. You can use the X version of the GNU debugger by running xxgdb like this:

```
$ xxgdb xdebug
```

But, even though the target program is an X client, you can debug the program using the command-line debugger. To do that, enter the command

```
$ gdb xdebug
```

List some lines to find the one that calls XNextEvent(), and then set a breakpoint there with a command such as this:

```
(gdb) b 79
Breakpoint 1 at 0x8048918: file xdebug.cpp, line 79.
```

Run the program up to the breakpoint and use a *print* command to view each event's data, which might extend several pages. Be sure to fasten your seat belt before entering the second command:

```
(gdb) run
(gdb) print event
```

SUMMARY

X programming adds a new dimension to C++ programming for Linux and also for other UNIX systems that support X. Under Linux, XFree86 provides several X servers that are optimized for PC, Intel hardware. X uses a client/server model to provide a graphical user interface, or GUI. However, unlike Microsoft Windows, X is hardware-independent and can run client applications on a wide variety of video displays and computer systems. Because X uses the client/server model, the X server and client applications can run on a user's workstation or at separate locations across a network. Developing X applications requires learning new techniques for network communication, event-driven asynchronous programming, and Xlib fundamentals. This and the next two chapters introduce Xlib programming so that you'll be able to understand higher-level toolkits such as Motif widgets, the Gnome project, and the V C++ class library presented in this book's last two chapters.

For more information on subjects introduced in this chapter, turn to the following chapters:

- Chapter 2, "Installing Linux"
- Chapter 28, "Breaking Out of Xlib Fundamentals"
- Chapter 29, "Introducing the V Class Library"

## CHAPTER 27

CONTROLLING XLIB INPUT AND OUTPUT

Responding to mouse and keyboard input and displaying text and graphics are demanding tasks in X programming. For one, the user's input arrives asynchronously in the form of events from the X server, and that input might be interspersed with other events that require handling. For another, an X client's window is merely a blank canvas waiting for you to fill it. Even displaying a single character means learning new programming techniques such as loading fonts, determining character sizes and positions in display pixels, and displaying text in reference to a graphics context for the X server's display.

Other complications in graphics output arise due to the interaction of the client's window with others. The most important rule, as you learn in this chapter, is that a client must be prepared to redraw its window's contents at any time. It's not enough simply to draw a shape in a window. If the window is covered and then uncovered, the application must redraw the shape (or a portion of it) to maintain the illusion of a virtual desktop of overlapping windows.

This chapter explores mouse and keyboard techniques for X clients and also shows methods for displaying text and graphics. You also learn how to use window attributes to create visual effects such as tiling the background with a pixmap and changing the cursor shape when the mouse pointer moves into the window's interior.

MOUSE INPUT EVENTS

There are probably more types of mouse input devices than there are, well, species of mice. But all share two characteristics—they report directional movement through a little ball rolling over a flat surface, and they report the clicking and releasing of one or more buttons. Two- and three-button mice are common, but one-button creatures are not unheard of. I include trackballs in this category because, as far as the program is concerned, these are nothing more than upside-down mice.

> **Note**
>
> X recognizes up to five mouse buttons, presumably one for each finger. I've never seen a mouse with more than three buttons, but I'm told four-button mice are sometimes found on computer-aided design (CAD) systems.

Before explaining more about mouse input events, it helps to get a few terms straight. The *mouse* is the physical device that you cup in your hand. It has one or more *buttons* that you can click or double-click. The mouse *pointer* is a conceptual object that, internally to a program, refers to a location onscreen. The mouse *cursor* is the visible pixmap image that shows the location of the mouse pointer. The *hotspot* is a single pixel in the cursor that determines the exact location of the mouse pointer. The hotspot can be anywhere in the mouse cursor. In an arrow cursor, the hotspot is on the tip. In a crosshair cursor, the hotspot is dead center.

Note An X *pixmap* is an image composed of individual pixels, or picture elements, either stored in a file or created from program data, in a format suitable for display on an X server screen. A *bitmap* is generally considered to be any collection of bits that represent graphical information. Typically, a client converts bitmap data into a pixmap for display.

MOUSE EVENTS

The X server reports three types of events for all mouse activities. The three mouse input events are as follows:

- ButtonPress   This event reports that the user clicked a mouse button. The event.xbutton.button field indicates the button number, equal to one of the X symbolic constants Button1, Button2, Button3, Button4, or Button5.

- ButtonRelease   This event reports that the user released a mouse button. The event.xbutton.button field indicates the button number.

- MotionNotify   This event reports a mouse movement, with or without a button held down (that is, a click-and-drag event).

Note A two-button mouse numbers its buttons with the symbols Button1 and Button3. Button2 represents a third, center button, which might or might not be available on a typical Linux PC-based system.

SAMPLE MOUSE CLIENT

Listing 27.1 shows the event loop for xmouse.cpp, a program that demonstrates how to respond to mouse button and movement events. Although the program might seem simple, it sets the stage for some finer points about mouse activities explained after the listing. For example, by changing the event mask, you can obtain all mouse movement events, or just those generated when the user also clicks and holds a button—a so-called *click-and-drag* operation.

PART
V
CH
27

LISTING 27.1   XMOUSE.CPP (EVENT LOOP)

```
// Specify the types of events we want to receive
//
XSelectInput(display, win,
ExposureMask ¦ KeyPressMask ¦
ButtonPressMask ¦ ButtonReleaseMask ¦ Button1MotionMask);
// The event loop
//
bool done = false;'
int intMouseX = 0, intMouseY = 0;
XEvent event;
```

continues

LISTING 27.1   CONTINUED

```
while (!done) {
  XNextEvent(display, &event);
  switch (event.type) {
  case ButtonPress:
    cout << "ButtonPress event" << endl;
    cout << "  button == " << event.xbutton.button << endl;
    intMouseX = event.xbutton.x;
    intMouseY = event.xbutton.y;
    ShowMousePosition(gc, win, intMouseX, intMouseY);
    break;
  case ButtonRelease:
    XBell(display, 50);   // i.e. 50% volume
    break;
  case MotionNotify:
    intMouseX = event.xbutton.x;
    intMouseY = event.xbutton.y;
    ShowMousePosition(gc, win, intMouseX, intMouseY);
    break;
  case Expose:
    ShowMousePosition(gc, win, intMouseX, intMouseY);
    break;
  case KeyPress:
    cout << "Keypress detected" << endl;
    done = true;   // Exit on any keypress
    break;
  }
}
```

Compile the xmouse.cpp program by changing to its directory and running *make* for the Makefile stored there. Enter these commands:

```
$ cd src/c27/xmouse
$ make
...
$ ./xmouse
```

Note

Compile other programs in this chapter similarly. Also see the sidebar "Compiling X Clients" in Chapter 26, "Introducing X Programming."

Running the xmouse.cpp program displays a small window that shows the mouse pointer's location relative to the window (see Figure 27.1). Click and drag the mouse cursor inside the window to see other locations. Clicking and dragging is enabled only for Button1, but you can also click Button3. Releasing either button sounds a bell (which sounds more like a buzzer on my system). Press any key to end the program, or click the window's close button. The program reports events in the terminal window, showing button clicks and keypresses:

```
ButtonPress event
button == 1
ButtonPress event
button == 3
Keypress detected
```

Figure 27.1
The xmouse.cpp program shows the mouse pointer's coordinate values relative to the client window.

ButtonPress EVENTS

As for all events, the client application specifies the types of mouse events it wants to receive from the X server. In Listing 27.1, xmouse.cpp, a call to XSelectInput() specifies the mouse and other event masks for the current display and window:

```
XSelectInput(display, win,
  ExposureMask ¦ KeyPressMask ¦
  ButtonPressMask ¦ ButtonReleaseMask ¦ Button1MotionMask);
```

To obtain mouse button events, logically OR the ButtonPressMask symbol into the function's third argument. To obtain mouse button release events, add ButtonReleaseMask. These two events are reported for all buttons. Mouse-movement events, however, are a little more complex, and there are a variety of possible masks you can use for detecting mouse movements. More on that in the next section.

After getting the next event with XNextEvent(), if the event.type field equals ButtonPress, then the user has clicked a mouse button. The sample program intercepts this event using a switch case, displays the button number, and saves the mouse pointer location with these statements:

```
case ButtonPress:
  cout << "ButtonPress event" << endl;
  cout << "  button == " << event.xbutton.button << endl;
  intMouseX = event.xbutton.x;
  intMouseY = event.xbutton.y;
```

The xbutton.x and xbutton.y fields in the event structure represent the location, relative to the window, of the mouse cursor's hotspot. The sample program saves this information in two variables for use in displaying the location (this requires techniques introduced later in this chapter under "Graphics Output Functions").

A button release is just as easily detected as a button press. For fun, the sample program calls XBell() to make a sound when you release a button. The value 50 in the following statement represents the volume as a percentage, although the argument might or might not have any effect:

```
case ButtonRelease:
  XBell(display, 50);
```

MOUSE MOVEMENT EVENTS

Mouse movement, or motion, events are divided into three general categories. You can elect to receive all motion events when the mouse cursor is inside a client window, all click-and-drag events when the user holds down a button while moving the mouse, or click-and-drag

PART
V

CH
27

events only for specific mouse buttons. Xlib provides seven masks to indicate the types of mouse movement events you want to receive:

```
Button1MotionMask
Button2MotionMask
Button3MotionMask
Button4MotionMask
Button5MotionMask
ButtonMotionMask
PointerMotionMask
```

To try the effects of different masks, change `Button1MotionMask` to any of the preceding symbols in the following xmouse.cpp statement:

```
XSelectInput(display, win,
  ExposureMask ¦ KeyPressMask ¦
  ButtonPressMask ¦ ButtonReleaseMask ¦ Button1MotionMask);
```

To receive all mouse movement events, use the `PointerMotionMask`. To receive all click-and-drag events for any button, use `ButtonMotionMask`. To receive click-and-drag events for a specific button, use one of the numbered masks. Whatever mask you specify, the event arrives as a `MotionNotify` message. The sample program uses a `switch case` statement to intercept this type of event and record the mouse position:

```
case MotionNotify:
  intMouseX = event.xbutton.x;
  intMouseY = event.xbutton.y;
  ShowMousePosition(gc, win, intMouseX, intMouseY);
  break;
```

The client continues to receive `MotionNotify` events for as long as the user holds down the mouse button. This is true even if the cursor travels outside the window because, when the X server generates a `ButtonPress` event, it *grabs* the mouse for the window until the user releases the button. Because the mouse is grabbed for a specific window, all mouse events continue to go to that window even if the mouse pointer leaves the window's area. You can also grab the mouse pointer explicitly by calling `XGrabPointer()`, although for most click-and-drag operations this shouldn't be necessary because of the way the X server grabs the pointer automatically. (Enter ***info XGrabPointer*** for additional online information about this topic.)

TEXT OUTPUT

All X graphics operations boil down to one of two concerns: displaying text and displaying graphical shapes. In both cases, objects are drawn onscreen because, unlike most character-based terminals, an X window has no predefined character shapes. As a prelude to displaying text, a client application must load a font into the X server and then use special techniques to ensure that text is positioned properly in a window. Because user displays vary widely in resolution, producing good-looking text output in a window is a nontrivial task.

FINDING FONT NAMES

The first step in displaying text in an X window is to load a font. Listing 27.2, xfont.cpp, demonstrates how to obtain a list of available font names. This is a relatively short X client program that displays its results in a terminal window, so unlike other sample programs in this chapter, it's listed in full here.

LISTING 27.2 XFONT.CPP

```cpp
#include <iostream.h>
#include <stdlib.h>       // Nood exit()

#include <X11/Xlib.h>     // Most X programs need these headers
#include <X11/Xutil.h>
#include <X11/Xos.h>

#define MAXNAMES 1000     // Maximum number of names listed

Display *display;         // X server display structure

int main(int argc, char *argv[])
{
  // Attempt to establish communications with the X Server
//
  display = XOpenDisplay(NULL);
  if (display == NULL) {
    cerr << "Failure connecting to X Server";
    exit(1);
  }

  // Some variables needed by XListFonts()
  //
  char **fontNames;
  char *pattern;
  if (argc > 1)
    pattern = argv[1];
  else
    pattern = "*";
  int count = 0;
  // Display matching font names
  //
  fontNames = XListFonts(display, pattern, MAXNAMES, &count);
  cout << count << " fonts found" << endl;
  for (int i = 0; i < count; i++)
    cout << fontNames[i] << endl;
  XFreeFontNames(fontNames);       // Dispose allocated memory
  // Disconnect X server connection and exit.
  // (Program may never get to here)
  //
  XCloseDisplay(display);
  return 0;
}
```

The xfont.cpp program lists up to 1,000 font names (this should be adequate for most Linux installations), and it also recognizes wildcard command-line arguments. Compile and run the program using commands such as these:

```
$ cd src/c27/xfont
$ make
...
$ ./xfont *courier*
68 fonts found
-adobe-courier-bold-i-normal--   0-0-0-0-m-0-iso8859-1
-adobe-courier-bold-r-normal--   0-0-0-0-m-0-iso8859-1
...
-adobe-courier-medium-r-normal--   0-0-100-100-m-0-iso8859-1
```

The argument *courier* locates all font names containing the word "courier." As the program's output shows, many font names are lengthy strings that include source, style, size, and other information. In general, however, you don't need to understand every piece of this information to use a font. (Many X and Xlib books and other sources detail the intricacies of fonts and font names.)

Other types of fonts are more simply named, and in many cases, they are perfectly adequate for most output needs. These types of fonts are named according to their pixel dimensions such as the names "9x15," "10x20," and "12x24." Some of these are available in bold such as "9x15bold."

DISPLAYING TEXT

Armed with a font name, you can display text in that font as Listing 27.3, xtext.cpp, demonstrates. This is a partial listing that shows only the statements related to loading fonts and displaying text. Figure 27.2 shows the program's window.

Figure 27.2
The text output of
xtext.cpp.

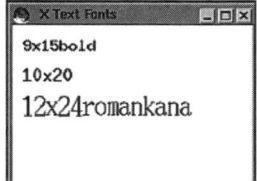

LISTING 27.3   XTEXT.CPP (PARTIAL)

```
void GetFont(char *fontName, XFontStruct** font);
void ShowFontName(GC& gc, Window win, int& y,
  XFontStruct* font, char *fontName);

int main()
{

  // Get a default graphics context for our window
  //
  GC gc = XCreateGC(display, win, 0, NULL);
  XSetForeground(display, gc, intBlackColor);  // Optional
```

```
    // Load some fonts. You might have to change the strings.
    // Run the xfont program to list them. Program ends if any
    // named font is unavailable.
    //
    XFontStruct *font1, *font2, *font3;  // Structure pointers
    char *fontName1 = "9x15bold";
    GetFont(fontName1, &font1);
    char *fontName2 = "10x20";
    GetFont(fontName2, &font2);
    char *fontName3 = "12x24romankana";
    GetFont(fontName3, &font3);

    // The event loop
    //
    bool done = false;
    XEvent event;
    int y;
    if (font1 != NULL && font2 != NULL && font3 != NULL)
    while (!done) {
      XNextEvent(display, &event);
      switch (event.type) {
      case Expose:
        y = 0;
        ShowFontName(gc, win, y, font1, fontName1);
        ShowFontName(gc, win, y, font2, fontName2);
        ShowFontName(gc, win, y, font3, fontName3);
        break;
      case ConfigureNotify:
        break;
      case KeyPress:
        cout << "Keypress detected" << endl;
        done = true;   // Exit on any keypress
        break;
      }
    }

    // Unload all fonts loaded by GetFont
    //
    if (font1 != NULL) XUnloadFont(display, font1->fid);
    if (font2 != NULL) XUnloadFont(display, font2->fid);
    if (font3 != NULL) XUnloadFont(display, font3->fid);

    // Disconnect X server connection and exit.
    // (Program may never get to here)
    //
    XCloseDisplay(display);
    return 0;
}

// Load font from X server.
// On many servers, a default font is loaded if the specified
// one is unavailable, so the error message is rarely seen.
void GetFont(char *fontName, XFontStruct** font)
{
  *font = XLoadQueryFont(display, fontName);
```

continues

LISTING 27.3   CONTINUED

```
  if (font == NULL)
    cerr << "Font " << fontName << " is not available" << endl;
}

// Display font name and update y coordinate value
void ShowFontName(GC& gc, Window win, int& y,
  XFontStruct* font, char *fontName)
{
  y += font->ascent + font->descent + 10;
  XSetFont(display, gc, font->fid);
  XDrawString(display, win, gc, 10, y, fontName,
  strlen(fontName));
}
```

A font is described by the XFontStruct type, addressed by a pointer. The sample program declares three such pointers as follows:

```
XFontStruct *font1, *font2, *font3;
```

To load each font, the program assigns a font name to a char* string and then calls a local function to load that font into the X server:

```
char *fontName1 = "9x15bold";
GetFont(fontName1, &font1);
```

The GetFont() function calls the Xlib XLoadQueryFont() function with the current display pointer and font name arguments. The function result is saved in the XFontStruct pointer:

```
*font = XLoadQueryFont(display, fontName);
```

If the result is NULL, then the font could not be loaded. Because unrecognized fonts typically default to other standard fonts, this should be rare under most X servers. However, you should always test the result of XLoadQueryFont() as in the sample listing. There are other ways to load fonts, but XLoadQueryFont() is most commonly used. (See the info page for this function for other font loaders.)

After loading a font, you can display text using its character shapes by calling the XDrawString() function. However, this requires a few other setup operations. First, you must obtain a graphics context, GC, for the window. The GC specifies various attributes to use for displaying text and graphics, and also style information such as the width of lines and patterns to use for filled shapes. The sample xfont.cpp program (refer to Listing 27.2) shows the simplest way to obtain a GC for a specific window:

```
GC gc = XCreateGC(display, win, 0, NULL);
XSetForeground(display, gc, intBlackColor);  // Optional
```

A GC is just an integer ID value—the actual structure is stored in the X server. Given the arguments shown here, XCreateGC() creates a *default* GC for the specified display and window. The final two arguments, 0 and NULL, tell the X server to use default values for all GC settings. (Chapter 28, "Breaking Out of Xlib Fundamentals," explains how to set individual GC parameters.) You might also want to call XSetForegound() as shown here to select a color for displayed text, but this step is optional.

The next step, shown in the sample listing in local function ShowFontName(), is to determine where in the window you want text to appear. For displaying lines of text, this means determining the relative y coordinate value for the text's height in pixels. Two values—ascent and descent—combined equal the maximum height of any character in the font. Adding a little to this value separates multiple lines. There are many other schemes for calculating text coordinate values relative to the window, but this formula works well enough in many cases:

```
y += font->ascent + font->descent + 10;
```

The next step sets the font into the GC obtained earlier. You don't have to do this every time before displaying a string—once set, the font remains in the GC until changed. Call XSetFont() to select a font loaded by XLoadQueryFont():

```
XSetFont(display, gc, font->fid);
```

Pass three arguments to the function: the X server display pointer, the gc variable obtained earlier for the window, and the fid (font ID) field for the loaded font. Finally, you are ready to display text in the selected font. Calling XDrawString() is the simplest method. It takes several arguments as shown here:

```
XDrawString(display, win, gc, 10, y, fontName, strlen(fontName));
```

Pass the display pointer, window ID, and graphics context variables as the first three arguments. The next two arguments are the x and y coordinate values of the pixel in the window where you want the string to appear. This pixel is typically located at the font's *origin*, a point just to the left of a character's *base line*. The ascent value mentioned earlier counts the pixels above this line; the descent counts those below. As a general rule, however, unless you really want to be fancy in positioning text, you can consider the coordinate values passed to XDrawString() to be about in the middle of lowercase letters with tails and smack on the bottom line of capitals. The last two arguments passed to XDrawString() are the string and its length in characters. You always must specify the length even when displaying an entire string.

> **Note**
>
> Don't assume that a graphics context refers to a default font in the X server. This might be true of some servers, but for best results, you should always load a font as explained in this section before displaying text by calling XDrawString() and other Xlib text-output functions.

GRAPHICS OUTPUT FUNCTIONS

Xlib provides a number of functions, called *graphics primitives*, for drawing lines and shapes in windows. In general, to draw graphics, a client application performs three essential steps:

- It initializes a graphics context (GC) for the display and window.
- It calls Xlib graphics primitive functions such as XDrawLine().
- It stores information needed to redraw the window's contents—for example, when it is uncovered by another window.

Those three steps are needed by any client application that draws graphics in a window. Because just about every client does that—even text, remember, is drawn graphically—all X clients perform these steps in one way or another.

GRAPHICS PRIMITIVES

Table 27.1 lists some of Xlib's graphics primitive functions. This chapter and the next show several of the functions in action, but for more information on them, look them up using the info utility. The table also includes string and text drawing functions.

TABLE 27.1   A FEW X PRIMITIVE GRAPHICS FUNCTIONS

Xlib Function	Description
XClearArea()	Clears a portion of a window
XClearWindow()	Clears the entire window
XCopyArea()	Copies an area of a window
XCopyPlane()	Copies an area using a bit-plane mask
XDrawArc()*	Draws a circular or elliptical arc
XDrawLine()*	Draws a line
XDrawPoint()*	Draws a point (a single pixel)
XDrawRectangle()*	Draws a rectangle or square
XDrawSegments()	Draws multiple unconnected lines
XDrawString()	Draws a single string
XDrawString16()	Draws a string of 16-bit characters
XDrawText()	Draws text with spacing and font data
XDrawText16()	Draws 16-bit character text
XFillArc()*	Fills an arc using the GC's arc_mode
XFillPolygon()	Fills a closed polygon
XFillRectangle()*	Fills a rectangle

These drawing functions have plural counterparts that can draw a list of two or more objects. For example, XDrawLines() can draw multiple connected lines stored in an array of coordinate values.

Note

Many graphics functions refer to a parameter of type Drawable. This is often treated as a window's visible surface (the so-called canvas), represented by a Window ID value, but a Drawable can be any pixmap having the same depth as the window's GC. For example, a Drawable might refer to a pixmap for drawing offscreen. To draw visible shapes, in most cases you can simply pass a Window ID to the function's Drawable parameter.

Decent Exposures

Combining the mouse button and movement events described at the beginning of this chapter with a simple graphics primitive, XDrawLine(), results in a program that lets users sketch simple graphics into a window. Compile and run the program, Listing 27.4, xsketch.cpp, and then click and drag the mouse cursor inside the client's window to sketch. Double-click the primary mouse button (probably the right one) to erase the image. Figure 27.3 shows a sample of the program's display. Email about my artistic skills will *not* be appreciated.

Figure 27.3
Sample xsketch window.

> **Note**
>
> The xsketch program doesn't include programming to redraw its contents. If you cover and uncover the window, it erases the covered portions of the drawing. The next section explains how to solve this problem.

LISTING 27.4   XSKETCH.CPP (EVENT LOOP)

```
// Get a default graphics context for our window
//
GC gc = XCreateGC(display, win, 0, NULL);

// Specify the types of events we want to receive
//
XSelectInput(display, win,
  ExposureMask | KeyPressMask |
  ButtonPressMask | ButtonReleaseMask | Button1MotionMask);

// Mouse movement and button event loop
// with double-clicking.
//
bool done = false;
bool mouseDown = false;
int x1, x2, y1, y2;
Time lastTime = 0;
XEvent event;
while (!done) {
  XNextEvent(display, &event);
  switch (event.type) {
```

continues

LISTING 27.4   CONTINUED

```
    case ButtonPress:
      x1 = event.xbutton.x;
      y1 = event.xbutton.y;
      mouseDown = true;
      break;
    case ButtonRelease:
      if (event.xbutton.time - lastTime < 250)
        XClearWindow(display, win);
      else
        lastTime = event.xbutton.time;
      mouseDown = false;
      break;
    case MotionNotify:
      if (mouseDown) {
        x2 = event.xbutton.x;
        y2 = event.xbutton.y;
        XDrawLine(display, win, gc, x1, y1, x2, y2);
        x1 = x2;
        y1 = y2;
      }
      break;
    case Expose:
      // Should redraw lines here
      break;
    case KeyPress:
      cout << "Keypress detected" << endl;
      done = true;   // Exit on any keypress
      break;
  }
}
```

In all cases, to prepare for drawing into a window, the first step is to obtain a GC for that window by calling XCreateCG(). As before, a default GC is obtained by passing the display, window ID, plus zero and NULL arguments as shown in the listing. This selects default values for the graphics context, in particular, specifying the window's background and foreground colors for graphical output.

To enable click-and-drag operations for the window, the program calls XSelectInput() with three mouse events, ButtonPressMask, ButtonReleaseMask, and Button1MotionMask. In addition, the program specifies ExposureMask and KeyPressMask to obtain window Expose and KeyPress events.

The event loop shows a few new techniques. To indicate internally that the user has clicked a mouse button, the ButtonPress event saves the mouse pointer coordinate values and sets a local bool mouseDown variable to true. This demonstrates a good way to communicate information between two or more events—in this case, telling the MotionNotify event logic that the user is holding down the mouse button.

That event calls the Xlib graphics primitive function XDrawLine() to draw a line from the previously saved coordinate to the current one. Although it might seem more appropriate to call XDrawPoint(), XDrawLine() is best in this case because the user might move the mouse pointer several pixels between MotionNotify events. But to see the difference, replace XDrawLine() with this statement:

```
XDrawPoint(display, win, gc, x2, y2);
```

DOUBLE BUTTON CLICKS

The xsketch.cpp program in Listing 27.4 also demonstrates one way to recognize a double mouse-button click. It does this by examining the time between ButtonRelease events. If that time is less than a certain threshold, the program assumes that the user double-clicked the mouse. In response, the sample program calls an Xlib graphics function to erase the window to the GC's background color. To use this method, define a variable of type Time, a data type provided by Xlib:

```
Time lastTime = 0;
```

A Time value is an unsigned 32-bit integer equal to the event's time in milliseconds. Time values wrap around after about 49 days, so for all practical purposes, these values are usable for determining the time between two events. (All events carry a time field.) The xsketch.cpp program's ButtonRelease event compares the last known time with the current time, and if the difference is less than 250 milliseconds, assumes that the user double-clicked the mouse:

```
case ButtonRelease:
  if (event.xbutton.time - lastTime < 250)
    XClearWindow(display, win);
  else
    lastTime = event.xbutton.time;
  mouseDown = false;
  break;
```

The call to XClearWindow() erases the window's interior to the current background color. This is a rare drawing routine that does not specify a GC because the window structure itself in the X server already records the background color, and it is the server's duty to paint window backgrounds.

Note

The double-click method described here works well enough in a variety of situations, but the method is less than perfect because it can miss a single click. A more robust double-click method would use an external timer to trigger single-click logic if a second mouse button event were not to arrive within a specified time.

SAVING GRAPHICS INFORMATION

One problem with the xsketch.cpp program in Listing 27.4 is that it does not save any information about the window's drawing. Because of this, covering and uncovering the client window causes its contents to disappear. This graphically illustrates one of the key requirements of an X window—a client must always be prepared to redraw its contents when an Expose event arrives.

That rule holds true even for X servers that implement a feature called the *backing store*. With this feature, the X server automatically preserves and restores a window's contents, and therefore does not necessarily post an Expose event to the client when the window becomes uncovered. To determine whether your server implements this feature, call the DoesBackingStore() macro. One of three return values tells you whether the server backs up mapped windows (WhenMapped), does not implement a backing store (NotUseful), or provides this feature for all windows (Always). Regardless of this function's value, however, you must redraw a client's contents in response to an Expose event. Even if the X server implements a backing store feature, it's still possible for a window's contents to require redrawing—for example, in response to a resizing operation that, due to the window's *gravity* attribute, affects the position of graphics relative to the window's origin (for more on this, see "Gravitational Considerations" later in this chapter).

It's totally your choice how to preserve the information your program needs to draw its graphical content. But remember to take advantage of other tools available to you. For example, the container classes and algorithms in the C++ standard template library (STL) make good choices for storing graphics information. To demonstrate, Listing 27.5, xlines.cpp, stores line coordinates in an STL vector container. To save space, the listing shows only the portions of the program that demonstrate its graphical techniques. Compile and run the program as you have others in this and the preceding chapter. Click and drag the mouse inside the window to draw some lines, and then cover and uncover the window. The uncovered portions of the drawing are redisplayed, although this happens so fast, you can't see it happen. The program also demonstrates a graphical technique called *rubber banding*. This animates the line while you drag the mouse—only when you release the mouse button is the line drawn in its final position.

LISTING 27.5   XLINES.CPP (PARTIAL)

```
#include <vector>        // Need vector<> template
#include <algorithm>     // Need for_each() algorithm

#include <X11/Xlib.h>    // Most X programs need these headers
#include <X11/Xutil.h>
#include <X11/Xos.h>

class TLine {
private:
  int _x1, _y1, _x2, _y2;
public:
  TLine(int x1=0, int y1=0, int x2=0, int y2=0):
_   x1(x1), _y1(y1), _x2(x2), _y2(y2) { }
  inline int GetX1() { return _x1; }
  inline int GetY1() { return _y1; }
  inline int GetX2() { return _x2; }
  inline int GetY2() { return _y2; }
};

Display *display;        // X server display structure
void DrawRubberLine(Display* display, Window win, GC gc,
```

```
    int x1, int y1, int x2, int y2);

// Define an STL vector of TLine objects
//
vector<TLine> lines(100);  // Grows larger if needed

int main()
{
  // Get a default graphics context for our window
  //
  GC gc = XCreateGC(display, win, 0, NULL);
  XSetLineAttributes(display, gc, 1, LineSolid, CapRound,
  JoinRound);

  // Specify the types of events we want to receive
  //
  XSelectInput(display, win,
    ExposureMask | KeyPressMask |
    ButtonPressMask | ButtonReleaseMask | Button1MotionMask);

  // Mouse movement and button event loop
  // with double-clicking.
  //
  bool done = false;
  bool mouseDown = false;
  int x1, x2, y1, y2;
  XEvent event;
  while (!done) {
    XNextEvent(display, &event);
    switch (event.type) {
    case ButtonPress:
      x1 = event.xbutton.x;
      y1 = event.xbutton.y;
      x2 = x1;
      y2 = y1;
      mouseDown = true;
      break;
    case ButtonRelease:
      if (x1 != x2 || y1 != y2) {
        DrawRubberLine(display, win, gc, x1, y1, x2, y2);
        x2 = event.xbutton.x;
        y2 = event.xbutton.y;
        XDrawLine(display, win, gc, x1, y1, x2, y2);
        lines.push_back(TLine(x1, y1, x2, y2));
      }
      mouseDown = false;
      break;
    case MotionNotify:
      if (mouseDown) {
        if (x1 != x2 || y1 != y2)  // Erase old line
          DrawRubberLine(display, win, gc, x1, y1, x2, y2);
        x2 = event.xbutton.x;
        y2 = event.xbutton.y;
        DrawRubberLine(display, win, gc, x1, y1, x2, y2);
      }
```

PART

V

CH

27

continues

LISTING 27.5   CONTINUED

```
      break;
    case Expose:
      vector<TLine>::iterator it;
      for (it = lines.begin(); it != lines.end(); it++)
        XDrawLine(display, win, gc,
          it->GetX1(), it->GetY1(), it->GetX2(), it->GetY2());
      break;
    case KeyPress:
      cout << "Keypress detected" << endl;
      done = true;    // Exit on any keypress
      break;
    }
  }

  // Disconnect X server connection and exit.
  // (Program may never get to here)
  //
  XCloseDisplay(display);
  return 0;
}

// Draw an erasable line using XOR logic
void DrawRubberLine(Display* display, Window win, GC gc,
  int x1, int y1, int x2, int y2)
{
  XSetFunction(display, gc, GXorReverse);
  XDrawLine(display, win, gc, x1, y1, x2, y2);
  XSetFunction(display, gc, GXcopy);
}
```

The program's TLine class saves two pairs of coordinate values marking the end points of a line. Because we haven't yet covered colormaps (see Chapter 28, "Breaking Out of Xlib Fundamentals"), this is the only saved information; however, another program might save the line's color, width, and other characteristics for redrawing. Creating a container for saving TLine objects is a simple matter of including the vector header and declaring an object named lines like this:

```
vector<TLine> lines(100);  // Grows larger if needed
```

I arbitrarily picked a capacity of 100 TLine objects, but the vector automatically grows as needed to accommodate more objects. After the usual initializations, the X client creates a graphics context by calling XCreateGC(). This time, however, the program modifies the GC's properties by calling XSetLineAttributes():

```
GC gc = XCreateGC(display, win, 0, NULL);
XSetLineAttributes(display, gc, 1, LineSolid, CapRound,
  JoinRound);
```

This is but one way to change the nature of visual graphics. You can also specify a variety of values directly when creating the GC. In this case, the second statement selects the line's attributes. For example, change 1 to 2 or 3 for wider lines.

Note

A line width of zero selects a fast, thin line but uses an algorithm that might not allow previously drawn lines to be erased by overdrawing–the technique used in this case to create rubber-band lines that appear to move along with the mouse pointer.

The program's event loop works much like the one in xsketch.cpp in Listing 27.4. However, in this case, the program displays and saves a line in response to a ButtonRelease event by executing these commands:

```
XDrawLine(display, win, gc, x1, y1, x2, y2);
lines.push_back(TLine(x1, y1, x2, y2));
```

When the X server posts an Expose event to the client, the program redraws the saved lines by using the following statements:

```
case Expose:
  vector<TLine>::iterator it;
  for (it = lines.begin(); it != lines.end(); it++)
    XDrawLine(display, win, gc,
      it->GetX1(), it->GetY1(), it->GetX2(), it->GetY2());
  break;
```

An iterator exported by the vector<TLine> class references each saved TLine object. Calling the GetX1() and similar class functions for each such object retrieves each line's coordinate values, passed to XDrawLine() for redrawing. Don't be concerned about the apparent complexity here. All functions are implemented inline, and the end result is fairly efficient. See Chapter 23, "Using the Standard Template Library (STL)," and Chapter 24, "Building Standard Containers," for more information about container templates.

The program does one other drawing operation in a local function, DrawRubberLine(), programmed using the following statements:

```
XSetFunction(display, gc, GXorReverse);
XDrawLine(display, win, gc, x1, y1, x2, y2);
XSetFunction(display, gc, GXcopy);
```

The first statement shows how to change an aspect of a GC, here setting the display logic to the value GXorReverse. This selects exclusive OR as the mechanism used for combining pixels on display. As a result, redrawing the line over the top of itself causes it to disappear. GXcopy is the default drawing method—it copies pixels—in this case, those in a line, directly to a specified Drawable. Table 27.2 lists other display modes you can pass to XSetFunction() and details the logical effect on source and destination pixels.

PART
V

CH
27

TABLE 27.2 XSetFunction() MODES

Mode	Logic
GXclear	0
GXand	source AND destination

continues

Table 27.2	Continued
GXandReverse	source AND NOT destination
GXcopy	source
GXandInverted	NOT source AND destination
GXnoop	destination
GXxor	source XOR destination
GXor	source OR destination
GXnor	NOT source AND NOT destination
GXequiv	NOT source XOR destination
GXinvert	NOT destination
GXorReverse	source OR NOT destination
GXcopyInverted	NOT source
GXorInverted	NOT source OR destination
GXnand	NOT source OR NOT destination
GXset	1

Keyboard Input Events

Of the two keyboard input events, KeyPress and KeyRelease, only the first is guaranteed to be available. The X server reports KeyRelease events only on hardware that provides the necessary signal from the keyboard. So, never count on obtaining KeyRelease events (most, if not all, Linux PC installations should support this event, however).

Because of great differences among keyboards on UNIX and Linux hardware, you cannot simply look up a key code as reported in a KeyPress or KeyRelease event. Instead, you must go through an intermediate step to map a key's event code with a value in the server's data tables for a value that represents a specific key. The result is a symbol such as XK_Up and XK_Home. Listing 27.6, xkey.cpp, demonstrates how to detect KeyPress events, look up the symbolic value in the server's key mapping, and display the key's name if it has one. As in most of this chapter's listings, to save space, only the relevant statements are printed here. Compile and run the program, and press any key to see its string name and translated, symbolic value in decimal. Press Esc to quit. Figure 27.4 shows a sample output window.

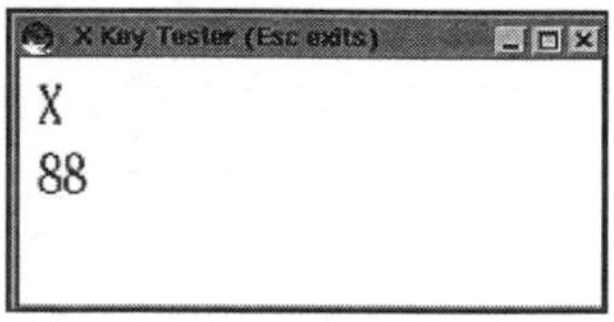

Figure 27.4
Sample xkey window.

LISTING 27.6 XKEY.CPP (PARTIAL)

```cpp
#include <X11/Xlib.h>    // Most X programs need these headers
#include <X11/Xutil.h>
#include <X11/Xos.h>
#include <X11/keysym.h>

void ShowKey(Display* display, Window win, GC gc,
XFontStruct* font, char *keyName, KeySym& key);

int main()
{
  XFontStruct *font;  // Font structure pointer
  char *fontName = "12x24";
  GetFont("12x24", &font);
  if (font == NULL)
    GetFont("9x15", &font);
  if (font == NULL)
    exit(1);
  XSetFont(display, gc, font->fid);

  // Specify the types of events we want to receive
  //
  XSelectInput(display, win,
    ExposureMask | KeyPressMask | KeyReleaseMask |
    StructureNotifyMask);

  // The event loop
  //
  bool done = false;
  KeySym key;
  XComposeStatus cstat;
  int size = 32;
  char keyname[size];
  keyname[0] = 0;
  XEvent event;
  while (!done) {
    XNextEvent(display, &event);
    switch (event.type) {
    case Expose:
      ShowKey(display, win, gc, font, keyname, key);
      break;
    case ConfigureNotify:
      break;
    case KeyPress:
      XClearWindow(display, win);
      XLookupString(&event.xkey, keyname, size, &key, &cstat);
      ShowKey(display, win, gc, font, keyname, key);
      if (key == XK_Escape)
        done = true;    // Exit on escape key
      break;
    case KeyRelease:    // Not available on all systems
      XBell(display, 50);
      break;
    }
```

continues

LISTING 27.6   CONTINUED

```
  }

  XUnloadFont(display, font->fid);
  XCloseDisplay(display);
  return 0;
}

// Load font from X server.
// On many servers, a default font is loaded if the specified
// one is unavailable, so the error message is rarely seen.
void GetFont(char *fontName, XFontStruct** font)
{
  *font = XLoadQueryFont(display, fontName);
  if (font == NULL)
    cerr << "Font " << fontName << " is not available" << endl;
}

// Display key name and value in decimal
void ShowKey(Display* display, Window win, GC gc,
  XFontStruct* font, char *keyName, KeySym& key)
{
  int y = font->ascent + font->descent + 10;
  int x = 10;
  char buf[10];
  XDrawString(display, win, gc, x, y,
    keyName, strlen(keyName));
  sprintf(buf, "%d", key);
  XDrawString(display, win, gc, x, y * 2,
    buf, strlen(buf));
}
```

DETECTING KEYBOARD EVENTS

So that your programs can recognize Xlib keyboard symbols such as XK_Escape, include the keysym.h header file using the following directive:

```
#include <X11/keysym.h>
```

This loads the actual definitions found in keysymdef.h. But don't load that file directly. You must include keysym.h to define certain other symbols that affect the symbolic names loaded into your program. To prepare for receiving KeyPress and KeyRelease events, call XSelectInput() with a mask as follows:

```
XSelectInput(display, win,
  ExposureMask | KeyPressMask | KeyReleaseMask |
  StructureNotifyMask);
```

Remember that even though you specify KeyReleaseMask, there is no guarantee that the client will receive KeyRelease events. An X display must have a keyboard, however, so it's safe to assume that KeyPress events are generated.

> **Note**
>
> On systems that implement an automatic repeat-key feature, the client may receive multiple `KeyPress` and `KeyRelease` events when the user presses and holds down a key. If this is a concern, you might be able to detect the automatically generated events by checking how much time passes between them, although in most cases you can probably ignore this feature with no harmful effects.

RESPONDING TO KEYBOARD EVENTS

The sample program's event loop shows how to respond to a `KeyPress` event and look up its symbolic value. For this, we need a couple of variables declared as

```
KeySym key;
XComposeStatus cstat;
int size = 32;
char keyname[size];
keyname[0] = 0;
```

A `KeySym` variable equals an `XK_` symbol as defined in keysymdef.h. `XComposeStatus` isn't used in this program, and it is meaningful only on systems with a *Compose* or similarly named key that selects an alternate character set. This might be found on computers such as desktop publishing systems that support multiple languages, or that need special symbols for some other purpose. In most cases, you can ignore the `XComposeStatus` value, but you have to define it anyway for the key mapping lookup function, `XLookupString()`, described next.

MAPPING KEYBOARD EVENT CODES

The `XLookupString()` function takes several arguments and returns two important values: a character string equal to the name of the event's key code and a symbolic value for that key. Never use the event's key code value directly. To ensure portability, all key values must be obtained by calling `XLookupString()`. This consults the X server's key mapping table for the user's hardware. Remember that your client might be shared among multiple servers all running on different kinds of hardware. If you use an event's key code directly, your program is almost sure to fail. In response to a `KeyPress` or `KeyRelease` event, call `XLookupString()` as follows:

```
XLookupString(&event.xkey, keyname, size, &key, &cstat);
```

The first argument refers to the `xkey` union that provides the fields specific to a `KeyPress` or `KeyRelease` event object. Next comes a pointer, `keyname`, to a `char` buffer followed by the size of that buffer in bytes. The function copies the key's string name into this buffer. Most key names are only one character long—the name of the `XK_A` key, for example, is the string `"A"`. However, it's possible that function keys and others have longer names depending on the server in use.

The last two arguments passed to `XLookupString()` are the addresses of `KeySym` and `XComposeStatus` variables. The function assigns to the `KeySym` variable the symbolic value for the event's key code. As mentioned, the `XComposeStatus` value is ignored.

After looking up the key's name and symbolic value, you can use it to display text or select a program function. The sample program does both. It calls a local function, ShowKey(), to display the key's name and symbolic value in decimal. Following the call to XLookupString(), the reported KeySym value can be compared to any XK_ constant in keysymdef.h. The sample program uses this technique to detect the Esc key and end the event loop when you press that key:

```
if (key == XK_Escape)
  done = true;   // Exit on escape key
```

Tip

When you don't need a key's string name, you can call the function XLookupKeysym() to obtain its symbolic value. The sample programming in the next section shows how to use this function.

WINDOW ATTRIBUTES

A window's attributes specify various display characteristics such as the background and foreground colors, a cursor shape, and border width. There are three ways to set attributes for a window:

- At creation by calling XCreateWindow()
- After creating by calling XSetWindowBorder() and similar utility functions
- After creation by calling XChangeWindowAttributes()

In most cases, clients select a window's attributes when they create the Window structure, but you can always change any attribute later. Keep in mind, however, that every such change results in an increase in network traffic. For best results, specify as many attributes as possible when you first create a new window. The following three sections show examples of each of the three window-attribute techniques.

Tip

You can freely use any of the methods described here to change a window's attributes after creation. Because Xlib combines all such techniques into a single network request, no one method is more efficient than another in terms of its impact on network performance.

CREATING WINDOWS WITH ATTRIBUTES

To specify attributes during a window's creation, follow these general steps after making the connection to the X server:

1. Declare a variable of the Xlib XSetWindowAttributes structure.
2. Assign values to the structure's fields.

3. Prepare a mask of type unsigned long with bits set for each field in the XSetWindowAttribute structure.

4. Create the window by calling XCreateWindow().

Listing 27.7, xattrib.cpp, shows how to use this method to create a window with a dark background—a so-called "reverse-video" effect, often used by pseudo character-based terminal windows. Only the statements relating to the window's creation are shown in the printed listing—the other statements duplicate programming discussed elsewhere in this chapter.

LISTING 27.7 XATTRIB.CPP (PARTIAL)

```
// Attempt to establish communications with the X Server
//
display = XOpenDisplay(NULL);
if (display == NULL) {
  cerr << "Failure connecting to X Server";
  exit(1);
}

// Calculate window's dimensions and position
//
int intScreenNum = DefaultScreen(display);
int intDisplayWidth = DisplayWidth(display, intScreenNum);
int intDisplayHeight = DisplayHeight(display, intScreenNum);
int intWidth = intDisplayWidth / 4;
int intHeight = intDisplayHeight / 3;
int intXPos = 0;
int intYPos = 0;

// Get the most basic of colors (black and white)
//
int intBlackColor, intWhiteColor;
intBlackColor = BlackPixel(display, DefaultScreen(display));
intWhiteColor = WhitePixel(display, DefaultScreen(display));

// Fill window attributes structure with values
// This should create a "reverse-video" window
//
XSetWindowAttributes attributes;
attributes.background_pixel = intBlackColor;
attributes.border_pixel = intWhiteColor;

// Set attribute mask that tells XCreateWindow() which
// fields to use for the preceding structure. Values not
// specified are ignored, and require no initialization.
//
unsigned long valuemask = CWBackPixel | CWBorderPixel;

// Create window the "hard" way by specifying the
// preceding attribute values (plus other arguments).
//
```

continues

LISTING 27.7   CONTINUED

```
Window win =
XCreateWindow(
  display,                      // X Server connection
  DefaultRootWindow(display),   // Parent Window ID
  intXPos, intYPos,             // Position
  intWidth, intHeight,          // Width and height
  8,                            // Border width
  CopyFromParent,               // Screen depth
  InputOutput,                  // Window "class"
  CopyFromParent,               // Visual type
  valuemask,                    // Attribute bit mask
  &attributes                   // Attribute value structure
);

// Assign a name for the window title bar (probably)
//
XStoreName(display, win, "Window Attributes");

// Map the window to the display
// Window is visible when first Expose event is received
//
XMapWindow(display, win);

// Get a default graphics context for our window
//
GC gc = XCreateGC(display, win, 0, NULL);
XSetForeground(display, gc, intWhiteColor);
```

The sample program creates a structure of type XSetWindowAttributes and then assigns a couple of values to the structure's fields using these statements:

```
XSetWindowAttributes attributes;
attributes.background_pixel = intBlackColor;
attributes.border_pixel = intWhiteColor;
```

The intBlackColor and intWhiteColor values are obtained from the X server's display information. You can set only the background and border colors during the window's creation. The foreground color is specified by the graphics context (GC), not the window itself. For each assignment to an attribute field, there must be a corresponding bit mask logically ORed into an unsigned long variable. To specify the mask value, the program follows the preceding statement with this:

```
unsigned long valuemask = CWBackPixel | CWBorderPixel;
```

Tip

Type *info XCreateWindow* and also view the X.h header for information about other CW bit masks.

Only the specified fields are changed in the window structure. The other values are ignored and set to default values (usually inherited from the parent window). With the structure and bit mask in place, call XCreateWindow() as shown in the listing and save the function result in a `Window` ID variable. Comments in the listing show the purpose of the other arguments passed to `XCreateWindow()`.

> **Note**
>
> A window's border width is usually set to zero because the window manager creates window borders using its own design parameters. In most cases, you can't create window borders of varying widths, and the `border_width` field in the window attribute structure is effectively unused.

CALLING WINDOW ATTRIBUTE FUNCTIONS

The easiest way to change a window attribute after the window's creation is to call an Xlib function designed to alter a specific attribute value. As an example, the event loop in xattrib.cpp (refer to Listing 27.7) flops the window's background and foreground colors when you click the mouse cursor inside the window. Listing 27.8 shows this portion of the event loop.

LISTING 27.8   XATTRIB.CPP (PARTIAL EVENT LOOP)

```
case ButtonPress:
  SwapColors();
  XSetWindowBackground(display, win, intBackgroundColor);
  XClearWindow(display, win);  // Make changes visible
  XFlush(display);  // Do it now
  break;
```

Local function `SwapColors()` exchanges the `intBackgroundColor` and `intForegroundColor` variables set during the program's startup phase. Three separate Xlib function calls are needed to change the display background and to make that change visible. First, `XSetWindowBackground()` changes the background attribute in the specified window. However, this produces no visual effect. Calling `XClearWindow()` redisplays the window's background, an action that takes place directly in the X server, not as a result of an event posted to the client. But this still might not have any immediate visual effect.

Finally, `XFlush()` sends all pending requests to the X server including those generated by the preceding function calls. At this time, the window is painted to the new background color. In this case, it isn't strictly necessary to call `XFlush()` because, when the event loop calls `XNextEvent()`, that function flushes any pending commands in the request buffer. However, there's no harm in calling `XFlush()` to force requests to be sent to the X server, although doing so too often could have a negative impact on network performance.

CHANGING ATTRIBUTE VALUES

The third way to change window attribute values resembles the method described for setting those values during the window's creation. After doing that, call the `XChangeWindowAttributes()` function to alter specific attributes. You may do this at any time, either before or after the window has been mapped and displayed. The xattrib.cpp

PART
V
CH
27

program demonstrates this technique in the portion of its event loop that responds to
KeyPress events. Listing 27.9 shows this portion of the program's event loop.

LISTING 27.9   XATTRIB.CPP (PARTIAL EVENT LOOP)

```
case KeyPress:
  key = XLookupKeysym(&event.xkey, 0);
  switch (key) {
case XK_Return:
  SwapColors();
  attributes.background_pixel = intBackgroundColor;
  attributes.border_pixel = intForegroundColor;
  valuemask = CWBackPixel | CWBorderPixel;
  XChangeWindowAttributes(display, win,
    valuemask, &attributes);
  XClearWindow(display, win);  // Make changes visible
  XFlush(display);  // Do it now
  break;
case XK_Escape:
  done = true;   // Exit on escape key
  break;
}
```

As you can see, this method is a bit more complex, although it accomplishes the same effect
as the code for ButtonPress events. The first step is to call XLookupKeysym() for the symbolic
code of the key value reported for the KeyPress event. A second switch statement compares
the resulting KeySym value to the constant XK_Return. If there's a match, the user pressed the
Enter or Return key, and the statements for that case swap the background and foreground
colors. Using the XSetWindowAttributes structure defined earlier, the program next assigns
the two swapped colors to the background_pixel and foreground_pixel fields. In addition,
valuemask (also defined earlier) is assigned bit-mask values to indicate which fields in the
attribute structure are valid. Although valuemask is already initialized in this example, it's
always a good idea to assign its values immediately before calling
XChangeWindowAttributes().

Note

Keep in mind that, on typical PC keyboards, the usual Enter key does not produce the same
key codes as a numeric keypad's Enter key. You might want to alert users to this difference
in your program's documentation.

That function assigns the new values to the window structure held in the X server. This isn't
enough, however, to cause a visual change onscreen. As explained in the preceding section,
to repaint the window's background, the program must clear the window and flush the
request buffer. (The last step isn't strictly necessary, however.) To see the effect of this
programming, run the sample xattrib.cpp program and press Enter. Press Esc to quit.

OTHER WINDOW ATTRIBUTES

Following are some additional attributes that you can set to control aspects of a window's appearance. You won't use these features in all clients, but they can produce useful visual effects that might improve your program's graphical interface.

CHANGING THE CURSOR SHAPE

Changing the cursor shape when the user moves the mouse pointer into a window is a great way to indicate the types of operations allowed. As you probably know, clients change the cursor shape to an *I-beam* to indicate that users can type text, and to a clock or hourglass shape to indicate that a lengthy process is going on, such as reading a file.

There are two ways to specify cursor shapes. You can select from a set of predefined cursors, or you can create your own by using pixmaps. In most cases, it's best to choose a default cursor because the X server typically provides patterns optimized for specific hardware and different resolutions. For that purpose, Xlib provides standard cursor constants listed in Table 27.3. For simplicity in loading the cursor images, the shapes are implemented as a standard font declared in the cursorfont.h header file. Load this file into your program with the following directive:

```
#include <X11/cursorfont.h>
```

TABLE 27.3 STANDARD CURSOR CONSTANTS			
XC_X_cursor	XC_dotbox	XC_lr_angle	XC_sb_v_double_arrow
XC_arrow	XC_double_arrow	XC_man	XC_shuttle
XC_based_arrow_down	XC_draft_large	XC_middlebutton	XC_sizing
XC_based_arrow_up	XC_draft_small	XC_mouse	XC_spider
XC_boat	XC_draped_box	XC_pencil	XC_spraycan
XC_bogosity	XC_exchange	XC_pirate	XC_star
XC_bottom_left_corner	XC_fleur	XC_plus	XC_target
XC_bottom_right_corner	XC_gobbler	XC_question_arrow	XC_tcross
XC_bottom_side	XC_gumby	XC_right_ptr	XC_top_left_arrow
XC_bottom_tee	XC_hand1	XC_right_side	XC_top_left_corner
XC_box_spiral	XC_hand2	XC_right_tee	XC_top_right_corner
XC_center_ptr	XC_heart	XC_rightbutton	XC_top_side
XC_circle	XC_icon	XC_rtl_logo	XC_top_tee
XC_clock	XC_iron_cross	XC_sailboat	XC_trek

PART

V

CH

27

continues

TABLE 27.3   CONTINUED

XC_coffee_mug	XC_left_ptr	XC_sb_down_arrow	XC_ul_angle
XC_cross	XC_left_side	XC_sb_h_double_arrow	XC_umbrella
XC_cross_reverse	XC_left_tee	XC_sb_left_arrow	XC_ur_angle
XC_crosshair	XC_leftbutton	XC_sb_right_arrow	XC_watch
XC_diamond_cross	XC_ll_angle	XC_sb_up_arrow	XC_xterm
XC_dot			

Two Xlib functions are needed to define a cursor shape for a window. Listing 27.10, xcursor.cpp, shows the necessary steps.

LISTING 27.10   XCURSOR.CPP (PARTIAL)

```
#include <X11/Xlib.h>    // Most X programs need these headers
#include <X11/Xutil.h>
#include <X11/Xos.h>
#include <X11/cursorfont.h>

Display *display;        // X server display structure

int main()
{
  ...
  // Specify cursor to appear when mouse pointer moves
  // into the window's area
  Cursor cursor =
    XCreateFontCursor(display, XC_coffee_mug);
  XDefineCursor(display, win, cursor);
}
```

The first step in defining a standard cursor is to call XCreateFontCursor() passing the X server's display pointer and one of the constants from Table 27.3. This loads the font character having that value and returns a Cursor ID for the cursor image stored in the server.

The second step is to call XDefineCursor(), passing the display pointer, Window ID, and result from XCreateFontCursor(). After these steps, moving the mouse pointer into the window automatically causes the new cursor shape to appear.

Call XUndefineCursor() to reset a cursor to none and therefore show the default arrow pointer. Except when creating a window for the first time, changing the window's cursor is best followed by a call to XFlush() to be sure the X server receives the requests as soon as possible.

GRAVITATIONAL CONSIDERATIONS

There are two kinds of gravity in X programming—*bit gravity* and *window gravity*. A window's bit gravity refers to the relative positioning of its content area, or canvas, to the window's frame. Window gravity refers to the relative positioning of one or more child windows to its parent. Gravity values are expressed as compass points so that a SouthWestGravity references the window's lower-left corner, and NorthGravity positions a window's content or a subwindow at the top of its parent. Normally, both kinds of gravity default to none, represented by the Xlib constant ForgetGravity—exactly what I wish I could do after eating too much for dinner.

Note

Setting a window's gravity to ForgetGravity tells the X server not to preserve the window's contents, even if the server implements a backing store feature. To use the server's backing store capabilities, if available, gravity must be set to a compass point such as SouthWestGravity, or to one of the related values CenterGravity or StaticGravity.

To demonstrate gravitational considerations, Listing 27.11, xgravity.cpp, displays a client parent window with a "sticky" subwindow as a child. The child window's gravity is set to NorthGravity, causing it to adhere as though glued to the top of its parent. This demonstrates the rudiments of creating a window that might be used as a panel for other objects such as a collection of buttons. When the main client window is moved or resized, the X server automatically repositions the panel child window so that it always sticks to the top of its parent. Figure 27.5 shows a sample of the program's output.

Figure 27.5
Sample output of
xgravity.cpp program.

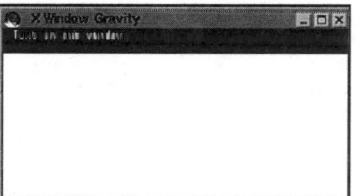

LISTING 27.11 XGRAVITY.CPP (PARTIAL)

```cpp
// Create subwindow "glued" to the parent using
// window gravity.
XSetWindowAttributes attributes;
attributes.win_gravity = NorthGravity;
attributes.background_pixel = intBlackColor;
unsigned long valuemask = CWWinGravity | CWBackPixel;

Window panel =
XCreateWindow(
  display,                  // X Server connection
  win,                      // Parent Window ID
  0, 0,                     // Position
  intWidth, intHeight / 8,  // Width and height
  0,                        // Border width
  CopyFromParent,           // Screen depth
```

PART

V

CH

27

continues

LISTING 27.11   CONTINUED

```cpp
    InputOutput,               // Window "class"
    CopyFromParent,            // Visual type
    valuemask,                 // Attribute bit mask
    &attributes                // Attribute value structure
);
XMapWindow(display, panel);

GC gcpanel = XCreateGC(display, panel, 0, NULL);
XSetForeground(display, gcpanel, intWhiteColor);
char * panelString = "Text in sub-window";

// Specify the types of events we want to receive
//
XSelectInput(display, win,
  ExposureMask | KeyPressMask | StructureNotifyMask);
XSelectInput(display, panel,
  ExposureMask | StructureNotifyMask);

// Mouse movement and button event loop
// with double-clicking.
//
bool done = false;
XEvent event;
while (!done) {
  XNextEvent(display, &event);
  switch (event.type) {
  case Expose:
    if (event.xexpose.window == panel) {
      // Sub window graphics go here
      XDrawString(display, panel, gcpanel, 10, 10,
        panelString, strlen(panelString));
    } else {
      // Main window graphics go here
    }
    break;
  case ConfigureNotify:
    break;
  case KeyPress:
    cout << "Keypress detected" << endl;
    done = true;   // Exit on any keypress
    break;
  }
}
```

The listing for xgravity.cpp shows only the portions that relate to the creation of the client's child window and its gravitational specification. The program also demonstrates how a client can respond to events for more than one window—techniques useful for displaying other kinds of child windows such as a status bar or a dialog box. The child window must be created the "hard way" using XCreateWindow() so that we can specify its gravity setting. This is done by creating an XSetWindowAttributes structure and setting the win_gravity field to an Xlib constant such as NorthGravity:

```cpp
XSetWindowAttributes attributes;
attributes.win_gravity = NorthGravity;
```

Try different `win_gravity` settings here to see their effects. For example, to glue the child window to the bottom of its parent, set its gravity to `SouthGravity`. However, if you try this, you might be surprised to see the child window still appear at the top of its parent. To display the child at the bottom, you must also set its initial X and Y coordinate values to something like this:

```
0, intHeight - (intHeight / 8),
```

After creating the subwindow, identified in the sample program by the `Window` ID variable named `panel`, map the window to the display as you do the main client window. Also create a GC for the panel and set its foreground color if necessary using these statements:

```
XMapWindow(display, panel);
GC gcpanel = XCreateGC(display, panel, 0, NULL);
XSetForeground(display, gcpanel, intWhiteColor);
```

Remember also to select the types of events you want the child window to receive. These events arrive in the same Xlib queue as for the main client window, and they are processed by the same event loop. In this case, we specify `Expose` and `ConfigureNotify` events for the panel window using the following statement:

```
XSelectInput(display, panel,
  ExposureMask | StructureNotifyMask);
```

The main event loop now receives events for both of the sample program's windows. To determine to which window an event refers, examine the event's `window` field. For example, the sample program's `Expose` event displays text in the panel window by calling `XDrawString()` as follows:

```
case Expose:
  if (event.xexpose.window == panel) {
    // Sub window graphics go here
    XDrawString(display, panel, gcpanel, 10, 10,
      panelString, strlen(panelString));
  }
```

If the `xexpose.window` field equals the `Window` ID assigned to `panel`, then we know the X server has requested that the client redraw the child window's contents. If the field equals the client `Window` ID, then the program would display the main window's graphics (there are none, however, in this example).

Not shown here is the code that resizes the child window relative to its parent. This illustrates that gravity affects *only* the window's relative position.

TILING A BACKGROUND PIXMAP

Normally, a window's background is a solid color, often white or black. Instead of a pixel value, however, you can also specify a pixmap to use for the window's background. The pixmap is *tiled* (replicated in rows and columns) so that only one small image is needed to fill the entire window. Typically, a 16-by-16-pixel image works fine, but you can use a pixmap of any dimensions.

PART

V

CH

27

> **Tip**
>
> Certain pixmap dimensions might display faster on specific X servers. To find the ideal dimensions for your system, call XQueryBestTile().

The steps for creating a pixmap and using it to tile a window's background are complicated by the concept of depth in color displays. To be used for a window's background, a pixmap must have the same depth as the screen on which a window is displayed. There are some ways to subvert that rule by copying pixmaps to selected bit planes, but for most cases, the steps shown here are the ones to use for creating pixmaps that work on all types of X hardware.

Listing 27.12, xtile.cpp, shows the steps needed to read a bitmap file and convert it into a pixmap suitable for painting a window's background. Due to a possibly swelled ego coupled with a lack of artistic drawing skills, as Figure 27.6 shows, I demonstrate the basic steps for painting a window's background with a pixmap of my initials. (I always admire artists who can create credible-looking images in a 16-by-16 bitmap!) After the listing, I explain how to use the same technique with any pixmap image. Run the program and resize the window to see how it paints the entire background regardless of the window's size. Only a small 16-by-16 pixel bitmap is needed to produce this effect.

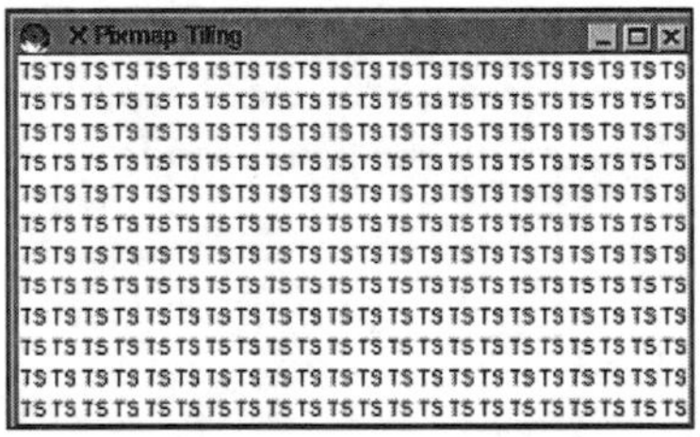

Figure 27.6
Sample window tiled with a pixmap of the author's initials.

LISTING 27.12   XTILE.CPP (PARTIAL)

```
// Load bitmap from file for use as window background
//
unsigned int bmWidth, bmHeight;   // Bitmap width and height
int bmXhot, bmYhot;               // Bitmap hotspot (ignored)
unsigned char * p;                // Pointer to raw bitmap data
int result = XReadBitmapFileData(
  "ts.xbm",
  &bmWidth, &bmHeight,
  &p,
  &bmXhot, &bmYhot );
if (result != BitmapSuccess) {
  cerr << "Failed to open ts.bmp file" << endl;
  exit(1);
}

// Construct a pixmap using the raw bitmap data
//
Pixmap pixmap =
  XCreatePixmapFromBitmapData(
```

```
        display,
        win,
        (char *) p,
        bmWidth, bmHeight,
        intBlackColor, intWhiteColor,
        DefaultDepth(display, intScreenNum));

// Use the pixmap as the window background "tile"
//
XSetWindowBackgroundPixmap(display, win, pixmap);

// The X server maintains a copy of the pixmap so we can
// now free the pixmap image and the raw bitmap data:
XFreePixmap(display, pixmap);
XFree(p);
```

The first step in using a pixmap for tiling a window is to create the bitmap image. Probably the easiest method for creating a new image is to use the standard X utility bitmap program. To run it, enter **bitmap** at a terminal window prompt and then create your image (or load one from disk and modify it). The program's buttons and commands are easy to figure out. Bitmap files created with the bitmap utility should be named with the filename extension .xbm. A sample ts.xbm file is in the c27/xtile directory on the CD-ROM. (See also "Bitmap File Format" at the end of this chapter.)

After creating the image you want to use, you need to load it into the client application. To make the bitmap compatible with the window's screen, and therefore suitable for use as its background, the client must convert the raw bitmap image into a pixmap having the same depth as the screen, a process sometimes called *rendering*. The rendered image is then passed to the X server for use in tiling the window's background. Two structures allocated memory by this process must also be freed to prevent a memory leak. Once passed to the X server, unless the bitmap and pixmap images are used in other ways, it is safe to destroy these structures.

Load a bitmap file by calling the XReadBitmapFileData() function as shown in the listing and repeated here:

```
int result = XReadBitmapFileData(
  "ts.xbm",
  &bmWidth, &bmHeight,
  &p,
  &bmXhot, &bmYhot);
```

The first argument is the filename string, ts.xbm in this case. The next two arguments are pointers to width and height integer variables, to which the function assigns the bitmap's size. The pointer p, passed by reference, should be of type unsigned char*. The function allocates memory to this pointer for holding the bitmap image data loaded from disk. The final two arguments are references to two other integers that identify the hotspot in a cursor image but are unused in this case.

If the result of XReadBitmapFileData() is not BitmapSuccess, then an error occurred. For small bitmaps, the likely cause is a bad or missing filename. When loading larger images, however, you might want to inspect the function result more closely. This result can equal `BitmapOpenFailed` if the file cannot be opened, `BitmapFileInvalid` if the file contains unrecognized data, or `BitmapNoMemory` if enough memory is not available for allocating space to hold the image data.

After successfully loading a bitmap image, the next step converts it into a pixmap in a form that the X server can use to paint the window's background. To do this, call `XCreatePixmapFromBitmapData()` as shown here:

```
Pixmap pixmap =
  XCreatePixmapFromBitmapData(
    display,
    win,
    (char *) p,
    bmWidth, bmHeight,
    intBlackColor, intWhiteColor,
    DefaultDepth(display, intScreenNum));
```

The function result is a value of type `Pixmap`, which is merely an integer ID that identifies the converted image held in the X server. Pass the initialized server display pointer and `Window` ID to this function. The third argument is a `char` pointer to the raw bitmap image data loaded by `XReadBitmapFileData()`. (It could also be a pointer to image data created by other means—for example, a static array of byte values.)

Note

> The type cast expression (`char*`) in the preceding statement avoids a compiler warning. Apparently, `XReadBitmapFileData()` is designed to use an `unsigned char*` while `XCreatePixmapFromBitmapData()` uses a `char*` declaration for its bitmap pointer parameter. Because the `char` type is signed by default in ANSI C++, this results in a type-mismatch warning. This is a small discrepancy of no consequence, although both functions probably should declare their parameters simply as type `char*`.

The final arguments passed to `XCreatePixmapFromBitmapData()` are the width and height of the raw bitmap image, the background and foreground colors to use, and the depth of the screen obtained here by calling the `DefaultDepth()` macro for the X server `display` pointer and default screen number. The resulting pixmap is now ready for use in tiling the window's background. Call the following function to tell the server to use the image this way:

```
XSetWindowBackgroundPixmap(display, win, pixmap);
```

You can perform the preceding steps after creating and mapping the window before it first appears, or at anytime later. However, after the client has received at least one `Expose` event for the window, to make a change to the background visible, follow the preceding statement with calls to `XClearWindow()` and `XFlush()`. This forces the X server to repaint the window's background immediately and also results in a new `Expose` event sent to the client for the window. At that time, the client can repaint any graphics over the new tiled background.

As mentioned, because the X server maintains a copy of the pixmap image data, following the preceding steps, you should probably destroy the raw bitmap and pixmap images. To do this, execute the following two statements:

```
XFreePixmap(display, pixmap);
XFree(p);
```

Never use the standard library's `free()` function or the C++ `delete` operator to free these objects. Always call the Xlib `XFreePixmap()` and `XFree()` functions as shown here.

BITMAP FILE FORMAT

The X bitmap utility creates an .xbm file in a format that you can include directly into a C or C++ source code file. A bitmap file is actually a text file containing declarations that describe the bitmap's size and its data. Listing 27.13, ts.xbm, shows the sample bitmap file used to tile the window in the preceding section. (I edited the ts_bits array data to save space.)

LISTING 27.13   TS.XBM

```
#define ts_width 16
#define ts_height 16
static unsigned char ts_bits[] = {
  0x00, 0x00, 0x00, 0x00, 0x00, 0x00,
  0x00, 0x00, 0x7c, 0x1c, 0x10, 0x22,
  0x10, 0x02, 0x10, 0x1c, 0x10, 0x20,
  0x10, 0x20, 0x10, 0x22, 0x10, 0x1c,
  0x00, 0x00, 0x00, 0x00, 0x00, 0x00,
  0x00, 0x00};
```

Instead of calling the `XReadBitmapFileData()` function to load a bitmap file in this format, you may use an `#include` directive to insert the file's text into a program source file:

```
#include <ts.xbm>
```

You can then call `XCreatePixmapFromBitmapData()` to convert the bitmap data identified as the array `ts_bits[]` to a pixmap and use it to tile a window's background as explained in the preceding section. You might want to use this technique to create a self-contained executable code file that does not depend on other files to be available at runtime.

SUMMARY

Programmers enter a brave new world when they begin programming an X client application's input and output. Unlike conventional programs that prompt for input, wait for the user to respond, and then take action accordingly, an X client's I/O occurs asynchronously in the form of requests to the X server and events from the server back to the client. This chapter introduced keyboard and mouse input techniques and also explained methods for drawing text and graphics in X windows. The chapter also detailed techniques for selecting window attributes such as background and foreground colors, changing the cursor shape, and tiling a window's background using a pixmap image.

PART
V

CH
27

For more information on subjects introduced in this chapter, turn to the following chapters:

- Chapter 23, "Using the Standard Template Library (STL)"
- Chapter 24, "Building Standard Containers"
- Chapter 26, "Introducing X Programming"

X Window Development

## CHAPTER 28

BREAKING OUT OF XLIB FUNDAMENTALS

With the information in Chapters 26 and 27, you now have enough basic knowledge to begin writing X client applications. In a short time, however, you are likely to discover the need for more facts and tools. Consider this chapter as a kind of bridge between the fundamentals you have learned and the next chapters, in which you build Linux and X applications based on the V class library complete with menus, buttons, status bars, and dialog boxes. Before then, however, you need to master a few more X subjects.

This chapter explains how to use colormaps to allocate colors and to draw colored graphics. The chapter also covers the subject of *atoms*—symbolic strings stored by the X server—that you can use for a variety of purposes such as inter-client communications. (The X cut buffer, or Clipboard, is implemented this way.) Finally in this chapter are some additional explanations of X graphics techniques for creating styled lines and painting filled shapes using colors and pixmap images.

INTRODUCING COLORMAPS

The subject of X colormaps could easily fill two or more chapters in this book. For that reason, instead of trying to explore every nook and cranny on the subject, this section covers only the essential highlights that most clients can use to add color graphics to their windows. Although there are many ways to use colormaps, unless you need to develop photo-quality graphics, the techniques described here should work in most applications.

WHAT IS A COLORMAP?

In a nutshell, a colormap is a database of values that cause pixels to be colored in specific hues. The word "color" here is somewhat misleading because, on a monochrome video system, a colormap might specify grayscale levels. In fact, the only time a colormap is *not* used in X graphics is on a monochrome flat screen with contrasting pixels of only two colors, black and white. However, as mentioned in Chapter 26, "Introducing X Programming," even those two colors are not guaranteed. On some video screens, for example, the contrasting colors might be dark orange and light orange. Nevertheless, in the program, they are called black and white.

Internally, a colormap is basically a lookup table of red, green, and blue (RGB) color values, or grayscale levels. When an X client needs to use a color, it *allocates* a cell in the colormap, called a *colorcell*, which might be shared by other clients. A pixel's value in memory is used as an index into the colormap to find the values that cause a pixel of a certain color or grayscale intensity to appear at a specific location.

BIT PLANES

All video screens possess some memory (or they use a portion of the system's memory) to store bits that represent the pixels on display. A system that uses 1 bit per pixel is said to have a single *bit plane* (or just *plane*). A system that uses 2 bits per pixel has two planes. One with 8 bits per pixel has eight planes. Systems commonly in use today offer 8 or 16 planes, although 24-bit true-color systems are fast becoming the norm.

As you might suspect, the number of colors that an X screen can show is related to the number of video planes. However, the relationship between the number of *possible* colors and those actually displayed at one time is a function, not of the video memory, but of the colormap's colorcells. For example, if eight planes are available, you would expect the display to be able to show 2^8 or 256 colors. However, if each color is represented as red, green, and blue (RGB) color values each from 0 to 255, an 8-plane system can actually show more than 16 million (256^3) colors—but only up to 256 colors at once. That number might be further reduced if two or more identical colors are allocated by the different clients in such a way that the associated colorcells cannot be shared. Figure 28.1 shows how bits in this type of system are used as indexes into a colormap to obtain actual RGB pixel values.

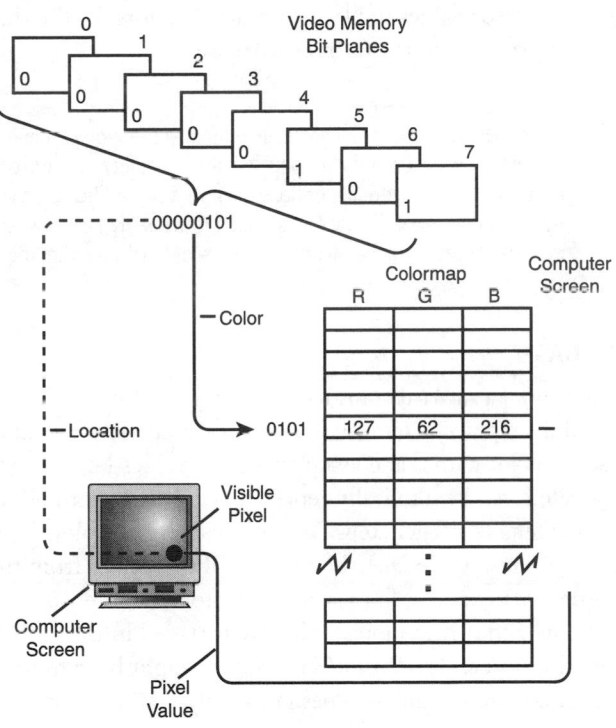

Figure 28.1
An 8-plane video screen's bits are used as indexes into a colormap to obtain RGB pixel values.

The relationship between bit plane values and colormaps begins to change in the world of 24-bit true-color systems. If a colormap in this system were created for every possible color combination, the structure would be impossibly huge. For this reason, in some cases, each third of a 24-bit-plane pixel is used as an index into a database of red, green, and blue level values, the combination of which results in a visible hue onscreen. In the extreme case, there is only one hardware colormap in existence, and the video bit planes map directly to RGB values. These so-called *true-color* displays can show more than 16 million *distinct* hues onscreen at the same time—more than the human eye can discern.

Regardless of the amount of video memory available and the number of possible planes, we can break down all types of screens into one of three basic categories:

- Monochrome single-plane systems
- Monochrome grayscale systems
- Color systems

For the purposes of programming X color graphics, it is usually only necessary to determine which of these categories best describes your system. In the first case, the client can use black and white for all its colors. However, if the client needs more than two colors, it has no choice but to display an error message and exit. In the second case, the client application can allocate grayscale color values in place of its usual colors. In the third case, the program can use color values provided in an X server database.

Note

Various techniques are possible for investigating the type of video system available, but in most cases, it is best simply to give users the capability to choose their own color values, perhaps using command-line options or from a setup file. Color graphics programming in X involves an amount of guesswork, and it is probably not possible to write software that works exactly the same on all possible types of hardware running UNIX and Linux.

THE X COLOR DATABASE

In most cases, by using a standard color name, your program has the best chance of producing predictable color graphics. Colors are defined in a database stored in file rgb.txt. This file contains a set of color names and associated RGB values known to the X server. Also in this file are grayscale levels symbolically represented as gray0 through gray100 (or grey0 through grey100) in single-integer steps. You may use these "colors" on color or monochrome grayscale systems. Table 28.1 shows some of the colors from the rgb.txt database in their declared order. Many colors have synonyms—for example, hot pink and HotPink are the same color. Some authorities indicate this file is stored in the path /usr/lib/X11, but on my system, I found it in /usr/X11R6/lib/X11, so you might have to hunt for it. The X server uses a compiled version of this file—it doesn't actually read the text.

TABLE 28.1   SELECTED X COLOR NAMES FROM RGB.TXT

snow	DarkSlateGrey	LightCoral
ghost white	dim gray	tomato
GhostWhite	DimGray	orange red
white smoke	navy blue	OrangeRed
WhiteSmoke	NavyBlue	red
antique white	cornflower blue	hot pink
AntiqueWhite	CornflowerBlue	HotPink

papaya whip	cyan	violet
PapayaWhip	light cyan	plum
blanched almond	LightCyan	blue violet
BlanchedAlmond	dark sea green	BlueViolet
bisque	DarkSeaGreen	purple
peach puff	sea green	medium purple
PeachPuff	SeaGreen	MediumPurple
seashell	forest green	thistle
honeydew	ForestGreen	gray0
mint cream	sandy brown	grey0
MintCream	SandyBrown	gray1
azure	tan	grey1
dark slate gray	chocolate	gray100
DarkSlateGray	firebrick	grey100
dark slate grey	light coral	

Using color names from rgb.txt doesn't guarantee that a client's graphics are displayed in any particular hue. However, using the standard names puts the responsibility of selecting actual colors on the heads of the system administrator and user. On a monochrome system, for instance, each color can be given grayscale levels, although in that case it is still good idea for the client itself to select grayN (or greyN) symbols to ensure that adjacent graphics are distinct. More importantly, because actual colors vary somewhat from one display to another, the database gives system administrators the opportunity to tweak color values appropriately—a process sometimes obscurely termed "gamma correction." Using color names from rgb.txt, then, helps ensure that ForestGreen really looks as lushly green as it should, even though the actual RGB values for that color may differ from one system to another.

ALLOCATING COLORS

Each entry in a colormap is called a *colorcell*. Each colorcell can be one of two types— read-only, or read-write. A read-only colorcell is *sharable* between two or more clients. A read-write colorcell is usable only by the client that allocates the cell. As its name implies, a read-write colorcell is changeable, but only by the allocating client. A read-only colorcell is allocated similarly by a client but can be shared by multiple clients. Once allocated, a read-only colorcell can never be changed. The only way to change a read-only colorcell is to delete it, allocate a new color, and redraw the client's graphics.

Many programmers assume that read-write colorcells are preferable because they can be easily altered, but this is generally not so. Because read-write colorcells cannot be shared among clients, they use up valuable space in the colormap and might cause the system to run out of colors for new applications. Also, true-color 24-bit systems that have only a single read-only hardware colormap can allocate only read-only, sharable colorcells. The only real advantage in using a read-write colorcell is that a client can instantly alter onscreen colors simply by changing the colorcell's RGB values. This is why read-write colorcells are not sharable—colorful chaos would likely result if one client could instantly alter colors shared by other clients.

Read-only colorcells, which a client can allocate but not change, help make more colors available to multiple clients. For example, if a client allocates the color PapayaWhip—a tasty sounding color—the X server returns a colormap index for that color that is the same for all clients using this hue. This is another good reason for specifying colors by name instead of by RGB value—you are more likely to share a named colorcell than one specified by its component pixel hues, although some X servers can return shared colorcells that are close matches to those requested.

In any case, to allocate a colorcell, a client calls one of two Xlib functions: XAllocColor() or XAllocNamedColor(). The result is inserted into a graphics context (GC) and then used to paint graphics or text using the color. It can also be used to create a pixmap for displaying color images (more on that in the section "Fill Rules and Styles" near the end of this chapter). Listing 28.1, xcolor.cpp, shows the basic technique for allocating colorcells using XAllocNamedColor().

LISTING 28.1   XCOLOR.CPP (PARTIAL)

```
Display *display;        // X server display structure

int main()
{
  // Attempt to establish communications with the X Server
//
  display = XOpenDisplay(NULL);
  if (display == NULL) {
    cerr << "Failure connecting to X Server";
    exit(1);
  }

  // Get the most basic of colors (black and white)
  //
  int intBlackColor, intWhiteColor;
  intBlackColor = BlackPixel(display, DefaultScreen(display));
  intWhiteColor = WhitePixel(display, DefaultScreen(display));
  // Create variables needed for XAllocNamedColor()
  //
  Colormap colormap = DefaultColormap(display, intScreenNum);
  char * colorname = "ForestGreen";
  XColor screenColor, exactColor;

  // Allocate color. Exit if operation fails.
  //
  if (!XAllocNamedColor(display, colormap, colorname,
                        &screenColor, &exactColor)) {
    cerr << "Cannot allocate color " << colorname << endl;
```

```
    exit(1);
  }

  // Create a graphics context for our window
  //
  XGCValues gc_values;
  unsigned long gc_mask = GCForeground | GCLineWidth;
  gc_values.foreground = screenColor.pixel;
  gc_values.line_width = 3;
  GC gc = XCreateGC(display, win, gc_mask, &gc_values);
  // Map the window to the display
  // Window is visible when first Expose event is received
  //
  XMapWindow(display, win);
...
}
```

The sample xcolor.cpp program is a copy of xsketch.cpp from the Chapter 27, "Controlling Xlib Input and Output," but it lets you sketch in colored lines by clicking and dragging the mouse. The program might fail if you do not have a color display, but in a moment I explain the steps needed to make it work on any X system, even those with a single bit plane display.

After establishing communications with the X server—the first job in any client application—the program uses the `BlackPixel()` and `WhitePixel()` macros to obtain the simplest color values available on all systems. These steps are the same as described in Chapters 26 and 27—however, you should still perform these duties in case the client is run on a system with a monochrome screen.

To allocate a color, `ForestGreen` in the listing, the program calls `XAllocateNamedColor()` using five arguments. One of the arguments is the `display` pointer already obtained. The other four are declared as follows:

```
Colormap colormap = DefaultColormap(display, intScreenNum);
char * colorname = "ForestGreen";
XColor screenColor, exactColor;
```

Obtain the default `Colormap` for the given display and screen number (found by the `DefaultScreen()` macro). This value is treated similarly to a `Window` ID integer value but is actually a pointer to the X server's colormap structure. However, you never use a `Colormap` as an actual pointer. Also define the name of the color you want, using one of the names from the rgb.txt database. Try some other names from Table 28.1 here to see their effects on your system. The two `XColor` variables hold the results from `XAllocNamedColor()`, called as follows:

```
if (!XAllocNamedColor(display, colormap, colorname,
                      &screenColor, &exactColor)) {
  cerr << "Cannot allocate color " << colorname << endl;
  exit(1);
}
```

The function returns a true or false status value indicating whether the named color can be allocated a colorcell in the colormap. If the function returns true, the two variables screenColor and exactColor are filled in with values that the program can use to display colored graphics. The first value is most likely a shared pixel value for the closest matching color the X server could find. The exactColor represents the exact RGB values for the requested color. You may use either return value, but the first may produce more consistent results.

> **Note**
>
> The color selection techniques here are for demonstration purposes, and production software shouldn't set colors so rigidly. Instead, your program should display as many available colors as possible and let users choose the actual colors they want.

Ending the program if XAllocNamedColor() fails is, of course, a drastic measure. In most cases, your program probably should take other actions if the function returns false— selecting alternate colors that are more likely to be available (green instead of ForestGreen, for instance). Remember that you can always fall back on the BlackPixel() and WhitePixel() macros. These values work even on single-plane monochrome systems, so in the worst possible case, if XAllocNamedColor() fails, a well-written X client should simply display its graphics in black and white. Only if this is impractical should the program end if it cannot allocate a requested color.

After calling XAllocNamedColor() successfully, you can use the returned pixel value. Basically, there are two ways to use an allocated color. You can specify the returned pixel value in creating a window with the XCreateSimpleWindow() or XCreateWindow() functions, or you can set the foreground color in a graphics context. The sample program uses the latter technique to create a GC using these statements:

```
XGCValues gc_values;
unsigned long gc_mask = GCForeground | GCLineWidth;
gc_values.foreground = screenColor.pixel;
gc_values.line_width = 3;
GC gc = XCreateGC(display, win, gc_mask, &gc_values);
```

Those statements show the "hard way" of creating a GC using an XGCValues structure and an associated bit mask (gc_mask) that tells XCreateGC which structure members to override from their default values. In this case, we want to set the foreground color and line width, indicated by the bit masks GCForeground and GCLineWidth. The screenColor.pixel member, initialized by the earlier call to XAllocNamedColor(), selects the foreground color for subsequent graphics that use this GC.

Alternatively, if the GC is already created, you can change the foreground color by calling XSetForeground() like this:

```
XSetForeground(display, gc, screenColor.pixel);
```

You might use this method to let users select colors from a menu or a toolbar of colored buttons. Although the sample program allocates only a single color, most clients probably need several allocated pixel values. To do that, simply create an array of XColor structures and allocate each one by calling XAllocNamedColor(). Xlib declares the XColor structure as follows:

```
typedef struct {
  unsigned long pixel;
  unsigned short red, green, blue;
  char flags;   // do_red, do_green, do_blue
  char pad;
} XColor;
```

Normally, the pixel member in an XColor structure is all you need to save and use to draw graphics in allocated colors. The red, green, and blue values represent the RGB components of the allocated colorcell. Never assume, however, that symbolic color names (or even the word "color") have any relation to actual colors that users see. The flags field in an XColor structure is significant only for read-write colorcells to indicate which of the RGB components to change. In the color techniques described here, the flags field is meaningless. The final char member pad presumably fills the XColor structure to an even number of bytes.

Note

An XColor structure's red, green, and blue members represent color levels using unsigned int values from 0 to 65535. This is so even if the actual values in a colorcell are in the range of 0 to 255. XColor member values are scaled in the X server according to the hardware's and colormap's needs.

COLORING SCALED GRAPHICS

To demonstrate how to draw graphics using multiple colors, Listing 28.2, xrainbow.cpp, paints a colorful rainbow in a window. The program also demonstrates the important technique of scaling graphics to fit in a window regardless of its size. Using this method, when users resize a window, its contents adjust automatically to fit within the new window boundaries. Figure 28.2 shows the program's window, unfortunately not as colorful here as it is on your screen (assuming you have a color display, that is).

Figure 28.2
A colorful rainbow demonstrates how to paint graphics in multiple colors and also how to scale graphics to fit inside a window's boundaries.

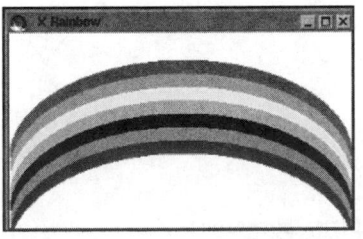

PART
VI

CH
28

LISTING 28.2   XRAINBOW.CPP (PARTIAL)

```
Display *display;      // X server display structure

#define MAXCOLORS 7    // Number of colors in following arrays

char *Roy_G_Biv[] = {
```

continues

LISTING 28.2 CONTINUED

```cpp
  "Red",
  "Orange",
  "Yellow",
  "Green",
  "Blue",
  "Violet",        // Indigo
  "DarkViolet"     // Violet
};

unsigned long colors[ MAXCOLORS ];
void GetColors(unsigned long intDefaultColor);
void PaintRainbow(Window win, GC gc,
int winWidth, int winHeight);

int main()
{
  // Attempt to establish communications with the X Server
//
  display = XOpenDisplay(NULL);
  if (display == NULL) {
    cerr << "Failure connecting to X Server";
    exit(1);
  }

...

  // Fill global colors array using intBlackColor for the
  // default color if any allocation fails.
  //
  GetColors(intBlackColor);
  // Specify the types of events we want to receive
  //
  XSelectInput(display, win,
    ExposureMask | KeyPressMask | StructureNotifyMask);
  // The event loop.
  //
  bool done = false;
  XEvent event;
  while (!done) {
    XNextEvent(display, &event);
    switch (event.type) {
    case Expose:
      if (event.xexpose.count == 0) {
        XClearWindow(display, win);
        PaintRainbow(win, gc, intWidth, intHeight);
      }
      break;
    case ConfigureNotify:
      intWidth = event.xconfigure.width;
      intHeight = event.xconfigure.height;
      break;
    case KeyPress:
      cout << "Keypress detected" << endl;
      done = true;   // Exit on any keypress
      break;
    }
```

```
  }

  // Disconnect X server connection and exit.
  // (Program may never get to here)
  //
  XCloseDisplay(display);
  return 0;
}

// Allocate global colors array using intDefaultColor if a
// named color cannot be allocated for any reason.
void GetColors(unsigned long intDefaultColor)
{
  Colormap colormap =
    DefaultColormap(display, DefaultScreen(display));
  XColor screenColor, exactColor;

  for (int i = 0; i < MAXCOLORS; i++) {
    if (!XAllocNamedColor(display, colormap, Roy_G_Biv[i],
                          &screenColor, &exactColor)) {
      cerr << "Color " << Roy_G_Biv[i]
           << " unavailable" << endl;
      cerr << "using 'black' in its place." << endl;
      colors[i] = intDefaultColor;
    } else {
      colors[i] = screenColor.pixel;
    }
  }
}

// Paint a colorful (we hope) rainbow in the window.
void PaintRainbow(Window win, GC gc,
  int winWidth, int winHeight)
{
  int x, y;
  unsigned int width, height;
  int angle1, angle2;
  int fudge = 10;        // A little "fudge" factor

  width = winWidth;
  height = winHeight / MAXCOLORS;
  angle1 = 0;                // 3 o'clock
  angle2 = 180 * 64;         // 9 o'clock
  x = 0;
  y = height;
  for (int i = 0; i < MAXCOLORS; i++) {
    XSetForeground(display, gc, colors[i]);
    XFillArc(display, win, gc, x, y,
      width, height * MAXCOLORS, angle1, angle2);
    y += (height / MAXCOLORS) + fudge;
  }
  XSetForeground(display, gc,
    WhitePixel(display, DefaultScreen(display)));
  XFillArc(display, win, gc, x, y,
    width, height * MAXCOLORS, angle1, angle2);
}
```

There are numerous ways to allocate multiple colors in an X client, but one of the most versatile is shown here. First, create an array of color name strings as in the listing. In this case, I named the array Roy_G_Biv in honor of the easily remembered acronym that stands for the basic colors of the rainbow: red, orange, yellow, green, blue, indigo, and violet. Unfortunately, however, X does not define Indigo, and the stock Violet color is too light—so I substituted two colors, Violet and DarkViolet, for the array's last two color names.

Along with the array of color name strings, also define an array of unsigned long values, one for each color:

```
unsigned long colors[ MAXCOLORS ];
```

You could instead create an array of XColor objects if you need access to other fields in that structure, but here we need to save only the pixel values returned by XAllocNamedColor(). After connecting to the X server, the sample program calls a local function, GetColors(), to fill the colors array. This function (located near the end of the listing) calls XAllocNamedColor() for each color-name string and assigns the returned pixel value to the colors array. If any colors cannot be allocated, the program assigns a default color (black in this case). This is probably inadequate in this example because on a monochrome system, if all colors default to black, the results won't look much like a rainbow. However, this just points out one of the difficulties in using color under X. It's never possible to predict the exact outcome of color graphics, and a little guesswork plus some faith is always necessary.

Because we are using color names, however, the program should work on most systems. To actually paint the rainbow, the program calls another local function, PaintRainbow(), when it receives an Expose event. The function merely paints half moons by calling the Xlib graphics primitive function XFillArc() with arguments set to fill the window with successive arcs, simulating a rainbow. The last call to XFillArc() erases the final half moon to the window's background color, completing the illusion. Notice how XSetForeground() assigns each pixel value from the colors array before drawing the arc shapes.

Tip

For online information on XFillArc(), type *info XFillArc*.

The xrainbow.cpp program also demonstrates how to scale graphics to fit the window regardless of its size. To see how this feature works, run the program and change the window's size. No matter how small or large you make the window, the rainbow fills it from corner to corner. (Sorry, but there's no pot of gold at either end!)

Scaling graphics isn't difficult as long as you design your drawing routines to calculate positions and other values based on the window's size. In this case, two integer variables, intWidth and intHeight, initialized before the window is created, record the window's size in pixels. To update these variables when the user resizes the window, add StructureNotifyMask to the event types passed to XSelectInput() before the program enters the event loop. Then, in the event loop, add a case for a ConfigureNotify event programmed like this:

```
case ConfigureNotify:
  intWidth = event.xconfigure.width;
  intHeight = event.xconfigure.height;
  break;
```

That's usually all you need to do to scale graphics—provided, that is, your graphics are drawn relative to window's size. You don't have to redraw graphics in response to this event. Just draw them as usual in response to an Expose event.

> **Note**
>
> Attempts to prevent users from resizing a window are strongly discouraged. It takes a little more work to scale graphics as described here, but users will appreciate your efforts in keeping your X applications as unrestrictive as possible.

ATOMIC ENERGY

Chapter 26, "Introducing X Programming," mentioned the topic of *atoms*. You may not need to use atoms in every application, but they are highly useful for specifying certain types of information and also for communicating between clients. The following sections explain how to create and use atoms.

SETTING AND GETTING ATOMS

In X programming, a *property* is a synonym for an *atom*. You have already seen one such atom, used to suggest a window title to the window manager. To assign a string for this purpose, programs such as xrainbow.cpp (refer to Listing 28.2) execute the following statement:

```
XStoreName(display, win, "X Rainbow");
```

That stores a copy of the specified string in the X server for this window and display. The string is in this case identified by the atomic symbol XA_WM_NAME. Other atomic symbols, all of which are capitalized beginning with XA, are found in the file Xatom.h in standard X11 include path. A specific string such as the suggested window title here is associated with its atomic symbol *and* a window ID; therefore, each window can have its own identically named atoms.

> **Note**
>
> As mentioned in the preceding chapters, a window title identified by the XA_WM_NAME atom is merely a suggestion or "hint" to the window manager. There is no guarantee that the window manager will actually display the title at any specific location, or at all. (Any window manager worth using, however, ought to at least make an attempt to display the window's title.)

Given any Window ID, you can obtain the name assigned to that window by calling XFetchName(). Use programming such as this (assume win is the Window ID):

```
char *wname = NULL;
if (XFetchName(display, win, &wname))
  cout << "Name is " << wname << endl;
```

XStoreName() and XFetchName() are called *convenience functions* because they translate to other Xlib function calls. XStoreName(), for example, calls XSetWMName(), which you also can use to set the window's name. XSetWMName() in turn calls XSetTextProperty(). Calling these lower-level functions is complicated by the need to construct an object of the Xlib structure, XTextProperty. Doing this requires calling another function, XStringListToTextProperty().

The reason for all this complexity is because XTextProperty is designed to work with a variety of data sizes as might exist on various host computers running X servers. Because the X server might need to communicate with clients also running on different machines over a network, atomic properties must be carefully managed to ensure that they are in the expected forms. In any event, you can usually use the techniques demonstrated in the next program to assign properties using an XTextProperty structure. The program in Listing 28.3, xatom.cpp, is the same as the xwelcome.cpp program in Chapter 26, "Introducing X Programming," but calls XSetWMName() to assign the window title. For demonstration, the program also calls XGetWMName() to retrieve the window's name property. The listing shows only the relevant statements.

LISTING 28.3   XATOM.CPP (PARTIAL)

```
//  XStoreName(display, win, "Easy-Method Window Title");
XTextProperty nameProp;    // Window name property
char *wname = "Window Name set by XSetWMName()";
int numStrings = 1;  // Only one string in above "list"
if (!XStringListToTextProperty(
    &wname, numStrings, &nameProp)) {
  cerr << "Unable to allocate XTextProperty" << endl;
  exit(1);
}
XSetWMName(display, win, &nameProp);
```

The comment at the head of the listing shows the easy way to assign the window's title property. To use the XSetWMName() function to do the same requires initializing an XTextProperty structure for one or more strings. You may use a list of strings or just one as demonstrated here. Call XStringListToTextProperty() as shown with three arguments:

- The address of the first string in the list (or the only one as in this case)
- The number of strings in the list
- The address of an XTextProperty structure

If the function returns zero (false), then the XTextProperty structure couldn't be initialized, and it's your choice what to do. If this is in the program's early stages, a failure here might indicate a severe memory shortage, or some other X server problem, and it's likely that the program won't be able to proceed. After initializing the XTextProperty structure, call XSetWMName() to assign the atom.

Note

> Although it is simpler to call XStoreName() to set the window title, you'll use the alternate method with other types of atoms. Type **info XSetTextProperty** for online information about this topic. Also try **info XSetWMProperties** for information on setting other types of window property atoms.

INTER-CLIENT COMMUNICATION

Atoms are the only reliable method for one client to communicate with another. Although you might be tempted to use other techniques, keep in mind that, in a networked environment, two clients might run on physically separated machines, possibly of different types. It isn't safe to use temporary files even for inter-client communications. Instead, consider using atom properties to transmit information. If the atom is associated with the root window, then you can be sure it is available to all clients running on the user's X server.

One of the best and easiest ways to pass information between clients is to use one of the eight *cut buffers* provided by the X server. A cut buffer—otherwise known as the Clipboard—is an atom property with the names XA_CUT_BUFFER0 through XA_CUT_BUFFER7. Most clients use the first cut buffer to transfer text information between them. Listing 28.4, xcut.cpp, demonstrates how a client can be notified when this cut buffer changes and also how to retrieve the buffer's contents.

Note

> Compile xcut by typing **make**, and then run the program. Keeping the original terminal window visible, switch to another terminal window (open a second one if necessary) and select text using the mouse. This notifies the xcut.cpp demonstration that one of the cut buffer atoms has changed. To verify that the client correctly picks up this information, the demonstration program echoes the buffered text in the terminal window. Note to Caldera Linux users: This doesn't seem to work properly with the KDE desktop KVT terminal, but it does work using Xterm.

LISTING 28.4   XCUT.CPP (PARTIAL)

```
// Specify the types of events we want to receive
//
XSelectInput(display, win,
ExposureMask | KeyPressMask | PropertyChangeMask );
XSelectInput(display, DefaultRootWindow(display),
PropertyChangeMask);

// The event loop
//
bool done = false;
XEvent event;
int nbytes = 0;
char *s = NULL;
while (!done) {
```

continues

PART

VI

CH

28

LISTING 28.4   CONTINUED

```
  XNextEvent(display, &event);
  switch (event.type) {
  case Expose:
    cout << "Expose event received" << endl;
    break;
  case PropertyNotify:
    cout << "PropertyNotify event" << endl;
    s = XFetchBytes(display, &nbytes);
    if (s != NULL && nbytes > 0) {
      cout << "Property changed: " << s << endl;
      XFree(s);
    }
    break;
  case KeyPress:
    cout << "Keypress detected" << endl;
    done = true;   // Exit on any keypress
    break;
  }
}
```

For a client to be notified that a cut buffer has been changed, it is necessary to specify the PropertyChangeMask for the root window. The root window owns the cut buffer atoms, so adding PropertyChangeMask to our window's events is alone not sufficient. Apparently, it doesn't hurt to select this event mask for the root and client windows, and this seems to ensure that the event is generated initially when the window comes into being. But if you don't want to do that, you may delete PropertyChangeMask from the first call to XSelectInput().

Note

You don't have to elect notification of a change to a cut buffer. Alternatively, you can access a cut buffer using the same techniques shown here in response to another type of event—for example, a mouse button click or a keypress. You might, however, want to use PropertyChangeMask to set a flag that indicates information is newly available in a cut buffer. Typically, a client does this to enable a Paste menu command or button, often called a Yank command in UNIX.

The switch case for the PropertyNotify event is selected when the user causes data to be inserted into the cut buffer. The program calls XFetchBytes() to retrieve the information—this always uses the first buffer identified as XA_CUT_BUFFER0. To use the other cut buffers, you can call the similar XFetchBuffer() function. To insert data into a buffer, call XStoreBytes() or XStoreBuffer().

Always call XFree() as shown in the sample program to delete string data returned by XFetchBytes() or XFetchBuffer(). This is a copy of the information held in the server, so deleting it does not prevent it from being used again.

LINE AND FILL STYLES

All graphics output in an X client application takes place in reference to a graphics context, or GC. This and the preceding two chapters show numerous examples of creating and using simple GCs, but this section explains some other more advanced features that you will undoubtedly want to use. With a GC, you can select the style of lines and also set a pixmap pattern to use for filled objects such as arcs and rectangles.

LINE WIDTH AND STYLE

The X server is capable of drawing lines in any practical width and in a variety of styles. Line styles affect not only straight lines but also the outlines of other shapes, so these concepts come into play in nearly every graphics program. Listing 28.5, xdash.cpp, shows the easiest way to create solid and dashed lines. The program also shows one way to change the width of dashes—an obscure feature that is neither obvious nor well explained in many tutorials. Figure 28.3 shows the program's window. (The third line's background color might or might not be visible on this page, but it should be a pale yellow onscreen.)

Figure 28.3
Sample xdash.cpp window showing three line styles: `LineSolid`, `LineOnOffDash`, and `LineDoubleDash`.

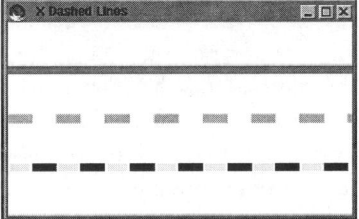

LISTING 28.5   XDASH.CPP (PARTIAL)

```
// Create a graphics context for our window
//
XGCValues gc_values;
unsigned long gc_mask = GCDashList;
gc_values.dashes = 24;   // Width of dashes and spaces
GC gc = XCreateGC(display, win, gc_mask, &gc_values);

// Paint lines in different styles
void PaintLines(Window win, GC gc,
  int winWidth, int winHeight)
{
  int x1, y1, x2, y2;
  unsigned int lineWidth = 8;

  x1 = 0;;
  y1 = lineWidth * 6;
  x2 = winWidth;
  y2 = y1;

  XSetForeground(display, gc, colors[0]);
```

PART
VI
CH
28

continues

LISTING 28.5 CONTINUED

```
XSetLineAttributes(display, gc,
lineWidth, LineSolid, CapButt, JoinBevel);
XDrawLine(display, win, gc, x1, y1, x2, y2);
y1 += (lineWidth * 6);
y2 = y1;

XSetForeground(display, gc, colors[1]);
XSetLineAttributes(display, gc,
lineWidth, LineOnOffDash, CapButt, JoinBevel);
XDrawLine(display, win, gc, x1, y1, x2, y2);
y1 += (lineWidth * 6);
y2 = y1;

XSetForeground(display, gc, colors[2]);
XSetLineAttributes(display, gc,
lineWidth, LineDoubleDash, CapButt, JoinBevel);
XDrawLine(display, win, gc, x1, y1, x2, y2);
}
```

The listing for xdash.cpp starts with the statements from main() needed to change the width of dashes and the spaces between them for line styles LineOnOffDash and LineDoubleDash. Naturally, this change doesn't affect solid lines of type LineSolid. The dashes field in the XGCValues structure is of type char, so the width of a dash is apparently limited to 255 pixels using this method. Use the mask GCDashList to inform XCreateGC() to use the setting assigned to the dashes field. I don't know why this mask value has the word *List* in it—dash widths set using this method are a single char value, not a list of values.

Later in the program is a local function, PaintLines(), listed in full here. This function changes the color of each line using the method and values from the xrainbow.cpp program earlier in this chapter (see Listing 28.2). After calling XSetForeground() to select the line's color, the program calls XSetLineAttributes() to select the line's style. The possible styles are as follows:

- lineWidth This can be any integer value including zero.*
- lineStyle This can be LineSolid, LineOnOffDash, or LineDoubleDash. The sample program's window displays lines in each style in that order.
- capStyle This value affects the style of line endings and can be any of the values CapNotLast, CapButt, CapRound, or CapProjecting. In general, the line-end style is more important with closed shapes such as rectangles.
- joinStyle This value specifies how the ends of two lines are combined when they meet in closed shapes. The value can be one of the constants JoinMiter, JoinRound, or JoinBevel.

*Note: A lineWidth of zero selects a so-called "fast" line of one pixel in width that may not be erasable by overdrawing and that may appear differently depending on the direction the line is drawn. Unless you must use fast lines—for example, as temporary outlines for complex shapes—it's usually best to set lineWidth to 1 or greater.

It's also possible to customize a dashed line's appearance, similar to the way a word processor lets you select tab spacings. Basically, to do this, you need to provide a list of dash and space width values and call the Xlib XSetDashes() function to insert this information into a GC before drawing your lines. Enter *info XSetDashes* for more information about this topic.

FILL RULES AND STYLES

Unlike with many graphics libraries, even complex shapes such as filled polygons are drawn by the X server, not by code linked to the client application. Although accessed through Xlib function calls, graphics primitives are intrinsic properties of X. The importance of this feature might not be realized until you consider that your client application can run on a wide range of hardware without requiring linking to system-dependent object code.

Even the most complex of graphical operations such as filling a polygon with a color pixmap are handled in the X server. The next two programs (see Listings 28.6 and 28.7) demonstrate these features and explain some other options you can select to fine-tune your program's graphical output.

Listing 28.6, xfill.cpp, displays polygons filled with solid colors. The polygon coordinates and colors are selected at random using the standard C library's random() function. Run the program and click the mouse inside the window to display a new polygon in one of several possible colors. Figure 28.4 shows a sample of the program's output.

Figure 28.4
The xfill.cpp program displays polygons filled with solid colors.

LISTING 28.6   XFILL.CPP (PARTIAL)

```
#define MAXPOINTS 12 // Num XPoint objects in points array
XPoint points[ MAXPOINTS ];
unsigned long polyColor;

void GetColors(unsigned long intDefaultColor);
void GetPoints(int winWidth, int winHeight);
void Paint(Window win, GC gc, int winWidth, int winHeight);

int main()
{
  srandom( time(NULL) );  // Seed random generator

  ...
```

PART

VI

CH

28

continues

LISTING 28.6 CONTINUED

```
    // Fill global colors array using intBlackColor for the
    // default color if any allocation fails.
    //
    GetColors(intBlackColor);

    // Fill global points array with random coordinates
    //
    GetPoints(intWidth, intHeight);  // Also sets polyColor

...

    // The event loop.
    //
    bool done = false;
    XEvent event;
    while (!done) {
      XNextEvent(display, &event);
      switch (event.type) {
      case Expose:
        if (event.xexpose.count == 0) {
          XClearWindow(display, win);
          Paint(win, gc, intWidth, intHeight);
        }
        break;
      case ConfigureNotify:
        intWidth = event.xconfigure.width;
        intHeight = event.xconfigure.height;
        break;
      case ButtonPress:
        GetPoints(intWidth, intHeight);
        XClearWindow(display, win);
        Paint(win, gc, intWidth, intHeight);
        break;
      case KeyPress:
        cout << "Keypress detected" << endl;
        done = true;   // Exit on any keypress
        break;
      }
    }

    // Disconnect X server connection and exit.
    // (Program may never get to here)
    //
    XCloseDisplay(display);
    return 0;
}

...

// Fill global points array with random coordinate values
void GetPoints(int winWidth, int winHeight)
{
  for (int i = 0; i < MAXPOINTS; i++) {
```

```
      points[i].x = random() % winWidth;
      points[i].y = random() % winHeight;
    }
    int colorIndex = random() % MAXCOLORS;
    polyColor = colors[colorIndex];

    // Display coordinate values in the terminal window
    // for debugging. You can remove these statements.
    //
    cout << endl;
    cout << "Color == " << Roy_G_Biv[colorIndex] << endl;
    cout << "GetPoints() points[]:" << endl;
    for (int i = 0; i < MAXPOINTS; i++) {
      cout << "x:" << points[i].x << ", y:"
           << points[i].y << endl;
    }
}

// Paint a colorful polygon
void Paint(Window win, GC gc, int winWidth, int winHeight)
{
  XSetForeground(display, gc, polyColor);
  XSetFillRule(display, gc, EvenOddRule);
  XSetFillStyle(display, gc, FillSolid);
  XFillPolygon(display, win, gc, points, MAXPOINTS,
    Nonconvex, CoordModeOrigin);
}
```

The xfill.cpp program initializes a `colors` array using the same values as in xrainbow.cpp (refer to Listing 28.2). Local function `GetPoints()` fills another array of `XPoint` structures with coordinate values selected at random and constrained to the window's width and height. This tends to make the finished polygon fill the window (more or less). The `GetPoints()` function also assigns a color selected at random to the global `polyColor` variable. For debugging purposes, the function writes the selected color and generated coordinate values to the terminal window. To see this output, arrange the program's window and the terminal so that you can see both. For each polygon, the terminal displays text such as the following:

```
Color == Green
GetPoints() points[]:
x:323, y:15
...
x:142, y:29
```

Xlib defines as follows the `XPoint` structure stored in the program's `points` array. You can use this structure to define any coordinate or an array of coordinates as in the sample program:

```
typedef struct {
  short x, y;
} XPoint;
```

To draw and fill a polygon using an array of XPoint structures, local function Paint() begins with three preparatory statements:

```
XSetForeground(display, gc, polyColor);
XSetFillRule(display, gc, EvenOddRule);
XSetFillStyle(display, gc, FillSolid);
```

The GC's foreground in this case specifies the solid color used to paint the polygon's interior. The foreground color, however, is valid only if the GC's fill style is set to FillSolid, done here in the third statement's call to XSetFillStyle(). The second statement sets the GC's fill rule to EvenOddRule, although this is the default setting. When filling polygons where lines cross, this rule determines whether an enclosed area is part of the pattern or belongs to the background. The other possible rule is WindingRule, which fills overlapping areas. (Change the fill rule to WindingRule to see the difference in the sample program.)

The GC's fill style can be one of four values (these apply to all filled shapes, not just polygons):

- FillSolid   This style uses the GC's foreground color to fill the shape.
- FillStippled   This style replicates a single-plane bitmap using the foreground color to fill the shape for each bit that is set to 1 in the bitmap.
- FillOpaqueStippled   This style is the same as FillStippled but also uses the GC's background color to paint bits set to 0 in the bitmap.
- FillTiled   This style replicates a pixmap of the screen's depth to fill the shape. (See Listing 28.7, xpatt.cpp, later in this section for an example of this style.)

Keep in mind that the GC's fill rule and style control the outcome of the XFillPolygon() function (and other filled shapes). To select fill rules and styles, first initialize the GC and then pass it to the graphics function, as the local Paint() function demonstrates with its final statement:

```
XFillPolygon(display, win, gc, points, MAXPOINTS,
  Nonconvex, CoordModeOrigin);
```

To the function, pass the global display pointer, Window ID, GC (after configuring it as described), a pointer to an array of XPoint objects, and the number of objects in that array. The final two arguments select two more features available for drawing and filling polygons. The first of these values is the polygon's *shape*, which can be one of three symbols: Complex, Convex, or Nonconvex. These values are merely hints to the X server that may or may not improve display performance, and only if the server takes the hint to use different drawing algorithms based on the type of polygon. These values seem to produce the same effects on my system, but in a critical application, you might want to give users the option to select one of these settings.

The last argument passed to XFillPolygon() selects the *mode* used to connect its XPoint coordinates. This can be one of the two values, which have somewhat misleading names:

- CoordModeOrigin   Considers all XPoint coordinate values to be relative to the window's origin.

■ CoordModePrevious Considers all XPoint coordinate values except the first to be relative to the preceding XPoint object.

The sample program uses the first setting so that all XPoint values are relative to the window's origin. If you use the second mode setting, the drawing "walks" off the screen because each new point except for the first is considered to be relative to the previous one. In other words, with the setting CoordModePrevious, if point A is (100, 100) and B is (50, 50), then B is actually at (150, 150) relative to the window. Normally, you should use CoordModeOrigin to connect polygon lines.

Another way to fill a polygon is to use a pixmap to fill the shape's interior with a pattern. This requires some additional techniques that are useful in a variety of graphical programs. For example, you might use these methods to create a button with a shaded surface. Listing 28.7, xpatt.cpp, demonstrates how to load and use a pixmap to paint a filled polygon with background colors selected at random. As with the previous example (Listing 28.6), run xpatt.cpp and click the mouse pointer in the window to change the image. The pixmap is created from the same bitmap image from the xtile.cpp program in Chapter 27, "Controlling Xlib Input and Output." Figure 28.5 shows a sample of the program's output.

Figure 28.5
The xpatt.cpp program displays polygons filled with a pixmap image and a background color selected at random.

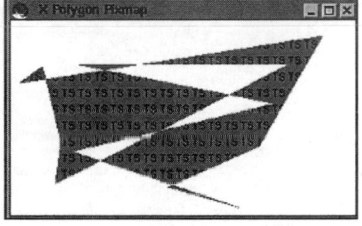

LISTING 28.7   XPATT.CPP (PARTIAL)

```
#define MAXPOINTS 12   // Num XPoint objects in points array
XPoint points[ MAXPOINTS ];
unsigned long polyColor;
unsigned int bmWidth, bmHeight; // Bitmap width and height
unsigned char * bitmap;         // Pointer to raw bitmap data
Pixmap pixmap;                  // Pixmap of same screen depth

void GetColors(unsigned long intDefaultColor);
void GetPoints(Window win, int winWidth, int winHeight);
void Paint(Window win, GC gc, int winWidth, int winHeight);

int main()
{
  srandom( time(NULL) );  // Seed random generator

...

  // Load bitmap from file for use as window background
```

continues

LISTING 28.7 CONTINUED

```
//
int bmXhot, bmYhot;    // Bitmap hotspot (ignored)
int result = XReadBitmapFileData(
  "ts.xbm",
  &bmWidth, &bmHeight,
  &bitmap,
  &bmXhot, &bmYhot );
if (result != BitmapSuccess) {
  cerr << "Failed to open ts.bmp file" << endl;
  exit(1);
}

// Fill global colors array using intBlackColor for the
// default color if any allocation fails.
//
GetColors(intBlackColor);

// Fill global points array with random coordinates
//
GetPoints(win, intWidth, intHeight); // Also sets polyColor

// The event loop.
//
bool done = false;
XEvent event;
while (!done) {
  XNextEvent(display, &event);
  switch (event.type) {
  case Expose:
    if (event.xexpose.count == 0) {
      XClearWindow(display, win);
      Paint(win, gc, intWidth, intHeight);
    }
    break;
  case ConfigureNotify:
    intWidth = event.xconfigure.width;
    intHeight = event.xconfigure.height;
    break;
  case ButtonPress:
    XFreePixmap(display, pixmap);
    GetPoints(win, intWidth, intHeight);
    XClearWindow(display, win);
    Paint(win, gc, intWidth, intHeight);
    break;
  case KeyPress:
    cout << "Keypress detected" << endl;
    done = true;    // Exit on any keypress
    break;
  }
}

// Free the pixmap and bitmap structures
//
XFreePixmap(display, pixmap);
XFree(bitmap);
```

```
  // Disconnect X server connection and exit.
  // (Program may never get to here)
  //
  XCloseDisplay(display);
  return 0;
}

...

// Paint a colorful polygon
void Paint(Window win, GC gc, int winWidth, int winHeight)
{
  XSetTile(display, gc, pixmap);
  XSetFillRule(display, gc, EvenOddRule);
  XSetFillStyle(display, gc, FillTiled);
  XFillPolygon(display, win, gc, points, MAXPOINTS,
    Nonconvex, CoordModeOrigin);
}
```

To keep the program simple, I moved a few variables out of main() and made them global variables. The program uses the same color techniques as in xrainbow.cpp (see Listing 28.2) and xfill.cpp (see Listing 28.6) in this chapter. To read the bitmap image file ts.xbm, the program calls XReadBitmapFileData() as described for xtile.cpp (refer to Listing 27.12) in Chapter 27. Not shown in the book listing (but included in the file on the CD-ROM) is an additional step in local function GetPoints() that fills the global points array and selects a color at random for the global polyColor variable. The additional programming converts the loaded bitmap image to a pixmap suitable for use in filling a graphical shape:

```
int screenNum = DefaultScreen(display);
pixmap =
  XCreatePixmapFromBitmapData(
    display,
    win,
    (char *) bitmap,
    bmWidth, bmHeight,
    BlackPixel(display, screenNum),   // Foreground
    polyColor,                         // Background
    DefaultDepth(display, screenNum));
```

The pixmap variable is a global object of type Pixmap. This step performs two important jobs. It converts the single-plane bitmap, also called a *stipple*, into a structure that is configured for display on the client's screen. It also specifies the foreground and background colors to use for this image. Although black is used for the foreground, this could also be a color pixel value. Unlike when filling a polygon (or other shape) with a solid color, the pixmap itself determines the foreground and background pixel values, not the GC.

The final step in the process is to paint the polygon, carried out in local function Paint(). This function is similar to the one in xfill.cpp (see Listing 28.6), but in addition to selecting a fill rule and style, performs the additional step of specifying the pixmap for the GC:

```
XSetTile(display, gc, pixmap);
XSetFillStyle(display, gc, FillTiled);
```

PART

VI

CH

28

The style must be set to `FillTiled` in this case to use the pixmap for the polygon's background. Calling `XFillPolygon()` now paints the shape by tiling the pixmap in the specified colors according to the fill rule in effect.

> **Note**
>
> If the GC's style is set to `FillStippled` or `FillOpaqueStippled`, then the GC's bitmap would be used as set by `XSetStipple()`. This is similar to the way a pixmap is used, but because a stipple is a single-plane bitmap, the GC's foreground and background colors are used for the displayed pixel values.

SUMMARY

This chapter introduced some advanced X programming subjects such as colormaps and filled polygons. A colormap is a lookup table that translates video bit plane values into RGB colors or grayscale intensity levels. Due to the use of colormaps, X client applications can be written to work on a wide variety of hardware, from single bit plane monochrome systems to 24-bit true-color displays, which are fast becoming the norm, especially in Linux installations. The chapter ended with details on selecting line styles and filling polygons with solid colors and pixmap images.

For more information on subjects introduced in this chapter, turn to the following chapters:

- Chapter 26, "Introducing X Programming"
- Chapter 27, "Controlling Xlib Input and Output"

## CHAPTER 29

INTRODUCING THE V CLASS LIBRARY

Chapters 26–28 introduce X programming and show many of the features provided by the Xlib API for C and C++ programming. But even with all the information in those chapters, developing a finished X application complete with windows, menus, buttons, and other graphical features might still seem an impossible task.

While researching available tools for creating finished X software, I quickly realized how difficult it would be to provide a useful guide to X software development in only a few chapters. Fortunately, during a late-night session on the Internet, I stumbled across a class library called V that simplifies X programming while also serving as an excellent example of how, using C++ classes and object-oriented techniques, it's possible to greatly reduce software complexity. And it's hard to find any task more complex than X programming! What's more, V is cross-compatible with Microsoft Windows and OS/2. This means that, with the software on this book's CD-ROM and the information in this and the next chapter, you can write applications that are source-code compatible between Linux and Microsoft Windows.

Note

To compile a finished V application for another operating system such as Microsoft Windows, you need to acquire or purchase a suitable compiler and development system such as Borland C++ or Watcom C++. By basing your X application on V classes, your program's source files can be compiled for another platform without requiring any changes, but the resulting executable code files are not transferable from one system to another.

WHAT IS V?

V is a streamlined set of C++ classes that put an object-oriented face on X programming. Developed by Bruce E. Wampler, a well-known software developer, V is freely distributed under the GNU General Public License (see Appendix E, "Copyright Information—The GNU General Public License"). On Linux, V is based on 3D Athena widgets (also known as the Xaw3d toolkit), but V can also use other Xlib toolkits such as Open GL and Motif.

V is distributed in source code form and is provided on this book's CD-ROM. You can also download the latest version and any updates from the Web site: `http://www.objectcentral.com`. As of this writing, version 1.22 is the latest release. The following sections explain how to install and compile the library, and also introduce some of its directories and sample programs. After that, you develop an X application using V, complete with pull-down menus and dialog boxes.

Note

A visual development system is in the works for V as I write these words. See the aforementioned Web site for more information.

INSTALLATION

After obtaining V's distribution file either from this book's CD-ROM or by downloading from the Internet, follow the next steps to install and compile the library and its example programs. On the CD-ROM, V's distribution file is stored in the src/v directory in the file v-1_22_tar.gz. This is a "tarred and zipped" file that requires unpacking to install V's numerous files. Copy this file to your home or another directory and then enter the following commands to unpack the distribution file into an automatically created subdirectory named v:

```
$ cp v-1_22_tar.gz /home/yourname
$ cd /home/yourname
$ gunzip v-1_22_tar.gz
$ tar -xvf v-1_22_tar
```

The gunzip utility removes the .gz filename extension and expands the compressed file. The tar utility unpacks the individually archived files into various subdirectories. To inspect these filenames before unpacking, use the following command:

```
$ tar -tf v-1_22_tar
```

After tar finishes, you may remove the original distribution file. Next, you need to configure V for compiling under Linux. To do that, change to V's newly created home directory and look for a file named Config.mk. In this file are directory and other settings that V's Makefile needs for compiling the library. You might also want to read V's Readme file for additional installation notes.

V is provided in source code form—you must compile the library before you can use it. This isn't difficult to do if you are careful to use the correct Config.mk file. You'll find several sample configurations in the v/Configs subdirectory for different operating systems and compilers. The one for Linux and GNU C++ is named ConfigX.mk. Copy this file to the V home directory using the following commands:

```
$ cd /home/yourname/v
$ mv Config.mk Config.old
$ cp Configs/ConfigX.mk Config.mk
```

That copies ConfigX.mk and renames it Config.mk in V's home directory. (You don't have to preserve the original Config.mk file, but it's probably a good idea to do so in case something goes wrong.) Load Config.mk into your text editor and locate the following definitions:

```
ARCH = linux
TOOLKIT = Athena
X11RV = X11R6
DEBUG = no
DEVEL = no
```

Those settings should be correct for Linux and GNU C++. You can probably ignore other definitions in Config.mk, but you might want to glance at them just to see what's there. Change DEBUG to yes if you want to create a library with debugging information for the GNU debugger. This lets you trace into the library and learn more about how V works with the underlying tools and Xlib function calls. However, you don't need to do this when just getting started with V programming. When you are finished checking out Config.mk, save any changes and return to V's home directory. Enter this command to compile the library:

```
$ make
```

Be prepared to wait 5 or 10 minutes while the make utility compiles the library's numerous modules and example programs. You might notice some error messages if you do not have Open GL installed. Don't worry about these—you don't need Open GL to use V, and you can safely ignore the errors. When finished, you should see the message "library, test, utils, examples, and tutorial made."

> **Note**
>
> Compiling V does *not* install any files into /usr or other system directories. You do not have to be root (the superuser) to compile V. This also means you can remove V entirely from your system simply by deleting its home directory.

V's SAMPLE PROGRAMS

After compiling V, the first thing you'll want to do is try some of its sample programs. Change to the v/bin directory and run the executable files you find there. Figure 29.1 shows a sample of the ./tutappx tutorial application. Notice that the program comes complete with a menu bar, a toolbar of buttons, a status bar, a dialog window, and some other features. Table 29.1 lists all sample programs provided with V and shows where to find their source code files. (In part because V works on different platforms, the executable sample files don't always match their source directory names, so I prepared this table to simplify browsing through the examples.)

Figure 29.1
A sample V application, tutappx, complete with graphical features such as a pull-down menu bar, toolbar, and dialog window.

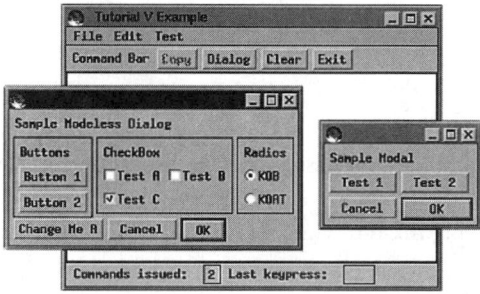

TABLE 29.1   V'S SAMPLE APPLICATIONS

Name	Source Path	Description
b2v	v/bmp2vbm	Bitmap to V Bitmap converter
icondemox	v/icons	Displays icons on button faces
protox	v/examp	Prototype suitable as a shell

Name	Source Path	Description
tutappx	v/tutor	Online documentation tutorial
vdrawexx	v/drawex	Simple color sketch example
vdrawx	v/draw	Object drawing demonstration
vgenx	v/appgen	V Application Generator
viconedx	v/iconed	Color icon editor
videx	v/vide	V integrated development environment
vtestlibx	v/tcot	V test program

Note

Using vdrawx, try opening the .drw sample graphics files in the directory v/draw. The vgenx V-application generator is described in more detail in the section "Creating a V Application." The videx program provides a kind of project manager for creating and maintaining V applications, but watch V's Internet Web site for a more sophisticated visual IDE currently being developed.

DOCUMENTATION

V comes with a well-written tutorial and reference to its many classes. I've tried in this chapter and in Chapter 30, "Developing X Software with V," not to duplicate V's online documentation but to supplement that information with a hands-on guide to programming X client applications. For a full understanding of the library, you need to read the online documentation as well as the information in this book.

Browse the online tutorial and reference now to become familiar with its layout. Use Netscape or another Web browser to open the file index.htm in the directory v/vrefman. Follow the hypertext links to other files.

CREATING A V APPLICATION

Now, let's create a V application and inspect some of its parts. The easiest way to start using V is to run its application generator, vgenx, which was written entirely using V. After you become a V expert, you might want to create new applications from scratch, or you can base them on one of the sample programs provided with V. But when just starting out, you'll find the application generator easy to use and especially helpful for defining various structures used for menus and dialog boxes that are otherwise tedious to create manually.

USING VGENX

The V application generator is named vgenx under UNIX and Linux, or vgen under Microsoft Windows. Run the program as follows to display the window in Figure 29.2:

```
$ cd v/bin
$ ./vgenx
```

Figure 29.2
The vgenx application generator window and Standard Application dialog box.

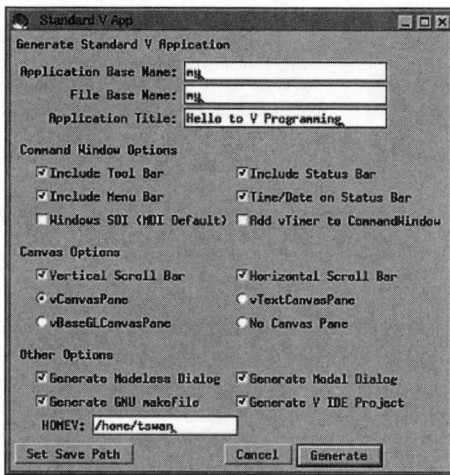

The figure shows the result of selecting the program's *Generate, Standard Application* command. Clicking the toolbar's *Standard App* button brings up the same dialog box. Disable the *Generator V IDE Project* check box. We won't use V's IDE here. Also change the application title string and elect to create a GNU Makefile. To follow along, use Figure 29.2 as a guide to select the generator's options. Your pathnames are probably different from mine.

In addition, you must specify the path where you installed V. The generator needs this path to create the application's Makefile. To set V's home path, click in the text-input box next to the label HOMEV and enter the base directory where you installed V. I entered /home/tswan/v as the pathname.

> **Tip**
>
> If you use the application generator often, consider modifying it to set V's home path according to your installation so that you don't need to change this setting for each new application you create.

Also click the *Set Save Path* button and select the directory where you want the generator to store the application's files and a Makefile. You can create this directory from a shell terminal window, or click the *mkdir* button in the file-open dialog box. In either case, be sure to set the save path before clicking the *Generate* button to create the application files. To follow along, click *Generate Now*. If you are not following along, you'll find the sample files I created in the src/c29/vmyapp directory on the CD-ROM.

> **Note**
>
> I modified the generated Makefile in src/c29/vmyapp to use the settings in the outer directory's src/c29 Config.mk file. This file assumes that you have installed V in your home directory. If not, edit Config.mk accordingly before trying to compile vmyapp.cpp using its associated Makefile.

EDITING THE GENERATED MAKEFILE

I've usually found it necessary to make small changes to the Makefile created by the V application generator vgenx. By default, this file is named something like makefile.my, so the first step is to rename it to Makefile using these commands:

```
$ cd /home/yourname/vmyapp
$ mv makefile.my Makefile
```

You can now try to compile the application by typing *make*, but if that doesn't work, you probably have to make some changes inside Makefile. If you are following along, load that file into your text editor and add "x" to the two include pathnames defined as follows:

```
VPATH  = $(HOMEV)/includex
CFLAGS = -O -I$(X11INC) -I$(HOMEV)/includex
```

Actually, the VPATH symbol appears to be defined but never used. These changes should allow you to type *make* to compile and link the generated application and then run it as follows:

```
$ make
...
$ ./my
```

Figure 29.3 shows the resulting window after I opened the sample program's modal and modeless dialog boxes (more on these topics in the following section, "Anatomy of a V Application"). The program is a complete X client application ready for modifying with your own menu commands and other features. Feel free to play with the menus—their commands simply display a verification window and don't do anything. The following section explains some of the generated files and classes to give an overview of how the generated V application is organized.

Figure 29.3
The sample application's modal and modeless dialog boxes.

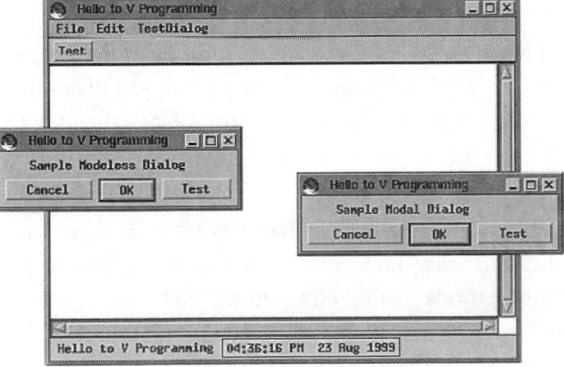

Note

Chapter 30, "Developing X Software with V," shows my own Makefile commands and sample programs for creating V applications without using vgenx.

ANATOMY OF A V APPLICATION

Browsing through the files created by V's application generator as described in the preceding sections gives a good overview of how a typical V application is organized. You don't need to memorize these notes—just read the following sections to gain a general feel for a V application's parts and pieces. To follow along, change to the src/c29/vmyapp directory and view the source files located there, or you can use the files from your own application if you created one.

GENERATED FILES

The V application generator typically creates several source code files plus associated header files. Depending on the options you select in the generator, it might create fewer or more files than listed here, but the main ones are as follows (each file has a corresponding header file named the same but ending in .h):

- **myapp.cpp**   This is the main application file. It derives a class, named myApp, from the vApp base class. All applications need one and only one similar main application class.

- **mycmdw.cpp**   This file derives a class, myCmdWindow, from the vCmdWindow base class. An object of this class represents the program's top-level window, called a *command window*. To this window are attached add-ons such as a menu bar, toolbar, and status line using static struct definitions. All V applications have at least one main command window class derived from vCmdWindow. However, a program may create as many windows as it needs.

- **mycnv.cpp**   This file defines the window's *canvas*. You might think of the canvas as the window's drawing surface or interior. To create your application's output, you modify various member functions in this file's class, myCanvasPane, derived from the vCanvasPane base class. Most V applications define at least one canvas object for each of their command windows.

- **mydlg.cpp**   This file derives the class, myDialog, from the vDialog base class. Using a struct defined in the mydlg.h header file, the result is a dialog box for user input. The dialog box is *modeless*, meaning that it does not prevent the user from executing other commands such as in the main command window's pull-down menus. Many V applications have at least one dialog box, but none is required.

- **mymdlg.cpp**   This file also creates a dialog box but declares the class, myModalDialog, derived from vModalDialog. This creates a *modal* dialog box, which captures all input until closed. While a modal dialog box is in use, other program operations are temporarily suspended. Most V applications have at least one modal dialog box—for example, to select program options.

The remaining sections in the chapter discuss the contents of the preceding files in more detail. Again, don't try to memorize any of this information—just get a general feel for the organization and class names. In Chapter 30, I walk through the steps for creating a V application from scratch.

MAIN APPLICATION

A V program's engine is its main application object. This object initializes the program using a class constructor and starts the program's ball rolling. The application class destructor performs any clean-up duties such as disengaging the client from the X server. Every V application must have one and only one main application object.

To create the application object, derive an application class from vApp and fill in a few member functions. Listing 29.1 shows the generated main application class declaration (with my apologies to the author for reformatting the code and removing some extraneous comments to save space).

LISTING 29.1   MYAPP.H (PARTIAL)

```
#include <v/vapp.h>
#include <v/vawinfo.h>

class myApp : public vApp {
  friend int AppMain(int, char**); // allow AppMain access
public:
  myApp(char* name, int sdi = 0, int h = 0, int w = 0);
  virtual ~myApp();
// Routines from vApp that are normally overridden
  virtual vWindow* NewAppWin(vWindow* win, char* name,
    int w, int h, vAppWinInfo* winInfo);
  virtual void Exit(void);
  virtual int CloseAppWin(vWindow*);
  virtual void AppCommand(vWindow* win,
    ItemVal id, ItemVal val, CmdType cType);
  virtual void KeyIn(vWindow*, vKey, unsigned int);
protected:
private:
  myCmdWindow* _myCmdWin; // Pointer to first window instance
};
```

The vApp class is declared in V's vapp.h header file. Include that header and also vawinfo.h in your program's main application file. The second header declares a class, vAppWinInfo, which apparently has little practical value but is included for backward compatibility with earlier V releases (see the online documentation for more about this class).

Derive your application class from vApp as shown in the listing. You can name your class as you like, but for clarity it should end with App. The first item in the derived class is a friend function declaration for AppMain(), giving that function access to myApp's private and protected declarations. AppMain() is the equivalent of a C or C++ program's main() function. V applications are totally object-oriented, and they use objects to construct and destroy the application. A V application does not have a main() function.

The other declarations in the myApp class override various member functions from the vApp base class. Depending on your needs, you might add or subtract from the generated functions—but these are typically needed in most applications. You can add other declarations to the class's protected section, which is empty by default. A single private data member defines a pointer to an object of the myCmdWindow class discussed in the next section.

Through this pointer the main application object accesses the program's top-level command window.

By convention, V prefaces private data members such as _myCmdWin with an underscore. When you come across a similarly spelled variable, you know it is a private member of a class and therefore accessible only from that class's member functions.

Listing 29.2, myapp.cpp, shows some of the function implementations for the prototypes in the class declaration. I deleted some functions that perform no new actions, and again, I reformatted the text to save space.

LISTING 29.2   MYAPP.CPP (PARTIAL)

```
#include "myapp.h"  // Header file

myApp::myApp(char* name, int sdi, int h, int w) :

vApp(name, sdi, h, w)
{
  // Constructor
  _myCmdWin = 0;
}

myApp::~myApp()
{
  // Destructor
}

vWindow* myApp::NewAppWin(vWindow* win, char* name,
  int w, int h, vAppWinInfo* winInfo)
{
  vAppWinInfo* awinfo = winInfo;
  char *appname = name;

  if (!*name) {
    appname = "Hello to V Programming";  // Default name
  }

  UserDebug1(Build,"myApp::NewAppWin(%s)\n",appname);

  // Create the first window using provided CmdWindow
  myCmdWin = (myCmdWindow*) win;
  if (!_myCmdWin) {
   _myCmdWin = new myCmdWindow(appname, w, h);
  }

  if (!awinfo)
    awinfo = new vAppWinInfo(appname);
  return vApp::NewAppWin(_myCmdWin, appname, w, h, awinfo);
}

void myApp::Exit(void)
{
```

```
    // This is called to close all windows.
    UserDebug(Build,"myApp::Exit()\n");
    vApp::Exit();  // Default behavior
}

...

//#######################

// The instance of the app
static myApp my_App("Hello to V Programming");

int AppMain(int argc, char** argv)
{
    // Use AppMain to create the main window
    (void) theApp->NewAppWin(0, "Hello to V Programming",
      450, 250);
    return 0;
}
```

The first two functions implemented in myapp.cpp are the myApp class constructor and destructor. In this case, the functions have little to do. As should all good class constructors, myApp's constructor initializes its private data member, setting the command window pointer _myCmdWin to NULL (zero). The constructor also calls its ancestor constructor in the vApp class, which carries out other initializations that don't concern us here. The myApp destructor does nothing new in this case, but you could insert statements to perform any shutdown duties such as closing a file. Because the myApp destructor is virtual, the base class destructor carries out its own duties unassisted (in case you're interested, the myApp destructor deletes any Clipboard data remaining before the program ends).

Next in the application class is probably its most important member function, NewAppWin(). This function is declared as follows:

```
vWindow* myApp::NewAppWin(vWindow* win, char* name,
  int w, int h, vAppWinInfo* winInfo)
```

The function returns a pointer to a vWindow object. This class, vWindow, is the base class for the vCmdWindow class, from which the application's own window classes are derived. The NewAppWin() function is responsible for constructing an object for each of the program's windows. It is designed to use an existing vWindow pointer, or if parameter win is NULL, to create a new instance of the application's command window. The name parameter is the window's default title, and the two integers suggest an initial width and height, although the window manager may alter these values. The final parameter must be supplied but is effectively unused.

Included among the statements in the NewAppWin() function is a macro UserDebug1() used as follows:

```
UserDebug1(Build,"myApp::NewAppWin(%s)\n",appname);
```

You'll find similar uses of this macro throughout the generated application files. If the symbol vDEBUG is defined (using the compiler option -DvDEBUG), the macro inserts a trace string that may help you debug a running (or runaway) V application. If vDEBUG is not defined, the macro defaults to nil (no associated text) and is effectively commented-out of the final code. This works similarly to the standard library's assert() macro.

The myapp.cpp module ends with two critical items present in all V applications. First is a static definition of the main application object:

```
static myApp my_App("Hello to V Programming");
```

The object, named my_App here, is of the myApp class derived from vApp. It specifies the main window's title string, which you can edit in the file or set using the application generator's dialog box. Because global objects are initialized automatically by C++, defining the object is all you need to do to initialize and run a V application—a good example of object-oriented programming at its best.

The final item in myapp.cpp is function AppMain(), which is declared as a friend to the myApp class (see myapp.h in Listing 29.1). The function is the equivalent to the main() function in a conventional C or C++ program, and it defines the usual argc and argv parameters for accessing any command-line strings. You may add statements to AppMain(), but in keeping with object-oriented design, the function needs only to create the program's top-level window using the following statement:

```
 (void) theApp->NewAppWin(0, "Hello to V Programming",
  450, 250);
```

The (void) preface isn't strictly needed, but indicates that the statement purposely ignores the value returned by NewAppWin(). Parameter theApp is a global variable defined in the V header file vapp.h. It is set to the application object when that object (my_App) is created. You could use either my_App or theApp in this case—they refer to the same object—but using theApp is in keeping with V's general design. This also gives you the option to create the main application object in a different way, or even in a separate file, and still be able to use that object throughout the application via the global theApp pointer.

MAIN COMMAND WINDOW

If the main application object is the program's engine, its main command window is its seat, windshield, and steering wheel. Listing 29.3, mycmdw.h, shows this module's class declaration (again, I edited the text to save space).

LISTING 29.3   MYCMDW.H (PARTIAL)

```
#include "mycnv.h"    // myCanvasPane
#include "mydlg.h"    // myDialog
#include "mymdlg.h"   // myModalDialog

class myCmdWindow;
class myTimer : public vTimer {
public:
  myTimer(myCmdWindow* cw) { cmdw = cw; }
  ~myTimer() {}
  virtual void TimerTick();
```

```
private:
  myCmdWindow* cmdw;
};

class myCmdWindow : public vCmdWindow {
  friend int AppMain(int, char**);  // allow AppMain access
public:
  myCmdWindow(char*, int, int);
  virtual ~myCmdWindow();
  virtual void WindowCommand(ItemVal id, ItemVal val,
    CmdType cType);
  virtual void KeyIn(vKey keysym, unsigned int shift);
protected:
private:
  // Standard elements
  vMenuPane* myMenu;           // For the menu bar
  myCanvasPane* myCanvas;      // For the canvas
  vCommandPane* myCmdPane;     // for the command pane
  vStatusPane* myStatus;       // For the status bar
  myTimer* _timer;             // Timer for Date/Time

  // Dialogs associated with CmdWindow
  myDialog* myDlg;
  myModalDialog* myMDlg;
};
```

The header file includes V headers needed for deriving our main application window's class. First, however, the listing derives myTimer from vTimer to provide for the status bar's date and time display. This class is generated only if you select that option in the application generator's dialog. (More on status bars in Chapter 30.)

The myCmdWindow class, derived from vCmdWindow, contains the programming for the application's top-level command window. As in the application class, the class declares AppMain() as a friend function, giving it access to myCmdWindow's protected and private members.

As generated, the derived command-window class overrides several member functions and also provides the usual constructor and destructor. You may add or subtract from the list of prototyped functions according to your needs.

Most important in the myCmdWindow class are the private declarations at its end. Each visual object associated with the window has a pointer to an object of an appropriate class. For example, myMenu points to an object of type vMenuPane, representing the window's menu bar. The number of pointers depends on the options you select in the application generator. In addition to the standard-element pointers, the generator includes declarations for a timer object and two other pointers for the program's modeless and modal dialog windows.

Inside the mycmdw.cpp module, Listing 29.4, is where you find the program's event-driven logic. The listing shows only a portion of the entire module, and once more, I reformatted the lines to save space. Not shown are the static definitions that define the window's pull-down menu bar, toolbar, and status bar. In Chapter 30, you learn how to create these elements.

LISTING 29.4   MYCMDW.CPP (PARTIAL)

```
#include <v/vnotice.h>  // for vNoticeDialog
#include <v/vkeys.h>    // to map keys
#include "mycmdw.h"     // our header

void myTimer::TimerTick()
{
  // update clock
  cmdw->WindowCommand(lblCurTime, lblCurTime, C_Button);
}

myCmdWindow::myCmdWindow(char* name, int width, int height) :
  vCmdWindow(name, width, height)
{
  // The Menu Bar
  myMenu = new vMenuPane(StandardMenu);
  AddPane(myMenu);
  // The Command Pane
  myCmdPane = new vCommandPane(ToolBar);
  AddPane(myCmdPane);
  // The Canvas
  myCanvas = new myCanvasPane;
  AddPane(myCanvas);
  // The Status Bar
  myStatus = new vStatusPane(StatBar);
  AddPane(myStatus);
 _timer = new myTimer(this);  // create timer
 _timer->TimerSet(1000);      // 1 second intervals
  // Associated dialogs
  myDlg = new myDialog(this,name);
  myMDlg = new myModalDialog(this,name);
  // Show Window
  ShowWindow();
  WindowCommand(lblCurTime,lblCurTime,C_Button);// update clock
  myCanvas->ShowVScroll(1);  // Show Vert Scroll
  myCanvas->ShowHScroll(1);  // Show Horiz Scroll
}

myCmdWindow::~myCmdWindow()
{
  delete myMenu;
  delete myCanvas;
  delete myCmdPane;
  delete myStatus;
 _timer->TimerStop();  // end it
  delete _timer;  // free it
  delete myDlg;
  delete myMDlg;
}

void myCmdWindow::KeyIn(vKey keysym, unsigned int shift)
{
  vCmdWindow::KeyIn(keysym, shift);
}

void myCmdWindow::WindowCommand(ItemVal id,
```

```
    ItemVal val, CmdType cType)
{
  switch (id) {
  //@V@:Case M_New
  case M_New:
    {
      vNoticeDialog note(this);
      note.Notice("New");
      break;
    }  //@V@:EndCase
  //@V@:Case M_Open
  case M_Open:
    {
      vNoticeDialog note(this);
      note.Notice("Open");
      break;
    }  //@V@:EndCase
  ...
  default:  // route unhandled commands up
    {
      vCmdWindow::WindowCommand(id, val, cType);
      break;
    }
  }
}
```

The lone statement in the myTimer class's TimerTick() function updates the main command window's status bar time display. This shows how one V object can communicate with another by calling its WindowCommand() function. Before such events can take place, however, the window object initializes its variables in the myCmdWindow constructor shown in the listing. The constructor's key duty is to construct visual objects associated with the window. For example, to create a menu bar, the myCmdWindow constructor executes these statements:

```
myMenu = new vMenuPane(StandardMenu);
AddPane(myMenu);
```

This uses new to initialize the private myMenu pointer as an object of the vMenuPane class to obtain a new menu bar. StandardMenu is the name of a struct (not shown here) that defines the actual menu and command strings. To add the menu *pane* to the current window, the myCmdWindow constructor simply calls the inherited AddPane() member function. Other panes such as a toolbar and status bar are added similarly. In addition, the constructor creates a dialog box object with these statements:

```
myDlg = new myDialog(this, name);
myMDlg = new myModalDialog(this, name);
```

It's not strictly necessary to create dialog box objects at the same time as the window, but this makes them readily available. They are not displayed at this time but are easily made visible by calling their ShowWindow() functions. The program's main command window is similarly made visible by calling ShowWindow() as follows:

```
ShowWindow();
```

At this point, the program's window is displayed, but as you learned in the preceding chapters on Xlib programming, it actually appears only after the server posts an Expose event for the window. V takes care of this detail, however, and for all practical purposes, you may consider the window to be usable after calling ShowWindow().

Corresponding to the main command window's constructor is a destructor. As shown in mycmdw.cpp, Listing 29.4, the destructor is expected to delete each pointer initialized in the constructor. This is merely standard object-oriented programming—but don't forget this step, or you can create serious memory leaks, especially in programs that create multiple child windows.

Finally in the main command window module is the WindowCommand() function. Here you program the application's main event-driven logic. Unlike in a pure Xlib client, however, instead of getting events, you branch to various statements according to the ItemVal id parameter passed to the function. To handle other events such as keypresses, you override functions such as KeyIn() (see Listing 29.4). V calls this function in response to a KeyPress event from the X server.

Inside WindowCommand(), as created by the application generator, you find a large switch statement that I reduced in the printed listing. The statement's main purpose is to respond to user menu selections. For example, selecting the sample program's *File, New* command causes V to issue a message id M_New to WindowCommand(). A case statement responds as follows:

```
case M_New:
{
  vNoticeDialog note(this);
  note.Notice("New");
  break;
}
```

The vNoticeDialog is a class that you can use to display a message. Simply create an object of the class and call its Notice() member function to display your message. This is a modal dialog, so users must close it before continuing. The this argument passed to the vNoticeDialog constructor provides it with a parent window—in this case, the main command window. Because the vNoticeDialog object is created inside a compound statement block delimited with braces, it is automatically deleted after the break statement—another great example of how C++ classes and objects greatly simplify complex programming. (If you don't believe me, try doing this with Xlib function calls!)

In many cases, messages sent to a window's WindowCommand() function might need to be passed to default logic in a base class. To ensure that all messages are properly handled, the switch statement in WindowCommand() should end with a default case that calls the ancestor's function like this:

```
vCmdWindow::WindowCommand(id, val, cType);
```

WINDOW CANVAS

Much of a window's visual activity is handled by painting graphics and text on a window's *canvas*. To provide for this, the application creates a window canvas object of a class derived from one of several that V provides.

In the sample generated application, the main window's canvas object is of a class named myCanvasPane, derived from the vCanvasPane base class. Listing 29.5 shows this class's declaration (edited for prime-time viewing here).

LISTING 29.5   MYCNV.H (PARTIAL)

```
#include <v/vcanvas.h>

class myCanvasPane : public vCanvasPane {
public:
  myCanvasPane();
  virtual ~myCanvasPane();

  // Scrolling
  virtual void HPage(int shown, int top);
  virtual void VPage(int shown, int top);
  virtual void HScroll(int step);
  virtual void VScroll(int step);

  // Events
  virtual void MouseDown(int x, int y, int button);
  virtual void MouseUp(int x, int y, int button);
  virtual void MouseMove(int x, int y, int button);
  virtual void Redraw(int x, int y, int width, int height);
  virtual void Resize(int newW, int newH);
...
};
```

The myCanvasPane class declares the usual constructor and destructor, along with some member functions for scrolling and handling input and output events. To respond to the user clicking the mouse inside the window's canvas area, simply override the MouseDown() function and provide whatever programming you need.

Handle graphics similarly. To paint graphics in a window, override Redraw() and call the graphical output functions you need (more on this in Chapter 30). Don't be concerned at this stage with how to draw actual objects. Be aware only that Redraw() is where you add this code for a specific window. It is the V equivalent of an Xlib program's response to an Expose event. If the window needs repainting—for example, on being exposed by the user moving another window aside—V calls Redraw() as needed to update the window's canvas. The four parameters indicate the portion of the window that requires redrawing, but except for highly complex graphics, you can simply draw everything and ignore these values. The Resize() function corresponds with the Xlib ConfigureNotify event.

> **Note**
>
> Scrolling is beyond this book's introduction to V programming but essentially requires the program to alter its *view* of information actually shown on the canvas, not to move any pixels. In other words, the program might have a logical drawing surface many times larger than the canvas's physical size. In response to the window's scrolling functions, the program simply adjusts the relative area of the logical surface displayed by `Redraw()`.

The canvas module, mycnv.cpp, isn't listed here because it contains no new programming. All member functions overridden in the `myCanvasPane` class merely call their ancestor class counterparts. However, this module is where you insert statements to add actual input and output to your application.

Modal and Modeless Dialog Boxes

The rest of the main files for the generated V application implement the program's sample modal and modeless dialog boxes. Creating these objects is beyond the scope of this introduction. However, you might want to examine the associated files: mydlg.h, mydlg.cpp, mymdlg.h, and mymdlg.cpp.

On browsing through those files, notice that static structures are used to define dialog box buttons, labels, and other items. As you might suspect, dialog boxes are merely specialized window objects, and they work much like the command windows described earlier. For example, each has a `DialogCommand()` function that, like `WindowCommand()`, responds to user input—clicking a button, for instance. To program a dialog box, you simply derive a class from the `vDialog` or `vModalDialog` base classes, provide static structures to define the dialog box's components, and initialize the object in a constructor. You then override `DialogCommand()` to respond to user input.

Summary

V is a class library that greatly simplifies developing X applications. Freely distributed under the GNU General Public License, V is completely object-oriented. It is also cross-compatible with Microsoft Windows and OS/2. If you write an application using V for X, you simply have to recompile it using a suitable development system such as Borland C++ or Watcom C++ to run under Microsoft Windows.

For more information on subjects introduced in this chapter, turn to the following chapters:

- Chapter 26, "Introducing X Programming"
- Chapter 30, "Developing X Software with V"

DEVELOPING X SOFTWARE WITH V

Chapter 29 introduced the V class library for X programming. This chapter walks you through several basic techniques needed by most X client applications, and it shows some ways you can use V to develop finished X software for Linux and other supported operating systems. After reading this chapter, you should be able to better understand V's online tutorials and references, and you also should be able to read and understand the sample programs provided with the library.

COMPILING THIS CHAPTER'S PROGRAMS

The programs in this chapter are divided into separate modules, and for that reason they are stored individually in subdirectories. To compile the programs in this chapter, change to a named directory (src/c30/vwelcome for instance) and type *make*. If you receive errors, edit the Config.mk file in the src/c30 directory and shown here in Listing 30.1.

LISTING 30.1   CONFIG.MK

```
# Edit the following for your installation (esp HOMEV)
CC       =    g++
HOMEV    =    $(HOME)/v
VIncDir  =    $(HOMEV)/includex
VLibDir  =    $(HOMEV)/lib
X11INC   =    /usr/X11R6/include
X11LIB   =    /usr/X11R6/lib
LIBS     =    -lVx -lXaw -lXmu -lXt -lXext -lX11


#===============================================================
# Compiler and linker flags
CFLAGS   =    -O -I$(X11INC) -I$(VIncDir)
LFLAGS   =    -O -L$(X11LIB) -L$(VLibDir)
```

Change HOMEV if necessary to the directory where you installed V as described in Chapter 29. By default, Config.mk uses the HOME environment variable defined for your shell. Most readers should have to make few if any changes to the file as listed here.

Note

If you already have an earlier version of V installed, you might have to change the LIBS setting -lVx to -lV and also set the VLibDir to /lib/linux. The other settings should work as shown here. For best results, however, you should install the newer version of V provided on this book's CD-ROM and also available via the Internet as described in Chapter 29, "Introducing the V Class Library."

UNDERSTANDING V CLASSES

V's online documentation comes with well-drawn charts that illustrate the library's class hierarchy. I doubt that I can improve on these diagrams, so rather than duplicate them here, Table 30.1 lists V's main classes and the header files in which they are declared. This is by no means a complete list but shows the classes and headers most often used in applications along with many of those described in this chapter. To use a class, include its header file into your program's modules. For more information about these and other V classes, use your Web browser to open V's online documentation starting with the file v/vrefman/index.html.

TABLE 30.1   V's MAIN CLASSES

Class	Header File	Creates
vApp	vapp.h	Main application
vBrush	vbrush.h	Painting (fill) brush
vCanvasPane	vcanvas.h	Window drawing canvas
vCmd	vcmd.h	Dialog and toolbar object
vCmdWindow	vcmdwin.h	Command (main or child) window
vColor	vcolor.h	Standard color object
vCommandPane	vcmdpane.h	Toolbar (pane)
vDC	vdc.h	Device (graphics) context
vDialog	vdialog.h	Modeless dialog box
vFont	vfont.h	Standard text font object
vMenuPane	vmenu.h	Menu bar (pane)
vModalDialog	vmodald.h	Modal dialog box
vPen	vpen.h	Outline pen
vStatusPane	vstatusp.h	Status bar (pane)

All V classes begin with lowercase v. As a convention, I derive my own classes from these using a capital T, meaning "Type." In this chapter, then, the class TCanvasPane is a class derived from V's vCanvasPane base class. You don't have to use my naming convention, but it's a good idea to adopt a consistent style so that you can identify the origins of your own classes.

Most V programming involves inheriting classes and overriding virtual functions to respond to X server events such as mouse button clicks, and also providing new functions for your program's input and output. When just getting started with V, concentrate on identifying the correct places to add your own code. Remember to *think objects*. Program your classes to perform on their own as much as possible and let V handle the communications with the X server.

V WELCOME PROGRAM

A simple program welcomes you to V programming and shows the minimum requirements for creating an application based on the class library. Although Chapter 29 lists parts of a program created by V's application generator, the program in this section (and all others in this chapter) is written from scratch using my own Makefile and source code conventions.

> **Note**
>
> Many of the modules for this chapter's programs have the same filenames, and for that reason, these modules are prefaced by their directory names in numbered listings.

The vWelcome program discussed in this section is divided into three modules: the main application, the application class, and the command window class. The following sections describe each of these modules and list the source code files in full. Other programs in this chapter build on this basic program and to save room do not list duplicated programming. Always refer to the files on disk for the complete source code.

Change to the src/c30/vwelcome directory now and type **make** to compile the program. Then enter *./vwelcome* to run the finished code file. Figure 30.1 shows the program's window. Use the mouse to select the *File, Exit* command to close the window and end the program. Compile, run, and exit all programs in this chapter similarly.

Figure 30.1
The vWelcome application shows the basic steps for creating a V application, complete with graphical window and menu bar.

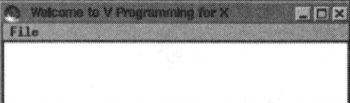

> **Note**
>
> The Makefiles for this chapter's programs understand several options. Type **make** with no arguments to compile and link all modules, or you can type **make all** to do the same. Type **make objs** to create only the object code files but not to link them into the final executable. (In a larger application, this option might be useful to check for syntax errors after a massive editing job.) To compile only a specific module, enter its object code filename—for example, type **make app.o** to compile only the app.cpp module. Type **make clean** to erase backup, object code, core, and the finished executable code files, returning the directory to its original state. You might want to copy the executable code file to another directory before typing **make clean**.

THE MAIN APPLICATION

The first file for vWelcome contains programming that is roughly equivalent to the main() function in a conventional C or C++ program. V applications have no main() function. Instead, as Listing 30.2, vwelcome.cpp, shows, a V application constructs an *application object* that initializes and runs the program. This makes the main application module fairly simple—consider it as the kickstarter that gets the X client's engine going.

LISTING 30.2 VWELCOME.CPP

```
#include "cmdwin.h"      // Include command window header
#include "app.h"         // Include application module header

// Construct the application object
static TWelcomeApp WelcomeApp(APPNAME);

// Main function
int AppMain(int argc, char* argv[])
{
  theApp->NewAppWin(0, TITLE, 325, 50);
  return 0;
}
```

The application object is a global, static variable of a class derived from vApp. In this case, I name the application class TWelcomeApp and the global object WelcomeApp. APPNAME is a string constant that represents the application name. TITLE is the window title string.

Function AppMain() resembles the main() function in a conventional program. It has argc and argv parameters for using any command-line options, although the sample program ignores these variables. Inside AppMain(), the first statement calls the NewAppWin() member function for an object addressed by theApp. This is a global V pointer that addresses the main application object—in this case, WelcomeApp. The four arguments passed to NewAppWin() are as follows:

- 0   This is a null vWindow* pointer value, but it could address an existing window (perhaps of the derived class vCmdWindow) if for some reason you want to create that object before initializing the application.
- TITLE   This is a standard C-style, null-terminated string that represents the window title. Because V is based on widgets (at least in UNIX and Linux), you can count on the window title appearing atop its frame, unlike in pure Xlib programming, which gives no similar guarantee.
- 325   This is a suggested width in pixels for the window frame.
- 50   This is a suggested height in pixels for the window frame.

There are two main reasons for using theApp pointer instead of the object directly. First, many other modules need to refer to this critical object, and second, in a larger program, you might define the application object in a separate module perhaps to hide it from view. In any case, you can always use theApp to address the main application object.

Note

Because of the way the X server, client applications, and the window manager work, you can't count on AppMain() returning. However, you *can* count on the main application object's class destructor being called before control returns to the process that started your client program. This means that your main application object always gets one last opportunity to perform critical tasks just before a program ends—saving a file, for example.

THE APPLICATION CLASS

The main application object is constructed from a class declared and implemented in this section's module. Listing 30.3, app.h, shows the declaration for the TWelcomeApp class.

LISTING 30.3   VWELCOME/APP.H

```
#include <v/vapp.h>   // Need vApp class

#define APPNAME "VWelcome"
#define TITLE "Welcome to V Programming for X"

// Application class
//
class TWelcomeApp : public vApp {
public:
  TWelcomeApp(char* name) : vApp(name) { }
  virtual ~TWelcomeApp() { }
  virtual vWindow* NewAppWin(vWindow* win, char* name,
    int h, int w, vAppWinInfo* winInfo);
};
```

Include the vapp.h header to make the vApp base class available. Also define application and title strings, used in the vwelcome.cpp module to initialize the program and give the window a title.

Derive your application class as shown for TWelcomeApp. At a minimum, the derived class needs a constructor, a virtual destructor, and a virtual member function NewAppWin(). In this example, the constructor and destructor have no new duties to perform and are implemented inline. The constructor calls its ancestor constructor, vApp(). Virtual base class destructors are called automatically. As mentioned in the prior section, the main application module calls NewAppWin() to create the program's main window.

> **Note**
>
> Strictly speaking, you can delete the word `virtual` from the derived application class destructor and other functions. This is because, even if a base class declares a member function `virtual`, a derived class needs to do the same only if another class will be derived from that one. I mention this tidbit because, while browsing V source code examples, you might come across member functions declared both ways.

Listing 30.4, app.cpp, shows the TWelcomeApp class's implementation. Because this class's constructor and destructor are implemented inline, the app.cpp file contains the programming for only one function, NewAppWin().

LISTING 30.4   VWELCOME/APP.CPP

```cpp
#include "app.h"        // Need TWelcomeApp
#include "cmdwin.h"      // Need TCmdWindow
#include <v/vawinfo.h>   // Need unused vAppWinInfo class

// Construct a new application window
vWindow* TWelcomeApp::NewAppWin(vWindow* win, char* name,
  int w, int h, vAppWinInfo* winInfo)
{
  vWindow* localWin = win;          // Local parameter copies
  vAppWinInfo* localInfo = winInfo;
  char *localName = name;

  if (!*localName)
    localName = TITLE;
  if (!localWin)
    localWin = new TCmdWindow(localName, w, h);
  if (!localInfo)
    localInfo = new vAppWinInfo(localName);
  return vApp::NewAppWin(localWin, localName, w, h, localInfo);
}
```

The module includes three header files. First is its own header, which declares the TWelcomeApp class. Next is the header, cmdwin.h, that declares the program's TCmdWindow class for representing the main window—more on this in the next section. The third header, vawinfo.h, declares a class, vAppWinInfo, that is needed for the NewAppWin() function but is essentially unused.

The NewAppWin() member function creates two objects. The first is one of the TCmdWindow class. The second is of the vAppWinInfo class. Arguments to these class constructors provide a suggested width and height for the window and the application name string. Using the resulting object pointers, the final step is to call the ancestor class's NewAppWin() function. Regardless of how complex your program, these steps are all your NewAppWin() function likely needs to perform.

Readers who are new to object-oriented programming might think something is missing at this stage. But remember to *think objects*. Trust the ancestor NewAppWin() function in the vApp class to do whatever is necessary to finish creating the program's window. On the application level, your code needs to do only the *additional* chores needed by your program. As a good example of this design approach, our vWelcome application object needs only to create the program's window object—exactly what that window does is the window class's responsibility, as described next.

THE COMMAND WINDOW CLASS

The final module in the vWelcome application declares and implements the program's command window class. A command window in V is one that can receive input and show graphical output. In X, windows are where the action is, and you might consider a V command window to be your program's action module. Listing 30.5, cmdwin.h, shows the declaration for vWelcome's TCmdWindow class.

LISTING 30.5   VWELCOME/CMDWIN.H

```
#include <v/vcanvas.h>  // Need vCanvasPane class
#include <v/vmenu.h>     // Need vMenuPane class
#include <v/vcmdwin.h>   // Need vCmdWindow class

// Command window class
class TCmdWindow : public vCmdWindow {
private:
  vCanvasPane* myCanvas;  // Pointer to window's canvas
  vMenuPane* myMenu;       // Pointer to window's menu
public:
  TCmdWindow(char* name, int width, int height);
  virtual ~TCmdWindow();
  virtual void WindowCommand(ItemVal id, ItemVal val,
    CmdType cType);
};
```

A command window class module usually needs at least the three headers included here. The first, vcanvas.h, declares the vCanvasPane, used to represent the window's interior drawing surface—or "canvas" for short. The vmenu.h header declares the vMenuPane class to represent the window's menu bar. This isn't strictly required, but most X applications should have a pull-down menu bar. The third header file includes vcmdwin.h, which declares the vCmdWindow class from which our class is derived.

That class, TCmdWindow, begins with two private data member declarations. The first of these, myCanvas, is a pointer to a vCanvasPane object. Any output to this window is directed through this pointer. The second private member is a pointer, myMenu, to a vMenuPane object. This pointer, as you can no doubt guess, addresses the object that represents the window's pull-down menus.

Because the pointers are private to the class, a TCmdWindow object *owns* the addressed objects. In this way, a V command window owns its canvas and menu bar and, as you learn later, other elements such as tool and status bars. This is a sensible and easy-to-use design. Because a command window owns its menu bar and other elements, the place to control those items is in the command window module.

> **Tip**
>
> Keep in mind that when an object owns another, this does not imply any relationship on the class level. In learning any new class library, the difference between classes related through inheritance and those related through object ownership is one of the most important distinctions to make. (V's online class hierarchy diagrams clearly show these relationships.)

In addition to its private data members, the TCmdWindow class declares three functions: a constructor, a virtual destructor, and a virtual function WindowCommand(). As its name suggests, the function is responsible for responding to commands directed at this window—for example, in response to a user selecting a pull-down menu command. Listing 30.6, cmdwin.cpp, implements vWelcome's TCmdWindow class.

LISTING 30.6   VWELCOME/CMDWIN.CPP

```cpp
#include "cmdwin.h"
#include <v/v_defs.h>    // Need standard definitions

// Define a simple menu command item
static vMenu FileMenu[] =
{
  {"E&xit", M_Exit, isSens, notChk, noKeyLbl, noKey, noSub},
  {NULL}
};

// Define a simple top-level menu item
static vMenu StandardMenu[] =
{
  {"&File", M_File, isSens, notUsed, notUsed, noKey,
➥&FileMenu[0]},
  {NULL}
};

// Our command window constructor
TCmdWindow::TCmdWindow(char* name, int width, int height) :
  vCmdWindow(name, width, height)  // Call ancestor constructor
{
  myMenu = new vMenuPane(StandardMenu);   // Create menu pane
  AddPane(myMenu);                         // Add it to our window
  myCanvas = new vCanvasPane;              // Create window canvas
  AddPane(myCanvas);                       // Add it to our window
  ShowWindow();                            // Make window visible
]

// Our command window destructor
TCmdWindow::~TCmdWindow()
{
  delete myMenu;    // One for each "new" in constructor
  delete myCanvas;
}

// Respond to menu selections and other commands
void TCmdWindow::WindowCommand(
  ItemVal id, ItemVal val, CmdType cType)
{
  switch (id) {
  case M_Exit:        // User selected File¦Exit command
    theApp->Exit();   // Exit the application
    break;
  default:            // Route unhandled commands
    vCmdWindow::WindowCommand(id, val, cType);
    break;
  }
}
```

The implementation for the TCmdWindow class is the largest in the bunch, and this fact is probably true for most V applications. The first two items are common C++ struct declarations that create the strings and other options for the program's pull-down menu bar. V uses similar structures for menus, toolbars, status bars, and dialog boxes. This differs from some other X (and also Microsoft Windows) development systems that rely on *resources* for these types of items. In V, you create all program elements in the program's source code files. Other sections in this chapter explain these structures in more detail, so I won't go into them here.

The TCmdWindow constructor and destructor functions come next in the module. The constructor has two important duties—to create objects for the class's private data member pointers and to call a function ShowWindow() that makes the window visible. The window constructor might also perform other operations—initializing a container object, for example, to store information about the program's window. (More on this in the next section.)

The TCmdWindow destructor should perform any shut-down duties related to the destruction of this window. In this case, the destructor deletes all pointers initialized by new in the constructor.

Finally in this module, is the implementation of the WindowCommand() member function. Because this is only a simple example, this function is not large—in practice, however, it typically contains a long switch statement for responding to the many input events directed at this window. Here, only one such event is possible—identified by parameter id equal to the constant M_Exit when the user selects the menu's *File*, *Exit* command.

M_Exit and other constants beginning with M_ are defined in the v_defs.h header file, included at the beginning of the TCmdWindow implementation module. You may use predefined menu command constants such as this one (there are dozens available), or you may create your own constants. By convention, to distinguish between the two types, preface your own menu constants with a lowercase m_.

CommandWindow()'s switch statement has two cases. The one for M_Exit calls the Exit() function for the global application object addressed by theApp. This is the correct way to end a V application. The default case calls the ancestor class's CommandWindow() function to process any events not handled at the application level. The three arguments passed to CommandWindow() are of the following types. Because programming a V application mainly involves writing code to respond to events (just as in all X applications), study these argument types carefully:

- ItemVal id   This value identifies the command event such as a menu selection or a button click. It is a unique integer value that is usually used in a switch statement as a case selector.

- ItemVal val   This value contains additional information for some but not all types of command events. For example, val might be the value returned from a spinner button selected by the user clicking the button's up or down arrows.

- CmdType cType   This value tells you the type of object that was selected for this command event. For example, if id refers to a menu command, cType equals C_Menu. CmdType is an enumeration declared in v_defs.h. It is typically used to identify objects such as check boxes (C_CheckBox), labels (C_Label), and many other sorts of visual objects in dialog boxes and toolbars.

And that's it—a complete V application ready to fill with your own code. Before continuing to the next sections for a look at how to implement menus, toolbars, status bars, graphics, and other features, you might want to review the preceding discussion. As mentioned, all other sample programs in this chapter build on vWelcome's modules.

> **Note**
>
> Not counting comments and conditional directives, the total number of lines in vWelcome is about 110 versus 158 lines for the similar xWelcome Xlib application in Chapter 26, "Introducing X Programming." Even ignoring its pull-down menu and potential for other GUI elements, the V application's source code is about one-third smaller than the Xlib equivalent—another good example of how C++ classes and object-oriented programming can reduce complexity in software development.

SOFTWARE DEVELOPMENT WITH V

As with most programming tools, after you learn how to get a V application up and running, you might wonder how to handle input and output. Because a V application is, of course, an X client, the same observations made for Xlib programming in Chapters 26 through 28 apply. However, instead of making requests to the X server and responding to server events, a V application uses two input and output techniques: responding to command events such as menu selections in a window's CommandWindow() function and overriding virtual member functions to handle specific actions such as mouse button clicks and cursor movements. The following sections show examples of both methods.

GRAPHICS

All graphics output in a V application is made in reference to an object of the vDC class. The DC in this class name stands for "Device Context," but in Xlib programming, this is called a GC for "Graphics Context." No matter—DCs and GCs are conceptually the same, although a vDC object is much more convenient to create and use.

The vDC class provides for the characteristics of graphical output including colors, outline widths, and the pattern and color used in filled shapes. As a C++ class, vDC provides graphics functions for creating output. For example, if pDC is a pointer to a vDC object, a program can draw a line using the following statement:

```
pDC->DrawLine(x1, y1, x2, y2);
```

Although that's one way to draw graphics, another more common way is to call similarly named functions in a window's canvas object. Most windows own a canvas object of a class derived from vCanvasPane. By deriving a new class from that one and creating this object for a window, you provide a simple way to create graphical output. The next program demonstrates how to do this in a sketch application that lets you draw lines by clicking and dragging the mouse. The program also demonstrates how to respond to mouse button and movement events.

> **Note**
>
> See the vDC class online documentation, and also its header file vdc.h, for a list of available graphics functions. In general, there is a vDC member function for each Xlib graphics primitive. These same member functions are also available to any canvas object.

MOUSE INPUT

The vSketch application demonstrates how to create graphical output and also respond to mouse activity. The program is based on the vWelcome application in the previous sections, and only the new programming is listed here. Except for the program's title, window name, and a few other parameters, the application and window modules are nearly identical in both programs. Figure 30.2 shows a sample of the program's output (I think my art skills are improving).

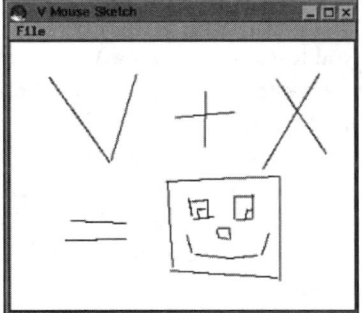

Figure 30.2
Sample window from the vSketch application, which lets you sketch lines by clicking and dragging the mouse.

A V window is but a frame that can hold other objects, generally referred to as *panes*. One type of pane is a canvas on which you can draw a program's graphical output. There are several types of pane classes in V, but for a window's output, you'll normally use the vCanvasPane class. Listing 30.7, canvas.h, shows the declaration of the derived TCanvasPane class used in the vSketch application.

LISTING 30.7   VSKETCH/CANVAS.H

```
#include <v/vcanvas.h>  // Need vCanvasPane class
#include <vector>       // Need vector<> template

class TLine {
private:
  int _x1, _y1, _x2, _y2;
public:
  TLine(int x1=0, int y1=0, int x2=0, int y2=0):
    _x1(x1), _y1(y1), _x2(x2), _y2(y2) { }
  inline int GetX1() { return _x1; }
  inline int GetY1() { return _y1; }
  inline int GetX2() { return _x2; }
```

```
    inline int GetY2() { return _y2; }
};

class TCanvasPane : public vCanvasPane {
private:
  bool mouseDown;        // True while mouse button down
  int x1, y1, x2, y2;    // Line coordinates
  vector<TLine> lines;   // Array of TLine objects
public:
  TCanvasPane();   // Constructor
  ~TCanvasPane();  // Destructor
// Override some inherited functions
  virtual void MouseDown(int x, int y, int button);
  virtual void MouseUp(int x, int y, int button);
  virtual void MouseMove(int x, int y, int button);
  virtual void Redraw(int x, int y, int w, int h);
};
```

To store the coordinate values of each line—needed to redraw the canvas if the window is uncovered or resized—the module declares a TLine class. It's up to you how to store graphics information for your application, but I used a class here because a more extensive graphics program might base all its shapes using a hierarchy of related classes.

The TCanvasPane class, derived from V's vCanvasPane, begins with some private data members needed to maintain graphical output. Variable mouseDown is true while the user holds down a mouse button, and the integer variables represent the line being drawn. The vector<TLine> class instantiates the standard template library's vector template to create a container for keeping track of line coordinates.

Declarations in the TCanvasPane's public section include the usual constructor and destructor used in most classes and four other functions. The first three of these obviously relate to mouse button clicks and movements. The fourth, Redraw(), draws the canvas's output.

Those function prototypes override functions of those same names inherited from the vCanvasPane class. Each function is tied to a specific type of event. A button press event, for example, causes V to call the canvas's MouseDown() virtual function. This is a good example of how, using virtual C++ functions, you can easily alter the behavior of an object. In this case, we want to draw lines when the user clicks and drags the mouse, so we simply override the virtual mouse functions for the window's canvas and let V figure out how and when to call those functions.

The Redraw() function is one of the most critical in all V applications. It is equivalent to the Xlib Expose event, which requires the window to re-create its contents. In general, to create graphical output in a window, you simply add drawing commands to the canvas's Redraw() function. The next module, Listing 30.8, canvas.cpp, shows how this is done in vSketch.

LISTING 30.8   VSKETCH/CANVAS.CPP

```cpp
#include "canvas.h"

// Constructor
TCanvasPane::TCanvasPane():
  vCanvasPane(),  // Call ancestor constructor
  lines()         // Construct lines vector (grows as needed)
{
  mouseDown = false;
  x1 = y1 = x2 = y2 = 0;
}

// Destructor
TCanvasPane::~TCanvasPane()
{
  // Nothing to do!
}

// Respond to mouse button click event
// Prepares for drawing the next line
void TCanvasPane::MouseDown(int x, int y, int button)
{
  mouseDown = true;    // Set mouse down flag
  x1 = x;              // Remember starting location
  y1 = y;
  x2 = x1;             // Set end point == beginning
  y2 = y1;             // as a "do nothing" flag
}

// Respond to mouse button release event
// Save current line in the lines vector
void TCanvasPane::MouseUp(int x, int y, int button)
{
  mouseDown = false;  // Reset mouse down flag
  if (x1 != x2 || y1 != y2) {
    DrawRubberLine(x1, y1, x2, y2);  // Erase old line
    x2 = x;            // Save line end point
    y2 = y;
    DrawLine(x1, y1, x2, y2);  // Draw fixed line
    lines.push_back(TLine(x1, y1, x2, y2)); // Save line
  }
}

// Respond to mouse movement event
// Draws a "rubber line" (i.e. an erasable line)
void TCanvasPane::MouseMove(int x, int y, int button)
{
  if (mouseDown) {
    if (x1 != x2 || y1 != y2)
      DrawRubberLine(x1, y1, x2, y2);  // Erase old line
    x2 = x;   // Save line end point so far
    y2 = y;
    DrawRubberLine(x1, y1, x2, y2);    // Draw new line
  }
}
```

```
// Draw graphics using saved information
// Uses STL iterator and vector-template techniques
void TCanvasPane::Redraw(int x, int y, int w, int h)
{
  vector<TLine>::iterator it;
  for (it = lines.begin(); it != lines.end(); it++)
    DrawLine(it->GetX1(), it->GetY1(),
             it->GetX2(), it->GetY2());
}
```

As usual, the TCanvasPane class constructor initializes an object of this class. The constructor should always call its ancestor constructor as shown to ensure that any inherited members are properly initialized. Also initialize any class objects such as the lines container. Like all good containers, this vector template expands as needed to hold more objects and is therefore much easier to use than a standard array. The TCanvasPane constructor also sets other data members to sensible starting values. The destructor has nothing to do, but I included it anyway just for the sake of good form.

The rest of the modules show the implementations for the overridden virtual canvas functions. Each is fairly simple to understand. When the user clicks the mouse inside the window's canvas, V calls the MouseDown() function and passes the relative coordinate of the mouse pointer's hotspot in parameters x and y. Parameter button equals the button number, but the sample program ignores this value, and you can use any active button to draw.

MouseMove() shows how to draw a rubber line—one that appears to stretch and move while you click and drag the mouse. In Xlib programming, this requires setting a display mode into the graphics context, but in V, you can simply call the DrawRubberLine() function as shown. Calling that function with the same coordinate values erases a previously drawn line, thus creating the illusion of a moving line. Other rubbery functions in the vCanvasPane class include DrawRubberEllipse() and DrawRubberRectangle(). They work similarly, but, of course, draw different shapes.

MouseUp() fixes a line in place by first calling DrawRubberLine() to erase the current temporary line and then calling DrawLine() to draw the final one. The function also saves the line coordinates by storing a TLine object in the lines vector container. None of this takes place if the beginning and ending line coordinates are the same—as they are, for example, if the user simply clicks the mouse without dragging it.

Finally in the canvas module is the code that draws all lines if the window is uncovered, either in whole or in part. In your own code, do whatever is necessary in Redraw() to draw your window's contents. Here, I use the standard template library technique of obtaining an iterator for the lines container and then call V's DrawLine() function for each stored TLine object.

V passes to DrawLine() four integer coordinates that represent a rectangular region relative to the window's origin (0,0 at upper left) of the area that needs redrawing. In simple programs such as this one, you can simply ignore these variables and draw everything. If the window is complex, however, you might use these variables to draw only those objects that fall inside the exposed region.

KEYBOARD INPUT

There are two main ways to intercept keyboard activity in V programs. You can receive key-press input at the window level, or you can do the same in the application object. The window gets first crack at incoming keypresses, so this is the usual method. Also, unless you need to program a global key that works the same regardless of which window is active, you probably want to process keypresses only for the window that has the input focus.

The next sample program, vKey, demonstrates how to intercept keypresses. For reference, the program displays two values—one that represents the key itself and another that indicates whether the Shift, Control, or Alt key is held down for keys that are not otherwise uniquely identified. Figure 30.3 shows a sample of the program's window. The values in the window are for the M-F1 (Alt-F1) key on my keyboard.

Figure 30.3
The vKey application shows key and shift values for keypresses—in this case, M-F1 (Alt-F1).

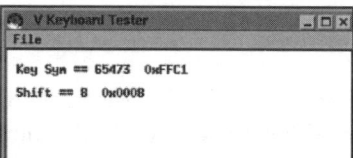

After color graphics, probably the second most hazardous programming job in X programming is dealing with keyboard input. (Programmers who deal with colormaps ought to receive combat pay.) Fortunately, V defines virtual key codes that should be the same regardless of the hardware. You might not have access to specialized keys in some cases, but you should have plenty of function, keypad, control, and alphanumeric keys for just about any application. Listing 30.9, cmdwin.cpp, shows the programming in vKey's command window module that intercepts keypresses.

LISTING 30.9   VKEY/CMDWIN.CPP (PARTIAL)

```
#include <v/v_defs.h>    // Need standard definitions

// Intercept keyboard events
void TCmdWindow::KeyIn(vKey keysym, unsigned int shift)
{
  myCanvas->SaveKeyValues(keysym, shift);  // Pass to canvas
  // Call ancestor function to handle unprocessed keystrokes
  vWindow::KeyIn(keysym, shift);
}
```

To get keypresses in a window object, override the KeyIn() function inherited from the vWindow class, usually through its descendant vCmdWindow. Add the following declaration to your window class's public section and implement the function as shown in the listing:

```
virtual void KeyIn(vKey keysym, unsigned int shift);
```

The vKey value represents the key that was pressed. This might be an ASCII alphanumeric code, a control key value, or one of the symbols defined in V's vkeys.h header file. These are virtual key values such as vk_Backspace, vk_Right, and vk_Enter that have obvious meanings but might be associated with keys labeled differently. For example, a user's Return key might generate the vk_Enter value.

In the sample cmdwin.cpp listing, KeyIn() calls the canvas object's SaveKeyValues() function, discussed in a moment. This prepares the canvas for displaying the key's values. To handle any keys not processed, be sure to call the ancestor KeyIn() function as shown. This is optional, but if you don't do this, the keyboard is effectively "captured" for this window, and even system keys might become disabled. However, menu accelerator keys (also sometimes called hot keys) are handled in V at a another level and are not seen in KeyIn().

PART

VI

CH

30

Note

Because V uses a PC keyboard as its keyboard standard, a fact that is most convenient for Linux programmers, it defines 12 function key symbols vk_F1 through vk_F12. However, other UNIX systems might not have the same number of function keys available. For this reason, you might want to provide a setup utility or command so that users can specify what keys they have and their values.

To display each keypress, vKey's canvas object uses a technique that is generally useful in graphical programming. Listing 30.10, canvas.h, shows this module's header file.

LISTING 30.10   VKEY/CANVAS.H (PARTIAL)

```
#include <v/vcanvas.h>   // Need vCanvasPane class
#include <v/v_defs.h>    // Need vKey type

class TCanvasPane : public vCanvasPane {
private:
  vKey _keysym;
  unsigned int _shift;
public:
  TCanvasPane();      // Constructor
  ~TCanvasPane();     // Destructor
  virtual void Redraw(int x, int y, int w, int h);
public:
  void SaveKeyValues(vKey keysym, unsigned int shift);
  void Paint();
};
```

Our customized window canvas class, TCanvasPane, is derived as usual from vCanvasPane. Two private values, _keysym and _shift, save the values of the current key. This is in keeping with the general rule in X programming that *all* graphical information must be saved in some way for redrawing at any time.

The class's first public section declares the usual constructor and destructor, and also the all important Redraw() function that is responsible for updating the canvas's contents. A second public section declares two new functions, SaveKeyValues() and Paint(). The first function is called from the window object's KeyIn() class member function to save the current keypress values. The second function creates the program's graphical output. The reason for not doing this in `Redraw()` becomes apparent in the next listing. By the way, I like to use two public sections as shown here to separate functions inherited and overridden in a derived class from new ones added to the class. This is merely my own convention, however, and not required. Listing 30.11, canvas.cpp, implements the class's functions.

LISTING 30.11 VKEY/CANVAS.CPP

```
#include "canvas.h"
#include <v/vkeys.h>      // Need keyboard symbols
#include <stdio.h>        // Need sprintf()

// Constructor
TCanvasPane::TCanvasPane():
  vCanvasPane()  // Call ancestor constructor
{
  _keysym = vk_None;
  _shift = 0;
}

// Destructor
TCanvasPane::~TCanvasPane()
{
  // Nothing to do!
}

// Save key values and update display
void TCanvasPane::SaveKeyValues(
  vKey keysym, unsigned int shift)
{
  _keysym = keysym;
  _shift = shift;
  Paint();  // Update window
}

// Draw graphics using saved key information
void TCanvasPane::Redraw(int x, int y, int w, int h)
{
  Paint();  // Update window
}

// Display saved key values
// Called when key values are changed and when
// window needs updating.
void TCanvasPane::Paint()
{
  int ascent, descent, spacing, x, y;
  char buffer[32];

  Clear();  // Erase window

  // Initialize text positioning variables
  TextHeight(ascent, descent);
```

```
    spacing = ascent + descent + 10;
    x = 10;
    y = spacing;

    // Display keysym value in decimal and hex
    sprintf(buffer, "Key Sym == %d  0x%04X", _keysym, _keysym);
    DrawText(x, y, buffer);

    // Display shift value in decimal and hex
    y += spacing;
    sprintf(buffer, "Shift == %d  0x%04X", _shift, _shift);
    DrawText(x, y, buffer);
}
```

The constructor initializes the two private data members. Notice that _keysym is set to vk_None, a reserved value that stands for no key. Function SaveKeyValues() merely assigns new values to these variables and then, to update the display, calls the local Paint() function.

Redraw() does the same, simply calling Paint() to draw the program's canvas output if, for example, the window is uncovered. The reason for doing this in Paint() and not in Redraw() is simply to avoid duplication of effort. In many programs, you need to update the screen as a result of user input (a new keypress in this case) and also as a result of the X server sending an Expose event to the client, and it is often convenient to create a separate function such as Paint() that handles both instances.

The first step in Paint() clears the window's current contents by calling the inherited Clear() function. Alternatively, you can pass coordinate values to ClearRect() to clear only a portion of the window's interior, using the values that V passes to Redraw(). However, in this small example, Paint() simply redraws all its output.

Remember always that text is drawn just like other graphics, and, therefore, the positioning of text output is more difficult than on a character terminal. Two integer values, ascent and descent, when combined, equal the maximum height of a letter in the current font. Find these values by calling the inherited TextHeight() function like this:

```
TextHeight(ascent, descent);
```

That assigns both values to the variables passed as reference arguments. As shown in the listing, you might want to add a little "fudge factor" to the sum of these values to separate lines of text with some whitespace.

Prepare your program's text output using whatever means works in your application. Here, I elected to use the standard C library's sprintf() function to prepare a character buffer with the decimal and hexadecimal values of the saved _keysym. To display this text, the program calls the inherited DrawText() function as follows:

```
sprintf(buffer, "Key Sym == %d  0x%04X", _keysym, _keysym);
DrawText(x, y, buffer);
```

Note

> For more information on creating text output in V programs, see the online documentation for the vDC class's member functions DrawText(), DrawAttrText(), GetFont(), SetFont(), TextWidth(), and TextHeight(). See also the vFont class, as well as vTextCanvasPane, derived from vCanvasPane, for more advanced text output tasks such as creating scrollable text.

V STANDARD COMPONENTS

V provides three of the most common elements found in most GUI applications: menus, toolbars, and status bars. The following sections introduce these components and show the basics for creating them in V programs.

MENUS

V provides easy-to-use tools for creating pull-down menus complete with optional accelerator keys and submenus. Any window may have a menu bar, but usually, only the program's main top-level window provides pull-down menus. To create a menu bar in V, you design its elements using V's vMenu struct, and then construct an object of the vMenuPane class and attach it to the window. Rarely, if ever, do you need to derive a new class from vMenuPane—the stock version is more than adequate for most applications.

To demonstrate how to create a menu bar with commands activated by the mouse and also selectable by pressing accelerator keys, I added some new code to the vSketch program in this chapter to create a new example, vMenu. Figure 30.4 shows the resulting program's display with its *Width* menu visible. Run the program and use the mouse to select a line width from 1 to 9 from the new menu. Or you can press function keys F1 through F9 to do the same. The program also has a new *File, New* command that erases the window. ("File" is used only by convention here—the sample program has no file capabilities.) Select *File, Exit* or press its accelerator key M-X (Alt-X) to exit the program.

Figure 30.4
The expanded sketch program, vMenu, has a *Width* menu for selecting line widths.

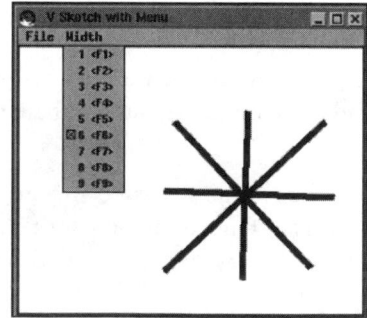

Because a menu bar is a "pane" type component owned by a window object, the place to create the menu structures is naturally in the command-window module. Listing 30.12, cmdwin.cpp, shows this programming for the vMenu sample program.

LISTING 30.12   VMENU/CMDWIN.CPP

```cpp
#include "cmdwin.h"
#include <v/v_defs.h>    // Need standard definitions
#include <v/vkeys.h>     // Need virtual key symbols

// Define menu item constants not in v_defs.h
const ItemVal m_Width  = 100;
const ItemVal m_Width1 = 101;
const ItemVal m_Width2 = 102;
const ItemVal m_Width3 = 103;
const ItemVal m_Width4 = 104;
const ItemVal m_Width5 = 105;
const ItemVal m_Width6 = 106;
const ItemVal m_Width7 = 107;
const ItemVal m_Width8 = 108;
const ItemVal m_Width9 = 109;

// Define the File menu's commands
static vMenu FileMenu[] =
{
  {"New", M_New, isSens, notChk, noKeyLbl, noKey, noSub},
  {"-", M_Line, notSens, notChk, noKeyLbl, noKey, noSub},
  {"E&xit", M_Exit, isSens, notChk, "Alt-X", 'x', noSub,
    VKM_Alt},
  {NULL}
};

static vMenu WidthMenu[] =
{
{"1", m_Width1, isSens, isChk,  "F1", vk_F1, noSub},
{"2", m_Width2, isSens, notChk, "F2", vk_F2, noSub},
{"3", m_Width3, isSens, notChk, "F3", vk_F3, noSub},
{"4", m_Width4, isSens, notChk, "F4", vk_F4, noSub},
{"5", m_Width5, isSens, notChk, "F5", vk_F5, noSub},
{"6", m_Width6, isSens, notChk, "F6", vk_F6, noSub},
{"7", m_Width7, isSens, notChk, "F7", vk_F7, noSub},
{"8", m_Width8, isSens, notChk, "F8", vk_F8, noSub},
{"9", m_Width9, isSens, notChk, "F9", vk_F9, noSub},
  {NULL}
};

// Define the top-level menu bar
vMenu MenuBar[] =
{
  {"&File", M_File, isSens, notUsed, notUsed, noKey,
    &FileMenu[0]},
  {"&Width", m_Width, isSens, notUsed, notUsed, noKey,
    &WidthMenu[0]},
  {NULL}
};

// Our command window constructor
TCmdWindow::TCmdWindow(char* name, int width, int height) :
```

continues

LISTING 30.12 CONTINUED

```
  vCmdWindow(name, width, height)  // Call ancestor constructor
{
  widthMenuItem = m_Width1;         // Remember checked menu
  myMenu = new vMenuPane(MenuBar);  // Create menu pane
  AddPane(myMenu);                  // Add it to our window
  myCanvas = new TCanvasPane;       // Create our canvas object
  AddPane(myCanvas);                // Add it to our window
  pen.SetColor(0, 0, 0);            // Set pen color to black
  pen.SetWidth(1);                  // Set initial pen width
  myCanvas->SetPen(pen);            // Set pen into canvas
  ShowWindow();                     // Make window visible
}

// Our command window destructor
TCmdWindow::~TCmdWindow()
{
  delete myMenu;     // One for each "new" in constructor
  delete myCanvas;
}

// Respond to menu selections and other commands
void TCmdWindow::WindowCommand(
  ItemVal id, ItemVal val, CmdType cType)
{
  switch (id) {
  case M_New:
    myCanvas->Clear(); // Erase window's canvas
    break;
  case m_Width1:       // Fall-through cases for Window menu
  case m_Width2:
  case m_Width3:
  case m_Width4:
  case m_Width5:
  case m_Width6:
  case m_Width7:
  case m_Width8:
  case m_Width9:
    pen.SetWidth(id - m_Width1 + 1);    // Change pen width
    myCanvas->SetPen(pen);              // Insert in canvas
    SetValue(widthMenuItem, 0, Checked); // Uncheck old cmd
    widthMenuItem = id;
    SetValue(widthMenuItem, 1, Checked); // Check new cmd
    break;
  case M_Exit:              // User selected File¦Exit command
    theApp->Exit();   // Exit the application
    break;
  default:                  // Route unhandled commands
    vCmdWindow::WindowCommand(id, val, cType);
    break;
  }
}
```

For most menus, include the V headers v_defs.h and vkeys.h. The first header makes standard menu command values such as M_Exit available. The second header includes virtual key codes used in defining accelerator keys.

For consistency among applications, you are urged to use V's standard symbols when possible. However, you are free to invent your own. In this case, I defined new symbols for the program's *Width* menu as follows:

```
const ItemVal m_Width  = 100;
const ItemVal m_Width1 = 101;
. . .
const ItemVal m_Width9 = 109;
```

The first value represents the menu item; the others identify each command in the menu. You may use any names, but they should be of type ItemValue and to lessen confusion are best prefaced with lowercase m_. By convention, start your own symbols at 100 and increase by one.

PART

VI

CH

30

> **Note**
>
> Standard values are reserved from 30,000 and up. Assign values less than 30,000 to all your own symbolic menu and other component constants. (In the program's source code, however, don't insert a comma in numbers such as 30,000.)

The next step is to create a static struct object for each of your program's pull-down menus. These structs represent the commands in each menu, not the top-level menu name such as *File* or *Width* in the sample program. For example, the program defines its *File* menu commands with the following struct array:

```
static vMenu FileMenu[] =
{
 {"New", M_New, isSens, notChk, noKeyLbl, noKey, noSub},
 {"-", M_Line, notSens, notChk, noKeyLbl, noKey, noSub},
 {"E&xit", M_Exit, isSens, notChk, "Alt-X", 'x', noSub,
   VKM_Alt},
 {NULL}
};
```

Each item in the vMenu struct array may consist of seven or eight items. The list must end with {NULL}. First is a string to display in the menu. Next is the item's symbolic identifier—either a standard one such as M_New, or one of your own. The isSens value indicates whether this item is user-selectable at runtime or is disabled by default. To create a separator line, assign a single dash string as its name and use the M_Line symbol along with notSens as shown (you don't want users selecting a separator line). The notChk label indicates no check mark next to this item. The noKeyLbl indicates no additional accelerator key label. Notice that the *Exit* command specifies Alt-X as this value—it's shown in brackets in the window (at least in my window manager). To indicate the accelerator key value, use noKey if there is none, or an ASCII character constant such as 'x' here. The noSub label indicates there is no submenu—you can use the name of another vMenu struct here to create a submenu, opened by selecting this command. Finally, specify an optional shift key such as VKM_Alt. This is combined with the accelerator key so that, in this example, pressing M-X (Alt-X) selects the *File, Exit* command to end the program.

The program's *Width* menu is created similarly. Here's a portion of the associated structure:

```
static vMenu WidthMenu[] =
{
  {"1", m_Width1, isSens, isChk,  "F1", vk_F1, noSub},
...
  {NULL}
};
```

In this case, I wanted function keys to select each width value, so I use the vk_F1 symbols for the accelerator keys but specify no optional Shift key. Because this is a nonstandard menu, it uses constants m_Width1 and others defined in the module. The isChk value indicates that the first command should have a check mark at startup. (In a moment, I show how to add a check mark to new items when selected.)

After defining each set of menu commands, a final vMenu struct defines the top-level menu names that are to appear on the menu bar. It's interesting that V uses the same vMenu struct for this purpose, as shown in the sample program's main menu structure:

```
vMenu MenuBar[] =
{
 {"&File", M_File, isSens, notUsed, notUsed, noKey,
    &FileMenu[0]},
 {"&Width", m_Width, isSens, notUsed, notUsed, noKey,
    &WidthMenu[0]},
 {NULL}
};
```

The ampersands are supposed to underline significant hotkeys in each menu item, but in some X window managers, this feature might not work as expected. The fields are identical to those in the menu command structures, but the notUsed symbol indicates values that don't apply to top-level menus—specifically check marks and alternate accelerator key labels. The final item in each entry should be the zero-indexed address of the associated command structure. End the whole shebang with a {NULL} entry, and you're done with the design phase of your program's menu bar.

To construct the menu bar at runtime, construct an object of the vMenuPane class, passing as an argument the top-level menu structure. Because this structure refers to all the others in your menu's design, a simple statement brings in all your menu command entries. For any menus with check-marked items, you should also create a variable of type ItemVal for remembering which item is selected. The sample program's TCmdWindow constructor shows the necessary steps repeated here:

```
widthMenuItem = m_Width1;        // Remember checked menu
myMenu = new vMenuPane(MenuBar); // Create menu pane
AddPane(myMenu);                 // Add it to our window
```

The first statement records the initially checked menu item. Next, a new object of type vMenuPane is constructed for the MenuBar struct defined earlier. Finally, call the inherited

AddPane() function to add the menu bar pane to this window. The rest is automatic. (Be sure, however, to delete myMenu, and all other objects created by new, in the class destructor.)

Using pull-down menu commands is the easiest part of all. Simply add a case to the WindowCommand() function's switch statement for an id value equal to each menu's constant. For example, the following case for M_New clears the window when the user selects the *File*, *New* command:

```
case M_New:
  myCanvas->Clear(); // Erase window's canvas
  break;
```

To respond to *Width* menu selections, and in similar menus that select one of several possible options, you can use a "fall-through" case for each command as shown here:

```
case m_Width1:      // Fall-through cases for Window menu
...
case m_Width9:
  pen.SetWidth(id - m_Width1 + 1);      // Change pen width
  myCanvas->SetPen(pen);                // Insert in canvas
  SetValue(widthMenuItem, 0, Checked);  // Uncheck old cmd
  widthMenuItem = id;
  SetValue(widthMenuItem, 1, Checked);  // Check new cmd
  break;
```

The pen object of V's vPen class is a private data member added to our TCmdWindow class. Calling this class's SetWidth() function changes the width of lines created by DrawLine() (as well as the outline width of other shapes). To use the pen, the program calls SetPen() for the window's canvas. The other statements show how to uncheck an old menu item and then check the new one so that the current selection is properly shown in the menu. This doesn't happen automatically—you have to be sure that the proper item is checked using similar code.

TOOLBARS

Toolbars with selectable buttons have become standard fare in most GUI applications. Typically, a toolbar's buttons provide alternative ways to select menu commands. For example, many users find it easier to click a *Save* button than to pull down the *File* menu and select *Save*. To demonstrate how to create a V toolbar, I further expanded the vSketch program (using vMenu's modules) to add a toolbar with buttons to clear the window and exit the program, and also a spinner button for selecting line widths. Figure 30.5 shows the window of the new program, vTool.

Note

The figure shows a well-known child's game—try to draw the house without lifting your "pen" and without crossing any lines. (I'm stretching my artistic talents to the limit here.)

Figure 30.5
The vSketch and vMenu programs are further enhanced in vTool with a toolbar of selectable button objects.

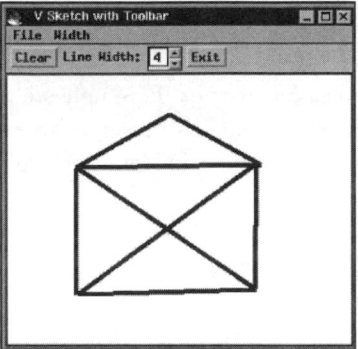

The techniques for creating a toolbar are similar to those for creating a pull-down menu. The vTool program demonstrates the proper steps in its cmdwin.cpp module, shown in Listing 30.13. To save room, the listing shows only the statements relating to the creation and use of the toolbar.

LISTING 30.13 VTOOL/CMDWIN.CPP (PARTIAL)

```
const ItemVal m_SpinWidth = 199;
const ItemVal m_Clear = M_New;  // Button == menu command
...

// Define data for the toolbar's spinner component
static int spinnerData[3] = {1, 9, 1};  // Min, max, step

// Define toolbar (command bar) structure
static CommandObject Toolbar[] =
{
  { C_Button, m_Clear, 0, "Clear", NoList,
    CA_None, isSens, NoFrame, 0, 0 },
  { C_Label, 999, 0 , "Line Width:", NoList,
    CA_None, isSens, NoFrame, 0, 0 },
  { C_Spinner, m_SpinWidth, 1, "" , (void*) &spinnerData[0],
    CA_None, isSens, NoFrame, 0, 0 },
  { C_Button, M_Exit, 0, "Exit", NoList,
    CA_None, isSens, NoFrame, 0, 0 },
  { C_EndOfList, 0, 0, 0, 0, CA_None, 0, 0, 0 }
};

// Our command window constructor
// Note: Add the toolbar after the menu but before the
// canvas to make it appear under the menu bar.
TCmdWindow::TCmdWindow(char* name, int width, int height) :
  vCmdWindow(name, width, height)  // Call ancestor constructor
{
  widthMenuItem = m_Width1;            // Remember checked menu
  myMenu = new vMenuPane(MenuBar);     // Create menu pane
  AddPane(myMenu);                     // Add it to our window
  myToolbar = new vCommandPane(Toolbar); // Create toolbar pane
  AddPane(myToolbar);                  // Add it to our window
  myCanvas = new TCanvasPane;          // Create our canvas object
```

```
    AddPane(myCanvas);                  // Add it to our window
    pen.SetColor(0, 0, 0);              // Set pen color to black
    pen.SetWidth(1);                    // Set initial pen width
    myCanvas->SetPen(pen);              // Set pen into canvas
    ShowWindow();                       // Make window visible
}

// Respond to menu selections and other commands
void TCmdWindow::WindowCommand(
    ItemVal id, ItemVal val, CmdType cType)
{
    switch (id) {
    case M_New:
      myCanvas->Clear(); // Erase window's canvas
      break;
    case m_Width1:        // Fall-through cases for Window menu
...
    case m_SpinWidth:
      {
      if (id == m_SpinWidth)           // Simulate menu command
        id = m_Width1 + (val - 1);
      int newWidth = id - m_Width1 + 1;       // Calculate width
      pen.SetWidth(newWidth);                 // Change pen width
      myCanvas->SetPen(pen);                  // Insert in canvas
      SetValue(widthMenuItem, 0, Checked);    // Uncheck old cmd
      widthMenuItem = id;                     // Remember new cmd
      SetValue(widthMenuItem, 1, Checked);    // Check new cmd
      SetValue(m_SpinWidth, newWidth, Value); // Update spinner
      break;
      }
...
    }
}
```

V calls a toolbar a *command pane*. In it are one or more *command objects* such as buttons, spinners, and other visual components. Some of those objects need associated structures, as demonstrated for the spinner object that lets you select line widths using the mouse. To identify the component, the module defines a new constant, m_SpinWidth, with a value unique from others, including any menu items. The spinner object's data is stored as a small array of int values that specify the minimum value, maximum value, and step size for each mouse click:

```
static int spinnerData[3] = {1, 9, 1};  // Min, max, step
```

Other command objects that require data structures are detailed in V's online reference. Look up *Command Objects* in the index for more information. After creating any such required structures, define the toolbar object of type CommandObject like this:

```
static CommandObject Toolbar[] =
```

Follow that declaration with one bracketed definition for each toolbar item. The sample structure includes definitions for a button (*Clear*), a label, the spinner component, and another button (*Exit*). V positions each object in the order listed, and there's no way (except perhaps creating an invisible label or a similar object) to alter the default positions—the small price we pay for V's portability. (Remember, all this code compiles under all supported platforms, including Microsoft Windows.)

To create the toolbar at runtime and add it to the command window, construct an object of type vCommandPane and pass as an argument your CommandObject structure. Next, call AddPane() as shown here:

```
myToolbar = new vCommandPane(Toolbar);
AddPane(myToolbar);
```

Be sure also to delete myToolbar in the class destructor (this isn't shown in the listing):

```
delete myToolbar;
```

Responding to toolbar component selections is a simple matter of adding their identifiers to the WindowCommand() function's switch statement. In some cases, you can merely assign the identical value used for a menu command and let that section of the program carry out the associated operation. For example, the sample toolbar's *Clear* button identifier is equated to M_New using the following statement:

```
const ItemVal m_Clear = M_New;
```

As a result, clicking the *Clear* button simulates that menu command selection, and no new programming is needed to clear the screen.

The code for the spinner component is a little more involved. You could add a new case for this object's identifier (m_SpinWidth), but I decided to combine its code with the *Width* menu cases to keep both items in synch. When the user selects a *Width* menu command, the spinner's value needs to be updated; when selecting a spinner value, the *Width* menu item for that value needs to be check-marked. The trick for doing operations like that in V is to call the inherited SetValue() function as follows:

```
SetValue(m_SpinWidth, newWidth, Value);
```

In this case, newWidth is the width value. The first argument identifies the component to update. Value is a symbol that tells V what to do with the passed argument value—it is not a variable. See the online documentation for "Command Objects" for more about the SetValue() function. It has a different effect depending on the type of component involved.

STATUS BARS

The third standard V component, and another expected element of most GUI applications, is usually called a status bar (or a status line). It is typically aligned to the window's bottom edge and is used for showing labels, plus information such as line numbers and the date and time.

To demonstrate how to create a status bar, I enhanced the growing vSketch program (using the files from vTool) to display the mouse position and the number of lines drawn in the program's window. Figure 30.6 shows the window for the new program, vStat. (The image in the figure also gives the answer to the previous house-drawing puzzle.) Run the program and draw some lines to see how the status bar is updated.

Figure 30.6
The vSketch application is further enhanced by a status bar in vStat's window that shows the mouse position and number of lines drawn.

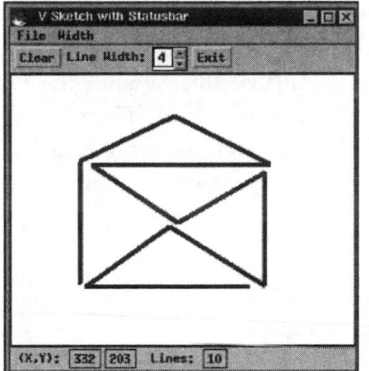

Because in this case the information needed to update the status bar—namely the mouse (x,y) position and the number of lines drawn—comes from the program's canvas object, this poses a dilemma for the program. The command window, as you recall, owns the canvas as an object. Because the command window also owns the status bar pane, the canvas must tell its owning window to update the information in the status bar. In other words, the window class must refer to the canvas class, and the canvas class must refer back to the window class. This "chicken and egg" problem presents a problem in the logistics of declaring both classes so that each can refer to the other—but this is easily solved, as you will see, by using a so-called *forward class declaration.* Listing 30.14, canvas.h, shows the necessary declarations. (The listing doesn't show the TLine class used to save line information. This class is unchanged from the previous examples.)

LISTING 30.14   VSTAT/CANVAS.H (PARTIAL)

```cpp
#include <v/vcanvas.h>  // Need vCanvasPane class

class TCmdWindow;   // Forward declaration

class TCanvasPane : public vCanvasPane {
private:
  bool mouseDown;        // True while mouse button down
  int x1, y1, x2, y2;    // Line coordinates
  vector<TLine> lines;   // Array of TLine objects
  TCmdWindow* cwOwner;   // Command window owner
public:
  TCanvasPane( TCmdWindow* owner );   // Constructor
  ~TCanvasPane();   // Destructor
  // Override some inherited functions
  virtual void Clear();
  virtual void MouseDown(int x, int y, int button);
  virtual void MouseUp(int x, int y, int button);
  virtual void MouseMove(int x, int y, int button);
  virtual void MouseMotion(int x, int y);
  virtual void Redraw(int x, int y, int w, int h);
};
```

The forward declaration for TCmdWindow permits the TCanvasPane to use this class name in two ways. First, it declares a pointer to a TCmdWindow object, cwOwner, that refers to the canvas object's owning command window. To initialize this variable, the TCanvasPane constructor also declares a pointer of the same type as a parameter. These are all the changes necessary to make the canvas aware of its owner and, therefore, able to call public functions for that window object. Listing 30.15, cmdwin.h, shows the command window class, TCmdWindow, declaration.

LISTING 30.15   VSTAT/CMDWIN.H (PARTIAL)

```
#include <v/vstatusp.h> // Need vStatusPane
#include "canvas.h"      // Need TCanvasPane class

class TCmdWindow : public vCmdWindow {
private:
  TCanvasPane* myCanvas;     // Pointer to our canvas object
  vMenuPane* myMenu;         // Pointer to window's menu
  vCommandPane* myToolbar;   // Pointer to window's toolbar
  vStatusPane* myStatus;     // Pointer to window's statusbar
  ItemVal widthMenuItem;     // Checked Width-menu command
  vPen pen;                  // Drawing pen
public:
  TCmdWindow(char* name, int width, int height);
  virtual ~TCmdWindow();
  virtual void WindowCommand(ItemVal id, ItemVal val,
    CmdType cType);
public:
  // Status bar update info functions called by canvas
  void UpdateMouseInfo(int x, int y);
  void UpdateNumLines(int n);
};
```

In addition to other headers not shown in the listing, the header file for the TCmdWindow class includes vstatusp.h for the vStatusPane class, used to create the status bar. A pointer to this class is declared in the private section. In addition, two new functions, UpdateMouseInfo() and UpdateNumLines() are declared. These functions are called by the canvas object to update the command window's status bar display. Listing 30.16, canvas.cpp, shows the functions where this happens. Remember, the mouse events occur in the canvas object—so, to update the window's status bar, the canvas must call its owner window's functions as declared in TCmdWindow.

LISTING 30.16   VSTAT/CANVAS.CPP (PARTIAL)

```
#include "canvas.h"   // Our header
#include "cmdwin.h"   // Need our TCmdWindow class

// Constructor
TCanvasPane::TCanvasPane( TCmdWindow* owner ) :
  vCanvasPane(),  // Call ancestor constructor
  lines()         // Construct lines vector (grows as needed)
{
```

```
    mouseDown = false;
    x1 = y1 = x2 = y2 = 0;
    cwOwner = owner;   // Remember who owns this object
}

// Erase window's canvas and lines vector
void TCanvasPane::Clear()
{
    vCanvasPane::Clear();   // Call ancestor function
    lines.erase(lines.begin(), lines.end());
    cwOwner->UpdateNumLines(lines.size());   // Update Status bar
}

// Respond to mouse button click event
// Prepares for drawing the next line
void TCanvasPane::MouseDown(int x, int y, int button)
{
    mouseDown = true;     // Set mouse down flag
    x1 = x;               // Remember starting location
    y1 = y;
    x2 = x1;              // Set end point == beginning
    y2 = y1;              // as a "do nothing" flag
    cwOwner->UpdateMouseInfo(x, y);   // Update status bar
}

// Respond to mouse button release event
// Save current line in the lines vector
void TCanvasPane::MouseUp(int x, int y, int button)
{
    mouseDown = false;   // Reset mouse down flag
    if (x1 != x2 || y1 != y2) {
        DrawRubberLine(x1, y1, x2, y2);   // Erase old line
        x2 = x;            // Save line end point
        y2 = y;
        DrawLine(x1, y1, x2, y2);   // Draw fixed line
        lines.push_back(TLine(GetPen(), x1, y1, x2, y2));
        // Update status bar information
        cwOwner->UpdateMouseInfo(x, y);
        cwOwner->UpdateNumLines(lines.size());
    }
}

// Respond to mouse movement button-down event
// Draws a "rubber line" (i.e. an erasable line)
void TCanvasPane::MouseMove(int x, int y, int button)
{
    if (mouseDown) {
        if (x1 != x2 || y1 != y2)
            DrawRubberLine(x1, y1, x2, y2);   // Erase old line
        x2 = x;   // Save line end point so far
        y2 = y;
        DrawRubberLine(x1, y1, x2, y2);       // Draw new line
    }
    // Update status bar information
    cwOwner->UpdateMouseInfo(x, y);
```

continues

LISTING 30.16   CONTINUED

```
}

// Respond to all mouse motion events
void TCanvasPane::MouseMotion(int x, int y)
{
  // Update status bar information
  cwOwner->UpdateMouseInfo(x, y);
}
```

In addition to responding to mouse movements when the mouse button is held down, the new class also overrides function MouseMotion() so that it can show the mouse pointer coordinate values whenever the cursor enters the canvas area. To update the status bar, the canvas simply calls the owning window's UpdateMouseInfo() and UpdateNumLines() functions as shown in the listing. Notice that the TCanvasPane() constructor saves the pointer to its owning window object to make these calls. Be sure to include the command window header file (cmdwin.h) in the canvas module so that you can call these functions.

The final step in programming a status bar is to create its structure and implement functions that display values in the status bar's components. Usually, the best place for this programming is in the command window module along with the menu and toolbar declarations you've seen in prior sample listings. Listing 30.17, cmdwin.cpp, shows the portions of the module that relate to the new status bar pane.

LISTING 30.17   VSTAT/CMDWIN.CPP (PARTIAL)

```
#include "cmdwin.h"
#include <v/v_defs.h>      // Need standard definitions
#include <v/vkeys.h>       // Need virtual key symbols
#include <v/vutil.h>       // Need IntToStr()
#include <stdio.h>         // Need sprintf()
...

// Define status bar component constants
const ItemVal m_StatLabel     = 200;
const ItemVal m_XPosition      = 201;
const ItemVal m_YPosition      = 202;
const ItemVal m_NumLines       = 203;
...

vStatus Statusbar[] =
{
  { "(X,Y):", m_StatLabel, CA_NoBorder, isSens, 0 },
  { "000", m_XPosition, CA_None, isSens, 0 },
  { "000", m_YPosition, CA_None, isSens, 0 },
  { " Lines:", m_StatLabel, CA_NoBorder, isSens, 0 },
  { "0", m_NumLines,  CA_None, isSens, 0 },
  { NULL, 0, 0, 0, 0 }
};

// Our command window constructor
// Note: Add the toolbar after the menu but before the
```

```
// canvas to make it appear under the menu bar.
TCmdWindow::TCmdWindow(char* name, int width, int height) :
  vCmdWindow(name, width, height)   // Call ancestor constructor
{
  widthMenuItem = m_Width1;              // Remember checked menu
  myMenu = new vMenuPane(MenuBar);       // Create menu pane
  AddPane(myMenu);                       // Add it to our window
  myToolbar = new vCommandPane(Toolbar); // Create toolbar pane
  AddPane(myToolbar);                    // Add it to our window

  myCanvas = new TCanvasPane(this);      // Create our canvas object
  AddPane(myCanvas);                     // Add it to our window
  myStatus = new vStatusPane(Statusbar); // Create statbar pane
  AddPane(myStatus);                     // Add it to our window

  pen.SetColor(0, 0, 0);                 // Set pen color to black
  pen.SetWidth(1);                       // Set initial pen width
  myCanvas->SetPen(pen);                 // Set pen into canvas
  ShowWindow();                          // Make window visible
}
...

// The canvas object calls this to update the status
// bar's mouse x,y position information when the mouse
// pointer moves inside the window.
void TCmdWindow::UpdateMouseInfo(int x, int y)
{
  char buffer[8];  // Temporary text buffer

  sprintf(buffer, "%03d", x);
  SetString(m_XPosition, buffer);  // Show X info
  sprintf(buffer, "%03d", y);
  SetString(m_YPosition, buffer);  // Show Y info
}

// Similarly, this function updates the number of
// lines drawn in the window. It too is called by
// the canvas object.
void TCmdWindow::UpdateNumLines(int n)
{
  char buffer[8];

  IntToStr(n, buffer);
  SetString(m_NumLines, buffer);
}
```

Define unique constants for each item in your status bar. Labels may all be defined using the same constant, such as m_StatLabel here. I used the range of 200 to 203 for these values, but any unique integers are fine as long as they are less than 30,000. These values must be unique for *all* components, including menu commands and toolbar items.

The status bar itself, like menus and toolbars, is a struct composed of a V type declared in v_defs.h. Define your status bar of type vStatus like this:

```
vStatus Statusbar[] =
```

Each bracketed item that follows specifies a text label, a unique identifier, whether you want a border, and isSens (to display the item normally, not dimmed). The final zero is an unused placeholder. End the array with a NULL entry as shown.

To create the status bar, create an object of the vStatusPane class passing the Statusbar structure as an argument. Save this pointer in a variable such as myStatus here. Also add a corresponding delete statement to the class destructor (not shown in the listing):

```
delete myStatus;
```

You also have to create the canvas object a little differently because it needs to know who its owner is. Do this by passing the this pointer to the canvas constructor:

```
myCanvas = new TCanvasPane(this);
```

The this pointer here refers to the command window object that is under construction. The statement permits the canvas to call the window's functions, UpdateMouseInfo() and UpdateNumLines(), shown next in the listing.

For demonstration purposes, I used two different methods to convert numeric information such as the mouse coordinate values to strings for display in the status bar. UpdateMouseInfo() calls the standard library's sprintf() function to convert the x and y values passed by the canvas object to a temporary string buffer. Calling the inherited SetText() function for each status bar component identifier updates the information shown in the window.

The other function, UpdateNumLines(), calls the V utility function IntToStr() (prototyped in header vutil.h) to convert the number of lines to a temporary string. Calling SetText() updates this value in the status bar.

> **Note**
>
> The status bar automatically takes care of updating its display if the window is exposed—you don't have to do this in the canvas's Redraw() function.

FINAL NOTE

There are many other subjects I'd like to cover about C++, X, Xlib, and V programming, but this book has to end at some place, and, I suppose, this place is as good as any. If you have read this book from cover to cover, you have come a long way from writing simple C++ programs to fully developed object-oriented X applications. I can only hope that your questions are answered somewhere in this book's pages and that you have enough information to carry you on to the next step in your quest to master C++ programming and Linux software development. Please write to me in care of the publisher and let me know any subjects you'd like to see in a future edition, or another book, and also accept my sincere wishes for successful, bug-free code in all your programming projects!

SUMMARY

This chapter showed how to develop object-oriented V applications for X, complete with pull-down menu bars, toolbars, status bars, and graphics. Be sure to check out V's Web site for updates and future add-ons for this excellent class library for X programming.

For more information on subjects introduced in this chapter, turn to the following chapters:

- Chapter 24, "Building Standard Containers"
- Chapter 26, "Introducing X Programming"
- Chapter 29, "Introducing the V Class Library"

PART

VI

CH

30

PART **VII**

APPENDIXES

APPENDIX

GNU C++ Reserved Words

GNU C++ RESERVED WORDS

_ _alignof	_ _const_ _	_ _inline	reinterpret_c	try
_ _alignof_ _	const	_ _inline_ _	return	typedef
and	const_cast	inline	short	typeid
and_eq	continue	int	_ _signature_ _	typename
_ _asm	default	_ _label_ _	signature	_ _typeof
_ _asm_ _	delete	long	_ _signed	_ _typeof_ _
asm	do	mutable	_ _signed_ _	typeof
_ _attribute	double	namespace	signed	union
_ _attribute_ _	dynamic_case	new	_ _sigof_ _	unsigned
auto	else	not	sigof	using
bitand	enum	not_eq	sizeof	virtual
bitor	explicit	operator	static	void
bool	_ _extension_ _	or	static_cast	_ _volatile
break	extern	or_eq	struct	_ _volatile_ _
case	false	overload	switch	volatile
catch	float	private	template	_ _wchar_t
char	for	protected	this	while
class	friend	public	throw	xor
compl	goto	register	true	xor_eq
_ _const	if			

C++ OPERATOR PRECEDENCE AND ASSOCIATIVITY

C++ OPERATOR PRECEDENCE AND ASSOCIATIVITY

Level	Operators	Evaluation Order
1 (high)	`() . [] -> ::`	left-to-right
2	`* & ! ~ ++ -- + - sizeof new delete`	right-to-left
3	`.* ->*`	left-to-right
4	`* / %`	left-to-right
5	`+ -`	left-to-right
6	`<< >>`	left-to-right
7	`< <= > >=`	left-to-right
8	`== !=`	left-to-right
9	`&`	left-to-right
10	`^`	left-to-right
11	`¦`	left-to-right
12	`&&`	left-to-right
13	`¦¦`	left-to-right
14	`?:`	right-to-left
15	`= *= = += -= %= <<= >>= &= ^= ¦=`	right-to-left
16 (low)	`,`	left-to-right

Operators at the top of the table have higher precedence over operators below. C++ evaluates expressions with operators of higher precedence before it evaluates expressions with operators of lower precedence. Given an expression with operators of equal precedence, C++ evaluates any subexpressions in the given order of associativity.

Some symbols in the table are ambiguous, but C++ uses the context of an expression to know what operation to perform. For example, in the table, unary plus (+) and unary minus (-) are at level 2 and have precedence over arithmetic plus and minus at level 5. The & symbol at level 2 is the address-of operator; the & operator at level 9 is the bitwise AND operator. The * operator at level 2 is the pointer-dereference operator; the * characters at level 3 are part of the two-character .* and three-character ->* member-pointer-dereference operators; the * symbol at level 4 is the multiplication operator.

Note

See Chapter 7, "Applying Fundamental Operators," for more about using precedence and associativity.

APPENDIX

WEB AND FTP SITES

WEB AND FTP SITES

Numerous Web and FTP (file transfer protocol) sites are available with enough files to keep a Linux and GNU C++ fanatic busy for a lifetime. Following are a few of the sites that I've found highly useful in writing this book, and also just for fun. You can find hundreds of additional links to other sites by starting with those listed here.

Your key source for information and files for GNU C++, and for other GNU Free Software Foundation projects, is this Web site:

`http://www.gnu.org/`

Turn to the page labeled "software" for information on GNU C++ and other languages. There's tons of software on this site complete with source code, and much of it written in C and C++. Another great source of information about GNU C++ is found on the following Web site:

`http://egcs.cygnus.com`

Cygnus Solutions is a main contributor to GCC (the GNU Compiler Collection) and EGCS. This site also provides lots of information and additional links to related UNIX and Linux sites. For more information about the Mandrake-Linux software on this book's CD-ROM, log on to this Web site:

`http://www.linux-mandrake.com`

Using your browser's FTP capabilities, or other FTP software, you'll find numerous help, source code, and other files at this related FTP address:

`ftp://ftp.linux-mandrake.com`

This book also introduces the C++ class library, V, for X programming. The library supports cross development for Microsoft Windows, X, and OS/2 (and possibly other platforms). For the source files to the latest version of V, and for information about a soon-to-be-released visual development system based on V, log on to the following Web site, which also supports pages for other C++ and Linux topics:

`http://www.objectcentral.com/`

My secret fantasy is to be a pilot. Not needing another expensive hobby, however, I'll settle for my sailboat. But when I want to dream, I log on to the following site. This is absolutely the coolest flight simulator project around, and it's written using C++ for Linux and Microsoft Windows:

`http://www.flightgear.org/`

Here are some additional Linux, UNIX, and GNU C++ sites you might find interesting.

`http://www.redhat.com`
`http://www.calderasystems.com`
`http://www.sunsite.unc.edu/pub/Linux`
`http://www.ssc.com/linux`
`http://www.linuxjournal.com`

And last but not least, here's my favorite. Let me know if you have any feedback!

`http://www.tomswan.com`

APPENDIX

USING THE CD-ROM

USING THE CD-ROM

To install the Linux-Mandrake 6.0 operating system, insert the included CD-ROM and reboot. Follow instructions onscreen. If you cannot boot to the CD-ROM, you'll have to use another method to install Linux. If you can boot to MS-DOS, insert the CD-ROM (shown here as drive D:), and enter these commands:

```
d:
cd \dosutils
autoboot.bat
```

You must be running *only* MS-DOS for those commands to work—you cannot, for example, use these commands from a DOS window opened in Microsoft Windows. If you can't boot to MS-DOS, you have to create a special boot floppy disk to install Linux. Complete instructions for creating this disk are in the file Readme on the CD-ROM. View this file using the Microsoft Windows WordPad accessory application.

As when installing any operating system software, installing Linux deletes any existing files on your system (unless you take other measures, not described here, to protect your hard drive's partitions). Make a complete backup of all files before installing this book's CD-ROM.

Note

See Chapter 2, "Installing Linux," for more information on installing and configuring Linux for use with this book. See Chapter 3, "Installing GNU C++," for additional installation suggestions, and for instructions on installing this book's sample listing files.

APPENDIX

E

COPYRIGHT INFORMATION—
THE GNU GENERAL PUBLIC LICENSE

COPYRIGHT INFORMATION—THE GNU GENERAL PUBLIC LICENSE

GNU GENERAL PUBLIC LICENSE

Version 2, June 1991

Copyright © 1989, 1991 Free Software Foundation, Inc.

675 Mass Ave., Cambridge, MA 02139, USA

Everyone is permitted to copy and distribute verbatim copies of this license document, but changing it is not allowed.

PREAMBLE

The licenses for most software are designed to take away your freedom to share and change it. By contrast, the GNU General Public License is intended to guarantee your freedom to share and change free software—to make sure the software is free for all its users. This General Public License applies to most of the Free Software Foundation's software and to any other program whose authors commit to using it. (Some other Free Software Foundation software is covered by the GNU Library General Public License instead.) You can apply it to your programs, too.

When we speak of free software, we are referring to freedom, not price. Our General Public Licenses are designed to make sure that you have the freedom to distribute copies of free software (and charge for this service if you wish), that you receive source code or can get it if you want it, that you can change the software or use pieces of it in new free programs; and that you know you can do these things.

To protect your rights, we need to make restrictions that forbid anyone to deny you these rights or to ask you to surrender the rights. These restrictions translate to certain responsibilities for you if you distribute copies of the software, or if you modify it.

For example, if you distribute copies of such a program, whether gratis or for a fee, you must give the recipients all the rights that you have. You must make sure that they, too, receive or can get the source code. And you must show them these terms so they know their rights.

We protect your rights with two steps: (1) copyright the software, and (2) offer you this license which gives you legal permission to copy, distribute and/or modify the software.

Also, for each author's protection and ours, we want to make certain that everyone understands that there is no warranty for this free software. If the software is modified by someone else and passed on, we want its recipients to know that what they have is not the original, so that any problems introduced by others will not reflect on the original authors' reputations.

Finally, any free program is threatened constantly by software patents. We wish to avoid the danger that redistributors of a free program will individually obtain patent licenses, in effect making the program proprietary. To prevent this, we have made it clear that any patent must be licensed for everyone's free use or not licensed at all.

The precise terms and conditions for copying, distribution and modification follow.

GNU GENERAL PUBLIC LICENSE

TERMS AND CONDITIONS FOR COPYING, DISTRIBUTION AND

MODIFICATION

This License applies to any program or other work which contains a notice placed by the copyright holder saying it may be distributed under the terms of this General Public License. The "Program", below, refers to any such program or work, and a "work based on the Program" means either the Program or any derivative work under copyright law: that is to say, a work containing the Program or a portion of it, either verbatim or with modifications and/or translated into another language. (Hereinafter, translation is included without limitation in the term "modification".) Each licensee is addressed as "you".

Activities other than copying, distribution and modification are not covered by this License; they are outside its scope. The act of running the Program is not restricted, and the output from the Program is covered only if its contents constitute a work based on the Program (independent of having been made by running the Program). Whether that is true depends on what the Program does.

1. You may copy and distribute verbatim copies of the Program's source code as you receive it, in any medium, provided that you conspicuously and appropriately publish on each copy an appropriate copyright notice and disclaimer of warranty; keep intact all the notices that refer to this License and to the absence of any warranty; and give any other recipients of the Program a copy of this License along with the Program.

   You may charge a fee for the physical act of transferring a copy, and you may at your option offer warranty protection in exchange for a fee.

2. You may modify your copy or copies of the Program or any portion of it, thus forming a work based on the Program, and copy and distribute such modifications or work under the terms of Section 1 above, provided that you also meet all of these conditions:

   a) You must cause the modified files to carry prominent notices stating that you changed the files and the date of any change.

   b) You must cause any work that you distribute or publish, that in whole or in part contains or is derived from the Program or any part thereof, to be licensed as a whole at no charge to all third parties under the terms of this License.

   c) If the modified program normally reads commands interactively when run, you must cause it, when started running for such interactive use in the most ordinary way, to print or display an announcement including an appropriate copyright notice and a notice that there is no warranty (or else, saying that you provide a warranty) and that users may redistribute the program under these conditions, and telling the user how to view a copy of this License. (Exception: if the Program itself is interactive but does not normally print such an announcement, your work based on the Program is not required to print an announcement.)

These requirements apply to the modified work as a whole. If identifiable sections of that work are not derived from the Program, and can be reasonably considered independent and separate works in themselves, then this License, and its terms, do not apply to those sections when you distribute them as separate works. But when you distribute the same sections as part of a whole which is a work based on the Program, the distribution of the whole must be on the terms of this License, whose permissions for other licensees extend to the entire whole, and thus to each and every part regardless of who wrote it.

Thus, it is not the intent of this section to claim rights or contest your rights to work written entirely by you; rather, the intent is to exercise the right to control the distribution of derivative or collective works based on the Program.

In addition, mere aggregation of another work not based on the Program with the Program (or with a work based on the Program) on a volume of a storage or distribution medium does not bring the other work under the scope of this License.

3. You may copy and distribute the Program (or a work based on it, under Section 2) in object code or executable form under the terms of Sections 1 and 2 above provided that you also do one of the following:

   a) Accompany it with the complete corresponding machine-readable source code, which must be distributed under the terms of Sections 1 and 2 above on a medium customarily used for software interchange; or,

   b) Accompany it with a written offer, valid for at least three years, to give any third party, for a charge no more than your cost of physically performing source distribution, a complete machine-readable copy of the corresponding source code, to be distributed under the terms of Sections 1 and 2 above on a medium customarily used for software interchange; or,

   c) Accompany it with the information you received as to the offer to distribute corresponding source code. (This alternative is allowed only for noncommercial distribution and only if you received the program in object code or executable form with such an offer, in accord with Subsection b above.)

The source code for a work means the preferred form of the work for making modifications to it. For an executable work, complete source code means all the source code for all modules it contains, plus any associated interface definition files, plus the scripts used to control compilation and installation of the executable. However, as a special exception, the source code distributed need not include anything that is normally distributed (in either source or binary form) with the major components (compiler, kernel, and so on) of the operating system on which the executable runs, unless that component itself accompanies the executable.

If distribution of executable or object code is made by offering access to copy from a designated place, then offering equivalent access to copy the source code from the same place counts as distribution of the source code, even though third parties are not compelled to copy the source along with the object code.

4. You may not copy, modify, sublicense, or distribute the Program except as expressly provided under this License. Any attempt otherwise to copy, modify, sublicense or distribute the Program is void, and will automatically terminate your rights under this License. However, parties who have received copies, or rights, from you under this License will not have their licenses terminated so long as such parties remain in full compliance.

5. You are not required to accept this License, since you have not signed it. However, nothing else grants you permission to modify or distribute the Program or its derivative works. These actions are prohibited by law if you do not accept this License. Therefore, by modifying or distributing the Program (or any work based on the Program), you indicate your acceptance of this License to do so, and all its terms and conditions for copying, distributing or modifying the Program or works based on it.

6. Each time you redistribute the Program (or any work based on the Program), the recipient automatically receives a license from the original licensor to copy, distribute or modify the Program subject to these terms and conditions. You may not impose any further restrictions on the recipients' exercise of the rights granted herein. You are not responsible for enforcing compliance by third parties to this License.

7. If, as a consequence of a court judgment or allegation of patent infringement or for any other reason (not limited to patent issues), conditions are imposed on you (whether by court order, agreement or otherwise) that contradict the conditions of this License, they do not excuse you from the conditions of this License. If you cannot distribute so as to satisfy simultaneously your obligations under this License and any other pertinent obligations, then as a consequence you may not distribute the Program at all. For example, if a patent license would not permit royalty-free redistribution of the Program by all those who receive copies directly or indirectly through you, then the only way you could satisfy both it and this License would be to refrain entirely from distribution of the Program.

   If any portion of this section is held invalid or unenforceable under any particular circumstance, the balance of the section is intended to apply and the section as a whole is intended to apply in other circumstances.

   It is not the purpose of this section to induce you to infringe any patents or other property right claims or to contest validity of any such claims; this section has the sole purpose of protecting the integrity of the free software distribution system, which is implemented by public license practices. Many people have made generous contributions to the wide range of software distributed through that system in reliance on consistent application of that system; it is up to the author/donor to decide if he or she is willing to distribute software through any other system and a licensee cannot impose that choice.

   This section is intended to make thoroughly clear what is believed to be a consequence of the rest of this License.

8. If the distribution and/or use of the Program is restricted in certain countries either by patents or by copyrighted interfaces, the original copyright holder who places the Program under this License may add an explicit geographical distribution limitation

excluding those countries, so that distribution is permitted only in or among countries not thus excluded. In such case, this License incorporates the limitation as if written in the body of this License.

9. The Free Software Foundation may publish revised and/or new versions of the General Public License from time to time. Such new versions will be similar in spirit to the present version, but may differ in detail to address new problems or concerns.

   Each version is given a distinguishing version number. If the Program specifies a version number of this License which applies to it and "any later version", you have the option of following the terms and conditions either of that version or of any later version published by the Free Software Foundation. If the Program does not specify a version number of this License, you may choose any version ever published by the Free Software Foundation.

10. If you wish to incorporate parts of the Program into other free programs whose distribution conditions are different, write to the author to ask for permission. For software which is copyrighted by the Free Software Foundation, write to the Free Software Foundation; we sometimes make exceptions for this. Our decision will be guided by the two goals of preserving the free status of all derivatives of our free software and of promoting the sharing and reuse of software generally.

NO WARRANTY

11. BECAUSE THE PROGRAM IS LICENSED FREE OF CHARGE, THERE IS NO WARRANTY FOR THE PROGRAM, TO THE EXTENT PERMITTED BY APPLICABLE LAW. EXCEPT WHEN OTHERWISE STATED IN WRITING THE COPYRIGHT HOLDERS AND/OR OTHER PARTIES PROVIDE THE PROGRAM "AS IS" WITHOUT WARRANTY OF ANY KIND, EITHER EXPRESSED OR IMPLIED, INCLUDING, BUT NOT LIMITED TO, THE IMPLIED WARRANTIES OF MERCHANTABILITY AND FITNESS FOR A PARTICULAR PURPOSE. THE ENTIRE RISK AS TO THE QUALITY AND PERFORMANCE OF THE PROGRAM IS WITH YOU. SHOULD THE PROGRAM PROVE DEFECTIVE, YOU ASSUME THE COST OF ALL NECESSARY SERVICING, REPAIR OR CORRECTION.

12. IN NO EVENT UNLESS REQUIRED BY APPLICABLE LAW OR AGREED TO IN WRITING WILL ANY COPYRIGHT HOLDER, OR ANY OTHER PARTY WHO MAY MODIFY AND/OR REDISTRIBUTE THE PROGRAM AS PERMITTED ABOVE, BE LIABLE TO YOU FOR DAMAGES, INCLUDING ANY GENERAL, SPECIAL, INCIDENTAL OR CONSEQUENTIAL DAMAGES ARISING OUT OF THE USE OR INABILITY TO USE THE PROGRAM (INCLUDING BUT NOT LIMITED TO LOSS OF DATA OR DATA BEING RENDERED INACCURATE OR LOSSES SUSTAINED BY YOU OR THIRD PARTIES OR A FAILURE OF THE PROGRAM TO OPERATE WITH ANY OTHER PROGRAMS), EVEN IF SUCH HOLDER OR OTHER PARTY HAS BEEN ADVISED OF THE POSSIBILITY OF SUCH DAMAGES.

END OF TERMS AND CONDITIONS

LINUX AND THE GNU SYSTEM

The GNU project started 12 years ago with the goal of developing a complete free UNIX-like operating system. "Free" refers to freedom, not price; it means you are free to run, copy, distribute, study, change, and improve the software.

A UNIX-like system consists of many different programs. We found some components already available as free software—for example, X Window and TeX. We obtained other components by helping to convince their developers to make them free—for example, the Berkeley network utilities. Other components we wrote specifically for GNU—for example, GNU Emacs, the GNU C compiler, the GNU C library, Bash, and Ghostscript. The components in this last category are "GNU software."

The GNU system consists of all three categories together.

The GNU project is not just about developing and distributing free software. The heart of the GNU project is an idea: that software should be free, and that the users' freedom is worth defending. For if people have freedom but do not value it, they will not keep it for long. In order to make freedom last, we have to teach people to value it.

The GNU project's method is that free software and the idea of users' freedom support each other. We develop GNU software, and as people encounter GNU programs or the GNU system and start to use them, they also think about the GNU idea. The software shows that the idea can work in practice. People who come to agree with the idea are likely to write additional free software. Thus, the software embodies the idea, spreads the idea, and grows from the idea.

This method was working well—until someone combined the Linux kernel with the GNU system (which still lacked a kernel), and called the combination a "Linux system."

The Linux kernel is a free UNIX-compatible kernel written by Linus Torvalds. It was not written specifically for the GNU project, but the Linux kernel and the GNU system work together well. In fact, adding Linux to the GNU system brought the system to completion: it made a free UNIX-compatible operating system available for use.

But ironically, the practice of calling it a "Linux system" undermines our method of communicating the GNU idea. At first impression, a "Linux system" sounds like something completely distinct from the "GNU system." And that is what most users think it is.

Most introductions to the "Linux system" acknowledge the role played by the GNU software components. But they don't say that the system as a whole is more or less the same GNU system that the GNU project has been compiling for a decade. They don't say that the idea of a free UNIX-like system originates from the GNU project. So, most users don't know these things.

This leads many of those users to identify themselves as a separate community of "Linux users," distinct from the GNU user community.

They use all of the GNU software; in fact, they use almost all of the GNU system; but they don't think of themselves as GNU users, and they may not think about the GNU idea.

It leads to other problems as well—even hampering cooperation on software maintenance. Normally when users change a GNU program to make it work better on a particular system, they send the change to the maintainer of that program; then they work with the maintainer, explaining the change, arguing for it and sometimes rewriting it, to get it installed.

But people who think of themselves as "Linux users" are more likely to release a forked "Linux-only" version of the GNU program, and consider the job done. We want each and every GNU program to work "out of the box" on Linux-based systems; but if the users do not help, that goal becomes much harder to achieve.

So, how should the GNU project respond? What should we do now to spread the idea that freedom for computer users is important?

We should continue to talk about the freedom to share and change software—and to teach other users to value these freedoms. If we enjoy having a free operating system, it makes sense for us to think about preserving those freedoms for the long term. If we enjoy having a variety of free software, it makes sense for to think about encouraging others to write additional free software, instead of additional proprietary software.

We should not accept the splitting of the community in two. Instead we should spread the word that "Linux systems" are variant GNU systems—that users of these systems are GNU users, and that they ought to consider the GNU philosophy which brought these systems into existence.

This article is one way of doing that. Another way is to use the terms "Linux-based GNU system" (or "GNU/Linux system" or "Lignux" for short) to refer to the combination of the Linux kernel and the GNU system.

Copyright ® 1996 Richard Stallman

(Verbatim copying and redistribution is permitted without royalty as long as this notice is preserved.)

The Linux kernel is Copyright ® 1991, 1992, 1993, 1994 Linus Torvalds (others hold copyrights on some of the drivers, file systems, and other parts of the kernel) and is licensed under the terms of the GNU General Public License.

THE FREEBSD COPYRIGHT

All of the documentation and software included in the 4.4BSD and 4.4BSD-Lite Releases is copyrighted by The Regents of the University of California.

Copyright ®1979, 1980, 1983, 1986, 1988, 1989, 1991, 1992, 1993, 1994 The Regents of the University of California. All rights reserved.

Redistribution and use in source and binary forms, with or without modification, are permitted provided that the following conditions are met:

1. Redistributions of source code must retain the above copyright notice, this list of conditions and the following disclaimer.
2. Redistributions in binary form must reproduce the above copyright notice, this list of conditions and the following disclaimer in the documentation and/or other materials provided with the distribution.
3. All advertising materials mentioning features or use of this software must display the following acknowledgement:

   This product includes software developed by the University of California, Berkeley and its contributors.
4. Neither the name of the University nor the names of its contributors may be used to endorse or promote products derived from this software without specific prior written permission.

THIS SOFTWARE IS PROVIDED BY THE REGENTS AND CONTRIBUTORS "AS IS" AND ANY EXPRESS OR IMPLIED WARRANTIES, INCLUDING, BUT NOT LIMITED TO, THE IMPLIED WARRANTIES OF MERCHANTABILITY AND FITNESS FOR A PARTICULAR PURPOSE ARE DISCLAIMED. IN NO EVENT SHALL THE REGENTS OR CONTRIBUTORS BE LIABLE FOR ANY DIRECT, INDIRECT, INCIDENTAL, SPECIAL, EXEMPLARY, OR CONSEQUENTIAL DAMAGES (INCLUDING, BUT NOT LIMITED TO, PROCUREMENT OF SUBSTITUTE GOODS OR SERVICES; LOSS OF USE, DATA, OR PROFITS; OR BUSINESS INTERRUPTION) HOWEVER CAUSED AND ON ANY THEORY OF LIABILITY, WHETHER IN CONTRACT, STRICT LIABILITY, OR

TORT (INCLUDING NEGLIGENCE OR OTHERWISE) ARISING IN ANY WAY OUT OF THE USE OF THIS SOFTWARE, EVEN IF ADVISED OF THE POSSIBILITY OF SUCH DAMAGE.

The Institute of Electrical and Electronics Engineers and the American National Standards Committee X3, on Information Processing Systems have given us permission to reprint portions of their documentation.

In the following statement, the phrase "this text" refers to portions of the system documentation.

Portions of this text are reprinted and reproduced in electronic form in the second BSD Networking Software Release, from IEEE Std 1003.1-1988, IEEE Standard Portable Operating System Interface for Computer Environments (POSIX), copyright C 1988 by the Institute of Electrical and Electronics Engineers, Inc. In the event of any discrepancy between these versions and the original IEEE Standard, the original IEEE Standard is the referee document.

In the following statement, the phrase "This material" refers to portions of the system documentation.

This material is reproduced with permission from American National Standards Committee X3, on Information Processing Systems. Computer and Business Equipment Manufacturers Association (CBEMA), 311 First St., NW, Suite 500, Washington, DC 20001-2178. The developmental work of Programming Language C was completed by the X3J11 Technical Committee.

The views and conclusions contained in the software and documentation are those of the authors and should not be interpreted as representing official policies, either expressed or implied, of the Regents of the University of California.

www@FreeBSD.ORG

$Date: 1997/07/01 03:52:05 $

INDEX

F

W